THE DAILY STUDY BIBLE

THE GOSPEL OF LUKE

D—I

THE GOSPEL OF LUKE

The Rev. WILLIAM BARCLAY, D.D.

*Lecturer in New Testament Language and Literature,
and in Hellenistic Greek, in the University of Glasgow*

THE SAINT ANDREW PRESS
EDINBURGH

Published by The Saint Andrew Press
121 George Street, Edinburgh, 2
and printed in Scotland by
McCorquodale & Co., Ltd., Glasgow

First Edition	-	September, 1953
Second Edition	-	February, 1956
Third Edition	-	September, 1956
Second Impression	-	May, 1957
Third Impression	-	January, 1958
Fourth Impression	-	November, 1958
Fifth Impression	-	May, 1960

GENERAL INTRODUCTION

IT may truly be said that this series of Daily Bible Studies began almost accidently. A series which the Church of Scotland was using came to an end, and another series was immediately required. I was asked to write a volume on *Acts*, and, at the moment, had no intention beyond that. But one volume followed another, until the demand for one volume became a plan to write on the whole New Testament.

The translation which is given in each volume claims no special merit. It was included in order that the reader might be able to carry both the text of the New Testament and the comments on it wherever he went, and that he might be able to read it anywhere. While I was making the translation, the translations of Moffatt, Weymouth, and Knox were ever beside me. *The American Revised Standard Version, The Twentieth Century New Testament,* and *The New Testament in Plain English,* by Charles Kingsley Williams, have been in constant use. Since its publication, I have consistently consulted *The Authentic New Testament,* translated by Hugh J. Schonfield.

I cannot see another edition of these books going out to the public without expressing my very deep and sincere gratitude to the Church of Scotland Publications Committee for allowing me the privilege of first beginning, and then continuing, this series. And in particular I wish to express my very great gratitude to the convener, Rev. R. G. Macdonald, O.B.E., M.A., D.D., and to the committee's secretary and manager, Rev. Andrew McCosh, M.A., S.T.M., for constant encouragement and never-failing sympathy and help.

As these volumes went on, the idea of the whole series developed. The aim is to make the results of modern scholarship available to the non-technical reader in a form that it does not require a theological education to understand; and then to seek to make the teaching of the New Testament books relevant to life and work to-day. The whole aim of these books is summed up in Richard of Chichester's famous prayer; they are meant to enable men and women to know Jesus Christ more clearly, to love Him more dearly, and to follow Him more nearly. It is my prayer that they may do something to make that possible.

FOREWORD

ANYONE who writes a book like this has necessarily many debts. The commentaries on *Luke* by Alfred Plummer, in the International Critical Commentary, and by J. M. Creed in the Macmillan Commentary, have been constantly beside me. These are commentaries on the Greek text. The commentaries on the English text by H. Balmforth, in the Clarendon Bible, and by W. Manson, in the Moffatt Commentary, have been in constant use.

It is my hope and my prayer that something of the loveliness of what is to many the loveliest of all the gospels may shine through this book.

WILLIAM BARCLAY

TRINITY COLLEGE, GLASGOW
November, 1955

CONTENTS

THE GOSPEL OF LUKE

CONTENTS

THE GOSPEL OF LUKE

CONTENTS

THE GOSPEL OF LUKE

CONTENTS

INTRODUCTION

A lovely Book and its Author

The gospel according to St. Luke has been called the loveliest book in the world. Once an American asked Denney if he could recommend a good life of Christ, and Denney answered, " Have you tried the one that Luke wrote? " There is a legend that Luke was a skilled painter; there is even a painting of Mary in a Spanish cathedral to this day which purports to be by him. Certainly he had an eye for vivid things. It would not be far wrong to say that the third gospel is the best life of Christ ever written. Tradition has always believed that Luke was the author and we need have no qualms in accepting tradition in this case. In the ancient world it was the regular thing to attach books to famous names; no one thought it wrong. But Luke was never one of the famous figures of the early Church. If he had not written the gospel very certainly no one would have attached it to his name. Luke was a Gentile; and he has the unique distinction of being the only New Testament writer who was not a Jew. He was a doctor to profession (Colossians 4: 14) and maybe that very fact gave him the wide sympathy that he possessed. It has been said that a minister sees men at their best; a lawyer sees men at their worst; and a doctor sees men as they are. Luke saw men and loved them all. The book was written to a man called Theophilus. He is called *most excellent Theophilus* and the title given to him is the normal title for a high official in the Roman government. No doubt Luke wrote it to tell an earnest inquirer more about Jesus; and he succeeded in giving Theophilus a picture which must have thirled his heart even closer to the Jesus of whom he had heard.

The Symbols of the Gospels

Every one of the four gospels was written from a certain point of view. Very often on stained glass windows the writers of the gospels are pictured; and usually to each of them there is attached a symbol. The symbols vary but one of the commonest allocations of them is this. The emblem of *Mark* is a *man*. Mark is the simplest and the most straightforward of the gospels. It has been well said that its characteristic is *realism*. It is the nearest to being a report of Jesus' life. The emblem of *Matthew* is a *lion*. Matthew was a Jew writing for Jews and he saw in Jesus the Messiah, the Lion of the tribe of Judah, the one whom all the prophets had predicted. The emblem of *John* is the *eagle*. The eagle can fly higher than any other bird. It is said that of all creatures only the eagle can look straight into the sun. John is the theological gospel; its flights of thought are higher than those of any of the others. It is the gospel where the philosopher can find themes to think about for a lifetime and to solve only in eternity. But the symbol of *Luke* is the *calf*. The calf is the animal for sacrifice; and Luke saw in Jesus the sacrifice for all the world. In Luke above all the barriers are broken down and Jesus is for Jew and Gentile, saint and sinner alike. He is the Saviour of the World. Keeping that in mind, let us now set down the characteristics of Luke's gospel.

An Historian's Care

First and foremost, Luke's gospel is an exceedingly careful bit of work. His Greek is notably good. The first four verses are well-nigh the best Greek in the New Testament. In these verses he claims that his work is the product of the most careful research. His opportunities were ample and his sources must have been good. As the trusted companion of Paul he must have known all the great figures of the Church, and we may be sure that he made them tell their story to him. For two years he was Paul's companion in imprisonment in Caesarea. In the long days Luke had every opportunity for study and research and he must have used them well. An example of Luke's care is the way in which he dates the emergence of John the

Baptist. He dates it by no fewer than six contemporary datings. " Now in the fifteenth year of Tiberius Caesar (1), Pontius Pilate being governor of Judaea (2), Herod being tetrarch of Galilee (3), and his brother Philip being tetrarch of Ituraea and of the regions of Trachonitis (4), and Lysanias the tetrarch of Abilene (5), Annas and Caiaphas being the high priests (6), the word of God came unto John " (Luke 3: 1, 2). Here is a man who is writing with care and who will be as accurate as it is possible for him to be.

The Gospel for the Gentiles

It is clear that Luke wrote mainly for Gentiles. Theophilus was a Gentile, as was Luke himself, and there is nothing in the gospel that a Gentile could not grasp and understand. (*a*) As we have seen Luke begins his dating from the reigning *Roman* Emperor and the current *Roman* governor. The *Roman* date comes first. (*b*) Unlike Matthew, he is not greatly interested in the life of Jesus as the fulfilment of Jewish prophecy. (*c*) He very seldom quotes the Old Testament at all. (*d*) He has a habit of giving Hebrew words in their Greek equivalent so that a Greek would understand. Simon the *Cananaean* becomes Simon the *Zealot*. (cp. Luke 6: 15 and Matthew 10: 4, where *Canaanite* should be *Cananaean*). In Luke *Calvary* is called not by its Hebrew name, *Golgotha*, but by its Greek name, *Kranion*. Both mean *the place of a skull*. He never uses the Jewish term *Rabbi* of Jesus but always a Greek term meaning *Master*. When he is tracing the descent of Jesus, he traces it not to Abraham, the founder of the Jewish race, as Matthew does, but to Adam, the founder of the human race. (cp. Matthew 1: 2 and Luke 3: 38). It is just because of this that Luke is the easiest of all the gospels to read. He was writing, not for Jews, but for people very like ourselves.

The Gospel of Prayer

Luke's gospel is specially the gospel of prayer. At all

the great moments of His life, Luke shows us Jesus at prayer. Jesus prayed at His Baptism (3: 2); before His first collision with the Pharisees (5: 16); before He chooses the Twelve (6: 12); before He questions His disciples as to who they think He is and before His first prediction of His own death (9: 18); at the Transfiguration (9: 29); and upon the Cross (23: 40). Only Luke tells us that Jesus prayed for Peter in his hour of testing (22: 32). Only he tells us the prayer parables of the Friend at Midnight (11: 5-13) and the Unjust Judge (18: 1-8). To Luke the unclosed door of prayer was one of the most precious doors in all the world.

The Gospel of Women

In Palestine the place of women was low. In the Jewish morning prayer a man thanks God that God has not made him " a Gentile, a slave or a woman." But Luke in his gospel gives a very special place to women. The Birth narrative is told from Mary's point of view. It is in Luke that we read of Elizabeth, of Anna, of the widow at Nain, of the woman who anointed Jesus' feet in the house of Simon the Pharisee. It is Luke who makes vivid the picture of Martha and of Mary, and of Mary Magdalene. It is very likely that Luke was a native of Macedonia. In Macedonia women held a more emancipated position than anywhere else, and that may have something to do with it.

The Gospel of Praise

In the gospel of Luke the phrase *praising God* occurs oftener than in all the rest of the New Testament put together. This praise reaches its peak in the three great hymns that the Church has sung throughout all her generations—*The Magnificat* (1: 46-55); the *Benedictus* (1: 68-79); and the *Nunc Dimittis* (2: 29-32). There is a radiance in Luke's gospel which is a lovely thing, as if the sheen of heaven had touched the things of earth.

The Universal Gospel

But the outstanding characteristic of Luke is that his is the universal gospel. All the barriers are down; Jesus Christ is for all men without distinction. (a) The Kingdom of Heaven is not shut to the Samaritans (Luke 9: 51-56). Luke alone tells the parable of the Good Samaritan (10: 30-37). The one grateful leper was a Samaritan (Luke 17: 11-19). John can record a saying that the Jews have no dealings with the Samaritans (John 4: 9). But Luke refuses to shut the door on any man. (b) Luke shows Jesus speaking with approval of Gentiles whom the orthodox Jew would have considered unclean. He shows us Jesus citing the widow of Sarepta and Naaman the Syrian as shining examples (4: 25-27). The Roman centurion is praised for the greatness of his faith (7: 9). Luke tells us of that great word of Jesus, " They shall come from the east and from the west and from the north and from the south, and shall sit down in the Kingdom of God " (13: 29). (c) Luke is supremely interested in the poor. When Mary brought her offering for her purification it was the offering of the poor (2: 24). When Jesus is, as it were, setting out His credentials to the emissaries of John, the climax is, " The poor have the gospel preached to them " (7: 22). He alone tells the Parable of the Rich Man and the Poor Man (16: 19-31). In Luke's account of the Beatitudes the saying of Jesus runs, not, as in Matthew (5: 3), " Blessed are the poor in spirit," but simply, " Blessed are ye poor " (Luke 6: 20). Luke's gospel has been called " the gospel of the underdog." His heart ran out to everyone for whom life was an unequal struggle. (d) But above all Luke shows Jesus as the friend of outcasts and sinners. He alone tells the story of the woman who anointed Jesus' feet and bathed them with her tears and wiped them with her hair in the house of Simon the Pharisee (7: 36-50); of Zacchaeus, the quisling tax-gatherer (19: 1-10); the parable of the Pharisee and the Tax-gatherer (18: 9-14). Luke alone tells the story of the Penitent Thief

(23: 43); and Luke alone has the immortal story of the Prodigal Son and the Loving Father (15: 11-32). When Matthew tells how Jesus sent His disciples out to preach, he says that Jesus told them not to go to the Samaritans or the Gentiles (Matthew 10: 5); but Luke omits that altogether. All the four gospel writers quote from Isaiah 40 when they give the message of John the Baptist, " Prepare ye the way of the Lord; make straight in the desert a highway for our God "; but only Luke continues the quotation to its triumphant conclusion, " And all flesh shall see the salvation of God " (Isaiah 40: 3-5; Matthew 3: 3; Mark 1: 3; John 1: 23; Luke 3: 4). Luke of all the gospel writers saw no limits to the love of God.

The Book Beautiful

As we study this book we must look for these characteristics. Somehow of all the gospel writers one would have liked to meet Luke best of all, for this Gentile doctor who had the tremendous vision of the infinite sweep of the love of God must have been a lovely soul. Faber wrote the lines,

> There's a wideness in God's mercy,
>   Like the wideness of the sea;
> There's a kindness in His justice,
>   Which is more than liberty.
>
> For the love of God is broader
>   Than the measures of man's mind;
> And the heart of the Eternal
>   Is most wonderfully kind.

And Luke's gospel is the demonstration that that is true.

ST. LUKE

AN HISTORIAN'S INTRODUCTION

Luke I: I-4

> Since many have set their hands to the task of drawing
> up an account of the events which were completed
> amongst us, telling the story just as those who were
> the original eye-witnesses and who became the servants
> of the word handed it down to us, I too made up my
> mind to carry out a careful investigation of all things
> from the beginning, and to write to you, Theophilus,
> your excellency, an orderly account of them, so that
> you might have in your mind a full and reliable account
> of the things in which you have been instructed.

LUKE'S introduction is unique in the first three gospels
because it is the only place in them where the author
steps out upon the stage and when the writer uses the
pronoun " I." There are three things to note in this passage.
(i) It is the best bit of Greek in the New Testament.
Luke uses here the very form of introduction which the
great Greek historians all used. Herodotus, the famous
writer of Greek history, begins, " These are the researches
of Herodotus of Halicarnassus." A much later historian,
Dionysius of Halicarnassus, tells us at the beginning of his
history, " Before beginning to write I gathered information,
partly from the lips of the most learned men with whom
I came into contact, and partly from histories written by
Romans of whom they spoke with praise." So Luke, as
he began his gospel story, in the most sonorous Greek
followed the highest models he could find. It is as if Luke
said to himself, " I am writing the greatest story in the
world, and nothing but the best is good enough for that
story." Some of the ancient manuscripts are very beautiful
productions, written in silver ink on purple vellum; and
often the scribe, when he came to the name of God or of
Jesus, wrote it in gold. Dr. Boreham tells of an old workman
who, every Friday night, took the newest and the shiniest

coins out of his pay packet for Sunday's offering in Church. The historian, the scribe and the workman were all filled with the same idea—only the best is good enough for Jesus. They would always give their utmost for the highest. (ii) It is a most significant thing that Luke was not satisfied with anyone else's story of Christ He must have his own. Real religion is never a second hand thing, a carried story, a repeated tale. It is a personal discovery. Dr. Gossip used to say that the four gospels are important, but beyond them all comes the gospel of personal experience. Luke had to rediscover Jesus Christ for himself. (iii) There is no passage of the Bible which sheds such a flood light on the doctrine of the inspiration of scripture. No one will deny that the gospel of Luke is an inspired document; and yet Luke begins by affirming that it is the product of the most careful historical research. God's inspiration does not come to the man who sits with folded hands and lazy mind and only waits, but to the mind which thinks and seeks and searches. True inspiration comes when the seeking mind of man meets the revealing Spirit of God. The word of God is given, but it is given to the man who is seeking for it. " Seek and ye shall find."

A SON IS PROMISED

Luke I: 5-25

In the time of Herod, the king of Judaea, there was a priest called Zacharias, who belonged to the section of Abia. His wife was also a direct descendant of Aaron and her name was Elizabeth. Both of them were good people before God, for they walked blamelessly in all the commandments and ordinances of the Lord. They had no child because Elizabeth was barren and both of them were far advanced in years. When he was acting as priest before God, when his section was on duty, in accordance with the custom of priestly duty, it fell to him by lot to go into the Temple of the Lord to burn the incense. The whole congregation

of the people was praying outside at the hour when
incense was offered. The angel of the Lord appeared
to him, standing at the right side of the altar of incense.
When Zacharias saw him he was deeply moved and
awe fell upon him. The angel said to him, " Do not be
afraid, Zacharias, because your request has been heard
and your wife Elizabeth will bear you a son and you
must call him by the name of John. You will have
joy and exultation and many will rejoice at his birth.
He will be great in God's sight; he must not drink
wine or strong drink and, even from the time he is in
his mother's womb, he will be filled with the Holy
Spirit. He will turn many sons of Israel to the Lord
their God; and he himself will go before His face in
the spirit and the power of Elijah, to turn the hearts
of the fathers to the children, and the disobedient
to the wisdom of the just, to get ready a people
prepared for the Lord." Zacharias said to the angel,
" How will I know that this is going to happen?
For I am an old man and my wife is far advanced in
years." " I am Gabriel," the angel answered, " who
stands before God, and I have been sent to speak to
you and to tell you this good news. And—look you—
you will be silent and unable to speak until the day
these things happen, because you did not believe my
words which will be fulfilled in their own time."
The people were waiting for Zacharias and they were
surprised that he was lingering so long in the Temple.
When he came out he was not able to speak to them
and they realized that he had seen a vision in the
Temple. He kept making signs to them but he remained
unable to speak. When the days of his time of service
were completed he went away to his own home. After
these days Elizabeth his wife conceived; and she
hid herself for five months. " This is God's doing
for me," she said, " when He looked upon me to take
away my shame among men."

ZACHARIAS, the central character in this scene, was a
priest. He belonged to the section of Abia. Every direct
descendant of Aaron was automatically a priest. That
meant that for all ordinary purposes, there were far too
many priests. They were therefore divided into twenty-
four sections. Only at the Passover, at Pentecost and at
the Feast of Tabernacles did all the priests serve. For the

3

rest of the year each course served one week twice a year.
Priests who loved their work looked forward to that week
of service above all things; it was the high-light of their
lives. A priest might only marry a woman of absolutely
pure Jewish lineage. It was specially meritorious to marry
a woman who was also a descendant of Aaron, as Elizabeth,
the wife of Zacharias, was. There were as many as twenty
thousand priests altogether and so there were not far short
of a thousand in each section. So within the sections all
the duties were allocated by lot. Every morning and
evening, sacrifice was made for the whole nation. A burnt
offering of a male lamb, one year old, without spot or
blemish was offered, together with a meat offering of
flour and oil and a drink offering of wine. Before the morning
sacrifice and after the evening sacrifice incense was burned
on the altar of incense so that, as it were, the sacrifices
might go up to God wrapped in an envelope of sweet-
smelling incense. It was quite possible that many a priest
would never have the privilege of burning incense all his
life; but if the lot did fall on any priest that day was the
greatest day in all his life, the day he longed for and dreamed
of. On this day the lot fell on Zacharias and very certainly
he would be thrilled to the core of his being. But in
Zacharias' life there was a tragedy. He and Elizabeth
were childless. The Jewish Rabbis said that seven people
were excommunicated from God and the list began, " A
Jew who has no wife, or a Jew who has a wife and who has no
child." Childlessness was a valid ground for divorce.
Not unnaturally Zacharias, even on his great day, was
thinking of his personal and domestic tragedy and was
praying about it. And then the wondrous vision came and
the glad message that, even when hope was dead, a son
would be born to him. The incense was burned and the
offering made in the inmost court of the Temple, the
Court of the Priests. While the sacrifice was being made,
the congregation thronged the next court, the Court of the
Israelites. It was the privilege of the priest at the evening

sacrifice to come to the rail between the two courts after the incense had been burned to bless the people. And the people marvelled that Zacharias was so long delayed. When he came he could not speak and the people knew that he had seen a vision. So in a wordless daze of joy Zacharias finished his week's duty and went home; and then the message of God came true and Elizabeth knew that she was going to have a child. One thing stands out here. *It was in God's house that God's message came to Zacharias.* We often wish that a message from God would come to us. In Shaw's play, *Saint Joan*, Joan hears the voices from God. The Dauphin is annoyed. " Oh, your voices, your voices," he said, " Why don't your voices come to me ? I am the king not you." " They do come," said Joan, " but you do not hear them. You have not sat in the field in the evening listening for them. When the angelus rings you cross yourself and have done with it, but if you prayed from your heart and listened to the thrilling of the bells in the air after they stopped ringing, you would hear the voices as well as I do." Joan gave herself the chance to hear God's voice. Zacharias was in the Temple waiting on God. God's voice comes to those who listen for it—as Zacharias did—in God's house.

GOD'S MESSAGE TO MARY

Luke I: 26-38

In the sixth month the angel Gabriel was sent from God to a town of Galilee called Nazareth, to a maiden who was betrothed to a man called Joseph, who belonged to the house of David. The maiden's name was Mary. He came in to her and said, " Greetings, most favoured one. The Lord is with you." She was deeply moved at this word and wondered what a greeting like that could mean. The angel said to her, " Do not be afraid, Mary, for you have found favour in God's sight. Look you—you will conceive and you will bear a son and you must call him by the name of Jesus.

5

He will be great and He will be called the Son of the Most High; and the Lord God will give Him the throne of David His father; and He will rule over the house of Jacob forever, and there will be no end to His Kingdom." Mary said to the angel, "How can this be since I do not know a man?" The angel answered, "The Holy Spirit will come upon you and the Spirit of the Most High will overshadow you, and so the child who will be born will be called holy, the Son of God, and—look you—Elizabeth, too, your kinswoman has also conceived in her old age; and this is now the sixth month for her who is called barren, because there is nothing which is impossible with God." Mary said, "I am the Lord's servant. Whatever He says, I accept." And the angel went away from her.

MARY was betrothed to Joseph. Betrothal lasted for a year, and it was quite as binding as marriage. It could only be dissolved by divorce. Should the man to whom a girl was betrothed die, in the eyes of the law she was a widow. In the law there occurs the strange-sounding phrase, "a virgin who is a widow." Once two people were betrothed there was a bond between them which nothing but death could break. Here in this passage we are face to face with one of the great controversial doctrines of the Christian faith—the Virgin Birth. The Church does not insist that we believe in this doctrine. Let us look at the reasons for and against believing in it, and then we may make our own decision. There are two great reasons for accepting it literally. (i) If we read this passage, and still more if we read Matthew 1: 18-25, the literal meaning is that Jesus was to be born of Mary, without a human father. (ii) It is very natural to argue that if Jesus was, as we believe, so very special a person, He would have a special entry into the world. And now let us look at the things which may make us wonder if the story of the Virgin Birth is to be taken as literally as all that. (i) The genealogies of Jesus both in Luke and in Matthew (Luke 3: 23-38; Matthew 1: 1-17) both trace the genealogy of Jesus through *Joseph*, which is strange if Joseph was not His real father.

(ii) When Mary was looking for Jesus on the occasion that He lingered behind in the Temple, she said, " Your father and I have been searching for you and we were very worried " (Luke 2: 48). There the name *father* is very definitely given by Mary to Joseph. (iii) Repeatedly Jesus is referred to as Joseph's son (Matthew 13: 35; John 6: 42). (iv) The rest of the New Testament knows nothing of the Virgin Birth. True, in Galatians 4: 4 Paul speaks of Jesus as " born of a woman." But this is the natural phrase for any mortal man. (cp. Job 14: 1; 15: 14; 25: 4). But let us ask, " If we do not take the story of the Virgin Birth literally, how did it arise? " The Jews had a saying that in the birth of *every* child there are three partners—the father, the mother and the Spirit of God. They believed that no child could ever be born without the Spirit. And it may well be that the New Testament stories of the Birth of Jesus are lovely, poetical ways of saying that, even if He had a human father, the Holy Spirit of God was operative in His Birth in the most unique and special way. In this matter we may make our own decision. It may be that we will desire to cling to the literal doctrine of the Virgin Birth; it may be that we will prefer to think of it as a beautiful way of stressing the presence of the Spirit of God in family life.

Mary's submission is a very lovely thing. " Whatever God says, I accept." Mary had learned to forget the world's commonest prayer—" Thy will be *changed* "—and to pray the world's greatest prayer—" Thy will be *done*."

THE PARADOX OF BLESSEDNESS

Luke 1: 39-45

In those days Mary arose and went eagerly to the hill country, to a city of Judah, and went into the house of Zacharias and greeted Elizabeth. When Elizabeth heard Mary's greeting the babe leaped in her womb and Elizabeth was filled with the Holy Spirit, and she lifted up her voice with a great cry and said, " Blessed are you among women and blessed is the fruit of your womb. Why has this been granted to me—that the mother of my Lord should come to me? For—look you—when the voice of your greeting came to my ears the babe in my womb leaped with exultation. Blessed is she who believed that the things spoken to her from the Lord would find their fulfilment."

THIS whole passage is a kind of lyrical song on the blessedness of Mary. Nowhere can we better see the paradox of blessedness than in the life of Mary. To Mary was granted the blessedness of being the mother of the Son of God. Well might her heart be filled with a wondering, tremulous, amazed joy at so great a privilege. And yet that very blessedness was to be a sword to pierce her heart. That very glory was to break her heart. She was blessed and that very blessedness meant that some day she would see that Son of hers hanging on a cross. To be chosen by God so often means at one and the same time a crown of joy and a cross of sorrow. The piercing truth is that God does not choose a person for ease and comfort and selfish joy but for a great task that will take all that head and heart and hand can bring to it. *God chooses a person to use that person.* When Joan of Arc knew that her time was short she prayed, " I shall only last a year; use me as you can." When that is realized then the sorrows and the hardships that serving God may bring are not matters for lamentation; they are our glory, for all is done and suffered for God. When Richard Cameron was caught by the dragoons they killed him. He had very beautiful hands and they cut off these hands and sent them to his father with a message asking if he recognized them. " They are my son's," he said, " my own dear son's. Good is the will of the Lord who can never wrong me or mine." The tears of life were lit by the sense that this too was in the plan of God. A great Spanish saint prayed for his people, " May God deny

8

you peace and give you glory." A great modern preacher said, "Jesus Christ came not to make life easy but to make men great." It is the paradox of blessedness that it confers on a person at one and the same time the greatest joy in all the world and the greatest task in all the world.

A WONDROUS HYMN

Luke I: 46-56

> And Mary said, "My soul magnifies the Lord, and my spirit has exulted in God, my Saviour, because He looked graciously on the humble estate of His servant. For—look you—from now on all generations shall call me blessed, for the Mighty One has done great things for me and His name is holy. His mercy is from generation to generation to those who fear Him. He demonstrates His power with His arm. He scatters the proud in the plans of their hearts. He casts down the mighty from their seats of power. He exalts the humble. He fills those who are hungry with good things and He sends away empty those who are rich. He has helped Israel, His son, in that He has remembered His mercy—as He said to our fathers that He would—to Abraham and to his descendants forever."

HERE we have a passage which has become one of the great hymns of the Church—the *Magnificat*. It is a passage which is saturated in the Old Testament. It is specially kin to Hannah's song of praise in I Samuel 2: I-IO. It has been said that religion is dope, the opiate of the people; but, as Stanley Jones said, "the *Magnificat* is the most revolutionary document in the world." The *Magnificat* speaks of three of the revolutions of God. (i) *He scatters the proud in the plans of their hearts.* That is a *moral* revolution. Christianity is the death of pride. Why? Because if a man sets his life beside the life of Christ it tears the last vestiges of pride from him. Sometimes something

happens to a man which with a vivid, blinding, revealing
light shames him. O. Henry has a short story like this.
There was a lad who was brought up in a village. In school
he used to sit beside a girl and they were fond of each
other. He went to the city and he fell on evil ways. He
became a pickpocket and a petty thief. One day he had
just snatched an old lady's wallet. It was clever work,
and he was pleased. And then he saw coming down the
street the girl whom he used to know, still sweet with the
radiance of innocence. And suddenly he saw himself for
the cheap, vile thing he was. Burning with shame, he leaned
his head against the cool iron of a lamp standard. " God,"
he said, " I wish I could die." He saw himself. Christ
enables a man to see himself. It is the deathblow to pride.
The moral revolution has begun. (ii) *He casts down the
mighty—he exalts the humble*. That is a *social* revolution.
Christianity puts an end to the world's labels and prestige.
Muretus was a wandering scholar of the middle ages.
He was poor. In an Italian town he took ill and was taken
to a hospital for waifs and strays. The doctors were dis-
cussing his case in Latin, never dreaming he could understand. They suggested that since he was such a worthless
wanderer they might use him for medical experiments.
He looked up and answered them in their own learned
tongue, " Call no man worthless for whom Christ died."
When we have realized what Christ did for all men, it is
no longer possible to speak about a *common* man. The
social grades and ranks are gone. (iii) *He has filled those
who are hungry . . . those who are rich he has sent empty away.*
That is an *economic* revolution. A non-Christian society
is an acquisitive society where each man is out to amass
as much as he can get. A Christian society is a society
where no man dares to have too much while others have
too little, where every man must get only to give away.
There is loveliness in the *Magnificat* but in that loveliness
there is dynamite. Christianity begets a revolution in
each man, and a revolution in the world.

HIS NAME IS JOHN

Luke I: 57-66

> When Elizabeth's time to bear the child was completed
> she brought forth a son. When her neighbours and
> kinsfolk heard that the Lord had shown great mercy
> to her they rejoiced with her. On the eighth day they
> went to circumcise the child and it was their intention
> to call him Zacharias after his father. But his mother
> said, " No; he must be called John." They said to
> her, " There is no one in your connection who is
> called by this name." They asked his father by signs
> by what name he wished him to be called. He asked
> for a writing tablet and wrote, " John is his name."
> Immediately his mouth was opened and his tongue
> was loosed and he kept on praising God. And great
> awe fell upon all the neighbours, and all these events
> were talked about in all the hill country of Judaea;
> and all those who heard them kept them in their
> hearts and said, " What will this child turn out to be,
> for the hand of the Lord is with him? "

IN Palestine the birth of a child was an occasion of great
joy, especially if the child was a boy. When the time of
the birth was near at hand, the friends and the local
musicians gathered near the house. When the birth was
announced, if it was a boy, the musicians broke into music
and song, and there was universal congratulation and
rejoicing. If it was a girl the musicians went silently
and regretfully away! There was a saying, " The birth
of a male child causes universal joy, but the birth of a
female child causes universal sorrow." So in Elizabeth's
house there was a double joy. At last she had a child and
that child was a son. On the eighth day the boy was
circumcised and on that day he received his name. Girls
could be named any time within thirty days of their birth.
In Palestine names were descriptive. They sometimes
described a circumstance attending the birth as *Esau*
and *Jacob* do (Exodus 25: 26). They sometimes describe
the child. *Laban*, for instance, means *white* or *blonde*.
Sometimes the child received the parental name. Often

the name describes the parents' joy. *Saul* and *Samuel*, for instance, both mean *asked for*. Sometimes the name was a declaration of the parents' faith. *Elijah* for instance, means *Jehovah is my* God. Thus in a time of Baal worship Elijah's parents asserted their faith in the true God. Elizabeth, to the neighbours' surprise, said that her son must be called John and Zacharias indicated that that was also his desire. *John* is a shorter form of the name *Jehohanan*, which means *Jehovah's gift* or *God is gracious*. It was the name which God had ordered to be given to the child and it described the parents' gratitude for an all-unexpected joy. It was the question of the neighbours and of all who had heard the amazing story, " What will this child turn out to be? " Every child is a bundle of possibilities. There was an old Latin schoolmaster who always bowed gravely to his class before he taught them. When he was asked why, he answered, " Because you never know what one of these lads will turn out to be." The entry of a child into a family is two things. First, it is the greatest privilege which life can offer a man and a wife. It is something for which to thank God. Second, it is one of life's supreme responsibilities, for that child is a bundle of possibilities, and on parents and teachers depends how these possibilities will or will not be realized.

A FATHER'S JOY

Luke I: 67-80

His father Zacharias was filled with the Holy Spirit and prophesied like this: " Blessed be the Lord, the God of Israel, because He has graciously visited His people and wrought deliverance for them. He has raised the horn of salvation for us in the house of David, His servant—as long ago He said He would through the mouth of His holy prophets—even deliverance from our enemies and from the hand of all who hate us, in that He has shown mercy to us as He did to our fathers and has remembered His holy covenant, the pledge which He gave to Abraham our father, to grant to us that we, being delivered from the hands of our enemies, should fearlessly serve Him, in holiness and righteousness before Him, all our days. And you, child, shall be called the prophet of the Most High; for you will walk before the Lord to prepare His ways, in order to give the knowledge of salvation to His people together with forgiveness of their sins, through the mercy of our God, in which the dawn from on high has graciously visited us, to shine upon those who sit in darkness and in the shadow of death, and to direct our feet in the way of peace."

And the child grew and was strengthened by the Spirit; and he lived in the desert places until the day when he was displayed to Israel.

ZACHARIAS had a great vision for his son. He thought of him as the prophet and the forerunner who would prepare the way of the Lord. All devout Jews hoped and longed for the day when the Messiah, God's Anointed King, would come. Most of them believed that, before He came, a forerunner would come to announce His coming and to prepare His way. The usual belief was that Elijah would return to do so (Malachi 4: 5). Zacharias saw in his son the one who would prepare the way for the coming of God's King. Verses 75-77 give a great picture of the steps of the Christian way. (i) There must be a *preparation*. All life is a preparation to lead us to Christ. When Sir Walter Scott was young his aim was to be a soldier. An accident made him slightly lame and that dream had to be abandoned. He took to reading the old Scottish histories and romances and he so became the master novelist. An old man said of him, " He was makin' himsell a' the time; but he didna ken maybe what he was about till years had passed." In life God is working all things together to bring us to Christ. (ii) There must be *knowledge*. It is the simple fact that men did not know what God was like until Jesus came. The Greeks thought of a passionless God, beyond all joy and sorrow, looking on men in calm unmoved detachment—no help there. The Jews thought of a demanding God, whose name was law and whose function was that of judge—nothing but terror there. Jesus came to tell of a God who was love, and in staggered amazement men could only say, " We never knew that God was like that." One of the great functions of the incarnation is to bring to men the knowledge of God. (iii) There is *forgiveness*. We must be clear about one thing regarding forgiveness. Forgiveness is not so much the remission of penalty as the restoration of a relationship. Nothing can deliver us from certain consequences of our sins; the clock cannot be put back; but the estrangement from God is turned to friendship. The distant God is become near and the God we feared has become the lover of the souls of men. (iv) There is a *new walk in life* in the ways of peace. *Peace* in Hebrew does not mean merely freedom from trouble; it means all that makes for a man's highest good; and through Christ a man is enabled to walk in the ways that lead to everything that means life, and no longer to all that means death.

JOURNEY TO BETHLEHEM

Luke 2: 1-7

In these days a decree went out from Caesar Augustus that a census should be taken of all the world. The census first took place when Quirinius was governor of Syria; and everyone went to enrol himself, each man to his own town. So Joseph went up from Galilee, from the town of Nazareth, to Judaea, to David's town, which is called Bethlehem, because he belonged to the house and the line of David, to enrol himself with Mary who was betrothed to him and she was with child. When they arrived there her time to bear the child was completed; and she bore her first-born son and wrapped him in swaddling clothes and laid him in a manger because there was no room for them in the place where they had meant to lodge.

IN the Roman Empire periodical censuses were taken with the double object of assessing taxation and discovering those who were liable for compulsory military service. The Jews were exempt from military service, and, therefore, in Palestine a census would be predominantly for taxation purposes. Regarding these censuses, we have definite information as to what happened in Egypt; and almost certainly what happened in Egypt happened in Syria too and Judaea was part of the province of Syria. The information we have comes from actual census documents written on papyrus and then discovered in the dust-heaps of Egyptian towns and villages and in the sands of the desert. Such censuses were taken every fourteen years. And from A.D. 20 until about A.D. 270 we possess actual documents from every census taken. If the fourteen year cycle held good in Syria then this census must have been in 8 B.C. and that year was the year in which Jesus was born. It may be that Luke has made one slight mistake. Quirinius did not actually become governor of Syria until A.D. 6; but he held an official post previously in those regions from 10 B.C. until 7 B.C. and it was during that first period that this census must have been taken. Critics used to question the fact that every man had to go to his own city to be enrolled; but here is an actual government edict from Egypt:

> "Gaius Vibius Maximus, Prefect of Egypt orders: 'Seeing that the time has come for the house to house census, it is necessary to compel all those, who for any cause whatsoever are residing outside their districts to return to their own homes, that they may both carry out the regular order of the census, and may also diligently attend to the cultivation of their allotments.'"

If that was the case in Egypt, it may well be that in Judaea, where the old tribal ancestries still held good, men had to go to the headquarters of their tribe. Here is an instance where further knowledge has shown the accuracy of the New Testament.

The journey from Nazareth to Bethlehem was 80 miles in length. The accommodation for travellers was in any case most primitive. The eastern khan was like a series of stalls opening off a common courtyard. Travellers brought their own food; all that the innkeeper provided was fodder for the animals and a fire to cook. The town was crowded and there was no room for Joseph and Mary. So it was in the common courtyard that Mary's child was born. Swaddling clothes were like this—they consisted of a square of cloth with a long, bandage-like strip coming diagonally off from one corner. The child was first wrapped in the square of cloth and then the long strip was wound round and round about him. The word which is translated *manger* means, quite generally, a place where animals feed; and therefore it can be either the stable or the manger which is meant. That there was no room in the inn was symbolic of what was to happen to Jesus. The only place where there was room for Him was on a cross. He sought an entry to the over-crowded hearts of men; He could not find it; and still His search—and His rejection—go on.

SHEPHERDS AND ANGELS

Luke 2: 8-20

In this country there were shepherds who were in the fields, keeping watch over their flock by night. An angel of the Lord appeared to them and the glory of the Lord shone round about them and they were much afraid. The angel said to them, " Do not be afraid; for—look you—I am bringing you good news of great joy, which will be to every people, for to-day a Saviour has been born for you, in David's town, who is Christ the Lord. You will recognize Him by this sign. You will find the Babe wrapped in swaddling clothes and laid in a manger." And suddenly with the angel there was a crowd of heaven's host, praising God and saying, " In the highest heights glory to God; and on earth peace to the men whose welfare He ever seeks." When the angels had left them and gone away to heaven, the shepherds said to each other, " Come! Let us go across to Bethlehem and let us see this thing which has happened which the Lord has made known to us." So they hurried on and they discovered Mary and Joseph, and the Babe lying in a manger. When they had seen Him they told everyone about the word which had been spoken to them about this child; and all who heard were amazed at what was told them by the shepherds. But Mary stored up these things in her memory and in her heart kept wondering what they meant. So the shepherds returned glorifying and praising God for all that they had seen, just as it had been told to them.

IT is a wonderful thing that the story should tell that the first announcement of God should come to the shepherds. The shepherds were despised by the orthodox good people of the day. Shepherds were quite unable to keep the details of the ceremonial law; they could not observe all the meticulous hand-washings and rules and regulations. Their flocks made far too constant demands on them; and so the orthodox looked down on them as very common people. It was to simple men of the fields that God's message first came. But these shepherds were in all likelihood very special shepherds. We have already seen how in the Temple, morning and evening, an unblemished lamb was offered as a sacrifice to God. To see that the supply of perfect and unblemished offerings was always available the Temple authorities had their own private sheep flocks; and we know that these flocks were pastured near Bethlehem. It is most likely that these shepherds were in charge of the flocks from which the Temple offerings were chosen. It is a lovely thought that the shepherds who looked after the Temple lambs were the first to see the Lamb of God who takes away the sin of the world.

We have already seen that when a child was born the local musicians congregated at the house to greet him with simple music. Jesus was born in a stable in Bethlehem and therefore that ceremony could not have been carried out. It is a lovely thought that the minstrelsy of heaven took the place of the minstrels of earth, and angels sang the songs for Jesus that it was impossible for the earthly singers to sing.

All through these readings we must have been thinking of the rough simplicity of the birth of the Son of God. We might have expected that, if the Son of God had to be born into this world at all, it would be in a palace or a mansion. There was a European monarch who worried his court by often disappearing and walking incognito amongst his people. When he was asked not to do so for security's sake, he answered, " I cannot rule my people unless I know how they live." It is the great thought of the Christian faith that we have a God who knows this life we live because He too lived it, and claimed no special advantage over common men.

THE ANCIENT CEREMONIES ARE OBSERVED

Luke 2: 21-24

> When the eight days necessarily prior to circumcision had elapsed, He was called by the name of Jesus, the name by which He had been called by the angel before He had been conceived in the womb. When the time which, according to the law of Moses, must precede the ceremony of purification had elapsed, they brought Him up to Jerusalem to present Him to the Lord (in accordance with the regulation in the Lord's law, " Every male creature which opens the womb must be called sacred to the Lord ") and to make the sacrifice which the regulation in the Lord's law lays down, that is, a pair of doves or two young pigeons.

IN this passage we see Jesus undergoing three ancient ceremonies which every Jewish boy had to undergo. (i) *Circumcision.* Every Jewish boy was circumcised on the eighth day after his birth. So sacred was that ceremony that it could be carried out even on a Sabbath when the law forbade almost every act which was not absolutely essential; and, as we have seen, on that day a boy received his name. (ii) *The Redemption of the First-born.* According to the law (Exodus 3: 2) every firstborn male, both of human beings and of cattle, was sacred to God. That law may have been a recognition of the gracious power of God in giving human life, or it may even have been a relic of the day when children were sacrificed to the gods. Clearly if it had been carried out literally life would have been disrupted. There was therefore a ceremony called the Redemption of the Firstborn (Numbers 18: 16). It is laid down that for the sum of five shekels—approximately fifteen shillings—parents could, as it were, buy back their son from God. The sum had to be paid to the priests. It could not be paid sooner than thirty-one days after the birth of the child and it might not be long delayed after that. (iii) *The Purification after Childbirth.* When a woman had borne a child, if it was a boy she was unclean for forty days, if it was a girl, for eighty days. She could go about her household and her daily business but she could not enter the Temple or share in any religious ceremony (Leviticus 12). At the end of that time she had to bring to the Temple a lamb for a burnt offering and a young pigeon for a sin offering. That was a somewhat expensive sacrifice, and so the law laid it down (Leviticus 12: 8) that if she could not afford the lamb she might bring another pigeon. The offering of the two pigeons instead of the lamb and the pigeon was technically called *The Offering of the Poor.* It was the offering of the poor which Mary brought. Again we see that it was into an ordinary home that Jesus was born, a home where there were no luxuries, a home where every penny had to be looked at twice, a home where the members of the family knew all about the difficulties of making a living and the haunting insecurity of life. When life is worrying for us we must remember that Jesus knew what the difficulties of making ends meet can be.

These three ceremonies are strange old ceremonies; but all three have at the back of them the conviction that a child is a gift of God. The Stoics used to say that a child was not *given* to a parent but only *lent* by God. Of all God's gifts there is none for which we shall be so answerable as the gift of a child.

A DREAM REALIZED

Luke 2: 25-35

> Now—look you—there was a man in Jerusalem called Simeon. This man was good and pious. He was waiting for the comforting of Israel and the Holy Spirit was upon him. He had received a message from the Holy Spirit that he would not see death until he had seen the Lord's Anointed One. So he came in the Spirit to the Temple precincts. When His parents brought in the child Jesus, to do regarding Him the customary ceremonies laid down by the law, he took Him into his arms and blessed God and said, " Now, O Lord, as you said, let your servant depart in peace, because my eyes have seen your instrument of salvation, which you have prepared before all the people, a light to bring your revelation to the Gentiles, and the glory of your people Israel." His father and mother were amazed at what was said about Him. Simeon blessed them and said to Mary His mother, " Look you, this child is appointed to be the cause whereby many in Israel will fall and many rise and for a sign which will meet with much opposition. As for you— a sword will pierce your soul—and all this will happen that the inner thoughts of many hearts may be revealed."

THERE was no Jew who did not regard his own nation as the chosen people. But the Jews saw quite clearly that by human means their nation could never attain to the supreme world greatness which they believed that their destiny involved. By far the greater number of them believed that because the Jews were the chosen people they were bound some day to become masters of the world and lords of all the nation. To bring in that day some believed that some great, celestial champion would descend upon the earth; some believed that there would arise another king of David's line and that all the old glories would revive; some believed that God Himself would break directly into history by supernatural means. But in contrast to all that there were some few people who were known as *the Quiet in the Land*. They had no dreams of violence and of power and of armies with banners; they believed in a life of constant prayer and quiet watchfulness until God should come. All their lives they waited quietly and patiently upon God. Simeon was like that; in prayer, in worship, in humble and faithful expectation he was waiting for the day when God would comfort His people. God had promised to him through the Holy Spirit that life would not end for him before he had seen God's own Anointed King. In the baby Jesus he recognized that King and he was glad. Now he was ready to depart in peace and his words have become the *Nunc Dimittis*, another of the great and precious hymns of the Church.

In verse 34 Simeon gives a kind of summary of the work and fate of Jesus. (i) Jesus will be the cause whereby *many will fall*. This is a strange and a hard saying but it is true. It is not so much God who judges a man; a man judges himself; and his judgment is his reaction to Jesus Christ. If, when he is confronted with that goodness and that loveliness, his heart runs out in answering love he is within the Kingdom. If, when so confronted, he remains coldly unmoved or actively hostile, he is condemned. There is a great refusal just as there is a great acceptance. (ii) Jesus will be the cause whereby *many will rise*. Long ago Seneca said that what men needed above all was a hand let down to lift them up. It is the hand of Jesus which lifts a man out of the old life and into the new, out of the sin into the goodness, out of the shame into the glory. (iii) Jesus would meet with *much opposition*. Towards Jesus Christ there can be no neutrality. We either surrender to Him or are at war with Him. And it is the tragedy of life that the pride of man keeps us from making that surrender wherein is victory.

A LOVELY OLD AGE

Luke 2: 36-40

> There was a prophetess called Anna. She was the daughter of Phanuel and she belonged to the tribe of Asher. She was far advanced in years. She had lived with her husband ever since seven years after she came to womanhood; and now she was a widow of eighty-four years of age. She never left the Temple and day and night she worshipped with fastings and with prayers. At that very time she came up and she began to give thanks to God and she kept speaking about Him to all those who were waiting expectantly for the deliverance of Jerusalem. When they had completed everything which the Lord's law lays down they returned to Galilee to their own town of Nazareth. And the child grew bigger and stronger and He was filled with wisdom, and God's grace was on Him.

ANNA, too, was one of the Quiet in the Land. We know nothing about her except what these verses tell but even in this brief compass Luke has drawn us a complete character sketch. (i) Anna was a widow. *She had known sorrow and she had not grown bitter.* Sorrow can do one of two things to us. It can make us hard, bitter, resentful, rebellious against God. Or, it can make us kinder, softer, more sympathetic. It can despoil us of our faith. Or, it can root faith ever deeper and more immovable. It all depends how we think of God. If we think of God as a tyrant we will resent God. If we think of God as Father we too will be sure that

> A Father's hand will never cause
> His child a needless tear.

(ii) She was eighty-four years of age. *She was old and she had never ceased to hope.* Age can take away the bloom and the strength of our bodies; but age can do worse—the years can take away the life of our hearts until the hopes that once we cherished die and we become dully contented and grimly resigned to things as they are. Again it all depends on how we think of God. If we think of God as

distant and remote and detached we may well despair;
but if we think of God as intimately connected with life,
as having His hand on the helm of life we too will be sure
that the best is yet to be, and the years will never kill
our hope. How then was Anna such as she was? (i) *She
never ceased to worship*. She spent her life in God's house
with God's people. God gave us His Church to be our
mother in the faith. We rob ourselves of a priceless treasure
when we neglect to be one with God's worshipping people.
(ii) *She never ceased to pray*. Public worship is great;
but private worship is also great. As someone has truly
said, " They pray best together who first pray alone."
The years had left Anna without bitterness and in unshak-
able hope because day by day she kept her contact with
Him who is the source of strength and in whose strength
our weakness is made perfect.

THE DAWNING REALIZATION

Luke 2: 41-52

Every year His parents used to go to Jerusalem for
the feast of the Passover. When He was twelve years
of age, when they went up according to the custom
of the feast, and when they had completed the days
of the feast, when they returned home the child Jesus
stayed on in Jerusalem. His parents were not aware
of this. They thought He was in the caravan and when
they had gone a day's journey they looked for Him
amongst their kinsfolk and acquaintances. When
they did not find Him they turned back to Jerusalem,
looking for Him all the time. After three days they
found Him in the Temple precincts, sitting in the
middle of the Rabbis, listening to them and asking
them questions. All who were listening were astonished
at His understanding and at His answers. When
they saw Him they were amazed. His mother said
to Him, " Child, why did you do this to us? Look
you, your father and I have been looking for you and
we have been very worried." He said to them, " Why
were you looking for me? Did you not know that I
was bound to be in my Father's house?" They did

not understand the meaning of what He said to them. So He came home with them and went to Nazareth and He was obedient to them. His mother kept all these things in her heart. And Jesus grew wise and grew bigger and increased in favour with God and man.

THIS is one of the supremely important passages in the gospel story. It was laid down by law that every adult male Jew who lived within twenty miles of Jerusalem must attend the Passover. In point of fact it was the aim of every Jew in all the world at least once in a lifetime to attend that feast. A Jewish boy became a man when he was twelve years of age. Then he became *a son of the law* and had to take the obligations of the law upon him. So at twelve Jesus for the first time went to the Passover. We may well imagine how the holy city and the Temple and the sacred ritual fascinated Him. When His parents returned He lingered behind. It was not through carelessness that they did not miss Him. Usually the women in a caravan started out much earlier than the men for they travelled more slowly. The men started later and travelled faster and the two sections would not meet until the evening encampment was reached. It was Jesus' first Passover. No doubt Joseph thought He was with Mary and Mary thought that He was with Joseph and not till the evening camp did they miss Him. They returned to Jerusalem to search for Him. For the Passover season it was the custom for the Sanhedrin to meet in public in the Temple court to discuss, in the presence of all who would listen, religious and theological questions. It was there that they found Jesus. We must not think of it as a scene where a precocious boy was dominating a crowd of his seniors. *Hearing and asking questions* is the regular Jewish phrase for a student learning from his teachers. Jesus was listening to the discussions and eagerly searching for knowledge like an avid student. And now there comes one of the key passages in the life of Jesus. " *Your father* and I," said Mary, " have been searching for you." " Did you not realize," said Jesus, " that you would find me in *my Father's* house "?

See how very gently but very definitely Jesus takes the name *father* from Joseph and gives it to God. At some time Jesus must have discovered His own unique relationship to God. He cannot have known it when He was a child in the manger and a baby at His mother's breast or He would be a monstrosity and an abnormality. As the years went on He must have thought; and then at this first Passover, with manhood dawning on Him, there came in a sudden blaze of realization the consciousness that He was not as other men are, that in a unique and special sense He was the Son of God. Here we have the story of the day when Jesus discovered who He was. And mark one thing—the discovery did not make Him proud. It did not make Him look down on His humble parents, the gentle Mary and the hard-working Joseph. He went home and *He was obedient to them.* The very fact that He was God's Son made Him the perfect son of His human parents. The real man of God does not despise earthly ties; just because he is God's man he discharges human duties with supreme fidelity.

THE COURIER OF THE KING

Luke 3: 1-6

In the fifteenth year of the reign of Tiberius Caesar, when Pontius Pilate was governor of Judaea, and when Herod was tetrarch of Galilee, his brother Philip, tetrarch of Ituraea and the district of Trachonitis, and Lysanias, tetrarch of Abilene, in the high-priesthood of Annas and Caiaphas, the word of God came to John, the son of Zacharias, when he was in the desert. So he came into the territory around Jordan, preaching a baptism of repentance whereby sins might be forgiven—as it stands written in the book of the words Isaiah, the prophet, " The voice of one crying in the wilderness, ' Get ready the road of the Lord, make His paths straight; every ravine shall be filled up; every mountain and hill will be made low; the twisted places will be made into straight roads and the rough places into smooth; and all flesh shall see God's instrument of salvation.' "

To Luke the emergence of John the Baptist was one of the hinges on which history turned. So much so is that the case that he dates it in no fewer than six different ways. (i) Tiberius was the successor of Augustus and therefore the second of the Roman Emperors. As early as A.D. 11 or 12 Augustus had made him his colleague in the imperial power but he did not become sole emperor until A.D. 14. The fifteenth year of his reign would therefore be A.D. 28-29. Luke then begins by setting the emergence of John against a world background, the background of the Roman Empire. (ii) The next three dates Luke gives are connected with the political organisation of Palestine. The title tetrarch literally means *governor of a fourth part*. In such provinces as Thessaly and Galatia, which were divided into four sections or areas, the governor of each part was known as a *tetrarch*; but later the word widened its meaning and came to mean the governor of any part. Herod the Great died in 4 B.C. after a reign of about forty years. He divided his kingdom between three of his sons and in the first instance the Romans approved the decision. (a) To Herod Antipas he left Galilee and Peraea. He reigned from 4 B.C. to A.D. 39 and therefore Jesus' life was lived in Herod's reign and very largely in Herod's dominions in Galilee. (b) To Herod Philip he left Ituraea and Trachonitis. He reigned from 4 B.C. to A.D. 33. Caesarea Philippi was called after him and was actually built by him. (c) To Archelaus he left Judaea, Samaria and Edom. He was a thoroughly bad king. The Jews in the end actually petitioned Rome for his removal; and Rome, impatient of the continual troubles in Judaea, installed a procurator or Roman governor. That is how the Romans came directly to rule Judaea. At this time Pilate, who was in power from A.D. 25 until A.D. 37, was the Roman governor. So in this one sentence Luke gives us a panoramic view of the division of the Kingdom which had once belonged to Herod the Great. (iii) Of Lysanias we know practically nothing. (iv) Having dealt with the world situation and the

Palestinian political situation, Luke turns to the religious situation and he dates John's emergence as being in the priesthood of Annas and Caiaphas. There never at any time were two high-priests at the one time. What then does Luke mean by giving these two names? The high-priest was at one and the same time the civil and the religious head of the community. In the old days the office of high-priest had been hereditary and for life. But with the coming of the Romans the office was the object of all kinds of intrigue. The result was that between 37 B.C. and A.D. 26 there were no fewer than twenty-eight different high-priests. Now Annas was actually high-priest from A.D. 7 until A.D. 14. He was therefore at this time out of office; but he was succeeded by no fewer than four of his sons and Caiaphas was his son-in-law. Therefore, although Caiaphas was the reigning high-priest, Annas was the power behind the throne. That is in fact why Jesus was brought first to him after His arrest (John 18:13) although at that time he was not in office at all. Luke associates his name with Caiaphas because, although Caiaphas was actually high-priest, Annas was still the most influential priestly figure in the land.

Verses 4-6 are a quotation from Isaiah 40:3-5. When a king proposed to tour a part of his dominions in the east, he sent a courier before him to tell the people to prepare the roads. During the Coronation Service in Westminster Abbey there happened a kind of modern parallel to this. When all the congregation was seated, a squad of cleaners unexpectedly emerged with brushes and vacuum cleaners and proceeded to sweep the carpets so that they would be absolutely clean for the coming of the Queen. So John is regarded as the courier of the King. But the preparation on which he insisted was a preparation of the heart and of the life. " The King is coming," he said. " Mend, not your roads, but your lives." There is laid on everyone of us the perennial duty of seeking to make life fit for the King to see.

JOHN'S SUMMONS TO REPENTANCE

Luke 3: 7-18

> To the crowds who came out to be baptized by him, John used to say, " You spawn of vipers, who put it into your heads to flee from the coming wrath? Produce fruits to match repentance. Do not begin to say among yourselves, ' We have Abraham as our father.' I tell you that God is able to raise up children to Abraham from these stones. Even now the axe is laid at the root of the trees. Every tree that does not bear good fruit is cut down and thrown into the fire." The crowds asked him, " What are we to do? " He answered them, " Let him who has two robes give one to one who has none and let him who has food do likewise." The tax-collectors came to be baptized and said to him, " Teacher, what are we to do? " He said to them, " Exact no more beyond what your instructions lay down." The soldiers, too, asked him, " What are we to do? " He said to them, " Treat no man with violence and do not play the false informer and be content with your pay."
>
> When the people were in a state of expectancy and when they were all wondering in their hearts about John, as to whether he could be the Anointed One, John answered them all, " I baptize you with water, but the One who is stronger than I is coming, the latchet of whose sandals I am not worthy to unloose. He will baptize you with the Holy Spirit and with fire. His winnowing fan is in His hand to cleanse His threshing floor and He will gather the corn into His store but He will burn the chaff with unquenchable fire."

HERE we have the message of John to the people. Nowhere does the difference between John and Jesus stand out so clearly because, whatever the message of John was it was not a gospel. It was not good news; it was news of terror. John had lived in the desert. The face of the desert was covered with stubble and brushwood, as dry as tinder. Sometimes a spark set the face of the desert alight and out from their crannies came the vipers and the snakes, scurrying in terror from the menacing flames. It was to them that John likened the people who came to

28

be baptized. The Jews had not the slightest doubt that in God's economy there was a most favoured nation clause. They held that God would judge the nations with one standard but the Jews with another. They, in fact, held that a man was safe from judgment simply in virtue of the fact that he was a Jew. A son of Abraham was exempt from judgment. John told them that racial privilege meant nothing; that life not lineage was God's standard of judgment. There are three outstanding things about John's message. (i) It began by demanding that men should share with one another. It was a social gospel which laid it down that God will never absolve the man who is content to have too much while others have too little. (ii) It ordered a man, not to leave his job, but to work out his own salvation by doing that job as it should be done. Let the tax-collector be a good tax-collector; let the soldier be a good soldier. It was a man's duty to serve God where God had set him. There is a negro spiritual like this:

> There's a king and captain high,
> And he's coming by and by,
> And he'll find me hoeing cotton when he comes.
> You can hear his legions charging in the regions of the sky,
> And he'll find me hoeing cotton when he comes.
> There's a man they thrust aside,
> Who was tortured till he died,
> And he'll find me hoeing cotton when he comes.
>
> He was hated and rejected,
> He was scorned and crucified,
> And he'll find me hoeing cotton when he comes.
> When he comes ! when he comes !
> He'll be crowned by saints and angels when he comes,
> They'll be shouting out Hosanna ! to the man that men denied,
> And I'll kneel among my cotton when he comes.

It was John's conviction that nowhere can a man serve God better than in his day's work. (iii) John was quite sure that he himself was only the forerunner. The King was still to come and with Him there would come judgment. The winnowing fan was a great flat wooden shovel; with it the grain was tossed into the air; the heavy grain fell to the ground and the chaff was blown away. And just as the chaff was separated from the grain so the King would separate the good and bad. So John painted a picture of judgment, but it was a judgment which a man could meet with confidence if he had discharged his duty to his neighbour and if he had faithfully done his day's work.

John was one of the world's supremely effective preachers. Once Chalmers was congratulated on a sermon. " Yes," he said, " *but what did it do?* " It is clear that John preached for action and produced action. He did not deal in theological subtleties but in life.

THE ARREST OF JOHN

Luke 3: 19, 20

So then, urging the people with many other pleas, John preached the gospel to them. But, when Herod the tetrarch was rebuked by him concerning the matter of Herodias, his brother's wife, and concerning all the other wicked things he had done, he added this also to them all—he shut up John in prison.

JOHN was so plain and blunt a preacher of righteousness that he was bound to run into trouble. In the end Herod arrested him. Josephus, the Jewish historian, says that the reason of the arrest was that Herod " feared lest the great influence John had over the people might put it in his power and inclination to raise a rebellion; for they seemed ready to do anything he should advise." That is no doubt true but the New Testament writers give a much more personal and immediate cause. Herod Antipas had

30

married Herodias and John rebuked him for it. Now the relationships involved in this marriage are extremely complicated. Herod the Great was a much-married man. Herod Antipas, who married Herodias and who arrested John, was the son of Herod the Great by a woman called Malthake. Herodias herself was the daughter of Aristobulus, who was also the son of Herod the Great by Mariamne, commonly called the Hasmonean. Now, as we have seen, Herod had divided up his realm between Archelaus, Herod Antipas and Herod Philip. He had another son, also called Herod, who was his son by another Mariamne, the daughter of a high priest. This Herod had no share in his father's realms and lived as a private citizen in Rome. This Herod married Herodias. He was in fact her half-uncle, because her father, Aristobulus, and he were both sons of Herod by different wives. Herod Antipas, on a visit to Rome, seduced her from his half-brother and married her. She was at one and the same time his sister-in-law, because she was married to his half-brother, and his niece because she was the daughter of Aristobulus, another half-brother. The whole proceeding was utterly revolting to Jewish opinion and quite contrary to Jewish law, and indeed improper on any standards. It is a dangerous thing to rebuke an eastern tyrant, but John did so. The result was that he was arrested and imprisoned in the dungeon castle of Machaerus on the shores of the Dead Sea. There could be no greater cruelty than to take this child of the desert and shut him up in the confines of a dungeon cell. Ultimately he was beheaded to gratify the resentment of Herodias (Matthew 14: 5-12; Mark 6: 17-29).

It is always a dangerous thing to speak the truth; and yet the man who allies himself with the truth, may for the moment end in gaol or on the scaffold, but in the final count he is the victor. Once the Earl of Morton, who was the regent of Scotland, threatened Andrew Melville, the reformer. " There will never," he said menacingly, " be

quietness in this country till half a dozen of you be hanged
or banished the country." Melville answered him, " Tush!
sir, threaten your courtiers in that fashion. It is the same
to me whether I rot in the air or in the ground . . . God be
glorified, it will not lie in your power to hang nor exile
His truth." Plato once said that the wise man will always
choose to suffer wrong rather than to do wrong. We need
only ask ourselves whether in the last analysis and at the
final assize we would prefer to be Herod Antipas or John
the Baptist.

THE HOUR STRIKES FOR JESUS

Luke 3: 21, 22

> When all the people had been baptized and when
> Jesus too had been baptized, as He was praying, the
> heaven was opened and the Holy Spirit in bodily
> form like a dove came down upon Him and there was a
> voice from heaven, " You are my beloved son; in
> you I am well pleased."

THE thinkers of the Church have always sought an answer
to the problem, " Why did Jesus go to John to be baptized?"
The baptism of John was a baptism of repentance and it is
our conviction that Jesus was without sin. Why then
did He offer Himself for this baptism? In the early Church
it was sometimes suggested, with a homely touch, that
He did it to please Mary, His mother, and in answer to
her entreaties; but we would need a better reason than
that. In the life of every man there are certain definite
stages, certain hinges on which his whole life turns. It
was so in the life of Jesus and, every now and again, we
must stop and try to see the life of Jesus as a whole. The
first great hinge, as we have already seen, was the visit
to the Temple when He was twelve, when He discovered
His unique relationship to God. By the time of the emergence of John Jesus was about thirty (Luke 3: 23). That
is to say at least eighteen years had passed. All through
these years Jesus must have been thinking and realizing

more and more His own uniqueness. But still He remained the village carpenter of Nazareth. He must have known that a day must come when He must say good-bye to Nazareth and go out upon His larger task. He must have waited for some sign that that day had come. Now when John emerged the people flocked out to hear him and to be baptized. That is to say, throughout the whole country there was an unprecedented *movement towards God*. When Jesus saw that He knew that *His hour had struck*. It was not that He was conscious of sin and of the need of repentance. It was that He knew that now He too must identify Himself with this movement towards God. For Jesus the emergence of John was God's call to action; and His first action was to identify Himself with the people in their search for God.

But in Jesus' baptism something happened. Before He could take this tremendous step He had to be sure that He was right; and in the moment of the baptism *God spoke to Him*. Make no mistake, what happened in the baptism was an experience personal to Jesus. The voice of God came to Him and the voice of God told Him that He had taken the right decision. But more—far more—that very same voice of God mapped out all His course for Him. God said to Him, " You are my beloved Son; in you I am well pleased." That saying is composed of two texts. *You are my beloved Son*—that is from Psalm 2: 7 and was always accepted as a description of the Messianic King. *In whom I am well pleased*—that is part of Isaiah 42: 1 and is from a description of the servant of the Lord whose portrait culminates in the sufferings of Isaiah 53. Therefore in His baptism Jesus realized, first, that He was the Messiah, God's Anointed King; and, second, that that involved not power and glory, but suffering and a Cross. The Cross did not come on Jesus unawares; from the first moment of realization He saw that Cross ahead. The baptism shows us Jesus asking for God's approval and receiving the destiny of the Cross.

THE GOSPEL OF LUKE

THE LINEAGE OF JESUS

Luke 3: 23-38

When Jesus began His ministry He was about thirty years of age. He was the son (as it was supposed) of Joseph, the son of Heli, the son of Matthat, the son of Levi, the son of Melchi, the son of Jannai, the son of Joseph, the son of Mattathias, the son of Amos, the son of Nahum, the son of Esli, the son of Naggai, the son of Maath, the son of Mattathias, the son of Semein, the son of Josech, the son of Joda, the son of Joanan, the son of Rhesa, the son of Zerubbabel, the son of Shealtiel, the son of Neri, the son of Melchi, the son of Addi, the son of Cosam, the son of Elmadam, the son of Er, the son of Jesus, the son of Eliezer, the son of Jorim, the son of Matthat, the son of Levi, the son of Symeon, the son of Judas, the son of Joseph, the son of Jonam, the son of Eliakim, the son of Melea, the son of Menna, the son of Mattatha, the son of Nathan, the son of David, the son of Jesse, the son of Obed, the son of Boaz, the son of Salmon, the son of Nashon, the son of Amminadab, the son of Arni, the son of Hezron, the son of Perez, the son of Judah, the son of Jacob, the son of Isaac, the son of Abraham, the son of Terah, the son of Nahor, the son of Serug, the son of Reu, the son of Pelag, the son of Eber, the son of Shelah, the son of Cainan, the son of Arphaxad, the son of Shem, the son of Noah, the son of Lamech, the son of Methuselah, the son of Enoch, the son of Jared, the son of Mahalaleel, the son of Cainan, the son of Enos, the son of Seth, the son of Adam, the son of God.

THIS passage begins with one most suggestive statement. It tells us that when Jesus began His ministry He was no less than about thirty years of age. Why did Jesus spend thirty years in Nazareth when He had come to be the Saviour of the world? It is commonly said that Joseph died fairly young and that Jesus had to take upon Himself the support of Mary and of His younger brothers and sisters, and that not until they were old enough to take the business on their own shoulders did He feel free to leave Nazareth and to go out into the wider world. Whether that be so or not three things are true. (i) It was essential that Jesus should carry out with the utmost fidelity the more limited tasks of family duty before He could be entrusted by God with the universal task of saving the world. It was by His fidelity, His conscientiousness, His performance of the narrow duties of home that Jesus fitted Himself for the great task He had to do. When Jesus Himself told the Parable of the Talents, the word of God to the faithful servants was, " Well done good and faithful servant; you have been faithful over a few things, I will make you ruler over many things " (Matthew 25: 21, 23). Beyond a doubt Jesus was putting His own experience into words when He said that. When Sir James Barrie's mother died, he said, " I can look back and I cannot see the smallest thing undone." It was because Jesus faithfully performed the smallest duties that the greatest task in all the world was given to Him. (ii) It gave Him the opportunity to live out His own teaching. Had He always been a homeless, wandering teacher with no human ties or obligations, men might have said to Him, " What right have you to talk about human duties and human relationships, you, who never fulfilled them? " But Jesus was able to say to others, not, " Do as I say," but, " Do as I have done." Tolstoi was the man who always talked about living the way of love; but his wife wrote poignantly of him, " There is so little genuine warmth about him; his kindness does not come from the heart, but merely from his principles. His biographies will tell of how he helped the labourers to carry buckets of water, but no one will ever know that he never gave his wife a rest and never— in all these thirty-two years—gave his child a drink of water or spent five minutes by his bedside to give me a chance to rest a little from all my labours." But no one could ever say that of Jesus. He lived at home what He preached abroad. (iii) If Jesus was to help men He had to know how men lived. And because He spent these thirty years in Nazareth, He knew the problems of making a living, the haunting insecurity of the life of the working man, the ill-natured customer, the man who would not pay his debts. It is the glory of the incarnation that there is no problem in life and living which we face which Jesus did not also face.

Here we have Luke's genealogy of Jesus. The Jews were interested in genealogies. Genealogies, especially of the priests, who had to prove unbroken descent from Aaron, were kept amongst the public records. In the time of Ezra and Nehemiah we read of priests who lost their office because they could not produce their genealogy (Ezra 2: 61-63; Nehemiah 7: 63-65). But the problem of this genealogy is its relationship with that in Matthew 1: 1-17. The facts are these—only Luke gives the section from Adam to Abraham; the section from Abraham to David is the same in both; but the section from David to Joseph is almost completely different. Ever since men studied the New Testament they have tried to explain the differences. (i) It is said that both genealogies are symbolic and that Matthew gives the *royal* descent of Jesus and Luke the *priestly* descent. (ii) One of the earliest suggestions of all was that Matthew in fact gives the genealogy of *Joseph* and Luke of *Mary*. (iii) The most ingenious explanation is as follows. In Matthew 1: 16 Joseph's father is *Jacob*; Luke 3: 23 it is *Heli*. According to the Jewish law of levirate marriage (Deuteronomy 25: 5f) if a man died his brother must, if free to do so, marry the widow and ensure the continuance of the line. Now when that happened a son of such a marriage could be called the son either of the first or the second husband. It is suggested that Joseph's mother married twice. Joseph was in actual fact the son of Heli, the second husband, but he was in the eyes of the law the son of Jacob, the first husband who had died. It is then suggested that while Heli and Jacob had the same mother they had different fathers and that Jacob's father was descended from David through Solomon and Heli's father was descended from David through Nathan. This ingenious theory would mean that *both* genealogies are correct. In fact, all that we can say is that we do not know.

Two things are to be noted about the genealogy of Jesus which Luke gives. (i) It stresses the real humanity of Jesus. It stresses the fact that He was a man amongst men. He was no phantom or demi-god. To save men He became in the most real sense a man. (ii) Matthew stops at Abraham; Luke goes right back to Adam. To Matthew, Jesus was the possession of the Jews; to Luke, He was the possession of all mankind, because His line is traced back not to the founder of the Jewish nation but to the founder of the human race. It is one of Luke's great thoughts that he removes the national and racial boundaries even from the ancestry of Jesus.

THE BATTLE WITH TEMPTATION

Luke 4: 1-13

Jesus came back from the Jordan full of the Holy Spirit. He was led by the Spirit into the wilderness, and for forty days He was tempted by the devil; and in those days He ate nothing, and when they were completed He was hungry. The devil said to Him, " If you really are the Son of God, tell these stones to become bread." Jesus answered him, " It stands written, ' Man shall not live by bread alone.' " He took Him up and showed Him in an instant of time all the kingdoms of the inhabited world. The devil said to Him, " I will give you all this power and the glory of them, because it has been handed over to me, and I can give it to whomsoever I wish. If then you worship me all of it will be yours." Jesus answered him, " It stands written, ' You must worship the Lord God and Him only must you serve.' " He brought Him to Jerusalem and set Him on a pinnacle of the Temple, and said to Him, " If you really are the Son of God throw yourself down from here, for it stands written, ' He has given His angels instructions concerning you, to take care of you, and they will bear you up in their hands lest you dash your foot against a stone.' " Jesus answered him, " It has been said, ' You must not try to test the Lord your God.' " So when He had gone through the whole gamut of temptation, the devil left Him for a time.

WE have already seen how there were certain great mile-
stones in the life of Jesus and here is one of the greatest of all.
In the Temple when He was twelve there had come the
dawning realization that God was His Father in the most
unique way. In the emergence of John, for Him the hour
had struck and in His baptism God's approval had come
to Him. So at this time Jesus was just about to begin
His campaign. Before a man begins a campaign he must
choose the methods he will use. The Temptation Story
shows us Jesus choosing once and for all the method by
which He proposed to seek to win men to God. It shows us
Jesus rejecting the way of power and glory and accepting
the way of suffering and the Cross.

Before we go on to think of this story in detail there are
two general points we must note. (i) This is the most
sacred of stories, for it can have come from no other source
than His own lips. At some time He must have Himself
told His disciples about this most intimate experience of
His soul. (ii) Even at this time Jesus must have been
conscious of quite exceptional powers. The whole point
of the Temptations is that they could only have come to a
man who could do astonishing things. It is no temptation
to us to turn stones into bread or leap from a Temple
pinnacle, for the simple reason that it is impossible. These
are temptations which could only have come to a man whose
powers were unique and who had to decide how to use them.

First of all let us think of the scene. It happened in the
wilderness. The inhabited part of Judaea stood on the
central plateau which was the backbone of Southern
Palestine. Between it and the Dead Sea there stretched a
terrible wilderness, thirty-five by fifteen miles. It was
called Jeshimmon, which means "The Devastation."
The hills were like dust heaps; the limestone looked
blistered and peeling; the rocks were bare and jagged;
the ground sounded hollow to the horses' hooves; it
glowed with heat like a vast furnace and it ran out to the
precipices, 1,200 feet high, which swooped down to the

Dead Sea. It was there in that awesome devastation that Jesus was tempted.

We must not think that the three temptations came and went like scenes in a play. We must think of Jesus deliberately retiring to this lonely place and for forty days wrestling with the problem of how He could win men. It was a long battle and a battle which never ended until the Cross, for the story ends by saying that the Tempter left Jesus—*for a season*.

(i) The first temptation was to turn stones into bread. This wilderness was not a wilderness of sand. It was covered by little bits of limestone exactly like loaves. The Tempter said to Jesus, " If you want people to follow you, use your wonderful powers to give them material things." The Tempter was suggesting that Jesus should *bribe people with material gifts* into following Him. Back came Jesus' answer which is a quotation of Deuteronomy 8: 3. " A man," He said, " will never find life in material things." The task of Christianity is not to produce new conditions, although the weight and voice of the Church must be behind all efforts to make life better for men. But the real task is to produce *new men*; and given the new men the new conditions will follow.

(ii) In the second temptation Jesus in imagination stood upon a mountain from which the whole civilized world could be seen. The Tempter said, " Worship me, and all will be yours." *That is the temptation to compromise.* The devil said, " I have got people in my grip. Don't set your standards so high. Strike a bargain with me. Just compromise a little with evil and men will follow you." Back comes Jesus' answer, " God is God, and right is right and wrong is wrong. There can be no compromise in the war with evil." Once again Jesus quotes scripture (Deuteronomy 6: 13; 10: 20). It is a constant temptation to seek to win men by compromising with the standards of the world. G. K. Chesterton said that the tendency of the world it to see things in terms of an indeterminate gray; but the duty of the Christian is to see things in terms of black and white. As Carlyle said, " The Christian must be consumed by the conviction of the infinite beauty of holiness and the infinite damnability of sin."

(iii) In the third temptation Jesus in imagination saw Himself on the pinnacle of the Temple where Solomon's Porch and the Royal Porch met. There was a sheer drop of 450 feet down into the Kedron Valley below. This temptation was the temptation *to give the people sensations.* " No," said Jesus, " you must not make senseless experiments with the power of God " (Deuteronomy 6: 16). Jesus saw quite clearly that if He produced sensations He could be a nine days' wonder. But the sensationalist never lasts. It is the hard way of service and of suffering which leads to the Cross, but after the Cross to the crown.

THE GALILAEAN SPRINGTIME

Luke 4: 14, 15

> So Jesus returned in the power of the Spirit to Galilee; and the story of Him spread throughout the whole countryside. He kept on teaching in their synagogues; and He was held in high reputation by all.

No sooner had Jesus left the wilderness but He was faced with another decision. He knew that for Him the hour had struck; He had settled once and for all the method which He was going to take. Now He had to decide, *Where would He start?*

(i) He began in *Galilee.* Galilee was an area in the north of Palestine about fifty miles from north to south and twenty-five miles from east to west. The name itself means a circle and comes from the Hebrew word *Galil.* It was so called because it was encircled by non-Jewish nations. Just because of that new influences had always played upon Galilee and it was the most forward-looking and the least conservative part of Palestine. It was an extraordinarily densely populated part of Palestine. Josephus, who was himself at one time governor of the area, says that it had 204 villages or towns, none with a population less than 15,000. It seems incredible that there could be about 3,000,000 people congregated in Galilee. It was a land of extraordinary fertility. There was a proverb which said that, " It is easier to raise a legion of olive trees in Galilee than to bring up one child in Judaea." The wonderful climate and the superb water supply made it the garden of Palestine. The very list of trees which grew there shows how amazingly fertile it was—the vine, the olive, the fig, the oak, the walnut, the terebinth, the palm, the cedar, the cypress, the balsam, the firtree, the pine, the sycomore, the baytree, the myrtle, the almond, the pomegranate, the citron and the oleander. The Galilaeans themselves were the Highlanders of Palestine. Josephus says of them, " They were ever fond of innovations and by nature disposed to changes, and delighted in seditions. They were ever ready to follow a leader who would begin an insurrection. They were quick in temper and given to quarrelling." " The Galilaeans," it was said, " have never been destitute of courage." " They were ever more anxious for honour than for gain." So that is the land in which Jesus began. It was His own land; and it would give Him, at least at the beginning, an audience who would listen and kindle at His message.

(ii) *He began in the Synagogue.* The Synagogue was the real centre of religious life in Palestine. There was only one Temple; but the law said that wherever there were ten Jewish families there must be a Synagogue; and so in every town and village it was in the Synagogue that the people met to worship. There were no sacrifices in the Synagogue. The Temple was designed for sacrifice; the Synagogue for teaching. But how could Jesus gain an entry into the Synagogue and how could he, a layman, the carpenter from Nazareth, deliver His message there?

In the Synagogue service there were three parts. (*a*) The worship part in prayer was offered. (*b*) The reading of the scriptures. Seven people from the congregation read. As they read the ancient Hebrew, which was no longer widely understood, was translated by the Targumist into Aramaic or Greek, in the case of the Law, one verse at a time, in the case of the prophets three verses at a time. (c) The teaching part of the service. In the Synagogue there was no professional ministry; there was no one person to give the address; the president would invite any distinguished person present to speak and then discussion and talk would follow. That is how Jesus got His chance. The Synagogue and its platform at this stage were open to Him.

(iii) The passage ends by saying that He was held in high reputation by all. This period of Jesus' ministry has been called the Galilaean springtime. He had come like a breath of the very wind of God. The opposition had not yet crystallised. Men's hearts were hungry for the word of life, and they had not yet realized what a blow He was to strike at the orthodoxy of His time. A man with a message will always command an audience.

WITHOUT HONOUR IN HIS OWN COUNTRY

Luke 4: 16-30

> So Jesus came to Nazareth where He had been brought up; and, as was His habit, He went into the Synagogue on the Sabbath day, and He stood up to read the lesson. The roll of the prophet Isaiah was given to Him. He opened the roll and found the passage where it is written, " The Spirit of the Lord is upon me because He has anointed me to bring the Good News to the poor. He has sent me to announce release to the captives, and recovering of sight to the blind, to set at liberty those who have been bruised, to proclaim that the year which everyone is waiting for has come." And He folded up the roll and handed it back to the officer and sat down ; and the eyes of all in the

Synagogue were fixed intently on Him. He began to say
to them, " To-day this scripture has been fulfilled
in your ears." And all witnessed to Him and were
amazed at the words of grace that came from His
mouth. And they said, " Is this not the son of Joseph?"
He said to them, " You are bound to quote the proverb
to me, ' Physician, heal yourself; we have heard about
all that happened in Capernaum; do the same kind
of things in your own home country.' " He said, " This
is the truth that I tell you. No prophet is accepted in
his own home country. In truth I tell you there were
many widows in Israel in the days of Elijah, when the
heaven was shut up for three years and six months
and when there was a great famine all over the earth.
And to none of them was Elijah sent but he was sent
to Sarepta, to a widow of Sidon. There were many
lepers in Israel in the times of Elisha the prophet;
and none of them was healed; but Naaman the Syrian
was." And the people in the Synagogue were filled
with anger as they listened to these things; and they
rose up and hustled Him out of the town. They took
Him to the brow of the hill on which their town is
built, to throw Him down; but He passed through
the midst of them and went upon His way.

ONE of Jesus' very early visits was to Nazareth, His
home town. Nazareth was not a village. It is called a
polis which means a town or city; and it may well have
had as many as 20,000 inhabitants. It stood in a little
hollow in the hills on the lower slopes of Galilee near the
Plain of Jezreel. But a boy had only to climb to the hilltop above the town and he could see an amazing panorama
for miles around. Sir George Adam Smith describes the
scene from the hilltop. The history of Israel stretched
out before the watcher's eye. There was the plain of Esdra-
leon where Deborah and Barak had fought; where Gideon
had won his victories; where Saul had crashed to disaster
and where Josiah had been killed in battle; there was
Naboth's vineyard and the place where Jehu slaughtered
Jezebel; there was Shunem where Elisha had lived; there
was Carmel where Elijah had fought his epic battle with
the prophets of Baal; and, blue in the distance, there was

43

the Mediterranean and the isles of the sea. But not only the history of Israel was there; the world itself unfolded itself from the hilltop in Nazareth. Three great roads skirted it. There was the road from the south with the pilgrims to Jerusalem on it. There was the great Way of the Sea which led from Egypt to Damascus with the laden caravans moving along it. There was the great road to the east with the caravans from Arabia on it and the Roman legions marching out to the eastern frontiers of the Empire. It is quite wrong to think of Jesus as being brought up in a backwater; He was brought up in a town in sight of history and with the traffic of the world almost at its doors.

We have already described the Synagogue service and this passage gives us a vivid picture of it in action. It was not a book which Jesus took, for at this time everything was written on rolls. It was from Isaiah 61 that He read. In verse 20 the Authorised Version speaks misleadingly of *the minister*. The official in question was the *Chazzan*. He had many duties. He had to take out and put back the sacred rolls of scripture; he had to keep the Synagogue clean; he had to announce the coming of the Sabbath with three blasts of the silver trumpet from the Synagogue roof; and he was also the teacher in the village school. Verse 20 says that Jesus sat down. That gives us the impression that He was finished. In point of fact it means that He was about to start because the speaker gave the address seated and Rabbis taught sitting down. (cp. Our own phrase, a professor's *chair*).

What angered the people was the apparent compliment that Jesus paid to Gentiles. The Jews were so sure that they were God's people that they utterly despised all other peoples. They believed that " God had created the Gentiles to be fuel for the fires of hell." And here was this young Jesus, whom they all knew, preaching as if the *Gentiles* were specially favoured by God. It was beginning to dawn upon them that there were things in this new message the like of which they had never dreamed of.

44

THE GOSPEL OF LUKE

We must note two other things before we leave this passage.

(i) It was Jesus' habit to go to the Synagogue on the Sabbath Day. There must have been many things with which He radically disagreed and which grated on Him—*yet He went*. The worship of the Synagogue might be far from perfect; yet Jesus never omitted to join Himself to God's worshipping people on God's day.

(ii) We have only to read the passage of Isaiah that Jesus read to see the difference between Jesus and John the Baptist. John was the preacher of doom and at his message men must have shuddered with terror. It was a *gospel*—Good News—which Jesus brought. Jesus too knew the wrath of God but it was always the wrath of love.

THE SPIRIT OF AN UNCLEAN DEVIL

Luke 4: 31-37

> Jesus came down to Capernaum, a town in Galilee, and He was teaching them on the Sabbath day; and they were astonished at His teaching because His speech was with authority. There was in the Synagogue a man who had a spirit of an unclean demon and he cried out with a loud voice, " What have we to do with you, Jesus of Nazareth? Have you come to destroy us? I know who you are—the Holy One of God." So Jesus rebuked it. " Be muzzled," He said, " and come out of him." And after the demon had thrown him into the midst of them, it came out of him and it did him no harm. Astonishment fell on them all and they kept saying to each other, " What word is this? because He gives orders to unclean spirits with authority and with power and they come out." And the story of Him went out to every place in the surrounding district.

WE would have liked to know as much about Capernaum as we do about Nazareth, but it is the strange fact that there is even doubt as to the site of this lake-side town where so much of Jesus' mighty work was done.

This passage is specially interesting because it is the first passage in Luke where we encounter demon possession. The ancient world believed that the air was thickly populated with evil spirits. These spirits, they believed, sought an entry into men. Often they did enter a man through either food or drink. All illness was caused by these evil spirits. The Egyptians believed that there were thirty-six different parts of the human body and any of them could be entered and controlled by one of these evil spirits. There could be a spirit of deafness, of dumbness, of fever; spirits which took a man's sanity and wits away; spirits of lying and of deceit and of uncleanness. It was such a spirit that Jesus, in this passage, exorcised from this man. To many people this is a problem. On the whole, modern thought regards this belief in spirits as primitive and superstitious and as something which men have outgrown. And yet Jesus seemed to believe in them. There are three possibilities. (i) Jesus actually did believe in them. If that is so, Jesus as far as scientific knowledge went was nothing in advance of His own age; He was under all the limitations of contemporary medical thought. There is no need to refuse such a conclusion for, if Jesus was really a man, in scientific things He must have had the knowledge then open to a man. (ii) Jesus Himself did not believe in them, but the sufferer did believe, and most intensely. Therefore Jesus could only cure people by assuming their beliefs about themselves to be true. If a person is ill and someone says to him, " There's nothing wrong with you," that is no help. The reality of the pain has to be admitted before a cure can follow. The people believed they were possessed of devils and Jesus, like a wise doctor, knew He could not heal them unless He assumed that their view of their own trouble was real. (iii) Modern thought has been swinging round to the admission that perhaps there is something in demons after all. There are certain troubles which have no bodily cause at all, as far as can be discovered. There is no reason why the man is ill, but he is ill. Since there is no physical explanation some now think that there must be a spiritual one and that demons are not so unreal after all.

The people were astonished at Jesus' power—and no wonder. The east was full of people who could exorcise demons. But their methods were weird and wonderful. An exorcist would put a ring under the afflicted person's nose. He would recite a long spell; and then all of a sudden there would be a splash in a basin of water which he had put near to hand—and the demon was out ! A magical root called Baaras was specially effective. When a man approached it, it shrank into the ground unless gripped, and to grip it was certain death. So the ground round it was dug away; a dog was tied to it; the struggles of the dog tore up the root; and when the root was torn up the dog died, as a substitute for a man. What a difference between all this hysterical paraphernalia and the calm single word of command of Jesus ! It was the sheer authority which staggered them.

Jesus' authority was something quite new. When the Rabbis taught they supported every statement with quotations. They always said, " There is a saying that . . ." Rabbi so and so said " that . . ." They always appealed to authority. When the prophets spoke, they said, " Thus saith the Lord." Theirs was a delegated authority. When Jesus spoke, He said, " I say to you." He needed no authorities to buttress Him; He did not enjoy a delegated authority; He was authority incarnate. Here was something new; here was a man who spoke as one who knew.

In every sphere of life the expert bears an air of authority. A musician tells how when Toscanini mounts the rostrum authority flows from him and the orchestra feels it. When we need technical advice we call in the expert and we take his word for it. *Jesus is the expert in life.* He speaks and men know that this is beyond human argument— this is God.

A MIRACLE IN A COTTAGE

Luke 4: 38, 39

> Jesus left the Synagogue and came into Simon's house; and Simon's mother-in-law was in the grip of a major fever. They asked Him to do something for her. He stood over her and rebuked the fever and it left her. Immediately she got up and began to serve them.

HERE Luke, the doctor, writes. *In the grip of a major fever*—every word is a medical word. *In the grip of* is the medical Greek for someone who is very definitely laid up with some illness. The Greek medical writers divided fevers into two classes—major and minor. Luke knew just how to describe this illness.

There are three great truths in this short incident.

(i) Jesus was always ready to serve. He had just left the Synagogue. Every preacher knows what he feels like after a service. Virtue is gone out of him; he has need of rest. The last thing he wants is a crowd of people and a fresh call upon him. But no sooner had Jesus left the Synagogue and entered Peter's house than the insistent cry of human need was at him. He did not claim that He was tired and must rest. He answered it without complaint. The Salvation Army people tell of a Mrs. Berwick in the days of the London blitzes. She had been in charge of the Army's social work in Liverpool and she had retired to London. People had queer ideas in the time of the blitzes and they had the idea that somehow Mrs. Berwick's house was safe; and so they gathered there. Though she had retired, the instinct to help was there. She got together a simple first-aid box and then she put a notice in her window, " If you need help knock here." Always Jesus was ready to help; His followers must be the same.

(ii) Jesus did not need a crowd to work a miracle. Many a man will put out an effort in a crowd that he will not make among his own private circle. Many a man is at his best in society and at his worst at home. All too commonly we are gracious, courteous, obliging to strangers and the very opposite when there is no one but our own folk to see. But Jesus was prepared to put out all His power in a village cottage in Capernaum when the crowds were gone.

(iii) Whenever Peter's mother-in-law was cured *immediately she began to serve them*. She realized that she had been given back her health to spend it in the service of others. She wanted no fussing and no petting; she wanted to get on with cooking and serving her own folk and Jesus. Mothers are always like that. We would do well to remember that if God gave us the priceless gift of health and strength, He gave us it that we might use it always in the service of others.

THE INSISTENT CROWDS

Luke 4: 40-44

> When the sun was setting all who had friends who were ill with all kinds of sicknesses brought them to Jesus; and He laid His hands upon each one of them and cured them. Out of many there came demons, shouting out and saying, " You are the Son of God." And He rebuked them and would not allow them to speak, because they knew that He was the Anointed One. When day came, He went out and went to a desert place; and the crowds kept looking for Him and they tried to restrain Him so that He would not go away from them; but He said to them, " I must tell the Good News of the Kingdom of God to other towns too, because that is what I was sent to do."

(i) Early in the morning Jesus went out to be alone. He was only able to meet the insistent needs of men because He first companied with God. Once, in the 1914-18 war, there was a staff conference due to begin. All were present except one—Marshal Foch, the commander-in-chief himself. At last an officer who knew him well said, " I think I know where we may find him." He led them round to a ruined chapel which was close beside General Headquarters and there, before the shattered altar, the great soldier was kneeling in prayer. He knew that before he met men he must first meet God.

(ii) And yet there is no word of complaint or resentment when Jesus' privacy was invaded by the crowds. Prayer is great but in the last analysis human need is greater. Florence Allshorn, the great missionary teacher, used to run a training college for missionaries. She knew human nature and she had no time for people who suddenly discovered that their quiet hour was due just when the dishes were to be washed ! Pray we must; but prayer must never be an escape from reality. Prayer cannot preserve a man from the insistent cry of human need. It must prepare him for it; and sometimes, too soon, and in a hurry, he will need to rise from his knees and get to work—even when he does not want to.

(iii) Jesus would not let the demons speak. Over and over again we will get on Jesus' lips this injunction to silence. Why? For this very good reason—the Jews had their own popular ideas of the Messiah. To them the Messiah was to be a conquering king who would set his foot upon the eagle's neck and sweep the Romans from Palestine. Palestine was in an inflammable condition. Rebellion was always just below the surface and often broke out. Jesus knew that if the report went out that He was the Messiah these revolutionaries would be ready to flare up. Before men could call Him Messiah, He had to teach them what being Messiah meant, that it meant not being the conquering king but the suffering servant. Jesus' injunctions to silence were given because people did not yet know what Messiahship meant, and if they started out with the wrong ideas death and destruction would surely follow.

(iv) Here is the first mention of the Kingdom of God in Luke's gospel. Jesus came preaching the Kingdom of God (Mark I: 15). That was the essence of His message. What did He mean by the Kingdom of God? When we look at this we find an amazing paradox. For Jesus the

Kingdom was three things at the same time. (*a*) It was *past*. Abraham, Isaac and Jacob were in the Kingdom and they had lived centuries ago (Luke 13: 28). (*b*) It was *present*. " The Kingdom," He said, " is within you, or among you " (Luke 17: 21). (*c*) It was *future*. It was something which God was still to give and for which men must ever pray. How can the Kingdom be all these things at the same time? Turn to the Lord's Prayer. There are two petitions in it side by side. Thy Kingdom come; Thy will be done in earth as it is in Heaven (Matthew 6: 10, 11). Now the Hebrews, as any verse of the psalms will show, had a way of saying things twice; and always the second way explained, or developed, or amplified the first way. Now put these two phrases together—Thy Kingdom come; Thy will be done in earth as it is in heaven. The second explains the first; and therefore, *The Kingdom of God is a society upon earth where God's will is as perfectly done as it is in heaven.* So then if any man in the past has perfectly done God's will, He is in the Kingdom; if any man does it now, He is in the Kingdom; but the day when all men will do that will is still far distant; therefore the consummation is still to come; and so the Kingdom is past and present and future all at the same time. Other men do that will spasmodically, sometimes obeying, sometimes disobeying. Only Jesus always and at all times did it perfectly. That is why He is the foundation and the incarnation of the Kingdom. He came to enable all men to do the same. To do God's will is to be a citizen of the Kingdom of God. We may well pray—" Lord, bring in Thy Kingdom, beginning with me."

THE CONDITIONS OF A MIRACLE

Luke 5: 1-11

Jesus was standing on the shore of the Lake of Gennesaret while the crowds pressed in upon Him to listen to the word of God. He saw two boats riding close to the shore. The fishermen had disembarked from them and were washing their nets. He embarked on one of the boats, which belonged to Simon, and asked him to push out a little from the land. He sat down and continued to teach the crowds from the boat. When He stopped speaking, He said to Simon, " Push out into the deep water and let down your nets for a catch." Simon answered, " Master, we have toiled all night long and we caught nothing; but, if you say so, I will let down the nets." When they had done so they enclosed a great crowd of fishes; their nets were torn with the numbers; so they signalled to their partners in the other boat to come and help them. They came and they filled both the boats so that they began to sink. When Simon Peter saw this he fell at Jesus' knees. " Leave me, Lord," he said, " because I am a sinful man." Wonder gripped him and all who were with him at the number of fishes they had caught. It was the same with James and John, Zebedee's sons, who were partners with Simon. Jesus said to Simon, " From now on you will be catching men." So they brought the boats to land and they left everything and followed Him.

THE famous sheet of water in Galilee is called by three names—the Sea of Galilee, the Sea of Tiberias and the Lake of Gennesaret. It was thirteen miles long by eight miles wide. It lies in a dip in the earth's surface and is 680 feet below sea level. That fact gives it its almost tropical climate. Nowadays it is almost deserted, but in the days of Jesus is had nine townships clustered round its shores, none of them with fewer than 15,000 people. Gennesaret is really the name of the lovely plain on the west side of the lake. It is a most fertile piece of land. The Jews loved to play with derivations, and they had three derivations for Gennesaret all of which show how beautiful it was. (i) From *kinnor*, which means a harp because " its fruit is as sweet as the sound of a harp." (ii) From *gan*, a garden, and *sar*, a prince—hence " the prince of gardens." (iii) From *gan*, a garden, and *asher*, riches—hence " the garden of riches."

We have to note, first of all, that, without anything being said, we are here confronted with a turning point

in the career of Jesus. Last time we heard Him preach
He was in the Synagogue; now He is at the lakeside.
True, He will be back in the Synagogue again; but the
time is coming when the door of the Synagogue will be
shut to Him and when His Church will be the lakeside and
the open road, and His pulpit a boat. He would go anywhere where men would listen to Him. " Our societies,"
said John Wesley, " were formed from those who were
wandering upon the dark mountains, that belonged to no
Christian Church; but were awakened by the preaching
of the Methodists, who had pursued them through the
wilderness of this world to the High-ways and the Hedges—
to the Markets and the Fairs—to the Hills and the Dales—
who set up the Standard of the Cross in the Streets and
Lanes of the Cities, in the Villages, in the Barns, and
Farmers' Kitchens, etc.—and all this done in such a way,
and to such an extent, as never had been done before since
the Apostolic age." " I love a commodious room," said
Wesley, " a soft cushion and a handsome pulpit, but
field preaching saves souls." When the Synagogue was
shut Jesus took to the open road.

There is in this story what we might call a list of the
conditions of a miracle. (i) There is the eye that sees.
There is no need to think that Jesus *created* a shoal of
fishes for the occasion. In the Sea of Galilee there were
phenomenal shoals which covered the sea as if it was
solid for as much as an acre. Most likely Jesus' keen eye
saw just such a shoal and His keen sight made it look
like a miracle. We need the eye that really sees. Many
people have seen the steam raise the lid of a kettle; only
James Watt saw it and thought of a steam engine. Many
people have seen an apple fall; only Isaac Newton saw
it and went on to think out the law of gravity. The earth
is full of miracles for the eye that sees. (ii) There is the
spirit that will make an effort. If Jesus said it, tired as he
was, Peter was prepared to try again. For most people
the disaster of life is that they give up just one effort too

soon. (iii) There is the spirit which will attempt what seems hopeless. The night was past and the night was the time for fishing. All the circumstances were unfavourable, but Peter says, " Let circumstances be what they may, if you say so, we will try again." Too often we wait because the time is not opportune. If we wait for a perfect set of circumstances we will never begin at all. If we want a miracle we must take Jesus at His word when He bids us attempt the impossible.

TOUCHING THE UNTOUCHABLE
Luke 5: 12-15

While Jesus was in one of the towns—look you—a man who was a severe case of leprosy saw Him. He fell before Him and besought Him, " Lord, if you are willing to do so you are able to cleanse me." Jesus stretched out His hand and touched him. " I am willing," He said. " Be cleansed." Immediately the leprosy left him. Jesus enjoined him to tell no one. " But," He said, " go and show yourself to the priest, and bring the offering for cleansing, as Moses' law laid it down, to prove to them that you are cured." Talk about Him spread all the more; and many crowds assembled to listen to Him and to be cured of their illnesses.

IN Palestine there were two kinds of leprosy. There was one which was rather like a very bad skin disease, and it was the less serious of the two. There was one in which the disease, starting from a small spot, ate away the flesh until the wretched sufferer was left with only the stump of a hand or a leg. It was literally a living death. The regulations concerning leprosy are in Leviticus, chapters 13 and 14. The most terrible thing about leprosy was the isolation it brought. The leper was to cry " Unclean! Unclean!" wherever he went; he was to dwell alone; " without the camp shall be his habitation " (Leviticus 13: 45, 46). He was banished from the society of men and exiled from home. The result was, and still is, that the psychological consequences of leprosy were as serious as the physical. Dr. A. B. MacDonald, in an article on the leper colony in Itu, of which he is in charge, writes, " The leper is sick in mind as well as body. For some reason there is an attitude to leprosy different from the attitude to any other disfiguring disease. It is associated with shame and horror, and carries, in some mysterious way, a sense of guilt, although innocently acquired like most contagious troubles. Shunned and despised, frequently do lepers consider taking their own lives and some do." The leper was hated by others until he came to hate himself. That is the kind of man who came to Jesus; he was unclean; *and Jesus touched him.*

(i) Here is a tremendous truth—*Jesus touched the untouchable.* Jesus' hand went out to the man from whom everyone else would have shrunk away. Two things emerge. First, when we despise ourselves, when our hearts are filled with bitter shame, let us remember, that, in spite of the shame, Christ's hand is still stretched out. Mark Rutherford wished to add a new beatitude, " Blessed are those who heal us of our self-despisings." That is what Jesus did and does. Second, it is of the very essence of Christianity to touch the untouchable, to love the unlovable, to forgive the unforgivable. Jesus did so—and so must we.

(ii) Jesus sent the man to carry out the normal, prescribed routine for cleansing. The regulations are described in Leviticus 14. That is to say a miracle did not dispense with what medical science of the time could do. It did not absolve the man from carrying out the prescribed rules and regulations. We will never get miracles by neglecting the gifts and the sciences and the wisdom God has given us. It is when man's skill combines with God's grace that the wonder happened—and still happens.

(iii) Verse 15 tells us of the popularity Jesus enjoyed. But it was only because people wanted something out of Him. There are so many who desire the gifts of God but who repudiate the demands of God—and, than that, there could be nothing more dishonourable.

THE OPPOSITION INTENSIFIES

Luke 5: 16, 17

> Jesus withdrew into the desert places and He continued in prayer. On a certain day He was teaching and, sitting listening, there were Pharisees and experts in the law who had come from every village in Galilee and from Judaea and Jerusalem. And the power of the Lord was there to enable Him to heal.

THERE are only two verses here; but as we read them we must pause, for this indeed is a milestone. The Scribes and the Pharisees had arrived on the scene. The opposition which would never be satisfied until it had killed Jesus had emerged into the open.

If we are to understand what happened to Jesus we must understand something about the Law, and the relationship of the Scribes and the Pharisees to it. When the Jews returned from Babylon about 440 B.C. they knew well that, humanly speaking, their hopes of national greatness were gone. They therefore deliberately decided that they would find their greatness in being a people of the law. They would bend all their energies to knowing and keeping God's law. The basis of the law was the Ten Commandments. These commandments are great wide principles for life. They are not rules and regulations; they do not legislate for each event and for every circumstance. For a certain section of the Jews that was not enough. They desired not great principles; they sought a rule to cover every conceivable situation in life. From the Ten Commandments they proceeded to develop and elaborate these rules. Let us take an example. The commandment says, " Remember the Sabbath day to keep it holy "; and then goes on to lay it down that on the Sabbath no work must be done (Exodus 20: 8-11). But that was not enough for the Jews. They asked, " What is work? " They went on to define work under thirty-nine different heads which they called " Fathers of Work." Even that was not enough. Each of these heads was infinitely sub-divided. Literally thousands of rules and regulations began to emerge. These were called the Oral Law, and they began to be set not only at level with the Ten Commandments but even above them. Again, let us take an actual example. One of the works forbidden on the Sabbath was carrying a burden. Jeremiah 17: 21-24 says, " Take heed to yourselves and bear no burden on the Sabbath day." But, these legalists insisted, a burden must be defined. So the definition was given. A burden is " food equal in weight to a dried fig, enough wine for mixing in a goblet, milk enough for one swallow, oil enough to anoint a small member, water enough to moisten an eye-salve, paper enough to write a custom-house notice upon, ink enough to write two letters, reed enough to make a pen " . . . and so on endlessly. So for a tailor to leave a pin or needle in his robe on the Sabbath was to break the law and to sin; to pick up a stone big enough to fling at a bird on the Sabbath was to sin. Goodness became identified with these endless rules and regulations. Let us take another example. To heal on the Sabbath was to work. It was laid down that only if life was in actual danger could healing be done; and then steps could only be taken to keep the sufferer from getting worse, not to improve his condition. So a plain bandage could be put on a wound, but not any ointment; plain wadding could be put into a sore ear, but not medicated. It is easy to see that there is no limit to this. The Scribes were the experts in the law who knew all these rules and regulations, and who deduced them from the law. The name Pharisee means " The Separated One "; and the Pharisees were those who had separated themselves from ordinary people and ordinary life in order to keep these rules and regu- lations. Note two things. First, for the Scribes and Pharisees these rules were a matter of life and death; to break one of them was deadly sin. Second, only people desperately in earnest would ever have tried to keep them, for they must have made life supremely uncomfortable.

It was only the best people who would even make the attempt. Jesus had no use for rules and regulations like that. For Him, the cry of human need superseded all such things. But to the Scribes and Pharisees He was a law-breaker, a bad man who broke the law and taught others to do the same. That is why they hated Him, and in the end killed Him. It is the tragedy of the life of Jesus that those who were most in earnest about their religion drove Him to the Cross. It was the irony of things that the best people of the day ultimately crucified Him. From this time on there was to be no rest for Him. Always He was to be under the scrutiny of these hostile and critical eyes. The opposition had crystallised and there was but one end.

Jesus knew this and before He met the opposition He withdrew to pray. The love in the eyes of God comforted Him for the hate in the eyes of men. The approval of God nerved Him to meet the criticism of men. He drew strength for the battle of life from the peace of God— and it is enough for the disciple that he should be as his Lord.

FORGIVEN AND HEALED

Luke 5: 18-26

Now—look you—there came men bearing on a bed a man who was paralysed, and they were trying to carry him in and to lay him before Jesus. When they could find no way to carry him in because of the crowd they climbed up on to the roof and they let him down, bed and all, through the tiles right into the middle of them in front of Jesus. When Jesus saw their faith, He said, " Man, your sins are forgiven you." The Scribes and Pharisees began to raise questions. " Who," they said, " is this who insults God? Who can forgive sins but God alone? " Jesus was well aware of what they were thinking. He answered, " What are you thinking about in your hearts? Which is easier—to say, ' Your sins are

forgiven you,' or to say, ' Rise and walk '?   But that
you may know that the Son of Man has authority on
earth to forgive sins (He said to the paralysed man),
I tell you, rise, take up your bed, and go to your own
house."   And immediately he stood up in front of
them and lifted up the bedding on which he was lying
and went away to his house, glorifying God. Astonish-
ment gripped them all and they glorified God and
were filled with awe.   " To-day," they said, " we have
seen amazing things."

HERE we have a vivid story. Jesus was in a house teaching.
The Palestinian house was flat-roofed. The roof had only
the slightest tilt, sufficient to make the rain water run off.
It was composed of beams laid from wall to wall and quite
a short distance apart. The space between the beams was
filled with close packed twigs, compacted together with
mortar and then marled over. It was the easiest thing in
the world to take out the packing between two beams.
In fact coffins were very often taken in and out of a house
via the roof.

What does the passage about forgiving sins mean?
To understand it we must remember that sin and suffering
were in Palestine inextricably connected. It was implicitly
believed that if a man was suffering he had sinned. And
therefore the sufferer very often had an even morbid sense
of sin. That is why Jesus began by telling the man that
his sins were forgiven. Without that the man would never
believe that he could be cured. This shows how in debate
the Scribes and Pharisees were completely routed. They
objected to Jesus claiming to extend forgiveness to the man.
But on their own arguments and assumptions the man was
ill because he had sinned; and if he was cured that was the
final proof that his sins were forgiven. The complaint
of the Pharisees had recoiled on them and left them speechless.

The wonderful thing about this story is that here is
a man who was saved by the faith of his friends. *When
Jesus saw their faith*—the eager faith of those who had

stopped at nothing to bring their friend to Jesus won that cure. It still happens. (i) There are those who have been saved by the faith of their parents. Carlyle used to say, that still across the years there came his mother's voice to him, " Trust in God and do the right." When Augustine was living a reckless and immoral life his devout mother came to ask the help of a Christian bishop. " It is impossible," he said, " that the child of such prayers and tears should perish." Many of us would gladly witness that we owe all that we are and ever will be to the faith of godly parents. (ii) There are those who are daily saved by the faith of those who love them. When H. G. Wells was newly married, and when success was bringing new temptations to him, he said, " It was as well for me that behind the folding doors at 12 Mornington Road there slept one so sweet and clean that it was unthinkable that I should appear before her squalid or drunken or base." Many of us would do the shameful thing but for the fact that we could not meet the pain and sorrow in someone's eyes.

In the very structure of life and love—blessed be God— there are the precious influences which save men's souls.

THE GUEST OF AN OUTCAST

Luke 5: 27-32

> After that Jesus went out, and He saw a tax-collector, called Levi, sitting at his tax-collector's table. He said to him, " Follow Me! " He left everything and rose and followed Him. And Levi made a great feast for Him in his house; and a great crowd of tax-collectors and others who were their friends sat down at table with them. The Pharisees and Scribes complained at this, and said to the disciples, " Why do you eat and drink with tax-collectors and sinners? " Jesus answered, " Those who are healthy have no need of a doctor but those who are ill have. I did not come to invite the righteous but sinners to repentance."

HERE we have the call of Matthew (cp. Matthew 9: 9-13). Of all people in Palestine the tax-collectors were the best hated. At this time Palestine was a country subject to the Romans. The tax-collectors had taken service under the Roman government; and therefore, they were regarded as quislings, and renegades and traitors. The taxation system lent itself to abuse. The Roman custom was to farm out the taxes. They assessed a district at a certain figure, and then they sold the right to collect the taxes within it to the highest bidder. So long as the buyer handed over the assessed figure at the end of the year he was entitled to retain whatever else he could extract from the people; and since there were no newspapers or wireless, and no ways of making public announcements which would reach everyone, the common people had no real idea of what they had to pay. There were two types of taxes. First, there were stated taxes. There was a poll tax which all men from 14 to 65, and all women from 12 to 65, had to pay simply for the privilege of existing. There was a ground tax which consisted of one-tenth of all grain grown, and one-fifth of wine and oil. This could be paid in kind or commuted into money. There was income tax, which was one per cent. of a man's income. In these taxes there was not a great deal of room for extortion. Second, there were all kinds of duties. A tax was payable for using the main roads, the harbours, the markets. A tax was payable on a cart, on each wheel of it, and on the animal which drew it. There was purchase tax on certain articles, and there were import and export duties. A tax-collector could bid a man stop on the road and unpack his bundles and could charge him well nigh what he liked. If a man could not pay sometimes the tax-collector would offer to lend him money at an exorbitant rate of interest and so get him further into his clutches. Robbers, murderers and tax-collectors were classed together. A tax-collector was barred from the Synagogue. A Roman writer tells us that he once saw a monument to an honest tax-collector.

An honest specimen of this renegade profession was so rare that when he occurred he received a monument. Matthew was like that, and Jesus chose him as an apostle.

(i) The first thing that Matthew did was to invite Jesus to a feast—he could well afford it—and to invite his fellow tax-collectors and their outcast friends to meet Jesus. Matthew's first instinct was to share the wonder he had found. John Wesley once said, " No man ever went to Heaven alone; he must either find friends or make them." It is a Christian duty to share the blessedness that we have found.

(ii) The Scribes and Pharisees objected. The Pharisees— the Separated Ones—would not even have let the skirt of their robe touch the like of Matthew. Jesus made the perfect answer. Once Epictetus called his teaching " the medicine of salvation." Jesus pointed out that it is only sick people who need doctors; and people like Matthew and his friends were the very people who needed Him most of all. It would be well if we were to regard the sinner not as a criminal but as a sick man; and if we were to look on the man who has made a mistake not as someone deserving contempt and condemnation but as needing love and help to find the right way.

THE HAPPY COMPANY

Luke 5: 33-35

> They said to Him, " John's disciples fast frequently and pray. So do the disciples of the Pharisees; but your disciples eat and drink." Jesus said to them, " You cannot make the children of the bridechamber fast while the bridegroom is with them. But the days will come—and when the bridegroom is taken away from them in those days they will fast."

WHAT amazed and shocked the Scribes and the Pharisees was the normality of the followers of Jesus. Collie Knox tells how once a well-loved chaplain said to him, " Young Knox, don't make an agony of your religion." It was said of Burns that he was haunted rather than helped by his religion. The orthodox Jews had an idea—not yet altogether dead—that a man was not being religious unless he was being uncomfortable. They had systematised their religious observances. They fasted on Mondays and Thursdays; and often they whitened their faces so that no one could fail to see that they were fasting. True, fasting was not so very serious because it lasted only from sunrise to sunset and after that ordinary food could be taken. The idea was to call God's attention to the faster. Sometimes they even thought of it in terms of sacrifice. By fasting a man was in essence offering nothing less than his own flesh to God. Even prayer was systematised. Prayer was to be offered at 12 midday, 3 p.m. and 6 p.m. Jesus was in any event opposed radically to religion by rule. He used a vivid picture. When two young people married in Palestine they did not go away for a honeymoon; they stayed at home; and for a week they kept open house. They dressed in their best; sometimes they even wore crowns; for the week they were king and queen and their word was law. They would never have a week in their hard-wrought lives like that again. And the favoured guests who shared this festive week were called the children of the bridechamber.

(i) It is extremely suggestive that more than once Jesus likens the Christian life to a wedding feast. Joy is a primary Christian characteristic. It was said of a famous American teacher by one of her students, " She made me feel as if I was bathed in sunshine." Far too many people think of Christianity as something which compels them to do all the things they do not want to do and hinders them from doing all the things they do want to do. Laughter has become a sin, instead of—as a famous philosopher called it—" a sudden glory." Robert Louis Stevenson was right, when he wrote in *The Celestial Surgeon,*

" If I have faltered more or less
    In my great task of happiness;
    If I have moved among my race
    And shown no glorious morning face;
    If beams from happy human eyes
    Have moved me not; if morning skies,
    Books, and my food, and summer rain
    Knocked on my sullen heart in vain:
    Lord, thy most pointed pleasure take
    And stab my spirit broad awake;
    Or, Lord, if too obdurate I,
    Choose Thou, before that spirit die,
    A piercing pain, a killing sin,
    And to my dead heart run them in ! "

(ii) But at the same time Jesus knew that there would come a day when the bridegroom would be taken away. He was not caught unawares by death. Ahead He saw the Cross; but even on the way to the Cross He knew that joy that no man taketh from us, because it is the joy of the presence of God.

THE NEW IDEA

Luke 5: 36-39

> He spoke a parable to them like this: " Nobody puts a patch from a new garment on an old garment. If he does the new will tear it and the patch from the new will not match the old. No one puts new wine into old skins. If he does the new wine will burst the skins and it will be spilled and the skins will be ruined. But new wine must be put into new skins, and no one who drinks old wine wishes for new for he says, ' The old is good.' "

THERE is in religious people a kind of passion for the old. Nothing moves more slowly than a Church. The trouble with the Pharisees was that the whole religious outlook of Jesus was so startling new that they simply could not adjust themselves to it. The mind soon looses the quality of elasticity and will not accept new ideas. Jesus used two illustrations. " You cannot put a new patch on an old garment," He said. The strong new cloth will only rip the rent in the old cloth wider. Bottles in Palestine were made of skin. When new wine was put into them it fermented and gave off gas. If the bottle was new there was a certain elasticity in the skin and it gave with the pressure; but if it was old the skin was dry and hard and it would burst. " Don't," says Jesus, " let your mind become like an old wineskin. People say of wine, ' The old is better.' It may be at the moment, but they forget that it is a mistake to despise the new wine, for the day will come when it has matured and it will be best of all." The whole passage is Jesus' condemnation of the shut mind and his plea that men should not reject new ideas.

(i) We should never be afraid of adventurous thought. If there is such a person as the Holy Spirit God must ever be leading us into new truth. Fosdick somewhere asks, " How would medicine fare if doctors were restricted to drugs and methods and techniques three hundred years old? " And yet our standards of orthodoxy are far older than that. The man with something new has always to fight. Galileo was branded a heretic when he held that the sun moved round the earth. Lister had to fight for antiseptic technique in surgical operations. Simpson had to battle against opposition in the merciful use of chloroform. Let us have a care that when we resent new thought we are not simply demonstrating that our minds are grown old and inelastic and let us never shirk the adventure of thought.

(ii) We should never be afraid of new methods. That a thing has *always* been done may very well be the best reason for stopping doing it. That a thing has *never* been done may very well be the best reason for trying it. No business could exist on outworn methods—and yet the Church tries to. Any business which had lost as many customers as the Church has would have tried new ways long ago—but the Church resents all that is new. Once on a world tour Rudyard Kipling saw General Booth come aboard the ship. He came aboard to the beating of tambourines which Kipling's orthodox soul resented. Kipling got to know the General and told him how he disliked tambourines and all their kindred. Booth looked at him. " Young man," he said, " if I thought I could win one more soul for Christ by standing on my head and beating a tambourine with my feet I would learn how to do it." There is a wise and an unwise conservatism. Let us have a care that in thought and in action we are not hidebound reactionaries when we ought, as Christians, to be gallant adventurers.

THE INCREASING OPPOSITION

Luke 6: 1-5

> One Sabbath day, Jesus happened to be going through the corn fields, and His disciples were plucking the ears of corn and rubbing them in their hands and eating them. Some of the Pharisees said, " Why are you doing what it is illegal to do on the Sabbath? " Jesus answered, " Have you not read what David did when he and his comrades were hungry?—how he went into the house of God and took the loaves of the presence and ate them and gave them to his comrades, although it is not legal for any but the priests to eat them. The Son of Man," He said to them, " is the Lord of the Sabbath."

THIS is the first of two incidents which show the opposition to Jesus rapidly coming out into the open and which make it clear that the immediate charge against Jesus was that He was a breaker of the Sabbath law. He and His disciples were passing along one of the paths which intersected the corn fields. The fact that the disciples plucked the ears of corn was in itself no crime. One of the merciful laws of the Old Testament laid it down that anyone passing through a corn field was free to pluck the corn so long as he did not put a sickle into it (Deuteronomy 23: 25). On any other day there would have been no complaint; but this was the Sabbath. Four of the forbidden kinds of work were reaping, threshing, winnowing, and preparing food; and technically the disciples had broken every one of them. By plucking the corn they were guilty of reaping; by rubbing it in their hands, of threshing; by flinging away the husks, of winnowing; and the very fact that they ate it showed that they had prepared food on the Sabbath. To us the whole thing seems fantastic; but we must remember that to a strict Pharisee this was a deadly sin; one of the little rules and regulations had been broken; this to them was a matter of life and death.

They made their accusation and Jesus quoted the Old Testament to them. He quoted the incident in I Samuel 21: 1-6 when David and his comrades, when they were very hungry, ate the shewbread of the Tabernacle. A better name for it is The Bread of the Presence. Every Sabbath morning there were laid before God twelve wheaten loaves baked of flour sieved no fewer than eleven times. There was one loaf for every tribe. In the time of Jesus these loaves were laid on a table of solid gold, three feet long, one and a half feet broad, and nine inches high. The table stood lengthwise along the northern side of the Holy Place. The bread stood for the very presence of God and none but the priests might eat of it (Leviticus 24: 5-9). But David's need had taken precedence over rules and regulations. The Rabbis themselves said, " The Sabbath is made for you and not you for the Sabbath." That is to say at their highest and their best the Rabbis admitted that human need abrogated ritual law. If that be so, how much more is the Son of Man, with His heart of love and mercy, Lord of the Sabbath? How much more can He use it for His purposes of love? But the Pharisees had forgotten the claims of mercy because they were immersed in their rules and regulations. It is a most suggestive thing that they were watching Jesus and His disciples as they passed through the corn fields. Clearly they were spying; from now on every act of Jesus' life was to be watched and scrutinised by these bleak and critical and hostile eyes.

In this passage there is one great general truth. Jesus said to the Pharisees, " Have you not read what David did? " The answer of course was, " Yes "—but they had never seen what it meant. It is possible to read scripture meticulously, to know the Bible inside out from cover to cover, to be able to quote it verbatim and to pass any examination on it—and yet completely to miss its real meaning. Why did the Pharisees miss the meaning—and why do we so often miss it? (i) They did not bring to scripture *an open mind*. They came to scripture not to learn God's will, but to find proof texts to buttress up their own ideas. Far too often men have taken a theology to the Bible instead of finding their theology in the Bible. When we read scripture we must come saying, not, " Listen, Lord, for Thy servant is speaking," but, " Speak, Lord, for Thy servant is listening." (ii) They did not bring *a needy heart*. The man who comes with no sense of need always misses the deepest meaning of scripture. When need awakens, the Bible is a new book. When Bishop Butler was dying he was troubled. " Have you forgotten, my lord," said his chaplain, " that Jesus Christ is a Saviour? " " But," said the dying bishop, " how can I know that He is a Saviour for me? " " It is written," said the chaplain, " him that cometh unto Me I will in nowise cast out." And Butler answered, " I have read these words a thousand times and I never saw their meaning until now. Now I die in peace." The sense of need unlocked for him the treasury of scripture.

When we read God's book we must bring to it the open mind and the needy heart—and then to us also it will be the greatest book in the world.

THE DEFIANCE OF JESUS

Luke 6: 6-12

On another Sabbath Jesus went into the Synagogue and was teaching, and there was a man there whose right hand was withered. The Scribes and the Pharisees watched Him to see if He would heal on the Sabbath day in order to find a charge against Him. He knew well what they were thinking. He said to the man with the withered hand, " Rise, and stand in the midst." He rose and stood. Jesus said to them, " Here is a question for you—is it legal to do good on the Sabbath day or to do evil? To save a life or to destroy it? " He looked round on them and said to him, " Stretch out your hand." He did so and his hand was restored. They were filled with insane anger, and they discussed with each other what they could do to Jesus.

BY this time the opposition to Jesus was quite open. Jesus was teaching in the Synagogue on the Sabbath day and the Scribes and Pharisees were there with the set purpose of watching Him so that, if He healed, they could charge Him with breaking the Sabbath. There is one interesting touch in the story. If we compare the story in Matthew 12: 10-13 and Mark 3: 1-6 with Luke's version of it, we find that only Luke tells us that it was the man's *right* hand which was withered. There speaks the doctor, interested in the details of the case. In this incident Jesus quite openly broke the law. To heal was to work, and work was prohibited on the Sabbath day. True, if there was any danger to life steps might be taken to help a sufferer. For instance, it was always legal to treat diseases of the eye or throat. But this man was in no danger of his life; he might have waited until the next day without peril. But Jesus laid down the great principle that, whatever the rules and regulations may say, it is always right to do a good thing on the Sabbath day. Jesus asked the piercing questions, " Is it legal to save life or to destroy it on the Sabbath? " That must have struck home, for while He was seeking to help the life of the man, they were doing all they could to destroy him. It was He who was seeking to save and they who were seeking to destroy.

In this story there are three characters.

(i) There is *the man with the withered hand*. We can tell two things about him. (*a*) One of the apocryphal gospels, that is, one of the gospels which never gained admission into the New Testament, tells us that he was a stone mason, and he came to Jesus, beseeching His help and saying, " I was a stone mason earning my living with my hand; I beseech you, Jesus, give me back my health that I may not have to beg my bread with shame." *He was a man who wanted to work*. Gods always looks with approval on the man who wants to do an honest day's work. (*b*) *He was a man who was prepared to attempt the impossible*. He did not argue when Jesus told him to stretch out his useless hand; he tried and, in the strength Jesus gave him, he succeeded. *Impossible* is a word which should be banished from the vocabulary of the Christian. As a famous scientist said, " The difference between the difficult and the impossible is only that the impossible takes a little longer to do."

(ii) There is *Jesus*. There is in this story a glorious atmosphere of defiance. Jesus knew that He was being watched, but without hesitation He healed. He bade the man stand out in the midst. This thing was not going to be done in a corner. There is a story of one of Wesley's preachers who proposed to preach in a hostile town. He hired the town-crier to announce the meeting, and the town-crier announced it in a terrified whisper. The preacher took the bell from him and rang it and thundered out. " Mr. So and So will preach in such and such a place and at such and such a time to-night—*and I am the man*." The real Christian displays with pride the banner of his faith and bids the opposition do its worst.

(iii) There were *the Pharisees*. Here were men who took the quite extraordinary course of hating a man who had just cured a sufferer. They are the outstanding example of men who loved their system more than they loved God. Their rules and regulations were dearer to them than God. We see this happen in Churches over and over again.

Disputes are not about the great matters of the faith but about matters of Church government and the like. Leighton once said, "The mode of Church government is unconstrained; but peace and concord, kindness and goodwill are indispensable." There is an ever-present danger of setting loyalty to a system above loyalty to God.

JESUS CHOOSES HIS MEN

Luke 6: 12-19

> In these days Jesus went away into a mountain to pray; and He spent the whole night in prayer to God. When day came He called His disciples. From them He chose twelve, whom He also called Apostles— Simon, whom He named Peter, and Andrew his brother, and James, and John, and Philip, and Bartholomew, and Matthew, and Thomas, and James the son of Alphaeus, and Simon who was called the Zealot, and Judas the son of James, and Judas Iscariot, who became a traitor. He came down with them and took His stand with them on a place in the plain; and there was a great crowd of His disciples there, and a great crowd of people from all Judaea and Jerusalem and from the coastal district of Tyre and Sidon, who had come to listen to Him and to be healed from their diseases; and those who were distressed by unclean spirits were healed and the whole crowd sought to touch Him because power went out from Him, and He healed all.

HERE we see Jesus choosing His men. It is interesting and salutary to see why He chose them, because it is for the same reasons and purposes that He still wants and needs men.

(i) Mark 3: 14 tells us that He chose them *that they might be with Him*. That means two things. (*a*) Jesus chose them to be His friends. It is the amazing thing that Jesus needed human friendship. It is of the very essence of the Christian faith that we can say in all reverence and in all humility that God cannot be happy without men.

Just because God is Father there is a blank in God's heart until the last man comes home. (*b*) Jesus knew that the end was coming. Had Jesus lived in a later age He might have written a book which would have carried His teaching all over the world. But, living when He did, Jesus chose these men that He might write His message upon them. They were to be His living books. They were to company with Him that they might some day take His message to all men.

(ii) Jesus chose them *from His disciples*. The word disciple means *a learner*. They were to be those who were always learning more and more about Him. A Christian is a man whose whole life is spent learning about that Lord whom He will some day meet face to face and will know even as He is known.

(iii) Jesus chose them to be *His apostles*. The Greek word *apostolos* means *someone who is sent out*. It can be used for an envoy or an ambassador. So they were to be His ambassadors to men. A little girl received in the Sunday School a lesson on the disciples. She did not get the word quite right, because she was very young; and she came home and told her parents that she had been learning about Jesus' *samples*. The ambassador is the man who in a foreign land stands for and speaks for and represents his country. He is supremely the sample of his country. The Christian is ever sent to be an ambassador for Christ, not by his words, but by his life and deeds.

About the Twelve themselves we may note two things.

(i) They were very *ordinary men*. There was not a wealthy, nor a famous, nor an influential man amongst them; they had no special education; they were men of the common folk. It is as if Jesus said, " Give me twelve ordinary men and I will change the world." The work of Jesus is not in the hands of men whom the world calls great, but in the hands of ordinary people like ourselves.

(ii) They were *a strange mixture*. To take but two of them—Matthew was a tax-collector, and, therefore, a traitor and a renegade to his own country. Simon was a Zealot, and the Zealots were fanatical nationalists, men who were sworn to assassinate every traitor and every Roman they could lay hands on. It is one of the miracles of the power of Christ that Matthew and Simon the Zealot could live at peace in the close company of the apostolic band. When men are really Christian the most diverse and divergent characters and types can live at peace together. It was said of Gilbert Chesterton and his brother Cecil, "They always argued, they never quarrelled." It is only in Christ that we can solve the problem of living together; and that is so because even the most opposite people are united because they both love Him. If we really love Him we will also love each other.

THE END OF THE WORLD'S VALUES

Luke 6: 20-26

> Jesus lifted up His eyes upon His disciples and said, "Happy are you poor, because yours is the Kingdom of God. Happy are you who are hungry now because you will be filled. Happy are you who weep now because you will laugh. Happy are you when men will hate you and shut you off from their company and insult you and cast out your name as an evil name, for the sake of the Son of Man; for—look you—your reward in heaven will be great. Their fathers used to treat the prophets in the same way. But woe to you who are rich because you have all the comfort you are going to get. Woe to you who are filled because you will be hungry. Woe to you who laugh now because you will grieve and weep. Woe to you when all men speak well of you, for that is what your fathers used to do to the false prophets."

LUKE'S Sermon on the Plain and Matthew's Sermon on the Mount (Matthew, chapters 5 to 7) closely correspond. Both start with a series of Beatitudes. There are differences between the versions of Matthew and Luke, but this one thing is clear—they are a series of bombshells. It may well be that we have read them so often that we have forgotten how revolutionary they are. They are quite unlike the laws which a philosopher or a typical wise man might lay down. Each one is a challenge. As Deissmann said, " They are spoken in an electric atmosphere. They are not quiet stars but flashes of lightning followed by a thunder of surprise and amazement." Quite literally they take the accepted standards and turn them upside down. The people whom Jesus called happy the world would call wretched; and the people Jesus called wretched the world would call happy. Just imagine anyone say, " Happy are the poor, and, Woe to the rich ! " To talk like that is to put an end to the world's values altogether.

Where then is the key to this? The key comes in verse 24. There Jesus says, " Woe to you who are rich because you have all the comfort you are going to get." The word Jesus uses there for *have* is the word which is used for receiving payment in full of an account. It is a business word, the word which a tradesman wrote on an account when he had received payment in full. What Jesus is saying is this, " If you set your heart and bend your whole energies to obtain the things which the world values, you will get them—but that is all you will ever get." In the expressive modern phrase, literally, you have had it! But if on the other hand you set your heart and bend all your energies to be utterly loyal to God and true to Christ, you will run into all kinds of trouble; you may by the world's standards look unhappy, but your payment is still to come; and when it comes it will be joy eternal.

We are here face to face with an eternal choice. It is a choice which begins in childhood and never ends till life ends. Will you take the easy way, and the way which yields immediate pleasure and profit? or, Will you take the hard way which yields immediate toil and sometimes suffering? Will you seize on the pleasure and the profit of the moment? or, Are you willing to look ahead and sacrifice them for the greater good? Will you concentrate

on the world's rewards? or, Will you concentrate on
Christ? If you take the world's way you must abandon
the values of Christ. If you take Christ's way you must
abandon the values of the world. Jesus had no doubt
which way in the end brought happiness. F. R. Maltby
said, " Jesus promised His disciples three things—that
they would be completely fearless, absurdly happy and
in constant trouble." G. K. Chesterton, whose principles
constantly got him into trouble, once said, " I like getting
into hot water. It keeps you clean! " It is Jesus' teaching
that the joy of heaven will amply compensate for the trouble
of earth. As Paul said, " Our light affliction is but for a
moment and works for us a far more exceeding and eternal
weight of glory " (2 Corinthians 4: 17). The challenge of
the Beatitudes is, " Will you be happy in the world's way,
or in Christ's way? "

THE GOLDEN RULE

Luke 6: 27-38

> Jesus said, " But to you who are listening I say, Love
> your enemies, do good to those who hate you, bless
> those who curse you, pray for those who ill-use you.
> To him who strikes you on one cheek offer the other
> cheek also. If anyone takes away your cloak, do not
> stop him taking your tunic too. Give to everyone
> who asks you; if anyone takes away your belongings
> do not demand them back again. As you would like
> men to act towards you, so do you act towards them.
> If you love those who love you, what special grace
> is there in that? Even sinners love those who love
> them. If you are kind to those who are kind to you,
> what special grace is there in that? Even sinners do
> that. If you lend to those from whom you wish to get,
> what special grace is in that? Even sinners lend to
> sinners in order to get as much back again. But you
> must love your enemies; and do good to them; and
> lend with no hope of getting anything in return.
> Your reward will be great and you will be the sons of
> the Most High, because He is kind both to the thankless

> and to the wicked. Be merciful as your Father in
> heaven is merciful; do not judge and you will not be
> judged; do not condemn and you will not be con-
> demned; forgive and you will be forgiven. Give and it
> will be given to you. People will give into your bosom,
> good measure pressed together, shaken down, running
> over; for with what measure you measure it will be
> measured to you back again."

THERE is no commandment of Jesus which has caused so
much discussion and debate as the commandment to
love our enemies. Before we can obey it we must discover
what it means. In Greek there are three words for to love.
There is *eran*, which describes passionate love, the love
of a man for a maid. There is *philein*, which describes
our love for our nearest and dearest, the warm affection of
the heart. Now neither of these two words is used here.
The word used here is *agapan*, which needs a whole para-
graph to translate it. *Agapan* describes an active feeling
of benevolence towards the other person; it means that
no matter what that person does to us we will never allow
ourselves to desire anything but his highest good; and
we will deliberately and of set purpose go out of our way
to be good and kind to him. This is most suggestive.
We cannot love our enemies as we love our nearest and
dearest. To do so would be unnatural, impossible and even
wrong. But we can see to it that, no matter what a man
does to us, even if he insults, ill-treats and injures us, we
will seek nothing but his highest good. One thing emerges
from this. The love we bear to our dear ones is something
we cannot help. We speak of *falling* in love; it is something
which happens to us. But this love towards our enemies
is not only something of the heart; it is something of the
will. It is something which by the grace of Christ we will
ourselves to do.

This passage has in it two great facts about the Christian
ethic.

(i) The Christian ethic is *positive*. It does not consist in
not doing things but in *doing* them. Jesus gave us the

THE GOSPEL OF LUKE

Golden Rule which bids us do to others as we would have them do to us. That rule exists in many writers of many creeds in its *negative* form. Hillel, one of the great Jewish Rabbis, was asked by a man to teach him the whole law while he stood on one leg. He answered, " What is hateful to thee, do not to another. That is the whole law and all else is explanation." Philo, the great Jew of Alexandria, said, " What you hate to suffer, do not do to anyone else." Isocrates, the Greek orator, said, " What things make you angry when you suffer them at the hands of others, do not you do to other people." The Stoics had as one of their basic rules, " What you do not wish to be done to yourself, do not you do to any other." When Confucius was asked, " Is there one word which may serve as a rule of practice for all one's life? " he answered, " Is not Reciprocity such a word? What you do not want done to yourself, do not do to others." *Everyone of these forms is negative.* It is not unduly difficult to keep oneself from such action; but it is a very different thing to go out of your way to do to others what you would want them to do to you. The very essence of Christian conduct is that it does not consist in not doing bad things, but in actively doing good things.

(ii) The Christian ethic is based on *the extra thing*. Jesus described the common ways of sensible conduct and then dismissed them with the question, " What special grace is in that? " So often people claim to be just as good as their neighbours. Very likely they are. But the question of Jesus is, " How much *better* are you than the ordinary person? " It is not our neighbour with whom we must compare ourselves; we may well stand that comparison very adequately; it is *God* with whom we must compare ourselves; and in that comparison we are all in default.

(iii) What is the reason for this Christian conduct? The reason is that it makes us like God, for that is the way in which God acts. God sends His rain on the just and the unjust. He is kind to the man who brings Him joy and equally kind to the man who grieves His heart. God's love embraces saint and sinner alike. It is that love that we must copy; if we, too, seek nothing but even our enemy's highest good we will in truth be the children of God.

Verse 38 has the strange phrase, " People will give into your bosom." The Jew wore a long loose robe down to the feet, and round the waist a girdle. The robe could be pulled up so that the bosom of the robe above the girdle formed a kind of outsize pocket in which things could be carried. So the modern equivalent of the phrase would be, " People will fill your pocket."

RULES FOR LIFE AND LIVING

Luke 6: 39-46

> Jesus spoke a parable to them: " Surely a blind man cannot lead a blind man? If he tries to do so will not both fall into the ditch? The disciple cannot advance beyond his teacher, but every disciple will be equipped as his teacher is. Why do you look at the speck of dust that is in your brother's eye and never notice the plank that is in your own eye? Or, how can you say to your brother, ' Brother, let me take out the speck of dust that is in your eye,' when you yourself do not notice the plank in your own eye? You hypocrite! First put the plank out of your own eye and then you will see clearly to put out the speck of dust that is in your brother's eye. There is no good tree which produces rotten fruit, nor again, is there a rotten tree which produces good fruit. Each tree is recognized by its own fruit. People do not gather figs from thistles nor do they gather grapes from a bramble bush. The good man produces good from the treasure of his heart. The evil man produces evil from the evil. The mouth speaks out of whatever abounds in the heart."

To us this reads like a disconnected series of separate sayings. Two things are possible. It may well be that Luke is collecting together here sayings of Jesus which were

78

spoken on different occasions and is giving us a kind of compendium of rules for life and living. Or, this may be an instance of the Jewish method of preaching. The Jews called preaching *Charaz*, which means *stringing beads*. The Rabbis held that the preacher must never linger more than a few moments on any topic but, in order to maintain interest, must move quickly from one topic to another. Jewish preaching, therefore, often seems to us to be disconnected.

The passage falls into four sections.

(i) Verses 39 and 40. Jesus warned those who listen that no teacher can lead his scholars beyond that stage which he himself has reached. That is a double warning to us. In our learning we must seek only the best teacher of all for only He can lead us farthest on. In our teaching we must ever remember that we cannot teach what we do not know.

(ii) Verses 41 and 42. Here is an example of the humour of Jesus. It must have been with a smile that Jesus drew the picture of a man with a plank in his own eye trying to extract a speck of dust from someone else's eye. Jesus taught that we have no right to criticise unless we ourselves are free of faults. That simply means that we have no right to criticise at all, because " there is so much bad in the best of us and so much good in the worst of us that it ill becomes any of us to find fault with the rest of us."

(iii) Verses 43 and 44 remind us that a man cannot be judged in any other way than by his deeds. It was said to a teacher, " I cannot hear what you say for listening to what you are." Teaching and preaching are both " truth through personality." Fine words will never take the place of fine deeds. That is very relevant to-day. We fear the menace of Communism and of other secular movements. We will never defeat these movements by writing books and pamphlets and holding discussion groups. The only way to prove the superiority of Christianity is to show by our lives that it produces better men and women.

(iv) Verse 45. In this verse Jesus reminded men that the words of their lips are in the last analysis the product of their hearts. No man can speak of God with his mouth unless the Spirit of God be in his heart. Nothing shows the state of a man's heart so well as the words he speaks when he is not being careful and considering his words, but when he is talking freely and saying, as we say, the first thing which comes into his head. If you ask a person to direct you to a certain place, one person may tell you it is near such and such a *church*; another, that it is near such and such a *cinema*; another, that it is near such and such a *football ground*; another, that it is near such and such a *public house*. The very words of the answer to a chance question show where a man's thoughts most naturally turn and where the interests of his heart lie. Always our speech betrays us.

THE ONLY SURE FOUNDATION

Luke 6: 47-49

> Jesus said, " Why do you call me, Lord, Lord, and do not what I say? I will show you what everyone who comes to me and listens to my words and does them is like. He is like a man building a house, who dug deep down into the earth and laid the foundation on a rock. When the flood rose the river dashed against that house but it could not shake it because it was well founded. But he who has listened to me and has not done what I say is like a man who built his house on the top of earth without any foundation. The river dashed against it and immediately it collapsed, and great was the fall of it."

To get the real picture behind this parable we have to read Matthew's version of it as well in Matthew 7: 24-27. In Luke's version the river does not seem to make sense;

that is because Luke was not a native of Palestine and had not a clear picture of the circumstances in his own mind; whereas Matthew did belong to Palestine and knew just what the picture was. In Palestine in summer many of the rivers dried up altogether and left a sandy river bed empty of water. But in winter, after the September rains had come, the empty river bed became a raging torrent. Now many a man, looking for a site for a house, found an inviting stretch of sand and built there, only to discover when the winter came that he had built his house in the middle of a raging river which swept the house away. But the wise man searched for rock, where it was much more difficult to build and where it was hard labour to cut out the foundations. But when the wild winter weather came his toil was amply repaid, for his house stood strong and firm and secure. In either form the parable teaches us the importance of laying the right foundation for life. The only true foundation for life is obedience to the teaching of Jesus.

What made the foolish builder choose so unwisely?

(i) The foolish builder wanted *to avoid toil.* He could not be bothered to dig into the rock. The sand was much easier, and much more attractive, and much less trouble. He wanted the easy way. It may be easier to take our way than it is to take Jesus' way but the end is ruin. It may seem hard to take Jesus' but it is the way to security here and hereafter.

(ii) The foolish builder was *short-sighted.* He never troubled to think what his chosen site would be like six months afterwards. In every decision in life there is a short view and a long view. Happy is the man who never barters future good for present pleasure. Happy is the man who sees things, not in the light of the moment, but in the light of eternity.

When we learn that the hard way is often the best way, and that the long view is always the right view, then we will found our lives upon the teaching of Jesus and no storms will ever shake them.

A SOLDIER'S FAITH

Luke 7: 1-10

When Jesus had completed all His words in the hearing of the people, He went into Capernaum. The servant of a certain centurion was so ill that he was going to die, and he was very dear to him. When he heard about Jesus he sent some Jewish elders to Him and asked Him to come and save his servant's life. They came to Jesus and strenuously urged Him to come. " He is," they said, " a man who deserves that you should do this for him, for he loves our nation and has himself built us our Synagogue." So Jesus went with them. When He was now quite near the house the centurion sent friends to Him. " Sir," he said, " do not trouble yourself. I am not worthy that you should come under my roof; nor do I count myself fit to come to you; but just speak a word and my servant will be cured. For I myself am a man under orders, and I have soldiers under me, and I say to one, ' Go,' and he goes; and to another, ' Come,' and he comes; and I say to my servant, ' Do this,' and he does it." When Jesus heard this He was amazed at him. He turned to the crowd who were following Him and said, " I tell you I have not found such great faith not even in Israel." And those who had been sent returned to the house and found the servant completely cured.

THE central character in this story is a Roman centurion. This centurion was no ordinary man.

(i) First and foremost, *he was a centurion*, and no centurion was an ordinary man. A centurion was the equivalent of a company sergeant-major; and the centurions were the backbone of the Roman army. Wherever centurions are spoken of in the New Testament they are spoken of well (cp. Luke 23: 47; Acts 10: 22; 22: 26; 23: 17, 23, 24; 24: 23; 27: 43). Polybius, the historian, describes the qualifications of centurions. They must be not so much " seekers after danger as men who can command, steady in action, and reliable; they ought not to be over anxious to rush into the fight; but when hard pressed they must be ready to hold their ground and die at their posts."

The centurion must have been a man amongst men or he would never have held the post which was his.

(ii) *He had a completely unusual attitude to his slave.* He loved this slave and would go to any trouble to save him. In the eyes of Roman law, a slave was defined as a living tool; he had no rights; a master could ill-treat him and even kill him if he chose. A Roman writer on estate management recommends the farmer to examine his implements every year and to throw out those which are old and broken, and to do the same with his slaves. Normally when a slave was past his work he would have been thrown out to die. The attitude of this centurion to his slave was quite unusual.

(iii) *He was clearly a deeply religious man.* A man needs to be more than superficially interested before he will go the length of building a Synagogue. It is true that the Romans encouraged religion from the cynical motive that it kept people in order. They regarded it as the opiate of the people. Augustus recommended the building of Synagogues for that very reason. As Gibbon said in a famous sentence, " The various modes of religion which prevailed in the Roman world were all considered by the people as equally true; by the philosopher as equally false; *and by the magistrate as equally useful.*" But this centurion was no administrative cynic; he was a sincerely religious man.

(iv) *He had an extremely unusual attitude to the Jews.* If the Jews despised the Gentiles, the Gentiles hated the Jews. Anti-semitism is not a new thing. The Romans called the Jews a filthy race; they spoke of Judaism as a barbarous superstition; they spoke of the Jewish hatred of mankind; they accused the Jews of worshipping an ass's head and annually sacrificing a Gentile stranger to their God. True, many of the Gentiles, weary of the many gods and the loose morals of paganism, had accepted the Jewish doctrine of the one God and the austere Jewish ethic. But the whole atmosphere of this story implies a close bond of friendship between this centurion and the Jews.

(v) *He was a humble man.* He knew quite well that a strict Jew was forbidden by the law to enter the house of a Gentile (Acts 10: 28). He knew that a strict Jew would not allow a Gentile into his house, nor have any communication with him. He would not even come to Jesus himself. He persuaded his Jewish friends to approach the Master. This man who was accustomed to command had an amazing humility in the presence of true greatness.

(vi) *He was a man of faith.* His faith is based on the soundest argument. He argued from the here and now to reach the there and then. He argued from his own experience to God. If his authority produced the results it did, how much more must that of Jesus? He came with that perfect confidence which looks up and says, " Lord, I *know* you can do this." If we only had a faith like that for us too the miracle would happen and life would become new.

THE COMPASSION OF CHRIST

Luke 7: 11-17

Next, after that, Jesus was on His way to a town called Nain; and His disciples and a great crowd accompanied Him on the journey. When He came near the gate of the town—look you—a man who had died was being carried out to burial. He was his mother's only son, and she was a widow. There was a great crowd of townspeople with her. When the Lord saw her He was moved to the depths of His heart for her and said to her, " Don't go on weeping!" He went up and touched the bier. Those who were carrying it stood still. " Young man," He said, " I tell you, rise!" And the dead man sat up and began to speak. And He gave him back to his mother. And awe gripped them all. They glorified God saying, " A great prophet has been raised up amongst us," and, " God has graciously visited His people." This story about Him went out in all Judaea and all the surrounding countryside.

IN this passage, and in the one immediately preceding it, once again Luke, the doctor, speaks. In verse 10 the word which we translated *completely cured* is the technical medical term for *sound in wind and limb*. In verse 15 the word which is used for *sitting up* is the technical term for a patient *sitting up in bed*.

This incident happened at Nain, which was a day's journey from Capernaum. Nain lies between Endor and Shunem, where Elisha, as the old story runs, raised another widow's son (2 Kings 4: 18-37). To this day, ten minutes' walk from Nain out on the road to Endor, there is a cemetery of rock tombs in which the dead are laid.

In many ways this is the loveliest story in all the gospels.

(i) It tells us of *the pathos and the poignancy of human life*. The funeral procession would be headed by the band of professional mourners with their flutes and their cymbals, uttering in a kind of frenzy their shrill cries of grief. There is all the ageless sorrow of the world in the austere and simple sentence, " He was his mother's only son and she was a widow."

" Never morning wore to evening
But some heart did break."

In Shelley's *Adonais*, his lament for Keats, he writes,

" As long as skies are blue, and fields are green,
Evening must usher night, night urge the morrow,
Month follow month with woe, and year wake year
to sorrow."

Virgil, the Roman poet, in an immortal phrase spoke about " The tears of things "—*sunt lacrimae rerum*. It is in the nature of things that we live in a world of broken hearts.

(ii) But to the pathos of human life, *Luke adds the compassion of Christ*. Jesus was moved to the depths of His heart. There is no stronger word in the Greek language for pity and sympathy and feeling, and it is a word which, again and again in the gospel story, is used of Jesus (Matthew 14: 14; 15: 32; 20: 34; Mark 1: 41; 8: 2). Here to the ancient world must have been a staggering thing. The noblest faith in antiquity was that of Stoicism. The Stoics believed that the primary characteristic of God was *apathy*. By *apathy* they meant *incapability of feeling*. If someone can make another sad or sorry, glad or joyful, it means that, at least for the moment, he can influence the other person. If he can influence him that means that, at least for the moment, he is greater than he and superior to him. Now, no one can be greater than God; therefore, no one must influence God; therefore, in the nature of things, God must be incapable of feeling. And here men were presented with the amazing conception of one who was the Son of God and who was moved to the depths of His being.

> " In ev'ry pang that rends the heart,
>   The Man of sorrows has a part."

For many that is the most precious thing about the God who was the God and Father of our Lord Jesus Christ.

(iii) But to the compassion of Jesus, Luke adds *the power of Jesus*. Jesus went up and touched the bier. It was not a coffin, for coffins were not used in the east. Very often long wicker work baskets were used for carrying the body to the grave. It was a dramatic moment. As one great commentator says, " Jesus claimed as His own what death had seized as his prey." It may well be that here we have a miracle of diagnosis; that Jesus with these keen eyes of His saw that the lad was in a cataleptic trance and saved him from being buried alive, as so many were in Palestine. It does not matter; the fact remains that Jesus claimed for life a lad who had been marked for death. Jesus is not only the Lord of life; He is the Lord of death who Himself triumphed over the grave and who has promised that, because He lives, we shall live also (John 14: 19).

THE FINAL PROOF

Luke 7: 18-29

> John's disciples told him about all these things; so John called two of his disciples and sent them to the Lord saying, " Are you He who is to come, or, are we to look for another? " When they arrived, the men said to Him, " John, the Baptiser, has sent us to you. Are you the One who is to come," he asks, " or are we to look for another? " At that time He cured many of their diseases and afflictions and of evil spirits, and to many blind people He gave the gift of sight. " Go," He answered them, " and tell John what you have seen and heard. The blind recover their sight; the lame walk; the lepers are cleansed; the deaf hear; the dead are raised up; the poor have the Good News told to them; and blessed is he who does not find a stumbling-block in me."
>
> When John's messengers had gone away, Jesus began to say to the crowds concerning John, " What did you go out into the desert to see? A reed shaken by the wind? But what did you go out to see? A man dressed in soft clothes? Look you—those who wear expensive clothes and live in luxury are in royal palaces. But what did you go out to see? A prophet? Yes, I say to you, and something more than a prophet. This is he of whom it stands written—' Look you, I send my messenger before you to prepare your way before you.' I tell you there is no one greater amongst those born of women than John. But he who is least in the Kingdom of God is greater than he." When the people and the tax-collectors heard this they called God righteous for they had been baptized with John's baptism.

THERE was a day when John sent emissaries to Jesus to ask if He really was the Messiah, God's Anointed King, or if they must look for someone else.

(i) This incident has worried many thinkers because they have been surprised at the apparent doubt in the mind of John. Various explanations have been advanced. (*a*) It is suggested that John took this step, not for his own sake, but *for the sake of his disciples*. He was sure enough; but they had their qualms and he desired that they should be confronted with proof unanswerable. (*b*) It is suggested that John wished to hurry Jesus on, that he thought that it was time that Jesus moved towards decisive action. (*c*) The simplest explanation is the best. Think what was happening to John. John, the child of the desert and of the wide-open spaces, was confined in a dungeon cell in the castle of Machaerus. Once one of the Macdonalds, a Highland chieftain, was confined in a little cell in Carlisle Castle. In his cell there was one little window. To this day you may see the marks in the sandstone of the feet and the hands of the Highlander as he lifted himself up and clung to the window ledge, as day by day he gazed with infinite longing out upon the border hills and valleys that he would never walk again. Shut in his cell, choked by the narrow walls, John asked this question because his cruel captivity had put tremors in his heart.

(ii) Note the proof that Jesus offered. He pointed at the facts. The sick and the suffering and the humble poor were experiencing the power and hearing the word of the Good News. Here is a point which is seldom realized—*this is not the answer John expected*. If Jesus was God's Anointed One, John would have expected Jesus to say, " My armies are massing. Caesarea, the headquarters of the Roman government, is about to fall. The sinners are being obliterated. And judgment has begun." John would have expected Jesus to say, " The wrath of God is on the march." Jesus said, " The mercy of God is here." Let us remember that where pain is soothed and sorrow turned to joy, where sorrow and suffering and death are vanquished, there is the Kingdom of God. Jesus answer was, " Go back and tell John that the love of God is here."

(iii) After John's emissaries had gone, Jesus paid His own tribute to John. People had crowded out into the desert to see and hear John. They had not gone out to see a reed shaken in the wind. That may mean one of two things. (*a*) Nothing was commoner by Jordan's banks than a reed shaken in the wind. It was in fact a proverbial phrase for the commonest of sights. It may then mean that the crowds went out to see no ordinary sight. (*b*) It may stand for fickleness. It was no vacillating, swaying character men went out to see, not a man like a swaying reed, but a man immovable as a mighty tree. They had not gone out to see some soft effeminate soul, like the silk-clad courtiers of the royal palace. What then had they gone out to see? (*a*) First, Jesus pays John a great tribute. All men expected that before God's Anointed King arrived upon the earth, Elijah would return to prepare the way and to act as His herald (Malachi 4: 5). John was the herald of the Highest. (*b*) Second, Jesus states quite clearly the limitations of John. The least in the Kingdom of Heaven was greater than he. Why? Some have said that it was because John had wavered, if but for a moment, in his faith. It was not that. It was because John marked a dividing line in history. Since John's proclamation had been made Jesus had come; eternity had invaded time; heaven had invaded earth; God had arrived in Jesus; and therefore life could never be the same again. We date all time as before Christ and after Christ—B.C. and A.D. Jesus is the dividing line. And, therefore, all who come after Him and who receive Him are of necessity granted a greater blessing than all who went before. The entry of Jesus into the world divided all time into two; and the entry of Jesus into our lives divided all life in two. If any man be in Christ he is a new creature (2 Corinthians 5: 17). He is created all over again.

As Bilney, the martyr said, " When I read that Christ Jesus came into the world to save sinners, it was as if day suddenly broke on a dark night."

THE PERVERSITY OF MEN

Luke 7: 30-35

But the Pharisees and the Scribes frustrated God's purpose for themselves because they were not baptized by Him. " To whom," asked Jesus, " will I compare the men of this generation? And to whom are they like? They are like children seated in the market place and called to one another. ' We have piped to you,' they say, ' and you did not dance. We have sung you a dirge and you did not weep.' John the Baptiser came neither eating bread nor drinking wine, and you say, ' He has a demon.' The Son of Man came eating and drinking and you say, ' Look! a gluttonous man and a wine-drinker, the friend of tax-collectors and sinners.' But wisdom is justified by her children."

THIS is a passage which has two great warnings in it.

(i) It tells us of the perils of free-will. The Scribes and the Pharisees had succeeded in frustrating God's purpose for themselves. The tremendous truth of Christianity is that the coercion of God is not the coercion of force but the coercion of love. It is precisely there that we can glimpse the sorrow of God. It is always love's greatest tragedy to look upon some loved one who has taken the wrong way and to see what might have been, what could have been and what was meant to have been. That is life's greatest heartbreak. Sir William Watson has a poem called *Lux Perdita*, the " Lost Light."

" These were the weak, slight hands
That might have taken this strong soul, and bent
Its stubborn substance to thy soft intent,
And bound it unresisting with such bands
As not the arm of envious heaven had rent.

These were the calming eyes
That round my pinnace could have stilled the sea,
And drawn thy voyager home, and bid him be
Pure with their pureness, with their wisdom wise,
Merged in their light, and greatly lost in thee.

90

But thou—thou passedst on,
With whiteness clothed of dedicated days,
Cold, like a star; and me in alien ways
Thou leftest, following life's chance lure, where shone
The wandering gleam that beckons and betrays."

It is true that,

" Of all sad words of tongue and pen
The saddest are those, ' It might have been.' "

God's tragedy, too, is the might have been of life. As G. K. Chesterton said, " God had written not so much a poem, but rather a play; a play He had planned as perfect, but which had necessarily been left to human actors and stage managers, who had since made a great mess of it." God save us from making shipwreck of life and bringing heartbreak to God by using our freewill to frustrate His purposes.

(ii) It tells of the sheer perversity of men. John had come, living with a hermit's austerity, and the Scribes and Pharisees had said that he was a mad eccentric, that some demon had taken his wits away. Jesus had come, living the life of men and entering into all their activities, and they had taunted Him with loving earth's pleasures far too much. We all know the days when a child will girn at anything; we all know the moods when nothing will please us. The human heart can be lost in a perversity in which any appeal that God may make will be met with wilful and wayward and childish discontent.

(iii) But there are the few who answer; and God's wisdom is in the end justified by those who are God's children. Man may misuse their freewill to frustrate God's purposes; men in their perversity may be blind and deaf to all God's appeal. Had God used the force of coercion and laid on man the iron bonds of a will that could not be denied then there would have been a world of automata and a world without trouble. But God chose the dangerous way of love, and love in the end will triumph.

A SINNER'S LOVE

Luke 7: 36-50

> One of the Pharisees invited Jesus to eat with him. He went into the Pharisee's house and reclined at table; and—look you—there was a woman in the town, a bad woman. She knew that He was at table in the Pharisee's house, so she took an alabaster phial of perfume and stood behind Him, beside His feet, weeping. She began to wash His feet with tears, and she wiped them with the hairs of her head; and she kept kissing His feet and anointing them with the perfume. When the Pharisee, who had invited Him, saw this, he said to himself, " If this fellow was a prophet, He would have known who and what kind of a person this woman is who keeps touching Him, for she is a bad woman." Jesus answered him, " Simon, I have something to say to you." He said, " Master, say it." Jesus said, " There were two men who were in debt to a certain lender. The one owed him £20, the other £2. Since they were unable to pay he cancelled the debt to both. Who then will love him the more? " Simon answered, " I presume, he to whom the greater favour was shown." He said to him, " Your judgment is correct." He turned to the woman and said to Simon, " Do you see this woman? I came into your house—you gave me no water for my feet. She has washed my feet with her tears, and wiped them with the hairs of her head. You did not give me any kiss. But she, from the time I came in, has not ceased to kiss my feet. You did not anoint my head with oil. She has anointed my feet with perfume. Wherefore, I tell you, her sins—her many sins—are forgiven for she loved much. He to whom little is forgiven loves little." He said to her, " Your sins are forgiven." Those who were at table with Him began to say to themselves, " Who is this who forgives even sins? " He said to the woman, " Your faith has saved you. Go in peace."

THIS is one of the stories which is so vivid that it makes one believe that Luke may well have been an artist.

(i) The scene is in the courtyard of the house of Simon the Pharisee. The houses of well-to-do people were built

round an open courtyard in the form of a hollow square.
Often in the courtyard there was a garden and a fountain;
and there in the warm weather meals were eaten. It was
the custom in the east that when a Rabbi was at a meal
in such a house, all kinds of people came in—they were
quite free to do so—to listen to the pearls of wisdom which
fell from his lips. That explains the presence of the woman.
When a guest entered such a house three things were
always done. The host placed his hand on the guest's
shoulder and gave him the kiss of peace. That would be
a mark of respect which was never omitted in the case of a
distinguished Rabbi. The roads were only dust tracks,
and shoes were only soles held in place by straps across
the foot. So always cool water was poured over the guest's
feet to cleanse and comfort them. Either a pinch of sweet-
smelling incense was burned or a drop of attar of roses was
placed on the guest's head. These things good manners
demanded, and in this case not one of them was done.
In the east the guests did not sit, but reclined, at table.
They lay on low couches, resting on the left elbow, leaving
the right arm free, with the feet stretched out behind;
and during the meal the sandals were taken off. That
explains how the woman could be standing at Jesus' feet.

(ii) Simon was a Pharisee, one of The Separated Ones.
Why should such a man invite Jesus to his house at all?
There are three possible reasons. (*a*) It is just possible
that he was an admirer and a sympathiser with Jesus,
for not all the Pharisees were His enemies (cp. Luke 13 : 31).
But the whole atmosphere of discourtesy makes that
unlikely. (*b*) It could be that Simon had invited Jesus
to His house with the deliberate intention of enticing
Him into some word or action which might have been made
the basis of a charge against Him. Simon may have been
an *agent provocateur*. Again, it is not likely, because in
verse 40 Simon gives Jesus the title, Rabbi. (*c*) Most
likely, Simon was a collector of celebrities; and with a half-

patronising contempt had invited this startling young Galilaean to have a meal with him. That would best explain the strange combination of a certain respect with the omission of the courtesies of the occasion. Simon was a man who tried to patronise Jesus.

(iii) The woman was a bad woman, and a notoriously bad woman. She was a prostitute. No doubt she had listened to Jesus speak from the edge of the crowd, and had glimpsed in Him the hand which would lift her from the mire of her ways. Round her neck she wore, like all Jewish women, a little phial of concentrated perfume; they were called alabasters; and they were very costly. She wished to pour it on His feet, for it was all she had to offer. But as she saw Him the tears came and fell upon His feet. For a Jewish woman to appear with hair unbound was an act of the gravest immodesty. On her wedding day a girl bound up her hair and never would she appear with it unbound again. The fact that this woman loosed her long hair in public showed how she had forgotten everyone except Jesus.

The whole story demonstrates a contrast between two attitudes of mind and heart. (i) Simon was conscious of no need and therefore felt no love, and therefore received no forgiveness. Simon's impression of himself was that he was a good man in the sight of men and of God. (ii) The woman was conscious of nothing else than a clamant need, and therefore was overwhelmed with love for Him who could supply it, and therefore received forgiveness.

The one thing which shuts a man off from God is self-sufficiency. And the strange thing is that the better a man is the more he feels his sin. Paul could speak of sinners " of whom I am chief " (2 Timothy I: 15). Francis of Assisi could say, " There is nowhere a more wretched and a more miserable sinner than I." It is true to say that the greatest of sins is to be conscious of no sin; but a sense of need will open the door to the forgiveness of God, because God is love, and love's greatest glory is to be needed.

ON THE ROAD

Luke 8: 1-3

> After that, Jesus travelled through the country, town by town, and village by village, preaching the Good News of the Kingdom of God. The Twelve were with Him, as were certain women, who had been cured from evil spirits and from illnesses. There was Mary, who is called Mary Magdalene, out of whom there went seven devils, and Joanna, the wife of Chuza, who was Herod's agent, and Susanna and many others. It was their habit to minister to their needs out of their resources.

THE time which we saw coming has now come. Jesus is on the road. The Synagogues were not now open to Him, as once they had been. He had begun, as it were, in the Church, where any man with a message from God might justly expect to find a responsive and receptive audience. Instead of a welcome He had found opposition; instead of eager listeners He had found the Scribes and Pharisees bleakly waiting to catch Him out in His words and deeds; so now He took to the open road, and the hillside and the lake shore.

(i) Once more we are confronted with a fact which we have already noted. This passage lists a little group of women who served Him out of their resources. It was always considered to be a pious act to support a Rabbi, and the fact that the devoted followers of Jesus helped Him in this way was in direct line with ordinary custom and practice. But, as with the disciples, so with these women, we cannot fail to see how mixed a company they were. There was Mary Magdalene, that is Mary from the town of Magdala, out of whom He had cast seven devils. Clearly she had a past that was a dark and terrible thing. There was Joanna. She was the wife of Chuza, Herod's *epitropos*. A king had many perquisites and much private property; his *epitropos* was the official who looked after the king's financial interests. In the Roman Empire, even in provinces which were governed by proconsuls appointed by the senate, the Emperor still had his *epitropos* to safeguard his interests. So then there could be no more trusted and important official. It is an amazing thing to find Mary Magdalene, with the dark past, and Joanna, the lady of the court, in the one company. It is one of the supreme achievements of Jesus that He can enable the most diverse people to live together without in the least losing their own personalities or qualities. G. K. Chesterton writes about the text which says that the lion will lie down with the lamb. " But remember that this text is too lightly interpreted. It is constantly assumed . . . that when the lion lies down with the lamb the lion becomes lamb-like. But that is brutal annexation and imperialism on the part of the lamb. That is simply the lamb absorbing the lion instead of the lion eating the lamb. The real problem is— Can the lion lie down with the lamb and still retain his royal ferocity? *That* is the problem the Church attempted; *that* is the miracle she achieved." There is nothing which the Church needs more than to learn how to yoke in common harness the diverse temperaments and qualities of different people. If we are failing it is our own fault, for, in Christ, it can be done—it has been done.

(ii) In this list of women we have a group whose help was practical. Being women, they would not in Palestine be allowed to preach; but they gave the gifts they had. There was an old shoemaker who once had wished to become a minister, but the way had never opened up. He was the friend of a young divinity student; and when the lad one day was called to his first charge the old man asked him for one favour. He asked to be allowed always to make the lad's shoes, as long as life remained to him, so that he might feel that the preacher was wearing his shoes in the pulpit into which he could never come himself. It is not always the person in the foreground who is doing the greatest work. How many a man who occupies a public position could not sustain it for one week without the privacy of the home behind him! There is no gift which cannot be used in the service of Christ. Many of His greatest servants are in the background, unseen but essential to His cause.

THE SOWER AND THE SEED

Luke 8: 4-15

When a great crowd had gathered, and when they came to Him from every city, Jesus spoke to them by means of a parable. The sower went out to sow his seed. As he sowed some seed fell by the wayside. It was trampled upon and the birds of the heaven devoured it. Other seed fell on rocky ground where it grew up and withered because there was no moisture. Other seed fell in the middle of thorns and the thorns grew up along with it and choked the life out of it. Other seed fell into good ground and it produced a crop a hundredfold. As He told the story He said, " He that has an ear to hear let him hear."

The disciples asked Him what the parable meant. He said, " It is given to you to know the secrets of the Kingdom of God. To the others it is presented in parables, so that they may see, and yet not see, and so that they may hear and yet not understand."

The meaning of the parable is this. The seed is the word of God. Those by the wayside stand for those who have heard, and then the devil comes and takes the word from their hearts so that they may not believe and be saved. Those on the rocky ground stand for those, who, whenever they hear the word, gladly receive it; but they have no root; they believe for a time; but when a time of trial comes they fall away. The seed that fell among thorns stands for those, who, when they have heard, go their way and are suffocated by the cares, the wealth and the pleasures of this life, and so never complete their crop. The seed that is in the good ground stands for those who have heard the word and keep hold of it in a heart that is fine and good and bear fruit with fortitude.

IN this parable Jesus used a picture that all His hearers would recognize. It is in fact quite likely that He was looking at some sower sowing his seed as He spoke.

The parable speaks of four kinds of ground. (i) The common ground in Palestine was split into long narrow strips; between the strips there were paths which were rights of way; when the seed fell on these paths which were as hard as the road it had no chance of getting it. (ii) There was the rocky ground. This does not mean ground that was full of stones. It means ground which was only a thin skin of earth over a shelf of limestone rock. In such ground there was no moisture and no nourishment, and the growing plant was bound to wither and die. (iii) The ground which was full of thorns was ground which at the moment looked clean enough. It is possible to make any bit of ground *look* clean simply by turning it over. But the seeds of the weeds and the fibrous roots of the wild grasses had been left in it. The good seed and the weeds grew together, and weeds always grow more strongly than good plants; and so the life was choked out of the good seed. (iv) The good ground was ground that was deep and clean and well-prepared.

Verses 9 and 10 have always been puzzling verses. It sounds as if Jesus was saying that He spoke in parables so that people would not be able to understand; and we cannot believe that Jesus would deliberately cloak His meaning to hide it from His listeners. Various explanations have been suggested. (i) Matthew (13: 13) puts it slightly different. He says that Jesus spoke in parables *because* people could not rightly see and understand. Matthew seems to say that it was not to hinder people from seeing and understanding but to help them that Jesus so spoke. (ii) Matthew quotes immediately after this a saying of Isaiah 6: 9, 10. Isaiah in effect says, " I have spoken to them the word of God and the only effect in fact is that they have not understood a word of it." So then the saying of Jesus may indicate not the object of His teaching in parables but the result of it. The net result was that people just did not understand. (iii) What Jesus really meant is this—people can become so dull and heavy and blunted in mind that when God's truth comes to them they cannot see it. It is not God's fault. They have become so mentally lazy, so blinded by prejudice, so unwilling to see anything they do not want to see, that the result is that they have become incapable of assimilating God's truth.

There are two interpretations of this parable.

(i) It is suggested that the parable means that the fate of the word of God depends on the heart into which it is sown. (*a*) The hard path represents the shut mind, the mind which, as we put it, will not take it in. (*b*) The shallow ground represents those who accept the word but who never think it out and who never realize its consequences and who therefore collapse when the strain comes. (*c*) The thorny ground stands for those whose lives are so busy that the things of God get crowded out. We must ever remember that the things which crowd out the highest need not necessarily be bad things. They may in themselves be good things. The worst enemy of the best is the second best. (*c*) The good ground stands for the good heart. The good hearer does three things. First, he listens attentively. Second, he keeps what he hears in his mind and heart and thinks over it until he discovers its meaning for himself. Third, he acts upon it. He translates what he has heard into terms of action.

(ii) It is suggested that the real interpretation of the parable is this. Think of the situation. Jesus has been banished from the Synagogues. The Scribes and the Pharisees and the religious leaders are up against Him. Inevitably the disciples would be disheartened. It is to them Jesus speaks this parable and in it He is saying, " Every farmer knows that some of his seed will be lost; it cannot all grow. But that does not discourage him or make him stop sowing because he knows that in spite of that the harvest is sure." It is Jesus saying to His disciples, " I know we have our setbacks and our

THE GOSPEL OF LUKE

discouragements; I know we have our enemies and our opponents; but, never despair; in the end the harvest is sure."

So this parable can be both a warning to us as to how we hear and receive the word of God and an encouragement to banish all despair in the certainty that not all the setbacks can defeat the ultimate harvest of God.

LAWS FOR LIFE

Luke 8: 16-18

> No one lights a lamp and then hides it under a vessel or puts it under a bed. No! he puts it on a lamp-stand so that those who come in may see the light. There is nothing hidden which will not be made manifest; there is nothing secret which will not be known and brought into the open. Take care, then, how you listen; for to him who has it will be given; and from him who has not there shall be taken away even what he thinks he has.

HERE we have three sayings, each with its own warning for life.

(i) Verse 16 stresses the essential conspicuousness of the Christian life. Christianity is in its very nature something which must be seen. It is easy to find prudential reasons why we should not flaunt our Christianity in the world's face. In almost every person there is an instinctive fear of being different. The world is always likely to persecute those who do not conform to pattern. A writer tells how he kept hens. In the hen-run all the hens were precisely the same in marking except one. The one different hen was pecked to death by the other occupants of the hen-run. Even in the animal world to be different is a crime. Hard as it may be, the duty is laid upon us of never being ashamed to show whose we are and whom we serve; and if we regard the matter in the right way it will be, not a duty, but a privilege. A short time before the Coronation most houses and shops were displaying their flags. I was out on a country road at that time; and in a little copse by the roadside I came upon a tinker's camp. It consisted of only one little tent, and beside the tent there fluttered on a pole a Union Jack nearly as big as the tent itself. It was as if that vagrant tinker said, " I haven't got much in this world; but I am going to attach my colours to what I have." The Christian, however humble his position and his sphere, must never be ashamed to show his colours.

(ii) Verse 17 stresses the impossibility of secrecy. There are three people from whom we try to hide things. (*a*) Sometimes we try to hide things from ourselves. We shut our eyes to the consequences of certain actions and habits, the consequences of which we are well aware. It is like a man deliberately shutting his eyes to symptoms of an illness which he knows he has. We have only to state that to see the incredible folly of it. (*b*) Sometimes we try to hide things from our fellow men. Things have a way of coming out. The man with a secret is an unhappy man. The happy man is the man with nothing to hide. It is told that once an architect offered to build for Plato a house in which every room would be hidden from the public eye. " I will give you twice the money," said Plato, " if you build me a house into every room of which all men's eyes can see." Happy is the man who can speak like that. (*c*) Sometimes we try to hide things from God. No man ever attempted a more impossible task. We would do well to have before our eyes forever the text which says, " Thou, God, seest me."

(iii) Verse 18 lays down the universal law that the man who has will get more; and that the man who has not will lose what he has. If a man is physically fit and keeps himself so his body will be ready for ever greater efforts ; if he lets himself go flabby he will lose even the abilities he has. The more a student learns the more he can learn; but if he refuses to go on learning then he will lose the knowledge he has. This is just another way of saying that there is no standing still in life. All the time we are either going forward or going back. The seeker will always find; but the man who stops seeking will lose even what he has.

TRUE KINSHIP

Luke 8: 19-21

> Jesus' mother and brothers came to Him, and they could not get at Him because of the crowd. He was given a message, " Your mother and your brothers are standing outside and they want to see you." " My mother and my brothers," He answered them, " are those who hear the word of God and do it."

IT is not difficult to see that, at least during His lifetime, Jesus' family were not in sympathy with Him. Mark 3: 21 tells us how His kinsmen came and tried to restrain Him because they believed Him to be mad. In Matthew 10: 36 Jesus warns His followers that a man's foes may well be those of his own household—and He was speaking out of hard and bitter experience.

There is in this passage a great and a practical truth. It may very well be that a man finds himself closer to people who are not related to him than he does to his own kith and kin. The deepest relationship of life is not merely a blood relationship; it is the relationship of mind to mind and heart to heart. It is when people have common aims, common principles, common interests, a common goal in life that they become really and truly kin. Now let us remember the definition of the Kingdom which we have already worked out. The Kingdom of God is a society upon earth where God's will is as perfectly done as it is in heaven. It was Jesus' supreme quality that He, of all people, alone succeeded in fully achieving that identity of His will and the will of God. Therefore, all whose one aim in life is to make God's will their will are the true kindred of Jesus. We speak of all men being the sons of

God; and in one very real and very precious sense that is true, because God loves saint and sinner; but the deepest kind of sonship is ethically conditioned. It is when a man puts his will in line with God's will, by the help of the Holy Spirit, that real kinship begins. The Stoics declared that that was the only way to happiness in this life. They had the conviction that everything that happens—joy and sorrow, triumph and disaster, gain and loss, sunshine and shadow— is the will of God. When a man refuses to accept it he batters his head against the walls of the universe and can bring himself nothing but pain and trouble of heart. When he looks up to God and says, " Do with me as you wish," then there is the way to joy.

If all that be so two things emerge.

(i) There is a loyalty which surpasses all earthly loyalties; there is something which takes precedence of the dearest things on earth. In that sense Jesus Christ is a demanding master, for He will share a man's heart with nothing and with no one. Love is necessarily exclusive. We can only love one person at a time and serve one master at a time. (ii) That is hard; but there is this great wonder— that when a man gives himself thus absolutely to Christ he becomes one of a family whose boundaries are the earth. Whatever loss he may experience is counterbalanced by his gain. As John Oxenham wrote:

> " In Christ there is no East or West,
>   In Him no South or North,
> But one great fellowship of love
>   Throughout the whole wide earth.
>
> In Him shall true hearts everywhere
>   Their high communion find,
> His service is the golden cord
>   Close-binding all mankind.
>
> Join hands, then, brother of the faith,
>   Whate'er your race may be!
> Who serves My Father as a son
>   Is surely kin to Me.

THE GOSPEL OF LUKE

In Christ now meet both East and West,
In Him meet South and North,
All Christly souls are one in Him,
    Throughout the whole wide earth."

The man who, through Jesus Christ, seeks the will of God has entered into a family which includes all the saints in earth and in heaven.

CALM AMIDST THE STORM

Luke 8: 22-25

One day Jesus and His disciples embarked upon a ship. "Let us go over," He said to them, "to the other side of the lake." So they set sail. As they sailed He fell asleep. A violent squall of wind came down upon the lake; and the boat began to fill with water; and they were in peril. They came to Him and woke Him. "Master, Master," they said, "we are perishing." When He awoke, He rebuked the wind and the surf of the water. They ceased their raging, and there was a calm. "Where is your faith?" He said to them. But they were awe-stricken and amazed. "Who can this be," they said to each other, "because He gives His orders even to the winds and the water, and they obey Him?"

LUKE tells this story with an extraordinary economy of words, and yet with an extraordinary vividness. It was no doubt for much needed rest and quiet that Jesus decided to cross the lake. As they sailed He fell asleep. It was a lovely thing to think of the sleeping Jesus. He was tired just as we become tired. He, too, could reach the point of exhaustion when the claim of sleep is imperative. He trusted His men. They were the fishermen of the lake; He was content to leave things to their skill and seamanship and to relax. He trusted God; He knew that He was as near to God by sea as ever He was by land.

And then the storm came down. The Sea of Galilee is famous for its sudden squalls. A traveller says, "The sun

104

had scarcely set when the wind began to rush down towards the lake, and it continued all night long with increasing violence, so that when we reached the shore next morning the face of the lake was like a huge boiling caldron." The reason of these storms is this. The Sea of Galilee is more than six hundred feet below sea level. It is surrounded by table lands beyond which the great mountains rise. The rivers have cut deep ravines through the table lands down into the sea. These ravines act like great funnels to draw down the cold winds from the mountains; and thus the storms arise. The same traveller tells how they tried to pitch their tents in such a gale, " We had to double-pin all the tent-ropes, and frequently were obliged to hang on with our whole weight upon them to keep the quivering tabernacle from being carried up bodily into the air." It was just such a sudden storm that struck the boat that day, and Jesus and His disciples were in peril of their lives. The disciples woke Jesus and with a word He calmed the storm.

Everything that Jesus did had more than a merely temporal significance. And the real meaning of this incident is that, *wherever Jesus is, the storm becomes a calm.*

(i) When Jesus comes, He calms *the storms of temptation.* Sometimes temptation comes to us with an almost over-mastering force. As Stevenson once said, " You know the Caledonian Railway Station in Edinburgh? One cold bleak morning I met Satan there." It comes to us all to meet Satan. If we meet that tempest of temptation alone we perish; but with Christ there comes the calm in which temptations lose their power.

(ii) When Jesus comes, He calms *the storms of passion.* Life is doubly difficult for the man with the hot heart and the blazing temper. A friend met such a man. " I see," he said, " that you have succeeded in conquering your temper." " No," said the man, " I didn't conquer it. Jesus conquered it for me."

" When deep within our swelling hearts
    The thoughts of pride and anger rise,
When bitter words are on our tongues
    And tears of passion in our eyes,
Then we may stay the angry blow,
    Then we may check the hasty word,
Give gentle answers back again,
    And fight a battle for our Lord."

But it is a losing battle unless Jesus be with us to give us
the calm of victory.

(iii) When Jesus comes, *He calms the storms of sorrow.*
Into every life some day the tempest of sorrow must come,
for sorrow is ever the penalty of love and if a man loves he
will sorrow. When Pusey's wife died, he said, " It was
as if there was a hand beneath my chin to hold me up."
In that day, in the presence of Jesus, the tears are wiped
away and the wounded heart is soothed.

THE DEFEAT OF THE DEMONS

Luke 8: 26-40

They came in their voyage to the district of the
Gerasenes, which is across the lake from Galilee.
When Jesus had disembarked on the land there met
Him a man from the town who had demons. For a
long time he had gone unclothed, and he did not
stay in a house but amongst the tombs. When he
saw Jesus he uttered a great cry and fell down before
Him and shouted, " What have you and I to do with
each other, Jesus, you Son of the Most High God?
I beseech you—don't torture me! "—for Jesus had
commanded the unclean spirit to come out of the man.
For many a time it had snatched at him, and he was
kept bound with chains and fetters, but when he
was driven into the deserted places by the demons,
he would burst the fetters. Jesus answered, " What
is your name? " He said, " A regiment "—because
many demons had entered into him, and they begged
Him not to order them to depart to the abyss. There

was a herd of many pigs there, feeding on the mountain-side. The demons asked Him to allow them to go into them. He did so. So the demons came out of the man and into the pigs, and the herd rushed down the precipice into the lake and were drowned. When those who were in charge of them saw what had happened, they fled and brought the story to the town and to the countryside round about. They came out to see what had happened. They came to Jesus and found the man from whom the demons had gone out sitting there at Jesus' feet, clothed and in his senses—and they were afraid. Those who had seen what had happened told them how the demon-possessed man had been cured; and the whole crowd from the Gerasene countryside asked Him to go away from them, because they were in the grip of a great fear. So He embarked on the ship and went away. The man from whom the demons had gone out begged to be allowed to go with Him; but He sent him away. " Go back," He said, " to your home and tell the story of all that God did for you." So he went away and proclaimed throughout the whole town all that God had done for him.

WE will never even begin to understand this story unless we realize that whatever we think about the demons, they were intensely real to the people of Gerasa and to the man whose mind was deranged. This man was a case of violent insanity. He was too dangerous to live amongst men and he lived amidst the tombs, which were believed to be the home and the haunt of demons. We may well note the sheer courage of Jesus in dealing with this man. The man had a maniacal strength which enabled him to snap his fetters. His fellow-men were very certainly so terrified of him that they would never try to do anything for him; but Jesus faced him calm and unafraid. When Jesus asked the man his name, he answered, " Legion." A Roman legion was a regiment of 6,000 soldiers. Doubtless this man had seen a Roman legion on the march, and his poor, afflicted mind felt that there was not one demon, but a whole regiment of demons inside him. It may well be that the very word haunted him, because very possibly he may have seen atrocities carried out by a Roman legion when he was a child. It is perfectly possible that it was these very atrocities which left a scar upon his mind and which ultimately sent him mad.

Far too much difficulty has been made out of the demons and the pigs. Jesus has been condemned for sending the demons into the innocent swine. That has been characterised as a cruel and immoral action. Again we must remember the intensity of the belief of these people in demons. The man, thinking the demons were speaking through him, besought Jesus not to send the demons into the abyss of hell to which they would be consigned in the final judgment. Let us see if we can form a picture of what happened. The man—and this is the essence of this part of the story—would never have believed that he was cured unless he had ocular and visible demonstration. Nothing less than the visible departure of the demons would have convinced him. Surely what happened was this. The herd of swine was feeding there on the mountain side. Jesus was exerting His power to cure what was a very stubborn case. Suddenly the man's wild cries and shouts and screams disturbed the swine and they went dashing down the steep place into the sea in blind terror. " Look! " said Jesus, " Look! There your demons are gone! " Jesus *had* to find a way to get into the mind of this poor man; and in that way He found it. In any event, can we compare the value of a herd of swine with the value of a man's immortal soul? If it cost the lives of these swine to save this man's soul, are we to complain? Is it not the case of a perverse fastidiousness which complains that swine were killed in order to heal a man? Surely we ought to preserve a sense of proportion. If the only way to convince this man of his cure was that the swine should perish, it seems a quite extraordinarily blind objection that the swine perished.

We must look at the reaction of two sets of people.

(i) There were *the Gerasenes*. They besought Jesus to

go away. (*a*) They hated having the routine of life disturbed. Life went peacefully on and then there arrived this disturbing Jesus and they hated Him. More people hate Jesus because He disturbs them than for any other reason. If Jesus says to a man, " You must give up this habit, you must change your life "; if Jesus says to an employer, " You can't be a Christian and make people work under conditions like that "; if Jesus says to a landlord, " You can't take money for slums like that "—one and all are liable to say to Him, " Go away and let me be in peace." That is an answer we are all liable to give. (*b*) They loved their swine more than they valued the soul of a man. One of life's supreme dangers is to value things above persons. That very tendency created the slums and created vicious working conditions. Much nearer home, that very tendency makes us selfishly demand our ease and comfort even if it means that someone who is tired has to slave and toil for us. No thing in this world can ever be as important as a person.

(ii) There was *the man who was cured*. Very naturally he wanted to come with Jesus, and Jesus sent him home. Christian witness, like Christian charity, begins at home. It would be so much easier to live and speak for Christ among people who do not know us. It is our duty, where Christ has set us, there to witness for Him. And if it should happen that we are the only Christian in the shop, the office, the school, the factory, the circle in which we live or work, that is not matter for lamentation. It is a challenge to us in which God says, " Go and tell the people you meet every day what I have done for you."

AN ONLY CHILD IS HEALED

Luke 8: 40-42 and 49-56

When Jesus came back the crowd welcomed Him for they were all waiting for Him. A man called Jairus came to Him. He was the president of the Synagogue.

He threw himself at Jesus' feet and asked Him to come to his house, because he had an only daughter who was about twelve years of age and she was dying. As He went the crowd pressed round about Him . . . While He was still speaking someone came from the president's house. " Your daughter is dead," he said. " Don't bother the Master any more." Jesus heard this. " Don't be afraid," He said. " Just have faith and she will be cured." When He had come to the house He allowed no one to come in with Him, except Peter and John and James, and the girl's father and mother. They were all weeping and wailing for her. " Stop weeping," He said, " for she is not dead but sleeping." They laughed Him down because they were sure she was dead. He took hold of her hand and said to her, " Child, rise! " Her breath came back to her and immediately she rose. He told them to give her something to eat. Her parents were out of themselves with amazement; but He enjoined them to tell no one what had happened.

HERE is all the pathos of life suddenly turned to gladness. Very keenly Luke felt the tragedy of this girl's death. There were three things which made it so poignant. (*a*) She was an only child. Only Luke tells us that. The light of her parents' life had gone out. (*b*) She was about twelve years of age. That is to say she was just at the dawn of womanhood because children in the East develop much more quickly than in the West. She could even have been contemplating marriage at that age. What should have been the morning of life had become the night. (*c*) Jairus was the president of the Synagogue. That is to say, he was the man who was responsible for the administration of the Synagogue and the ordering of public worship. He had reached the highest post that life could give him in the respect of his fellow men. No doubt he was well to do; no doubt he had climbed the ladder of earthly ambition and prestige. It seemed as if life—as it sometimes does— had given lavishly of many things but was about to take the most precious thing away. All the pathos of life— which we know so well—is in the background of this story.

The wailing women had already come. To us it sounds almost repulsively artificial. But to hire these wailing women was in Palestine a token of respect to the dead that would never have been omitted. They were sure she was dead, but Jesus said that she was asleep. It is perfectly possible that Jesus meant this quite literally. It may well be that here we have a real miracle of diagnosis; that Jesus saw that the girl was in a deep trance, and that she was just on the point of being buried alive. From the evidence of the tombs in Palestine it is clear that many were buried alive. It could happen the more easily because climatic conditions in Palestine make burial within a matter of hours a sheer necessity. However that may be Jesus by His power gave her back her life.

We must note one very practical touch. Jesus ordered that the girl should be given something to eat. Is it possible that He was thinking just as much of the mother as of the girl? The mother, with the pain of grief and the sudden shock of joy, must have been almost on the point of collapse. At such a time to do some practical thing with one's hands is a life-saver. And it may well be that Jesus, in His kindly wisdom which knew human nature so well, was giving the overwrought mother a job to do to calm her nerves.

But by far the most interesting character in this story is Jairus.

(i) Jairus was clearly *a man who could pocket his pride.* He was the president of the Synagogue. By this time the Synagogue doors were rapidly closing on Jesus, if they had not already closed. He could have had no love for Jesus, and he, too, must have regarded Jesus as a breaker of the law. But in his hour of need, he pocketed his pride and asked for help. There is a famous story of Roland, the paladin of Charlemagne. He was in charge of the rearguard of the army and he was suddenly caught by the Saracens at Roncesvalles. The battle raged fiercely against terrible odds. Now Roland had a horn called Olivant which he had taken from the giant Jatmund and its blast could be heard thirty miles away. So mighty was it that, as they said, the birds fell dead when its blast tore through the air. Oliver, his friend, besought him to blow the horn so that Charlemagne would hear and come back to help. But Roland was too proud to ask for help. One by one his men fell fighting till only he was left. Then at last with his dying breath he blew the horn, and when Charlemagne heard he came hasting back. But it was too late, for Roland, too, was dead. He was too proud to ask for help. It is easy to be like that, to think that we can handle life ourselves. But the way to find the miracles of the grace of God is to pocket our pride and humbly to confess our need and to ask. Ask and ye shall receive— but there is no receiving without asking.

(ii) Jairus was clearly *a man of a stubborn faith*. Whatever he felt, he did not wholly accept the verdict of the wailing women; for with his wife he went into the room where the girl lay. He hoped against hope. No doubt in his heart there was the unvoiced feeling, " You never know what this Jesus can do." And none of us knows all that Jesus can do. In the darkest day we can still hope in the unsearchable riches and the all-sufficient grace and the unconquerable power of God.

NOT LOST IN THE CROWD

Luke 8: 43-48

There was a woman who had had a flow of blood for twelve years. She had spent all her living on doctors and she could not be cured by any of them. She came up behind Jesus and she touched the tassel of His robe; and immediately her flow of blood was stayed. Jesus said, " Who touched me? " When they were all denying that they had done so, Peter and his companions said, " Master, the crowds are all round you and press in upon you." Jesus said, " Someone has touched me, for I know that power has gone out of me." The woman saw that she could not hide. She came all trembling; she threw herself at His feet;

and in front of everyone she told Him why she had touched Him, and that she had been cured there and then. " Daughter," He said to her, " your faith has cured you. Go in peace."

THIS story laid hold on the heart and the imagination of the early Church. It was believed that the woman was a Gentile from Caesarea Philippi. Eusebius, the great Church historian (A.D. 300), relates how it was said that the woman had at her own cost erected a statue commemorating her cure in her native city. It was said that that statue remained there until Julian, the Roman Emperor who tried to bring back the pagan gods, destroyed it, and erected his own in place of it, only to see his own statue blasted by a thunderbolt from God.

The shame of the woman was that ceremonially she was unclean (Leviticus 15: 19-33). Her issue of blood had cut her off from life. That was why she did not come openly to Jesus but crept up in the crowd; and that was why at first she was so embarrassed when Jesus asked who touched Him.

All devout Jews wore robes with fringes on them (Numbers 15: 37-41; Deuteronomy 22: 12). The fringes ended in four tassels of white thread with a blue thread woven through them. They were to remind the Jew every time he dressed and every time he saw them that he was a man of God and committed to the keeping of the laws of God. Later, when it was dangerous to be a Jew, these tassels were worn on the undergarments. Nowadays they still exist on the *talith* or shawl that the Jew wears round his head and shoulders when he is at prayer. But in the time of Jesus they were worn on the outer garment, and it was one of these the woman touched.

Luke, the doctor, here speaks again. Mark says of the woman that she had spent her all on the doctors and was no better, *but rather grew worse* (Mark 5: 26). But Luke misses out the final phrase because he did not like this gibe against the doctors!

The lovely thing about this story is that from the moment Jesus was face to face with the woman, there seems to be nobody there but He and she. It happened in the middle of the crowd; but the crowd was forgotten and Jesus spoke to that woman and treated her as if she was the only person in the world. She was a poor, unimportant sufferer, with a trouble that made her unclean, and yet to that one unimportant person, Jesus gave all of Himself.

We are very apt to attach labels to people and to treat them according to their relative importance. To Jesus a person had none of these man-made labels. He or she was simply a human soul in need. Love never thinks of people in terms of human importances. A distinguished visitor once came to call on Thomas Carlyle. He was working and could not be disturbed, but Jane, his wife, agreed to take this visitor up and open the door just a chink that he might at least see the sage. She did so, and as they looked in at Carlyle, immersed in his work and oblivious of all else, penning the books that made him famous all over the world, she said, " That's Tammas Carlyle about whom all the world is talking—*and he's my man.*" It was not in terms of the world's labels Jane thought, but in terms of love. A traveller tells how she was travelling in Georgia in the days before the Second World War. She was taken to see a very humble, poor, old woman in a little cottage. The old peasant woman asked her if she was going to Moscow. The traveller said she was. " Then," asked the woman, " would you mind delivering a parcel of home-made toffee to my son? " He could not get anything like it in Moscow. The son's name was Josef Stalin. We do not normally think of the late dictator of all the Russias as a man who liked toffee—but his mother did! For her the man-made labels did not matter.

Almost everybody would have regarded the woman in the crowd as totally unimportant. For Jesus she was someone in need, and therefore He, as it were, withdrew from the crowd, and gave Himself to her. " God loves each one of us as if there was only one of us to love."

EMISSARIES OF THE KING

Luke 9: 1-9

> Jesus called The Twelve together and gave them
> power and authority over all demons, and to cure
> diseases. He sent them out to proclaim the Kingdom
> of God, and to cure those who were ill. He said to
> them, " Take nothing for the road, neither a staff
> nor a wallet, nor bread nor money, nor two tunics.
> Whatever house you go into, stay there, and leave
> from there. As for whoever do not receive you—
> when you leave that town shake off the dust from
> your feet as evidence against them." So they went
> out, and they went through the villages, preaching
> and healing everywhere.
>
> Herod, the tetrarch, heard about the things which
> were going on. He did not know what to make of
> them, because it was said by some, " John is risen from
> the dead "; and by some, " Elijah has appeared ";
> and by others, " One of the prophets of the ancient
> days has risen again." But Herod said, " John I
> myself beheaded. Who is this about whom I hear
> such reports? " And he tried to see Him.

In the ancient days there was in effect only one way of
spreading a message abroad, and that was by word of
mouth. Newspapers did not exist; books had to be hand-
written, and a book the size of the New Testament would
have cost £40 per copy to produce. Wireless, that great
disseminator of news, had not even been dreamed of.
That is why Jesus sent out The Twelve on this mission.
He Himself was under the limitations of time and space.
His helpers had to be mouths to speak for Him.

They were to travel light. That was simply because
the man who travels light travels far and fast. The more
a man is cluttered up with material things the more he
is shackled to one place. God needs a settled ministry;
but God also needs those who will abandon earthly things
to adventure for Him.

If they were not received they were to shake off the dust
off their feet when they left the town. When Rabbis

entered Palestine after some journey in a Gentile land, they shook off the last particle of heathen dust from their feet. A village or town which would not receive them was to be treated as a strict Jew would treat a heathen country. It had refused its opportunity and had condemned itself.

That this ministry was mightily effective is plain from Herod's reaction. Things were happening. Perhaps Elijah, the forerunner, had at last come. Perhaps even the great promised prophet had arrived (Deuteronomy 18: 15). But " Conscience doth make cowards of us all," and there was a lingering fear in Herod's mind that John, the Baptiser, whom he thought he had eliminated, had come back to haunt him.

The one thing which stands out about the ministry which Jesus laid upon The Twelve is this—over and over again in this short passage *it joins preaching and healing.* It joins concern for men's bodies and men's souls. It was something which did not deal only in words, however comforting; it dealt in deeds. It was a message which was not confined to news of eternity; it proposed to change conditions on earth. It was the reverse of a religion of " pie in the sky." It insisted that health to men's bodies was as integral a part of God's purpose as health to their souls. Nothing has done the Church more harm than the repeated statement that the things of this world do not matter. In the middle thirties of our own times there was unemployment, and unemployment which invaded respectable and decent homes. The father's skill was rusting in idleness; the mother was trying to make a shilling do what a pound ought to do; children could not understand what was going on except that they went hungry. Men grew bitter or grew dully broken. To go and tell such people that material things makes no difference was an unforgiveable thing, especially if the teller was in reasonable comfort himself. General Booth was once blamed for offering food and meals to poor people instead of the simple gospel. The old warrior flashed back, " It is impossible to comfort men's hearts with the love of God when their feet are perishing with cold." Of course, it is possible to overstress material things. But it is equally possible to neglect them. The Church will forget only at her peril that Jesus first sent out His men *to preach the Kingdom and to heal*, to save men in body and in soul.

FOOD FOR THE HUNGRY

Luke 9: 10-17

> When the apostles returned they told Jesus all that they had done. So He took them and withdrew privately to a place called Bethsaida. When the crowds found out where He was they followed Him; and He welcomed them, and talked to them about the Kingdom of God, and healed those who had need of healing. The day began to draw to a close. The Twelve came to Him. "Send the crowd away," they said, "that they may go to the surrounding villages and countryside and find some place to stay and get food because here we are in a desert place." He said to them, "Do you give them food to eat." They said, "All we have is five loaves and two fishes— unless we go and buy food for all this people." For there were about five thousand men. He said to His disciples. "Make them sit down in companies of fifty." They did so, and they got them all seated. He took the five loaves and the two fishes and looked up into heaven and blessed them and broke them and gave them to His disciples to set before the crowd. And all of them ate and were satisfied; and what they had left over was taken up and there were twelve baskets of the fragments.

THIS is the only miracle of Jesus which is related in all the four gospels (cp. Matthew 14: 13; Mark 6: 30; John 6: 1). It begins with a lovely thing. The Twelve had come back from their tour. Never was a time when Jesus needed more to be alone with them, so He took them to the neighbourhood of Bethsaida, which was a village on the far side of the Jordan to the north of the Sea of Galilee. When the people discovered where He had gone they followed Him out in their hordes—*and He welcomed them*. There is all the divine compassion here. Most people would have resented the invasion of their hard-won privacy. How would we feel if we had sought out some lonely place to be with our most intimate friends and suddenly a clamorous mob of people turned up with their insistent demands? Sometimes we are too busy to be disturbed. But, to Jesus, human need took precedence over everything.

The evening came; home was far away; and the people were tired and hungry. Jesus, astonishingly, ordered His disciples to give the people a meal. There are two ways in which a man can quite honestly look at this miracle. First, he can see in it simply a miracle in which Jesus created food for this vast multitude. Second, some people think that this is what happened. The people were hungry—*and they were utterly selfish*. They all had something with them, but they would not even produce it for themselves in case they had to share it with others. The Twelve laid before the multitude their little store, and thereupon others were moved to produce their little store, and in the end there was more than enough for everyone. So it may be regarded as a miracle which turned selfish, suspicious folk into generous people, a miracle of what happens, when moved by Christ, people are moved to share.

Before Jesus distributed the food He blessed it; He said grace. There was a Jewish saying that " he who enjoys anything without thanksgiving is as though he robbed God." The blessing which was said in every home in Palestine before every meal ran like this, " Blessed art Thou, Jehovah, our God, King of the world, who causest bread to come forth from the earth." Jesus would not eat without giving thanks to the Giver of all good gifts.

This is a story which tells us many things.

(i) *Jesus was concerned that men were hungry*. It would be a most interesting thing to try to work out how much time Jesus spent, not talking, but easing men's pain and satisfying men's hunger. Jesus still needs the service of men's hands. The mother who has spent a lifetime cooking meals for a hungry family; the nurse, the doctor, the friend, relation or parent, who has sacrificed life and time to ease another's pain; the social reformer who has burned himself out to seek better conditions for men and women— they have all preached a far more effective sermon than the man who talks, even if he is an orator.

(ii) *The help which Jesus gives is generous.* There was enough, and more than enough. In love there is no nice calculation of the less and more. God is like that. When we sow a packet of seeds we usually have to thin the plants out, and we often have to throw away far more than we can keep. God has created a world where there is more than enough for all if men will share it.

(iii) As always there is a permanent truth in an action in time. *In Jesus all men's needs are supplied.* There is a hunger of the soul; there is in every man, sometimes at least, a longing to find something in which he may invest his life. Our hearts are restless until they rest in Him. " My God shall supply all your need," said Paul (Philippians 4: 19)—even in the desert places of this life.

THE GREAT DISCOVERY

Luke 9: 18-22

> It happened that when Jesus was praying alone His disciples were with Him. He asked them, " Who do the crowds say that I am? " They answered, " Some say that you are John the Baptiser; others that you are Elijah; others that one of the prophets of the ancient days has risen again." He said to them, " But *you*—who do you say that I am? " Peter answered, " The Anointed One of God." Jesus warned and enjoined them to tell this to no one. " The Son of Man," He said, " must suffer many things, and must be rejected by the elders and chief priests and scribes, and must be killed, and must be raised again on the third day."

THIS is one of the most crucial moments in the whole life of Jesus. He asked this question when He was already turning His face to go to Jerusalem (Luke 9: 51). He well knew what awaited Him there, and the answer to this question was of supreme importance. What Jesus *knew* was that He Himself was going to a Cross to die. What He *wanted to know* before He went was, " Was there anyone who had really discovered who He was? " The answer would make all the difference. If there was no answer, but dull incomprehension, it meant that all His work had gone for nothing. If there was an answer of realization, however incomplete, it meant that He had lit such a torch in the hearts of men as time would never put out. How Jesus' heart must have lifted when Peter's sudden discovery rushed to his lips—" You are the Anointed One of God! " When Jesus heard that He knew He had not failed.

But not only had The Twelve to discover that fact; they had also to discover what that fact meant. They had grown up against a background of thought in which they had been taught to expect from God a conquering King who would lead them to world dominion. Peter's eyes would blaze with flaming excitement when he said this. But Jesus had to teach them that God's Anointed One had come to die upon a Cross. He had to take their ideas of God and of God's purposes and turn them upside down; and from this time that is what He set Himself to do. They had discovered who He was; now they had to discover what that discovery meant.

There are two great general truths in this passage.

(i) Jesus began by asking what men were saying about Him; and then, suddenly, He flashes the question at The Twelve, " Who do *you* say that I am? " It is never enough to know what other people have said about Jesus. A man might be able to pass any examination on what has been said and thought about Jesus; he might have read every book about Christology which has been written in every language upon earth and still not be a Christian. Jesus must always be our own personal discovery. Our religion can never be a carried tale. To every man Jesus comes asking, not, " Can you tell me what others have said and written about me? " but, " Who do *you* say that I am? " Paul did not say, " I know *what* I have believed "; he said, " I know *whom* I have believed " (2 Timothy 1 : 12). Christianity does not mean reciting a creed; it means knowing a person.

(ii) In this passage we listen to the word *must* on the lips of Jesus. " I must," He said, "go to Jerusalem and die." It is of the greatest interest to look at the times in Luke's gospel when Jesus said *must*. " I *must* be in my Father's house," He said (2 : 49). " I *must preach* the Kingdom," He said (4 : 43). " I *must* walk to-day and to-morrow," He said (13 : 33). Over and over again He told His disciples how He *must* go to His Cross (9 : 22; 17 : 25; 24 : 7). Jesus was one who knew that He had a destiny to fulfil. God's will was His will. He had no other object but to do upon earth what God had sent Him to do. The Christian, like His Lord, is a man under orders.

THE CONDITIONS OF SERVICE

Luke 9: 23-27

> Jesus said to them all, " If any man wishes to come after me, let him deny himself, and day by day let him take up his cross and follow me. Whoever wishes to save his life will lose it. Whoever loses his life for my sake will save it. What profit is it to a man if he gains the whole world and loses himself or has himself confiscated? Whoever is ashamed of me and of my words, of him shall the Son of Man be ashamed when He shall come in His own glory, and in the glory of His Father and of the holy angels. I tell you truly that there are some of these who are standing here who will not taste death until they see the Kingdom of God."

HERE Jesus lays down the conditions of service for those who would follow Him.

(i) A man must deny himself. What does that mean? A great scholar comes at the meaning in this way. Peter once *denied* his Lord. That is to say, he said of Jesus, " I do not know the man." To deny ourselves is to say, " I do not know myself." It is to ignore the very existence of oneself. It is to treat the self as if it did not exist. Usually we treat ourselves as if our self was far and away the most important thing in the world. If we are to follow Jesus we must obliterate self and forget that self exists.

(ii) A man must take up his cross. What does that mean? Jesus well knew what crucifixion meant. When He was a lad of about eleven years of age Judas the Galilaean had led a rebellion against Rome. He had raided the royal armoury at Sepphoris, which was only four miles from Nazareth. The Roman vengeance was swift and sudden. Sepphoris was burned to the ground; its inhabitants were sold into slavery; and two thousand of the rebels were crucified on crosses which were set in lines along the road-side that they might be a dreadful warning to others tempted to rebel. To take up our cross means to be prepared to face things like that for loyalty to God; it means to be ready to endure the worst that man can do to us for the sake of being true to God.

(iii) A man must spend his life, not hoard it. The whole gamut of the world's standards must be changed. The questions are not, " How much can I *get*? " but, " How much can I *give*? " Not, " What is the *safe* thing to do? " but, " What is the *right* thing to do? " Not, " What is the minimum permissible in the way of work? " but, " What is the maximum possible? " The Christian must realize that he is given life, not to keep it for himself, but to spend it for others; not to husband its flame, but to burn himself out for Christ and for men.

(iv) Loyalty to Jesus will have its reward, and disloyalty its punishment. If we are true to Him in time, He will be true to us in eternity. If we seek to follow Him in this world, in the next world He will point to us as one of His people. But if by our lives we disown Him, even though with our lips we confess Him, the day must come when He cannot do other than disown us.

(v) In the last verse of this passage, Jesus says that some of those standing there will see the Kingdom of God before they die. Some people wish to maintain that when Jesus said this He was looking forward to His return in glory, that He declared that that would happen within the lifetime of some of those standing there, and that therefore He was completely mistaken. That is not so. What Jesus was saying is this, "Before this generation has passed away you will see signs that the Kingdom of God is on the way." Beyond a doubt that was true. Something came into the world which, like leaven in dough, began to change the world. It would be well if, sometimes, we turned from our pessimism and thought rather of the light that has been slowly breaking on the world.

As A. H. Clough wrote,

" Say not the struggle naught availeth,
    The labour and the wounds are vain,
The enemy faints not, nor faileth,
    And as things have been they remain.

If hopes were dupes, fears may be liars;
    It may be, in yon smoke conceal'd,
Your comrades chase e'en now the fliers,
    And, but for you, possess the field.

For while the tired waves, vainly breaking,
    Seem here no painful inch to gain,
Far back, through creeks and inlets making,
    Comes silent, flooding in, the main.

And not by eastern windows only,
    When daylight comes, comes in the light;
In front the sun climbs slow, how slowly!
    But westward, look, the land is bright! "

Be of good cheer—The Kingdom is on the way—and we do well to thank God for every sign of its dawning.

THE MOUNTAIN TOP OF GLORY

Luke 9: 28-36

> About eight days after these words, Jesus took Peter
> and John and James and went up into a mountain
> to pray.   While He was praying the appearance of
> His face became different and His clothing became
> white as the lightning's flash.   And—look you—
> two men were talking with Him, who were Moses and
> Elijah.   They appeared in glory, and they talked
> about the departure which He was going to accomplish
> in Jerusalem.   Peter and his friends were heavy with
> sleep.   When they were fully awake they saw His
> glory, and the two men standing with Him.   And
> when they were going to leave Him, Peter said,
> " Master, it is good for us to be here.   So let us make
> three booths, one for you and one for Moses and one
> for Elijah," for he did not know what he was saying.
> As he was saying this a cloud came and overshadowed
> them and they feared as they entered into the cloud.
> A voice came from the cloud saying, " This is My
> Beloved Son, My Chosen One!   Hear Him! "   And
> when the voice had passed, Jesus was found alone.
> They kept silent in those days and did not tell anyone
> anything about what they had seen.

HERE we have another of the great hinges in Jesus' life
upon earth.   We must remember that He was just about
to set out to Jerusalem and to the Cross.   We have already
looked at one great moment when He asked His disciples
who they believed Him to be in order that He might discover
if anyone had realized who He was.   But there was one
thing which Jesus would never do—He would never take
any step without the approval of God.   In this scene that
is what we see Him seeking and receiving.   What happened
on the Mount of Transfiguration we can never know, but
we do know that something tremendous did happen.
Jesus had gone there to seek the approval of God for the
decisive step that He was about to take. There Moses and
Elijah appeared to Him.   Moses was the great law-giver of
the people of Israel; Elijah was the greatest of the prophets.
It was as if the princes of Israel's life and thought and

religion told Jesus to go on. Jesus could set out to Jerusalem now, certain that at least one little group of men knew who He was, certain that what He was doing was the consummation of all the life and thought and work of His nation, and certain that God approved of the step that He was taking.

There is one vivid sentence here. It says of the three apostles, " When they were fully awake they saw His glory."

(i) In life we miss so much because our minds are asleep. There are certain things which are very liable to keep our minds asleep. (*a*) There is *prejudice*. We may be so set in our ideas that our minds are shut. A new idea knocks at the door of them but we are like sleepers who will not awake. (*b*) There is mental *lethargy*. There are so many who refuse the strenuous struggle of thought. " The unexamined life," said Plato, " is the life not worth living." But how many of us have really thought things out and thought them through? It was said of someone that he had skirted the howling deserts of infidelity, whereat a wiser man said that he would have been better to have fought his way through them. Sometimes we are so lethargic that we will not even face our questions and our doubts. (*c*) There is *the love of ease*. There is a kind of defence mechanism in us that makes us automatically shut the door against any disturbing thought. A man can drug himself mentally until his mind is sound asleep.

(ii) But life is full of things which are designed to waken us. (*a*) There is *sorrow*. Once Elgar said of a young singer, who was technically perfect, but quite without feeling and expression, " She will be great when something breaks her heart." Often sorrow can rudely awaken a man, but in that moment, through the tears he will see the glory. (*b*) There is *love*. Somewhere Browning tells of two people who fell in love. She looked at him. He looked at her as a lover can—" and suddenly life awoke." Real love is an awakening to horizons which we never dreamed were there.

(c) There is *the sense of need*. For long enough a man may live the routine of life, half asleep; and then all of a sudden into life there comes some completely insoluble problem, some quite unanswerable question, some overmastering temptation, some summons to an effort which he feels is beyond his strength. In that day there is nothing left for him to do but to " cry, clinging heaven by the hems." And that sense of need awakens him to God.

We would do well to pray, " Lord, keep me always awake to Thee."

COMING DOWN FROM THE MOUNT

Luke 9: 37-45

> On the next day, when they had come down from the mountain, a great crowd of people met Him. And—look you—a man shouted from the crowd, " Teacher, I beg you to look with pity upon my son, because he is my only child. And—look you—a spirit seizes him and he suddenly shouts out; he convulses him until he foams at the mouth; he shatters him and will hardly leave him. I begged your disciples to cast out the spirit but they could not do it." Jesus answered, " O faithless and twisted generation! How long will I be with you? How long will I bear you? Bring your son here." While he was coming the demon dashed him down and convulsed him. Jesus rebuked the unclean spirit and healed the boy, and gave him back to his father; and everyone was astonished at the majesty of God.
> While they were all wondering at the things which He kept doing, He said to His disciples, " Let these words sink into your ears—the Son of Man is going to be delivered into the hands of men." They did not know what this word meant; and its meaning was concealed from them so that they did not perceive it; and they were afraid to ask Him about this word.

No sooner had Jesus descended from the mountain top than the demands and the disappointments of life were upon Him. A man had come to the disciples seeking their help, for his only son was an epileptic. Of course his epilepsy was attributed to the malign activity of a demon. The word used in verse 42 is very vivid. As he was coming to Jesus, the demon *dashed him down.* It is the word which is used of a boxer dealing a knock-out blow to his opponent or of a wrestler throwing someone. It must have been a pitiful sight to see the lad convulsed; and the disciples were quite helpless to cure him. But when Jesus came He dealt with the situation with calm mastery and gave the boy back to his father, cured and healed.

In this passage two things stand out.

(i) The moment on the mount is absolutely necessary, but it cannot be prolonged beyond its own time. If the ascent to the mountain is essential the descent from the mountain is just as imperative. Peter, not really knowing what he was saying, would have liked to linger on the mountain top. He wished to build three tabernacles there that they might stay there in all the glory. Often there comes to us moments that we would like to prolong indefinitely. But after the time on the mountain top we must come back to the battle and the routine of life. We are not meant to live withdrawn upon the mountain top; that time is meant to give us strength for life's everyday. After the great struggle at Mount Carmel with the prophets of Baal, Elijah, in reaction, ran away. Out into the desert he went, and there as the old story runs, as he lay under a juniper tree asleep, an angel twice prepared a meal for him. And then there comes the sentence, " And he arose and did eat and drink and went in the strength of that meat forty days and forty nights " (I Kings 19: 1-8). To the mountain top of the presence of God we must go, but not to remain there, but to go in the strength of that time for many days. It was said of Captain Scott, the great explorer, that he was " a strange mixture of the dreamy and the practical, and never more practical than immediately after he had been dreamy." We cannot live forever in the moment on the mountain but we cannot live at all without it.

(ii) In no incident is the sheer competence of Jesus so clearly shown. When He came down from the mountain the whole situation was quite out of hand. The whole impression is that of people running about not knowing what to do. The disciples were helplessly baffled; the boy's father was bitterly disappointed and upset. Into this scene of disorder came Jesus. He gripped the whole situation in a flash, and in His mastery the disorder became a calm. So often we feel that life is out of control; that we have lost our grip on things. Only the Master of life can deal with life with this calm competence which brings everything under control.

(iii) But once again the incident finished with Jesus pointing at the Cross. Here was triumph; here Jesus had mastered the demons and astonished the people. And in that very moment when they were ready to acclaim Him, Jesus told them that He was on the way to die. It would have been so easy for Jesus to take the way of popular success; it was His greatness that He rejected it and chose the Cross. He would not Himself shirk that Cross to which He called others.

TRUE GREATNESS

Luke 9: 46-48

There arose an argument amongst them as to which of them should be the greatest. But when Jesus knew the thoughts of their hearts He took a child and set him beside Him. "Whoever," He said to them, " receives this child in my name, receives me; and whoever receives me, receives Him that sent me. He who is least among you, he it is who is the greatest."

So long as The Twelve thought of Jesus' Kingdom as an earthly kingdom it was quite inevitable that they should be in competition for the highest places in it. Long ago the Venerable Bede suggested that this particular quarrel arose because Jesus had taken Peter, John and James up into the mountain top with Him, and because the others were jealous.

Jesus knew what was going on in their hearts. He took a child and placed him beside Himself; that seat would be the seat of highest honour. He went on to say that whoever received a little child, received Him; and whoever received Him, received God. What did He mean? The child was quite unimportant. The Twelve were the chosen lieutenants of Jesus; but this child occupied no place of honour and held no official position. So Jesus said, " If you are prepared to spend your lives serving people, helping people, loving people who, in the eyes of the world, do not matter at all, you are serving me and you are serving God." Jesus said, " If you are prepared to spend your life doing the apparently unimportant things and never trying to be what the world calls great, then you will be great in the eyes of God." There are so many wrong motives for service.

(i) There is the desire for *prestige*. A. J. Cronin tells of a district nurse he knew when he was in practice as a doctor. For twenty years, single-handed, she had served a ten-mile district. " I marvelled," he says, " at her patience, her fortitude and her cheerfulness. She was never too tired at night to rise for an urgent call. Her salary was most inadequate, and late one night, after a particularly strenuous day, I ventured to protest to her, ' Nurse, why don't you make them pay you more? God knows you are worth it.' ' If God knows I'm worth it,' she answered, ' that's all that matters to me.' " She was working, not for men, but for God. And when we work for God prestige will be the last thing that enters into our mind for we will know that our best is not good enough for God.

(ii) There is the desire for *place*. If ever a man is given a task or a position or an office in the Church, he should regard it not as an honour but as a responsibility. There are those who serve within the Church, not thinking really of those they serve, but thinking of themselves. A certain English Prime Minister was offered congratulations on attaining to that office. " I do not want your congratulations," he said, " but I do want your prayers." To be chosen for office is to be set apart for service, not elevated to honour in the eyes of men.

(iii) There is the desire for *prominence*. Many a person will serve or give so long as his service and his generosity are known, so long as he is thanked and praised. It is Jesus' own instruction that we should not let our left hand know what our right hand is doing. If we give, only to gain something out of the giving for ourselves, we have undone all the good we might have done.

TWO LESSONS IN TOLERANCE

Luke 9: 49-56

> John said to Jesus, " Master, we saw a man casting out demons in your name; and we stopped him because he does not follow with us." Jesus said to him, " Don't try to stop him, for he who is not against us is for us."
> When the days that He should be received up were on their way to being completed He fixed His face firmly to go to Jerusalem. He sent messengers on ahead. When they had gone on they went into a village of the Samaritans to make ready for Him; and they refused to receive them because His face was set in the direction of Jerusalem. When His disciples, James and John, learned of this they said, " Lord, would you like us to order fire to come down from heaven and destroy them? " He turned to them and rebuked them; and they went on to another village.

HERE we have two lessons in tolerance.

There were many exorcists in Palestine, all claiming to be able to cast out demons; and no doubt John regarded this man as a competitor and wished to eliminate him.

The direct way from Galilee to Jerusalem led through Samaria; but most Jews avoided it. There was a centuries' old quarrel between the Jews and the Samaritans (John 4: 9). The Samaritans in fact did everything they could to hinder and even to injure any bands of pilgrims who attempted to pass through their territory. For Jesus to take that way to Jerusalem was unusual; and to attempt to find hospitality in a Samaritan village was still more unusual. When Jesus did this He was extending a hand of friendship to a people who were enemies. In this case not only was hospitality refused, but the offer of friendship was spurned. No doubt James and John believed they were doing a most praiseworthy thing when they offered to call in divine aid to blot out the village.

There is no passage in which Jesus so directly teaches the duty of tolerance as in this. In many ways tolerance is a lost virtue, and, where it does exist, it exists from the wrong cause. Of all the greatest religious leaders none was such a pattern of tolerance as John Wesley. " I have no more right," he said, " to object to a man for holding a different opinion from mine that I have to differ with a man because he wears a wig and I wear my own hair; but if he takes his wig off and shakes the powder in my face, I shall consider it my duty to get quit of him as soon as possible." " The thing," he said, " which I resolved to use every possible method of preventing was a narrowness of spirit, a party zeal, a being straitened in our own bowels—that miserable bigotry which makes many so unready to believe that there is any work of God but among themselves." " We think," he said, " and let think." When his nephew, Samuel, the son of his brother Charles, entered the Roman Catholic Church, John Wesley wrote to him, " Whether in this Church or that I care not. You may be saved in either or damned in either; but I fear you are not born again." The Methodist invitation to the sacrament is simply, " Let all who love the Lord come here." The conviction that our beliefs and our methods alone are correct has been the cause of more tragedy and distress in the Church than almost any other thing. Oliver Cromwell wrote once to the intransigent Scots, " I beseech you by the bowels of Christ, think it possible that you may be mistaken." T. R. Glover somewhere quotes a saying, " Remember that whatever your hand finds to do, some-one thinks differently! "

There are many ways to God. God has His own secret stairway into every heart. God fulfils Himself in many ways; and no man and no Church has a monopoly of the truth of God.

But—and this is intensely important—our tolerance must be based not on indifference but on love. We are not tolerant because—as the modern phrase has it—we could not care less; but because we look at the other person, not with the eyes of criticism, but with the eyes of love. When Abraham Lincoln was criticized for being too cour-teous to his enemies and when he was reminded that it was his duty to destroy them, he gave the great answer, " Do I not destroy my enemies when I make them my friends? " Even if a man be utterly mistaken we must never regard him as an enemy to be destroyed, but as a strayed friend to be recovered by love.

THE HONESTY OF JESUS

Luke 9: 57-62

> As they were journeying along the road, a man said to Jesus, " I will follow you wherever you go." Jesus said to him, " The foxes have dens; the birds of the air have places to roost; but the Son of Man has nowhere to lay His head."
>
> He said to another man, " Follow Me! " " Lord," he said, " let me go first and bury my father." He said to him, " Let the dead bury their dead; but do you go and tell abroad the news of the Kingdom of God."
>
> Another man said to Him, " Lord, I will follow you; but let me first say good-bye to the folk at home." Jesus said to him, " No man who puts his hand to the plough and looks back is the right kind of man for the Kingdom of God."

HERE we have the words of Jesus to three would-be followers.

(i) To the first man, Jesus' advice was, " Before you follow me, count the cost." No one can ever say that he was induced to follow Jesus under false pretences. Jesus paid men the compliment of pitching His demands so high that they cannot be higher. It may well be that we have hurt the Church very seriously by trying to tell people that Church membership need not make so very much difference; we would be better to tell them that it must make all the difference in the world. We might have fewer people; but those we had would be totally pledged to Christ.

(ii) Jesus' words to the second man sound harsh, but they need not be so. In all probability the man's father was not dead, and not even nearly dead. His saying most likely meant, " I will follow you after my father has died." An English official in the East tells of a very brilliant Arab young man. So brilliant was he that it would have been perfectly possible for him to come to Oxford or Cambridge on a scholarship. Such a scholarship was offered to him. His answer was, " I will take it after I have buried my father." At the time his father was not much more than forty years of age. The point that Jesus was making is that in everything there is a crucial moment; if that moment is missed the thing most likely will never be done at all. This man in the story had stirrings in his heart to get out of his spiritually dead surroundings. If he missed the moment he would never get out. The psychologists tell us that every time we have a fine feeling, if we do not act on that feeling at once, the less likely we are to act on it each time. The emotion becomes a substitute for the action. Take one example—sometimes we feel that we would like to write a letter, perhaps of sympathy, perhaps of thanks, perhaps of congratulations, to someone. Unless we do it on the moment, if we put it off until to-morrow, it will in all likelihood never be written at all. It is Jesus' insistence that we must act at once when our hearts are stirred within us.

(iii) Jesus' words to the third man state a truth which no one can deny. No ploughman ever ploughed a straight furrow looking back over his shoulder. There are some whose hearts are in the past. They walk forever looking backwards and thinking wistfully of the good old days. Watkinson, the great preacher, tells how once at the seaside, when he was with his little grandson, they met an old minister. The old man was very disgruntled and, to add to all his troubles, he had a slight touch of sunstroke. The little boy had been listening, but had not picked it up quite correctly; and when they left the grumbling complaints of the old man, he turned to Watkinson and said, " Granddad, I hope *you* never suffer from a *sunset*! " The Christian marches on, not to the sunset, but to the dawn. The watchword of the Kingdom is not, " Backwards!" but, "Forwards!" To this man Jesus did not say either, " Follow!" or, " Return! " He said, " I accept no lukewarm service," and left the man to make his own decision.

LABOURERS FOR THE HARVEST

Luke 10: 1-16

> After these things the Lord appointed other seventy men and sent them out in twos ahead of Him into every town and place where He intended to go. " The harvest is great," He said to them, " but the workers are few. Pray then the Lord of the harvest to send out workers for the harvest. Go! Look you—I am sending you out as sheep in the midst of wolves, Do not take a purse or a wallet or sandals. Greet no one on the road. Into whatever house you go. say first of all, ' Peace to this house! ' If it is a son of peace who lives there your peace will remain upon it; but if not it will return to you. Remain in the same house eating and drinking whatever they give you; for the workman deserves his pay. Do not go from house to house. If you go into any town and

they receive you, eat what is put before you. Heal those in it who are ill, and keep saying to them, ' The Kingdom of God has come near you! ' If you go into any town and they do not receive you, go out into its streets and say, ' The very dust which clings to our feet from this town, we wipe off against you. But realize this—the Kingdom of God has come near you!' I tell you, things will be easier for Sodom in that day than for that town. Woe to you Chorazin! Woe to you Bethsaida! For if the mighty works which have been done in you had been done in Tyre and Sidon, they would long ago have sat in dust and ashes and repented. But at the judgment things will be easier for Tyre and Sidon than for you. And you Capernaum—will you be exalted to Heaven? You will be cast down to Hell. He who listens to you, listens to me; and he who sets no value on you, sets no value on me; and he who sets no value on me, sets no value on Him that sent me."

THIS passage describes a wider mission than the first mission of The Twelve. The number seventy was to the Jews a symbolic number. (*a*) It was the number of the elders who were chosen to help Moses with the task of leading and directing the people in the wilderness (Numbers 11: 16, 17, 24, 25). (*b*) It was the number of the Sanhedrin, the supreme council of the Jews. If we relate The Seventy to either of these bodies they will be the helpers of Jesus. (*c*) It was held to be the number of nations in the world. Luke was the man with the universalist view, and it may well be that he was thinking of the day when every nation in the world would know and love his Lord.

There is one interesting sidelight here. One of the towns on which woe is pronounced is Chorazin. It is implied that Jesus did many mighty works there. In the gospel history as we have it Chorazin is never even mentioned, and we do not know one thing that Jesus did or one word that Jesus spoke there. Nothing could show so vividly how much we do not know about the life of Jesus. The gospels are not biographies; they are only sketches of the life of Jesus (cp. John 21: 25).

This passage tells us certain supremely important things about both the preacher and the hearer.

(i) The preacher is not to be cluttered up with material things; he is to travel light. It is easy to get entangled and enmeshed in the things of this life. Once Dr. Johnson, after seeing through a great castle and its policies, remarked grimly, " These are the things which make it difficult to die." Earth must never blot out heaven.

(ii) The preacher is to concentrate on his task. He is to greet no man on the way. This goes back to Elisha's instruction to Gehazi in 2 Kings 4: 19. It is not an instruction to discourtesy; but it does mean that the man of God must not turn aside or linger on the lesser things while the great things call him.

(iii) The preacher must not be in the work for what he can get out of it. He is to eat what is put before him; he must not move from house to house seeking better and more comfortable quarters. It was not long before the Church has its spongers. There is a work called *The Teaching of the Twelve Apostles*. It was written about A.D. 100, and it is the Church's first book of order. In those days there were prophets who wandered from town to town. It is laid down that if a prophet wishes to stay in a place for more than three days without working he is a false prophet; and if a prophet in the Spirit asks for money or a meal he is a false prophet! The labourer is worthy of his hire, but the servant of a crucified Master cannot be a seeker for luxury.

(iv) Of the hearer, this passage tells us that to have heard God's word is a great responsibility. A man will be judged according to what he had the chance to know. We allow things in a child we condemn in an adult; we forgive things in a savage we would punish in a civilized man. Responsibility is the other side of privilege.

(v) It is a terrible thing to reject God's invitation. There is a sense in which every promise of God that a man has ever heard can become his condemnation. If he receives these promises they are his greatest glory, but each one that he has heard and rejected will some day be a witness against him.

A MAN'S TRUE GLORY

Luke 10: 17-20

> The Seventy returned with joy. " Lord," they said, " at your name the demons are subject to us." He said to them, " I saw Satan fall like lightning from Heaven. Look you—I have given you authority to walk upon snakes and scorpions and over all the power of the Enemy. Nothing will hurt you. But do not rejoice in this—that the spirits are subject to you; but rejoice that your names are written in Heaven."

WHEN The Seventy returned they were radiant with the triumphs which they had wrought in the name of Jesus. Jesus said to them, " I saw Satan fall like lightning from Heaven." That is a difficult phrase to understand. It can have two meanings.

(i) It may mean, " I saw the forces of darkness and evil defeated; the citadel of Satan is stormed and the Kingdom of God is on the way." It may mean that Jesus knew that the deathblow to Satan and all his powers had been struck, however long his final conquest might be delayed; that, as a great scholar put it, D day has been accomplished and sooner or later V day is bound to follow.

(ii) But equally well it may be a warning against pride. The legend was that it was for a pride which rebelled against God that Satan was cast out of Heaven where once he had been the chief of the angels. It may be that Jesus was saying to The Seventy, " You have had your triumphs; keep yourselves from pride, for once the chief of all the angels fell to pride and was cast from heaven."

Certainly Jesus went on to warn His disciples against pride and over-confidence. It was true that they were given all power, but their greatest glory was that their names were written in heaven.

It will always remain true that a man's greatest glory is not what he has done but what God has done for him. It might well be claimed that the discovery of the use of chloroform saved the world more pain than any other single medical discovery. Once someone asked Sir James Simpson, its discoverer, " What do you regard as your greatest discovery? " The questioner naturally expected the answer, " The discovery of chloroform." But Simpson answered, " My greatest discovery was when I discovered that Jesus Christ is my Saviour." Even the greatest man can only say in the presence of God,

> " Nothing in my hand I bring,
> Simply to Thy Cross I cling;
> Naked, come to Thee for dress;
> Helpless, look to Thee for grace;
> Foul, I to the fountain fly;
> Wash me, Saviour, or I die."

It is pride which bars from heaven; it is humility which is the passport to the presence of God.

THE UNSURPASSABLE CLAIM

Luke 10: 21-24

At that time Jesus rejoiced in the Holy Spirit. " I thank you, O Father, Lord of Heaven and earth," He said, " that you have hidden these things from the wise and clever and that you have revealed them to babes. Yes, O Father, for so it was your good pleasure in your sight. All things have been handed over to me by my Father. No one knows who the Son is except the Father; and no one knows who the Father is except the Son, and he to whom the Son wishes to reveal Him." He turned to His disciples when they were in private and said, " Happy are the eyes which see the things which you are seeing for I tell you that many prophets and kings desired to see the things that you are seeing and did not see them, and to hear the things that you are hearing and did not hear them."

THE GOSPEL OF LUKE

THERE are three great thoughts in this passage.

(i) Verse 21 tells us of the wisdom of simplicity. The simple mind could receive the truths that the learned mind could not take in. Once Arnold Bennet said that, " The only way to write a great book was to write it with the eyes of a child who sees things for the first time." It is possible to be too clever. It is quite possible to be so clever and so learned that in the end we cannot see the wood for the trees. Someone has said that the test of a really great scholar is how much he is able to forget. After all, we must always remember this—that Christianity does not mean knowing all the theories about the New Testament; still less does it mean knowing all the theologies and the Christologies; because Christianity does not mean *knowing about Christ*; it means *knowing Christ*; and to do that requires not earthly wisdom but heavenly grace.

(ii) Verse 22 tells of the unique relationship between Jesus and God. This is what the Fourth Gospel means when it says, " The Word became flesh " (John 1: 14), or when it makes Jesus say, " I and my Father are one," or, " He who hath seen me hath seen the Father " (John 10: 30; 14: 9). To the Greeks God was unknowable. There was a great gulf fixed between matter and spirit, man and God. " It is very difficult," they said, " to know God, and when you do know Him it is impossible to tell anyone else about Him." But when Jesus came He said, " If you want to know what God is like, look at me." Jesus did not so much tell men about God; He showed men God, because in Him were the mind and the heart of God towards men.

(iii) Verses 23 and 24 tell us that Jesus is the consummation of all history. In these verses Jesus said, " I am the One to whom all the prophets and the saints and the kings looked forward and for whom they longed." This is what Matthew means when over and over again in his gospel he wrote, " This was done that it might be fulfilled which was spoken by the prophet saying . . . "

cp. Matthew 2: 15, 17, 23). Jesus was the peak to which history had been climbing, the goal to which it had been marching, the dream which had ever haunted men of God. If we desire to express this in terms of modern thought we might dare to put it this way. We believe in evolution, the slow climb upwards of man from the level of the beasts Jesus is the end and climax of the evolutionary process because in Him, man met God, and He is at once the perfection of manhood and the fulness of godhead.

WHO IS MY NEIGHBOUR?

Luke 10: 25-37

Look you—an expert in the law stood up and asked Jesus a test question. " Teacher," he said, " What is it that, if I do it, I will become the possessor of eternal life? " He said to him, " What stands written in the law? How do you read? " He answered, " You must love the Lord your God with your whole heart, and with your whole soul, and with your whole strength, and with your whole mind, and your neighbour as yourself." " Your answer is correct," said Jesus. But he, wishing to put himself in the right, said to Jesus, " And who is my neighbour? " Jesus answered, " There was a man who went down from Jerusalem to Jericho. He fell amongst brigands who stripped him and laid blows upon him, and went away and left him half-dead. Now, by chance, a priest came down by that road. He looked at him and passed by on the other side. In the same way when a Levite came to the place he looked at him and passed by on the other side. A Samaritan who was on the road came to where he was. He looked at him and was moved to the depths of his being with pity. So he came up to him and bound up his wounds, pouring in wine and oil; and he put him on his own beast and brought him to an inn and cared for him. On the next day he put down two shillings and gave them to the inn-keeper. ' Look after him,' he said, ' and whatever more you are out of pocket, when I come back this way, I'll square up with you in full.' Which of these

three, do you think, was neighbour to the man who
fell into the hands of brigands?" He said, "He who
showed mercy on him." "Go," said Jesus to him,
"and do likewise."

FIRST, let us look at *the scene* of this story. The road from
Jerusalem to Jericho was a notoriously dangerous road.
Jerusalem is 2,300 feet above sea-level; the Dead Sea
near which Jericho stood, is 1,300 feet below sea-level.
So then, in little more than 20 miles, this road dropped
3,600 feet. It was a road of narrow, rocky defiles, and of
sudden turnings which made it the happy hunting-ground
of brigands. In the fifth century Jerome tells us that it
was still called "The Red, or Bloody Way." In the 19th
century it was still necessary to pay safety money to the
local Sheiks before one could travel on it. As late as the
early 1930's H. V. Morton tells us that he was warned
to get home before dark, if he intended to use the road,
because a certain Abu Jildah was an adept at holding up
cars and robbing travellers and tourists, and escaping
to the hills before the police could arrive. When Jesus
told this story, He was telling about the kind of thing that
was constantly happening on this Jerusalem to Jericho road.

Second, let us look at the *characters*. (*a*) There was
the traveller. He was obviously a reckless and foolhardy
character. People seldom attempted the Jerusalem to
Jericho road alone if they were carrying goods or valuables.
Seeking safety in numbers, they always travelled in convoys
or caravans. This man had no one but himself to blame
for the plight in which he found himself. (*b*) There was
the priest. The priest hastened past the man. No doubt
he was remembering that he who touched a dead man was
unclean for seven days (Numbers 19: 11). He could not
be sure, but he feared that the man was dead; and if
he touched him, he would lose his turn of duty in the
Temple; and he refused to risk that. He was a man who
set the claims of ceremonial above those of charity. The
Temple and its liturgy meant more to him than the pain

of man. (c) There was *the Levite*. He seems to have gone nearer to the man before he passed on. The bandits were in the habit of using decoys. One of their number would act the part of a wounded man; and when some unsuspecting traveller stopped over him, the others would rush upon him and overpower him. The Levite was a man whose motto was, " Safety first." He would take no risks to help anyone else. (d) There was *the Samaritan*. The listeners would obviously expect that with his arrival the villain had arrived. He may not have been *racially* a Samaritan at all. The Jews had no dealings with the Samaritans, and yet this man seems to have been a kind of commercial traveller who was a regular visitor to the inn. In John 8: 48 the Jews call Jesus a Samaritan. The name was sometimes used to describe a man who was a heretic and a breaker of the ceremonial law. Perhaps this man was a Samaritan in the sense of being a man whom all orthodox good people despised. We note two things about him. (i) His credit was good! Clearly the innkeeper was prepared to trust him. He may have been theologically unsound, but he was an honest man. (ii) He alone was prepared to help. A heretic he may have been, but the charity of God was in his heart. It is no new experience to find the orthodox more interested in dogmas than in help and to find the man the orthodox despise to be the man who loves his fellow men. In the end we will be judged not by the creed we hold but by the life we live.

Third, let us look at *the teaching* of the parable. The Scribe who asked this question was in earnest. Jesus asked him what was written in the law, and then said, " How do you read? " Strict orthodox Jews wore round their wrists little leather boxes called phylacteries, which contained certain passages of scripture—Exodus 13: 1-10; 11-16; Deuteronomy 6: 4-9; 11: 13-20. " Thou shalt love the Lord thy God " is from Deuteronomy 6: 3 and 11: 13. So Jesus said to the Scribe, " Look at the phylactery on your own wrist and it will answer your question."

To that the Scribes added Leviticus 18: 19, which bids a man love his neighbour as himself; but with their passion for definition the Rabbis sought to define who a man's neighbour was; and at their worst and their narrowest they confined the word *neighbour* to their *fellow Jews*. For instance, some of them said that it was illegal to help a Gentile woman in her sorest time, the time of childbirth, for that would only have been to bring another "Gentile into the world. So then the Scribe's question, "Who is my neighbour?" was a genuine question. Jesus' answer involves three things. (i) We must help a man even when he has brought his trouble on himself, as the traveller by his recklessness had done. (ii) Any man of any nation who is in need is our neighbour. Our help must be as wide as the love of God. (iii) The help must be practical, and must not consist merely in *feeling* sorry. No doubt the priest and the Levite felt a pang of pity for the wounded man, but they *did* nothing. Compassion, to be real compassion, must issue in deeds.

What Jesus said to the Scribe, He says to us—"Go *you* and do the same."

THE CLASH OF TEMPERAMENTS

Luke 10: 38-42

> As they journeyed, Jesus entered into a village. A woman called Martha received Him into her house. She had a sister called Mary, and she sat at Jesus' feet and kept listening to His word. Martha was worried about much serving. She stood over them and said, "Lord, don't you care that my sister has left me alone to do the serving? Tell her to give me a hand." "Martha, Martha," the Lord answered her, "you are worried and troubled about many things. Only one thing is necessary. Mary has chosen the better part, and it is not going to be taken away from her."

IT would be hard to find more vivid character drawing in greater economy of words than we find in these verses.

(i) They show us *the clash of temperaments*. We have never allowed enough for the place of temperament in religion. Some people are naturally dynamos of activity; others are naturally quiet. It is hard for the active person to understand the person who sits and thinks and contemplates. And the person who is devoted to quiet times and to meditation is very apt to look down on the person who would rather be doing something. There is no right or wrong in this. God did not make everyone alike. One person may pray,

> " Lord of all pots and pans and things,
>   Since I've no time to be
> A saint by doing lovely things,
>   Or watching late with Thee,
> Or dreaming in the dawnlight,
>   or storming heaven's gates,
> Make me a saint by getting meals
>   And washing up the plates."

Another person may sit with folded hands but mind intense and think and pray, and both are serving God. God needs His Marys and His Marthas too.

(ii) But these verses show us something more—they show us *the wrong kind of kindness*. Think where Jesus was going when this happened. He was on His way to Jerusalem—to die. His whole being was taken up with the intensity of that inner battle to bend His will to the will of God. When Jesus came to that home in Bethany it was a great day; and Martha was eager to celebrate it by—as we say—laying on the best the house could give. So she rushed and fussed and cooked; *and that was precisely what Jesus did not want*. All He wanted was quiet. With the Cross before Him, and with the inner tension in His heart, He had turned aside to Bethany to find an oasis of calm away from the demanding crowds if only for an hour or two; and that is what Mary gave Him, and that is what Martha, in her kindness, did her best to destroy. " One thing is necessary " —quite possibly this means, " I don't want a big spread; one course, the simplest meal is all I want." It was simply that Mary understood and that Martha did not. Here is one of the great difficulties in life. So often we want to be kind to people—but we want to be kind to them *in our way*; and should it happen that our way is not the necessary way, we sometimes take offence and think that we are not appreciated. If we are trying to be kind the first necessity is to try to see into the heart of the person we desire to help—and then to forget all our own plans and to think only of what he or she needs. Jesus loved Martha, and Martha loved Him, but when Martha set out to be kind, it had to be her way of being kind, and she was really being unkind to Him whose heart cried for quiet. Jesus loved Mary and Mary loved Him, and Mary understood.

TEACH US TO PRAY

Luke 11: 1-4

> Jesus was praying in a certain place, and when He stopped, one of His disciples said to Him, " Lord, teach us to pray, as John taught his disciples." He said to them, " When you pray, say,
>
>> O Father, let your name be held in reverence.
>> Let your Kingdom come.
>> Give to us each day our bread for the day.
>> And forgive us our sins as we too forgive everyone
>>   who is in debt to us.
>> And lead us not into temptation."

IT was the regular custom for a Rabbi to teach his disciples a simple prayer which they might habitually use. John had done that for his disciples, and now Jesus' disciples came to Him asking Him to do the same for them. This is Luke's version of The Lord's Prayer. It is shorter than Matthew's, but it will teach us all we need to know about how to pray and what to pray for.

(i) It begins by calling God *Father*. That was the characteristic Christian address to God. (cp. Galatians 4: 6; Romans 8: 15; I Peter I: 17). The very first word tells us that in prayer we are not coming to someone out of whom gifts have to be unwillingly extracted, but to a Father who delights to supply His children's needs.

(ii) In Hebrew *the name* meant much more than merely the name by which a person is called. *The name* means the whole character of the person as it is revealed and known to us. Psalm 9: 10 says, "They that know *Thy name* will put their trust in Thee." That means far more than knowing that God's name is Jehovah. It means those who know the whole character and mind and heart of God will gladly put their trust in Him.

(iii) We must note particularly the order of the Lord's Prayer. Before anything is asked for ourselves, God and His glory, and the reverence due to Him, come first. Only when we give God His place will all other things take their proper place.

(iv) The prayer covers all life. (*a*) It covers *present need*. It tells us to pray for our daily bread; but note it is bread *for the day* for which we pray. This goes back to the old story of the manna in the wilderness (Exodus 16: 11-21). Only enough for the needs of the day might be gathered. We are not to worry about the unknown future, but to live a day at a time.

> " I do not ask to see
> The distant scene—one step enough for me."

(*b*) It covers *past sin*. When we pray we cannot do other than pray for forgiveness for the best of us is a sinful man coming before the purity of God. (*c*) It covers *future trials*. *Temptation* in the New Testament means any testing situation. It includes far more than the mere seduction to sin; it covers every situation which is a challenge to and a test of a person's manhood and integrity and fidelity. We cannot escape it, but we can meet it with God.

Someone has said that the Lord's Prayer has two great uses in our own private prayers. If we use it at the beginning of our devotions it awakens all kinds of holy desires which will lead us on into the right pathways of prayer. If we use it at the end of our devotions it sums up all that we ought to pray for in the presence of God.

ASK AND YOU WILL RECEIVE

Luke 11: 5-13

> Jesus said to them, " Suppose one of you has a friend and goes to him towards midnight and says to him, ' Friend, lend me three loaves because a friend of mine has arrived at my house from a journey and I have nothing to set before him '; and suppose his friend answers from within, ' Don't bother me; the door has already been shut and my children are in bed with me; I can't get up and supply you '—I tell you, if he will not rise and supply him because he is his friend, he will rise and give him as much as he needs because of his shameless persistence. For I say to you, ' Ask and it will be given to you; seek and you will find; knock and it will be opened to you. For everyone who asks receives; and he who seeks finds; and to him who knocks it will be opened. If a son asks any father among you for bread, will he give him a stone? Or, if he asks a fish, will he, instead of a fish, give him a serpent? Or if he asks an egg, will he give him a scorpion? If you then, who are evil, know to give good gifts to your children, how much more will your Father who is in Heaven give the Holy Spirit to those who ask Him? ' "

IN Palestine travellers often travelled late in the evening to avoid the heat of the midday sun. In Jesus' story just such a traveller had arrived towards midnight at his friend's house. In the east hospitality is a sacred duty; it was not enough to set before a man a bare sufficiency; the guest had to be confronted with an ample abundance. In the villages bread was baked at home. Only enough for the day's needs was baked, because, if it was kept and

became stale, no one would wish to eat it. So the late
arrival of the traveller confronted the householder with an
embarrassing situation, because his larder was empty and
he could not fulfil the sacred obligations of hospitality.
Late as it was, he went out to borrow from a friend. The
friend's door was shut. In the east no one would knock
on a shut door unless the need was imperative. In the
morning the door was opened and remained open all day,
for there was little privacy; but if the door was shut,
that was a definite sign that the householder did not wish
to be disturbed. But the seeking householder was not
deterred. He knocked, and kept on knocking. The poorer
Palestinian house consisted of one room with only one
little window. The floor was simply of beaten earth covered
with dried reeds and rushes. The room was divided into
two parts, not by a partition, but by a low platform.
Two-thirds of it were on ground level. The other third
was slightly raised. On the raised part the charcoal stove
burned all night, and round it the whole family slept,
not on raised beds, but on sleeping mats. Families were
large, and they slept close together for warmth. For one
to rise was inevitably to disturb the whole family. Further,
in the villages it was the custom to bring the livestock,
the hens and the cocks and the goats, into the house at
night. Is there any wonder that the man who was in bed
did not want to rise? But the determined borrower knocked
on with shameless persistence—that is what the Greek
word means—until at last the householder, knowing that
by this time the whole family was disturbed anyway, arose
and gave him what he needed.

 " That story," said Jesus, " will tell you about prayer."
The lesson of this parable is not that we must persist in
prayer; it is not that we must batter at God's door until
we finally compel God for very weariness to give us what
we want; until we coerce an unwilling God to answer.
A parable literally means *something laid alongside.* If
we lay something beside another thing to teach a lesson,

that lesson may be drawn from the fact that the things are like each other or from the fact that the things are a contrast to each other. The point here is based, not on likeness, but on *contrast*. What Jesus said is, " If a churlish and unwilling householder can in the end be coerced by a friend's shameless persistence into giving him what he needs, *how much more* will God who is a loving Father supply all His children's needs? " " If you," said Jesus, " who are evil, know that you are bound to supply your children's needs, *how much more* will God? "

This does not absolve us from intensity in prayer. After all, we can only guarantee the reality and sincerity of our desire by the passion with which we pray; but it does mean this, that we are not wringing gifts from an unwilling God, but that we are going to one who knows our needs better than we know them ourselves, and whose heart towards us is the heart of generous love. If we do not receive what we pray for, it is not because God grudgingly refuses to give it to us, but because He has some better thing for us. There is no such thing as unanswered prayer. The answer given may not be the answer we desired or expected. Even when it is a refusal of our wishes it is the answer of the love and the wisdom of God.

A MALICIOUS SLANDER

Luke 11: 14-23

Jesus was casting out a dumb demon. When the demon came out the dumb man spoke and the crowds were amazed. Some of them said, " He casts out demons by the help of Beelzebul, who is the prince of demons." Others, trying to put Him to the test, sought a sign from heaven from Him. He knew what they were thinking. " Every kingdom," He said, " that is divided against itself is devastated; and every house that is divided against itself falls; so if Satan is divided against himself how will his kingdom stand? You must answer that question because you say that I cast out demons

by the help of Beelzebul. If I cast out demons by the
power of Beelzebul, by whose power do your sons
cast them out? You have become your own judges.
But if it is by the finger of God that I cast out the
demons, then the Kingdom of God has come upon
you. When a strong man in full panoply guards his
own homestead, his goods are in peace. But when
a stronger man than he comes and conquers him, he
will take away the armour in which he trusted, and
will divide his spoil. He who is not with me is against
me; and he who does not gather with me scatters."

WHEN Jesus' enemies were helpless to oppose Him by
fair means they resorted to slander. They declared that
His power over the demons was due to the fact that He
was in league with the prince of demons. They attributed
His power not to God but to the devil. Jesus gave them a
double and a crushing answer. First, He struck them a
shrewd blow. There were many exorcists in Jesus' time in
Palestine. Josephus, the Jewish historian, traces this
power back to Solomon. Part of Solomon's wisdom was
that he was skilful with herbs, and that he had invented
incantations which drove out demons in such a way that
they never came back again; and Josephus states that he
had seen Solomon's methods used with success even in
his own day. (Josephus, *Antiquities of the Jews* ; 8 : 5 : 2)
So Jesus delivers a home-thrust. " If I," He said, " cast
out devils because I am in league with the prince of devils,
what of your own people who do the same thing? " " If
you condemn me," He said, " you are only condemning
yourselves." Second, He used a really unanswerable
argument. No kingdom in which there is a civil war can
survive. If the prince of devils is lending his power to
defeat his own emissaries he is finished. There is only one
way for a strong man to be defeated and that is for a still
stronger man to master him. " Therefore," said Jesus, " if
I cast out devils, so far from that proving that I am in
league with the prince of devils, it proves that the devil's
citadel is breached, the strong man of evil is mastered,
and the Kingdom of God is here."

Out of this passage there emerge certain permanent truths.

(i) It is by no means uncommon for people to resort to slander when honest opposition is helpless. Gladstone, the great prime minister, was interested in the reformation of the fallen women of the streets of London. His enemies suggested that he was interested in them for very different and very inferior reasons. There is nothing so cruel as slander, for slander is apt to stick because the human mind is such that it always tends to think the worst, and very often the human ear would prefer to hear the derogatory rather than the complimentary tale. We need not think that we are altogether free of that particular sin. How often do we tend to think the worst of other people? How often do we deliberately impute low motives to someone whom we dislike? How often do we repeat the slanderous and the malicious tale and murder reputations over the tea-cups? To think of this will not cause complacency but calls for self-examination.

(ii) Once again we must note that Jesus' proof that the Kingdom had come was the fact that sufferers were healed and that health walked where disease had been. In the modern phrase, Jesus' aim was not only *soul* salvation; it was also *whole* salvation.

(iii) Luke finishes this section with the saying of Jesus that he who was not with Him was against Him, and that he who did not help to gather the flock helped to scatter it abroad. There is no place for neutrality in the Christian life. The man who stands aloof from the good cause automatically helps the evil cause. A man is either on the way or in the way.

THE PERIL OF THE EMPTY SOUL

Luke 11: 24-28

When the unclean spirit goes out of a man, it goes through waterless places seeking for rest. And when it does not find it, it says, " I will go back to my house from which I came out." So it comes and finds the house swept and in order. Then it goes and gets in addition seven spirits worse than itself, and they enter in and settle there; and the last state of that man is worse than the first.

When He was speaking a woman lifted up her voice from the crowd and said, " Happy is the womb that bore you and the breasts at which you sucked." " But," He said, " rather, happy are those who hear the word of God and keep it."

HERE is a grim and terrible story. There was a man from whom an unclean spirit was expelled. The unclean spirit wandered seeking rest and found none. It determined to return to the man. It found the man's soul swept and garnished—but empty. So the spirit went and collected seven spirits worse than itself and came back and entered in; and the man's last state was worse than his first.

(i) Here is the fundamental truth that you cannot leave a man's soul empty. It is not enough to banish the evil thoughts and the evil habits and the old ways and leave the soul clean but empty. The empty soul is the soul in peril. Adam C. Welch liked to preach on the text, " Be not ye filled with new wine wherein is excess, but be filled with the Spirit " (Ephesians 5: 18). When he did so his opening sentence was, " You've got to fill a man with something." It is not enough to drive out the evil; the good must come in.

(ii) That means that we can never erect a real religion on negatives. We can never found a religion on a series of Thou shalt not's. Take a very clear example—one of the great problems of the modern world is the problem of Sunday observance. Too often the problem is approached with a tirade against the things which people allow themselves to do on the Sunday, and with a catalogue of prohibitions and of forbidden things. But the man to whom we speak has a perfect right to ask, " Well, what *may* I do? " And unless we tell him, his last state is worse than his first, for we have simply condemned him to idleness, and Satan is an adept at finding mischief for idle hands to do. It is always the peril of religion that it should present itself in a series of negatives. True, the cleansing is necessary; but after the rooting out of the evil there must come the filling with the good.

(iii) Herein is the great practical truth that the best way to avoid the evil is to do the good. The loveliest garden I ever saw was so full of flowers that there was scarcely room for a weed to grow. In no garden is it enough to uproot weeds; flowers must be sown and planted until the space which the weeds would have usurped is filled. Nowhere is this truer than in the world of thought and thoughts. Often we are troubled with wrong thoughts. If we go no further than to say to ourselves, " I must not think about that; I will not think about that," all that we do is to fix our thoughts upon it more and more. The cure is to think of something else, to banish the evil thought by thinking a good thought. We never become good by *not* doing things, but by filling life with lovely things.

Verses 27 and 28 show Jesus speaking sternly but truly. The woman who spoke was carried away by a moment of emotion. Jesus pulled her back to reality. The moment of emotion is a fine thing; but the greatest thing is a life of obedience in the routine things of everyday. No amount of fine feeling can take the place of faithful doing.

THE RESPONSIBILITY OF PRIVILEGE

Luke 11: 29-32

> When the crowds were thronging upon Him, He began to say, " This generation is a wicked generation. It seeks a sign, and no sign will be given to it except the sign of Jonah; for just as Jonah was a sign to the people of Nineveh so the Son of Man will be to this generation. The queen of the south will rise up in judgment with the men of this generation and will

condemn them, because she came from the ends of the earth to hear the wisdom of Solomon, and—look you—something greater than Solomon is here. The men of Nineveh will rise up in judgment with this generation and will condemn it, because they repented at the preaching of Jonah, and—look you—something greater than Jonah is here."

THE Jews wanted Jesus to do something sensational to prove that He really was the Anointed One of God. Later than this, about the year A.D. 45, a man called Theudas arose claiming to be the Messiah. He persuaded the people to follow him out to the Jordan with the promise that he would cleave the river in two and give them a pathway through it to the other side. Needless to say he failed, and the Romans dealt summarily with his rising; but that is the kind of thing that the people wanted Jesus to do to prove His claims. They could not see that the greatest sign that God could ever send was Jesus Himself. Just as once long ago Jonah had been God's sign to Nineveh, so now Jesus was God's sign to them—and they failed to recognize Him. When Solomon was king the Queen of Sheba recognized his wisdom and came from far to benefit from it; when Jonah preached the men of Nineveh recognized the authentic voice of God and responded to it. In the day of judgment these people would rise up and condemn the Jews of Jesus' time, because these Jews had had an opportunity and a privilege far beyond anything they had ever had and had refused to accept it. The condemnation of the Jews would be all the more complete because their privileges were so great. Privilege and responsibility go ever hand in hand. Think of two of our greatest privileges and think how we use them.

(i) We have available to everyone the Bible, the word of God. That did not cost nothing. There was a time when it was death to teach the English Bible. When Wycliff wrote to a certain scholar, about the year A.D. 1350, asking him to teach the common people the gospel stories in the English tongue, he answered, " I know well that I am holden by Christ's law to perform thy asking, but, natheless, we are now so far fallen away from Christ's law, that if I would answer to thy askings *I must in case undergo the death*; and thou wottest well that a man is beholden to keep his life as long as he may." Later on, Foxe was to tell us that in those days men sat up all night to read and hear the word of God in English. " Some gave five marks (equal to £40 of our money), some more, some less for a book; some gave a load of hay for a few chapters of St. James or St. Paul in English." It was Tyndale who gave England its first printed Bible. To do so, as he said himself, he suffered, " poverty, exile, bitter absence from friends, hunger and thirst and cold, great dangers and innumerable other hard and sharp fightings." In 1536 he was martyred. When, some years before, the authorities had burned the book, he said, " They did none other thing than I looked for; no more shall they do if they burn me also." There is no book which cost so much as the Bible. To-day it is in serious danger of deserving the cynical definition of a classic—a book of which everyone has heard and which no one reads. We have the privilege of possessing the Bible, and that privilege is a responsibility for which we shall answer.

(ii) We have freedom to worship as we think right; and that, too, is a privilege which cost the lives of men; and the tragic thing is that so many people have used that freedom in order not to worship at all. That privilege, too, is a responsibility for which we shall answer.

If a man possesses Christ, and Christ's Book, and Christ's Church, he is the heir of all the privileges of God; and if he neglects them or refuses them he, like the Jews in the time of Jesus, is a man under condemnation.

THE DARKENED HEART

Luke 11: 33-36

No one lights a lamp and puts it in a cellar or under a bushel, but upon a lamp-stand, so that those who come in may see the light. The lamp of the body is your eye. When your eye is sound your whole body is full of light; but if the eye is diseased the whole body is full of darkness. Take care, then, lest the light that is in you is darkness. If, then, your whole body is full of light, without any part of darkness, it will be altogether bright as when the lamp with its ray gives you light.

THIS is a passage the meaning of which it is not easy to grasp. Very probably the meaning is this—the light of the body depends on the eye. If the eye is healthy the body receives all the light it needs; if the eye is diseased then the light turns to darkness. Just so, *the light of life depends on the heart.* If the heart is right the whole life is irradiated with light; if the heart is wrong all life is darkened. Jesus urges us to see that the inner lamp is always burning.

What then is it that darkens the inner light? What is it that can go wrong with our hearts?

(i) Our hearts may become *hard.* Sometimes, if we have to do something unaccustomed with our hands, the skin is irritated and ruffled, and we have pain; but if we repeat the action often enough the skin becomes hardened and we can do what once hurt us without any trouble or pain. It is so with our hearts. The first time we do a wrong thing we do it with a tremor and sometimes with a sore heart. Each time we repeat it the tremor grows less, until in the end we can do it without a qualm. There is a terrible hardening power in sin. No man ever took the first step to sin without the warnings sounding in his heart; but if he sins often enough the time comes when he ceases to care. That which we were once afraid and hesitant and reluctant to do becomes a habit. We have nobody but ourselves to blame if we allow ourselves to reach that stage.

(ii) Our hearts may become *dull.* It is the experience of life that it is tragically easy to accept things. In the beginning our hearts may be sore at the sight of the world's suffering and pain; but in the end most people become so used to it that they accept it and feel nothing about it at all. It is all too true that for most people the feelings of youth are far more intense than those of age. That is specially true of the Cross of Jesus Christ. Florence Barclay tells how when she was a little girl she was taken to church for the first time. It was Good Friday, and the long story of the crucifixion was read and beautifully read. She heard Peter deny and Judas betray; she heard Pilate's bullying cross-examination; she saw the crown of thorns, the buffeting of the soldiers; she heard of Jesus being delivered to be crucified, and then there came the words with their terrible finality, " and there they crucified Him." No one in the church seemed to care; but suddenly the little girl's face was buried in her mother's coat, and she was sobbing her heart out, and her little voice rang through the silent church, " Why did they do it? Why did they do it?" That is how we all ought to feel about the Cross, but we have heard the story so often that we can listen to it with no reaction at all. God keep us from the heart which has lost the power to feel the agony of the Cross—borne for us.

(iii) Our hearts may be actively *rebellious*. It is quite possible for a man to know the right way and deliberately to take the wrong way. A man may actually feel God's hand upon his shoulder and twitch that shoulder away. With open eyes a man may take his way to the far country when God is calling him home.

God save us from the darkened heart.

THE WORSHIP OF DETAILS AND THE NEGLECT OF THE THINGS THAT MATTER

Luke 11: 37-44

After Jesus had spoken a Pharisee asked Him to dine with Him. He came in and reclined at the table. The Pharisee was surprised when he saw that He did not dip His hands in water before He ate. The Lord said to him, " You Pharisees cleanse the outside of the cup and the dish, but inside you are full of grasping and wickedness. Fools! Did He who made the outside not make the inside also? But cleanse the things that are within—and look you—all things will be pure for you.

But woe to you Pharisees! because you give tithes of mint and rue and every herb and pass by justice and the love of God. These you ought to have done without omitting the others. Woe to you Pharisees! because you love the chief seats in the Synagogues and greetings in the market places. Woe to you! because you are like tombs which are not seen, and the men who walk over them do not know that they are doing it."

THE Pharisee was surprised that Jesus did not wash His hands before eating. This was not a matter of cleanliness but of the ceremonial law. The law laid it down that before a man ate he must wash his hands in a certain way, and that he must also wash them between the courses. As usual every littlest detail was worked out. Large stone vessels of water were specially kept for the purpose because ordinary water might be unclean; the amount of water used must be at least a quarter of a log, that is enough to fill one and a half egg-shells. First the water must be poured over the hands beginning at the tips of the fingers and running right up to the wrist. Then the palm of each hand must be cleansed by rubbing the fist of the other into it. Finally, water must again be poured over the hand, this time beginning at the wrist and running down to the fingertips. To the Pharisee to omit the slightest detail of this was to sin. Jesus' comment was that if they were as particular about cleansing their hearts as they were about washing their hands they would be better men.

There were certain dues which the meticulously orthodox would never omit to pay. (*a*) *The first fruits of the soil.* The first fruits of the seven kinds—wheat, barley, vines, fig-trees, pomegranates, olives and honey—were offered in the Temple. (*b*) *There was the Terumah.* The first fruits

were given to God, but the Terumah was a contribution
to the upkeep of the priests. It was the presentation of
the first fruits of every growing thing. The amount to
be given was one-fiftieth of the total yield. (c) *There was
the tithe*. The tithe was paid directly to the Levites, who,
in turn, paid a tithe of what they received to the priests.
It was one-tenth of " everything that can be used as food
and is cultivated and grows out of the earth." The meti-
culousness of the Pharisees in tithing is shown by the fact
that even the law said it was not necessary to tithe rue.
No matter what their inner hearts and feelings were like,
however much they neglected justice and forgot love, they
never omitted the tithe.

The chief seats at the Synagogue were the seats out in
front facing the audience. In the congregation itself the
best seats were the front seats, and the seats decreased
in honour the further back they got. The advantage of
these seats was that they could be seen by all! The more
exaggerated the respect of the greetings the Pharisees
received in the streets the better they were pleased.

The point of verse 44 is this. Numbers 19: 16 lays it
down that, whosoever in the open fields touches a grave
shall be unclean for seven days. To be unclean was to be
debarred from all religious worship. Now, it might be that
a man might touch a grave without knowing that he was
doing it. That did not matter; its touch made him unclean.
Jesus said that the Pharisees were exactly like that.
Although men might not know it their influence could
do nothing but harm. All unawares, the man who came
in contact with them, was being touched for evil. Men might
not suspect the corruption but it was there; all the time
they were being infected with wrong ideas of God and of
the demands of God.

Two things stand out about the Pharisees and for these
two things Jesus condemned them.

(i) They concentrated on *externals*. So long as the
externals of religion were carried out that was all that

mattered. Their hearts might be as black as hell; they might be utterly lacking in charity and even justice; so long as they went through the correct motions at the correct time they considered that they were good in the eyes of God. A man may be regular in his church attendance; he may be a diligent student of his Bible; he may be a generous giver to the Church; but if in his heart there are thoughts of pride and of contempt, if he has no charity in his dealings with his fellow men in the life of the everyday, if he is unjust to his subordinates or dishonest to his employer, he is not a Christian man. No man is a Christian when he meticulously observes the conventions of religion and forgets the realities.

(ii) They concentrated on *details*. Compared with love and kindness, justice and generosity, the washings of hands and the giving of tithes with mathematical accuracy were mere unimportant details. Once a man came to Dr. Johnson with a tale of woe. He worked in a paper factory; he had taken for his own purposes a very little piece of paper and a very little bit of string, and he had convinced himself that he had committed a deadly sin and would not stop talking about it. At last Johnson broke out on him, " Sir, stop bothering about paper and packthread when we are all living together in a world that is bursting with sin and sorrow." How often church courts and church people get lost in totally unimportant details of church government and administration, and even argue and fight about them, and forget the great realities of the Christian life!

THE SINS OF THE LEGALISTS

Luke 11: 45-54

A Scribe answered, " Teacher, when you talk like that you are insulting us." Jesus said, " Woe to you Scribes too! because you bind burdens upon men that are hard to bear and you yourselves do not lay a finger on the burdens. Woe to you! because you build the tombs of the prophets whom your fathers killed! So you are witnesses that you agree with the deeds of your fathers, because they killed them and you build them tombs. Because of this God in His wisdom said, ' I will send prophets and apostles to them, some of whom they will slay and persecute, so that the blood of all the prophets, shed from the foundation of the world, will be required from this generation, from the blood of Abel to the blood of Zacharias who perished between the altar and the Temple.' Yes, I tell you, it will be required from this generation. Woe to you Scribes! You did not enter in yourselves and you hindered those who were trying to enter."

As Jesus went away from them, the Scribes and Pharisees began to watch Him intensely, and to try to provoke Him to discuss on many subjects, for they were laying traps for Him, to hunt for something out of His mouth which they could use as a charge against Him.

HERE three charges are levelled against the Scribes.

(i) They were experts in the law; they laid upon men the thousand and one burdens of the ceremonial law; but they did not keep them themselves, because they were experts in evasion. Here are some of their evasions. The limit of a Sabbath day's journey was 2,000 cubits (1,000 yards) from a man's residence. But if a rope was tied across the end of the street, the end of the street became his residence and he could go 1,000 yards beyond that; if on the Friday evening he left at any given point enough food for two meals that point technically became his residence and he could go 1,000 yards beyond that! One of the forbidden works on the Sabbath was the tying of knots, sailors' or camel drivers' knots, and knots in ropes. But a woman might tie the knot in her girdle. Therefore, if a bucket of water had to be raised from a well a rope could not be knotted to it, but a woman's girdle could, and it could be raised with that! To carry a burden was forbidden, but the codified written law lays it down,

" he who carries anything, whether it be in his right hand, or in his left hand, or in his bosom, or on his shoulder is guilty; but he who carries anything on the back of his hand, with his foot, or with his mouth, or with his elbow, or with his ear, or with his hair, or with his money bag turned upside down, or between his money bag and his shirt, or in the fold of his shirt or in his shoe, or in his sandal is guiltless, because he does not carry it in the usual way of carrying it out." It is incredible that men should ever have thought that God could have laid down laws like that, and that the working out of details like that was a religious service and that the keeping of them was a matter of life and death. But that was Scribal religion. Little wonder that Jesus turned on the Scribes, and that the Scribes regarded Him as an irreligious heretic.

(ii) The attitude of the Scribes to the prophets was paradoxical. They professed a lip service and a deep admiration for the prophets. But the only prophets they admired were dead prophets; when they met a living one they tried to kill him. They honoured the dead prophets with tombs and memorials, but they dishonoured the living ones with persecution and death. " Your new moons," said Isaiah, " and your appointed feasts my soul hateth." " He hath shewed thee, O man, what is good," said Micah; " and what doth the Lord require of thee but to do justly, to love mercy and to walk humbly with thy God? " That was the essence of the prophetic message; and that was the very antithesis of Scribal teaching. No wonder the Scribes, with their external details, hated the prophets, and Jesus walked in the prophetic line. The murder of Zacharias is described in 2 Chronicles 24: 20, 21.

(iii) The Scribes shut the people off from scripture. Their interpretation of scripture was so fantastic that it was impossible for the ordinary man to understand it. In their hands scripture became a book of riddles. In their mistaken ingenuity they refused to see its plain meaning themselves, and they would not let anyone else see it either. The scriptures had become the perquisite of the expert and a dark mystery to the common man.

None of this is so very out of date. There are still those who demand from others standards which they themselves refuse to satisfy. There are still those whose religion is nothing other than legalism. There are still those who make the word of God so difficult that the seeking mind of the common man is bewildered and does not know what to believe or to whom to listen.

THE CREED OF COURAGE AND OF TRUST
Luke 12: 1-12

In the meantime, when the people had been gathered together in their thousands, so that they trampled on each other, Jesus began to say first of all to His disciples, " Be on your guard against the leaven of the Pharisees, which is hypocrisy. There is nothing covered up which will not be unveiled, and there is nothing secret which shall not be known. All, therefore, that you have spoken in the dark shall be heard in the light; and what you have spoken into someone's ear in the inner room will be proclaimed on the house-tops. I tell you, my friends, do not be afraid of those who kill the body and who after that are not able to do anything further. I will warn you whom you are to fear—fear Him who after He has killed you has authority to cast you into hell. Yes, I tell you, fear Him! Are not five sparrows sold for two farthings? And yet not one of them is forgotten before God. But as for you—even the hairs of your head are all numbered. Do not be afraid. You are of more value than many sparrows. I tell you, everyone who acknow-ledges me before men, him will the Son of Man acknow-ledge before the angels of God; but he who denies me before men will be denied before the angels of God. If anyone speaks a word against the Son of Man it will be forgiven him; but he who speaks irreverently of the Holy Spirit will not be forgiven. When they bring you before Synagogues and rulers and those set in authority, do not worry how you will defend yourself or about what defence you will make, or about what you will say, for the Holy Spirit will teach you in that same hour what you ought to say."

163

WHEN we read this passage we are reminded again of the Jewish definition of preaching. As we saw, the Jews called preaching Charaz, which means *stringing pearls*. This passage, too, is a passage of pearls strung together, without the close connections which modern preaching demands. But in this passage there are certain dominant ideas.

(i) It tells us of the *forbidden sin*, which is *hypocrisy*. The word *hypocrite* began by meaning *someone who answers*; and *hypocrisy* originally meant *answering*. First the words were used of the ordinary flow of question and answer in any talk or in any dialogue; then they began to be connected with question and answer *in a play*. From that they went on to be connected with *acting a part*. *Hypocrisy is acting a part*. The hypocrite is never genuine; he is always play-acting. The basis of hypocrisy is insincerity. God would rather have a blunt, honest sinner, than someone who puts on an act of goodness.

(ii) It tells of the *correct attitude to life* which is an attitude of *fearlessness*. There are two reasons for that fearlessness. (*a*) Man's power over man is strictly limited to this life. A man can destroy another man's life *but not* his soul. In the 1914-18 war *Punch* had a famous cartoon in which it showed the German Emperor saying to King Albert of Belgium, " So now you have lost everything "; and back came Albert's answer, " But not my soul! " On the other hand, God's power is such that it can blot out a man's very self and soul. It is, therefore, only reasonable to fear God rather than to fear men. It was said of John Knox, as his body was being lowered into the grave, " Here lies one who feared God so much that he never feared the face of man." (*b*) God's care is the most detailed of all care. To God we are never lost in the crowd. Matthew says, "Are not two sparrows sold for a farthing? " (Matthew 10: 29). Here Luke says, "Are not *five* sparrows sold for *two farthings*? " If you were prepared to spend two farthings you got not four, but five sparrows. One was flung into the bargain as having no value at all. Not even the sparrow on which men set not a farthing's value is forgotten before God. The very hairs of our head are numbered. It has been computed that a blonde person has about 145,000 hairs; a dark-haired person, 120,000; and a person with red hair, 90,000! The Jews were so impressed with the individual care of God that they said that every blade of grass had its guardian angel. None of us needs to fear for each one of us can say, " God cares for *me*."

(iii) It tells us of *the unforgivable sin* which is the sin against the Holy Spirit. Both Matthew and Mark record that Jesus spoke about this sin immediately after the Scribes and Pharisees had attributed His cures to the prince of devils instead of to God (Matthew 12: 31, 32; Mark 3: 28, 29). These men could look at the very grace and power of God and call it the work of the devil. To understand this we must remember that Jesus was talking about the Holy Spirit as *the Jews* understood that conception, not in the full Christian sense, about which His audience at that time obviously knew nothing. To a Jew God's Spirit had two great functions. Through the Spirit God told His truth to men, and it was by the action of the Spirit in a man's mind and heart that he could recognize and grasp God's truth. Now, if a man for long enough refuses to use any faculty he will lose it. If we refuse to use any part of the body long enough it atrophies. Darwin tells how when he was a young man he loved poetry and music; but he so devoted himself to biology that he completely neglected them. The consequence was that in later life poetry meant nothing to him, and music was only a noise, and he said that if he had his life to live over again he would see to it that he would read poetry and listen to music so that he would not lose the faculty of enjoying them. Just so we can lose the faculty of recognizing God. By repeatedly refusing God's word, by repeatedly taking our own way, by repeatedly shutting our eyes to God and closing our ears to Him, we can come to a stage when we do not recognize God when we see Him, when to us evil becomes good and good becomes evil. That is what happened to the Scribes and Pharisees. They had so blinded and deafened themselves to God that when God came they called Him the devil. Why is that the unforgivable sin? Because in such a state *repentance is impossible*. If a man does not even realize that he is sinning, if goodness no longer makes any appeal to him, then he cannot repent. God has not shut him out. By his repeated refusals he has shut himself out. And that means that the one man who can never have committed the unforgivable sin is the man who fears that he has, for once a man has committed it, he is so dead to God that he would be conscious of no sin at all.

(iv) It tells us of *the rewarded loyalty*. The reward of loyalty is no material thing. The reward is that in heaven Jesus will say of us, " This was my man. Well done! "

(v) It tells us of *the help of the Holy Spirit*. In the Fourth Gospel the favourite title of the Holy Spirit is the *Paraclete*. *Parakletos* means *someone who stands by to help*. It can be used of a witness, or an advocate to plead our cause. In the day of trouble there need be no fear, for on such a day no less a person than the Holy Spirit of God stands by to help.

THE PLACE OF MATERIAL POSSESSIONS IN LIFE
Luke 12: 13-30

One of the crowd said to Jesus, " Teacher, tell my brother to divide the inheritance with me." He said to him, " Man, who appointed me a judge or an arbitrator over you? " He said to them, " Watch and guard yourself against the spirit which is always wanting more; for even if a man has an abundance his life does not come from his possessions." He spoke a parable to them. " The land," He said, " of a rich man bore good crops. He kept thinking what he would do. ' What will I do,' he said, ' because I have no room to gather in my crops? ' So he said, ' This is what I will do. I will pull down my barns and I will build bigger ones, and I will gather there all my corn and all my good things; and I will say to my soul, Soul, you have many good things laid up for many years. Take your rest, eat, drink and enjoy yourself.' But God said to him, ' Fool! This night your soul is demanded from you; and, the things you prepared—who will get them all?' So is he who heaps up treasure for himself and is not rich towards God."

Jesus said to His disciples, " I therefore tell you, do not worry about your life—about what you are to eat; nor about your body—about what you are to wear. For your life is something more than food, and your body than clothing. Look at the ravens. See how they do not sow or reap; they have no storehouse or barn; but God feeds them. How much more valuable are you than the birds? Which of you, by worrying about it, can add a few inches to his span of life? If, then, you cannot do the littlest thing why worry about the other things? Look at the lilies. See how they grow. They do not work; they do not spin; but, I tell you, not even Solomon in all his glory was clothed like one of these. If God so clothe the grass in the field, which is there to-day and which to-morrow is cast into the oven, how much more will He clothe you, O you of little faith? Do not you seek what you are to eat and what you are to drink; do not be tossed about in a storm of anxiety. The peoples of the world seek for all these things. Your Father knows that you need them. But seek His Kingdom and all these things will be added to you. Do not fear, little flock, because it is your Father's will to give you the Kingdom. Sell your possessions and give alms. Make yourselves purses which never grow old, a treasure in the heavens that does not fail, where a thief does not come near and a moth does not destroy. For where your treasure is there your heart will also be."

IT was not uncommon for people in Palestine to take their unsettled disputes to respected Rabbis; but Jesus refused to be mixed up in anyone's disputes about money. But out of that request there came to Jesus an opportunity to lay down what His followers' attitude to material things should be. Jesus had something to say both to those who had an abundant supply of material possessions and to those who had not.

(i) To those who had an abundant supply of possessions Jesus spoke this parable of the Rich Fool. Two things stand out about this man. (a) *He never saw beyond himself.* There is no parable which is full of the words, I, me, my and mine. A schoolboy was once asked what parts of speech *my* and *mine* are. He answered, " Agressive pronouns." The rich fool was aggressively self-centred. It was said of a self-centred young lady, "Edith lived in a little world, bounded on the north, south, east and west by Edith." The famous criticism was made of a self-centred person, " There is too much ego in his cosmos." When this man had a superfluity of goods the one thing that never even entered his head was to give any away. The man's whole attitude is the very reverse of Christianity. Instead of denying himself he aggressively affirmed himself; instead of finding his happiness in giving he tried to conserve it by keeping. John Wesley's rule of life was to *save* all he could and *give* all he could. When he was at Oxford he had an income of £30 a year. He lived on £28 and gave £2 away. When his income increased to £60, £90 and £120 a year, he still lived on £28 and gave the balance away. The Accountant-General for Household Plate demanded a return from him. His reply was, " I have two silver tea spoons at London and two at Bristol. This is all the plate which I have at present; and I shall not buy any more, while so many around me want bread." The Romans had a proverb which said that money was like sea-water; the more a man drank the thirstier he became. And so long as a man's attitude is that of the rich fool his desire will always be to get more—and that is the reverse of the Christian way. (b) *He never saw beyond this world.* All his plans were made on the basis of life in this world. There is a story of a conversation between a young and ambitious lad and an older man who knew life. " I will," said the young man, " learn my trade." " And then? " said the older man. " I will set up in business." " And then? " " I will make my fortune." " And then? " " I suppose that I shall grow old and retire and live on my money." "And then?" "Well, I suppose that some day I will die." "*And then?*" came the last stabbing question. The man who never remembers that there is another world is destined some day for the grimmest of grim shocks.

(ii) But Jesus had something to say to those who had few possessions. In all this passage the thought which Jesus forbids is *anxious thought* or *worry*. Jesus never ordered any man to live in a shiftless, thriftless, reckless way. What He did tell a man to do was to do his best and then to leave the rest to God. The lilies that Jesus spoke of were the scarlet anemones of the hills of Palestine. After one of the infrequent showers of summer rain, the mountain side would be scarlet with them; and they bloomed one day and died. Wood was scarce in Palestine, and it was the dried grasses and wild flowers that were used to feed the oven fire. " If," said Jesus, " God looks after the birds and the flowers, how much more will He care for you? " Jesus said, " Seek first the Kingdom of God." We saw that God's Kingdom was a state on earth in which God's will was as perfectly done as it is in heaven. So Jesus says, " Bend all your life to obeying God's will and rest content with that." Jesus said, " So many people give all their effort to heap up things which in their very nature cannot last. Work for the things which last forever. things which you need not leave behind when you leave this earth, but which you can take with you." In Palestine wealth was often in the form of costly raiment; the moths could get at the fine clothes and leave them ruined. But if a man clothes his soul with the garments of honour and purity and goodness, nothing on earth can injure them. if a man seeks the treasures of heaven his heart will be fixed on heaven; but if he seeks the treasures of earth his heart will be thirled to earth—and some day, inevitably, he must say good-bye to them, for, as the grim Spanish proverb has it, " There are no pockets in a shroud."

169

BE PREPARED

Luke 12: 35-48

" Let your loins be girt and your lamps burning. Be like men who are waiting for their master to come home from the wedding feast, so that, when he comes and knocks, they will open to him immediately. Happy are those servants whom the master will come and find awake. This is the truth that I tell you—he will gird himself; he will make them recline at table; and he will come and serve them. Happy are they if he finds them so, even if he comes in the second or third watch. Know this—that if the householder knew at what time the thief would come he would have been awake and he would not have allowed his home to be broken into. So you must show yourselves ready, for the Son of Man comes at an hour you do not expect."

Peter said, " Lord are you speaking this parable to us or to everyone? " The Lord said, " Who, then, is the faithful and wise steward, whom the master will set over the administration of his house to give them their ration of food at the right time? Happy is that servant whom the master will come and find acting like this. I tell you truly that he will put him in charge of all his possessions. But if that servant says in his heart, ' My master is delayed in coming,' and if he begins to beat the men servants and the maid servants, and to eat and drink and get drunk, the master of that servant will arrive on a day on which he is not expecting him and at an hour which he does not know, and he will cut him in pieces and he will place his part with the unfaithful. That servant who knew the will of his master, and who failed to have things ready, and to act in accordance with that will, will be beaten with many stripes. But he who did not know, even if he did things that deserved stripes, will be beaten with few stripes. To whom much is given, from him much will be required; and men will demand much from him to whom much was entrusted."

THIS passage has two senses. In its narrower sense it refers to the Second Coming of Jesus Christ; in its wider sense it refers to the time when God's summons enters

man's life. It is at its widest a call to prepare to meet our
God. The whole praise is for the servant who is ready.
The long flowing robes of the east were a hindrance to
work; and when a man prepared to work he gathered
up his robes under his girdle to leave himself free for activity.
The eastern lamp was like a cotton wick floating in a sauce-
boat of oil. Always the wick had to be kept trimmed, and
the lamp had to be kept replenished or the light would
go out. No man can tell the day or the hour when eternity
will invade time, and when God's summons will come.
How, then, would we like God to find us?

(i) We would like God to find us *with our work completed*.
Life for so many of us is filled with loose ends. There
are the things undone and the things half done; the things
put off and the things not even attempted. The great
men had always the sense of a task that must be finished.
Keats wrote,

> " When I have fears that I may cease to be
> Before my pen has glean'd my teeming brain."

Robert Louis Stevenson wrote,

> " The morning drum-call on my eager ear
> Thrills unforgotten yet; the morning dew
> Lies yet undried along my field of noon.
>
> But now I pause at whiles in what I do,
> And count the bell, and tremble lest I hear
> (My work untrimmed) the sunset gun too soon."

It was Jesus Himself who said, " I have finished the
work which Thou gavest me to do " (John 17: 4). No
man should ever lightly leave undone a task he ought to
have finished, or might have finished, before night falls.

(ii) We would like God to find us *at peace with our fellow-
men*. It would be a haunting thing to pass from this world
at bitterness with some fellow-man. No man should let
the sun go down upon his wrath (Ephesians 4: 26), least

of all the last sun of all, and he never knows which sun will be his last.

(iii) We should like God to find us *at peace with Himself*. It will make all the difference at the last whether we feel that we are going out to a stranger or to an enemy, or whether we are going to fall asleep in the arms of God.

In the second section of this passage Jesus drew the picture of the wise and the unwise steward. In the east the steward had almost unlimited power. He was himself a slave, yet he had control of all the other slaves. A trusted steward ran a master's house for him, and administered his estate. The unwise steward made two mistakes.

(i) He said, *I will do what I like while my master is away*. He forgot that the day of reckoning must come, and would come when he least expected it. We have a habit of dividing life into compartments. There is the part of life in which we remember that God is present; and there is the part of life in which we never think of God at all. We tend to draw a line between the activities which are sacred and the activities which are secular. But if we really know what Christianity means we will know that for us there is no part of life when the master is away. We are working and living forever in our great task-master's eye.

(ii) He said, *I have plenty of time to put things right before the master comes*. There is nothing so fatal as to feel that we have plenty of time. Jesus Himself said, " I must work the works of Him that sent me while it is day; the night cometh when no man can work " (John 9: 4). Dennis Mackail tells how, when Sir James Barrie was old, he would never make arrangements or give invitations for a distant date. " Short notice now! " he would say. One of the most dangerous days in a man's life is when he discovers the word to-morrow.

The passage finishes with the warning that knowledge and privilege always bring responsibility. Sin is doubly sinful to the man who knew better; failure is doubly blameworthy in the man who had every chance to do well.

THE COMING OF THE SWORD

Luke 12: 49-53

> Jesus said, " I came to cast fire upon the earth. And what do I wish? Would that it were already kindled! there is an experience through which I must pass; and now I am under tension until it is accomplished! Do you think I came to give peace in the earth? Not that, I tell you, but division! From now on in one house there will be five people divided—three against two, and two against three. They will be divided, father against son, and son against father, mother against daughter, and daughter against mother, mother-in-law against her daughter-in-law, and daughter-in-law against her mother-in-law."

To those who were learning to regard Jesus as the Messiah, The Anointed One of God, these words would come like a bleak shock. They regarded the Messiah as the conqueror and king; and they regarded the Messianic age as a golden time.

(i) In Jewish thought fire is almost always the symbol of *judgment*. So, then, Jesus regarded the coming of His Kingdom as a time of judgment. The Jews firmly believed that God would judge the nations by one standard and themselves by another; that, in fact, the very fact that a man was a Jew would be enough to absolve him from the judgment of God. However much our wishful thinking wishes to eliminate the element of judgment from the message of Jesus Christ it remains stubbornly and unalterably there.

(ii) The Authorised Version translates verse 50, " I have a baptism to be baptised with." The Greek verb *baptizein* means *to dip*. In the passive it means to be submerged. Often it is used metaphorically. For instance, it is used of a ship sunk beneath the waves and submerged. It can be used of a man submerged in drink, and therefore dead-drunk. It can be used of a scholar submerged by an examiner's questions, as we say in our modern idiom, *sunk*. But above all it is used of a man being submerged in passing through some grim and terrible experience—of someone who can say, " All the waves and billows are gone over me." That is the way in which Jesus uses it here. "I have," He said, "a terrible experience through which I must pass; and life is full of tension until I pass through it and emerge triumphantly from it." The Cross was ever before His eyes. How different from the Jewish idea of God's King! Jesus came, not with avenging armies and flying banners, but to give His life a ransom for many.

> There was a Knight of Bethlehem,
>   Whose wealth was tears and sorrows,
> His men-at-arms were little lambs,
>   His trumpeters were sparrows.
> His castle was a wooden Cross
>   On which He hung so high;
> His helmet was a crown of thorns,
>   Whose crest did touch the sky.

(iii) His coming would inevitably mean divisions. In point of fact it did. That was one of the great reasons why the Romans hated Christianity—because it tore families in two. Over and over again a man had to decide whether he loved his kith and kin or Christ better. The essence of Christianity is that loyalty to Christ has to take precedence of the dearest loyalties of this earth. A man must be prepared to count all things but loss for the excellence of Jesus Christ.

WHILE YET THERE IS TIME

Luke 12: 54-59

> Jesus said to the crowds, " When you see a cloud rising in the west, immediately you say, ' Rain is coming.' And so it happens. When you feel the south wind blowing, you say, ' There will be scorching heat.' And so it happens. Hypocrites! you can read the signs of the face of the earth and the sky. How can you not read the signs of this time? Why do you

not for yourselves judge what is right? When you are going with your adversary to the magistrate, make an effort to come to an agreement with him on the way, lest he drag you to the judge, and the judge will hand you over to the officer, and the officer will throw you into prison. I tell you, you will not come out from there until you have paid the last farthing."

THE Jews of Palestine were weatherwise. When they saw the clouds forming in the west, over the Mediterranean Sea, they knew that the rain was on the way. When the south wind blew from the desert they knew that the sirocco-like wind, was coming. But those who were so wise to read the signs of the sky could not, or would not, read the signs of the times. If they had been able to do so they would have seen that the Kingdom of God was on the way.

Jesus used a very vivid illustration. He said, " When you are threatened with a law-suit, come to an agreement with your adversary before the matter comes to court, for if you do not you will have imprisonment to endure and a fine to pay." Note that the whole assumption is that the defendant has a bad case which will inevitably go against him. " Every man," Jesus implied, " has a bad case in the presence of God; and if a man is wise, he will make his peace with God while yet there is time."

Jesus, and all His great servants, have always been obsessed with the urgency of time. Andrew Marvell spoke of always hearing " time's wingèd chariot hurrying near." There are some things a man cannot afford to put off; above all he cannot afford to delay making his peace with God.

We read in the last verse of paying to the last *farthing*. We have already come across several references to money; and it will be useful if we collect the information about Jewish coinage in the time of Jesus. In order of value the principal coins were as follows:

The *Lepton*; *Lepton* means the *thin one*; it was the smallest coin, and was worth one sixteenth of a penny. It was the widow's mite (Mark 12: 42). It is also the coin mentioned here.

The *Quadrans* was worth two lepta, therefore it was one-eighth of penny. It is mentioned in Matthew 5: 26.

The *Assarion* was worth a little more than a halfpenny. It is mentioned in Matthew 10: 29 and Luke 12: 6.

The *Denarius* was worth about 8d. It was a day's pay for a working man (Matthew 20: 2); and it was the coin that the Good Samaritan left with the innkeeper (Luke 10: 25).

The *Drachma* was a silver coin worth about 9d. It was the coin which the woman lost and searched for (Luke 15: 8).

The *Didrachma* or *Half-shekel* was worth about 2s. It was the amount of the Temple Tax which everyone had to pay. It was also for thirty didrachmae—about £3—that Judas betrayed Jesus.

The *Shekel* was worth about 4s., and was the coin found in the fish's mouth (Matthew 17: 27).

The *Mina* is the coin mentioned in the Parable of the Pounds (Luke 19: 11-27). It was equal to 100 drachmae; and was, therefore, worth about £4.

The *Talent* was not so much a coin but a weight of silver worth £240. It is mentioned in Matthew 18: 24 and in the Parable of the Talents (Matthew 25: 14-30).

SUFFERING AND SIN

Luke 13: 1-3

At this time some men came and told Jesus about the Galilaeans whose blood Pilate had mingled with their sacrifices. "Do you think," He answered, "that these Galilaeans were sinners above all the Galilaeans because this happened to them? I tell you, No! But unless you repent you will all perish in like manner.

> Or, as for the eighteen on whom the tower in Siloam
> fell—do you think they were debtors to God beyond
> all those who dwell in Jerusalem? I tell you, No!
> But unless you repent you will perish in the same way.''

WE have here references to two disasters about which
we have no definite information and about which we can
only speculate. First, there is the reference to the Galilaeans
whom Pilate murdered in the middle of their sacrifices.
As we have seen, Galilaeans were always liable to get
involved in any political trouble that might arise, because
they were a highly inflammable people. Just about this
time Pilate had been involved in serious trouble. He had
decided very rightly that Jerusalem needed a new and
improved water supply. He proposed to build it and,
to finance it, he proposed to use certain Temple monies.
It was a laudable object, and a more than justifiable expen-
diture. But at the very idea of spending Temple monies
like that, the Jews were up in arms. When the mobs
gathered, Pilate instructed his soldiers to mingle with them.
The soldiers had cloaks over their battle dress so that they
were disguised. They were instructed to carry cudgels
rather than swords. At a given signal they were to fall
on the mob and disperse them. This was done, but the
soldiers dealt with the mob with a violence far beyond
their instructions and a considerable number of people
lost their lives. Almost certainly Galilaeans would be
involved in that. We know that Pilate and Herod were at
enmity, and only became reconciled after Pilate had sent
Jesus to Herod for trial (Luke 23: 6-12). And it may well
be that it was just this incident, involving the murder of
Galilaeans by Pilate, which provoked that enmity. As
for the eighteen on whom the tower in Siloam fell, they
are still more obscure. The Authorised Version uses the
word *sinners* of them also; but, as the margin shows,
it should not be *sinners* but debtors. Maybe we have a
clue here. It has been suggested that they had actually
taken work on Pilate's hated aqueducts. If so, any money

they earned was due to God and should have been volun-
tarily handed over, because it had already been stolen
from God; and it may well be that popular talk had declared
that the tower had fallen on them because of the work they
had consented to do.

But there is far more than an historical problem in this
passage. The Jews rigidly connected sin and suffering.
Eliphaz had long ago said to Job, " Who ever perished
being innocent? " (Job 4: 7). This was a cruel and a heart-
breaking doctrine, as Job knew well. And Jesus utterly
denied it in the case of the individual person. As we all
know very well it is often the greatest saints who have
to suffer most. But Jesus went on to say that if His hearers
did not repent they too would perish. What did He mean
by that? One thing is clear—Jesus foresaw and foretold
the destruction of Jerusalem, which happened in A.D. 70
(cp. Luke 19: 21-24). Jesus knew well that if the Jews
went on with their intrigues, their rebellions, their plottings,
their political ambitions, they were simply going to commit
national suicide; He knew that in the end Rome would
step in and obliterate the nation; and that is precisely
what happened. So what Jesus meant was this, if the
Jewish nation kept on seeking an earthly kingdom and
rejecting the Kingdom of God they could only come to
one end.

To put the matter like that leaves a, at first sight,
paradoxical situation. It means that we cannot say that
individual suffering and sin are inevitably connected, but
we can say that national sin and suffering are so connected.
The nation which chooses the wrong ways will in the end
suffer for it. But the individual is in very different case.
The individual is not an isolated unit. He is bound up in
the bundle of life. Often he may object, and object violently,
to the course his nation is taking; but when the consequence
of that course comes he cannot escape being involved in it.
The individual is not an isolated unit, and is often caught
up in a situation which he did not make; his suffering is

often not his fault; but the nation is a unit and chooses its own policy and will reap the fruit of it. It is always dangerous to attribute human suffering to human sin; but it is always safe to say that the nation which rebels against God is on the way to disaster.

THE GOSPEL OF THE OTHER CHANCE AND THE THREAT OF THE LAST CHANCE

Luke 13: 6-10

> Jesus spoke this parable, " A man had a fig-tree planted in his vineyard. He came looking for fruit on it and did not find it. He said to the keeper of the vineyard, ' Look you—for the last three years I have been coming and looking for fruit on this fig-tree, and I still am not finding any. Cut it down! Why should it use up the ground? ' ' Lord,' he answered him, ' let it be this year too, until I dig round about it and manure it, and if it bears fruit in the coming year, well and good; but if not, you will cut it down.' "

HERE is a parable at one and the same time lit by grace and close packed with warnings.

(i) The fig-tree occupied *a specially favoured position.* In Palestine it was not unusual to see fig-trees, thorn-trees and apple-trees in vineyards. The soil was so shallow and poor that trees were grown wherever there was soil to grow them; but the fact remains the fig-tree had a more than average chance; and it had not proved worthy of it. Repeatedly, directly and by implication, Jesus reminded men that they would be judged according to the opportunities they had. C. E. M. Joad once said of this, our own generation, " We have the powers of gods and we use them like irresponsible schoolboys." Never was a generation entrusted with so much, and, therefore, never was a generation so answerable to God.

(ii) Clearly the parable teaches us that *uselessness invites disaster.* It has been claimed that the whole process of evolution in this world is to produce useful things, and that that which is useful will go on from strength to strength in the economy of evolution, while that which is useless will surely be eliminated. The most searching question we can be asked is, " Of what use were you in this world? "

(iii) Further, the parable teaches that *nothing which only takes out can survive*. The fig-tree was drawing strength and sustenance from the soil; and in return it was producing nothing. That was precisely its sin. In the last analysis, there are two kinds of people in this world— those who take out more than they put in, and those who put in more than they take out. In one sense we are all in debt to life. We came into life at the peril of someone else's life; and we would never have survived without the care of those who loved us. We have inherited a Christian civilization and a freedom which we did not create. There is laid on us the duty of handing things on even better than we found them. " Die when I may," said Abraham Lincoln, " I want it said of me that I plucked a weed and planted a flower wherever I thought a flower would grow." Once a student was being shown bacteria under the microscope. He could actually see one generation of these microscopic living things being born, dying and another being born to take its place. He saw, as he had never seen before, how one generation succeeds another. " After what I have seen," he said, " I pledge myself never to be a weak link." If we take that pledge we will fulfil the obligation of putting into life at least as much as we take out.

(iv) This parable tells us of *the gospel of the second chance*. A fig-tree normally takes three years to reach maturity. If it is not fruiting by that time it is not likely to fruit. But this fig-tree was given a second chance. It is always Jesus' way to give a man chance after chance. Peter and Mark and Paul would all gladly have witnessed to that. God is infinitely kind to the man who falls and rises again.

(v) But this parable makes it quite clear that *there is a final chance.* If we refuse chance after chance, if God's appeal and challenge come again and again in vain the day comes, not when God has shut us out, but when we by deliberate choice have shut ourselves out from God. God save us from that!

MERCY MORE THAN LAW

Luke 13: 13-17

Jesus was teaching in one of the Synagogues on the Sabbath; and—look you—there was a woman there who had a spirit of weakness for eighteen years. She was bent together and could not straighten up properly. When Jesus saw her He called her to Him. " Woman," He said, " you are set free from your weakness "; and He laid His hands upon her; and immediately she was straightened. The president of the Synagogue was vexed that Jesus had healed on the Sabbath. " Are there not six days," he said to the crowd, "in which work ought to be done? Come and be healed on them and not on the Sabbath day." " Hypocrites! " the Lord answered. " Does each one of you not loose his ox or his ass from the manger on the Sabbath, and lead him out and give him drink? And as for this woman, a daughter of Abraham, whom —look you—Satan bound for eighteen years, should she not have been loosed from this bond on the Sabbath day? " And, as He said this, His opponents were put to shame, and all the crowd rejoiced at the glorious things that were done by Him.

THIS is the last time that we ever hear of Jesus being in a Synagogue, and it is clear that, by this time, the authorities were watching His every action, and waiting to pounce upon Him whenever they got the chance. Jesus healed the woman who for eighteen years had not been able to straighten her bent body; and then the president of the Synagogue intervened. He had not even the courage to speak directly to Jesus. He addressed his protest to the waiting people, although it was meant for Jesus. Jesus had healed on the Sabbath; technically healing was work; and, therefore, Jesus had broken the Sabbath. But Jesus answered His opponents out of their own law. The Rabbis abhorred cruelty to dumb animals and, even on the Sabbath, it was perfectly legal to loose beasts from their stalls and to water them. Jesus demanded, " If you can loose a beast from a stall and water him on the Sabbath day, surely it is right in the sight of God to loose this poor woman from her infirmity."

(i) The president of the Synagogue, and those like him, were *people who loved systems more than they loved people*. They were more concerned that their own petty little laws should be observed than that a woman should be helped and healed. One of the great problems of a developed civilization is the relationship of the individual to the system. In times of war the individual vanishes. A man ceases to be a man and becomes a member of such and such an age group or the like. Certain men are lumped together, not as individuals, but as living ammunition who are, in the terrible word, expendable. A man becomes an item in a statistical list. Sidney and Beatrice Webb, afterwards Lord and Lady Passmore, were two great economists and statistical experts; but H. G. Wells said of Beatrice Webb that the trouble about her was that " she saw men as specimens walking." In Christianity the individual always comes before the system. It is true to say that without Christianity there can be no such thing as democracy, because Christianity alone guarantees and defends the value of the ordinary and the individual man. If ever Christian principles were banished from political and economic life there would be nothing left to keep at bay the totalitarian state where the individual is lost in the system, and only exists, not for his own sake, but for the sake of the system. Strangely enough, this worship of systems very commonly invades the Church. There are many Church people—it would be a mistake to call them

Christian people—who are more concerned with the method of Church government than they are with the worship of God and the service of men. It is all too tragically true that more trouble and strife arises in Churches over legalistic details of procedure than for any other reason. In the world, and in the Church, we are constantly in peril of loving systems more than we love God and more than we love men.

(ii) Jesus' whole action in this matter makes it clear that it is not God's will that any human being should suffer one moment longer than is absolutely necessary. The Jewish law was that it was perfectly legal to help someone on the Sabbath who was in actual danger of his life. If Jesus had postponed the healing of this woman until the morrow no one could have criticised Him; but Jesus insisted that suffering must not be allowed to continue until to-morrow if it could be helped to-day. Over and over again in life some good and kindly scheme is held up until this or that regulation is satisfied, or this or that technical detail worked out. He gives twice who gives quickly, as the Latin proverb has it. No helpful deed that we can do to-day should be postponed until to-morrow.

THE EMPIRE OF CHRIST

Luke 13: 18, 19

> So Jesus said to them, " To what is the Kingdom of God like, and to what will I compare it? It is like a grain of mustard seed, which a man took and cast into his garden; and it grew until it became a tree, and the birds of the air found a lodging in its branches."

THIS is an illustration which Jesus used more than once, and which He used for different purposes. In the east mustard is not a garden herb but a field plant. It does literally grow to be a tree. A height of seven or eight feet was common, and a traveller tells how once he came across a mustard plant which was twelve feet high, and which overtopped a horse and its rider. It is common to see a cloud of birds around such trees, for they love the little black mustard seeds.

Matthew (13: 31, 32) also relates this parable with a different emphasis. His version is,

> Jesus offered them another parable. " The Kingdom of Heaven is like a grain of mustard seed, which a man took and sowed in his field. It is the smallest of all seeds, but, when it has grown, it is greater than all herbs, and becomes a tree, so that the birds of the air come and find a lodging in its branches."

The point of the parable in Matthew and in Luke is quite different. Matthew stresses *the smallness of the seed* which Luke never even mentions; and Matthew's point is that the greatest things can, and do, start from the smallest beginnings and so does the Kingdom of Heaven. Luke's version leads up to the birds finding a lodging place in the branches. In the east the regular symbol of a great empire was a mighty tree; and the subject nations who found shelter and protection within it are typified by birds in the branches (cp. Ezekiel 31: 6; 17: 23). As we have seen more than once Luke is the universalist who dreamed of a world for Christ; and so Luke's point is that the Kingdom of God will grow into a vast empire in which all kinds of men and nations will come together, and in which they will find the shelter and the protection of God. There is much in Luke's conception that we would do well to learn.

(i) There is room in the Empire of the Kingdom for *a wide variety of beliefs*. No man and no Church has a monopoly of all truth. To think ourselves right and everyone else wrong can lead to nothing but trouble and bitterness and strife. So long as all these beliefs are stemmed in Christ they are all facets of God's truth.

(ii) There is room in the Empire of the Kingdom for *a wide variety of experiences*. We do infinite harm when we try to standardize Christian experience, and when we insist that all men must come to Christ in the same way. One man may have a sudden shattering experience and may be able to point to the day and the hour, and the very minute, when God invaded his life. Another man's heart may open to Christ normally and naturally, and without crisis, as the petal of the lint-bell opens to the sun. Both experiences come from God and both men belong to God.

(iii) There is room in the Empire of the Kingdom for *a wide variety of ways of worship*. One man finds touch with God in an elaborate ritual and in a splendid liturgy; another finds God in the bare simplicities. There is no right or wrong here. It is the glory of the Church that within its fellowship somewhere a man will find the worship that brings him to God. Let him find it, but let him not think his way the only way and let him not criticize another's way.

(iv) There is room in the Empire of the Kingdom for *all kinds of people*. The world has its labels and its distinctions and its barriers. But in the Kingdom there is no distinction between rich and poor, small and great, famous and unknown. The Church should be the only place in the world where all distinctions are gone.

(v) There is room in the Empire of God *for all nations*. There are still in the world barriers like the colour bar. A famous Test Match cricketer, whose autograph crowds struggle to get, can still be barred from a London hotel. A writer tells how in America she had lunch with Paul Robeson and his wife, and was thrilled to lunch with the great singer and actor. She moved on to stay with friends at Chicago. She was full of this experience, but her story of it was received very coldly. She asked why. The answer was, " If I were you, I would not talk too much about lunching with Paul Robeson." " Why? " she asked, " surely he is one of the world's great artists." " That may be," was the answer, " but Paul Robeson's a nigger."

In Revelation 21: 16 we are given the dimensions of the Holy City. It is a square each of whose sides is 12,000 furlongs. 12,000 furlongs is 1,500 miles; and the area of a square whose sides are 1,500 miles is 2,250,000 square miles! There is room in the city of God for all the world and more.

THE LEAVEN OF THE KINGDOM

Luke 13: 20, 21

> Again Jesus said, " To what will I liken the Kingdom of God? It is like leaven, which a woman took and hid in three measures of meal, until the whole was leavened."

THIS is an illustration which Jesus took from His own home. In those days bread was baked at home. Leaven was a little piece of fermented dough which had been kept over from the last baking and had fermented in the keeping. Leaven is regularly used in Jewish thought for influence. Usually it is used for bad influence, because the Jews identified fermentation with putrefaction, and leaven stood for rottenness. Jesus had seen Mary take a little bit of leaven and put it in the dough. He had seen the whole character of the dough changed by that little bit of leaven. " That," He said, " is how my Kingdom comes." There are two interpretations of this parable. From the first of them the following points emerge.

(i) The Kingdom of Heaven starts *from the smallest beginnings*. The leaven was very small but it changed the whole character of the mass of the dough. We well know how in any court, or committee, or board one person can be a focus of trouble or a centre of peace. The Kingdom of Heaven starts from the dedicated lives of individual men and women. It may be that in the place where we work or live we are the only professing Christian. That is God giving us the task to be the leaven of the Kingdom there.

THE GOSPEL OF LUKE

(ii) The Kingdom of Heaven *works unseen*. We cannot see the leaven working, but all the time it is doing its transforming work. The Kingdom is on the way. Anyone who knows a little history will be bound to see that. Seneca, than whom the Romans had no higher thinker, could write, " We strangle a mad dog; we slaughter a fierce ox; we plunge the knife into sickly cattle lest they taint the herd; children who are born weakly and deformed we drown." In A.D. 60 that was the normal thing. Things like that cannot happen to-day because slowly, but inevitably, the Kingdom is on the way.

(iii) The Kingdom of Heaven *works from inside*. Until the leaven got into the dough it was powerless to help; it had to get right inside. We will never change men from the outside. New houses, new conditions, better material things only change the surface. It is the task of Christianity to make, not new things, but new men. And once the new men are created the new world will surely follow. That is why the Church is the most important institution in the world, for it is the factory where *men* are produced.

(iv) The power of the Kingdom *comes from outside*. The dough had no power to change itself. Neither have we. We have tried and failed. To change life we need a power outside and beyond us. We need the master of life, and He is forever waiting to give to us also the secret of victorious living.

The second interpretation of this parable insists that so far from working unseen the work of the leaven is manifest to all because it turns the dough into a bubbling, seething mass. So, then, the leaven stands for the disturbing power of Christianity. In Thessalonica it was said of the Christians, " The people who have turned the world upside down have come here too " (Acts 17: 6). Religion is never dope; it never sends people comfortably to sleep; it never makes them placidly accept the evils that should be striven against. Real Christianity is the most revolutionary thing in the world, for it works a revolution in the

187

individual life and in all society. " May God," said Unamuno the great Spanish mystic, " deny you peace and give you glory." The Kingdom of Heaven is the leaven which fills a man at one and the same time with the peace of God and the divine discontent which will not rest until the evils of earth are swept away by the changing, revolutionizing power of God.

THE RISK OF BEING SHUT OUT
Luke 13: 22-30

> Jesus continued to go through towns and villages, teaching and making His way to Jerusalem. " Lord," someone said to Him, "are those who are to be saved few in number? " He said to them, " Keep on striving to enter through the narrow door, because many, I tell you, will seek to enter in and will not be able to. Once the master of the house has risen and shut the door, and when you begin to stand outside and knock, saying, ' Lord, open to us,' he will answer you, ' I do not know where you come from.' Then you will begin to say, ' We have eaten and drunk in your presence and you taught in our streets.' He will say, ' I tell you, I do not know where you come from. Depart from me all you who are workers of iniquity.' There will be weeping and gnashing of teeth there, when you will see Abraham and Isaac and Jacob in the Kingdom of God and yourselves cast out. And they will come from the east and from the west, and from the north and from the south, and take their places at table in the Kingdom of God. And—look you—there are those who are last who will be first, and there are those first who will be last."

WHEN this questioner asked his question he would certainly do so on the assumption that the Kingdom of God was for the Jews only, and that Gentiles would all be shut out. Jesus' answer must have come as a shock to him.

(i) Jesus declared that entry to the Kingdom can never be automatic, and that it is the result and the reward of a struggle. " Keep on striving to enter," said Jesus. The word that is used for *striving* is the word from which the English word *agony* is derived. The struggle to enter in must be so intense that it can be described as an agony of soul and spirit. We run a certain danger. It is easy to think that, once we have become members of the Church by profession, we have reached the end of the road, that then we can, as it were, sit back like those who have arrived and who have achieved their goal. There is no such finality in the Christian life. A man must ever be going forward or necessarily he is going backward. The Christian way is like a climb up a mountain pathway towards a peak which will never be reached in this world. It was said of two gallant climbers who died on Mount Everest, "When last seen they were going strong for the top." It was inscribed on the grave of an Alpine guide who had died on the mountain-side, " He died climbing." For the Christian life is ever an upward and an onward way.

(ii) The defence of these people was, " We ate and drank in your presence, and you taught in our streets." There are those who seem to think that just because they are members of a Christian civilisation all is well. They would differentiate between themselves and the poor heathen in their ignorance and their blindness. But the man who lives in a Christian civilisation is not necessarily a Christian. He may be enjoying all its benefits; he certainly is living on the Christian capital which others before him have built up; but that is no reason for sitting back content and sure that all is well. It is a challenge which asks us, " What did you do to initiate all this? What have you done to preserve and develop it? " We cannot live on borrowed goodness.

(iii) There will be surprises in the Kingdom of God. Those who were very prominent in this world may have to be very humble in the next; those whom no one noticed here may be the princes of the world to come. There is a story of a woman who in this world had been used to every luxury and to all respect. She died, and when she arrived

in heaven an angel was sent to conduct her to her house.
They passed many a lovely mansion, and the woman
thought that each one, as they came to it, must be the one
allotted to her. When they had passed through the main
streets of heaven they came to the suburbs and the outskirts where the houses were much smaller; and on the
very fringe they came to a house which was little more
than a hut. "That is your house," said the conducting
angel. "What," said the woman, "that! I cannot live
in that." "I am sorry," said the angel, "but that is all
that we could build for you with the materials you sent
up." The standards of heaven are not the standards of
earth. Earth's first will often be last, and earth's last will
often be first.

COURAGE AND TENDERNESS

Luke 13: 31-35

> At that hour some Pharisees came to Jesus. "Depart,"
> they said to Him, "and get on your way from this
> place, because Herod is out to kill you." "Go," He
> said, "and tell that fox, look you, I cast out demons
> and I work cures to-day and to-morrow, and on the
> third day my work is perfected. I must be on my way
> to-day, and to-morrow and the next day, because it
> is not possible for a prophet to perish out of Jerusalem.
> Jerusalem! Jerusalem! Killer of the prophets!
> Stoner of those who sent to you! How often I wanted
> to gather together your children as a hen gathers her
> brood under her wings—and you would not! Look
> you, your house is desolate. I tell you, you will not
> see me until you shall say, 'Blessed is He who comes in
> the name of the Lord.'"

BECAUSE of the insight that it gives to us into the life of
Jesus, as it were behind the scenes, this is one of the most
interesting passages in Luke's gospel.

(i) It gives us the, at first sight, surprising information
that not all the Pharisees were hostile to Jesus. Here we
have some of them actually warning Him that He was in

danger, and advising Him to seek safety. It is true that from the gospels we do get a one-sided picture of the Pharisees. The Jews themselves knew very well that there were good and bad Pharisees. They divided them into seven different classes. (i) *The Shoulder Pharisees*. These wore their good deeds on their shoulder, and performed them to be seen of men. (ii) *The Wait-a-little Pharisees*. They could always find a good excuse for putting off a good deed until to-morrow. (iii) *The Bruised or Bleeding Pharisees*. No Jewish Rabbi could be seen talking to any woman on the street, not even his wife, or mother or sister. But certain of the Pharisees went further. They would not even look at a woman on the street; they even shut their eyes to avoid seeing a woman; they, therefore, knocked into walls and houses and bruised themselves; and then exhibited their bruises as special badges of extraordinary piety. (iv) *The Pestle and Mortar or Hump-backed Pharisees*. They walked bent double in a false and cringing humility; they were the Uriah Heeps of Jewish religion. (v) *The Ever-reckoning Pharisees*. They were ever reckoning up their good deeds and, as it were, striking a balance-sheet of profit and loss with God. (vi) *The Timid or Fearing Pharisees*. They went ever in the fear of the wrath of God. They were, as it was said of Burns, not helped but haunted by their religion. (vii) *The God-loving Pharisees*. They were copies of Abraham and lived in faith and charity. There may have been six bad Pharisees for every good one; but this passage shows that even amongst the Pharisees there were those who admired and respected Jesus.

(ii) This passage shows us Jesus talking to a king. Herod Antipas, King of Galilee, was out to stop Jesus. To the Jew the fox was a symbol of three things. First, the fox was regarded as the sliest of animals. Second, it was regarded as the most destructive of animals. Third, the fox was the symbol of a worthless and insignificant man. It takes a brave man to call the reigning king a fox. It is told that Latimer was once preaching in Westminster

Abbey when Henry the king was one of the congregation. In the pulpit he soliloquised, "Latimer! Latimer! Latimer! Be careful what you say. The king of England is here!" Then he went on, "Latimer! Latimer! Latimer! Be careful what you say. The King of Kings is here." Jesus took His orders from God, and he would not shorten his work by one day to please or to escape any earthly king.

(iii) The lament over Jerusalem is a most important passage, because it is another of these passages which shows how little we really know of Jesus' life. It is quite clear that Jesus could never have spoken like this, unless, prior to this, He had more than once gone with His offer of love to Jerusalem; and in the first three gospels there is no word or indication of any such visits. Once again it is clear that in the gospels we have the merest sketch of Jesus' life. There is nothing which hurts so much as to go to someone and offer love, and to have that offer rejected and spurned. It is life's bitterest tragedy to give one's heart to someone only to have it broken. That is what happened to Jesus in Jerusalem; and still He comes to men, and still men reject Him. But the fact remains that to reject the love of God is in the end to be in peril of the wrath of God.

UNDER THE SCRUTINY OF HOSTILE MEN

Luke 14: 1-6

> On the Sabbath day Jesus had gone into the house of one of the rulers who belonged to the Pharisees to eat bread; and they were watching Him. And—look you—there was a man before Him who had dropsy. Jesus said to the Scribes and Pharisees, "Is it lawful to heal on the Sabbath? Or, is it not?" They kept silent. So He took him and healed him and sent him away. He said to them, "Suppose one of you has an ass or an ox, and it falls into a well, will he not immediately pull it out, even if it is on the Sabbath day?" And they had no answer to these things.

IN the gospel story there are seven incidents in which Jesus healed on the Sabbath day. In Luke's gospel we have already studied the story of the healing of Simon's wife's mother (4: 38); of the man with the withered hand (6: 6); and of the woman who was bent for eighteen years (13: 14). To these John adds the story of the healing of the paralytic at the pool of Bethesda (John 5: 9); and of the man born blind (John 9: 14). Mark adds one more— the healing of the demon-possessed man in the Synagogue at Capernaum (Mark 1: 21). Anyone would think that a record like that would have made a man beloved of all; but it is the tragic fact that every miracle of healing that Jesus wrought on the Sabbath day only made the Scribes and Pharisees more certain that He was a dangerous and irreligious law-breaker who must at all costs be stopped. If we are to understand what happened to Jesus it is essential to remember that the orthodox Jews of His day regarded Him as a law-breaker. He healed on the Sabbath; therefore He worked on the Sabbath; therefore He broke the law.

On this occasion a Pharisee invited Him to a meal on the Sabbath. The law had its meticulous and detailed regulations about Sabbath meals. Of course no food could be cooked on the Sabbath; that would have been to work. All food had to be cooked on the Friday; and, if it was necessary to keep it hot, it must be kept hot in such a way that it was not cooked any more! So it is laid down that food to be kept warm for the Sabbath must not be put into " oil dregs, manure, salt, chalk or sand, whether moist or dry, nor into straw, grape-skins, flock or vegetables, if these are damp, though it may be if they are dry. It may be, however, put into clothes, amidst fruits, pigeons' feathers and flax tow." It was the observance of regulations like that that the Pharisees and Scribes regarded as religion. No wonder they could not understand Jesus!

It is by no means impossible that the Pharisees " planted " the man with the dropsy in this house on this occasion to see what Jesus would do. They were watching Him; and the word used for *watching* is the word that is used for " interested and sinister espionage." Jesus was under scrutiny.

Without hesitation Jesus healed the man. He knew perfectly well what they were thinking; and He quoted their own law and practice to them. Open wells were quite common in Palestine, and were not infrequently the cause of accidents. (cp. Exodus 21: 33). It was perfectly allowable to rescue a beast which had fallen in. Jesus, with searing contempt, demands how, if it be right to help an animal on the Sabbath, it can be wrong to help a man.

This passage tells us certain things about Jesus and about His enemies.

(i) It shows us the serenity with which Jesus met life. There is nothing more trying than to be under constant and critical scrutiny. When that happens to most people they lose their nerve and, even more often, they lose their temper. They become irritable, and there may be greater sins than irritability, but there is none which causes more pain and heartbreak. But even in things which would have broken men's spirit Jesus remained serene. If we live with Him, He can make us like Himself.

(ii) It is to be noted that Jesus never refused any man's invitation of hospitality. To the end He never abandoned hope of men. To hope to change them, or even to appeal to them, might be the forlornest of forlorn hopes, but He would never let a chance go. He would not refuse even an enemy's invitation. It is as clear as daylight that we will never make our enemies our friends if we refuse to meet them and to talk with them.

(iii) The most amazing things about the Scribes and Pharisees is their staggering lack of a sense of proportion. They would go to endless trouble to formulate and to obey their petty rules and regulations; and yet they would count it a sin to ease a sufferer's pain on the Sabbath day. If a man had one prayer to pray he might well pray to be given a sense of proportion. The things which disturb the peace of congregations are seldom big things and are often trifles. The things which divide men from men, and which destroy friendships, are often little things to which no sensible man, in his saner moments, would allow any importance. The little things can bulk so largely that they can fill the whole horizon. Only if we put first things first will all things take their proper place—and love comes first.

THE NECESSITY OF HUMILITY

Luke 14: 7-11

> Jesus spoke a parable to the invited guests, for He noticed how they chose the first places at the table. "When you are bidden by someone to a marriage feast," He said, "do not take your place at table in the first seat, in case someone more distinguished than you has been invited by him, for in that case, the man who invited you will come and say to you, 'Give place to this man.' And then, with shame, you will begin to take the lowest place. But, when you have been invited, go and sit down in the lowest place, so that, when the man who has invited you comes he will say to you, 'Friend, come up higher.' Then you will gain honour in front of all who sit at table with you. For he who exalts himself will be humbled, and he who humbles himself will be exalted."

JESUS chose a homely illustration to point an eternal truth. If a quite undistinguished guest arrived early at a feast and annexed the top place, and if a more distinguished person then arrived, and the man who had usurped the first place was told to step down, a most embarrassing situation would result. If, on the other hand, a man deliberately slipped into the bottom place, and was then asked to occupy a more distinguished place, his humility would gain him all the more honour.

Humility has always been one of the inevitable characteristics of great men. When Thomas Hardy was so famous that any newspaper would gladly have paid enormous sums for his work, he used sometimes to send to a newspaper a poem; and always with it he enclosed a stamped and addressed envelope for the return of his manuscript should it be rejected. Even in his greatness he was humble enough to think that his work might be turned down. There are many stories and legends of the humility of Principal Cairns. He would never enter a room, or go on to a platform, first. He always said, " You first, I follow." Once, as he came on to a platform, there was a great burst of applause in welcome. He stood aside and let the man after him come first, and began himself to applaud. He never dreamed that the applause could possibly be for him; he thought that it must be for the other man. It is only the little man who is self-important.

How can we retain our humility?

(i) We can retain it by realizing the facts. How ever much we know we know very little compared with the sum total of knowledge. How ever much we have achieved we have achieved very little in the end. However important we may believe ourselves to be, when death removes us, or, when we retire from our position, life and work will go on just the same.

(ii) We can retain it by comparison with the perfect. It is when we go and see or hear the expert that we realize how poor our own performance is. Many a man has decided to burn his clubs after a day at the Golf Open Championship. Many a man has decided never to appear in public again after hearing a master musician perform. Many a preacher has been humbled almost to despair when he has heard a real saint of God speak. And if we set our lives beside the life of the Lord of all good life, if we see our unworthiness in comparison with the radiance of His stainless purity, then pride will die and self-satisfaction will be shrivelled up.

DISINTERESTED CHARITY

Luke 14: 12-14

> Jesus said to the man who had invited Him, " Whenever you give a dinner or a banquet, do not call your friends, or your brothers, or your kinsfolk or your rich neighbours, in case they invite you back again in return and you receive a repayment. But when you give a feast, invite the poor, the maimed, the lame and the blind. Then you will be happy, because they cannot repay you. You will receive your repayment at the resurrection of the righteous."

HERE is a searching passage, because it demands that we should examine the motives behind our generosity, and our charity and all our giving.

(i) A man may give from a sense of duty.

> He dropped a penny in the plate
> And meekly raised his eyes,
> Glad the week's rent was duly paid
> For mansions in the skies.

Our giving may be given to God and to man much in the same way as we pay our income tax—as the satisfaction of a grim duty which we cannot escape.

(ii) A man may give purely from motives of self-interest. Consciously or unconsciously he may regard his giving as an investment. He may regard each gift he gives as an entry on the credit side of his account in the ledger of God. Such giving, so far from being generosity, is simply rationalized selfishness.

(iii) A man may give in order to feel superior. Such giving can be a cruel thing. It can hurt the recipient much more than a blunt refusal would. When a man gives like that he stands on his little eminence and looks down. He may even with the gift throw in a short and smug lecture. It would be better not to give at all than to give merely to gratify one's own vanity and one's own desire for power. The Rabbis had a saying that the best kind of giving was when the giver did not know to whom he was giving, and when the receiver did not know from whom he was receiving.

(iv) A man may give because he cannot help it. That is the only real way to give. The law of the Kingdom is this—that if a man gives to gain a reward he will receive no reward; but if a man gives with no thought of reward his reward is certain. The only real giving is the giving which is the uncontrollable outflow of love. Once Dr. Johnson cynically described gratitude as " a lively sense of favours to come." The same definition could equally apply to certain forms of giving. God gave because God so loved the world—and so must we.

THE KING'S BANQUET AND THE KING'S GUESTS

Luke 14: 15-24

When one of those who were sitting at table with Jesus heard this, he said, " Happy is the man who eats bread in the Kingdom of God." Jesus said to him, " There was a man who made a great banquet, and who invited many people to it. At the time of the banquet he sent his servants to say to those who had been invited, ' Come, because everything is now ready.' With one accord they all began to make excuses. The first said to him, ' I have bought a field, and I must go out and see it. Please have me excused.' Another said, ' I have bought five yoke of oxen, and I am on my way to try them out. Please have me excused.' Another said, ' I have married a wife, and, therefore, I cannot come.' So the servant came and told his master these things. The master of the house was enraged, and said to his servant, ' Go out quickly to the streets and lanes of the town and bring here the poor, and the maimed, and the blind and the lame.' The servant said, ' Sir, your orders have been carried out and there is still room.' So the master said to his servant, ' Go out to the roads and to the hedges, and compel them to come in, so that my house may be filled. For I tell you that none of these men who were invited shall taste of my banquet.' "

THE Jews had a series of ever-recurring conventional pictures of what would happen when God broke into history, and when the golden days of the new age arrived. One of these pictures was the picture of the Messianic Banquet. On that day God would give a great feast to His own people at which Leviathan, the sea monster, would be part of the food. It is of that banquet that the man who spoke to Jesus was thinking. When he spoke of the happiness of those who would be guests at that banquet he was thinking of Jews, and of Jews only, for the average, orthodox Jew would never have dreamed that the Gentiles and the sinners would find a place at the feast of God. Jesus knew that, and that is why Jesus spoke this parable. In Palestine, when a man made a feast, the day of it was announced long beforehand, and the invitations were sent out and accepted; but the hour of it was not announced; and when the day came and all things were ready, servants were sent out to summon the already invited guests. To accept the invitation beforehand and then to refuse it when the day came was a grave and serious insult. In the parable the master stands for God. The originally invited guests stand for the Jews. Throughout all their history they had looked forward to the day when God would break in; and when He did, they tragically refused His invitation. The poor people from the streets and lanes stand for the tax-gatherers and sinners who welcomed Jesus in a way in which the orthodox never did. Those gathered in from the roads and the hedges stand for the Gentiles for whom there was still ample room at the feast of God. As Bengel, the great commentator put it, " both nature and grace abhor a vacuum," and when the Jews refused God's invitation and left His table empty, the invitation went out to the Gentiles.

There is one sentence in this parable which has been sadly misused. " Go out," said the master, " and compel them to come in." Long ago Augustine used that text as a justification for religious persecution. It was used as a defence, and even a command, to cœrce people into the Christian faith. It was used as a defence for the inquisition, the thumb-screw, the rack, the threat of death and imprisonment, the campaigns against the heretics, for all those things which are the shame of Christianity. Beside it we should always set another text—The love of Christ constrains us. (2 Corinthians 5: 14.) In the Kingdom of God there is only one compulsion—the compulsion of love.

But though this parable spoke with a threat to the Jews who had refused God's invitation, and with an undreamed of glory to the sinners and the outcasts, and the Gentiles who had never dreamed of receiving it, there are in it truths which are forever permanent, and which are as new as to-day. In the parable the invited guests made their excuses, and men's excuses do not differ so very much to-day.

(i) The first man said that he had bought a field, and was going to see it. He allowed the claims of business to usurp the claims of God. It is still possible for a man to be so immersed in this world that he has no time to worship, and even no time to pray.

(ii) The second man said that he had bought five yoke of oxen, and that he was going to try them out. He let the claims of novelty usurp the claims of Christ. It often happens that when people enter into new possessions they become so taken up with them that the claims of worship and of God get crowded out. People have been known to acquire a motor car, and then to say, " We used to go to Church on a Sunday, but now that we have got the car we go off to the country for the day." It is perilously easy for a new game, a new hobby, even a new friendship to take up even the time that should be kept for God.

(iii) The third man said, with even more finality than the others, " I have married a wife, and I cannot come." One of the wonderful merciful laws of the Old Testament laid it down, " When a man hath taken a new wife, he shall not go out to war, neither shall he be charged with any business, but he shall be free at home one year, and shall cheer up his wife which he hath taken." (Deuteronomy 24: 5.) No doubt that very law was in this man's mind. It is one of the tragedies of life when good things, the best of things, can crowd the claims of God out of life. There is no lovelier thing than a home, and yet a home was never meant to be used selfishly. They live best together who live with God; they serve each other best who also serve their fellow men; the atmosphere of a home is most lovely when those who dwell within it never forget that they are also members of the great family and household of God.

The Banquet of the Kingdom

Before we leave this passage we must note this, that the whole of it, verses I to 25, has all to do with feasts and banquets. It is a most significant thing that Jesus thought of His Kingdom and His service in terms of a feast. The symbol of the Kingdom was the happiest thing that human life can give. Surely this is the final condemnation of the Christian who is afraid to enjoy himself. There has always been a type of Christianity which has taken all the colour out of life. Julian spoke of those pale-faced, flat-breasted Christians for whom the sun shone and they never saw it. Swinburne slandered Christ by saying,

> " Thou hast conquered, O pale Galilæan,
> The world has grown gray at thy breath."

Ruskin, who was brought up in a rigid and a narrow home, tells how he was given a jumping-jack as a present, and how a pious aunt took it away from him, saying that toys were no things for a Christian child. Even so great and sane and healthy a scholar as A. B. Bruce said that you could not conceive of the child Jesus playing games when He was a boy, or smiling when He was a man. W. M. Macgregor, in his Warrack Lectures, speaks with the scorn, of which he was such a master, about one of John Wesley's few mistakes. He founded a school at Kingswood, near Bristol. He laid it down that no games were to be allowed in the school or in the grounds, because " he who plays when he is a child will play when he is a man." There were no holidays. The children rose at 4 a.m. and spent the first hour of the day in prayer and meditation, and on Friday they fasted until three in the afternoon. W. M. Macgregor characterizes the whole set up as " nature-defying foolishness." We must always remember that Jesus thought of the Kingdom in terms of a feast. A gloomy Christian is a contradiction in terms. Locke, the great philosopher, defined laughter as " a sudden glory." There is no healthy pleasure which is forbidden to a Christian man, for a Christian is like a man who is forever at a wedding feast.

ON COUNTING THE COST

Luke 14: 25-33

> Great crowds were on the way with Jesus. He turned and said to them, " If any man comes to me and does not hate his father and mother, and wife and children, and brothers and sisters, and even his own life too, he cannot be my disciple. Whoever does not carry his cross and come after me cannot be my disciple. Which of you, if he wishes to build a tower, does not first sit down and reckon up the expense, to see whether he has enough to finish it? This he does lest, when he has laid the foundation and is unable to complete the work, all who see him begin to mock him, saying, ' This man began to build and was unable to finish the job.' Or, what king when he is going to engage battle with another king, does not first sit down and take counsel, whether he is able with ten thousand men to meet him who comes against him with twenty thousand? If he finds he cannot, while he is still distant, he sends an embassy and asks for terms of peace. So, therefore, everyone of you who does not bid farewell to all his possessions cannot be my disciple."

WHEN Jesus said this He was on His way to Jerusalem. He knew that He was on His way to the Cross; the crowds who were with Him thought that He was on His way to an empire. That is why He spoke to them like this. In the most vivid way possible He told them that the man who would follow Him was not on the way to worldly power and glory, but must be ready for a loyalty which would sacrifice the dearest things in life, and for a suffering which would be like the agony of a man upon a cross. We must not take the words of Jesus with a cold and unimaginative literalness. Eastern language is always as vivid as the human mind can make it. When Jesus tells us to hate our nearest and dearest, he does not mean that literally. He means that no love in life can compare with the love we must bear to him.

There are two suggestive truths within this passage.

(i) It is possible to be a follower of Jesus without being a disciple; to be a camp-follower without being a soldier of the king; to be a hanger-on in some great work without pulling one's weight. Once someone was talking to a great scholar about a younger man. He said, " So and so tells me that he was one of your students." The teacher answered devastatingly, " He may have attended my lectures, but he was not one of my students." There is a world of difference between attending lectures and being a student. It is one of the supreme handicaps of the Church that in the Church there are so many distant followers of Jesus and so few real disciples.

(ii) It is a Christian's first duty to count the cost of following Christ. The tower which the man was going to build was probably a vineyard tower. Vineyards were often equipped with towers from which watch was kept against thieves who might steal the harvest. An un-finished building is always a humiliating thing. In Scotland, we can, for instance, think of that weird structure called " M'Caig's Folly " which stands behind Oban. In every sphere of life a man is called upon to count the cost. In the introduction to the marriage ceremony the minister states what marriage is, and then says, " It is, therefore, not to be entered upon lightly or unadvisedly, but thoughtfully, reverently, and in the fear of God." First a man and woman must count the cost. No man need become a student unless he will count the cost of learning. It is so with the Christian way. But if a man is daunted by the high demands of Christ let him remember that he is not left to fulfil them alone. He who called him to the steep road will walk with him every step of the way and will be there at the end to meet him.

THE INSIPID SALT

Luke 14: 34, 35

> Jesus said, " Salt is a fine thing; but if salt has become insipid, by what means shall its taste be restored? It is fit neither for the land nor the dunghill. Men throw it out. He who has an ear to hear, let him hear."

JUST sometimes Jesus speaks with a threat in His voice. When a person is always carping, and criticizing, and complaining, his irritable anger ceases to have any significance or any effect. But when someone whose accent is the accent of love suddenly speaks with a threat we are bound to listen. What Jesus is saying here is this—when a thing loses its essential quality, and when it fails to perform the essential duty for which it was created, it becomes useless and is fit for nothing but to be thrown away. In this passage Jesus uses salt as a symbol of the Christian life. What, then, are its essential qualities? In Palestine salt had three characteristic uses.

(i) Salt was used as *a preservative*. Salt is the earliest of all preservatives. The Greeks used to say that salt could put a new soul into dead things. Without salt the thing putrefied and went bad; with salt its freshness was preserved. That must mean that true Christianity must act as a preservative against the corruption of the world. The individual Christian must be the conscience of his fellows; and the Church must be the conscience of the nation. The Christian must be such that in his presence no doubtful language will be used, no questionable stories told, no dishonourable action suggested. He must be like a cleansing antiseptic in the circle in which he moves. The Church must be such that she speaks fearlessly against all evils, and supports fearlessly all good causes. She must be such that she will never hold her peace through fear or favour of men.

(ii) Salt was used as *a flavouring*. Food, without salt, can be revoltingly insipid. The Christian, then, must be the man who brings flavour into life. The Christianity which acts like a shadow of gloom and a wet blanket is no true Christianity. The Christian is the man who, by his courage, his hope, his cheerfulness and his kindness brings a new flavour into life.

(iii) Salt was used *on the land*. It was used to make it easier for all good things to grow. The Christian must be such that he makes it easier for people to be good, and harder to be bad. We all know people in whose company there are certain things we would not and could not do; and equally we all know people in whose company we might well stoop to things which by ourselves we would not do. There are those fine souls in whose company it is easier to be brave, and cheerful and good. The Christian must carry with him a breath of heaven in which the fine things flourish and in which the evil things shrivel up.

That is the function of the Christian; if he fails in his function there is no good reason why he should exist at all; and we have already seen that in the economy of God uselessness invites disaster. He who has an ear to hear, let him hear.

THE SHEPHERD'S JOY

Luke 15: 1-7

> The tax-collectors and sinners were all coming near to
> Jesus to hear Him, and the Pharisees and Scribes
> were murmuring, saying, " This man welcomes sinners
> and eats with them."
> He spoke this parable to them. " What man of
> you," he said, " who has a hundred sheep, and who
> hast lost one of them, does not leave the ninety-nine
> in the wilderness and go after the one that is lost
> until he finds it? And when he finds it, rejoicing he
> lays it on his shoulders; and when he comes home he
> calls together his friends and neighbours, saying to
> them, ' Rejoice with me because I have found my
> sheep which was lost.' I tell you that just so there
> will be joy in heaven over one sinner who repents
> more than over ninety-nine just people who have no
> need of repentance."

THERE is no chapter of the New Testament so well known
and so dearly loved as the fifteenth chapter of Luke's
gospel. It has been called " the gospel in the gospel,"
as if it contained the very distilled essence of the good
news which Jesus came to tell.

These parables of Jesus arose out of a perfectly definite
situation. It was an offence to the Scribes and Pharisees
that Jesus companied and associated with men and women
who, by the orthodox, were labelled as sinners. The
Pharisees gave to people who did not keep the law a general
classification. They called them *The People of the Land*.
There was a complete barrier between the Pharisees and
The People of the Land. To marry a daughter to one of
them was like exposing her, bound and helpless, to a lion.
The Pharisaic regulations laid it down, "When a man is
one of the People of the Land, entrust no money to him,
take no testimony from him, trust him with no secret, do
not appoint him guardian of an orphan, do not make him
the custodian of charitable funds, do not accompany him
on a journey." A Pharisee was forbidden to be the guest
of any such man, or to have him as his guest. He was

even forbidden, so far as it was possible, to have any business dealings with him, or to buy anything from him or sell anything to him. It was the deliberate Pharisaic aim to avoid every contact with The People of the Land, the people who did not observe the petty details of the law. Obviously, they would be shocked to the core at the way in which Jesus companied with people who were not only rank outsiders, but sinners, contact with whom would necessarily defile. We will understand these parables more fully if we remember that the strict Jews said, not " There is joy in heaven over one sinner who repents," but, " There is joy in heaven over one sinner who is obliterated before God." They looked sadistically forward not to the saving but to the destruction of the sinner.

So Jesus told them the parable of the lost sheep and the shepherd's joy. The shepherd in Judæa had a hard and dangerous task. Pasture was scarce. The narrow central plateau was only a few miles wide, and then it plunged down to the wild cliffs and the terrible devastation of the desert. There were no restraining walls, and the sheep would wander. George Adam Smith wrote of the shepherd, " On some high moor across which at night the hyænas howl, when you meet him, sleepless, far-sighted, weather-beaten, armed, leaning on his staff and looking out over his scattered sheep, everyone of them on his heart, you understand why the shepherd of Judæa sprang to the front in his people's history; why they gave his name to the king and made him the symbol of providence; why Christ took him as the type of self-sacrifice." The shepherd was personally responsible for the sheep. If a sheep was lost the shepherd must at least bring home the fleece to show how it had died. These shepherds were experts at tracking, and could follow the straying sheep's footprints for miles across the hills. There was not a shepherd for whom it was not all in the day's work to lay down his life for his sheep. Many of the flocks were communal flocks, belonging, not to individuals, but to villages. There would

THE GOSPEL OF LUKE

be two or three shepherds in charge. Those whose flocks
were safe would arrive home on time, and they would
bring news that one shepherd was still out on the mountain
side searching for a sheep which was lost. The whole
village would be upon the watch, and then, when, in the
distance, they saw the shepherd striding home with the
lost sheep across his shoulders there would rise from the
whole community a shout of joy and of thanksgiving.
That is the picture that Jesus drew of God; that, said
Jesus, is what God is like. God is as glad when a lost
sinner is found as a shepherd is when a strayed sheep is
brought home. As a great saint said, " God, too, knows
the joy of finding things that have gone lost."

There is a wondrous thought here. It is the truly
tremendous truth that God is kinder than men. The
orthodox would write off the tax-collectors and the sinners
as being beyond the pale, and as deserving of nothing but
destruction. Not so God. Men may give up hope of a
sinner. Not so God. God loves the folk who never stray
away; but in His heart there is the joy of joys when one
lost one is found and comes home; and it would be a
thousand times easier to come back to God than to come
home to the bleak criticism of men.

> Souls of men! why will ye scatter
>   Like a crowd of frightened sheep?
> Foolish hearts! why will ye wander
>   From a love so true and deep?
>
> Was there ever kindest shepherd
>   Half so gentle, half so sweet,
> As the Saviour who would have us
>   Come and gather round His feet?
>
> For the love of God is broader
>   Than the measure of man's mind;
> And the heart of the Eternal
>   Is most wonderfully kind.

THE COIN A WOMAN LOST AND FOUND

Luke 15: 8-10

> Or, what woman who has ten silver pieces, if she loses one piece, does not light a lamp and sweep the house and search carefully until she finds it? And when she has found it she calls together her friends and neighbours, saying, " Rejoice with me because I have found the silver piece which I lost." Even so, I tell you, there is joy in the presence of the angels of God over one sinner who repents.

THE coin in question in this parable was a silver drachma which was worth about 9d. It would not be difficult to lose a coin in a Palestinian peasant's house, and it might take a long search to find it. The Palestinian houses were very dark, for they were lit by one little circular window not much more than about eighteen inches across. The floor was beaten earth covered with dried reeds and rushes; and to look for a coin on a floor like that was very much like looking for a needle in a haystack. The woman swept the floor in the hope that she might see the coin glint, or hear it tinkle as it fell among the rushes.

There are two reasons why the woman may have been so eager to find the coin.

(i) It may have been a matter of sheer necessity. 9d. does not sound very much, but it was a little more than a whole day's wage for a working man in Palestine. These people lived always on the edge of things, and very little stood between them and real hunger and starvation. The woman may well have searched with intensity because if she did not find the family would not eat.

(ii) But there may be a much more romantic reason than that. In Palestine the mark of a married woman was a head-dress made of ten silver coins linked together by a silver chain. For years maybe a girl would scrape and save to amass her ten coins, for the head-dress was almost the equivalent of her wedding ring. When she had it it was so inalienably hers that it could not even be taken from her for debt. It may well be that it was one of these coins that the woman in the parable lost, and she searched for it as any woman would search if she had lost her marriage ring.

In either case it is easy to think of the joy of the woman when at last she saw the glint of the elusive coin, and when she held it in her hand again. God, said Jesus, is like that. The joy of God, and of all the angels, when one sinner comes home is like the joy of a home when a coin which has stood between them and starvation has been lost and is found; it is like the joy of a woman who loses her most precious possession, which had a value far beyond money, and then finds it again. No Pharisee had ever dreamed of a God like that. A great Jewish scholar has admitted that this is the one absolutely new thing which Jesus taught men about God—that God actually sought and searched for men. The Jew might have agreed that if a man came crawling home to God in self-abasement and knelt before God praying for pity he might find it; but the Jew would never have conceived of a God who went out to search for sinners. It is our glory that we believe in the seeking love of God, because we see that love incarnate in Jesus Christ, the Son of God, who came to seek and to save that which was lost.

THE STORY OF THE LOVING FATHER

Luke 15: 11-32

Jesus said, " There was a man who had two sons. The younger of them said to his father, ' Father, give me the part of the estate which falls to me.' So his father divided his living between them. Not many days after, the son realized it all and went away to a far country, and there in wanton recklessness scattered his substance. When he had spent everything a mighty famine arose throughout that country and he began to be in want. He went and attached himself to a citizen of that country, and he sent him into his fields to feed pigs; and he had a great desire to fill

himself with the husks the pigs were eating; and no
one gave anything to him. When he had come to
himself, he said, ' How many of my father's hired
servants have more than enough bread, and I—I am
perishing here with hunger. I will get up and I will
go to my father, and I will say to him, "Father, I have
sinned against heaven and before you. I am no
longer fit to be called your son. Make me as one of
your hired servants."' So he got up and went to his
father. While he was still a long way away his father
saw him, and was moved to the depths of his being
and ran and flung his arms round his neck and kissed
him tenderly. The son said to him, ' Father, I have
sinned against heaven and before you. I am no longer
fit to be called your son.' But the father said to his
servants, ' Quick! Bring out the best robe and put
it on him; put a ring on his finger; put shoes on his
feet; and bring the fatted calf and kill it and let us
eat and rejoice, for this my son was dead and has come
back to life again; he was lost and has been found.'
And they began to rejoice.

"Now the elder son was in the field. When he came
near the house he heard the sound of music and
dancing. He called one of the slaves and asked what
these things could mean. He said to him, ' Your
brother has come, and your father has killed the fatted
calf because he has got him back safe and sound.'
He was enraged and refused to come in. His father
went out and urged him to come in. He answered
his father, ' Look you, I have served you so many
years and I never transgressed your order, and to me
you never gave a kid that I might have a good time
with my friends. But when this son of yours—this
fellow who consumed your living with harlots—came,
you killed the fatted calf for him.' ' Child,' he said
to him, ' you are always with me. Everything that is
mine is yours. But we had to rejoice and be glad, for
your brother was dead and has come back to life
again; he was lost and has been found.'"

NOT without reason this has been called the greatest short
story in the world. Under Jewish law a father was not
free to leave his property as he liked. The elder son must
get two-thirds, and the younger one-third. (Deuteronomy
21: 17.) It was by no means unusual for a father to

distribute his estate before he died if he wished to retire from the actual management of affairs. But there is a certain heartless callousness in the request of the younger son. He said in effect, " Give me now the part of the estate I will get anyway when you are dead, and let me get out of this." The father did not argue. He knew that if the son was ever to learn he must learn the hard way; and he gave him his request. Without delay the son realized his share of the property and left home. He soon ran through the money; and he finished up feeding pigs, a task, that was forbidden to a Jew because the law said, " Cursed is he who feeds swine." Then Jesus paid sinning mankind the greatest compliment it has ever been paid. " When he came to himself," said Jesus. Jesus believed that so long as a man was away from God and against God he was not truly himself; he was only truly himself when he was on the way home. Beyond a doubt Jesus did not believe in total depravity; he never believed that you could glorify God by blackguarding man. He believed that man was never essentially himself until he came home to God. So the son decided to come home, and to plead to be taken back not as a son but in the lowest rank of slaves, the hired servants, the men who were only day labourers. The ordinary slave was in some sense a member of the family, but the hired servant could be dismissed at a day's notice. He was not one of the family at all. So he came home; and, according to the best Greek text, his father never gave him the chance to ask to be a servant. He broke in before that. That robe stands for honour; the ring stands for authority, for if a man gave to another his signet ring it was the same as giving him the power of attorney; the shoes stand for a son as opposed to a slave, for children of the family were shod and slaves were not. The slave's dream in the negro spiritual is of the time when " all God's chillun got shoes," for shoes were the sign of freedom. And a feast was made that all might rejoice at the wanderer's return.

Let us stop there, and let us see the truth so far in this parable.

(i) The parable should never have been called the Parable of the Prodigal Son, for the son is not the hero. It should be called the Parable of the Loving Father, for it tells us rather about a father's love than a son's sin.

(ii) The parable tells us much about the forgiveness of God. The father must have been waiting and watching for the son to come home, for he saw him a long way away. When he came he forgave him with no recriminations. There is a way of forgiving when forgiveness is conferred as a favour; and worse, when someone is forgiven, but always by hint and by word and by threat his sin is held over him. Once Lincoln was asked how he was going to treat the rebellious southerners when they had finally been defeated and had returned to the Union of the United States. The questioner expected that Lincoln would take a dire vengeance, but he answered, " I will treat them as if they had never been away." It is the wonder of the love of God that God treats us like that.

But that is not the end of the story. There enters the elder brother who was actually sorry that his brother had come home. The elder brother stands for the self-righteous Pharisees who would rather have seen a sinner destroyed than saved. Certain things stand out about the elder brother.

(i) His whole attitude shows that his years of obedience to his father had been years of grim duty and not of loving service.

(ii) His whole attitude is one of utter lack of sympathy. He refers to his brother, not as *my brother* but as *your son.* He was the kind of self-righteous character who would cheerfully have kicked a man farther into the gutter when he was already down.

(iii) He had a peculiarly nasty mind. There is no mention of harlots until he mentions them. He, no doubt, suspected and accused his brother of the sins he himself would have liked to commit.

Once again we have the same amazing truth here, that it is easier to confess to God than it is to many a man; that God is more merciful in his judgments than many an orthodox man is; that the love of God is far broader than the love of man; and that God can forgive when men refuse to forgive. In face of a love like that we cannot be other than lost in wonder, love and praise.

Three lost things

We must finally note that these three parables are not simply three ways of stating the same thing. There is a difference. The sheep went lost through *sheer foolishness*. It did not think, and many a man would escape sin if he thought in time. The coin did not go lost at all; it was lost *through no fault of its own*. Many a man is lead astray, and God will not hold him guiltless who has taught another to sin. The son *deliberately went lost,* callously turning his back on his father. But the love of God can defeat the foolishness of man, the seductions of the tempting voices, and even the deliberate rebellion of the heart.

A BAD MAN'S GOOD EXAMPLE

Luke 16: 1-13

Jesus said to His disciples, " There was a rich man who had a steward. He received information against the steward which alleged that he was dissipating his goods. He called him, and said to him, ' What is this that I hear about you? Give an account of your stewardship, for you can no longer be steward.' The steward said to himself, ' What am I to do? I have not the strength to dig, and I am ashamed to beg. I know what I will do, so that, when I am removed from my steward-ship, they will receive me into their houses.' So he summoned each of the people who owed debts to his master. To the first he said, ' How much do you owe

my master?' He said, 'Nine hundred gallons of oil.'
He said to him, 'Take your accounts and sit down
and write quickly, four hundred and fifty.' Then he
said to another 'And you—how much do you owe?'
He said, 'A thousand bushels of corn.' He said to
him, 'Take your accounts and write eight hundred.'
And the master praised the wicked steward because
he acted shrewdly; for the sons of this world are
shrewder in their own generation than the sons of
light. And, I tell you, make for yourselves friends
by means of your material possessions, even if they
have been unjustly acquired, so that when your money
goes done they will receive you into a dwelling which
lasts forever. He who is trustworthy in a very little
is also trustworthy in much; and he who is dishonest
in a very little is also dishonest in much. If you have
not shown yourself trustworthy in your ordinary
business dealings about material things, who will
trust you with the genuine wealth? If you have not
shown yourselves trustworthy in what belongs to
someone else, who will give you what is your own ?
No household slave can serve two masters, for either
he will hate the one and love the other, or he will hold
to the one and despise the other. You cannot be the
slave of God and of material things."

It is quite clear that this is a difficult parable to interpret.
It is a story about as choice a set of rascals as one could
meet anywhere. The steward was a rascal. He was a
slave, but he was nonetheless in charge of the running of
his master's whole estate. In Palestine there were many
absentee landlords. The master may well have been one
of these, and his whole business may well have been entrusted to his steward's hands. The steward had followed
a career of embezzlement. The debtors were also rascals.
No doubt what they owed was rent. Rent in Palestine
was often paid to a landlord, not in money, but in kind.
It was often an agreed proportion of the produce of the
part of the estate which had been rented. The steward
knew that he had lost his job. He, therefore, had a brilliant
idea. He falsified the entries in the books so that the
debtors were debited with far less than they owed. This

would have two effects. First, the debtors would be grateful to him; and second, and much more effective, he had involved the debtors in his own misdemeanours, and, if the worst came to the worst, he was now in a strong position to exercise a little judicious blackmail! The master himself was something of a rascal, for, instead of being shocked at the whole proceeding, he appreciated the shrewd brain behind it, and actually praised the steward for what he had done. The difficulty of the parable is clearly seen from the fact that Luke attaches no fewer than four different morals or lessons to it.

(i) In verse 8 the lesson is that children of this world are wiser in their generation that the children of light. That means that, if only the Christian was as eager and ingenious in his attempt to attain goodness as the man of the world is in his attempt to attain money and comfort, he would be a better man. If only men would give as much attention to the things which concern their souls as they do to the things which concern their business, they would be better men. It is quite true that over and over again a man will expend twenty times the amount of time and money and effort on his pleasure, his hobby, his golf, his garden, his sport as he does on his church. Our Christianity will only begin to become real and effective when we spend as much time and effort on it as we do on our worldly activities.

(ii) In verse 9 the lesson is that material possessions should be used to cement the friendships wherein the real and permanent value of life lies. That could be done in two ways. (a) It could be done as it affects eternity. The Rabbis had a saying, " The rich help the poor in this world, but the poor help the rich in the world to come." Ambrose, commenting on the rich fool who built bigger barns to store his goods, said, " The bosoms of the poor, the houses of widows, the mouths of children are the barns which last forever." It was in any event a Jewish belief that charity given to poor people would stand to a man's credit in the world to come. A man's true wealth would not be in what he kept, but in what he gave away. (*b*) It could be done as it affects this world. A man can use his wealth selfishly, or he can use it to make life easier, not only for himself, but for his friends and his fellow men. How many a poor scholar is forever grateful to a rich man who gave or left money to found bursaries and scholarships which made a university career possible! How many a man is grateful to a better-off friend who saw him through some time of need in the most practical way! Possessions are not in themselves a sin, but they *are* a great responsibility, and the man who uses them to help his friends has gone far to discharge that responsibility.

(iii) In verses 10 and 11 the lesson is that a man's way of fulfilling a small task is the best proof of his fitness or unfitness to be entrusted with a bigger task. That is clearly true of earthly things. No man will be advanced to a higher position until he has given proof of his honesty and ability in a smaller position. But Jesus extends the principle to eternity. He says, " Upon earth you are in charge of things which are not really yours. You cannot take them with you when you die. They are only lent to you. You are only a steward over them. They cannot, in the nature of things, be permanently yours. On the other hand in heaven you will get what is really and eternally and essentially yours. And what you get in heaven depends on how you used the things of earth. What you will be given as your very own will depend on how you used the things of which you were only steward."

(iv) Verse 13 lays down the rule that no slave can serve two masters. The master possessed the slave, and possessed him *exclusively*. Nowadays, a servant or a workman can quite easily do two jobs, and work for two people. He can do one job in his working time and another in his spare time. He could, for instance, be a clerk by day and a musician by night. Many a man augments his income or finds his real interest in a spare time occupation. But a slave had no spare time; every moment of his day, and every ounce of his energy, belonged to his master. He had no time which was his own. So, serving God, can never be a part time or a spare time job. Once a man chooses to serve God every moment of his time and every atom of his energy belongs to God. God is the most exclusive of masters. We either belong to God totally and altogether, or not at all.

THE LAW WHICH DOES NOT CHANGE

Luke 16: 14-18

> When the Pharisees, who were characteristically fond of money, heard these things, they derided Jesus. So He said to them, " You are those who make yourselves look righteous before men, but God knows your hearts, because that which is exalted amongst men is an abomination before God.
>
> " The law and the prophets were until John; from then the good news of the Kingdom of God is proclaimed; and every one forces his way into it; but it is easier for heaven and earth to pass away than for one dot of the law to become invalid.
>
> " Everyone who divorces his wife and marries another commits adultery, and he who marries a woman who has been divorced from her husband commits adultery."

THIS passage falls into three sections.

(i) It begins with a rebuke to the Pharisees. It says that they *derided* Jesus. The word literally means that they turned up their noses at Jesus. The Jew tended to connect earthly prosperity and goodness. Wealth was a sign that a man was a good man. The Pharisees put on a parade of goodness; and they regarded material prosperity as a reward of that goodness; but the more they exalted themselves before men, the more they became an abomination to God. It is bad enough for a man to think himself a good man; but it is worse when he points to material prosperity as an unanswerable proof of his goodness.

(ii) Before Jesus the law and the prophets had been the final word of God; but Jesus came preaching the Kingdom. When He did so the most unlikely people, the tax-collectors and the sinners, came storming their way into the Kingdom even when the Scribes and Pharisees would have set up barriers to keep them out. But Jesus emphasized one thing. The Kingdom was not the end of the law. True, the little details and regulations of the ceremonial law were wiped out. But let no man think that Christianity offered an easy way in which no laws remained. The great laws stood unaltered and unalterable. Certain Jewish letters are very like each other; they are distinguished only by the serif, which is the little line at the top or bottom of a letter. Not even a serif of the great laws would pass away.

(iii) As an illustration of the law that would never pass away Jesus took the law of chastity. This very definite statement of Jesus must be read against the contemporary background of Jewish life. The Jew glorified fidelity and chastity. The Rabbis said, " All things can God overlook except unchastity." " Unchastity causes the glory of God to depart." A Jew must surrender his life rather than commit idolatry, murder or adultery. But the tragedy was that at this time the marriage bond was on the way to being destroyed. We must always remember that in the eyes of Jewish law a woman was a thing. A woman could only divorce her husband if he became a leper, or an apostate, or if he ravished a virgin. Otherwise a woman had no rights whatever and no redress, other than that the marriage dowry must be repaid if she was divorced. The law said, " A woman may be divorced with or without her will; a man only with his will." The Mosaic law (Deuteronomy 24: 1) said, " When a man hath taken a wife and married her, and it come to pass that she find no favour in his eyes because he hath found some uncleanness in her, then let him write her a bill of divorcement, and give it in her hand, and send her out of his house." The bill of divorce had to be signed before two witnesses

THE GOSPEL OF LUKE

and ran, " Let this be from me thy writ of divorce and letter of dismissal and deed of liberation, that thou mayest marry whatsoever man thou wilt." Divorce was as simple and easy as that. The matter turned on the interpretation of the phrase *some uncleanness* in the Mosaic regulation. There were two schools of thought. The school of Shammai said that that meant adultery, and adultery alone. The school of Hillel said that it could mean " if she spoiled a dish of food; if she spun in the street; if she talked to a strange man; if she was guilty of speaking disrespectfully of her husband's relations in his hearing; if she was a brawling woman," which was defined as a woman whose voice could be heard in the next house. Rabbi Akiba went so far as to say that a man could divorce his wife if he found a woman who was fairer than she. Human nature being what it is, it was the school of Hillel which prevailed, so that, in the time of Jesus, things were so bad that women refused to marry at all, and family life was in danger. Jesus here lays down the sanctity of the marriage bond. The saying is repeated in Matthew 5: 31, 32 where adultery is made the sole exception to the universal rule. We some-times think that our own generation is bad, but Jesus lived in a generation when things were every bit as bad. If we destroy family life, we destroy the very basis of the Christian life; and Jesus here lays down the law which men will only relax at their peril.

THE PUNISHMENT OF THE MAN WHO NEVER NOTICED

Luke 16: 19-31

There was a rich man who dressed habitually in purple and fine linen, and who feasted in luxury every day. A poor man, called Lazarus, was laid at his gate. He was full of ulcerated sores, and he desired to satisfy his hunger from the things which fell from the rich man's table; more, the dogs used to come and lick his sores. The poor man died, and he was carried by the angels to the bosom of Abraham. The rich man died and was buried. And in hell, being in torture, he lifted up his eyes, and from far away he saw Abraham, and Lazarus in his bosom. He called out, " Father Abraham, have pity on me, and send Lazarus to me that he may dip the tip of his finger in water and cool my tongue, because I am in anguish in this fire." Abraham said, " Child, remember that you received in full your good things in your life-time, just as Lazarus received evil things. Now he is comforted, and you are in anguish; and, besides all this, between you and us a great gulf is fixed, so that those who wish to pass from here to you cannot do so, nor can any cross from there to us." He said, " Well then, I ask you, father, to send him to my father's house, that he may warn them, so that they, too, may not come to this place of torture." Abraham said, " They have Moses and the prophets. Let them listen to them." He said, " No, father Abraham; but if some one goes to them from the dead, they will repent." He said to them, " If they will not listen to Moses and the prophets, neither will they be convinced if some one should rise from the dead."

THIS is a parable constructed with such masterly skill that not one phrase is wasted. Let us look at the two characters in it.

(i) First, there is the rich man, who is usually called Dives, which is the Latin for rich. Every phrase adds something to the luxury in which he lived. He was clothed in purple and fine linen. That is the description of the robes of the High Priests, and such robes cost anything from £30 to £40, an immense sum in days when a working man's wage was about 9d. a day. He feasted in luxury every day. The word used for feasting is the word that is used for a glutton and a gourmet feeding on exotic and costly dishes. He did this *every day*. In so doing he definitely and positively broke the fourth commandment. That commandment does not only forbid work on the Sabbath; it also says *six days shalt thou labour* (Exodus 20: 9). In a country where the common people were fortunate if they ate meat once in the week and where they toiled for six days of the week, Dives is a figure of indolent self-indulgence. Lazarus was waiting for the crumbs that fell from Dives' table. In the time of Jesus there were neither knives nor forks nor napkins. Food was eaten with the hands and, in very wealthy houses, the hands were cleansed by wiping them on hunks of bread, and then the bread was thrown away. It was that bread which Lazarus was waiting for. Dives is the picture of wealthy luxury.

(ii) Second, there is Lazarus. Strangely enough Lazarus is the only character in any of the parables who is given a name. The name is the Latinized form of Eleazar, and means *God is my help*. He was a beggar. He was covered with ulcerated sores. So helpless was he that he could not even ward off the street dogs, unclean animals, who pestered him. Lazarus is the picture of helpless and abject poverty.

Such is the scene in this world, and then abruptly it changes to the next, and there Lazarus is in glory and Dives is in torment. What was the sin of Dives? He had not ordered Lazarus to be removed from his gate. He had had no objections to Lazarus receiving the bread that was flung away from his table. He did not kick Lazarus in the passing. He was not deliberately cruel to him. The sin of Dives was that he never noticed Lazarus, that he accepted Lazarus as part of the landscape, that he thought it perfectly natural and inevitable that Lazarus should lie in pain and hunger while he wallowed in luxury. As someone said, " It was not what Dives did that got him into gaol; it was what he did not do that got him into hell." The sin of Dives was that he could look on the world's suffering and need, and feel no answering sword of grief and pity pierce his heart; he looked at a fellow man, hungry and in pain, and did nothing about it. His was the punishment of the man who never noticed.

It seems hard that his request that his brothers should be warned was refused. But it is the plain fact that if men possess the truth of God's word, and if, wherever they look, there is sorrow to be comforted, need to be supplied, pain to be relieved, and if it moves them to no feeling and to no action, nothing will change them.

It is a terrible warning to remember that the sin of Dives was, not that he did wrong things, but that he did nothing.

LAWS OF THE CHRISTIAN LIFE

Luke 17: 1-10

> Jesus said to His disciples, " It is impossible that snares to sin should not arise; but woe to him through whom they do arise! It would be better for him if a millstone were hung around his neck and he were thrown into the sea rather than that he should cause one of these little ones to trip up.
>
> " Take heed to yourselves. If your brother sins, rebuke him; and if he repents, forgive him. Even if he sins against you seven times in the day, and if seven times he turns to you, saying, ' I repent,' you must forgive him."
>
> The apostles said to the Lord, " Give us also faith! " The Lord said, " If you have faith as a grain of mustard seed, you would say to this sycamine tree, ' Be rooted up and be planted in the sea, and it would obey you.'
>
> " If any of you has a slave ploughing or watching the flock, and the slave comes in from the field, will he say to him, ' Come at once and take your place at table '; or rather, will he not say to him, ' Get ready my evening meal, and gird yourself and serve me, until I eat and drink, and after that you shall eat and drink yourself '? Does he thank a servant because he has done what he was ordered to do? Even so, you too, when you have done everything you were ordered to do, say, ' We are unworthy servants. We have done what it was our duty to do.' "

THIS passage falls into four definite and disconnected sections.

(i) Verses 1 and 2 condemn the man who teaches others to sin. The Authorised Version talks in these verses about *offences*. The Greek word is exactly the same word as the

English word *scandal* (skandalon). This word has two meanings. (*a*) It originally meant the bait-stick in a trap, the stick which an animal, lured by the bait, might touch, and so be caught in the trap. (*b*) It then came to mean any stumbling-block placed in a man's way to trip him up. Jesus said that it was impossible to construct a world with no temptations; but woe to that man who taught another to sin, or who took away another's innocence. Every one must be given his first invitation to sin, his first push along the wrong way. Kennedy Williamson tells of an old man who was dying. Something was obviously worrying him. He told them at last what it was. " When I was a lad," he said, " I often played on a wide common. Near its centre two roads met and crossed, and, standing at the cross-roads, was an old ricketty sign-post. I remember one day twisting it round in its socket, thus altering the arms, and making them point in the wrong direction; and I've been wondering ever since how many travellers were sent on the wrong road by me." God will not hold the man guiltless, who, on the road of life, sends a younger or a weaker brother on the wrong way.

(ii) Verses 3 and 4 speak of the necessity of forgiveness in the Christian life. It tells us to forgive seven times. The Rabbis had a saying that if any man forgave another *three* times, he was a perfect man. The Christian standard takes the Rabbinic standard and doubles it and adds one. It is not a matter of calculated arithmetic. It simply means that the Christian standard of forgiveness must immeasurably exceed the best the world can achieve.

(iii) Verses 5 and 6 tell us that faith is the greatest force in the world. We must again remember that it was the eastern custom to use language in the most vivid possible way. This saying means that even that which looks completely impossible becomes possible, if it is approached with faith. We have only to think of the number of scientific marvels, of the number of surgical operations, of the feats of endurance which to-day have been achieved, and which less than fifty years ago would have been regarded as impossible. If we approach a thing, saying, ' It can't be done,' it will not be done; if we approach it, saying, ' It must be done,' the chances are that it will be done. We must always remember that we approach no task alone, but that with us there is God and all the power of God.

(iv) Verses 7-10 tell us that we can never put God in our debt, and that we can never have any claim on God. When we have done our best we have only done our duty; and a man who has done his duty has only done what, in any event, he could be compelled to do.

> Were the whole realm of Nature mine,
>   That were an offering far too small;
> Love so amazing, so divine,
>   Demands my soul, my life, my all.

It may be possible to satisfy the claims of *law*; but every lover knows that nothing he can ever do can satisfy the claims of *love*.

THE RARITY OF GRATITUDE

Luke 17: 11-19

> When Jesus was on the way to Jerusalem, He was going along between Samaria and Galilee; and, as He entered a village, ten lepers, who stood far off, met Him. They lifted up their voices and said, " Jesus, Master, have pity upon us." When He saw them, He said, " Go, and show yourselves to the priests." And as they went they were cleansed. When one of them saw that he was cured, he turned back, glorifying God with a great voice. He fell on his face at Jesus' feet and kept on thanking Him. And he was a Samaritan. Jesus said, " Were the ten not cleansed? The nine—where are they? Were none found to turn back and give glory to God except this foreigner? " And He said to him, " Rise and go! Your faith has made you well."

AT this time Jesus was on the border between Galilee and Samaria. He was met by a band of ten lepers. We know that the Jews had no dealings with the Samaritans, and yet in this band there was at least one Samaritan. Here is an example of one great law of life. A common misfortune had broken down the racial and the national barriers. In the common tragedy of their leprosy they had forgotten that they were Jews and Samaritans and remembered only that they were men in need. It is said that if a flood surges over a piece of country, and the wild animals congregate on some little bit of higher ground, you will see standing together animals who are natural enemies, and, who, at any other time, would have done their best to kill each other. Surely one of the things which should draw all men together is their common need of God.

The lepers stood afar off. (cp. Leviticus 13: 45, 46; Numbers 5: 2). There was no specified distance at which they should stand, but we know that at least one authority laid it down, that, when the wind was blowing from the leper to the healthy person, the leper should stand at least fifty yards away. Nothing could better show the utter isolation in which lepers lived.

There is no story in all the gospels which so poignantly shows man's ingratitude. The lepers had come to Jesus with a desperate longing; He had cured them, and nine never came back to give thanks. So often, once a man has got what he wants, he never comes back.

(i) So often children are ungrateful to their parents. There is a time in life when a week's neglect would have killed us. Of all living creatures man requires longest to become able to meet the needs which are essential for life. There were long years when we were dependent on parents for literally everything. And yet the day comes when an aged parent is a nuisance; and few young people ever think of repaying the debt they owe. As King Lear said in the day of his own tragedy,

" How sharper than a serpent's tooth it is
To have a thankless child! "

(ii) So often we are ungrateful to our fellow men. There
are few of us who have not at some time owed a very great
deal to some fellow man. There are few of us who, at the
moment, believed that we would ever forget; and there
are few of us who in the end satisfied the debt of gratitude
that we owe. If often happens that a friend, a teacher,
a doctor, a surgeon does something for us which it
is impossible to repay. The tragedy of life is that we do
not even try to repay it.

Blow, blow, thou winter wind,
Thou art not so unkind
As man's ingratitude.

(iii) So often we are ungrateful to God. In some time
of bitter need we pray with desperate intensity; the
time passes and we forget God. So many of us never even
give to God a grace before meat. He gave us His only
Son, and so often we never give to Him even a word of
thanks. The best thanks we can give God is to try to
deserve His goodness and His mercy a little better. " Bless
the Lord, O my soul, and *forget not all his benefits*." (Psalm
103: 2.)

THE SIGNS OF HIS COMING

Luke 17: 20-37

When Jesus was asked by the Pharisees when the
Kingdom of God was coming, He answered them,
" The Kingdom of God does not come with signs that
you can watch for; nor will they say, ' Look here!' or
' Look there!' For—look you—the Kingdom of God is
within you."
He said to His disciples, " Days will come when
you will long to see one of the days of the Son of Man
and you will not see it. And they will say to you,

'Look there! Look here!' Do not depart, and do not
follow them. For, as the flashing lightning lights up
the sky from one side to another, so shall be the Son
of Man in His day. But, first He must suffer many
things and must be rejected by this generation. Even
as it was in the days of Noah, so it will be in the days
of the Son of Man. They were eating, they were
drinking, they were marrying, they were being given
in marriage, until the day on which Noah entered
the ark and the flood came and wiped them all out.
In the same way, so it was in the days of Lot. They
were eating, they were drinking, they were buying,
they were selling, they were planting, they were
building, but, on the day on which Lot went out of
Sodom, fire and brimstone rained from heaven and
wiped them all out. It will be the same on the day
on which the Son of Man is revealed. If, on that day,
anyone is on the housetop, and his goods are in the
house, let him not come down to take them. In the
same way, if anyone is in the field, let him not turn
back. Remember Lot's wife! Whoever seeks to gain
his life will lose it, but whoever loses it will preserve
it alive. This is the truth I tell you—on that night
there will be two in one bed. One will be taken and
the other will be left. Two women will be grinding
together. One will be taken and the other left."
They said to Him, " Where, Lord? " He said to them,
" Where the body is, there the vultures will be gathered
together."

HERE are two very difficult passages.

In verses 20 and 21 Jesus answered the question of
the Pharisees as to when the Kingdom of God would come.
He said that it would not come with signs that you can
watch for. The word he used is the word that is used for
a doctor watching a patient for symptoms of some disease
which he suspects. We are not quite sure what Jesus
went on to say. The Greek may mean two things. (a) It
may mean, The Kingdom of God is within you. That is to
say, the Kingdom of God works in men's hearts. The
Kingdom of God is to produce not new things, but new
people. It is not a revolution in material things that we

are to look for, but a revolution in the hearts of men. (b) It may mean, The Kingdom of God is among you. That would refer to Jesus Himself. He was the very embodiment of the Kingdom, and they did not recognize Him. It was as if He said, " The whole offer and the whole secret of God are here—and you will not accept it."

Verses 22-37 speak of the Second Coming of Jesus. Out of this difficult passage we can only pick the things which are certain—and in truth they are enough.

(i) There will be times when the Christian will long for the coming of Christ. Like the martyred saints he will cry out, " How long? " (Revelation 6: 10.) But he will need to learn to light a candle of patience, and to wait. God takes His own time.

(ii) The coming of Christ is certain, but the time of that coming is quite unknown. Speculation is vain and useless People will come with false prophecies and false predictions. We must not leave our ordinary work to follow them. The best way that Christ can come upon a man is when a man is faithfully and humbly and watchfully doing his duty. As a great commentator said, " No man will foresee it, and all men will see it."

(iii) When that day comes the judgments of God will operate, and, of two people who, all their lives, lived side by side, one will be taken and the other will be left. There is a warning here. Intimacy with a good person does not necessarily guarantee our own salvation. " No man can deliver his brother." Is it not often true that a family is apt to leave the duties of church membership to one member of the family? Is it not often true that many a husband leaves the duties of the Church to his wife? The judgment of God is an individual judgment. We cannot discharge our duty to God by proxy, nor even by association. Often one will be taken and another left.

(iv) When they asked Jesus when all this would happen, He answered by quoting a well-known proverb. " Where the body is, there the vultures will be gathered together."

That simply meant that a thing would happen when the necessary conditions were fulfilled. That means for us that God will bring Jesus Christ again in His good time. We cannot know that time; we dare not speculate about it. We must live so that whenever He comes, at morning, at midday or at evening, He may find us ready.

UNWEARIED IN PRAYER

Luke 18: 1-8

Jesus spoke a parable to them to show that it is necessary always to pray and not to lose heart. " There was a judge," He said, " in a town who neither feared God nor respected man. There was a widow in the same town who kept coming to him and saying, ' Vindicate me against my adversary.' For some time he refused. But afterwards he said to himself, ' Even though I neither fear God nor respect man, because she bothers me, I will vindicate this widow, lest by her constant coming she exhausts me.' " The Lord said, " Listen to what the unjust judge says. And shall God not vindicate His own chosen ones who cry to Him day and night, even though He seem to wait for long? But when the Son of Man comes will He find faith on earth? "

THIS parable tells of the kind of thing which could, and often did, happen in Palestine. There are two characters in it.

(i) There is the judge. He was clearly not a Jewish judge. All ordinary Jewish disputes were taken before the elders, and not into the public courts at all. If, under Jewish law, a matter was taken to arbitration, one man could not constitute a court. There were always three judges, one chosen by the plaintiff, one by the defendant, and one independently appointed. This judge was one of these paid magistrates appointed either by Herod or by the Romans. Such judges were notorious. Unless a plaintiff had influence and money to bribe his way to a verdict he had no hope of ever getting his case settled.

They were said to pervert justice for a dish of meat. People even punned on their title. Officially they were called *Dayyaneh Gezeroth*, which means judges of prohibitions or punishments. Popularly they were called *Dayyaneh Gezeloth*, which means robber judges.

(ii) The widow was the symbol of all who were poor and defenceless. It was obvious that she, without resource of any kind, had no hope of ever extracting justice from such a judge. But she had one weapon—the weapon of persistence. It is quite possible that what the judge in the end feared was actual physical violence. The word translated, lest she *exhausts* me can, and does mean, lest she *give me a black eye*. It is possible to close a person's eye in two ways—either by sleep or assault and battery! In any event, in the end, her persistence won the day.

This parable is like the Parable of the Friend at Midnight. It does not *liken* God to an unjust judge; it *contrasts* God to such a person. In this parable Jesus was saying, " If, in the end, an unjust and rapacious judge can be wearied into giving a widow woman justice, *how much more* will God, who is a loving Father, give His children what they need? "

That is true, but we must ever remember that that is no reason why we should expect to get whatever we pray for. Often a father has to refuse the request of a child, because he knows that what the child asks would hurt rather than help. God is like that. We do not know what is to happen in the next hour, let alone the next week, or month, or year. Only God sees time whole, and, therefore, only God knows what is good for us *in the long run*. That is why Jesus said that we must never be discouraged in prayer. That is why He wondered if men's faith would stand the long delays before the Son of Man should come. We will never grow weary in prayer, and our faith will never falter if, after we have offered to God *our* prayers and requests, we add the perfect prayer, *Thy* will be done.

THE SIN OF PRIDE

Luke 18: 9-14

> Jesus spoke this parable to some who were self-confidently sure that they were righteous and who despised others. " Two men went up to the Temple to pray. The one was a Pharisee, the other, a tax-collector. The Pharisee stood and prayed thus with himself, ' O God, I thank Thee, that I am not as the rest of men, thieves, unjust, adulterers, or even as this tax-collector. I fast twice a week. I give a tenth of all that I get.' The tax-collector stood afar off, and would not lift even his eyes to heaven, and kept beating his breast and said, ' O God, be merciful, to me—the sinner.' I tell you, this man went down to his house accepted with God rather than the other, because everyone who exalts himself will be humbled, but he who humbles himself will be exalted."

In Palestine the devout observed three prayer times daily—9 a.m., 12 midday and 3 p.m. Prayer was held to be specially efficacious if it was offered in the Temple, and so at these hours many went up to the Temple courts to pray. Jesus told of two men who thus went to pray.

(i) There was a Pharisee. He did not really go to pray to God. He prayed *with himself*. True prayer is always offered to God and to God alone. A certain American cynically described a preacher's prayer as " the most eloquent prayer ever offered to a Boston audience." The Pharisee was really giving himself a testimonial before God. The Jewish law prescribed only one absolutely obligatory fast—that on the Day of Atonement. But those who wished to gain special merit fasted also on Mondays and Thursdays. It is noteworthy that these were the market days when Jerusalem was full of country people. Those who fasted whitened their faces and appeared in dishevelled clothes, and those days gave their piety the biggest possible audience. The Levites were to receive a tithe of all a man's produce (Numbers 18: 21; Deuteronomy 14: 22). But this Pharisee tithed everything, even things which there was no obligation to tithe.

His whole attitude was not untypical of the worst in Phariisaism. There is a recorded prayer of a certain Rabbi which runs like this, " I thank, Thee, O Lord my God, that Thou hast put my part with those who sit in the Academy, and not with those who sit at the street-corners. For I rise early, and they rise early; I rise early to the words of the law, and they to vain things. I labour, and they labour; I labour and receive a reward, and they labour and receive no reward. I run, and they run; I run to the life of the world to come, and they to the pit of destruction." It is on record that Rabbi Simeon ben Jochai once said, " If there are only two righteous men in the world, I and my son are these two; if there is only one, I am he! " The Pharisee did not really go to pray; he went to inform God how good he was.

(ii) There was the tax-collector. He stood afar off, and would not even lift his eyes to God. The Authorised Version does not even do justice to his humility for he prayed, " O God, be merciful to me—*the* sinner," as if he was not merely *a* sinner, but *the* sinner *par excellence*. " And," said Jesus, " it was that heart-broken, self-despising prayer which won him acceptance before God."

There are certain things about prayer which this parable unmistakably tells us.

(i) No man who is proud can pray. The gate of heaven is so low that none can enter it save upon his knees. All that a man can say is,

" None other Lamb, none other Name,
    None other Hope in heaven or earth or sea,
  None other Hiding-place from guilt and shame,
    None beside Thee."

(ii) No man who despises his fellow men can pray. In prayer we do not lift ourselves above our fellow men. We remember that we are one of a great army of sinning, suffering, sorrowing humanity, all kneeling before the throne of the mercy of God.

(iii) True prayer comes from setting our lives beside the life of God. No doubt all that the Pharisee said was true. He did fast; he did meticulously give tithes; he was not as other men are; still less was he like that tax-collector. But the question is not, " Am I as good as my fellow men? " The question is, " Am I as good as God? " Once I made a journey in the train down to England. As we passed through the Yorkshire moors I saw a little whitewashed cottage and it seemed to me to shine with an almost radiant whiteness. Some days later I made the journey back to Scotland. The snow had fallen, and was lying deep all around. We came again to the little white cottage, but this time its whiteness seemed drab and soiled and almost grey—in comparison with the virgin whiteness of the driven snow. It all depends what we compare ourselves with. And when we set our lives beside the wonder of the life of Jesus, and beside the holiness of God, then all that is left to say is, " God be merciful to me—the sinner."

THE MASTER AND THE CHILDREN

Luke 18: 15-17

> People were bringing even their babies to Jesus that He might touch them. When the disciples saw it they rebuked them. But Jesus called them to Him saying, " Let the little children come to me, and don't stop them, for of such is the Kingdom of God. This is the truth I tell you—whoever does not receive the Kingdom of God as a little child shall not enter into it."

IT was the custom in Palestine for mothers to bring their children to some distinguished Rabbi on their first birthday that he might bless them. That is what the mothers wanted for their children from Jesus. We are not to think that the disciples were hard and cruel. It was kindness that made them act as they did. Remember where Jesus was going. He was on the way to Jerusalem to die upon a Cross. The disciples could see upon His face the inner tension of His heart; and they did not want Jesus to be bothered. Often at home we say to some little child, "Don't bother your Daddy; he's tired and worried to-night." That is exactly how the disciples felt about Jesus. It is one of the loveliest things in all the gospel story that Jesus had time for the children when He was on the way to Jerusalem to die.

When Jesus said that it was of the child-like that the Kingdom of God was composed, what did He mean? What were the qualities of the child of which He was thinking?

(i) The child has not lost *the sense of wonder*. Tennyson tells of going, early one morning, into the bedroom of his little grandson, and of seeing the child "worshipping the sunbeam playing on the bedpost." As we grow older we begin to live in a world which has grown old and gray and tired. The child lives in a world with a sheen on it, a world in which God is always near.

(ii) The child's whole life is founded on *trust*. When we are young we never doubt where the next meal is to come from, or where our clothes will be found. We go out to school certain that the home will be there when we return, and all things ready for our comfort. When we go on a journey we never doubt that the fare will be paid, and that our parents know the way and will take us safely there. The child's trust in his parents is absolute—as ours should be in our great Father—God.

(iii) The child is naturally *obedient*. True, he often disobeys and grumbles at his parents' bidding. But his instinct is to obey. He knows very well that he should not disobey. He is not happy when he has been disobedient. In his heart of hearts his parents' word to him is law. Even so, so should we be with God.

(iv) The child has an amazing faculty of *forgiveness*. Almost all parents are unjust to their children. We demand from them a standard of obedience, of good manners, of refined language, of diligence which we seldom satisfy ourselves. Time and again we scold them for doing the very things we do ourselves. If others treated us in the way we treat our children in the matter of plain justice we would never forgive. But the child forgives and forgets, and does not even realize it when he is very young. It would be so much lovelier a world if we could forgive as a child forgives.

To keep alive the sense of wonder, to live in unquestioning trust, instinctively to obey, to forgive and to forget—that is the childlike spirit, and that is the passport to the Kingdom of God.

THE MAN WHO WOULD NOT PAY THE PRICE

Luke 18: 18-30

A ruler asked Jesus, " Good teacher, what shall I do to inherit eternal life? " Jesus said to him, " Why do you call me good? There is none good except one—God. You know the commandments—do not commit adultery, do not kill, do not steal, do not bear false witness, honour your father and your mother." He said, " From my youth I have kept all these." When Jesus heard that He said to him, " You still lack one thing. Sell everything you have got and distribute it to the poor, and you will have treasure in heaven. And come! Follow me!" When he heard these things he was very sad, because he was exceedingly rich. When Jesus saw him He said, " How hard it is for those who have riches to enter into the Kingdom of God! It is easier for a camel to go through the eye of a needle than for a rich man to enter the Kingdom of God." Those who heard Him said, " And who can be saved?" He said, " The things which are impossible with men are possible with God." Peter said, " Look you—we have left our private possessions and have followed you." He said to them, " This is the truth I tell you—there is no one who has left house, or wife, or brother, or parents or children for the sake of the Kingdom of God who will not get it all back many times over in this time, and, in the age that is coming, eternal life."

THIS ruler addressed Jesus in a way which, for a Jew, was without parallel. In all the religious Jewish literature there is no record of any Rabbi being addressed as, " Good teacher." The Rabbis always said " there is nothing that is good but the law." To address Jesus in such a way savoured of almost fulsome flattery. So Jesus began by driving him and his thoughts back to God. Jesus was always sure that His own power, and His own message, came to Him from God. When the nine lepers failed to return, Jesus' grief was, not that they had forgotten to come back to say thanks to Him, but that they had not come back to glorify God. (Luke 17: 18.)

It was indisputable that this ruler was a good man, but he felt within his heart and soul that in his life there was something lacking. Jesus' command to him was that if he wanted to find all that he was searching for in life he must sell all his possessions and distribute them to the poor and follow Him. Why did Jesus make this demand specially from this man? When the man whom Jesus had cured in the country of the Gerasenes wished to follow Him, He told him to stay at home. (Luke 8: 38, 39.) Why this very different advice to this ruler? There is a gospel called the *Gospel according to the Hebrews* most of which is lost; but in one of the fragments which remain there is an account of this incident which gives us a clue. " The other rich man said to Jesus, ' Master, what good thing must I do really to live?' Jesus said to him, ' Man, obey the law and the prophets.' He said, ' I have done so.' Jesus said to him, ' Go, sell all that you possess, distribute it among the poor, and come, follow me!' The rich man began to scratch his head because he did not like this command. The Lord said to him, ' Why do you say that you have obeyed the law and the prophets? For it is written in the law, " You must love your neighbour as yourself," and look you—there are many brothers of yours, sons of Abraham, who are dying of hunger, and your house is full of many good things, and not one single thing goes out of it to them.'

And He turned and said to Simon, his disciple, who was sitting beside Him, ' Simon, son of Jonas, it is easier for a camel to go through the eye of a needle than for a rich man to enter the Kingdom of Heaven.' '' There we have the secret and the tragedy of this rich ruler. He was living utterly selfishly. He was rich, and yet he gave nothing away. His real God was comfort, and the thing he really worshipped was his own possessions and his wealth. That is why Jesus told him to give it all away. There is many a man who uses such wealth as he has to bring comfort and joy and good to his fellow men; but this man used it for nobody but himself. If a man's god is that to which he gives all his time, his thought, his energy, his devotion, then wealth was his god. If he was ever to find happiness he must be done with all that and live for others with the same intensity as he had so long lived for himself.

Jesus went on to say that it was easier for a camel to go through the eye of a needle than for a rich man to enter the Kingdom of God. Quite often the rabbis talked of an elephant trying to get through the eye of a needle as a picture of something fantastically impossible. But Jesus' picture may have one of two origins. (i) It is said that beside the great gate into Jerusalem through which traffic went there was a little gate just wide and high enough for a man to get through. It is said that that little gate was called the needle's eye, and the picture is that of a camel trying to struggle through that little gate. (ii) The Greek word for a camel is *kamelos*. In this age of Greek there was a tendency for the vowel sounds to become very like each other, and there was another word which would sound almost exactly the same—the word *kamilos*, which means *a ship's hawser*. It may well be that what Jesus said was that it would be easier to thread a needle with a ship's hawser than for a rich man to enter the Kingdom of God. Why should it be so? The whole tendency of possessions is to shackle a man's thoughts to this earth. He has so big a stake in earth that he never wants to leave

it, and never thinks of anything else. It is not a sin to
have much wealth—but it is a great danger to the soul
and a great responsibility.

Peter pointed out that he and his fellow disciples had
left all to follow Jesus; and Jesus promised them that no
man would ever give up anything for the Kingdom of God
but he would be repaid many times over. It is the experience of all Christian folk that that is true. Once someone,
thinking of the trials he had endured, and the sorrows
he had borne, how he had lost his wife and ruined his health
in Africa, said to David Livingstone, " What sacrifices you
have made! " Livingstone answered, " Sacrifices? I never
made a sacrifice in all my life." For the man who walks
the Christian way there may be things the world calls
hard, but, beyond them all and through them all, there is
a peace which the world cannot give, and cannot take
away, and a joy that no man taketh from him.

THE WAITING CROSS

Luke 18: 31-34

> Jesus took The Twelve and said to them, " Look
> you—we are going up to Jerusalem, and everything
> that was written through the prophets about the
> Son of Man will be fulfilled. He will be handed over
> to the Gentiles; and He will be mocked and cruelly
> treated; and spat upon; and they will scourge Him
> and kill Him; and on the third day He will rise
> again." But they did not understand these things;
> this word was hidden from them; and they did not
> grasp what was being said.

THERE are two kinds of courage. There is the courage of
the man who, suddenly and without warning, is confronted
with some emergency or some crisis, and who unhesitatingly
and even recklessly flings himself into it without time to
think. There is the courage of the man who sees the
terrible situation looming ahead, and who knows that

nothing short of flight can avoid it, and who goes stead-
fastly and inflexibly on. There is no question which is the
higher courage. Many a man is capable of the heroic
action on the spur of the moment; it takes a man of
supreme courage to go on to face something which haunts
him for days ahead, and which, by turning back, he could
escape. In a novel a writer paints a picture of two children
walking along the road playing their children's games.
The one said to the other, " When you're walking along the
road, do you ever pretend that there is something terrible
just around the next corner waiting for you; and you've
got to go and face it? It makes it so exciting." With
Jesus it was no game of let's pretend. It was the grim
truth that there was something terrible waiting for Him.
He knew what crucifixion was like; He had seen it; and
yet He went on. If Jesus was nothing else He would still
be one of the most heroic figures of all time.

In face of Jesus' frequent warning of what was going to
happen to Him in Jerusalem we must often have wondered
why, when the Cross came, it was such a shock and such
a shattering blow to His disciples. The truth is that they
simply could not take in what He was saying to them.
They were obsessed with the idea of a conquering King;
they still clung to that hope that He would let loose His
power in Jerusalem and blast His enemies off the face of
the earth. Here is a great warning to every listener.
There are none so blind as those who refuse to see. The
human mind has a way of listening only to what it wants
to hear. There is a kind of wishful thinking which in its
heart of hearts believes that the unpleasant truth cannot
be true, and that the thing it does not want to happen
cannot happen. A man must ever struggle against the
human tendency to hear only what he wants to hear.

One thing more we must note. Jesus never foretold
the Cross without foretelling the Resurrection. He knew
that the shame lay before Him, but He was equally certain
that the glory lay before Him too. He knew what the

malice of men could do, but He knew also what the power of God could do. It was in the certainty of ultimate victory that He faced the apparent defeat of the Cross. He knew that without a cross there can never be any crown.

THE MAN WHO WOULD NOT BE SILENCED

Luke 18: 35-43

> When Jesus was approaching Jericho, a blind man was sitting by the wayside begging. When he heard the crowd passing through he asked what it meant. They told him, " Jesus of Nazareth is passing by." He shouted, " Jesus, Son of David, have pity on me! " Those who were going on in front rebuked him and told him to be quiet, but he cried all the more, " Son of David, have pity on me." Jesus stood, and ordered him to be brought to Him. When he had come near He asked him, " What do you want me to do for you? " He said, " Lord, that I may receive my sight." Jesus said to him, " Receive your sight; your faith has made you well." And immediately he received his sight and followed Him glorifying God, and, when the people saw it, they all gave praise to God.

THE one thing which stands out in this story is the sheer, desperate persistence of the blind man. Jesus was on His way to Jerusalem to the Passover. At such a time pilgrims travelled in bands together. One of the commonest ways for a Rabbi to teach was to discourse as he walked. That was what Jesus was doing, and the rest of the pilgrim band were crowding close around Him, not to miss anything that He might say. As such a pilgrim band passed through a village or a town those who themselves could not go to the feast lined the wayside to see the pilgrims pass and to bid them godspeed on the way. It was amongst the crowd that the blind man was sitting. When he heard the murmur of the crowd he asked what was happening, and he was told that Jesus was passing by. Immediately he cried out to Jesus for help and healing. Thereupon everyone tried to silence him. The people round Jesus were missing what Jesus was saying because of the clamour of this blind man. But the man would not be silenced. He shouted again. The word used for the shouts of the blind man is quite different in verse 39 from verse 38. In verse 38 the word describes an ordinary loud shout to attract attention. In verse 39 the word is the word used to describe the instinctive shout of ungovernable emotion, a scream, an almost animal cry. The word well shows the utter desperation of the man. So Jesus stopped, and the blind man found the healing he so passionately desired.

This story tells us two things.

(i) It tells us something about the blind man. He was determined to come face to face with Jesus. Nothing would stop him. He refused to be silent, and he refused to be restrained. His sense of need drove him relentlessly into the presence of Jesus. If a man wants a miracle that is the spirit that he must show. It is not just a gentle, sentimental longing that really taps the power of God; but the passionate, intense desire of the very depths of the human heart will never be disappointed.

(ii) It tells us something about Jesus. Jesus at the moment was discoursing to the crowd like any rabbi. But at the blind man's cry of need He stopped, the discourse forgotten. For Jesus it was always more important to act than to talk. Words always took second place to deeds. Here was a human soul in need. Discourse must end and action begin. Someone has said that so many teachers are like men throwing chatty remarks to a man drowning in a tempestuous sea. Jesus was never like that; He did not talk; He leaped to the rescue of the man. There is many a man who could not put two sentences together, but others love him for he is kind. Men may respect an orator, but they love a man with helping hands. Men admire a man with a great mind, but they love a man with a big heart.

THE GUEST OF THE MAN WHOM ALL MEN DESPISED

Luke 19: 1-10

Jesus entered Jericho and was passing through it. And—look you—there was a man called Zacchæus by name, and he was commissioner of taxes, and he was rich. He was seeking to see who Jesus was, and he could not for the crowd, because he was short in height. So he ran on ahead and climbed up into a sycomore tree, for He was to pass that way. When Jesus came to the place He looked up and said to him, "Zacchæus! Hurry and come down! for this very day I must stay at your house." So he hurried and came down, and welcomed Him gladly; and when they saw it they all murmured, "He has gone in to be the guest of a man who is a sinner." Zacchæus stood and said to the Lord, "Look you—half of my goods, Lord, I hereby give to the poor. If I have taken anything from any man by fraud I give it back to him four times over." Jesus said to him, "To-day salvation has come to this house, because he also is a son of Abraham; for the Son of Man came to seek and to save that which was lost."

JERICHO was a very wealthy, and a very important town. She lay in the Jordan valley, and she commanded both the approach to Jerusalem and the crossings of the river which gave access to the lands east of the Jordan. She had a great palm forest and world famous balsam groves which perfumed the air for miles around. Her gardens of roses were known far and wide. Men called her "The City of Palms." Josephus called her "a divine region," "the fattest in Palestine." The Romans carried her dates and balsam to world-wide trade and fame. All this combined to make her one of the greatest taxation centres in Palestine. We have already seen the taxes which the tax-collectors collected, and the wealth which they rapaciously acquired (Luke 5: 27-32). Zacchæus was a man who had reached the top of his profession, and he was also the best hated man in the district. There are three stages in the story of Zacchæus.

243

(i) Zacchæus was wealthy, but he was not happy. Inevitably he was lonely, for he had chosen a way that made him an outcast. He had heard of this Jesus who welcomed tax-collectors and sinners, and he wondered if He would have any word for him. Despised and hated by men, Zacchæus was reaching after the love of God.

(ii) Zacchæus determined to see Jesus, and he would let nothing stop him. For Zacchæus, to mingle with the crowd at all was a courageous thing to do, for many a man would take the chance to get a nudge, or kick, or push at this little tax-collector. It was an opportunity not to be missed. Zacchæus would be black and blue with bruises that day. He could not see—the crowd took an ill delight in making sure that he could not see. So he ran on ahead and climbed a fig-mulberry tree. A traveller describes the tree as being like " the English oak, and its shade is most pleasing. It is consequently a favourite wayside tree . . . It is very easy to climb, with its short trunk and its wide lateral branches forking out in all directions." Things were not easy for Zacchæus, but the little man had the courage of desperation.

(iii) Zacchæus took steps to show all the community that he was a changed man. When Jesus announced that He would stay that day at his house, and when he discovered that he had found a new and wonderful friend, immediately Zacchæus took a decision. He decided to give half of his goods to the poor; the other half he did not intend to keep to himself but to use to make restitution for the frauds of which he had been self-confessedly guilty. In his restitution he went far beyond what was legally necessary. Only if robbery was a deliberate and violent act of destruction was a fourfold restitution necessary. (Exodus 22: 1.) If it had been ordinary robbery, and the original goods were not restorable, double the value had to be repaid. (Exodus 22: 4, 7.) If voluntary confession was made, and voluntary restitution offered, the value of the original goods had to be paid, plus one-fifth. (Leviticus 6: 5;

THE GOSPEL OF LUKE

Numbers 5: 7.) Zacchæus was determined to do far more than the law demanded. He showed by his deeds that he was a changed man. Dr. Boreham has a terrible story. There was a meeting in progress at which several women were giving their testimony. One woman kept grimly silent. She was asked to testify, and she refused. She was asked why, and she answered, " Four of these women who have just given their testimony owe me money, and I and my family are half-starved because we cannot buy food." A testimony is utterly worthless unless it is backed by deeds which guarantee its sincerity. It is not a mere change of words which Jesus Christ demands, but a change of life.

(iv) So the story ends with the great words, The Son of Man came to seek and to save that which was lost. We must always be careful how we regard the meaning of this word *lost*. In the New Testament it does not mean damned or doomed. It simply means *in the wrong place*. A thing is lost when it has got out of its own place into the wrong place, and when we find such a thing, we return it to the place it ought to occupy. A man is lost when he has wandered away from God; and he is found when once again he takes his rightful place as an obedient child in the household and the family of his Father.

THE KING'S TRUST IN HIS SERVANTS

Luke 19: 11-27

> As they were listening to these things Jesus went on to tell them a parable because He was near Jerusalem, and they were thinking that the Kingdom of God was going to appear immediately. So He said, " There was a noble man who went into a distant country to receive a kingdom for himself and then to return. He called ten of his own servants and gave them £5 each and said to them, ' Trade with these until I come.' His citizens hated him, and they despatched an embassy after him, saying, ' We do not wish this man to be king over us.' When he had received the

245

kingdom and had returned, he ordered the servants to whom he had given the money to be called to him, that he might know what they had made by trading with it. The first came and said, ' Sir, your £5 has produced £50.' So he said to him, ' Well done, good servant! Because you have shown yourself faithful in a little thing, you shall have authority over ten cities.' And the second came and said to him also, ' Sir, your £5 has made £25.' He said to him also, ' You, too, are to be promoted over five cities.' Another came to him and said, ' Sir, here is your £5, which I was keeping laid away in a towel, for I was afraid of you, because I know that you are a hard man. You take up what you did not put down and you reap what you did not sow.' He said to him, ' Out of your own mouth I judge you, wicked servant. You knew that I am a hard man, taking up what I did not put down, and reaping what I did not sow. You ought, therefore, to have given my money to the bankers, so that when I came, I would have received it plus interest.' He said to those standing by, ' Take the £5 from him and give it to him who has £50.' ' They said to him, ' Sir, he has £50.' I tell you, that to everyone who has it will be given; but from him who has not, even what he has will be taken away. But as for these my enemies, who did not wish to have me as their king—bring them here and hew them to pieces in my presence.''

THIS parable is quite unique among the parables of Jesus, because it is the only parable part of whose story is based on an actual historical event. It tells about a king who went away to receive a kingdom, and whose subjects did their best to stop him receiving it. When Herod the Great died in 4 B.C. he left his kingdom divided between Herod Antipas, Herod Philip and Archelaus. That division had to be ratified by the Romans, who were the overlords of Palestine, before it became effective. Archelaus, to whom Judæa had been left, went to Rome to persuade Augustus to allow him to enter into his inheritance, whereupon the Jews sent an embassy of fifty men to Rome to inform Augustus that they did not wish to have him as king. In point of fact, Augustus confirmed him in his inheritance, though without the actual title of king. Anyone in Judæa, on hearing the parable, would immediately remember the historical circumstances on which it was based. The parable of the King and his servants tells us about certain great facts of the Christian life.

(i) It tells us of the king's *trust*. He gave his servants the money and then he went away and left them to use it as they could and as they thought best. He did not in any way interfere with them, or, as it were, stand over them. He left them entirely to their own devices. That is the way in which God trusts us. Someone has said, " The nicest thing about God is that He trusts us to do so much by ourselves."

(ii) It tells us of the king's *test*. As always, this trust was a test. The king's test was whether or not a man was faithful and reliable in little things. Sometimes a man justifies a certain large inefficiency in the ordinary routine affairs of life by claiming that " he has a mind above trifles." God has not. It is precisely in these routine duties that the tests of God are testing men. There is no example of this like Jesus Himself. Of His thirty-three years of life Jesus spent thirty in Nazareth. Had He not discharged with absolute fidelity the tasks of the carpenter's shop in Nazareth, and the obligation of being the bread-winner of the family, God could never have given Him the supreme task of being the Saviour of the world.

(iii) It tells us of the king's *reward*. The reward that the faithful servants received was not a reward which they could enjoy by sitting down and folding their hands and doing nothing. The one was put over ten cities and the other over five. The reward of work well done was more work to do. The greatest compliment we can pay a man is to give him ever greater, and ever harder tasks to do. The great reward of God to the man who has satisfied the test is more trust.

(iv) The parable concludes with one of the inexorable laws of life. To him who has, more will be given; from him who has not, what he has will be taken away. If a man plays a game, if he goes on practising at it, he will play it with ever greater efficiency; if he does not, he will lose even the small knack and ability he had. If we discipline and train our bodies they will grow ever fitter and stronger; if we do not they grow fat and flabby, and we lose even the strength we had. If a schoolboy is learning Latin, if he goes on with his learning, the wealth and riches of Latin literature will open wider and wider to him; if he does not go on learning, he will forget even the Latin he knew. If we really strive after goodness, if we master this and that temptation, new vistas and new heights of goodness are ever open to us; if we give up the battle and take the easy way even the resistance power we once possessed will be lost and we will slip from even the little height to which we had attained. There is no such thing as standing still in the Christian life. We either get more or lose what we had. We either advance to greater heights or slip back every day.

THE ENTRY OF THE KING

Luke 19: 28-40

When Jesus had said these things, He went on ahead on the way up to Jerusalem. When He had come near Bethphage and Bethany, which is near the mount called the Mount of Olives, He despatched two of His disciples. " Go to the village opposite," He said. " As you come into it, you will find tethered a colt upon which no man has ever sat. Loose it and bring it here. And if any one asks you, ' Why are you loosing this colt?' you will say, ' The Lord needs it.' " Those who had been despatched went off, and found everything exactly as He had told them. And as they were loosing the colt, its owners said to them, "Why are you loosing the colt?" They said, " The Lord needs it "; and they brought it to Jesus. They flung their garments on the colt, and mounted Jesus on it. As He went they strewed their garments on the road. When He was now drawing near, at the descent from the Mount of Olives, the whole crowd of the disciples began to rejoice, and to praise God with shouts for all the deeds of power they had seen, saying, " Blessed is the King who comes in the name of the Lord! Peace in heaven and glory in the heights! " Some of the Pharisees who were in the crowd said to Him, " Teacher, rebuke your disciples." " I tell you," He answered, " if these keep silent, the stones will cry out."

FROM Jerusalem to Jericho was only twenty miles, and now Jesus had almost reached His goal. Jerusalem, His journey's end, lay just ahead. The prophets had a regular custom of which they made use again and again. When words were of no effect, when people refused to take in and to understand the spoken message, the prophets resorted to some dramatic action which put their message into a picture which none could fail to see. We will get examples of such dramatic prophetic actions in I Kings 11: 29-31; Jeremiah 13: 1-11; 27: 1-11; Ezekiel 4: 1-3; 5: 1-4. It was just such a dramatic action which Jesus planned now. He proposed to ride into Jerusalem in such a way that the very action would be an unmistakable claim to be the Messiah, God's Anointed King. We have to note certain things about this entry into Jerusalem.

(i) It was carefully planned. It was no sudden, impulsive action. Jesus did not leave things until the last moment. He had His arrangement with the owners of the colt. *The Lord needs it* was a pass-word chosen long ago.

(ii) It was an act of glorious defiance, and of superlative courage. By this time there was a price on Jesus' head. (John 11: 57). It would have been natural that, if He was going into Jerusalem at all, He should have slipped in unseen and hidden Himself in some secret place in the back streets. But He entered in such a way as to focus the whole lime-light upon Himself, and to occupy the centre of the stage. It is a breath-taking thing to think of a man with a price upon his head, an outlaw, deliberately riding into a city in such a way that every eye was fixed upon him. It is impossible to exaggerate the sheer courage of Jesus.

(iii) It was a deliberate claim to be king. It was a deliberate fulfilling of the picture in Zechariah 9: 9. But even in this Jesus underlined the kind of kingship which He claimed. The ass in Palestine was not the lowly beast that it is in this country. It was a noble beast. Only in war did kings ride upon a horse; when they came in peace they came upon an ass. So Jesus by this action came as the king who comes to His people in love and in peace, and not as the conquering hero, in martial splendour, whom the mob expected and awaited.

(iv) It was one last appeal. In this action Jesus came, as it were with pleading hands outstretched, saying, " Even now, will you not take me as your King? " Before the hatred of men engulfed Him, once again He confronted men with love's last invitation.

THE PITY AND THE ANGER OF JESUS

Luke 19: 41-48

When Jesus had come near, and when He saw the city, He wept over it. " Would that, even to-day," He said, " you recognised the things which would give you peace! But as it is, they are hidden from your eyes; for days will come upon you when your enemies will cast a rampart around you, and will surround you, and will hem you in on every side, and they will dash you and your children within you to the ground, and they will not leave one stone upon another within you, because you did not recognise the day when God visited you."

And He entered into the Temple and began to cast out those who were selling. " It is written," He said to them, " My house shall be a house of prayer, but you have made it a brigands' cave."

And He taught daily in the Temple. The chief priests and the scribes sought to kill Him, as did the chief men of the nation; and they could not discover anything they could do to Him, for all the people, as they listened to Him, hung upon His words.

In this passage there are three separate incidents.

(i) There is Jesus' lament over Jerusalem. From the descent of the Mount of Olives there is a magnificent view of Jerusalem in which the whole city lies full displayed to the sight. As Jesus came to that turn in the road He stopped and wept over Jerusalem. Jesus knew what was going to happen to the city. The Jews were even then embarking upon a career of political manœuvre and intrigue which ended in the destruction of Jerusalem in A.D. 70, when the city was so devastated that a plough was drawn across the midst of it. The tragedy was that if only they had abandoned their dreams of political power and had taken the way of Christ it need never have happened. The tears of Jesus are the tears of God when He sees the needless pain and suffering in which men involve themselves through their foolish rebellion against His will.

(ii) There is the cleansing of the Temple. Luke's account of it is very summary. Matthew's is a little fuller (Matthew 21: 12, 13). Why did Jesus, who was the very incarnation of love, act with such violence to the money changers and the sellers of animals in the Temple courts? First, let us look at the money changers. Every male Jew had to pay a Temple tax every year of half a shekel. That was equal to about 1s. 2d., but, in evaluating it, it must be remembered that that was equal to two days' pay for a working man. A month before the Passover booths were set up in all the towns and villages and it could be paid there; but by far the greater part of it was actually paid by the pilgrims in Jerusalem when they came to the Passover Feast. In Palestine all kinds of currencies were in circulation, and, for ordinary purposes, they were all—Greek, Roman, Tyrian, Syrian, Egyptian—equally valid. But this tax had to be paid either in exact half shekels of the Sanctuary or in ordinary Galilæan shekels. That is where the money changers came in. To change a coin of exact value they charged one *maah*, which was equal to 2d. If a larger coin was tendered a charge of one *maah* was made for the requisite half shekel and of another *maah* for the giving of change. It has been computed that these money changers made a profit of between £8,000 and £9,000 per annum. It was a deliberate ramp, and an imposition on poor people who could least of all afford it. Second, let us look at the sellers of animals. Almost every visit to the Temple involved its sacrifice. Victims could be bought outside at very reasonable prices ; but the Temple authorities had appointed inspectors, for a victim must be without spot and blemish. It was, therefore, far safer to buy victims from the booths officially set up in the Temple. But there were times when a pair of doves would cost as much as 15s. inside the Temple and considerably less than 1s. outside. Again, it was a deliberately planned victimization of the poor pilgrims. It was nothing more or less than legalized robbery. Still worse, these Temple shops were known as the Booths of Annas, and were the property of the family of the High Priest. That is why Jesus was brought first before Annas when He was arrested (John 18: 13). Annas was delighted to gloat over this Jesus, who had struck such a blow at his evil monopoly. Jesus cleansed the Temple with such violence, because the Temple traffic was being used to exploit helpless men and women. It was not simply that the buying and selling interfered with the dignity and the solemnity of worship. It was that the very worship of the house of God was being used to exploit the worshippers. It was the passion for social justice which burned in Jesus' heart when He took this drastic step.

(iii) There is something almost incredibly audacious in the action of Jesus in teaching in the Temple courts when there was a price on His head. This was sheer defiance. At the moment the authorities could not arrest Him, for the people hung upon His every word. But every time He spoke He took His life in His hands, and He knew well that it was only a matter of time until the end should come. The courage of the Christian should match the courage of his Lord. He left us an example that we should never be ashamed to show whose we are and whom we serve.

BY WHAT AUTHORITY?

Luke 20: 1-8

One day, while Jesus was teaching the people in the Temple and telling them the good news, the chief priests and scribes, with the elders came up and said to Him, " Tell us, by what authority do you do these things? Or, who is it who gives you this authority? " He said to them, " I, too, will ask you for a statement. Tell me, was the baptism of John from heaven or from men? " They discussed it with each other. " If," they said to each other, " we say, ' From heaven,' He will say, ' Why did you not believe in him?' But, if we say, ' From men,' all the people will stone us, for they are convinced that John was a prophet." So they answered that they did not know where it was from. Jesus said to them, " Neither do I tell you by what authority I do these things."

THIS chapter describes what is usually called *The Day of Questions*. It was a day when the Jewish authorities, in all their different sections, came to Jesus with question after question designed to trap Him, and when, in His wisdom, He answered them in such a way that He routed them, and left them speechless, and without an answer.

The first question is put by the chief priests, the scribes and the elders. The chief priests were a body of men composed of ex-High Priests and of members of these families from which the High Priests were drawn. The phrase describes the religious aristocracy of the Temple. The three sets of men—chief priests, scribes and elders— were the component parts of the Sanhedrin, the supreme Council and governing body of the Jews; and we may well take it that this is a question concocted and raised by the Sanhedrin with a view to formulating a charge against Jesus.

No wonder they asked Him by what authority He did these things! To ride into Jerusalem as He did, and then to take the law into His own hands and cleanse the Temple as He did, required some explanation. To the orthodox Jews of the day, Jesus' calm assumption of authority was at all times an amazing thing. No Rabbi ever delivered a judgment or made a statement without giving his authorities. He would say, " There is a teaching that . . ." Or he would say, " This was confirmed by Rabbi So and So when he said . . ." But none would have claimed that utterly independent authority with which Jesus moved among men. What they wanted was that Jesus should say bluntly and directly that He was the Messiah and the Son of God. Then they would have a ready-made charge of blasphemy, and could arrest Him on the spot. But He would not give that answer, for His hour was not yet come.

The answer of Jesus is sometimes described as a clever debating answer, used simply to score a point like a shrewd debater. But it is far more than that. He asked them to answer the question, " Whence came the authority of John the Baptist? Was it human, or was it divine?" Now the whole point is that their answer to Jesus' question would answer their own question. Every one knew how John had regarded Jesus, and how he had considered himself only the fore-runner of the one who was the Messiah. If they agreed that John's authority was divine then they had also to agree that Jesus was the Messiah, because John had said so. If they denied it the people would rise against them. Jesus' answer in fact asks the question, " Tell me— where do you think yourself I got my authority?" He did not need to answer their question if they answered his.

To face the truth may confront a man with a sore and a difficult situation; but to refuse to face it confronts a man with a tangle out of which there is no escape. The emissaries of the Pharisees refused to face the truth, and they had to withdraw, frustrated and discredited with the crowd.

A PARABLE WHICH WAS A CONDEMNATION

Luke 20: 9-18

Jesus began to speak this parable to the people. " A man planted a vineyard and let it out to tenants, and went away for a long time. At the proper time he despatched a servant to the tenants so that they might give him his share of the fruit of the vineyard. The tenants beat him and sent him away empty-handed. He went on to send another servant. They beat him, too, and maltreated him, and sent him away empty-handed. He went on to send a third. This one they wounded and threw out. The owner of the vineyard said, ' What am I to do? I will send my beloved son. It may be they will respect him.' When the tenants saw him they said to each other, ' This is the heir. Let us kill him so that the inheritance will be ours.' And they flung him out of the vineyard and killed him. What, then, will the owner of the vineyard do to them? He will come, and he will destroy these tenants, and will give the vineyard to others." When they heard this, they said, " God forbid!" He looked at them and said, "What, then, is this which stands written—' The stone which the builders rejected, this has become the head of the corner? Everyone who falls against that stone will be shattered; but if it falls on anyone it will wipe him out as the wind blows the chaff away.' "

THIS is a parable whose meaning is crystal clear. The vineyard stands for the nation of Israel. (cp. Isaiah 5: 1-7.) The tenants are the rulers of Israel into whose hands the nation was entrusted. The messengers are the prophets who were disregarded, persecuted and killed. The son is Jesus Himself. And the doom is that the place which Israel should have occupied is to be given to others.

The story itself is the kind of story which could, and did happen. Judæa in the time of Jesus was in the throes of economic trouble and labour unrest. There was many an absentee landlord who let out his lands in just such a way. The rent was seldom paid in money. It was either a fixed amount of produce, irrespective of the success or the failure of the harvest, or, it was a percentage of the crop, whatever it might be.

In its teaching this is one of the richest of the parables. It tells us certain things about man.

(i) It tells us of *human privilege.* The tenants did not make the vineyard. They entered into possession of it.

The owner did not stand over them with a whip. He went away and left them to work in their own way.

(ii) It tells us of *human sin*. The sin of the tenants was that they refused to give the owner his due, and that they wished to control that which it was the sole right of the owner to control. Sin consists in the failure to give God His proper place in life and in usurping the power which should be His.

(iii) It tells of *human responsibility*. For long enough the tenants were left to their own devices; but the day of reckoning came. Soon or late a man is called upon to give account for that which was committed to his charge.

The parable tells us certain things about God.

(i) It tells us of the *patience* of God. The owner did not strike at the first sign of rebellion on the part of the tenants. He gave them chance after chance to do the right thing. There is nothing so wonderful as the patience of God. If any man had created the world he would have taken his hand, and, in exasperated despair, he would have wiped it out long ago.

(ii) It tells us of the *judgment* of God. The tenants thought that they could presume on the patience of the master, that, to use the modern phrase, they could get away with it. But God has not abdicated. However much a man may seem to get away with it, the day of reckoning comes. As the Romans put it, " Justice holds the scales with an even and a scrupulous balance and in the end she will prevail."

The parable tells us something about Jesus.

(i) It tells us that *He knew what was coming*. He did not come to Jerusalem hugging a dream that even yet He might escape the Cross. Open eyed, and unafraid, He went on. When Achilles, the great Greek hero, was warned by the prophetess Cassandra that, if he went out to battle, he would surely die, he answered, " Nevertheless I am for going on." For Jesus there was no turning back.

(ii) It tells us that *He never doubted God's ultimate triumph.* Beyond the power of wicked men there stood the undefeatable majesty of God. Wickedness may seem for a time to prevail, but it cannot in the end escape its punishment.

> Careless seems the great Avenger, history's pages but record
> One death grapple in the darkness, 'twixt old systems and the Word;
> Truth forever on the scaffold, Wrong forever on the throne,
> Yet that scaffold sways the future, and behind the dim unknown,
> Standeth God within the shadows, keeping watch above His own.

(iii) It lays down most unmistakably *Jesus' claim to be the Son of God.* In it deliberately He removes Himself from the succession of the prophets. They were servants. He is *the Son.* In this parable He made a claim that none could fail to see to be God's Chosen King.

The quotation about the stone which the builders rejected comes from Psalm 118: 22, 23. It was a favourite quotation in the early Church as a description of the death and resurrection of Jesus. (cp. Acts 4: 11; I Peter 2: 7.)

CAESAR AND GOD

Luke 20: 19-26

> The Scribes and chief priests tried to lay hands on Jesus at that very hour; and they feared the people, for they realized that He spoke this parable to them. They watched for an opportunity, and they despatched spies, who pretended that they were genuinely concerned about the right thing to do, so that they might fasten on what He said and be able to hand Him over to the power and the authority of the governor. They asked Him, " Teacher, we know that you speak and

teach rightly, and you are no respecter of persons.
Is it lawful for us to pay tribute to Cæsar? Or not?"
He saw their subtle deception and said to them,
"Show me a shilling piece. Whose image and inscription is on it?" They said, "Cæsar's." "Well
then," He said to them, "give to Cæsar what belongs
to Cæsar, and give to God what belongs to God."
There was nothing in this statement that they could
fasten on to in the presence of the people. They were
amazed at His answer, and they had nothing to say.

HERE the emissaries of the Sanhedrin returned to the
attack. They suborned men to go to Jesus and to ask a
question as if it was really troubling their consciences.
The tribute to be paid to Cæsar was a poll-tax of one
denarius, about 9d., per year. Everyone from 14 to 65
had to pay that simply for the privilege of existing. This
tribute was a burning question in Palestine, and had been
the cause of more than one rebellion. It was not the merely
financial question which was at stake. The tribute was not
regarded as a heavy imposition, and was in fact no real
burden at all. The issue at stake was this—the fanatical
Jews claimed that they had no king but God, and held
that it was wrong to pay tribute to anyone other than God.
The question was a religious question, for which there were
many who were willing to die. So, then, these emissaries
of the Sanhedrin attempted to impale Jesus on the horns
of a dilemma. If He said that the tribute should not be
paid, they would at once report Him to Pilate and arrest
would follow as the night the day. If He said that it should
be paid, He would alienate many of His supporters,
especially the Galilæans, whose support was so strong.
Jesus answered them on their own grounds. He asked to
be shown a *denarius*. Now, in the ancient world, the sign
of kingship was the issue of currency. For instance, the
Maccabees had immediately issued their own currency
whenever Jerusalem was freed from the Syrians. Further,
it was universally admitted that to have the right to issue
currency carried with it the right to impose taxation. If a

man had the right to put his image and superscription on a coin, *ipso facto* he had acquired the right to impose taxation. So Jesus said, " If you accept Cæsar's currency and use it, you are bound to accept Cæsar's right to impose taxes "; " *but*," He went on, " there is a domain in which Cæsar's writ does not run and which belongs wholly to God."

(i) If a man lives in a state, and enjoys all the privileges of a state, he cannot divorce himself from that state. The more honest a man is, the better citizen he will be. There should be no better and no more conscientious citizens of any state than Christians; and one of the tragedies of modern life is that Christians will not take their part in the government of the state. If they abandon their responsibilities, and leave materialistic politicians to govern the country, they cannot complain about what is happening and what will happen.

(ii) Nonetheless it remains true that in the life of the Christian, God has the last word and not the state. The voice of conscience is louder than the voice of any man-made laws. The Christian is at once the servant and the conscience of the state. Just because he is the best of citizens he will refuse to do what a Christian citizen cannot do. He will at one and the same time fear God and honour the king.

THE SADDUCEES' QUESTION

Luke 20: 27-40

> Some of the Sadducees, who say that there is no resurrection, came to Jesus and asked Him, " Teacher, Moses wrote to us that, if a man's married brother dies without leaving any children, his brother must take his wife and raise up descendants for his brother. Now there were seven brothers. The first took a wife and died childless. The second and the third also took her; and in the same way the whole seven left no children and died. Later the wife died too. Whose wife will she be at the resurrection, for the seven had

her to wife? " Jesus said to them, " The sons of this age marry and are married. But those who are deemed worthy to obtain that age and the resurrection from the dead neither marry or are married, for they cannot die any more, for they are like angels and they are sons of God, for they are the sons of the resurrection. That the dead are raised even Moses indicated in the passage about the bush, when he called the Lord, the God of Abraham, the God of Isaac and the God of Jacob. God is not the God of the dead but of the living, for all live to Him." Some of the Scribes said, " Teacher, you have spoken well "; and they no longer dared to ask Him any question.

WHEN the emissaries of the Sanhedrin had been finally silenced the Sadducees appeared on the scene. The whole point of their question depends on two things. (i) It depends upon the levirate law of marriage. (Deuteronomy 25: 5.) According to that law if a man died childless, his brother must marry the widow and beget children to carry on the line. It is far from likely that that law was operative in the time of Jesus, but it was included in the Mosaic regulations, and therefore the Sadducees regarded it as binding. (ii) It depends upon the beliefs of the Sadducees. Sadducees and Pharisees are often mentioned together, but in beliefs they were poles apart. (*a*) The Pharisees were entirely a religious body. They had no political ambitions, and were content with any government which allowed them to carry out the ceremonial law. The Sadducees were few but very wealthy. The priests and the aristocrats were nearly all Sadducees. They were the governing class; and they were largely collaborationist with Rome. It usually happens that the wealthy are collaborationist in any occupied country simply because they do not wish to lose their wealth, their comfort and their place, and are prepared to collaborate in order to keep them. (*b*) The Pharisees accepted the scriptures plus all the thousand detailed regulations and rules of the oral and ceremonial law, such as the Sabbath law and the laws about hand washing. The Sadducees accepted only the written law of the Old Testament. And in the Old Testament they stressed only the law of Moses and set no store on the prophetic books. (c) The Pharisees believed in the resurrection from the dead and in angels and spirits. The Sadducees held that there was no resurrection from the dead and that there were no angels or spirits. (d) The Pharisees believed in fate. They believed that a man's life was planned and ordered by God. The Sadducees believed in unrestricted free-will. (e) The Pharisees believed in and hoped for the coming of the Messiah; the Sadducees did not. For them the coming of the Messiah would have been a disturbance of their carefully ordered lives. The Sadducees, then, came with this question about who would be the husband in heaven of the woman who was married to seven different men. They regarded such a question as the kind of thing that made belief in the resurrection of the body ridiculous. Jesus gave them an answer which has a permanently valid truth in it. He said that we must not think of heaven in terms of this earth. Life there will be quite different, because we will be quite different. It would save a mass of misdirected ingenuity, and not a little heartbreak, if we ceased to speculate on what heaven is like and left things to the love of God.

But Jesus went further. As we have said, the Sadducees did not believe in the resurrection of the body. They declared they could not believe in it because there is no information about it, still less any proof of it, in the books of the law which Moses was held to have written. So far no Rabbi had been able to meet them on that ground; but Jesus did. He pointed out that Moses himself had heard God say, " I am the God of Abraham, the God of Isaac and the God of Jacob " (Exodus 3: 1-6), and that it was impossible that God should be the God of the dead. Therefore Abraham and Isaac and Jacob are still alive. Therefore there is such a thing as the resurrection of the body. No wonder the Scribes declared it to be a good answer, for Jesus had met the Sadducees on their own ground and had defeated them.

It may well be that we find this an arid passage. It deals with questions which were burning questions in the time of Jesus by arguments which a Rabbi would find completely convincing but which are not convincing to the modern mind. But out of this very aridity there emerges one great truth for anyone who teaches or who wishes to commend Christianity to his fellows. *Jesus used arguments that the people He was arguing with could understand.* He talked to people in their own language; He met them on their own grounds; and that is precisely why the common people heard Him gladly. Sometimes, when one reads religious and theological books, one feels that all this may be true but it would be quite impossible to present it to the non-theologically minded man who, in the world and the Church, is in an overwhelming majority. Jesus used language and arguments which people could, and did, understand; He met people with their own vocabulary, on their own grounds, and with their own ideas. We will be far better teachers of Christianity, and far better witnesses for Christ, when we learn to do the same.

THE WARNINGS OF JESUS

Luke 20: 41-44

Jesus said to them, " How does David say that the Christ is his son? For David himself says in the Book of Psalms, ' The Lord said to my Lord, sit at my right hand until I make your enemies your footstool.' So David calls Him Lord, and how can He be his son? "

IT is worth while taking this little passage by itself for it is a passage which to us is very difficult to understand. The most popular title of the Messiah was Son of David. That is what the blind man at Jericho called Jesus (Luke 18: 38, 39), and that is how the crowds addressed Him at

His entry into Jerusalem (Matthew 21: 9). Here Jesus seems to cast doubts on the validity of that title. The quotation is from Psalm 110: 1. In Jesus' time all the Psalms were attributed to David, and this Psalm was taken to refer to the Messiah. In it David says that He heard God speak to His Anointed One, and tell Him to sit at His right hand until His enemies became His footstool; and in it David calls the Messiah *My Lord*. How can the Messiah be at once David's son and David's Lord?

Jesus was doing here what He so often tried to do. He was trying to correct the popular ideas of the Messiah. The popular idea of the Messiah was that under him the golden age would come and Israel would become the greatest nation in the world. It was a dream of political power. How was that to happen? There were many ideas about that, but the popular idea was that some great descendant of David would come to this earth to be the invincible captain and king. So then the title *Son of David* was inextricably mixed up with world dominion, with military prowess, and with material conquest. Really what Jesus was saying here is, " You think of the coming Messiah as Son of David; so he is; *but He is far more.* He is Lord." He is telling men that they must revise their ideas of what Son of David means. They must abandon these fantastic dreams of world power, and visualize the Messiah as the Lord of the hearts and lives of men. He was implicitly blaming them for having too little an idea of God. It is always man's tendency to make God in his own image, and thereby to miss the full majesty of God.

THE LOVE OF HONOUR AMONG MEN

Luke 20: 45-47

> While all the people were listening, Jesus said to His disciples, " Beware of the Scribes who like to walk about in long robes, and who love greetings in the market places, and the chief seats in synagogues,

and the top place at banquets. They devour widows'
houses and pretend to offer long prayers. These will
receive the greater condemnation."

THE honours which the Scribes and Rabbis expected to
receive, and did receive were quite extraordinary. They
had rules of precedence all carefully drawn up. In the
college, the most learned Rabbi took precedence; at a
banquet, the oldest. It is on record that two Rabbis came
in, after walking on the street, grieved and bewildered
because more than one person had greeted them with,
" May your peace be great," without adding, " My masters!"
They claimed to rank even above parents. They said,
" Let your esteem for your friend border on your esteem
for your teacher, and let your respect for your teacher
border on your reverence for God." " Respect for a
teacher should exceed respect for a father, for both father
and son owe respect to a teacher." " If a man's father
and teacher have lost anything, the teacher's loss has the
precedence, for a man's father only brought him into this
world; his teacher, who taught him wisdom, brought him
into the life of the world to come. . . . If a man's father
and teacher are carrying burdens, he must first help his
teacher, and afterwards his father. If his father and
teacher are in captivity, he must first ransom his teacher,
and afterwards his father." Such claims are almost incredible; it was not good for a man to make them; it
was still less good for him to have them conceded to him.
It was claims like that that the Scribes and Rabbis made.

Jesus also accused the Scribes of devouring widows'
houses. A Rabbi was legally bound to teach for nothing.
All Rabbis were supposed to have trades, and to support
themselves by the work of their hands, while their teaching
was given free. That sounds very noble, but it was deliberately taught that to support a Rabbi was an act of
the greatest piety. " Whoever," they said, " puts part of
his income into the purse of the wise is counted worthy of
a seat in the heavenly academy." " Whosoever harbours a

disciple of the wise in his house is counted as if he offered a daily sacrifice." " Let thy house be a place of resort to wise men." It is by no means extraordinary that impressionable women were the legitimate prey of the less scrupulous and more comfort-loving rabbis. At their worst, they did devour widows' houses.

The whole unhealthy business shocked and revolted Jesus. It was worse, because these men knew so much better and held so responsible a place within the life of the community. It is always a thing which God will condemn when a man uses a position of trust to further his own ends and to pander to his own comfort.

THE PRECIOUS GIFT

Luke 21: 1-4

> Jesus looked up and saw those who were putting their gifts into the treasury—rich people—and He saw a poor widow putting in half a farthing. So He said, " I tell you truly that this poor widow has put in more than all, for all these contributed to the gifts out of their abundance, but she, out of her need, has put in everything she had to live on."

In the Court of the Women in the Temple there were thirteen collecting boxes known as The Trumpets. They were shaped like trumpets with the narrow part at the top and the wider part at the foot. Each of the thirteen was assigned to offerings for a different purpose—for instance, for the wood that was used to burn the sacrifice, for the incense that was burned on the altar, for the upkeep of the golden vessels, and so on. It was near The Trumpets that Jesus was sitting. After the strenuous debates with the emissaries of the Sanhedrin and the Sadducees He was tired, and His head drooped between His hands. He looked up and He saw many people flinging their offerings into The Trumpets; and then there came a poor widow. All she had in the world was two *lepta*, two mites. A *lepton* was the smallest of all coins; the name means "the thin one." It was worth one-sixteenth of a penny; and, therefore, the offering of the widow woman was only half a farthing. But Jesus said that it far outvalued all the other offerings, because it was everything that she had.

There are two things which determine the value of any gift.

(i) There is *the spirit in which it is given*. A gift which is unwillingly extracted, a gift which is given with a grudge, a gift that is given for the sake of prestige or of self-display loses more than half its value. The only real gift is the gift which is the inevitable outflow of the loving heart, the gift which is given because the giver cannot help giving it.

(ii) There is *the sacrifice which it involves*. That which is a mere trifle to one man may be a vast sum to another. The gifts of the rich, as they flung their offerings into The Trumpets, did not really cost them much; but the two mites of the widow woman cost her everything she had. They no doubt gave having nicely calculated how much they could afford to give; she gave with that utterly reckless generosity which could give no more. Giving does not begin to be giving until it hurts. A gift only shows our love when we ourselves have had to do without something, or have had to work doubly hard, in order to give it. How few people give to God like that! Someone draws a picture of a man in church, lustily singing,

> Were the whole realm of Nature mine
>   That were an offering far too small;
> Love so amazing, so divine
>   Demands my life, my soul, my all,

while, all the time, he is carefully feeling the coins in his pocket to make sure that it is a sixpence and not a shilling that he will put into the collection which is immediately to follow.

He is an insensate man who can read the story of the widow and her two mites without searching and humiliating self-examination.

TIDINGS OF TROUBLE

Luke 21: 5-24

When some were speaking about the Temple, how it was adorned with lovely stones and offerings, Jesus said, " As for these things at which you are looking —days will come in which not one stone here will be left upon another, which will not be pulled down." They asked Him, " Teacher, when, then, will these things be? And what will be the sign when these things are going to happen? " He said, " Take care that you are not led astray. Many will come in my name, saying, ' I am He! ' and, ' The time is at hand! ' Do not go after them. When you hear of wars and upheavals, do not be alarmed; for these things must happen first; but the end will not come at once."

Then He said to them, " Nation will rise against nation, and kingdom against kingdom. There will be great earthquakes; in some places there will be famines and pestilences; there will be terrifying things, and great signs from heaven. Before all these things, they will lay hands upon you, and they will hand you over to the synagogues and prisons, and you will be brought before kings and governors for the sake of my name. It will all be an opportunity for you to bear witness to me. So, then, make up your minds not to prepare your defence beforehand, for I will give you a mouth and wisdom against which all your opponents will be unable to stand or argue. You will be handed over even by parents, and brothers, and kinsfolk and friends; some of you will be put to death; and you will be hated by all for the sake of my name. But not one hair of your head will perish. By your endurance you will win your souls.

" When you shall see Jerusalem encircled by armies, then know that the time of the desolation is at hand. At that time let those in Jerusalem flee to the mountains; let those who are in the midst of her go out of her; and let not those in the country districts enter into her, because these are days of vengeance, to fulfil all that stands written. Woe to those who, in those days, are carrying a child in the womb, or who have a babe at the breast. For great distress will be upon the earth and wrath upon all the people. They

shall fall by the edge of the sword, and they will be
taken away captive to all nations. Jerusalem will be
trodden underfoot by the Gentiles, until the times
of Gentiles are completed."

The Background of the Chapter
FROM verse 5 onwards this becomes a very difficult chapter.
Its difficulty lies in the fact that beneath it there lie four
different conceptions.

(i) There is the conception of *The Day of the Lord*. The
Jews regarded time as being in two ages. There was
The Present Age, which was altogether bad and evil, incapable of being cured, and fit only for destruction. There
was *The Age to come*, which was the golden age of God
and of Jewish supremacy. But in between the two there
would be *The Day of the Lord*, which would be a terrible
time of cosmic upheaval and destruction, the desperate
birth-pangs of the new age. It would be a day of terror.
"Behold the Day of the Lord cometh, cruel both with
wrath and fierce anger, to lay the land desolate; and He
shall destroy the sinners thereof out of it." (Isaiah 13: 9;
cp. Joel 2: 1, 2; Amos 5: 18-20 ; Zephaniah 1: 14-18.)
It would come suddenly. " The Day of the Lord cometh as
a thief in the night." (I Thessalonians 5: 2; cp. 2 Peter
3: 10.) It would be a day when the world would be
shattered. " The stars of the heaven and the constellations
thereof shall not give their light; the sun shall be darkened
in his going forth, and the moon shall not cause her light
to shine. . . . Therefore will I shake the heavens, and the
earth shall remove out of her place, in the wrath of the
Lord of hosts, and in the day of His anger." (Isaiah 13:
10-13; cp. Joel 2: 30, 31; 2 Peter 3: 10.) The Day of
the Lord was one of the basic conceptions of religious
thought in the time of Jesus. Everyone knew these
terrible pictures. In this passage verses 9, 11, 25, 26 take
their imagery from that.

(ii) There is *the prophesied Fall of Jerusalem*. Jerusalem
fell to the Roman armies in A.D. 70 after a desperate

siege in which the inhabitants were actually reduced to cannibalism and in which the city had to be taken literally stone by stone. Josephus, the Jewish historian, says that the incredible numbers of 1,100,000 people perished in the siege, and 97,000 were carried away into captivity. The Jewish nation was obliterated; and the Temple was fired and became a desolation. In this passage verses 5, 6, 20-24 clearly refer to that event still to come.

(iii) There is *the Second Coming of Christ.* Jesus was sure that He was to come again, and the Early Church waited for that coming. It will often help us to understand the New Testament passages about the Second Coming if we remember that much of the older imagery which had to do with The Day of the Lord was taken and attached to it. In this passage verses 27 and 28 clearly refer to it. Before the Second Coming it was expected that many false claimants to be the Christ would arise, and great upheavals take place. In this passage verses 7, 8, 9 refer to that.

(iv) There is the idea of *persecution to come.* Jesus clearly foresaw and foretold the terrible things His people would have to suffer for His sake in the days to come. In this passage verses 12-19 refer to that.

This passage will become much more intelligible and valuable if we remember that beneath it there is not one consistent idea, but four allied conceptions.

The Passage

It was a comment on the splendour of the Temple that moved Jesus to prophesy. In the Temple the pillars of the porches and of the cloisters were columns of white marble, forty feet high, and each made of one single block of stone. Of the offerings, the most famous was the great vine made of solid gold, each of whose clusters was as tall as a man. The finest description of the Temple as it stood in the time of Jesus is in Josephus' book, *The Wars of the Jews,* in book 5, section 5. Josephus, at one point, writes, " The outward face of the Temple in its front wanted nothing that was likely to surprise either men's minds or their eyes, for it was covered all over with plates of gold of great weight, and, at the first rising of the sun, reflected back a very fiery splendour, and made those who forced themselves to look upon it to turn their eyes away, just as they would have done at the sun's own rays. But the Temple appeared to strangers, when they were at a distance, like a mountain covered with snow, for, as to those parts of it that were not gilt, they were exceeding white." To the Jews it was unthinkable that the glory of the Temple should be shattered to dust.

From this passage we learn certain basic things about Jesus and about the Christian life.

(i) Jesus could read the signs of history. Others might be blind to the approaching disaster but He saw the avalanche about to descend. It is only when a man sees things through the eyes of God that he sees them clearly.

(ii) Jesus was completely honest. "This," He said to His disciples, "is what you must expect if you choose to follow me." Once in the middle of a great struggle for righteousness, an heroic leader wrote to a friend, "Heads are rolling in the sand; come and add yours." Jesus believed in men enough to offer them, not an easy way, but a way for heroes.

(iii) Jesus promised that His disciples would never meet their tribulations alone. It is the sheer evidence of history that the great Christians have written over and over again, when their bodies were in torture, and when they were awaiting death, of sweet times with Christ. A prison can be like a palace, a scaffold like a throne, the storms of life like summer weather, when Christ is with us.

(iv) Jesus spoke of a safety that overpasses the threats of earth. "Not one hair of your head," He said, "will be harmed." In the days of the 1914-18 war Rupert Brooke, out of his faith and his ideal, wrote these lines:

We have found safety with all things undying,
    The winds, and morning, tears of men and mirth,
The deep night, and birds singing, and clouds flying,
    And sleep, and freedom, and the autumnal earth.
We have built a house which is not for Time's throwing,
    We have gained a peace unshaken by pain for ever.
War knows no power. Safe shall be my going,
    Secretly armed against all death's endeavour:
Safe though all safety's lost; safe where men fall;
And if these poor limbs die, safest of all.

The man who walks with Christ may lose his life, but he
can never lose his soul.

WATCH!

Luke 21: 25-37

And there will be signs in sun, and moon, and stars,
and on earth the nations will be in distress and will
not know what to do in the roaring of the sea and of
the wave, while men's hearts will swoon from fear
and from foreboding of the things that are coming
on the world. The power of the heavens will be shaken;
and then they will see the Son of Man coming in a
cloud, with power and much glory. When these
things begin to happen, look up and lift up your
hearts for your deliverance is near.

And He spoke this parable to them, " Look at the
fig-tree and all the trees; whenever they put out
their leaves, you see it for yourselves and you know that
the harvest is near. So, whenever you see these
things happening, you know that the Kingdom of
God is near. This is the truth I tell you, that this
generation will not pass away until all these things
have happened. The heaven and the earth will pass
away, but my words will not pass away."

Take care lest your hearts grow heavy with dissi-
pation and drunkenness and anxieties for the things
of this life, and lest that day come suddenly upon
you like a trap closing, for it will come upon all who
dwell upon the face of the earth. Be watchful at all
times, and keep praying that you may have strength

to escape all the things that are going to happen, and to be able to stand before the Son of Man.

During the days Jesus was teaching in the Temple, but at night He went out and stayed in the Mount called the Mount of Olives; and all the people came early in the morning to listen to Him in the Temple.

THERE are two main conceptions here.

(i) There is the conception of *the Second Coming of Jesus Christ*. There has always been much vain and useless argument and speculation about the Second Coming. When it will be, and what it will be like, are not ours to know. But the one great truth which it enshrines is this —that history is going somewhere. The Stoics regarded history as circular. They held that every three thousand years or so the world was consumed by a great conflagration, and that then it started all over again, and history repeated itself. That meant that history was going nowhere, and that men were tramping round on a kind of eternal tread-mill. The Christian conception of history is that it has a goal and, at that goal, Jesus Christ will be Lord of all. That is all we know, and all we need to know.

(ii) There is stressed *the need to be upon the watch*. The Christian must never come to think that he is living in a permanent situation. He must be a man who lives in a permanent state of expectation. A novelist, in one of her books, has a character who will not stoop to certain things that others do. " I know," she said, " that some day the great thing will come into my life, and I want to keep myself fit to take it." We must live forever in the shadow of eternity, in the certainty that we are men who are fitting or unfitting themselves to appear in the presence of God. There can be nothing so thrilling as the Christian life.

(iii) Jesus spent the day amidst the crowds of the Temple; He spent the night beneath the stars with God. He won His strength to meet the crowds through His quiet time alone; He could face men because He came to men from the presence of God.

AND SATAN ENTERED INTO JUDAS

Luke 22: 1-6

> The Feast of Unleavened Bread, which is called the
> Passover, was near, and the chief priests and the
> Scribes searched to find a way to destroy Jesus, for
> they were afraid of the people. And Satan entered
> into Judas, who was called Iscariot, who belonged to
> the number of The Twelve. So he went away and
> discussed with the chief priests and captains how he
> might betray Jesus to them. They were glad, and
> they undertook to give him money. So he agreed,
> and he began to look for a suitable time to betray
> Him, when the mob were not there.

IT was at the Passover time that Jesus came to Jerusalem
to die. The Feast of Unleavened Bread is not, strictly
speaking, the same thing as the Passover. The Feast of
Unleavened Bread lasted for a week, from 15th to 21st
Nisan (April), and the Passover itself was eaten on 15th
Nisan. It commemorated the deliverance of the people
of Israel from their slavery in Egypt (Exodus 12). On
that night the angel of death smote the first-born son in
every Egyptian family; but *he passed over* the homes of
the Israelites, because the lintel of their doors was smeared
with the blood of the lamb to distinguish them. On that
night they left so quickly that, at their last meal, there
was no time to bake bread with leaven. It was unleavened
cakes they ate.

There were elaborate preparations for the Passover.
Roads were repaired; bridges were made safe; wayside
tombs were whitewashed lest the pilgrim should fail to
see them, and so touch them and become unclean. For a
month before, the story and the meaning of the Passover
was the subject of the teaching of every Synagogue. Two
days before the Passover there was in every house a ceremonial search for leaven. The householder took a candle
and solemnly searched every nook and cranny in silence,
and the last particle of leaven was thrown out. Every

male Jew, who was of age, and who lived within 15 miles of Jerusalem, was bound by law to attend the Passover. But it was the ambition of every Jew in every part of the world, at least once in his lifetime, to come to the Passover in Jerusalem. To this day, when Jews keep the Passover, in every land they pray that they may keep it next year in Jerusalem. Because of this, vast numbers came to Jerusalem at the Passover time. Cestius was governor of Palestine in the time of Nero, and Nero tended to belittle the importance of the Jewish faith. To convince Nero of it Cestius took a census of the lambs slain at one particular Passover time. Josephus tells us that the number was 256,500. Now, the law laid it down that the minimum number for a Passover celebration was 10. And that means that on that occasion, if these figures are correct, there must have been more than 2,700,000 pilgrims to the Passover. It was in a city crowded like that that the drama of the last days of Jesus was played out.

The atmosphere of the Passover time was always inflammable. The headquarters of the Roman government was at Cæsarea, and, normally, only a small detachment of troops was stationed at Jerusalem; but at the Passover time many more were drafted in. The problem which faced the Jewish authorities was how to arrest Jesus without provoking a riot. It was solved for them by the treachery of Judas. Satan entered into Judas. Two things stand out.

(i) Just as God is ever looking for men to be His instruments, so is Satan. A man can be the instrument of good or of evil, of God or of the devil. The Zoroastrians see this whole universe as the battle ground between the god of the light and the god of the dark, and, in that battle, a man must choose his side. We, too, know that a man can be the servant of the light or of the dark.

(ii) But it remains true that Satan could not have entered into Judas unless Judas had opened the door. There is no handle on the outside of the door of the human heart. It must be opened from within.

To every man there openeth
A high way and a low;
And every man decideth
The way his soul shall go.

It is in our own decision whether we will choose to be
the instrument of Satan or the weapon in the hand of God.
We can enlist in either service. God help us to choose
aright!

THE LAST MEAL TOGETHER

Luke 22: 7-23

There came the day of the Feast of Unleavened
Bread, on which the Passover had to be sacrificed.
Jesus despatched Peter and John. "Go," He said,
"and make ready the Passover for us that we may
eat it." They said to Him, "Where do you want us
to make it ready?" "Look you," He said to them,
"when you have gone into the city, a man will meet
you, carrying a jar of water. Follow him to the house
into which he enters; and you will say to the master
of the house, 'The Teacher says to you, "Where is
the guest room that I may eat the Passover with my
disciples?"' And he will show you a big upper room,
ready furnished. There, get things ready." So they
went away and found everything just as He had told
them; and they made ready the Passover.
When the hour came He took His place at table,
and so did His disciples. "I have desired with all my
heart," He said to them, "to eat this Passover with
you before I suffer, for I tell you that I will not eat
it until it is fulfilled in the Kingdom of God." He
received the cup, and gave thanks, and said, "Take
this and divide it among yourselves. For I tell you
that from now on I will not drink of the fruit of the
vine until the Kingdom of God has come." And He
took the bread, and gave thanks, and broke it, and
gave it to them, saying, "This is my body which is
being given for you. Do this so that you will remember
me." In the same way, after the meal, He took the
cup saying, "This cup is the new covenant made at
the price of my blood, which is shed for you. But—

275

look you—the hand of him who betrays me is on the table with me, for the Son of Man goes as it has been determined. But woe to that man by whom He has been betrayed"; and they began to question one another who of them it could be who was going to do this.

ONCE again Jesus did not leave things until the last moment; His plans were made. The better class houses had two rooms. The one room was on the top of the other; the house looked exactly like a small box placed on the top of a large one. The upper room was reached by an outside stair. During the Passover time all lodging in Jerusalem was free. The only pay a host might receive for letting lodgings to the pilgrims was the skin of the lamb which was eaten at the feast. A very usual use of an upper room was that it was the place where a Rabbi met with his favourite disciples to talk things over with them, and to open his heart to them. Jesus had taken steps to procure such a room. He sent Peter and John into the city to look for a man bearing a jar of water. To carry water was a woman's task. A man carrying a jar of water would be as easy to pick out as, say, a man using a lady's umbrella on a wet day. This was a pre-arranged signal between Jesus and a friend.

So the feast went on; and Jesus used the ancient symbols to give them a new meaning.

(i) He said of the bread, " This is my body." Herein is exactly what we mean by a sacrament. A sacrament is something, usually a very ordinary thing, which has acquired a meaning far beyond itself for him who has eyes to see and a heart to understand. There is nothing specially theological or mysterious about this. In the house of everyone of us there is a drawer full of things which can only be called junk, and yet we will not throw them out; we cannot make ourselves do so, because when we touch and handle, and look at them, they bring back to us this or that person, or this or that occasion. They are common things, but they have a meaning far beyond themselves. That is a sacrament. When Sir James Barrie's mother died, and when they were clearing up her belongings, they found that she had kept all the envelopes in which her famous son had sent her the cheques he so faithfully and lovingly sent. They were only old envelopes, but they meant much to her. That is a sacrament. When Nelson was buried in St. Paul's Cathedral a party of his sailors bore his coffin to the tomb. One who saw the scene writes, " With reverence, and with efficiency, they lowered the body of the world's greatest admiral into its tomb. Then, as though answering to a sharp order from the quarter deck, they all seized the Union Jack with which the coffin had been covered and tore it to fragments, and each took his souvenir of the illustrious dead." All their lives that little bit of coloured cloth would speak to them of the Admiral they had loved. That is a sacrament. The bread which we eat at the sacrament is common bread, but, for him who has a heart to feel and understand, it is the very body of Christ.

(ii) He said of the cup, " This cup is the new covenant made at the price of my blood." In the biblical sense, a covenant is a relationship between man and God. God graciously approached man; and man promised to obey, and to keep God's law. The whole matter is set out in Exodus 24: 1-8. Now the continuance of that covenant depends on man's keeping his pledge and obeying this law. Man could not and cannot do that; man's sin interrupts the relationship between man and God. All the Jewish sacrificial system was designed to restore that relationship by the offering of sacrifice to God to atone for sin. What Jesus said was this—" By my life, and by my death, I have made possible a new relationship between you and God. You are sinners. That is true. But because I died for you, God is no longer your enemy but your friend." It cost the life of Christ to restore the lost relationship of friendship between God and man.

(iii) Jesus said, " Do this and it will make you remember me." Jesus knew how easily the human mind forgets. The Greeks had an adjective which they used to describe time—" time," they said, " which wipes all things out," as if the mind of man were a slate, and time a sponge which wiped it clean. Jesus was saying, " In the rush and press of things you will forget me. Man forgets because he must, and not because he will. Come in sometimes to the peace and stillness of my house and do this again with my people—and you will remember."

It made the tragedy all the more tragic that at that very table there was one who was a traitor. Jesus Christ has at every communion table those who betray Him, for if, in His house, we pledge ourselves to Him, and then if, by our lives, we go out to deny Him, we too are traitors to His cause.

STRIFE AMONG THE DISCIPLES OF CHRIST

Luke 22: 24-30

> Strife arose amongst them about which of them was to be considered greatest. Jesus said to them, " The kings of the Gentiles exercise lordship over them, and those who have authority over them claim the title of Benefactor. It must not be so with you; but let him who is greatest among you be as the youngest; and let him who is the leader be as him who serves. Who is the greater? He who sits at table, or he who serves? Is it not he who sits at table? But I am among you as one who serves. You are those who have stayed with me in my tribulations; and I assign to you a kingdom, just as my Father has assigned one to me, that you may eat and drink at my table in my Kingdom; and you will sit upon thrones judging the twelve tribes of Israel."

IT is one of the most poignantly tragic things in the gospel story that the disciples could quarrel about precedence in the very shadow of the Cross. The seating arrangements at a Jewish feast were very definite. The table was arranged like a square with one side left open. At the top side of the square, in the centre, sat the host. On his right sat the guest of first honour; on his left the second guest; second on his right, the third guest; second on his left the fourth guest; and so on round the table. The disciples had been quarrelling about where they were to sit, for they had not yet rid themselves of the idea of an earthly kingdom. Jesus told them bluntly that the standards of His Kingdom were not the standards of this world. A king on earth was evaluated by the power he exercised. One of the commonest titles for a king in the east was *Euergetes*, which is the Greek for *Benefactor*. Jesus said, " It is not the king but the servant who obtains that title in my Kingdom."

(i) What the world needs is service. The odd thing is that the business world knows this. Bruce Barton points out that you will find by the road-side, over and over again, the sign, *Service Station*. It was the claim of one firm, " We will crawl under your car oftener and get ourselves dirtier than any of our competitors." The strange thing is that there is more argument about precedence, and more concern about people's " places " in the Church, than anywhere else. The world needs and recognizes service.

(ii) It is only the man who will consent to serve more than anyone else who will really rise high. It frequently happens that the ordinary worker will go home at 5.30 p.m. to forget his or her job until next morning, while the light will be burning in the office of the chief executive long after everyone else has gone home. Often passers-by would see the light burning in John D. Rockefeller's office when the rest of the building was in darkness. It is a law of life that service leads to greatness; and that the higher a man rises the greater the servant he must be.

(iii) We can found our life on giving or on getting; but the plain fact is that if we found it on getting we shall miss both the friendship of man and the reward of God, for no one ever loved a man who was always out for himself.

(iv) Jesus finished His warning by promising His disciples that those who had stood by Him through thick and thin would in the end reign with Him. God will be in no man's debt. Those who have shared in the bearing of Christ's Cross will some day share in the wearing of Christ's crown.

PETER'S TRAGEDY

Luke 22: 31-38 *and* 54-62

" Simon, Simon," Jesus said, " Look you, Satan has been allowed to have you that he may sift you like wheat. But I have prayed for you that your faith may not wholly fail. And you—when you have turned again—strengthen your brothers." He said to Him, " Lord, I am ready to go with you to prison and to death." " Peter," He said, " I tell you, the cock will not crow to-day before you have three times denied that you know me."

And He said to them, " When I sent you out without purse or wallet or shoes, did you lack for anything?" They said, " For nothing." But He said to them, " But now, let him who has a purse take it, and so with a wallet; and let him who has no sword sell his cloak and buy one. For I tell you that this which stands written must be fulfilled in me—' And he was reckoned with the lawbreakers '—for that which was written of me is finding its fulfilment." They said, " Lord, here are two swords." He said to them, " It is enough." . . .

So they seized Jesus and led Him away, and brought Him to the High Priest's house. Peter followed a long way away. When they had kindled a fire in the middle of the courtyard, and were sitting there together, Peter sat in the midst of them. A maidservant saw him as he sat in the firelight. She looked intently at him. " This man, too," she said, " was with Him." He denied it. " Woman," he said, " I do not know Him." Soon after another man saw him and said, " You, too, were one of them." Peter said, " Man, I am not! " About an hour elapsed and another insisted, " Truly this man, too, was with Him. I know it for he is a Galilæan." Peter said, " Man, I don't know what you are talking about." And immediately —while he was still speaking—a cock crew. And the Lord turned and looked at Peter. And Peter remembered what the Lord had said, that He said to him, " Before the cock crows to-day you will deny me three times." And he went out and wept bitterly.

WE take the story of the tragedy of Peter all in one piece. Peter was a strange paradoxical mixture.

(i) Even in spite of his denial Peter was fundamentally loyal. H. G. Wells once said, " A man may be a bad musician, and yet be passionately in love with music.' No matter what Peter did, however terrible his failure, he was nonetheless passionately devoted to Jesus. There is hope for the man who even when he is sinning is still haunted by goodness.

(ii) Peter was well warned. Jesus warned him both directly and indirectly. Verses 33-38 with their talk of swords is a strange passage. But what they mean is this— Jesus was saying, " All the time so far you have had me with you. In a very short time you are going to be cast upon your own resources. What are you going to do about it? The danger in a very short time is not that you will possess nothing; but that you will have to fight for your very existence." This is not an incitement to armed force. It is simply a vivid eastern way of telling the disciples that their very lives are at stake. No one could say that the seriousness, and the danger of the situation, and his own liability to collapse were not presented to Peter.

(iii) Peter was over-confident. It is an odd and a warning thing to remember that if a man says, " That is one thing I will never do," that is the very thing against which he must most carefully guard. Again and again castles have been captured because the attackers took the route which seemed unattackable and unscalable, because, at that very spot, the defenders were off their guard. Satan is subtle. He can attack at the point at which a man is too sure of himself, for there the man is likeliest to be unprepared.

(iv) In all fairness it has to be noted that Peter was one of the two disciples (John 18: 15) who had the courage to follow Jesus into the courtyard of the High Priest's house at all. Peter fell to a temptation which could only have come to a brave man. The man of courage always runs more risks than the man who seeks a placid safety. Liability to temptation is the price that a man pays when he is adventurous in mind and in action. It may well be that it is better to fail in a gallant enterprise than to run away and not even to attempt it.

(v) It was not in anger that Jesus spoke to Peter, but in sorrow that He looked at Him. Peter could have stood it if Jesus had turned and reviled him; but that voiceless, grief-laden look went to Peter's heart like a sword, and opened the fountain of tears.

> I think I'd sooner frizzle up,
> I' the flames of a burnin' 'Ell,
> Than stand and look into 'Is face,
> And 'ear 'Is voice say—" Well? "

The penalty of sin is to face, not the anger of Jesus, but the heartbreak in His eyes.

(vi) Jesus said a very lovely thing to Peter. " When you have turned," He said, " strengthen your brothers." It is as if Jesus said to Peter, " You will deny me; and you will weep bitter tears; but the result will be that you will be better able to help your brothers who are going through it." We cannot really help a man until we have been in the same furnace of affliction, or the same abyss of shame, as he has been. It was said of Jesus, " He can help others who are going through it because He has been through it Himself." (Hebrews 2: 18, 19.) To experience the shame of failure and disloyalty is not all loss, because it gives us a sympathy and an understanding that otherwise we would never have won.

THY WILL BE DONE

Luke 22: 39-46

> Jesus went out, and, as His custom was, to the Mount
> of Olives. The disciples, too, accompanied Him.
> When he came to the place, He said to them, " Pray
> that you may not enter into temptation." And He
> was withdrawn from them, about a stone's throw,
> and He knelt and prayed. " Father," He said, " if it
> is your will, take this cup from me; but not my will,
> but yours be done." And an angel from heaven
> appeared strengthening Him. He was in an agony,
> and He prayed still more intensely, and His sweat
> was as drops of blood falling upon the ground. So
> He rose from prayer and came to His disciples, and
> found them sleeping from grief. " Why are you
> sleeping? " He said to them. " Rise and pray that
> you may not enter into temptation."

THE space within Jerusalem was so limited that there was
no room for gardens. Many well-to-do people had private
gardens out on the Mount of Olives. Some wealthy friend
had given Jesus the privilege of using such a garden, and
it was to it that Jesus went to fight His lonely battle.
Jesus was only thirty-three, and no one wants to die at
thirty-three. He knew what crucifixion was like; He had
seen it. He was in an *agony*; the Greek word is used of
someone who is fighting a battle with sheer fear. There
is no scene like this in all history. This was the very
hinge and turning point in Jesus' life. He could have
turned back even yet. He could have refused the Cross.
The salvation of the whole world hung in the balance as
the Son of God literally sweated it out in Gethsemane;
and He won.

A famous pianist said of Chopin's Nocturne in C sharp
minor, " I must tell you about it. Chopin told Liszt, and
Liszt told me. In this piece all is sorrow and trouble.
Oh such sorrow and trouble!—until he begins to speak to
God, to pray; then it is all right." That is the way it was
with Jesus. He went into Gethsemane in the dark; He
came out in the light—because He had talked with God.

THE GOSPEL OF LUKE

He went into Gethsemane in an agony; He came out with the victory won, and with peace in His soul—because He had talked with God.

It makes all the difference in what tone of voice a man says, " Thy will be done."

(i) He may say it in a tone of helpless submission, as one who is in the grip of a power against which it is hopeless to fight. The words may be the death-knell of hope.

(ii) He may say it as one who has been battered into submission. The words may be the admission of complete defeat.

(iii) He may say it as one who has been utterly frustrated, and who sees that the dream can never come true. The words may be the words of a bleak regret or even of a bitter anger, which is all the more bitter, because it cannot do anything about it.

(iv) He may say it with the accent of perfect trust. That is how Jesus said it. He was speaking to one who was Father; He was speaking to a God whose everlasting arms were underneath and about Him even on the Cross. He was submitting, but He was submitting to the love that would never let Him go. Life's hardest task is to accept what we cannot understand; but we can do even that if we are sure enough of the love of God.

> God, Thou art love! I build my faith on that . . .
> I know Thee, who has kept my path, and made
> Light for me in the darkness, tempering sorrow
> So that it reached me like a solemn joy:
> It were too strange that I should doubt Thy love.

Jesus spoke like that, and when a man can speak like that, he can look up and say in perfect trust, " Thy will be done."

THE TRAITOR'S KISS

Luke 22: 47-53

While Jesus was still speaking—look you—there came a crowd, and the man called Judas, one of The

Twelve, was leading them. He came up to Jesus to kiss Him; but Jesus said to him, " Judas, is it with a kiss that you would betray the Son of Man? " When those who were around Him saw what was going to happen, they said, " Lord, shall we strike with the sword? " And one of them struck the servant of the High Priest and cut off his ear. Jesus answered, " Let it come even to this! " And He touched the ear and healed him. Jesus said to the chief priests and the Temple captains, and to the elders who had come to Him, " Have you come out with swords and cudgels as against a brigand? When I was daily with you in the Temple you did not lift your hand against me; but this is your hour, and the power of darkness is here."

JUDAS had found a way to betray Jesus in such a way that the authorities could come upon Him when the crowd were not there. He knew that Jesus was in the habit of going at nights to the Garden on the Hill, and there he led the emissaries of the Sanhedrin. The Captain of the Temple, or the Sagan, as he was called, was the official who was responsible for the good order of the Temple; the captains of the Temple here referred to were his lieutenants who were responsible for carrying out the actual arrest of Jesus. When a disciple met a beloved Rabbi, he laid his right hand on the Rabbi's left shoulder and his left hand on the right shoulder and kissed him. It was the kiss of a disciple to a beloved master that Judas used as a sign of betrayal.

There are four different parties involved in this arrest, and their actions and reactions are very significant.

(i) There was Judas, the traitor. He was the man who had *abandoned God*, and who had entered into a league with Satan. It is only when a man has put God out of his life and taken Satan in that he can sink to selling Christ.

(ii) There were the Jews, who had come to arrest Jesus. They were the men who were *blind to God*. When God incarnate came to this earth, all that they could think of

285

was how to hustle Him to a Cross. They had so long chosen their own way, and had so long shut their ears to the voice of God, and their eyes to His guidance, that in the end they could not recognise Him when He came. It is a terrible thing to be blind and deaf to God. As Mrs. Browning wrote,

" I too have strength—
 Strength to behold Him and not worship Him,
 Strength to fall from Him and not to cry to Him."
God save us from a strength like that!

(iii) There were the disciples. They were the men who, *for the moment had forgotten God.* Their world had fallen in, and they were sure the end had come. The last thing they remembered at that moment was God; the only thing they thought of was the terrible situation into which they had fallen. Two things happen to the man who forgets God, and who leaves God out of the situation. He becomes utterly terrified and completely disorganized. He loses the power to face life and to cope with life. In the time of trial life is unlivable without God.

(iv) There was Jesus. And Jesus was the one person in the whole scene who *remembered God.* The amazing thing about Jesus in the last days is His absolute serenity once Gethsemane was over. In those days, even at His arrest, it is He who seems to be in control; and even at His trial, it is He who is the judge. The man who walks with God can cope with any situation and look any foe in the eyes, unbowed and unafraid. It is he, and he alone, who can ultimately say,

" In the fell clutch of circumstance,
 I have not winced nor cried aloud.
Under the bludgeonings of chance
 My head is bloody, but unbow'd.

It matters not how strait the gate,
 How charged with punishments the scroll,
I am the master of my fate:
 I am the captain of my soul."

It is only when a man has bowed to God that he can talk and act like a conqueror.

MOCKING AND SCOURGING AND TRIAL

Luke 22: 63-71

> The men who were holding Jesus mocked Him and
> beat Him. They blindfolded Him and asked Him,
> " Prophesy! Who is it who hit you? " And many
> another insulting word they spoke to Him.
> And when it was day, the assembly of the elders
> of the people came together, the chief priests and the
> scribes ; and they led Him away to the Sanhedrin,
> saying, " Tell us if you are God's Anointed One."
> He said to them, " If I tell you, you will not believe
> me; if I ask you, you will not answer. But from now
> on the Son of Man will be seated at the right hand of
> the power of God." They all said, " Are you then
> the Son of God? " He said to them, " You say that
> I am." They said, " What further evidence do we
> need? We ourselves have heard it from His own
> mouth."

THROUGHOUT the night Jesus had been brought before the
High Priest. That was a private and unofficial examination.
Its purpose was for the authorities to gloat over Him, and,
if possible, to trip Him up in cross-examination, so that a
charge could be formulated against Him. After that, He
was handed over to the Temple police for safe-keeping,
and they played their cruel jests upon Him. When the
morning came He was taken before the Sanhedrin.

The Sanhedrin was the supreme court of the Jews.
In particular it had complete jurisdiction over all religious
and theological matters. It was composed of seventy
members. Scribes, Rabbis and Pharisees, Priests and
Sadducees, and elders were all represented on it. It could
not meet during the hours of darkness. That is why they
held Jesus until the morning before they brought Him
before it. It could meet only in the Hall of Hewn Stone
in the Temple court. The High Priest was the president
of it. We possess the rules of procedure of the Sanhedrin.
Perhaps they are only the ideal, which was never fully
carried out; but at least they allow us to see, what the
Jews, at their best, conceived that the Sanhedrin should

be, and how far their actions fell short of their own ideals in the trial of Jesus. The court sat in a semi-circle, in which every member could see every other member. Facing the court there stood the prisoner dressed in mourning dress. Behind him there sat the rows of the students and disciples of the Rabbis. They might speak in defence of the prisoner but not against him. Vacancies in the court were probably filled by co-option from these students. All charges must be supported by the evidence of two witnesses independently examined. A member of the court might speak against the prisoner, and then change his mind and speak for him, but not *vice-versa*. When a verdict was due, each member had to give his individual judgment, beginning at the youngest and going on to the most senior. For acquittal a majority of one was all that was necessary; for condemnation there must be a majority of at least two. Sentence of death could never be carried out on the day on which it was given; a night must elapse so that the court might sleep on it, so that, perchance, their condemnation might turn to mercy. The whole procedure was designed for mercy; and, even from Luke's summary account, it is clear that the Sanhedrin when it tried Jesus was far from keeping its own rules and regulations.

It is to be very carefully noted that the charge that the Sanhedrin finally produced against Jesus was one of blasphemy. To claim to be the Son of God was an insult to God's majesty, and was therefore blasphemy, and punishable by death.

It is the tragic fact that when Jesus asked for love He did not even receive simple justice. It is the glorious fact that Jesus, even when He had emerged from a night of malignant questioning, even when He had been mocked and buffetted and scourged, still had the utter confidence that He would be set down at the right hand of God, and that His triumph was sure. His faith defied the facts. He never for a moment believed that men in the end could defeat the purposes of God.

TRIAL BEFORE PILATE AND SILENCE BEFORE HEROD

Luke 23: 1-12

The whole assembly rose up and brought Jesus to Pilate. They began to accuse Him. "We found this man," they said, "perverting our nation, and trying to stop men paying taxes to Cæsar, and saying that He Himself is the Anointed One, a king." Pilate asked Him, "Are you the king of the Jews?" He answered, "You say so." Pilate said to the chief priests and to the crowds, "I find nothing to condemn in this man." They were the more urgent. "He is setting the people in turmoil," they said, "throughout all Judæa, beginning from Galilee to this place." When Pilate heard this, he asked if the man was a Galilæan. When he realised that He was under Herod's jurisdiction, he referred Him to Herod, who was himself in Jerusalem in these days. When Herod saw Jesus he was very glad, because for a long time he had been wishing to see Him, because he had heard about Him; and he was hoping to see some sign done by Him. He questioned Him in many words; but He answered him nothing. The chief priests and the Scribes stood by vehemently hurling their accusations against Him. Herod with his soldiers treated Jesus contemptuously, and after he had mocked Him and arrayed Him in a gorgeous dress, he referred Him back again to Pilate. And Herod and Pilate became friends with each other that same day, for previously they had been at enmity with each other.

THE Jews in the time of Jesus had no power to carry out the death sentence. Such sentence had to be passed by the Roman governor and carried out by the Roman authorities. It was for that reason that the Jews brought Jesus before Pilate. Nothing better shows their conscience-less malignity than the crime with which they charged Him. In the Sanhedrin the charge had been one of blasphemy, that He had dared to call Himself the Son of God. Before Pilate that charge was never even mentioned. They knew well that it would have carried no weight with Pilate, and that he would never have proceeded on a charge which would have seemed to him a matter of Jewish religion and superstition. The charge they levelled against Jesus was an entirely political charge, and it has all the marks of the minds and ingenuity of the Sadducees. It was really the aristocratic, collaborationist Sadducees who achieved the crucifixion of Jesus, in their terror lest He should prove a disturbing element and produce a situation in which they would lose their wealth, their comfort and their power. Their charge before Pilate was really three-fold. They charged Jesus (a) with seditious agitation; (b) with encouraging men not to pay tribute to Cæsar; (c) with the assuming the title king. Every single item of the charge was a lie, and they knew it. They resorted to the most calculated and malicious lies in their well-nigh insane desire to eliminate Jesus.

Pilate was not an experienced Roman official for nothing; he saw through them; and he had no desire to gratify their wishes. But neither did he wish to offend them. They had dropped the information that Jesus came from Galilee; this they had intended as further fuel for their accusations, for Galilee was notoriously " the nurse of seditious men." But to Pilate it seemed a way out. Galilee was under the jurisdiction of Herod Antipas, who, at that very time, was in Jerusalem to keep the Passover. So to Herod, Pilate referred the case of Jesus. Herod is one of the very few people to whom Jesus had absolutely nothing to say. Why did Jesus believe that there was nothing to be said to Herod?

(i) Herod regarded Jesus as a sight to be gazed at. To Herod, Jesus was simply a spectacle. Jesus was not a sight to be stared at; He was a king to be submitted to. Epictetus, the famous Greek Stoic teacher, used to complain that people came from all over the world to his lectures, to stare at him, as if he had been a famous statue, but not to accept and to obey his teaching. Jesus is not a figure to be gazed at but a master to be obeyed.

(ii) Herod regarded Jesus—quite bluntly—as a joke. He jested at Him; He clothed Him in a king's robe as an imitation king. To put it in another way—Herod refused to take Jesus seriously. He would show Him off to his court as an amusing curiosity, but there his interest stopped. The plain fact is that the vast majority of men still refuse to take Jesus seriously. If they took Him seriously they would pay more attention than they do to His words and to His claims.

(iii) There is another possible translation of verse 11. " Herod with his soldiers treated Jesus contemptuously." That could be translated, " Herod, with his soldiers behind him, thought that Jesus was of no importance." Herod, secure in his position as king, strong with the power of his bodyguard behind him, believed that this Galilæan carpenter did not matter. There are still those who, consciously or unconsciously, have come to the conclusion that Jesus does not matter, that He is a factor which can well be omitted from life. They give Him no room in their hearts and no influence in their lives and believe that they can easily do without Him. To the Christian, so far from being of no importance, Jesus is the most important person in all the universe.

THE JEWS' BLACKMAIL OF PILATE

Luke 23: 13-25

Pilate summoned the chief priests, and the rulers, and the people and said to them, " You brought me this man as one who was seducing the people from their allegiance; and—look you—I have examined Him in your presence, and, of the accusations with which you charge Him, I have found nothing in this man to condemn; and neither has Herod; for he sent Him back to us. Look you—nothing deserving death has been done by Him. I will therefore scourge Him and release Him." All together they shouted out, " Take this man away! And release Barabbas for us." Barabbas had been thrown into prison

because a certain disorder had arisen in the city, and
because of murder. Again Pilate addressed them,
because he wished to release Jesus. But they kept
shouting, "Crucify, crucify Him!" The third time
he said to them, "Why? What evil has He done?
I have found nothing in Him which merits sentence
of death. I will chastise Him and release Him."
But they insisted with shouts, demanding that He
should be crucified; and their voices prevailed. So
Pilate gave sentence that their demand should be
granted. He released the man who had been thrown
into prison for disorder and murder, the man they
asked for, and Jesus he delivered to their will.

THIS is an amazing passage. One thing is crystal clear—
Pilate did not want to condemn Jesus. He was well aware
that to do so would be to betray that impartial justice
which was the glory of Rome. He made no fewer than
four attempts to avoid passing sentence of condemnation.
He told the Jews to settle the matter themselves. (John
19: 6, 7.) He tried to refer the whole case to Herod. He
tried to persuade the Jews to receive Jesus as the prisoner
who was granted release at the Passover time. (Mark 15: 6.)
He tried to effect a compromise, saying that he would
scourge Jesus and then release Him. It is clear that
Pilate was cœrced into sentencing Jesus to death. How
could a Jewish mob cœrce an experienced Roman governor
into sentencing Jesus to death? It is literally true that the
Jews blackmailed Pilate into sentencing Jesus to death.
The basic fact is that, under impartial Roman justice,
any province had the right to report a governor to Rome
for misgovernment, and such a governor would be severely
dealt with. Pilate had made two grave mistakes in his
government of Palestine. In Judæa the Roman headquarters were not at Jerusalem but at Cæsarea. But in
Jerusalem a certain number of troops were quartered.
Roman troops carried standards which were topped by
a little bust of the reigning emperor. The emperor was
at this time officially a god. The Jewish law forbade any
graven image, and, in deference to Jewish principles,

previous governors had always removed the imperial images before they marched their troops into Jerusalem. Pilate refused to do so. He marched his soldiers in by night with the imperial image on their standards. The Jews came in crowds to Cæsarea to request Pilate to remove the images. He refused. They persisted in their entreaties for days. On the sixth day he agreed to meet them in an open space surrounded by his troops. He informed them that unless they stopped disturbing him with their continuous requests the penalty would be immediate death. " They threw themselves on the ground, and laid their necks bare, and said they would take death very willingly rather than that the wisdom of their laws should be transgressed." Not even Pilate could slaughter men in cold blood like that, and he had to yield. Josephus tells the whole story in *The Antiquities of the Jews*, Book 18, chapter 3. Pilate followed this up by bringing into the city a new water supply, and financing the scheme with money taken from the Temple treasury, a story which we have already told in the commentary on Luke 13: 1-4. The one thing the Roman government could not afford to tolerate in their far-flung empire was civil disorder. Had the Jews officially reported either of these incidents there is little doubt that Pilate would have been summarily dismissed. It is John who tells us of the ominous hint the Jewish officials gave Pilate, when they said, " If you let this man go you are not Cæsar's friend." (John 19: 12.) The Jews compelled Pilate to sentence Jesus to death by holding the threat of an official report to Rome over his head.

Here we have the grim truth that a man's past can rise up and confront him and paralyse him. If a man has been guilty of certain actions and conduct there are certain things which he has no longer the right to say. If he says them his past will be flung in his face. We must have a care not to allow ourselves any conduct which will some day despoil us of the right to take the stand we know we ought to take, and which will entitle people to say, " You of all men, have no right to speak like that."

But if such a situation should arise there is only one thing to do—to have the courage to face it and its consequences. That is precisely what Pilate did not possess. He sacrificed justice rather than lose his post; he sentenced Jesus to death in order that he might remain the governor of Palestine. Had he been a man of real courage he would have done the right, and taken the consequences, but his past made him a coward.

THE ROAD TO CALVARY

Luke 23: 26-31

> As they lead Jesus away, they took Simon, a Cyrenian, who was coming in from the country, and on him they laid the cross to carry it behind Jesus.
> There followed Him a great crowd of the people and of women who bewailed and lamented Him. Jesus turned to them. " Daughters of Jerusalem," He said, " do not weep for me, but weep for yourselves, and for your children, because—look you— days are on the way in which they will say, ' Happy are those who are barren, and the wombs that never bore, and the breasts which never fed a child.' Then they will begin to say to the mountains, ' Fall upon us!' and to the hills, ' Cover us!' For if they do these things when the sap is in the wood, what will they do when the tree is dry? "

WHEN a criminal was condemned to be crucified, he was taken from the judgment hall and set in the middle of a hollow square of four Roman soldiers. His own cross was then laid upon his shoulders. And he was marched to the place of crucifixion by the longest possible route. He was made to march by every road and street, and lane and alley, while before him there marched another soldier bearing a placard with his crime inscribed upon it, so that he might be a terrible warning to anyone else who was

THE GOSPEL OF LUKE

contemplating such a crime. That is what they did with
Jesus. He began by carrying His own Cross (John 19: 17);
but under the weight of it His strength gave out, and He
could carry it no farther. Palestine was an occupied
country, and any citizen could be immediately impressed
into the service of the Roman government. The sign of
such impressment was a tap on the shoulder with the
flat of the blade of a Roman spear. When Jesus sank
beneath the weight of His Cross, the Roman centurion
in charge looked round for someone to carry it. Out of
the country into the city there came Simon from far off
Cyrene, which is the modern Tripoli. No doubt he was a
Jew who all his life had scraped and saved so that he
might be able to eat one Passover at Jerusalem. The flat
of the Roman spear touched him on the shoulder and he
found himself, willy-nilly, carrying a criminal's cross. Try
to imagine the feelings of Simon. He had come to Jerusalem
to realise the cherished ambition of a lifetime, and he
found himself walking to Calvary carrying a cross. His
heart was filled with bitterness towards the Romans and
towards this criminal who had involved him in His crime.
But if we can read between the lines the story does not
end there. J. A. Robertson saw in it one of the hidden
romances of the New Testament. Mark describes Simon
as the father of Alexander and Rufus. (Mark 15: 21.)
Now you do not identify a man by the name of his sons
unless these sons are well-known people in the community
to which you write. There is general agreement that
Mark wrote his gospel to the Church at Rome. Now turn
to Paul's letter to the Church at Rome. Amongst the
greetings at the end he writes, " Salute Rufus, chosen
in the Lord, and his mother and mine." (Romans 16: 13).
So in the Roman Church there is Rufus, so choice a Christian
that he can be called one of God's chosen ones, with a
mother so dear to Paul that he can call her his mother in
the faith. It may well be that this Rufus is the same Rufus
who was the son of Simon of Cyrene, and his mother was

Simon's wife. It may well be that as he looked on Jesus Simon's bitterness turned to wondering amazement and finally to faith; that he became a Christian; and that his family became some of the choicest souls in the Roman Church. It may well be that Simon from Tripoli thought he was going to realize a life's ambition, and that he was going to celebrate the Passover in Jerusalem at last; that he found himself sorely against his will carrying a criminal's cross; that, as he looked, his bitterness turned to wonder and to faith; and that in the thing that seemed to be his shame he found his Saviour.

Behind Jesus there came a band of women who were weeping for Him. He turned and bade them weep, not for Him, but for themselves. Days of terror were coming. In Judæa there was no tragedy like a childless marriage; in fact childlessness was a valid ground for divorce. But the day would come when the woman who had no child would be glad that it was so. Once again Jesus was seeing ahead the destruction of that city which had so often before, and which had now so finally, refused the invitation of God. Verse 31 is a proverbial phrase which could be used in many connections. Here it means, If they do this to one who is innocent, what will they some day do to those who are guilty and who deserve it?

THERE THEY CRUCIFIED HIM

Luke 23: 32-38

Two others who were criminals were brought to be put to death with Jesus. When they came to the place which is called the place of a skull, there they crucified Him, and the two criminals, one on His right hand, and one on His left. And Jesus said, " Father, forgive them, for they do not know what they are doing." And, as they divided His garments, they cast lots for them. The people stood watching

and the rulers gibed at Him. " He saved others,"
they said. " Let Him save Himself if He really is
the Anointed One of God, the Chosen One." The
soldiers also mocked Him, coming and offering vinegar
to Him, and saying, " If you are the King of the Jews
save yourself." There was also an inscription over
Him, " This is the King of the Jews."

WHEN a criminal reached the place of crucifixion his
cross was laid flat upon the ground. Usually it was a
cross shaped like a T with no top piece against which the
head could rest. It was quite low, so that the criminal's
feet were only two or three feet above the ground. There
was a company of pious women in Jerusalem who made it
their practice always to go to crucifixions and to give the
victim a drink of drugged wine which would deaden the
terrible pain. That drink was offered to Jesus and He
refused it. (Matthew 27: 34). He was determined to
face death at its worst, with a clear mind and senses un-
clouded. The victim's arms were stretched out upon the
cross bar, and the nails were driven through his hands.
The feet were not nailed, but only loosely bound to the
cross. Half way up the cross there was a projecting piece
of wood, called the saddle, which took the weight of the
criminal, or the nails would have torn through his hands.
And then the cross was lifted and set upright in its socket.
The terror of crucifixion was this—the pain of that terrible
process was bad enough, but it was not enough to kill a
man, and the victim was left to die of hunger and of thirst
beneath the blazing noontide sun and the frosts of the
night. Many a criminal was known to have hung for a
week upon his cross until he died raving mad.

The clothes of the criminal were the perquisites of the
four soldiers among whom he marched to the cross. Every
Jew wore five articles of apparel—the inner tunic, the
outer robe, the girdle, the sandals and the turban. Four
were divided among the four soldiers. There remained

the great outer robe. It was woven in one piece without a seam. (John 19: 23, 24.) To have cut it up and divided it would have ruined it; and so the soldiers gambled for it in the shadow of the Cross. It was nothing to them that another criminal was slowly dying in agony.

The inscription which was set upon the cross was the same placard as was carried before a man as he marched through the streets to the place of crucifixion.

Jesus said many wonderful things, but He rarely said anything more wonderful than, " Father, forgive them, for they know not what they are doing." Christian forgiveness is an amazing thing. When Stephen was being stoned to death he too prayed, " Lord, lay not this sin to their charge." (Acts 7: 60.) There is nothing so lovely, and there is nothing so rare, as Christian forgiveness. When the unforgiving spirit is threatening to turn our hearts to bitterness, let us hear again our Lord praying for forgiveness for those who crucified Him, and let us hear His servant Paul saying to his friends, " Be ye kind to one another, tender-hearted, forgiving one another, even as God for Christ's sake hath forgiven you." (Ephesians 4: 32).

The idea that this terrible thing was done in ignorance runs through the New Testament. Peter said to the people in after days, " I know that, through ignorance, you did it." (Acts 3: 17.) Paul said that they crucified Jesus because they did not know Him. (Acts 13: 27.) Marcus Aurelius, the great Roman Emperor and the Stoic saint, used to say to himself every morning, " To-day you will meet all kinds of unpleasant people; they will hurt you, and injure you, and insult you; but you cannot live like that; you know better, for you are a man in whom the spirit of God dwells." Others may have in their hearts the unforgiving spirit; others may sin in ignorance; but we know better; we are Christ's men and women; and we must forgive as He forgave.

THE PROMISE OF PARADISE

Luke 23: 39-43

> One of the criminals who were hanged kept hurling insults at Jesus. " Are You not the Anointed One? " he said. " Save yourself and us." The other rebuked him. " Do you not even fear God? " he said. " For we too are under the same sentence and justly so, for we have done things which deserve the reward that we are reaping; but this man has done nothing unseemly." And he said, " Jesus, remember me when you come into your Kingdom." He said to him, " This is the truth—I tell you—to-day you will be with me in Paradise."

IT was of set and deliberate purpose that the authorities crucified Jesus between two known criminals. It was deliberately so staged to humiliate Jesus in front of the crowd, and to rank Him with robbers. Legend has been busy with the penitent thief. He is called variously Dismas, Demas and Dumachus. One legend makes him a Judæan Robin Hood who robbed the rich to give to the poor. The loveliest legend tells how the holy family were attacked by robbers when they fled with Jesus, as a little child, from Bethlehem to Egypt. Jesus was saved by the kindness of a youth who was the son of the captain of the robber band. The little baby Jesus was so lovely that the young brigand could not bear to lay hands on Him but set Him free, saying, " O most blessed of children, if ever there come a time for having mercy on me, then remember me and forget not this hour." So, they say, that the robber youth who had saved Jesus when He was a baby, met Him again on a Cross on Calvary; and this time Jesus saved Him.

The word Paradise is a Persian word meaning *a walled garden.* When a Persian king wished to do one of his subjects a very special honour he made him a companion of the garden, and he was chosen to walk in the garden with the king. It was more than immortality that Jesus promised the penitent thief. He promised him the honoured place of a companion of the garden in the courts of heaven.

Surely this story tells us above all things that it is never too late to turn to Christ. There are other things of which we must say, " The time for that is past. I am grown too old for that now." But we can never say that of turning to Jesus Christ. So long as a man's heart beats, the invitation of Christ still stands. As the poet wrote of the man who was killed as he was thrown from his galloping horse,

> " Between the stirrup and the ground,
>   Mercy I asked, mercy I found."

For us it is literally true that while there is life there is hope.

THE LONG DAY CLOSES

Luke 23: 44-49

> By this time it was about midday, and there was darkness over the whole land until 3 o'clock in the afternoon, and the light of the sun failed. And the veil of the Temple was rent in the midst. When Jesus had cried with a great voice, He said, " Father, into your hands I commend my spirit." When He had said this He breathed His last. When the centurion saw what had happened, he glorified God. " Truly," he said, " this was a good man." All the crowds, who had come together to see the spectacle, when they saw the things that had happened, went home beating their breasts. And all His acquaintances, and the women who had accompanied Him from Galilee, stood far off and saw these things.

EVERY sentence of this passage is rich in meaning.

(i) There was a great darkness as Jesus died. It was as if the sun itself could not bear to look upon the deed men's hands had done. The world is ever dark in the day when men seek to eliminate and to banish Christ.

(ii) The Temple veil was rent in twain. The veil was the veil which hid the Holy of Holies, that place wherein there dwelt the very presence of God, into which no man might ever go except the High Priest, and he only once a year, on the great day of Atonement. It was as if the way to the secret of God's presence, hitherto barred to man, was thrown open to all. It was as if the heart of God, hitherto hidden, was laid bare to men. The coming of Jesus, the life of Jesus, and the death of Jesus, rent the veil which had concealed God from man. " He who hath seen me," said Jesus, " hath seen the Father." (John 14: 9.) On the Cross, as never before, and never again, men saw the love of God.

(iii) Jesus cried with a great voice. Three of the gospels tell us of this great cry. (cp. Matthew 27: 50; Mark 15: 37.) John, on the other hand, does not mention the great cry, but tells us that Jesus died saying, " It is finished." (John 19: 30.) In Greek and Aramaic *It is finished* is one word. *It is finished* and the great cry are one and the same thing. Jesus died with a shout of triumph on His lips. He did not say, " It is finished," as one who is battered to his knees and finally beaten, as one who admits defeat. He said it like a victor who has won his last engagement with the enemy, like one who has brought a tremendous task to its ultimate conclusion. Finished! It is the cry of the Christ, crucified and yet victorious.

(iv) Jesus died with a prayer on His lips. " Father, into your hands I commend my spirit." That is Psalm 31: 5 with one word added—the word *Father*. That verse was the first prayer that every Jewish mother taught her child to say last thing at night. Just as we were taught, maybe, to say, " This night I lay me down to sleep," so the Jewish mother taught her child to say, before the threatening dark came down, " Into thy hands I commend my spirit." And Jesus made it even more lovely for He began it with the word *Father*. Even on a Cross Jesus died like a child falling asleep in his father's arms.

(v) The centurion and the crowd were deeply moved as Jesus died. His death had done what even His life could not do; it had broken the hard hearts of men. Already Jesus' saying was coming true—" I, if I be lifted up from the earth, will draw all men unto Me." The magnet of the Cross had begun its work, even as He breathed His last.

THE MAN WHO GAVE JESUS A TOMB

Luke 23: 50-56

> Look you—there was a man named Joseph, a member of the Sanhedrin, a good and a just man. He had not consented to their counsel and their action. He came from Arimathæa, a town of the Jews, and he lived in expectation of the Kingdom of God. He went to Pilate and asked for the body of Jesus. He took it down, and wrapped it in linen, and laid it in a rock-hewn tomb where no one had ever yet been laid. It was the day of preparation, and the Sabbath was beginning. The women, who had accompanied Jesus from Galilee, followed and saw the tomb and how His body was laid in it. Then they went back home and prepared spices and ointments. And they rested on the Sabbath day according to the commandment.

IT was the custom that the bodies of criminals were not buried at all, but were left to the dogs and the vultures to dispose of; but Joseph of Arimathæa saved the body of Jesus from that indignity. There was not much time left that day. Jesus was crucified on the Friday; the Jewish Sabbath is our Saturday. But the Jewish day begins at 6 p.m. That is to say by Friday at 6 p.m. the Sabbath had begun. That is why the women had only time to see where the body was laid and to go home and prepare their spices and ointments for it and to do no more, for after 6 p.m. all work became illegal.

Joseph of Arimathæa is for us a figure of the greatest interest.

(i) Legend has it that in the year A.D. 6I he was sent by Philip to this country. He came to Glastonbury. With him he brought the chalice that had been used at the Last Supper, and in it the blood of Christ. That chalice became the Holy Grail, which it was the dream of King Arthur's knights to find and see. When Joseph arrived in Glastonbury they say that he drove his staff into the ground to rest on it in his weariness, and that the staff budded and became a bush which blooms every Christmas Day. St. Joseph's thorn still blooms at Glastonbury and, to this day, slips of it are sent all over the world. The first church in all England was built at Glastonbury, and the church, which legend links with the name of Joseph, is still a mecca of Christian pilgrims.

(ii) There is a certain tragedy about Joseph of Arimathæa. He is the man who gave Jesus a tomb. He was a member of the Sanhedrin; we are told that he did not agree with the verdict and the sentence of that court. But there is no word that he raised his voice in disagreement. Maybe he was silent; maybe he absented himself when he was powerless to stop a course of action with which he disagreed. What a difference it would have made if he had spoken! How it would have lifted up Jesus' heart if, in that grim assembly of bleak hatred, one lone voice had spoken for Him! But Joseph waited until Jesus was dead, and then he gave Him a tomb. It is one of the tragedies of life that we place on people's graves the flowers we should have given them when they were alive. We keep for their obituary notices, and for the tributes paid to them at memorial services and in committee minutes, the praise and thanks we should have given them when they were alive. Often, often we are haunted because we never spoke. A word to the living is worth a cataract of tributes to the dead.

THE WRONG PLACE TO LOOK

Luke 24: 1-12

On the first day of the week, at the first streaks of dawn, the women came to the tomb, bearing the spices which they had prepared. They found the stone rolled away from the tomb. They entered in, but they did not find the body of the Lord Jesus. While they were at a loss what to make of this—look you—two men stood by them in flashing raiment. They were afraid, and they bowed their faces to the ground. But they said to them, "Why are you looking for Him who is alive among the dead? He is not here; He is risen. Remember how He said to you, while He was still in Galilee, that the Son of Man must be betrayed into the hands of sinful men and that He must be crucified, and that on the third day He would rise again." Then they remembered His words; and they returned from the tomb and brought the news of all these things to the eleven and to the others. Mary Magdalene was there, and Joanna, and Mary, the mother of James. They, and the other women with them, kept telling these things to the apostles. But their words seemed to them an idle tale, and they refused to believe them. But Peter rose up and ran to the tomb; and he stooped down and saw the linen clothes lying all by themselves; and he went away wondering in himself at what had happened.

THE Jewish Sabbath was our Saturday; it was the last day of the week, and it commemorated the rest of God after the work of creation. The Christian Sunday is the first day of the week, and commemorates the Resurrection of Jesus. So on this first Christian Sunday, the women went to the tomb, as they thought, to carry out the last offices of love for the dear dead, and to embalm and anoint Jesus' body with their spices. In the east tombs were often carved out in caves in the rock. The body was wrapped in long linen strips like bandages, and then laid on a shelf in the rock tomb. The tomb was then closed by a great circular stone like a cart-wheel which ran in

THE GOSPEL OF LUKE

a groove across the opening. When the women came, the stone was rolled away. Now, just here, we have one of these discrepancies in the accounts of the Resurrection of which the critics and opponents of Christianity make so much. In Mark the messenger in the tomb is a young man in a long white robe (Mark 16: 5); in Matthew he is the Angel of the Lord (Matthew 28: 2). Here it is two men in flashing raiment; and in John it is two angels (John 20: 12). It is true that the differences are there; but it is also true that, whatever the attendant description, *the basic fact of the empty tomb never varies*, and that is the fact that matters. No two people ever described the same episode or incident in the same terms; nothing so wonderful as the Resurrection ever escaped a certain embroidery as it was repeatedly told and recounted. But at the heart of the story that one all-important fact of the empty tomb remains. The women returned with their story to the rest of the disciples, and they refused to believe them. They called it an idle tale. The word the rest used to describe it is a word that is used in Greek medical writers to describe the babbling of a fevered and insane mind. Only Peter went out to see if it might not possibly be true. The very fact that Peter was there says much for Peter. The story of his denial of his Master was not a thing that could be kept silent; and yet Peter had the moral courage to face those who knew his shame. There was something of the hero in Peter, as well as something of the coward. The man who was a fluttering dove is on the way to becoming a rock.

The all-important and the challenging question in this story is the question of the messengers in the tomb, " Why are you looking for Him who is alive among the dead?" There are many of us who still look for Jesus among the dead.

(i) There are those who regard Jesus as the greatest man and the noblest hero who ever lived, as one who

lived the loveliest life that has ever been lived on earth
and who then died. That will not do. Jesus is not dead;
He is alive. He is not a hero of the past; He is a living
presence to-day.

> Shakespeare is dust, and will not come
> To question from his Avon tomb,
> And Socrates and Shelley keep
> An Attic and Italian sleep.
>
> They see not. But, O Christians, who
> Throng Holborn and Fifth Avenue,
> May you not meet in spite of death,
> A traveller from Nazareth?

(ii) There are those who regard Jesus as a man whose
life must be studied, and whose words must be examined,
and whose teaching must be analysed. There is a tendency
to think of Christianity and Christ in terms of something
to be studied. The tendency may be seen in the quite
simple fact of the extension of the study group and the
extinction of the prayer meeting. Beyond a doubt study is
necessary; but Jesus is not only someone to be studied;
He is someone to be met and lived with every day in life
He is not only a figure in a book, even if that book be the
greatest book in the world; again, He is a living presence.

(iii) There are those who see in Jesus the perfect pattern
and example. He is that; but it remains true that a
perfect example can be the most heart-breaking thing in
the world. For centuries the birds gave men an example
of flight, and yet not till modern times could man fly.
We may remember that when we were young we were
presented at school with a writing book. At the top it
has a line of copperplate writing; below it had blank
lines on which we had to copy it. How utterly discouraging
were our efforts to reproduce that perfect pattern! But
then the teacher would come and, with her hand, would

guide our hand over the lines and we got nearer to it. That is what Jesus does. He is not only the pattern and the example. He helps us, and guides us, and strengthens us to follow that pattern and example. He is not simply a model for life; again, He is a living presence to help us to live.

It may well be that our Christianity has lacked the essential something, because we too have been looking for Him who is alive among the dead.

THE SUNSET ROAD THAT TURNED TO DAWN

Luke 24: 13-35

Now—look you—on that same day two of them were on the way to a village called Emmaus, which is about seven miles from Jerusalem; and they talked with each other about all the things which had happened. As they talked about them, and discussed them, Jesus Himself came up to them and joined them on their way. But their eyes were fastened so that they did not recognize Him. He said to them, " What words are these that you are exchanging with each other as you walk? " And they stood with faces twisted with grief. One of them, called Cleopas, answered, " Are you the only visitor in Jerusalem who does not know the things that happened in it in these days? " " What kind of things? " He said to them. They said to Him, " The story of Jesus of Nazareth, who was a prophet mighty in deed and in word before God and all the people; and how our chief priests and rulers handed Him over to sentence of death and how they crucified Him. As for us—we were hoping that He was the one who was going to rescue Israel. Yes—and to add to it all—this is the third day since these things happened. Yes and some women of our number astonished us, for they went early to the tomb, and, when they did not find His body, they came saying that they had seen a vision of angels, who said that He was alive. And some of our company went to the tomb and found it just as the women had said—but they did not see Him." He said to them, " O foolish ones and slow in heart to believe in all the things that the prophets said! Was it not necessary that the Anointed One should suffer and enter into His glory?" And beginning from Moses and all the prophets, He expounded to them the things concerning Himself in all the scriptures. As they came near the village to which they were going, He made as if He would have gone on; and they pressed Him. " Stay with us," they said, " because it is towards evening, and the day is already far spent." So He came in to stay with them. When He had taken His place at table with them, He took bread, and blessed it and broke it, and gave it to them; and their eyes were opened and they recognized Him; and He vanished out of their sight. They said to each other, " Was not our heart burning within us while He was talking to us on the road, as He opened the scriptures to us?" And they arose that very hour and went back to Jerusalem and found the eleven gathered together and those with them, and found that they were saying, " It is a fact that the Lord has risen, and He has appeared to Simon." So they recounted all that had happened on the road, and how He was known to them in the breaking of bread.

THIS is another of the immortal short stories of the world.

(i) It tells of two men who were walking towards the sunset. It has been suggested that that is the very reason why they did not recognize Jesus. Emmaus was west of Jerusalem. The sun was sinking, and the setting sun so dazzled them that they did not know their Lord. However that may be, it is true that the Christian is a man who walks not towards the sunset but to the sunrise. Long ago it was said to the children of Israel that they journeyed in the wilderness towards the sunrising. (Numbers 21: 11.) The Christian goes onwards, not to a night which falls, but to a dawn which breaks—and that is what, in their sorrow and their disappointment, the two on the Emmaus road had forgotten.

(ii) It tells us of the ability of Jesus to make sense of things. The whole situation seemed to these two men to have no explanation. Their hopes and dreams were shattered. There is all the poignant, wistful, bewildered regret in the world in their sorrowing words, " We were hoping that He was the one who was going to rescue Israel." They are the words of men whose hopes are dead and buried. And then Jesus came and talked with them, and the meaning of life became clear to them, and the darkness became light. A story-teller makes one of his characters say to the one with whom he has fallen in love, " I never knew what life meant until I saw it in your eyes." It is only in Jesus that, even in the bewildering times, we learn what life means.

(iii) It tells us of the courtesy of Jesus. He made as if He would have gone on. He would not force Himself upon them; He awaited their invitation to come in. God gave to men the greatest and the most perilous gift in the world, the gift of free-will; and we can use it to invite Christ to enter our hearts or to allow Him to pass on.

(iv) It tells how He was known to them in the breaking of bread. This always sounds a little as if it meant the sacrament; but it does not. It was at an ordinary meal in an ordinary house, when an ordinary loaf was being divided, that these men recognized Jesus. It has been beautifully suggested that perhaps they were present at the feeding of the five thousand, and, as He broke the bread in their cottage home, they recognized His hands again. It is not only at the communion table we can be with Christ; we can be with Him at the dinner table too. He is not only the host in His Church; He is the guest in every home. Fay Inchfawn wrote,

> " Sometimes, when everything goes wrong;
> When days are short and nights are long;
> When wash-day brings so dull a sky
> That not a single thing will dry.

And when the kitchen chimney smokes,
And when there's naught so " queer " as folks!
When friends deplore my faded youth,
And when the baby cuts a tooth.
While John, the baby last but one,
Clings round my skirts till day is done;
And fat, good-tempered Jane is glum,
And butcher's man forgets to come.
Sometimes I say on days like these,
I get a sudden gleam of bliss.
Not on some sunny day of ease,
He'll come . . . but on a day like this! "

The Christian lives for ever and everywhere in a Christ-filled world.

(v) It tells how these two men, when they received their own joy, hastened to share it. It was seven miles' tramp back to Jerusalem, but they could not keep the good news to themselves. The Christian message is never fully ours until we have shared it with someone else.

(vi) It tells how, when they reached Jerusalem, they found others who had already shared their experience. It is the glory of the Christian that he lives in a fellowship of people who have had the same experience as he has had. It has been said that true friendship only begins when people share a common memory and can say to each other, " Do you remember? " Each one of us is one of a great fellowship of people who share a common experience and common memory of their Lord.

(vii) It tells us how Jesus appeared to Peter. That must ever remain one of the great untold stories of the world. But surely it is a lovely thing that Jesus should make one of His first appearances to the man who had denied Him. It is the glory of Jesus that He can give the penitent sinner back his self-respect.

IN THE UPPER ROOM

Luke 24: 36-49

> While they were still speaking, Jesus stood in the midst of them, and said to them, " Peace to you!" They were terrified and afraid, because they thought that they were seeing a spirit. He said to them, " Why are you troubled? And why do the questions arise in your heart? See my hands and my feet— that it is I—myself. Handle me and see, for a spirit has not flesh and bones as you see that I have." And when He had said this He showed them His hands and His feet. When they still thought it too good to be true, and when they were astonished He said to them, " Have you anything to eat here?" They gave Him part of a cooked fish, and He took it and ate it before them.
>
> He said to them, " These are my words which I spoke to you while I was still with you—that all the things which stand written about me in the law of Moses, and in the prophets, and in the psalms must be fulfilled." Then He opened their minds so that they understood the scriptures; and He said to them, " Thus it is written, that the Anointed One should suffer and should rise from the dead on the third day; and that repentance in His name and forgiveness of sins should be proclaimed to all nations, beginning from Jerusalem. And—look you—I send out the promise of my Father upon you. But stay in this city until you will be clothed with power from on high."

HERE we read of how Jesus came to His own when they were gathered in the Upper Room. In this passage certain of the great notes of the Christian Faith are resonantly struck.

(i) It stresses *the reality of the Resurrection*. The Risen Lord was no phantom or ghost or hallucination. He was real. The Jesus who died was in truth the Christ who rose again. Christianity is not founded on the dreams of men's disordered minds, or the visions of their fevered eyes, but on one who in actual historical fact faced and fought and conquered death and rose again.

(ii) **It** stresses *the necessity of the Cross*. It was to the Cross that all the scriptures looked forward. The Cross was not forced on God; it was not an emergency measure when all else had failed and when the scheme of things had gone wrong. It was part of the plan of God, for the Cross is the one place on earth, where in a moment of time, we see the eternal love of God.

(iii) It stresses *the urgency of the task*. Out to all men had to go the call to repentance and the offer of forgiveness. The Church was not left to live forever in the Upper Room; it was sent out into all the world. After the Upper Room there came the world-wide mission of the Church. The days of sorrow were past and the tidings of joy must be taken to all men.

(iv) It stresses *the secret of power*. They had to wait in Jerusalem until power from on high came upon them, until Pentecost had come. There are times when the Christian may seem to be wasting time, when he must wait in a wise passivity. Action without preparation must of necessity fail. There is a time to wait on God and a time to work for God. Fay Inchfawn writes of the days when life is a losing contest with a thousand little things.

> " I wrestle—how I wrestle!—through the hours.
> Nay, not with principalities and powers—
> Dark spiritual foes of God's and man's—
> But with antagonistic pots and pans;
> With footmarks on the hall,
> With smears upon the wall,
> With doubtful ears and small unwashen hands,
> And with a babe's innumerable demands."

And then, even in the business, she lays aside her work to be for a moment with God.

> " With leisured feet and idle hands, I sat.
> I, foolish, fussy, blind as any bat,
> Sat down to listen, and to learn. And lo,
> My thousand tasks were done the better so."

The quiet times in which we wait on God are never wasted times; for it is in the time when we lay aside life's tasks that we are strengthened for the very tasks we laid aside.

THE HAPPY ENDING

Luke 24: 50-53

> Jesus led them out as far as Bethany; and He raised His hands and blessed them; and as He was blessing them He parted from them, and was borne up into heaven. And when they had worshipped Him they returned to Jerusalem with great joy; and they were continually in the Temple praising God.

THE Ascension must always remain a mystery, for it attempts to put into words what is beyond words and to describe what is beyond description. But that something such should happen was essential. It was unthinkable that the appearances of Jesus should grow fewer and fewer until finally they petered out. That would have effectively wrecked the faith of men. There had to come a day of dividing, when the Jesus of earth finally became the Christ of Heaven. But to the disciples the Ascension was obviously three things.

(i) It was *an ending*. One stage was past and another had begun. The day when their faith was faith in a flesh and blood person, and when it depended on the presence of that person's flesh and blood were ended. Now they were linked to someone who was forever independent of space and time.

(ii) But equally it was *a beginning*. The disciples did not leave the scene heart-broken; they left it with great joy. They left it so, because now they knew that they had a Master from which nothing could separate them any more.

> I know not where His islands lift
>   Their fronded palms in air;
> I only know I cannot drift
>   Beyond His love and care.

" I am persuaded," said Paul, " that nothing—nothing in life or in death—can separate me from the love of God in Christ Jesus my Lord." (Romans 8: 38, 39.)

(iii) Still, further, the Ascension gave the disciples the certainty that they had *a friend, not only on earth, but in heaven.* Surely it is the most priceless thing of all to know and to feel that in heaven there awaits us that self-same Jesus who on earth was wondrous kind. To die is not to go out into the dark; it is to go to Him.

So they went back to Jerusalem, and they were continually in the Temple praising God. It is not by accident that Luke's gospel ends where it began—in the House of God.

THE ARCHITECTURE
OF BRITAIN

Doreen Yarwood

THE ARCHITECTURE
OF BRITAIN

B. T. BATSFORD, LONDON

First published 1976
Second impression 1977
Copyright Doreen Yarwood 1976

Filmset by Servis Filmsetting Ltd, Manchester
and printed in Great Britain by
The Anchor Press Ltd, Tiptree, Essex
for the publishers B. T. Batsford Ltd
of 4 Fitzhardinge Street, London W1H 0AH

ISBN 0 7134 3118 0

Contents

PART TWO
CLASSICAL DOMINANCE

Preface

The text of this book presents a broad commentary on and description of architecture in Britain from Saxon times until the present day, relating the building activity to the life of the people and to their relationship with other countries of influence at the time. More than half the contents of the book is illustrative, in line drawings and half-tones. This pictorial coverage includes buildings of all types – ecclesiastical and secular, civic and domestic – as well as architectural and ornamental detail.

The line drawings were made by the author from her own photographic record. The author and publishers wish to thank J. M. Dent and Sons Ltd and and the Royal Institute of Architects for permission to reproduce 451 from the *Works in Architecture of R. and J. Adam*; also the following for permission to reproduce the photographic illustrations in this book : H.M. The Queen for 187; Robert Adam for 40 and 168; Aerofilms and Aero Pictorial Ltd for 184 and 132; G. Douglas Bolton for 234; J. Allan Cash for 103; B. C. Clayton for 55 and 169; Country Life for 347; John Dunbar for 439; Noel Habgood for 518; A. F. Kersting for 166–7, 308, 322, 345, 362, 382, 468 and 521; Ministry of Public Building and Works for 83; Paul Popper Ltd for 182; Kenneth Scowen for 186; Edwin Smith for 104, 118, 121 and 344; Scottish National Buildings Record for 303; J. Valentine and Sons Ltd for 236; Warburg Institute for 364; John Watt, Scottish Field for 170; John Yarwood for 14, 32, 36–8, 47, 57, 60, 75–82, 93, 97, 101–2, 116, 119, 132, 135, 138, 140, 142, 144–5, 147, 150–1, 156, 161, 185, 192–3, 195, 205–7, 216, 218, 220, 233, 247–8, 257, 276, 374–6, 410, 416–17, 421–5, 431–4, 436–7, 440, 442–4, 452, 497, 500, 519–20, 565–7.

339, 341 and 384 are from the publisher's collection.

London 1975   Doreen Yarwood

PART ONE

THE MIDDLE AGES

CHAPTER ONE

Britain before the coming of the Normans: AD 450–1066

The centuries between the departure of the Roman legions and the arrival of William of Normandy were years in which the British race was formed from a mingling of the successive waves of invaders who assailed her shores. While the Roman occupation lasted, barbarian raids from the Continent were kept within bounds. But, from the time in AD 409 when the Roman emperor notified Britain that henceforth her towns must defend themselves, because Rome herself was threatened, the British Isles became an easy prey to invaders. The south and east coasts were constantly attacked from the Continent by the Germanic peoples – themselves being pushed westwards – in particular, Angles, Saxons and Jutes, who settled respectively in East Anglia, Mercia, Northumbria; Essex, Sussex, Wessex; Kent and the Isle of Wight. These waves of invaders percolated westward and northward, confining the earlier Celtic peoples more and more to the fringes of Britain: Cornwall, Wales, Scotland and Ireland.

The appearance of Britain steadily returned to what it had been before the coming of the Romans. Roads were overgrown, towns, pavements and buildings were broken or destroyed and a primitive, nomad life was resumed. The arts – literature, painting, sculpture, architecture – were lost and, for some time, destruction was general.

New cultural beginnings emerged with the tentative spread of Christianity. The movement had been seeping slowly into Romanised Britain, but this had been rudely halted and destroyed by the Saxon invasions of the fifth and sixth centuries. The new spread of Christian teaching and culture came from a different direction, from the Celtic fringe areas which had escaped the Saxon onslaught.

The *monastic* way of life had evolved in Egypt, where monks pursued solitary lives, hermits in caves and huts. The movement spread westwards and soon monks began to establish communities, still living in huts, but grouping these to form larger units. In fifth-century Ireland, St Patrick, himself a British Christian, son of a Roman provincial official, came from Gaul to convert the Irish. Monasteries were built and flourished there in the sixth and seventh centuries. From Ireland these monks went forth indefatigably to spread the gospel to Scotland, Wales and Cornwall, from whence the light of Christian arts and learning was disseminated slowly to the rest of Britain. St Ninian founded the Celtic monastery at *Whithorn* (Scotland) in, it is thought, about 400 AD and, in 563, St Columba left Ireland to found the Celtic monastery on the island of *Iona*. From here, later, the Celtic Church spread to Northumbria, where St Aidan established the monastery at *Lindisfarne*.

Isolated and, often, island sites were favoured by these Celtic monks who wished to lead the contemplative life. They constructed small buildings in stone or wood, according to the availability of materials. These structures were generally of one cell or room and were rectangular or round, bee-hive shapes, low and simply roofed. The bee-hive cells were separate buildings, but often inter-communicated. The most usual method of construction in Scotland and in England was in dry masonry, each course corbelled out to converge at the top to make a domed vault. Remains of these in Britain are fragmentary, but

1 *Escomb, Durham, 7th century*

2 *The chancel arch, interior, Escomb*

3 *Plan, Brixworth*

4 *Plan, Boarhunt, Hampshire, 11th century*

5 *Interior, Brixworth*

6 *Brixworth Church, Northants, c.680 also 10th and 11th century. Later spire*

6A *Hexham Abbey Church, Northumberland. Built of stone from Roman Camp at Corstopitum (Corbridge), c.674*

6B *Repton Church, Derbyshire, 10th century*

in Ireland there are a number of examples in more complete condition. In the ruins of monastic settlements can be found a larger church or chapel building with the monks' cells clustered around it. One such instance is on the island of Skellig Michael, where there are nine buildings comprising two oratories, six huts and the church.

Remains of Celtic stonework in Britain also include the tall *round towers* and *carved crosses*. Both of these are more common in Ireland, but some examples exist in Britain. The stone round towers (like the one at *Brechin,* Angus), were built on the monastic sites, mainly during the times of the Viking raids; they acted as refuges and storage places for valuables. They were tall, delicately tapering and were capped by a conical stone roof. They contained a belfry as a means of warning the community in times of danger and they had doorways set well above ground level, accessible only by wooden ladders which could be withdrawn when under attack. A port was provided which made it possible to overturn the ladder put up by an attacker. Inside were floors of wood connected by spiral staircases (27).

The carved standing stones and *high crosses* can

also be found in Scotland and England. They were erected to mark a sacred site or a boundary, or might have been placed in commemoration of the dead. They vary in size and complexity of design; many are finely carved, the motifs of fret, plait and interlacing ornament being frequently employed as well as birds, animals, flowers and human figures (19, 22).

It was in AD 597, after nearly two centuries, that England again experienced the influence of the Christian Church from Rome. St Augustine, sent by the Pope, landed with his 40 Benedictine monks in Kent, to begin the re-establishment of Christianity in England. He built the first cathedral at Canterbury on the site remains of a Romano-British church. Like the early Christian churches in Rome, it was basilican in plan, with an apse, its nave flanked by aisles.

Anglo-Saxon Churches

Remains of Saxon building in England date from two different periods. The earlier work is seventh- and early eighth-century structures and the latter stems from the late ninth and the tenth century. Between these two periods took place the devastating Viking

7   *St Peter-on-the-Walls,*
    Bradwell, Essex, 10th century

9   *Bradford-on-Avon,*
    Wiltshire, 10th century

8   *Barton-on-Humber,*
    Lincolnshire, 10th century
    (belfry stage later)

10   *Deerhurst, Gloucestershire,*
     10th century

12   *Worth, Sussex, 10th century.*
     Later tower

11   *Plan, Worth*

raids, which destroyed the bulk of early Saxon culture. The majority of Saxon building was in wood, or even timber with wattle-and-daub construction, but the more important churches and monasteries were built in stone. The work of the earlier period was centred in two areas; the southern one in Kent followed the Roman Christian line stemming from St Augustine, while the northern, in Northumbria, was centred around Hexham and Lindisfarne, with closer affinities with Celtic monasticism. The architecture of the seventh century, though its remains are not numerous and, in many cases, are fragmentary, clearly reflects this difference of approach.

The Canterbury school in the south created churches on basilican plan, as in Rome. Most examples were simpler than the prototypes, presumably because of the lesser experience of British builders. Instead of a row of columns supporting the arcaded wall which divided nave from aisles, there were plain walls broken only by an opening on each side which led to a series of chambers. An example of this type of design can be seen in the ruined *Church of Reculver* in Kent. The *Church of St Peter and Paul at Canterbury* was of this type with the Roman pattern of apsidal chancel and, at the opposite end of the nave, the narthex (13).

The Northumbrian churches, in contrast, were built in the simpler, Celtic design of tall, narrow, aisleless nave and rectangular chancel, like the small church at *Escomb* in Co. Durham (1, 2). Even the great, seventh-century monastic churches of *Jarrow* and *Monkwearmouth* were of this pattern. In 664, after the Synod of Whitby, Northumbrian monasticism pursued the lines of Roman Christianity and, by the end of the century, impressive northern churches were being built which were basilican in plan. Those at *Hexham* and *York* and at *Ripon* were of this type and, according to written records, they were large, complex structures. In *Hexham Abbey Church* the crypt of the Saxon building survives, the prime example in England from this early period. Constructed in 674 of large blocks of stone, it is designed in barrel-vaulted chambers after the pattern in Rome (6A).

The best example surviving of this early period of Saxon church building is *Brixworth* in Northampton-shire. Both geographically and architecturally it is placed half-way between the Kentish and Northumbrian designs. This is a remarkable structure for so early a building. Nearly 100 feet long, it is constructed of rag-stone and re-used Roman bricks. Originally an arcade separated the aisles from nave and choir, while the latter ended in a polygonal apse. Despite the walling-in of the arcades and loss of the aisles, the remains constitute a fine example of early Saxon work* (3, 5, 6, 23).

While Carolingian architecture was being established on the Continent under the flourishing empire of Charlemagne in the ninth century, Britain was suffering the savage and repeated raids of the Norsemen, who came plundering, burning and looting round the coasts. The Saxons were unprepared and ill-equipped to fight; monasteries especially were unprotected and offered tempting riches at little cost in battle. The destruction at Lindisfarne in 793 was followed by that at Jarrow in 794 and Iona in 795. These early raids were precursors of longer and more adventurous visits which increased in intensity until 850. By 865 a Danish invasion army had arrived and was only finally controlled under King Alfred later in the century.

The majority of Saxon architecture surviving in Britain dates from the tenth and early eleventh centuries, the so-called 'golden age' of Saxon art. These buildings are stone, rubble and brick churches, important enough to have been constructed in durable materials, but none of them are the larger, impressive structures which we know were built (and rebuilt after Viking depredations) at such monasteries as Ely and Malmesbury. In these years over 30 Benedictine monasteries were built in Britain but little, apart from foundations, of these remain, due to the tremendous building activity initiated by the Normans after the Conquest. They then rebuilt the churches and cathedrals from the foundations upwards, usually on the same site.

The Saxon building which exists, therefore, is of second rank; the smaller churches. There are a number of these in different parts of the country, but in no case is the structure entirely unaltered and, in some instances, only the tower, a doorway or fenestration remains from the original work.

An interesting feature of these churches is that they

---

* The church was badly damaged by Viking attacks. It was in the tenth and eleventh centuries that it was built up again and when the west end stair turret was added, the side aisles with lean-to roof removed and the arcades blocked. The spire is fourteenth-century.

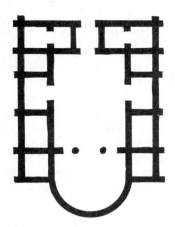

13　Plan, Reculver, Kent

14　St Benet, Cambridge

15　Earl's Barton, Northamptonshire, early 11th century

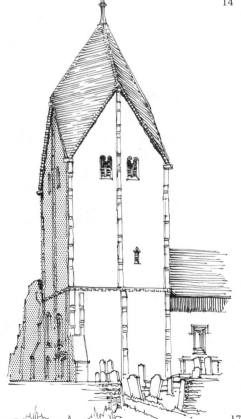

17　Sompting, Sussex, early 11th century

16　Greensted, Essex, 10th century

appear to have developed hardly at all, either in plan or structure, from those churches erected in the seventh century. A number of them are still very simple, merely a long, narrow, high nave or nave and chancel. Such churches have no aisles, no apse, no transepts. The best of these small churches is that dedicated to *St Lawrence* at *Bradford-on-Avon*, near Bath. This has a nave and chancel; its walls, some two and a half feet thick, are of large blocks of local stone, well cut and closely fitted. The chancel arch is typically narrow and the tiny, high nave is pierced by doorways on the other three sides. The small windows are set high in the otherwise unbroken walls (9). Other examples of the simple nave and chancel or single chamber church include those at *Boarhunt*, Hampshire (4) and *Bradwell*, Essex (7).

Many Saxon churches were built on the basilican plan with an apsidal-ended chancel, but these were rarely aisled; *Wing Church*, Buckinghamshire has a polygonal apse. The cruciform plan was unusual; two examples survive partly unaltered, that of *St Mary in Castro* in Dover Castle and *Worth Church* in Sussex. At Worth the chancel is apsidal; inside, the church is remarkably Saxon in appearance (11, 12, 20). The interior of *Deerhurst Church*, Gloucestershire retains its tall west wall, pierced by a small doorway and windows; the aisle arcades are later, Medieval, work (10, 21).

Characteristic of Saxon building style are the church *towers*, of which several survive. The one at *Earl's Barton* in Northamptonshire is the best known. It is an ornamented tower (15, 18, 29) with the typical stone pilaster strips in vertical line and chevron pattern. Several possible explanations have been put forward to account for these stone strips, which are also to be seen in the towers at *Sompting Church*, Sussex (17, 26), which retains its helm roof, *Barton-on-Humber Church*, Lincolnshire (8), *Barnack Church*, Northamptonshire, *Monkwearmouth Church*, Durham, *Dunham Magna Church*, Norfolk and *St Benet's Church*, Cambridge (14), as well as on the walling of *Worth Church* and *Bradford-on-Avon*, for example (9, 12). The strips are not of any structural significance and are probably only for decoration, though it has been suggested that the treatment is evocative of timber prototypes and represents a simulation of the wood and plaster structure. It seems more likely that it is the Saxon version of the Mediterranean blank wall arcading or a primitive attempt to portray the Carolingian neo-Roman treatment. At Bradford-on-Avon the simple arcading round the exterior walls is reeded, like classical pilasters.

Other characteristics of Saxon work which differentiate it from the later Norman structures are the long-and-short work, the unbuttressed, thinner walling and the window and doorway design. This so-called *'long-and-short work'* occurs where a tall, squared stone of up to four feet high is set vertically and this alternates with a flat stone slab set horizontally into the wall. This is a common construction for quoins, as in Earl's Barton, Barnack and Barton-on-Humber towers (8, 15).

Saxon *window openings* were round or triangular-headed, set singly or in pairs (21, 25, 29). They were often double splayed, that is, they had a narrow opening which splayed inwards and outwards. Earlier examples were generally set in the centre of the wall, later versions nearer the outer face, then, commonly, splayed inwards only. In the double window style, the two lights were often divided by a shaft or turned baluster (28), which supported the impost. This was a long rectangular block of stone, carried through the whole thickness of the wall, while the baluster was set nearer to the outer face (20). Some windows had narrow, round mouldings over the arch.

Belfry openings were cut straight through the wall thickness and were subdivided into two or more openings, each of which was covered by a round arch. A shaft or pilaster separated the openings. Shafts could be turned in baluster form with horizontal decorative bands or they were octagonal, oblong or square in section. *Capitals* were generally cubical, or, later, scalloped, while a few had volutes* (24, 26).

Doorways, like windows, were round or triangular-headed. Some examples were plain, others had simple mouldings or voussoir blocks. A number were finished with Roman bricks (23). Doorways were narrow in proportion to their height. At Earl's Barton, vertical pilaster strips are taken round the arch while the arch mouldings are set inside them. Square blocks form the imposts (18).

Few Saxon *crypts* survive in good condition though many of the larger churches possessed them. Apart

---

* All of these display crude derivations from classical, Byzantine and Carolingian work, as well as pre-dating Romanesque cushion capitals.

18 Tower doorway,
Earl's Barton Church

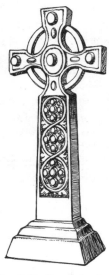

19 Celtic Cross, Scotland,
10th century

20 Window opening,
Worth Church

21 Window opening,
Deerhurst Church

22 Saxon cross, 8th century

23 Doorway, Brixworth Church

25 Saxon window using Roman
bricks

24 Saxon capital

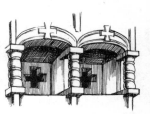

26 Sompting Church   27 Stone round tower, Ireland   28 Saxon baluster shaft   29 Tower window, Earl's
Barton Church

from the seventh-century one at *Hexham* (6A and page 6), there are traces of a basilican crypt at Brixworth Church and a tenth-century one at *Wing Church*. Here, under the polygonal-ended chancel, is an octagonal chamber with an ambulatory round it under the apse above. At *Repton Church* there is a square, tenth-century crypt with four columns supporting a stone vault (6B).

After the Viking raids, the Saxons, in the tenth and eleventh centuries, used more permanent *building materials* than previously. They re-used Roman stone from ruined buildings, and took Roman bricks for quoining and arch turning though, as at Brixworth, their skill was not sufficient to radiate brick voussoirs of the arches (23, 25). The Saxons quarried their own stone, such as Barnack stone in Northamptonshire, as well as different rag-stones, while in the chalk areas of the country they used flint for building. The majority of Saxon building was still of wood, of which almost nothing survives. One interesting exception is at the village church of *Greensted* in Essex, where remains of the tenth-century nave wall timbers still exist. This little church was built from the trunks of large oak trees, split and roughly hewn. They were set upright, close together and let into a sill at the bottom and a plate at the top, to form nave walls. They were fastened with wood pins. These timbers still form the nave walls of the little church, although they had to be removed in the nineteenth century, shortened and set into a brickwork plinth, because of decay at the foot. The church was originally nearly 30 feet long and 17 feet wide. A later tower, spire and roof have been added (16). It is interesting to compare this example at Greensted with the stave churches of Norway. In Essex the design is dictated by the availability of the limited length of the oak timbers whereas, in Norway, the structure is taken from tall pine trees.

The Saxons dug *earthworks* to protect their important homes and village groups, particularly after the commencement of the Viking raids. The chief hall or house was of timber with surrounding huts of timber and wattle-and-daub.* A wood palisade enclosed these and the whole site – planned on top of a natural hill or artificial mound – was surrounded by a circular ditch or two concentric ditches. The earth from these provided the mound or, alternatively, a bank beyond the ditch. Sometimes a double palisade was constructed with space for cattle between the two. Water filled the ditches which could be spanned with removable planks.

The Saxons lived in small communities. They built *homes* in most parts of the country of timber and wattle-and-daub, though in areas where stone was readily available it was used for walling. The common style of building was one used widely, even in Medieval times, and it can still be seen in England and in areas on the Continent from where it originated. This is the *cruck* form of house, built in bays. Each bay was about 16 feet wide and the number of these varied according to the wealth and importance of the owner. The bay divisions were marked by crucks or forks of massive timbers, in pairs. These crucks were bent tree trunks, meeting at the top in gable shape to support a ridge pole which ran horizontally along the ridge of the roof of the whole building. Smaller timbers between, called rafters, helped to hold up the roofing, which was of thatch or wood shingles. Such a building lacked head-room, as the walls and roof were in one curved piece. Inside, the great room or hall was divided into living and sleeping space for the family, servants, farm workers and animals. Such halls were for the *thegn* or lord (30). The majority of people lived in small huts of straw and branches, covered in turf, bracken, mud and heather, much as their prehistoric ancestors had done. Such huts could be abandoned and rebuilt if the inhabitants were harried to another part of the country by invaders and barbarian raids.

Cruck houses continued to be built in Britain throughout the Middle Ages. Then they were of half-timber and in the fourteenth and fifteenth centuries the roofs were raised and vertical walls inserted in order to give head-room. A number of examples from this time, still showing the cruck construction, can be seen in Britain (32).

Stone structures were built by the people of the tenth and eleventh centuries in the north of the country, in Scotland, Orkney and Shetland and in

---

* A type of construction where a row of vertical stakes or large branches are interwoven horizontally by smaller branches and reeds. Mud is plastered on one or both sides and dried out in the sun. A structural method used throughout the Middle Ages. In later times laths replaced branches and surfaces were plastered and painted on top of the mud. Hair or straw could be mixed with the mud to give greater strength and durability.

30 *Anglo-Saxon hall: a conjectural restoration*

31 *Dry-stone structure, Gallarus Oratory, Dingle, Ireland, 7th century or later*

32 *Medieval cruck construction, Weobley*

Ireland. The cruck shape was built in stone, as can be seen in the corbelled *Gallarus Oratory*, near Dingle in Ireland (31). The Norsemen also brought their form of house building with them and immigrant farmers interpreted this in stone from the ninth century onwards. In northern Scotland, Orkney and Shetland they built *long-houses*. These were low, long buildings with stone walls infilled with turf. Roofing was of thatch and timber weighted down, as Norwegian houses have been in country areas almost up till modern times, by heather ropes and stones. There was a door at each end of the long-house and windows in the lower roof slopes. A stone wall encircled the building, which was shared, like the southern, Saxon home, by family and livestock.

CHAPTER TWO

The Norman Conquest: Romanesque architecture 1066–1160

The Norman invasion of England, the last of its kind, was a princely conquest, led by Duke William of Normandy, who succeeded with a small army of only about 6000 men. In this it was unlike the earlier invasions by Saxons and Danes. These had been migrations of peoples, attracted by a rich, pleasant land, where they hoped to settle, farm and raise communities. Successive invaders who had come since the fifth century, when the Roman legions had left the British Isles undefended, had been unable totally to subdue the native peoples and weld them into one kingdom.

William was of different mould. He was of Viking stock, descendant of those Northmen (Norsemen) who had given their name to the part of north-west France to which they had come more than 150 years earlier from Scandinavia. They had retained their energy and fighting spirit; they had adopted the Latin culture, the French language and succeeded in combining their abilities in the arts of war and colonisation with those of administration and advanced political thinking. Being established in Normandy, these Norman aristocrats then turned their attention to Britain and Sicily.

Having conquered Harold's army, William proceeded unhesitatingly to subdue and unite his new colony and make it Norman. He parcelled out the land in estates to his Norman followers, so replacing the English aristocracy with one of his own. He then initiated the tremendous building programme to erect castles and fortified homes as strongpoints, to resist attempts at rebellion, and cathedrals and churches in support of the Christian religion which the Normans

had wholeheartedly embraced since early in the tenth century. These structures were, like the character of their builders, massive, ruthless, direct; they were only sparingly decorated. Stone had been readily available in Normandy and Norman builders were better masons than the Saxons though, for many years, most of the work was in wood, for speedy construction.

Many of the Saxon *towns* had been developed on Roman sites and, in turn, the Normans were attracted by similar suitable places to establish centres for defence and trade. These included towns such as Lincoln, York, Chester, Bath, Norwich, Southampton. London, from the days of Roman Londinium, was always the major city. One of the earliest stone buildings of William's reign was the keep of the Tower of London, now called the White Tower, erected as a sign of his dominance of the capital. Towns were small, buildings, even churches, were of wood, with thatch roofing and wattle walling. Most of them had gardens or open ground nearby. The streets were narrow and often steep so that excess water flowed down to the watercourse. Open drains ran down the centre while the passageways on either side were cobbled and sloped towards the drain. Cattle and pigs were driven over the cobblestones in streets which were dirty and dark.

The Romanesque style of architecture

The easiest way to define and to recognise an architectural style is by reference to its component parts and details. The style itself is a combination of all these parts, handled in such a manner as to present an overall scheme of specific character. Since each style owes something to others which have gone before, it may share components with these but yet, in totality, be something different and novel. This is so with Romanesque building. It is recognisable by its general and detailed characteristics where it appears in all parts of Europe, but its guise varies considerably from one area to another.

The two chief forms comprise the one developed in central Europe and that to be seen in the north and west. The former, as the name Romanesque suggests, springs from Roman classical design. It is in the central and southern areas such as northern Italy, south-east France, southern Germany and Spain that most examples of Roman building survive. From these, more numerous in the eleventh century than now, the Romanesque masons developed their own designs, using the round arch, the classical columns and capitals, arcading, tunnel vaults and the basilican church plan with its division into nave and aisles, its central timber roof and apsidal termination behind the high altar. These builders used the foliated motifs as well as animals, birds, human figures and devils. Their decoration was rich and vigorous, their façades and porticoes sculptured all over in biblical themes.

The strongest influence on Romanesque architecture in the north and west was the Norman style of work. Established in Normandy during the tenth century, the Normans brought their building methods and designs to Britain, also to southern Italy and Sicily, creating in these two widely dissimilar areas buildings of like character but adapted to the needs of the indigenous peoples.

Carolingian influence is apparent in Romanesque building design. This, characterised in its round and triangular-headed arches, simple shafts and brick-work patterning, had penetrated into Anglo-Saxon work. It also can be traced in Norman building but of stronger note is the pattern established in Normandy itself.

Here, in Caen, we can still see the two great churches of Duke William, the *Church of St Étienne* (L'Abbaye-aux-Hommes) and the *Church of La Trinité* (L'Abbaye-aux-Dames). St Étienne, built in 1066–77, illustrates the quality of northern Romanesque grouping in its masses and towers. The west front shows a strong vertical emphasis, with its twin, tall towers (capped by Gothic spires) flanking the plain

façade, broken only by unenriched round-headed windows and doorways. La Trinité, founded in 1062 by William's queen, Matilda, of Bayeux tapestry fame, has retained its original pattern even better. This is a massive, very Romanesque building, with a monumental façade of twin western towers in arcaded stages and, in between, a gabled centrepiece with deeply recessed round-headed doorway below; there is a square tower over the crossing, crowned by a stumpy spire. The interior is well preserved. It has a long nave with barrel-vaulted aisles and a fine apse covered by a groined vault. The nave is divided horizontally, on a northern pattern, into arcade, triforium and clerestory (35).

These two churches, though partly altered, display most clearly the structural pattern which the Normans brought to England. The buildings are massively constructed with very thick walling, especially at base, tall façades, little decoration, the round arch used for all openings and columns and piers solid and heavy with the plainest of capitals. Where decoration is used it is in abstract form – the chevron, the billet, the cushion. Unlike the central European models, the only Roman features used here are the arcade and round arch. The capitals are sternly formal, there is no sculpture, no richly ornamented portals. The Norman concept of Romanesque architecture, designed to suit the northern light and climate, as well as its religious needs, was for plainer, larger window area, solid, undecorated wall surfaces and an interior which is grouped to define and control the spatial qualities of the building. An important feature here was the Norman introduction of the tall, vertical shafts which extended from floor to wooden ceiling in the nave and choir. These divided the interior into bays and articulated the whole into compartments, creating a sense of progression from west doorway, up the aisle to eastern altar. This was a new concept and one which provided the basis for later Medieval building. The visual impact of the masses of solid walling is everywhere apparent. Even though these are pierced by arcades the effect is of carefully balanced power and weight (39).

Most Norman building in England before 1080 was in wood. This was the quickest means of erecting the secular buildings, in particular, which were needed to control and administer the country. After the initial rush to put up temporary castles, houses, churches and monasteries, the Normans settled down to constructing the great stone cathedrals, abbey churches and castles which still exist as testimony to their building skill, initiative and energy.

The earlier work had much in common with the corresponding structures in Normandy, but, just before the end of the century, the architectural style evolved from its early form into what may be termed High Romanesque: the zenith of its achievement. This is seen in the rediscovery of how to vault a tall, wide nave or hall with the groin and rib vaults, also in the increase of decoration on arch mouldings, capitals and columns. These features are still massive, strong and simple and the decoration is geometrical, but the deeply incised zig-zags, chevron cuts and cubiform capitals lend animation to the solidity of exterior portals and interior arcades not previously seen in Norman architecture. Towers especially were arcaded, generally in blind form, but imparting a plasticity which was new. The two great Norman buildings of this era in Britain are Durham Cathedral and the keep of the Tower of London. In a number of respects, Norman building in Britain was now moving ahead of its counterpart in northern France. Rib vaulting is the prime innovation and Durham is the prototype. In Normandy wooden ceilings remained the usual covering during the eleventh century.

It is especially interesting for students of Norman architecture in Britain to compare this version of northern Romanesque with the Norman work in their other kingdoms of *southern Italy* and *Sicily*. Here too, the Normans implanted their own style of work but, as in Britain, the buildings developed a somewhat different character from their Normandy prototypes. The south of Italy is now a region of poverty. In the tenth and eleventh centuries Apulia, its capital in Bari, became wealthy and powerful under Norman rule.

The great cathedral churches here – Trani, Troia, Bitonto, Molfetta, Canosa, as well as Bari itself – have the same Norman characteristics of power and solidity as in Normandy and Britain (38). Because of the brilliant sunlight, window openings are much smaller and the impression of immense areas of solid masonry walling is even more notable. The walls are equally thick but roof pitches are lower since it is unnecessary to throw off snow and heavy rains. Unlike the long, English naves, Italian ones are short and wide. Due to the width, roofing has to be of timber. Façades have the typical Norman form of tall,

twin towers but cupolas cover the crossing instead of a tower as in Britain while, inside, triforia are rare, the Italian fashion for a solid wall between nave arcade and larger clerestory windows above being adhered to. These differences are of surface character, the general impression being of the same fundamental source of style as in Britain and Normandy. The differences stem entirely from climatic variations and the people's temperament and needs.

The feature which creates the greatest difference between Apulian Norman Romanesque and the northern interpretation is the decoration. In Apulia, and even more in the Sicilian Norman kingdom, at Palermo, Cefalù and Monreale, for example, the craftsmen were Greek, from Byzantium, and the Saracenic influence from the Arabs was strong. Instead of English incised zig-zags, round arches and cubiform capitals, there are Saracenic arches, mosaic facing to walls and apses and a wealth of sculpture on capitals and portals based on plant and geometrical motifs. The sculpture is vigorous and the mosaics emit a rich glow of colour and gold to the darker interiors.

In Normandy *masons* had used chiefly their local Caen stone for important buildings. They introduced this material into England, transporting it from Normandy, for fine work on quoins, capitals and especially interiors. Caen stone is white and easy to carve. It was imported all through the Middle Ages but, because of the cost and effort of transportation, the Normans turned more to local materials for other building. They worked Bath stone, limestone, sandstones and rag-stones. Chalk and flint were included in walling. Such materials were used for cathedrals, churches, castles and monasteries. Most of the building in Britain was of the nearest convenient material and this, most commonly, was wood, wattle-and-daub, thatch with, possibly, stone foundations and bases.

Early Romanesque masonry by the Normans in England was massive. Fearful of collapse in the great buildings erected, masons built walls up to 24 feet thick at base. In general, they overestimated the thickness necessary for safety, though, since this work had wide joints and the mortar was poor and thin, the collapse of towers and roofs was not unknown. Windows were small, partly in order not to weaken the wall and partly for defence reasons. In castles and houses, the lowest row of windows was

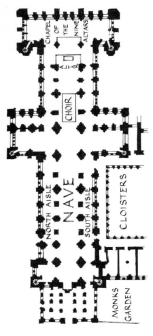

34   *Durham Cathedral,*
      12th century.
      Central Tower,
      15th century

33   *Plan, Durham Cathedral*

35   *Church of La Trinité, Caen, Normandy, 1063–1125*

36   *Nave capital, Hereford Cathedral*

37   *West doorway capitals, Rochester Cathedral*

above first-floor level.

Twelfth-century work was less massive. The masonry was by now fine jointed and more often carved in incised line or three-dimensional decoration. The knowledge and art of the mason increased and improved, enabling him to build with thinner walling and yet maintain stability. The Normans were prodigious builders and the quantity of work which they produced was immense. Even discounting the loss of all structures not of stone and the disappearance and alteration of many of the latter material, the amount of Norman Romanesque work which survives in Britain is a tribute to the strength and achievement of Norman construction.

The Cathedrals and Churches

Because of their importance in eleventh- and twelfth-century community life and the consequent care with which they were erected, it is ecclesiastical buildings which have survived in the greatest numbers. Of massive structure and durable material, the great cathedral, abbey, priory and parish churches exist all over the country. Most of them have been altered and enlarged in later years but a great deal of Norman workmanship remains, especially in the cathedrals. A tremendous effort was expended in building these. Many were erected on the sites of Saxon cathedral churches, but generally the Saxon building was demolished and the Norman one started from the foundation upwards.

The *plan* of early Romanesque cathedrals in western Europe was evolved on functional lines. The church was divided into two parts, east and west; the former devoted to use by the clergy, the latter for the lay public. From the tenth century onwards, the worship of saints became a growing custom and more chapels were needed for this in the eastern part of the cathedral. The French contribution to the Medieval church plan was either to build an ambulatory round an apsidal east end and design chapels which radiated from it, or to extend the choir aisles forwards to be almost flush with the apsidal end of the choir and also, sometimes, to build out chapels from the transepts.

The plan of an English cathedral developed from the Normandy design as set by the pattern of such churches as St Étienne in Caen. This has twin western towers, a long nave and short choir, both aisled, transepts and a semi-circular termination to the

eastern apse. (At St Étienne, as in many French churches, this was replaced later by the typical French chevet, wherein chapels were built radiating round a larger apse.) Often, in Norman examples, each transept was also finished on the eastern side by an apse, giving a tri-apsidal termination to the building.

The usual pattern in England was a cruciform structure, that is, a plan based on the cross. The western arm, the nave, was generally longer than the other three arms, which were quite short. This is known as the Latin cross plan, in distinction from the Greek cross plan with four equal arms, more common in eastern Europe and later Renaissance work. English cathedrals usually had a longer nave and choir than their Continental counterparts and early examples were not aisled.

After 1100, the English plan began to diverge from the Continental pattern by playing down the importance of the eastern apse or apses. Sometimes the transepts were built forward with chapels also flush with the central apse and, later still, the east ends of the majority of English cathedrals were altered to a square termination. *Ely, Winchester, Peterborough, Lincoln* and *Durham,* for example, have square ends (33). Generally, this was achieved by building on to the eastern arm a Lady Chapel or retro-choir. This provided greater space here, but at the same time it was no longer possible to walk round the ambulatory in the choir, behind the high altar. Among the English cathedrals which still preserve the ambulatory and apsidal east end are *Norwich* (41, 42) and *Canterbury,* while amongst churches, *St Bartholomew-the-Great* in *Smithfield* (London) is now restored to its original plan on this pattern. Again, in English cathedrals, the crossing was usually covered by a low, square, Norman tower, with or without a stumpy spire. On the Continent, a lantern or cupola was more common. The western towers were also square and these might be capped by low spires, as at Southwell* (46). Often, however, the Norman towers have suffered damage or collapse and have been replaced by slenderer Gothic ones.

Inside, the cathedral was usually designed in three horizontal stages. On the ground floor was the arcade (nave, choir or transept), above this was the triforium arcade and the third storey comprised a row of

_____

* These are modern replicas.

38   Trani Cathedral, Italy, c.1094

*39   One bay of nave arcade, Durham
Cathedral from 1093*

NAVE VAULT

CLERESTORY
WINDOWS

TRIFORIUM
ARCADE

TRIFORIUM
PASSAGE

VAULTING SHAFT
WHICH DIVIDES
THE BAYS

NAVE
ARCADE

NAVE
CAPITAL

AISLE
WINDOWS

NAVE
COLUMN

WALL
ARCADING

NAVE
BASE

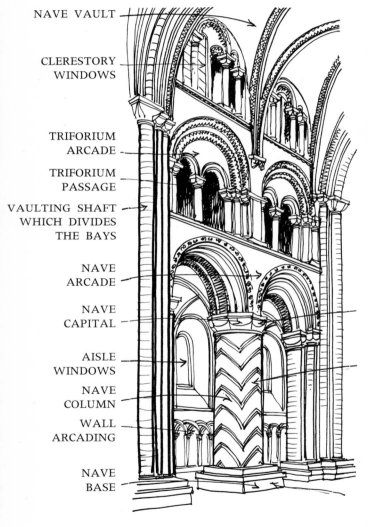

*40   Chapel and Tower of St Rule,
St Andrews, Scotland*

windows. These are termed clerestory (clearstory) windows, in contrast to the triforium arcade, which is also commonly known as the blind-storey. The clerestory windows light the building while behind the triforium arcade is a passage often extending all round the church. This backs on to the sloping roof which covers the aisles and extends from the lower part of the clerestory to the upper aisle arcade.

Reference has already been made to the Norman innovation of articulating the church into bays by means of a vertical, stone shaft extending from floor to nave or choir timber roof. Where a church was stone vaulted, this shaft, or group of shafts, terminated in a capital which supported the vault arch springing (*Durham*) (39); where the nave roof was timber spanned (*Ely*), the shaft(s) extended to the top of the nave wall on which the roof was supported. In cathedrals where bays were so articulated, the bay, usually contained one round arch at nave arcade level, two arches, or two small arches encompassed in a larger one, at triforium level, then one window in the clerestory stage; *Ely* (nave), *Peterborough* (nave and choir), and *Norwich* (transept) Cathedrals are like this. The nave arcade is then supported on piers of grouped shafts alternating with half columns. At *Durham* (nave and choir (39, 52)), the bay articulation is wider permitting two round arches in the nave arcade. Here, then, thick columns with incised decoration, alternate with shafted piers at this level, while in the triforium above, are two arches further subdivided into two.

In the naves of *Gloucester* and *Hereford Cathedrals*, and of *Tewkesbury Abbey Church*, it is the plain, heavy, round columns of the arcade which divide the bays and set the articulation pattern. The triforium arches and clerestory windows are then aligned above the centre of the round, nave arcade arches. A third variation comes in the aqueduct type of design as in *Southwell Minster* nave (48), wherein there are vertical shafts on the walls and each of the three stages is cut into deeply and widely by round-headed arches, one above the other. The stages are divided horizontally by string courses. Between the arches are the round columns at ground floor level, piers at triforium level and solid walling between the clerestory openings. This is an effective spatial design, dramatic, and characteristically Anglo-Norman Romanesque in its contrast of solid wall and column with deeply-shadowed round-arched open-

ings. On similar pattern are many of the Scottish Abbey Churches of this period, for instance the nave at *Dunfermline* (55). Of related design, also, is that at *Worksop Priory*, Nottinghamshire.

Many Norman cathedrals were built with *crypts* under the main floor of the building, and wholly or partly below ground level. These were often used to house the relics of saints and pilgrimages were held to visit them. Two of the finest examples remaining are those at *Canterbury* and *Rochester Cathedrals* (50, 51).

Durham Cathedral. Begun 1093

This is the prime example of Anglo-Norman Romanesque cathedral building in England. Many cathedrals possess extensive Norman workmanship but only at Durham is almost the whole structure in this style. The cathedral is sited magnificently above the River Wear, on a massive rock, appearing to grow out of it. The hill on which it stands is wooded. The differing greens blend superbly with the mellowed warmth of the stone when the rays of the evening sun fall upon the western façade. Although the building from this view is homogeneous, the three towers are not now all of Norman building. The massive central tower, which was originally capped by a low spire, dates from the fifteenth century, while the slenderer, twin western towers partly stem from c.1220 (34).

The cathedral was built, like many others at this time, as a monastic centre and as a fortification; in this case against the Scots. It was begun in 1093 on cruciform plan (33) and most of the interior, including the vault, is of Norman style. The cathedral interior, in its massive, powerful proportions and rows of differently incised columns, is superb. One can gain an impression of how Norman cathedrals must have appeared in the twelfth century, since this is one of the rare examples where clerestory windows have not been enlarged at a later date to give greater illumination (39).

Of greatest significance in architectural history are the stone vaults spanning nave and choir at Durham; the east end was vaulted by 1104 (later rebuilt) and the nave by 1135. These are thought to be the earliest rib vaults of Europe and of consequent importance in the development of Medieval architecture. Their ribs decorated with Romanesque ornament, these vaults give life and mystery to the cathedral design which

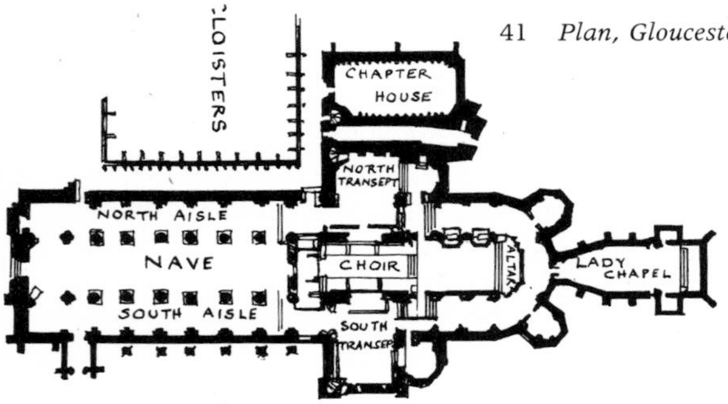

41   *Plan, Gloucester Cathedral*

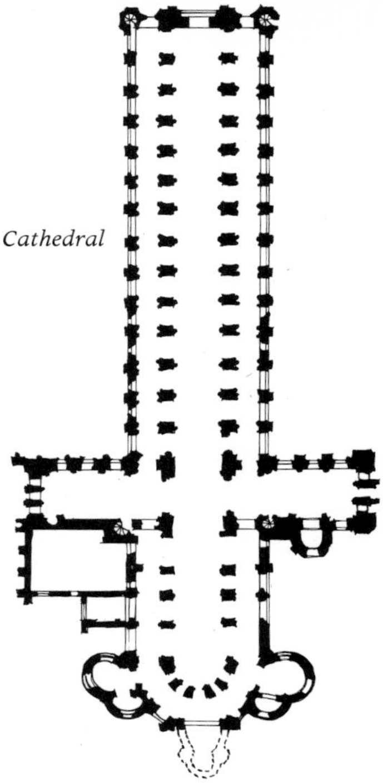

42   *Plan, Norwich Cathedral*

43   *Towered transept,*
Ely Cathedral,
begun 1083

44   *Central tower, St Alban's*
Cathedral, c.1077–88

45   *Norwich Cathedral from the*
east, 1096–1120 and later

46 *Southwell Minster,
c.1130 and later*

47 *Shaft detail, west doorway, Lincoln Cathedral, c.1150*

48 *Nave, Southwell Minster, c.1130*

50 *Crypt, Canterbury Cathedral, c.1096–1107. Groined vault*

49 *Crypt, Lastingham Church, Yorkshire, 1078–88*

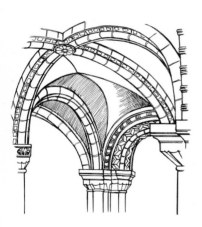

51 *Ribbed vault, monastic building, Canterbury Cathedral, 12th century*

52 *Nave and choir, Durham Cathedral, 1093–1133*

flat, timber roofs, rising on vertical walls, cannot do. They reiterate the rhythm of the vertical bays and round-arched masses, they extend the wall shafts upwards into curved planes, furthering the development of the spatial controlled design begun in the nave arcades. Durham is a powerful, homogeneous interior, dynamic, redolent of its age (52).

Churches

Parish churches were built all over the country at the same time as the cathedrals. Saxon churches were rebuilt as well as new churches on new sites. Similar styles of building and plan were attempted as in the cathedrals, though on a less ambitious scale. While some churches were simple, consisting only of aisleless nave and chancel, others were aisled, or had only one aisle, the other being added at a later date. The cruciform plan was most usual as was also a central tower, with short spire, over the crossing. Many chancels were apsidal, but these were frequently altered to a square termination when the eastern arm was extended in the Gothic period. The majority of Norman churches in England have been altered greatly or totally transformed. Of those which retain much of their character, especially in nave, tower and doorway or porch are *Kirkby Lonsdale Church*, Yorkshire, *Walsoken Church*, Norfolk, *Iffley Church*, Oxfordshire (58, 64), *Old Shoreham*, Sussex (67), *Barfreston*, Kent (81, 82), *Kilpeck,* Herefordshire (75, 76, 77, 78), and *St Bartholomew-the-Great*, Smithfield (72, 73). The last-named, already mentioned, has been considerably restored, mainly to the original design. In areas where stone was not easily available to bond the corners of a square tower, round towers were built. A number of these survive in Norfolk, where the lower courses are often of Saxon construction. Good examples include *Hales Church* and those at *Haddiscoe* and neighbouring *Thorpe-next-Haddiscoe*.

A few churches were built in England on centrally planned lines. They are based on the Early Christian church type like S. Costanza and S. Stefano Rotondo in Rome (fourth and fifth centuries) which, in turn, stemmed from the Ancient Roman mausoleum concept (59, 61). The English ones are Anglo-Norman Romanesque instead of classical like the Rome examples, but they have the same circular plan, with an inner ring of arcaded columns supporting triforium walling and arcade and, above, clerestory windows.

There is usually a conical roof over the central part above the clerestory windows, and a lower roof, at triforium level, over the circular aisle. The *Holy Sepulchre Church* at Cambridge dates from *c*.1130 and, though restored in the 1840s, is patterned on the original design (60). The *Temple Church* in London, dating from 1185, is another example. This was seriously damaged in the Second World War and has been rebuilt and added to.

Arches, columns, piers, arcades

The Romanesque *arch* is round. This can vary in form from the *semi-circular* shape, which is the most usual, and where the centre is on the diameter line, to the *segmental*, with a centre above diameter level, and the *stilted*, where it is below. The horseshoe arch, so common in southern Italy and Spain, is of Saracenic origin. Here, the curve is carried below the semi-circle; it is rarely used in England. Since Norman walling is thick, there is considerable depth between the two faces of the arch, inner and outer. In early work, the arch is not recessed; the edges are square in section and not moulded or ornamented (57, 87). Later work is moulded in deep rolls and rounds and often enriched with chevron (zig-zag), nail-head, billet, lozenge, cable or star decoration (48, 89, 90, 95, 97). Arches are constructed with radiating wedge-shaped blocks of stone, called *voussoirs* (77, 82). The central one at the top is the *keystone* and the horizontal ones at the sides, the *springers*. This is the point at which the arch springs from the capital. The under surface of an arch is termed the *soffit*, the upper surface, the *extrados*. Good examples of Norman arches are in *Durham Cathedral* nave (39, 52) and galilee, *Gloucester Cathedral* nave, *Ely Cathedral* nave.

Both columns and piers were used in Anglo-Norman building. The columns are circular in section (48, 74, 87, 89, 90, 95) and the piers square, often shafted with heavy half-columns and slenderer shafts (52, 73). They are all massive in scale and either plain, or decorated with incised carving in zig-zag, spiral or network patterns. *Durham Cathedral* (39, 52) and *Dunfermline Abbey Church* (55) have incised columns; *Gloucester* and *Tewkesbury*, plain versions.

The purpose of a capital is to give a larger area from which the arch may spring than the column or pier on which it stands. It also ornaments the junction (36). Early Norman examples are very plain and large. The

53   *Doorway, St Botolph's Priory, Colchester*

54   *Porch, Malmesbury Abbey, 12th century*

55   *Nave, Dunfermline Abbey, Scotland, 12th century*

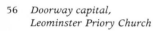

56   *Doorway capital,*
      Leominster Priory Church

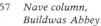

57   *Nave column,*
      Buildwas Abbey

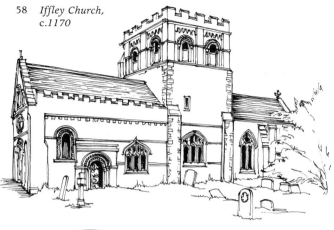

58 Iffley Church,
c.1170

60 Holy Sepulchre Church, Cambridge, c.1130

59 Plan, S. Costanza

61 Church of S. Costanza,
Rome, c.340

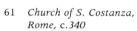
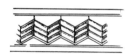

62 Chevron ornament   63 Star ornament

64 South doorway, Iffley Church

top member, the *abacus*, is a square or round block of stone and, in early work, constitutes the whole capital. Soon mouldings were added below and capitals were circular (*Tewkesbury Abbey*) and octagonal (*Durham Cathedral*) (39, 52). Cushion capitals were most typical (*Peterborough Cathedral* nave and *Kirkwall Cathedral* nave, Orkney); other designs were simply voluted at the corners in a rough imitation of the classical Ionic capital (*St John's Chapel*, Tower of London) (65, 87). From the cushion capital developed the scalloped design (57, 66, 89, 90) (*Holy Sepulchre Church*, Cambridge and *Hereford Cathedral* nave) and late Norman work includes some foliated capitals and others carved in figure and animal motifs (*Canterbury Cathedral* crypt), though these are rarer and never so vigorous and varied as those on the Continent (37, 56, 95).

Early Norman *bases* are plain and insignificant, consisting of an octagonal or square plinth and/or a quarter-round moulding (*Gloucester Cathedral* nave). Later examples have deeper and more complex mouldings, but all are round on a square or octagonal plinth (*St John's Chapel*, Tower of London) (39, 52, 57, 87, 89, 90, 95).

In Medieval architecture the arch is often used in arcading, where a row of columns or piers support arches (39, 52, 87, 89, 90, 95). These arcades may also be of decorative purpose only, standing in front of a plain wall surface. In these cases, the arches frequently interlace one another. They may be seen inside, at triforium level (48, 72) or for any wall decoration as in towers (43) and apses (choir aisle *Durham Cathedral*; south transept, *Ely Cathedral*; façade, *Castle Acre Priory*, Norfolk; façade, *Rochester Cathedral*; central lantern, exterior and interior, *Norwich Cathedral*, 45).

Roofs and Vaults

The exteriors of Norman *roofs* in Britain were covered by tiles or stone slates, wood shingles or thatch. The pitch was fairly steep to throw off water and snow. Later roofs were lead covered and so flatter. Roofs overhung the walls for drainage purposes and were supported by a cornice at the top of the wall. This, in turn, stood upon *corbels*, which are decoratively carved stone blocks. The complete member, cornice and corbels, is called a *corbel table*. A parapet might be built above this. These parapets were generally in the form of an inner and outer wall with lead-lined

passage between. These walls were pierced at intervals to let the water out. In order to project the water away from the wall face, lead spouts were fixed at these intervals and generally set into stone blocks which were carved into *gargoyles*. These were fashioned in many forms: devils, animals, birds, monsters, etc. The usual theory is that they represent the evil spirits which were captured and rendered harmless in stone by the Christian spirit of the building which they decorated. Some gargoyle spouts projected from aisle buttresses also.

The *interior* of the roofing was of timber or stone. Most Norman roofing was in wood, especially over the wider spans of nave or choir in a church or cathedral. In secular building and smaller churches the roof was left open to show the rafters and was of a fairly high pitch. The roof timbers were roughly trimmed heavy baulks, the possible width of span being determined by the length of timber available. Ridge ribs, purlins and wall plates ran horizontally, the latter being supported on stone corbels at the top of the walls. Rafters ran crosswise at right angles to the main beams. A heavy tie beam extended from wall to wall at intervals to counteract the outward thrust of the roof (48, 95).

In larger cathedrals and churches a flat boarded and painted ceiling was constructed underneath the open roof. A number of these buildings still possess such ceiled roofs, but these are usually replacements (the naves of *St Albans' Abbey Church, Rochester Cathedral*, and *Ely Cathedral*). Genuine Norman timber roofing of any kind is a rarity today.

An interior span covered by stone is called a *vault*. The Romans had known how to cover wide spans with stone and concrete and had used such vaults to roof their thermal baths and such domed buildings as the Pantheon in Rome. The art had been almost lost in the west in the years that followed the collapse of the Empire, though it was expanded in areas under Byzantine influence. In southern France and in Italy, where the classical trend persisted, the art of *barrel vaulting* was not abandoned. These barrel, or tunnel, vaults were continuous round arches of stone constructed on centering, that is, by building a wooden frame on the underside to the desired form, then setting stones and mortar in position on top. The framework was moved on to the next section when the mortar had set. Barrel vaults were used in England by Saxon and earlier Norman builders, where the span was fairly narrow. It was a method particularly suited to aisles. A good example survives in *St John's Chapel* in the Tower of London (87).

More common in England was the further development of the vault. Anglo-Norman builders were pace-setters in this field. At a time when barrel vaults were in general use in France and Italy, England had moved on to the *groined* and then the *rib vault*. The latter is generally regarded as a characteristic of Gothic architecture, but it was used with the round arch in England in Norman times. The groined vault is an intersecting barrel vault, where the two tunnels meet at right angles, giving four arches with different direction faces. Massive piers or columns are set at the intersections to support the vault. This was a common means of vaulting large crypts in Norman times. Those at *Canterbury* and *Rochester Cathedrals* are good examples (49, 50).

By the twelfth century builders were urgently seeking methods to cover the wider spans of cathedral naves with stone roofing, partly to enhance the interior design and partly to reduce the risk of fire damage. This problem was first solved at *Durham Cathedral* where the *ribbed vault* was built. In this system a skeleton of stone ribs for six arches is thrown over the span, supported on the pillars below. Two of the arches cross the square vaulting compartment diagonally, the others transverse from side to side from the span making four compartments in between. The arches are all built separately on centering. Infilling in stone was completed later between the ribs. The whole structure is lighter in weight than the barrel vault and, as at Durham, gives height and chiaroscuro to the interior of the building (39, 51, 52).

An essential complement to the subject of stone vaulting is that of *abutment*, though this did not fully develop till the Gothic period of building. A buttress is a reinforcement and projection to a wall. Its use makes the immensely thick wall less necessary. It enhances the design of the structure and economises on building materials. Norman builders constructed massive walls and used little abutment. Their buttresses were flat, of low projection and adhered to the exterior wall (70).

The chief need for abutment comes from the thrust and pressure set up from roofs and towers. With timber roofing and low towers, little abutment is needed, but as the Normans developed stone vaulting the matter of abutment increased in importance. In a timber roof the tie beam structure largely counteracts the outward thrust on walling. Barrel vaults create a uniform thrust along the whole wall so that the massive Norman wall with flat buttresses was adequate. With groined and ribbed vaulting, the maximum thrust is exerted via the diagonal ribs or groins, producing maximum force at points on the wall just above the arch springing. It is here that the buttress must provide the counterthrust needed. In between, the wall can safely be weakened by windows. The Normans, therefore, used a simple flying buttress system, but these are not visible on the exterior of the building (as in later Gothic architecture) but are internal, only to be seen in the triforia passages.

Doorways, porches, window openings

The *doorway* was the most richly ornamented feature in Anglo-Norman architecture; this was especially so in twelfth-century workmanship. It was deeply recessed and heavily moulded in concentric semi-circular arches. In order to concentrate the principal decoration on the exterior face, the door was set nearer to the inside wall surface. The mouldings were then continued down from the arch and impost moulding to the ground; they were often set with shafts, each of which possessed a decorative capital and base.

The actual door was of wood and was square-headed; few have survived. The space between the doorhead and the inner arch was filled by a stone slab called the *tympanum*. This acted as the focal centre of the doorway ornament, being carved in high relief in floral or animal sculpture or, in some cases, in a figure composition representing a scene from the bible. Since Norman doorways were large, it was not necessary to enlarge them greatly in later years (53, 97), so many fine examples are extant. Among the best of these are the façade entrance doorways at *Lincoln* (47) and *Rochester Cathedrals* (37), at *Malmesbury Abbey Church* (54) and at the churches of *Iffley* (64), *Barfreston* (81) and *Kilpeck* (75).

Norman *porches* are in similar style, the side often being arcaded. A very fine example survives from the monastic buildings at *Canterbury Cathedral* (74).

In contrast to the doorways, Norman *windows* are small and narrow. Early examples are little more than round-headed slits a few inches wide. The opening

65 *Capital, c.1080*

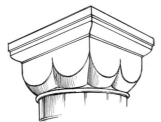

66 *Capital, c.1080*

67 *Old Shoreham Church,*
Sussex

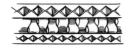

68 *Billet and lozenge*
ornament

69 *Window, Castle Rising*
Church, c.1160

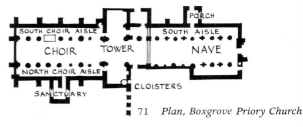

71 *Plan, Boxgrove Priory Church*

70 *Buttresses*

72 *Nave triforium,*
St Bartholomew-
the-Great, London

73 *Pier, St*
Bartholomew-the-
Great

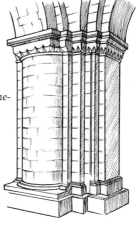

74 *Porch and*
staircase,
Canterbury
Cathedral,
c.1150–65

is set near to the outer wall face and is deeply splayed from the inside. They were made so narrow partly because of the lack of glass but chiefly for reasons of defence. These early window openings are usually undecorated (91, 92). Later examples are, like the doorways, round-headed, with carved mouldings in concentric semi-circles and with shafts set at the sides. *Iffley* and *Castle Rising Churches* (69) have windows like this. Not many examples survive as they were mostly enlarged in later Medieval times. A few openings were divided into two lights by a central shaft but tracery had not yet begun to develop. Small windows are also to be seen.

Towers and Steeples

Norman towers are wide and low. Later examples are richly ornamented on all four faces with arcading, which incorporates narrow, slit window and belfry openings. Round the top edge is an embattled parapet, set with gargoyle spouts and, at each corner, a decorative turret (44). Originally, most of these towers, which are set over the crossing and flanking the western façade or transepts of ecclesiastical buildings, had low pyramidal spires of wood. These have generally disappeared. The replacements at Southwell Minster are of this type of design. Many excellent examples of Norman towers exist all over the country. Among the finest are the transeptal towers at *Exeter Cathedral* (79), the central towers at *Tewkesbury Abbey Church, Norwich Cathedral* (45), *Winchester Cathedral* and *Southwell Minster* (46) and much of the western towers at Southwell, and also *Durham Cathedral* (34); *Canterbury Cathedral* has one early Norman tower on the south side.

Sculptural decoration is not common on Anglo-Norman ornamental work. Usually this is abstract or geometrical in form and applied to mouldings, capitals and columns. An exception to this can be seen in the one or two surviving tympana such as the Christ on the *Prior's doorway* at *Ely Cathedral* and the porch sculptures of the Apostles at *Malmesbury Abbey*. The Herefordshire school of sculpture is, therefore, of unusual interest in England, since it produced on a small scale sculptural carvings of vigour and imagination comparable to the richness and variety of French Burgundian work. *Kilpeck Church* is the chief example of this carving, especially on the south doorway (75, 76, 77, 78), while the font at *Eardisley Church* shows the lion enmeshed in magic plaitwork like the German examples of this time (80). In a different part of the country, *Barfreston Church* in Kent is also notable for its doorway carving (81, 82).

Monastic Building

The Church was the most important factor in the life of Medieval man. The Christian religion, as evidenced in the Church, touched his life in all its aspects, all the time. The Church was the moving spirit behind the tremendous building drive which created the great cathedrals, and the largest contribution in this field was in the monasteries. This is, above all, a religious architecture, though the buildings are practical, both in their arrangement and design, so as to enable the monks to live and work efficiently and harmoniously to the greater glory of God. During the Middle Ages the monastic communities provided education, shelter and guidance and the monks were themselves chief among the learned and educated members of society.

Many Orders built their monasteries in Britain. The mother houses of most of these were on the Continent, primarily in France. The building pattern varied in architectural design and detail but, in general, the layout was similar, so that a monk from one Order could easily find his way about the monastery of another. This was the result of years of developing the best and most convenient way of laying out a large, complex group of buildings.

The important structures of a monastery were first of all built in wood in a temporary manner then, over the years, rebuilt in stone. The church was always transferred first into permanent materials and other buildings followed later. Often large sections of the monastery were left in timber, with thatch roofing, for many years, rendering them liable to periodic, devastating fires. Thus, although the eleventh and twelfth centuries were the most energetic years of building, most monasteries today are the remains of later, Gothic styles of workmanship, replacing Norman building destroyed by fires.

The church was generally on cruciform plan with a central tower over the crossing.* This is, in most

---

* The Cistercian Abbey Churches were, in accordance with the dictates of their Order, very plain and simple. Early examples were aisleless and had no tower over the crossing. Later Norman Cistercian building, like *Fountains*

75   *South doorway, c.1140*

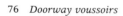

76   *Doorway voussoirs*

77   *Doorway detail*

78   *Doorway detail*

80 *Font, Eardisley Church*

81 *Doorway, Barfreston Church*

79 *North transeptal tower, Exeter Cathedral, c.1112–40*

82 *Doorway voussoirs, Barfreston*

instances, the only building surviving intact from many monasteries because, after the Dissolution in the time of Henry VIII, the church was converted into use as a parish church or cathedral for the lay community of the neighbouring town or village. Only those in remote areas, such as the Cistercian monasteries of Yorkshire – *Fountains, Rievaulx, Jervaulx, Kirkstall* – and those in Scotland, such as *Melrose*, or in the west country – *Tintern* – were left to ruin. But for the repair work of the nineteenth and twentieth centuries thse monuments would probably have disappeared by now. Among the abbey churches later converted to cathedral and parish use may be listed such famous buildings as *Canterbury, Winchester, Ely, Rochester* and *Norwich Cathedrals*; *Westminster* and *Sherborne Abbeys*.

The domestic buildings of the monastery were usually arranged round a quadrangle, one side of which was formed by the nave of the church, while its transept provided one right angle corner of the court. In the centre of this was generally a lawn – the *cloister garth*. On all four sides was a stone-flagged walk with an open, stone screen and lean-to roof covering it. This was called the *cloister* and has survived intact in many cathedrals and abbey churches. The cloister was often built on the south side of the church nave, to face the sun and to give protection from the north-east wind. Around it were then constructed the dormitory, refectory, chapter house, infirmary, almonry, library, calefactory and abbot's lodging. The dormitory was usually built next to the church transept. The monks could then enter the church undercover during the night, for services, by way of the night stairs. These still exist in a number of churches.

The Castle

Life was turbulent and insecure. Protection was equally important to the lord of the manor and his

---

Abbey Church, has a central tower and the nave has aisles. It is noteworthy, though, that the nave arcade (as is frequent in Cistercian Norman building) has pointed arches and a plain wall where the triforium stage is usually built. Cistercian churches almost invariably have square eastern terminations. The large numbers of churches built in this way by the Order was undoubtedly an influential factor in developing this characteristic in other ecclesiastical building in England.

meanest servants. Security was provided by the grouping together of the community in a fortified centre. This varied in size according to the wealth and lands owned by the nobleman, but the manner of living was similar, whatever the size of his estate. If this was important, a large castle was built, if small, then a modest house, but in each case fortified defences were essential.

Before 1100 most castles and houses were built of wood, with thatch roofing, on the *motte-and-bailey* principle. The *motte* was a large natural or artificially made hill or mound (94). A deep ditch was dug round its base. Round this was the *bailey*, an area of land enclosed by a wooden stockade which, in turn, was encircled by an earth rampart and a further, outer ditch. On top of the motte was built the house or castle, enclosed by a wooden fence. In this lived the lord, his family and servants. Inside the bailey were erected wooden buildings for storehouses and granaries, barns, smithy, kitchens, soldiers' quarters, villagers' cottages and stables. When under attack, everyone retreated to the castle, which could withstand a long siege. The only access route was via fortified bridges over the ditches and these were kept full of water.

In the twelfth century the wooden structures in important centres were replaced by stone ones. The hill castles were built in the form of keeps or strongpoints. These were of two types; the rectangular ones and the shell keeps. Both were built in large numbers but the latter were less strong and fewer have survived. The rectangular *keep* was an almost impregnable structure, large and heavy, too heavy to be constructed on an artificial mound, so it had to be sited on a natural eminence. The keep, up to 150 feet in height, was usually square in plan, with immensely thick walls, up to 20 feet thick at base, and with flat buttresses at the corners and in the centre of the four faces. These buttresses die away into the splayed base. Passages, bedrooms and garderobes were built into the thicknesses of these massive walls. Turrets were constructed at each corner of the keep, containing spiral stone staircases, with a central newel which extended through all the four or five floors. These staircases were designed so that one man could defend them against many ascending attackers as his right, sword hand would be free while those of the attackers were restricted by the newel.

The main entrance to the keep was on the first

83 *The White Tower, keep of the Tower of London, 1078–90*

87 *St John's Chapel, Tower of London, c.1080*

84 *The keep, Goodrich Castle, c.1160*

85 *Plan, Dover Castle keep*

86 *Plan, third floor of keep, Tower of London*

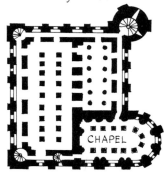

88   *Plan of second floor
      of keep*

89   *Second floor of keep
      as it is now*

90   *Impression of how 89 would have looked in the 12th century*

91   *Guildford Castle keep, 12th century*

92   *Malling Castle keep, c.1070*

93   *The Jew's House, Lincoln, c.1160*

94   *Keep and mound, Cardiff Castle, 11th century*

95   *Great Hall, Oakham Castle, c.1190*

96   *Carved moulding*

97   *Doorway, Jew's House*

floor; below this was an undercroft, used for storage, and this had a stone vaulted roof and solid, unpierced walls. The first floor was occupied by the garrison and servants and had only slit windows. The chief room in the castle was the great hall, which generally occupied the whole of the second floor. In larger keeps, this would be about 45 feet square and 30 feet high: a span too wide for timber baulks, so a stone dividing wall was built across the centre, pierced with open arches so that the room could still be used as one chamber. Ceiling timbers then spanned each half with great baulks slotted into holes in the stonework and smaller rafters crossing them at right-angles. This gave a flat roof to one storey and floor to the one above. *Fireplaces* were set into the outer walls with flues extending upwards at an angle to the exterior face. *Sanitation* was provided by the garde-robes built into the wall thicknesses. These had stone seats and a vent gave exit to the wall outside or a cesspool below.

The *great hall* was where everyone ate, lived and slept. Its stone walls were hung with woven fabrics, its floor strewn with rushes. There was no privacy. Small *bedchambers* were built into the thicknesses of the walls for the lord and his family but, even for these, the only access was through the arched door-ways in the hall. There were no doors. The windows in the outer walls corresponded with these openings, thus giving light to the hall. There was no glass, only wooden shutters which could shut out the cold air but only at the expense of cutting out the light as well. Bedsteads, in these bedchambers, were wood plat-forms piled with bedding – sheets, pillows, quilts and fur rugs. Curtains hung round to keep out the draughts were suspended from poles projecting from the walls on either side of the bed.

In the hall, there was little *furniture*. Oak chests, often only hollowed-out tree trunks, banded with iron, were used for storage of linen and silver as well as being seats. These are the oldest type of furniture. Trestle tables* and benches were set up at meal times. The lord and his guest sat at one end of the hall, their table often raised on a daïs. A wooden gallery for the musicians was usually built opposite to this, for music was an essential accompaniment to meals. At night guests and servants slept on the floor near the fireplaces. Artificial lighting was provided by sputter-ing torches, dipped in fat, and stuck in iron holders, lamps holding burning oil, home-made rushlights and, very costly, candles. The latter were set in iron candleholders, suspended from the ceiling beams. The hall was the centre of castle life for everyone from all social classes (89, 90, 95).

A number of the larger rectangular Norman keeps survive in Britain, as well as a few shell ones. The best preserved is the *White Tower*, keep of the Tower of London, built by William I c.1080 (83, 86). The *chapel* was an important chamber in larger keeps and *St John's Chapel* here is a magnificent example of its type (87). Other keeps of considerable interest include *Rochester Castle* (88, 89, 90), *Castle Hedingham*, Essex and *Dover* (85), *Porchester, Goodrich* (84) and *Colchester Castles*.

Little exists of domestic Norman building apart from the great castles. Most *houses* were of wood. The stone ones were fortified like the castles and the hall was the living and bedroom for everyone. It usually had a central hearth, logs piled against iron firedogs on a brick hearth. The smoke escaped through a louvre in the roof timbers. The *Jew's House* in Lincoln, c.1160, is a rare survivor, in much altered form (93, 97).

---

* The expression 'bed and board' had a literal meaning in Medieval times, signifying the two essentials for a traveller or guest.

CHAPTER THREE

The Gothic Style: Ecclesiastical Architecture 1150–1550

The Gothic form of architecture emerged from the Romanesque in a gradual transition. For some decades in the twelfth century, both in Britain and in France (where the new form was established first), characteristics of both types of building were present, side by side, in one structure. In Britain we refer to such work as 'transitional', where pointed arches are supported on heavy, round columns, as in Cistercian monastic churches, and ribbed stone vaults are carried on a Romanesque arcade, as at Durham, the flying buttresses being hidden from view behind the triforium arcade.

Gothic architecture is readily definable and recognised wherever it is to be found. Its characteristics are well known – the pointed arch, the stone ribbed vault and flying buttress. But none of these was previously unknown. The style is a fusion of these factors into a new concept, which evolved and grew to maturity over four whole centuries, adapting to the aesthetic ideals and needs of the people. In Britain, where the style developed early and was abandoned late, there are four distinct interpretations of the form. Each developed from the preceding one and made steady progress away from the solidity of the Romanesque towards the seeming ethereal fragility of the soaring spires and panelled stone and glass of the later fifteenth century.

Although Gothic architecture evolved gradually from the Romanesque, and it is not easy to ascribe a specific date to its emergence, it represents a completely new artistic and structural expression which was a reflection of the different spirit of the time in which it was born. The term 'Gothic' was coined in a later age as one of disapprobation and contempt. It was the sixteenth-century Italian artist and historian, Giorgio Vasari, who used the term and, in doing so, was merely expressing the thinking of his time, equating Medieval architecture with barbarism. To a post-Renaissance scholar, the Middle Ages had advanced only a small way beyond the sixth-century Goths; it was the Renaissance which brought greatness to architecture. The Romanesque style of building had been based upon the (Roman) classical tradition and, though no doubt regarded as a crude version by sixteenth-century Italy, it followed the basic, stable pattern.

The term 'Middle Ages' was similarly coined, in this case by a seventeenth-century German scholar, who likened it to an intermediate era between the collapse of the Roman Empire and the re-birth of classicism in the Renaissance ideals of the fifteenth century. To him also it represented a period of barbarism and decline.

Today, seen from a more distant perspective, we appreciate that Gothic architecture (for the term is now synonymous with Medieval building), was a great art form in its own right and one which had its birth and dominance in northern Europe not, as in the case of classicism, south of the Alps.

The all-pervasive influence during the Middle Ages was Christianity. The Church and its buildings were not only concerned with Sunday worship but formed an integral part of people's daily life. Everyone put tremendous effort into building the House of God, whether this was a great cathedral, a monastic structure or a simple, village church. This was the most important building of the community; it was in a durable material, and upon it was lavished the wealth, time and skill of the whole district. In return, the buildings and the men of God gave to the population security in times of danger, advice, interest and assistance in their daily lives, and they represented the chief source of education and knowledge for the community. To an illiterate population the decoration of the church gave a visible reality to their beliefs. On exterior and interior could be seen a pictorial record of the Bible story and teaching. The great sculptured portals of France, the wall and ceiling mosaics of Italy, the wall paintings and carved capitals and jambs of Britain, together with the beautiful coloured glass everywhere, all depict the theme so that the word of God could be passed from generation to generation and the intensity of faith kept alive.

It is difficult to pinpoint the exact time and place of the birth of a new movement. It is accepted that the earliest buildings completed in the Gothic style were in the Île de France, that small area in the vicinity of Paris, and that the classic pattern of the northern Gothic cathedral was established there in such examples as Notre Dame in Paris and at Amiens, Reims and Laon. It cannot be argued so categorically that this was the sole source of the style in the twelfth century or that it would not soon have developed in a similar manner elsewhere if the Île de France had not then produced it.

Great movements in all subjects – arts, sciences, medicine – begin and establish themselves because the climate is ready to receive them. The need is there and so is the ability to create the new development. The pointed arch was evolved because it became the key to constructing buildings which were then desirable. It was of vital importance that the House of God and its accompanying monastic buildings should be saved from the ravages of fire which were taking such toll of the timber-roofed Romanesque churches. Only a handful of these, for example Durham Cathedral, had stone vaults. It was the need for the development of the stone vault, to cover all ranges of height and width, which led to the evolution of Gothic architecture with its characteristic pointed arch. For the round Norman arch presents great problems in vaulting a church.

The pointed arch was not new. It had long been used in the Middle East and, in Europe, had been employed in areas subject to Moorish influence, such

as Spain and Sicily. It was being developed in such regions in the twelfth century, but northern France was, at this time, a more stable area, less troubled economically and by warfare. The stability of the Île de France region led to the creation of schools of artists and craftsmen, who travelled widely to execute commissions in different parts of Europe. Soon southern England too was creating its own schools of craftsmen.

The pointed arch is particularly suited to the stone vaulting of a church because of its flexibility of design. The problems arising from the use of the semi-circular arch stem from the fact that the nave and choir and their aisles often have different widths and heights. Vaulting is constructed in bays and the semi-circular arch lends itself to the square bay. The form of the bay is decided by the positioning of the supporting piers or columns. In Romanesque cathedrals the bay was transversed at roof level by two ribs which curved in diagonal line from nave pier to nave pier. As the diagonal ribs were longer than the four ribs connecting the four sides or faces of the bay, it was impossible for all those ribs to be semi-circular in section unless the vaults were dome-shaped and so making an uneven ridge line; alternatively, the side arches had to be stilted, not semi-circular or, more commonly, two bays were handled as one, making a longer, rectangular, not square, bay. Further problems arose because aisles were narrower and lower than nave and choir and this was even more difficult to reconcile with the rigid concept of the semi-circular arch. In consequence, few Romanesque buildings were stone vaulted. The pointed arch was more flexible for this purpose since it can be varied in proportion of width to height in order to accommodate differing spans and levels. The French aptly term this arch the *arc brisé*, the broken arch, which gives a clear picture of its function.

As the Gothic period advanced, churches became larger and higher: window and doorway openings increased in size so that the buildings were flooded with light. This was in contrast to the lower Romanesque churches, lit only by small, narrow windows. The knowledge of structure in masonry was extending quickly and, with this advance in technique, came the means to erect buildings which were mere shells of stone ribs and pillars. The area of solid wall shrank and the design became correspondingly more complex. Each individual member of the structure became more attenuated. Heavy columns and piers gave place to slender, lofty piers, encircled with clustered shafts, terminating in small moulded or foliated capitals. Towers became slenderer, many completed with equally elegant spires. The exterior of the church became a forest of vertical stone pinnacles stretching upwards into the vaults of heaven; the interior a mystic chiaroscuro in stone, gently illuminated by shafts of sunlight, gloriously coloured by their transition through the window glass.

This miracle of immense stone cathedrals pierced by great openings and carved into tracery was made structurally possible by the engineering development of the stone vault and its associated abutment. Both of these stem from the original adoption of the pointed arch. The basis of structures employing this form of arch, supported on piers, led, over many years, to great variety in vault design. In Britain especially many types of vault were designed, each evolving a stage further in delicacy and complexity, from the simple, ribbed, quadripartite vault, with four ribs and four compartments, of the thirteenth century, to the lierne and star designs of the fourteenth and the fan vault of the final phase. The Gothic buttress is the complement to the vault. As the latter progresses and becomes higher, wider and more complex, so must the abutment. The structure of a Gothic church, its arches, piers and vault, exerts an outward and downward pressure on the walls. In order to avoid thickening the whole wall area, as Romanesque builders had done, the Gothic mason provided reinforcement in the form of a stone buttress at the point on the wall where it was most needed. This point is just below the springing line of the vault. The abutment system moved, step by step, with that of vault design, from simple, wall buttresses to the forest of flying buttress pinnacles seen in fifteenth-century structures. Like all component parts of Gothic architecture, such abutment acquired an aesthetic and spiritual quality – an art form in itself – which stemmed from the original structural need.

The Cathedrals and Abbeys

The affinity between the fellow craftsmen grew closer during the Gothic period. The rapport among masons, glaziers, painters and metalworkers was complete and satisfying. No craftsman was of more vital importance than the sculptor. Carvers and modellers enjoyed freedom of expression and were presented with an immense architectural canvas on which to experiment and design. The Gothic cathedral façade was a supreme vehicle for such expression. The pattern was established in France in the early thirteenth century of a twin-towered façade with triple portico at base, spreading across the width of the elevation. The whole of this façade was decorated with symbolic sculpture, but it was the portals which were the focus of the design. On French cathedrals jamb and trumeau figures, tympanum scenes, archivolt groups, gargoyles and cresting, all played a part in relating the Bible story from Old and New Testaments. French sculptors were supreme and travelled widely in Europe, showing other nations how to enrich their cathedral façades.

In Britain there was much less sculpture. Carved decoration was largely restricted to capitals (foliated and with animals and birds), tympana and wall designs. The triple portal with its richly sculptured ornament is rare in Britain. At *Peterborough Cathedral*, for example, the west front has an immense triple portico, but the decoration is architectural, not sculptural. The great exception to this, in the thirteenth century, is *Wells Cathedral*, where in the niches of the west façade were over 300 statues and reliefs, of which about half remain (103). The general theme, representing the Fall and Redemption of Man, depicts this story from the Creation to the Enthronement of Christ. The sculptures still retain traces of the colour with which they were once vividly painted. There are a number of later Gothic porches and portals which are richly sculptured as, for instance, the south porch at Gloucester Cathedral (141).

The prototype of the Gothic cathedral is the Île de France pattern. Buildings like *Amiens Cathedral* represent, in Gothic form, a similar contribution to the architecture of their time as that made by the Parthenon to Hellenic Greece. One of the very first experiments in the Gothic style, using the pointed arch and vaulting system supported on slender columns, was the *Abbey Church of St Denis*, built between 1135 and 1145. Now in a Paris suburb, most of the church has been restored or rebuilt, but part of the original choir exists and the reconstructed west front still shows the early mixture of round and pointed arch heads.

In Britain it was not perceived for some time, in the twelfth century, that buildings such as St Denis and the *Cathedral of Paris*, begun in 1163, were creations of an entirely new structure and style in architecture. The British were using the pointed arch, but did not appreciate its structural possibilities. The Cistercians, for instance, preferred the pointed arch for its austere, aesthetic qualities and it can be seen in the nave arcades of such monastic churches as Fountains and Rievaulx Abbeys, set in a plain arcade upon massive Norman piers and columns. The pointed arch was also employed decoratively as a wall arcade.

The prototype equivalent in England to St Denis in France is the choir of *Canterbury Cathedral*. This, the first Gothic structure in Britain, was largely the work of a Frenchman, *William of Sens*. So called after the town of his birth, William had watched the *Cathedral of Sens* being built in Gothic design and when, in 1174, Canterbury Cathedral choir was severely damaged by fire and William was given the task of rebuilding, he constructed it in Gothic style. A revolutionary English structure for the time, William directed operations from 1175 until, five years later, he was crippled by a fall from some scaffolding and returned to France. The choir was completed by another William, known for distinctive reasons as the Englishman. The choir of Canterbury Cathedral is not only the first Gothic structure to be built in Britain, but it is entirely Gothic and owes nothing to Romanesque ancestry. Elegant columns and clustered piers, with foliated capitals, support the moulded, pointed-arched arcade. Above is the arcaded triforium and lancet clerestory windows, while the vaulting shafts, which carry the quadripartite vault, stand on the same nave capitals. The eastern termination of the choir is also of French design in that it is apsidal, with ambulatory behind the altar, while the circular eastern chapel is appropriately named Becket's crown (110).

It was *Thomas Rickman*, writer and ecclesiastical archaeologist, who, in 1817, classified the English styles of Gothic architecture under names which are still popularly used. He considered that Gothic architecture extended from 1066 until the middle of the sixteenth century and divided this long period into sections which replaced the previous divisions into centuries. His terms were Norman, Early English, Decorated and Perpendicular.

Since the time of Rickman many writers, both Victorian and twentieth-century, have given different classification, names and dates to Gothic architecture, but Rickman's description and nomenclature has

survived. By later study we have learnt that it is inaccurate to be too dogmatic in applying specific dates to these subdivisions because one style merged gradually into another. Each period evolved into the next during a transitional time, when some features of one style were used together with the newer one on a single structure. In different parts of Britain the onward progress was attained at different speeds and in different stages. One style of Gothic architecture did not prevail over the whole country at a given date. Gothic architecture is now thought to extend from the simple Lancet (or, as Rickman called it Early English) style, beginning with Canterbury Cathedral choir of 1175–84, until Elizabethan Mannerism took over from the Tudor version of Gothic about 1550.

The differing phases of the Gothic style are mirrored most richly and informatively in our cathedrals. These were the most important structures of their age and were therefore in the van of new ideas and art forms. Many of these cathedrals were built originally as the abbey churches of the monastery. After the Dissolution by Henry VIII, a large number of them survived as parish churches and later became cathedral churches. Some of the most famous of our cathedrals come into this category. None of the cathedrals in Britain is now in one style of Gothic architecture, though nearly all of them were built between 1066 and 1550. Most of them have some Norman workmanship, and some have vestiges of Saxon remains. The majority were added to and altered during the whole Medieval period, each retaining a larger proportion of one style in particular.

The *Lancet* or Early English type of Gothic architecture, often referred to as the springtime of the style, was fully developed between 1200 and 1275. It was a form of simplicity and grace. In Britain, where there was less sculptural decoration than on the Continent at this time, there is a certain austerity of form, but also a singular beauty of proportion, a freshness and unclutteredness. The characteristics of the architecture of these years are the plain, quadripartite ribbed vault, slender towers, with spires, replacing the square, squat Norman ones and thinner walls, now buttressed more strongly to offset a larger window area and the thrust of the stone vault. The windows are typically lancets, that is, narrow, pointed-arched lights, arranged singly or in groups of two, three or five. The vertical emphasis of the Gothic style is making itself felt (in contrast to the horizontal theme of both classical and Romanesque design). This can be seen in the higher vaults supported on taller nave and choir piers, which are slender and grouped in clustered shafts with delicate capitals and tall bases (100, 128).

As Durham Cathedral is the supreme example of Romanesque ecclesiastical architecture in Britain, so *Salisbury Cathedral* represents the early Gothic theme. It is the only British Gothic cathedral to be built largely in a single operation and, therefore, single style. On a new site, it was begun in 1220 and, by 1258, was mainly complete; the tower and spire are a little later. Salisbury is also unusual in that it is now surrounded by a green-swarded cathedral close and can be viewed from all angles. Medieval cathedrals were built where they were needed, that is, in the heart of the city, and were closely hemmed in by timber houses. In many instances these Medieval houses have been replaced by later brick and stone buildings, often now of a commercial nature. At Salisbury, the whole exterior of the cathedral can be seen and enjoyed at leisure; the views of it, across the meadows, have barely changed since Constable painted it from there (99, 142).

Apart from its situation and unity of style, Salisbury is also remarkable for its high standard of design and craftsmanship. It is built on the traditional English cruciform plan, with a central tower and spire* over the crossing. The plan itself is typically English in its widely projecting transepts and square east end, completed by a square Lady Chapel. This is in contrast to the French pattern where, by this time, the apsidal end had developed its chevet of radiating chapels, as at Le Mans Cathedral. This is only one instance of the fundamental divergence of the English Gothic from the Continental version. The narrow strip of sea between Britain and the Continent of Europe was sufficient to impede the easy passage of ideas. Britain was isolated from Continental thought and was evolving national characteristics in architecture, as in other fields. The lofty tower and spire over the crossing was another example of this national independence, seen most clearly at Salisbury. French nave and choir vaults were much higher than the English. They built their twin towers at the west end

and sometimes one over the crossing, but these are only seldom capped by spires. Partly this is because the money ran out at this stage and they were not built (or only one was completed, as at Strasbourg), but, more importantly, it was found that the high, wide vault would not take the strain of a tall crossing tower and spire.

At Salisbury, the nave and choir vault, much lower, is finely designed and there is the customary three-storeyed division of the wall structure into nave and triforium arcade with clerestory above. The windows of the latter are now much larger than their Norman predecessors though, sadly, at Salisbury little of the original coloured window glass survives. This gives to the interior here the cold, clinical appearance so at variance with its original thirteenth-century look. Colour was an integral part of Gothic architecture and the difference that this makes can be judged by the warmth given by the superb glass at Chartres Cathedral in France or León in Spain, both contemporary with Salisbury.

A quantity of early Gothic work in lancet style survives in other English *cathedrals*. The west façades of *Peterborough* and *Wells* have already been referred to (103); beautiful workmanship can also be seen in the nave at *Wells* (100). *Ripon Minster* has a thirteenth-century façade, with grouped lancet windows across the whole width of the gable and flanking towers (98, 143). At *Lincoln* the Norman cathedral on the summit of Lincoln Hill was largely rebuilt between 1185 and 1280, after a collapse following upon an earth tremor. The façade is unusual in that an immense stone screen was built, incorporating the earlier Norman front. Inside, the nave, transepts and choir are much of one style with ribbed vaults, moulded, pointed arches and foliated capitals arising from Purbeck marble shafts (144, 145). It is a homogeneous, impressive interior. At *Lichfield*, the cathedral nave, transepts and façade are largely in early Gothic style. The west front screen is enriched across the lower part by sculptured statues in niches. In reddish stone, this is a richly decorated example for English design.

One of the largest contributions to Medieval architecture was made by the *monastic orders*. Norman workmanship here has been discussed (page 29). During the whole Gothic period, until the Dissolution of Monasteries in the sixteenth century, building work proceeded in the founding of new monasteries and the rebuilding and enlarging of older

* This is the tallest in the country, 404 feet high.

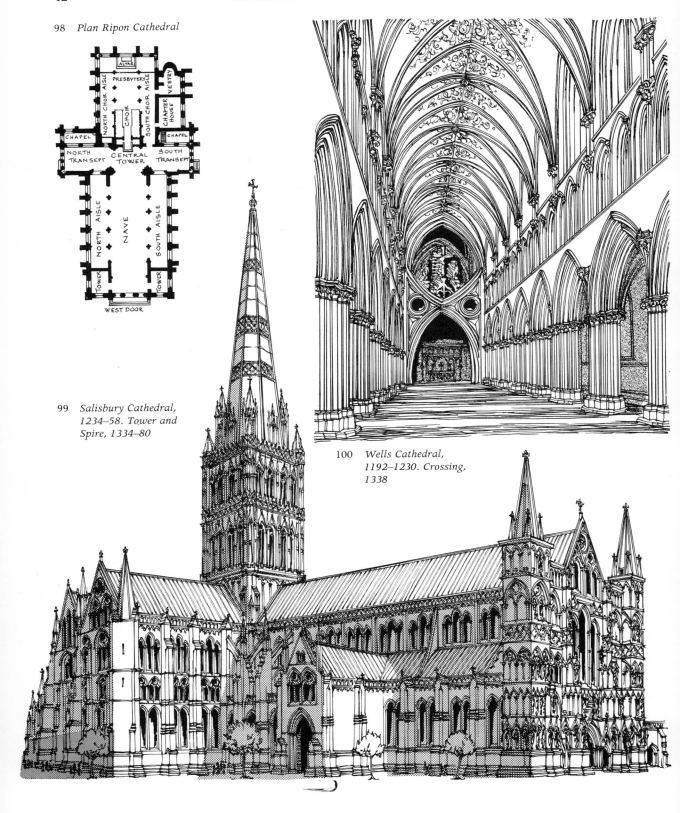

98   *Plan Ripon Cathedral*

99   *Salisbury Cathedral,*
1234–58. Tower and
Spire, 1334–80

100   *Wells Cathedral,*
1192–1230. Crossing,
1338

ones. Between 1000 and 1300 AD, 500 abbeys and priories were founded or re-established in Britain, under the jurisdiction of different orders; the chief of these were the Benedictine, Cistercian, Cluniac, Carthusian and Premonstratensian.

The Cistercian monasteries were probably the greatest loss as a result of the Dissolution because, by the nature of the order, they were set in remote sites and their churches could not, by reason of this remoteness, be used subsequently as cathedral or parish churches, as were those of so many other orders which had been built nearer to towns and villages. This circumstance has had the advantage, however, that the churches and coventual buildings, though in ruin, have not been partly rebuilt in later styles, as have their Continental counterparts, which are now frequently Baroque designs on a Gothic structure. During the sixteenth, seventeenth and eighteenth centuries such British monasteries fell into ruin, the stone being taken for local building and time and weather completing the decay. Since the mid-nineteenth century this process has been halted and repair work has saved the total loss of such superb structures as *Glastonbury Abbey*, Somerset, *Tintern Abbey*, Monmouthshire and *Fountains* and *Rievaulx*, Yorkshire in England and *Jedburgh* (167), *Dryburgh* and *Melrose Abbeys* (166) in Scotland.

Typical of Cistercian Abbeys was *Fountains*. The Norman workmanship here has been mentioned (page 29). In the thirteenth century the choir was extended and the transept known as the 'Chapel of the Nine Altars' was built. The remains of these give us some impression of the high quality of Early English workmanship in such abbeys. The fifteenth-century tower still dominates the Skell valley and many conventual buildings remain in part, such as the undercroft with its early ribbed vaulted roof (120).

Among the abbey churches still in use is *Hexham* in Northumberland, formerly an Augustinian Priory. The interior of the transepts, in particular, have retained their Early English characteristics in ground arcade, triforium and clerestory, and the façades are lit by six beautiful lancets. This church, earlier mentioned for its crypt (page 6), has also retained its midnight stair, a rare example and probably the finest in Britain. The Canons used to descend this stairway every night on the stroke of midnight for Matins. It is still used by the Abbey Choir.

The most famous of the abbey churches remaining to us is *Westminster* which, because of its importance, shows the imprint of every architectural style from Saxon to nineteenth century. A greater part of the abbey church was rebuilt under the direction of Henry III between 1245 and 1269, leaving us a heritage of pure early Gothic workmanship. Remaining of this work are much of the eastern arm, transepts and part of the nave. These show a strong French influence, since Henry had succeeded in attracting some of the finest artists from France, as well as from England, to work in his service. Westminster Abbey is the most French of our churches; this can be seen clearly in the great height of the vaults, the tall clerestory and lofty nave arcade with its high pointed arches. Especially French also is the north transept façade with its deep porches and rose window. The sculpture here also is French in its life and quality of movement.

The second stage in the steady development of Gothic architecture was called, by Rickman, 'Decorated'. It is thought of as the high summer of the style, a further stage in its evolution from the spring-like simplicity of lancet work. This second phase became established in the last quarter of the thirteenth century and lasted for about 100 years, until 1375. When we compare a fourteenth-century cathedral to a thirteenth-century one we note immediately three distinct changes: firstly, the larger window openings containing rich coloured glass and complex stone tracery in the head; secondly, the contracting area of plain wall, increasingly broken by more extensive abutment, and, thirdly, a greater variety and complexity in the design of stone vaulting.

These differences are the visible effects rather than the cause. Throughout the development of Gothic architecture, the aim of designers and builders was to create exteriors and interiors which would be more exciting, more three-dimensional, and to use their expanding knowledge to the full in order to obtain more varied effects. It was due to increased experience that builders were able safely to construct higher, wider and more delicate stone vaults. They supported these by an extended system of flying buttresses, which transferred the thrust to the aisle roofs and then down the wall buttress to the ground. At the same time, and for the same reasons, they were able to risk weakening the wall by larger window openings.

Designers experimented with new spatial forms

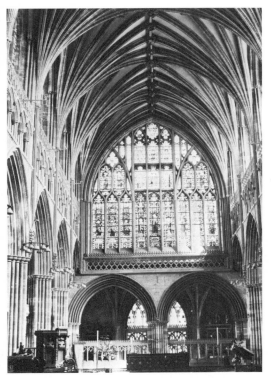

101   *Exeter Cathedral choir, 1328–90*

103   *Wells Cathedral, west front, c.1230–60*

102   *Exeter Cathedral, west front, 1328–75*

and lighting. The work at *Ely Cathedral* (1323–30) is an example of this. Here, the old central tower over the crossing was replaced by the unique octagon and lantern. From the interior, in particular, the effect is three-dimensional and remarkable; the tall crossing piers, with their alternating arch openings and windows, support the ribbed vault, which extends upwards on all eight sides to the panelled lantern. From directly underneath the view is of a star pattern in the centre of a radiating web of ribs, which culminates in the glowing coloured glass and curvilinear tracery of the windows (114).

Window tracery, though designed in many variations, is in one of two distinct types of pattern. The earlier style is termed *Geometric* and here the tracery of the window head incorporates motifs based upon the circle and its component parts. Later fourteenth-century work is termed *Curvilinear*, or flamboyant, and in this the window head tracery follows designs of complicated pattern in which the ogee curve is predominant.

Vaults also, though many variations are to be seen, fall into two distinct types. The earlier designs stem from the quadripartite vault. Here, intervening ribs are inserted, extending all the way from pier to ridge rib, between the structural quadripartite ribs. A fine example of this type of vault is to be seen in *Exeter Cathedral* (101). The other type of vault evolved from the proliferation of *lierne* ribs. These are ribs which do not extend from pier to ridge-piece, but run in any direction, crossing from one rib to another and making star patterns. Such ribs are not constructional but merely decorative. The term derives from the French *lier* – to bind or to tie. Beautiful examples of this type of vault are displayed in *York Minster* (104) and the choir of *Gloucester Cathedral*.

In the fourteenth century building work of all kinds was halted by the terrible visitation of plague, usually called the Black Death, of 1348–9. This was one of the recurring waves of infection which swept Britain and Europe in the Middle Ages. On this occasion it was so severe that about a third of the population died. Because of this, it is common to find in cathedrals and churches work of the two styles of Decorated architecture, side by side. A window head of pre-1348, often in Geometric design, will flank one of post-1349 – generally 1360 or later – in Curvilinear style. Characteristic of this later period also is the greater richness apparent in coloured glass and sculptural decoration.

Exeter Cathedral is the finest example of Decorated Gothic workmanship in Britain. The west façade is outstanding, with a richly sculptured entrance screen and, above it, the superb, traceried west window (137). The façade is flanked by the unusual (in Britain) two, earlier, transeptal towers (102). This is a construction more favoured in German work as in St Stephen's Cathedral in Vienna. Inside, Exeter Cathedral is also mainly in fourteenth-century style. Both nave and choir are covered uniformly by an impressive ribbed vault with carved bosses set at each intersection along the ridge rib. There are large traceried clerestory windows which beautifully illuminate the interior. The dignified piers, their clustered shafts of Purbeck marble, support deeply moulded arches on the small, moulded capitals. The triforium stage is shallow and delicately arcaded (101).

The west front of *York Minster* is also a first-class specimen of work of this period. Here, the wealth of decoration is in the form of tracery and window glass rather than sculpture, as exampled by the curvilinear centrepiece. This façade (apart from its fifteenth-century towers) dates from 1291–1345; the nave stems from the same time. Its impressively high vault is of lierne structure in distinction to that at Exeter, which has radiating ribs (104, 105, 106, 135).

Apart from these two superb specimens, extensive workmanship of the years 1275–1375 can be seen in a number of cathedrals. There is the spectacular Angel Choir (138) as well as the central tower (131) and Judgement Portal (140) at *Lincoln*, the curvilinear east window at *Carlisle* (134), much of *Bristol*, the choir of *Gloucester*, the façade of *Winchester* and *Salisbury's* chapter house and central tower and spire (99). At *Wells*, the central tower, the choir high vault (115) and the chapter house date from these years, as do *Hereford's* and *Worcester's* central towers and *St Albans'* Lady Chapel and nave.

The *final phase of Gothic architecture* in Britain evolved in the second half of the fourteenth century and lasted a long time, changing slowly but not greatly. It was not abandoned until after the middle of the sixteenth century, when Renaissance and Mannerist designs at last filtered through from the Continent. In this extended period, from about 1360 until 1550, the development of British architecture was in marked contrast to that of Continental countries. In previous stages of the Gothic evolution,

104   *Interior, 1291–1341*

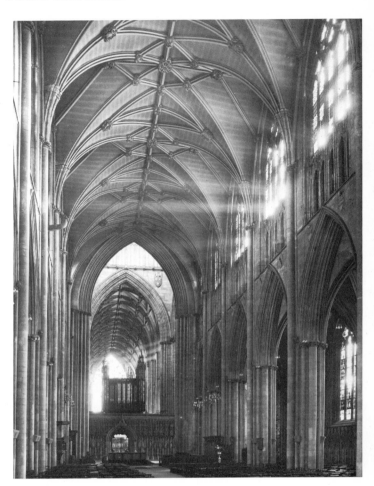

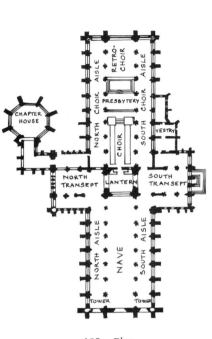

105   *Plan*

106   *The Minster from the south-east*

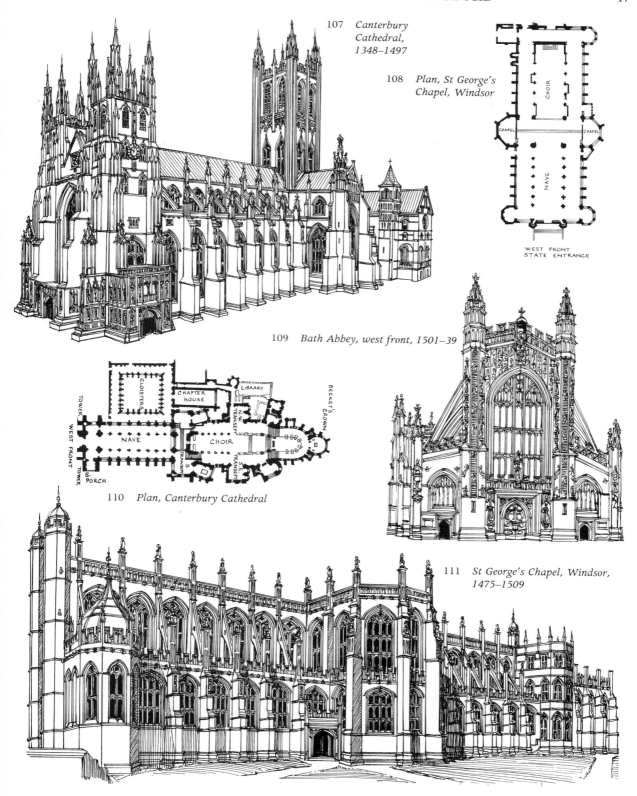

107 Canterbury Cathedral, 1348–1497

108 Plan, St George's Chapel, Windsor

WEST FRONT
STATE ENTRANCE

109 Bath Abbey, west front, 1501–39

110 Plan, Canterbury Cathedral

111 St George's Chapel, Windsor, 1475–1509

through Romanesque, Lancet and Decorated periods, there had been a parallel development in the different countries in Europe, although national characteristics had produced variations on the theme. From about 1360 onwards a separation occurred. Italy, the mainspring of the Renaissance, had no late Gothic development at all; France was also early affected by Renaissance ideas; Germany, Spain and Portugal continued Gothic building, but it was a further expression of fourteenth-century conceptions, becoming richer and richer in decoration which, in Spain, was carried to extremes in plateresque all-over ornament.

The English development is characterised by a restrained richness. *Perpendicular Gothic architecture* is, as its name indicates, an exercise in vertical lines, but there is also a new emphasis on the horizontal. The three principal features of this style are panelled decoration all over the building on windows, walls and vault alike; an increasing area of window space, and consequently of flying buttresses, in proportion to wall area and roofing by means of the fan vault. The best Perpendicular examples are not only cathedrals, as hitherto, but parish churches, chapels and houses. Of edifices which display in their entirety the new style, the royal and college chapels are supreme. These are mainly of later fifteenth-century construction. *Eton College Chapel* was begun in 1441, *King's College Chapel, Cambridge* (112) was built 1446–1515 and *St George's Chapel, Windsor* (108, 111, 136) in 1475–1509. These chapels all display the main features of Perpendicular Gothic: the plan is roughly rectangular and very simple (108); there are many windows along the side elevations and a gigantic multi-light one at each end. All have Perpendicular tracery and are separated by finialled flying buttresses, leaving only a small area of plain wall. Inside is a delicate but rich and complicated fan-vaulted roof and walls which are similarly stone panelled all over. These chapels are masterpieces of their time, supremely English, and represent the climax of craftsmanship and design in the Gothic style, achieving a harmonious balance of mass and space.

There is a quantity of work of this period in the *cathedrals*, but it is chiefly in the replacement of towers and vaults as well as in the enlargement of clerestory windows to increase the natural illumination. This, of course, is interesting as it affects the individual part replaced, but does not alter the concept or appearance of the building as a whole. As clerestory windows were enlarged, this had to be at the expense of the triforium, so, in cathedrals where such alterations to the fenestration were carried out, the windows became separated from the nave arcade by merely a band of carved decoration in sunk or pierced panelling. In the new Perpendicular windows not only was vertical panelled tracery substituted for the curves of Decorated work but the equilateral arch head was replaced by the flatter four-centred arch. This is especially typical of the years 1480–1540.

The principal examples of such work in cathedrals are at Canterbury, Winchester and Gloucester. The rebuilding of the nave at *Canterbury* was begun in 1378 and continued into the fifteenth century. Typically the clerestory was enlarged at the expense of the triforium and a lierne vault was constructed to roof the nave. The crowning glory of Canterbury is the central tower (its Angel Steeple), which rises over the crossing to 235 feet. This was completed in 1503 (107, 110). At *Winchester* the rebuilt nave is the finest work, completed in 1450. At *Gloucester* a very early instance of fan vaulting is to be seen in the reconstructed choir and cloisters, carried out in the mid-fourteenth century. It is on the exterior that the superb central tower, c.1450–7, shows the best Perpendicular work; it is dignified, solid, yet delicate and graceful. The great west window dates from 1437, the Lady Chapel 1499 and the richly sculptured porch c.1420 (141).

These years also saw the final phase in the building of and additions to the monastic structures. *Sherborne Abbey Church*, Dorset presents a complete example in Perpendicular style. The church was largely rebuilt in the fifteenth century in two stages between 1415 and 1504, introducing the large Perpendicular windows and fine flying buttresses and ornament (113). In 1539 the monastery was suppressed and the Abbey purchased by the parishioners of Sherborne from Sir John Horsey for £230, since which time it has served as the parish church. Other fifteenth-century monastic work includes the tower of *Fountains Abbey*, Yorkshire and that of *Christchurch Priory*, Hampshire, as well as the impressive flint and stone gateway to *St Osyth's Priory*, Essex.

In the *sixteenth century*, whilst France was imbibing Renaissance ideas from Italy and Francis I was gathering around him Italian artists and craftsmen, his contemporary English monarch, Henry VIII, tried to do the same. Britain was less attractive to Italians than

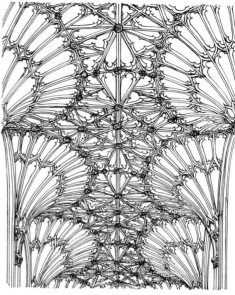

113 *Sherborne Abbey, nave fan vault, c.1475–1500*

112 *King's College Chapel, Cambridge, 1446–1515 (organ omitted)*

115 *Wells Cathedral, choir vault, lierne, c.1329*

114 *Ely Cathedral, lantern and octagon, 1330*

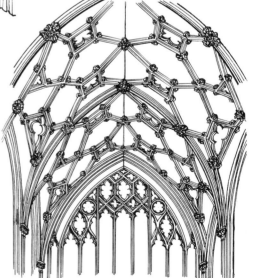

France, being further away and having a more intemperate climate, so Henry's success was limited. He succeeded in persuading *Pietro Torrigiano*, the Florentine sculptor, to come to design the tomb of the king's father, the late Henry VII, with consort, in the new chapel at *Westminster Abbey*. The tomb was completed in 1518, but it remains an isolated example for, after Henry VIII's break with Rome, England's tenuous links with Renaissance Italy were broken and the English retreated into isolationism. The English Renaissance was postponed and its form was also altered. Torrigiano's monument is Italian classical, the Elizabethan Renaissance forms are Mannerist, from Flanders and Germany.

The *Henry VII Chapel* at Westminster Abbey, which houses the tomb, is a masterpiece of panelled, fan-vaulted Perpendicular Gothic art (116, 121) and the outstanding instance in Britain of sixteenth-century chapel building.* Its counterpart in *abbey churches* is at *Bath*. Here, the essence of Perpendicular Gothic design is carried to its ultimate conclusion. The exterior is finely decorated with central tower, flying buttresses and ornamented turrets (109, 129). The whole interior is delicately fan vaulted; the perpendicular lines of the slender piers soar majestically towards these vaults (118).

Scotland

It was King David I who, in the twelfth century, laid the foundations of a stable Church and State in Scotland, which lasted through the Middle Ages. Monasticism, closely linked to the mother houses in France as well as to England, flourished and by the end of the thirteenth century a large number of foundations had been established, especially in the south and east of the country. The thirteenth century was Scotland's 'golden age' of *monastic building* and many abbeys survive in partial ruin from this time. The work was of fine quality which compared favourably with French and English contemporary building, but losses have been greater. Partly these were due to war, especially in the border monasteries which lay in the path of English armies, partly the buildings suffered from actual destruction in times of religious controversy, while neglect and use as convenient

---

* A later, excellent specimen was built at Trinity College, Cambridge.

stone quarries completed the sad tale. The abbey churches survive in part, walls, window openings, columns and fragments of vault, but little trace remains of their once rich carving, painting, ceramic and metalwork.

Although building continued during the fourteenth and fifteenth centuries in Scotland, the outstanding workmanship dates from the years 1150–1300. Earlier examples show fine quality transitional work with round and pointed arches used together in one building, such as the nave of the Augustinian *Abbey Church* at *Holyrood* in Edinburgh, which was founded by David I, also the remains of the Cistercian *Abbey Church* at *Dundrennan* in Galloway. Excellent specimens of the thirteenth-century Lancet style survive in quantity at *Jedburgh Abbey* in Roxburghshire (167) (though the fine west façade is of Transitional late twelfth-century design) and at *Dryburgh Abbey* in Berwickshire. One of the most famous Scottish *Abbey Churches* is *Melrose* in Roxburghshire (166). Founded by David I in 1136, this Cistercian Abbey endured a turbulent history. It was colonised from Rievaulx in Yorkshire and became one of the largest foundations in Britain, but suffered repeatedly in border wars. The finest remains date from the years 1380–1520 and these are fairly extensive.

Apart from the ruined abbeys, Scotland's Medieval heritage is not extensive. Again, the greatest building activity was in the thirteenth century, from which time some quality work survives at the *cathedrals* of Glasgow, Elgin and Dunblane (169). *Glasgow Cathedral* was begun, on the site of more than one earlier church, towards the middle of the thirteenth century. Despite the loss of its western towers in the nineteenth century, and other alterations, it remains the largest and best preserved Gothic building in Scotland. It is an interesting construction in that, although the thirteenth-century building was begun virtually from scratch, the original layout of the previous church was retained. This, like the early Christian basilicas in Rome, has an eastern arm on two levels, the upper one raised high to accommodate a large and splendid crypt or lower church, which houses the shrine of St Mungo, the patron saint (170). This type of structure is made possible by the uneven site on which the cathedral is built. Like most Gothic structures in Scotland, the east end is square, but the Scottish equivalent of the French chevet is obtained at Glasgow by extending the choir aisles round the eastern end behind the altar to form an ambulatory, then beyond this extend four chapels. The ambulatory plan is repeated in the lower church where, with the building of double staircases, the pilgrims visiting the shrine are able to circumnavigate it.

Glasgow Cathedral, despite the quality of its building, displays a solemn, dour appearance which characterises so much Scottish architecture. This is not so at *Elgin Cathedral*, possibly because it is partly ruined and, being roofless, permits the sunshine to enter. Also it did not survive as a cathedral, so did not suffer the heavy hands of nineteenth-century improvers. Elgin was a magnificent cathedral church (168), which suffered damage more than once by fire and attack and was repaired on each occasion. The structure was finally abandoned at the Reformation and, after the collapse of the central tower in 1711, suffered still further damage. The remains, which are still most impressive, date mainly from the thirteenth century.

After 1300 Scottish ecclesiastical architecture diverged from both Continental and English design and developed along its own individual lines, which were mainly backward glancing. There was a reversion to the Romanesque semi-circular arch and the solid column or clustered pier as well as a reintroduction of earlier styles of ornament. Ecclesiastical work on these lines is interesting for its individual and local character but, unlike the twelfth- and thirteenth-century work, is not of outstanding merit. The final Gothic phase in Scotland in the later fifteenth and early sixteenth centuries is marked by a florid, heavy decorative style with window tracery of curvilinear or flamboyant design and towers surmounted by crocketed and crowned open steeples.

Parish Churches in Britain

After the tremendous surge of building activity under the Normans, few new churches were constructed in the thirteenth century and much of this work was altered in the later Middle Ages. These early Medieval churches were built either on cruciform or simple rectangular plans. The Norman crossing tower was now often replaced by a single or twin western tower design. As in the case of Norman cathedral and abbey churches, the eastern apse was generally re-designed to give a square termination and the chancel lengthened to provide more space for chapels; grouped

lancet windows lit this eastern façade. Aisles were added to some naves and when these were roofed it became necessary to raise the nave wall to greater height and insert clerestory windows to illuminate the interior. Interesting thirteenth-century churches include *West Walton*, Norfolk, *St Denys, Sleaford*, Lincolnshire, *Uffington Church*, Berkshire and *Stoke Golding Church*, Leicestershire (124).

Through the fourteenth century, the process of enlarging parish churches, adding aisles and inserting larger windows continued. Most of these retained their timber roofs, covered by tiles, lead, wood shingles or thatch. Among the fine specimens of the time are *St Wulfram*, Grantham, *Heckington*, Lincolnshire, *Patrington*, Yorkshire (126), and *Holy Trinity*, Hull.

There exists a superb heritage in Britain of churches built or enlarged between 1375 and 1550 in Perpendicular Gothic style. Some are magnificent, almost of cathedral dimensions, a reflection of the new wealth and increased population in certain areas. Due largely to the cloth and wool trades, England was in the fifteenth century becoming a prosperous country and these churches are a symbol of this wealth. Most of them were crowned, usually at the west end, by tall towers and, in many instances, spires. A famous example is *St Botolph's Church*, at *Boston* in Lincolnshire, popularly called the 'Boston Stump' because its top storey was added so much later than the rest of the church and for many years the tower had a decapitated appearance (125). This tower is 295 feet high, while the spire of *Louth*, Lincolnshire, another fine parish church of the period, is 300 feet. Other beautiful spired churches are *St Mary Redcliffe*, Bristol and *Thaxted Church*, Essex (123), while *St Michael's*, Coventry, later the Cathedral, which was damaged in the Second World War and is now preserved as a memorial tower adjacent to the new cathedral, was one of the best of such churches (130).

There are also many towered churches (without spires) which exhibit the characteristics of the period, such as panelled walls, large, Perpendicular traceried windows, flying buttresses and lengthened chancels. In these years aisles were being added to existing nave, choir and transepts to give greater space, so the plan of such fifteenth-century churches is often rectangular, the cross being obscured by the increased width of the arms. These buildings are also noteworthy for their ornamentally carved, panelled

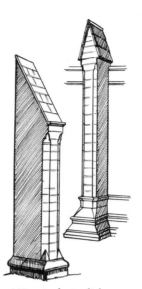

117 *Early English buttresses*

116 *Henry VII Chapel, Westminster Abbey, flying buttresses*

118 *Bath Abbey, 1501–39*

119 *St Mary's Church, Woolpit. Double hammerbeam roof, 1439–51*

120 *Fountains Abbey,
undercroft, 12th century*

122 *13th-century angle
and flying buttress*

121 *Henry VII Chapel, fan vault, 1503–19*

123   *Thaxted Church, 15th century*

124   *13th-century broach spire*

125   *St Botolph's Church, Boston, 1425–1520*

126   *St Patrick's Church, Patrington, 14th century*

127   *Church of St John the Baptist, Cirencester, c.1400–1500*

128 *Ely Cathedral, west tower, 1150–75*

129 *Bath Abbey, central tower, 1501–39*

130 *Old Coventry Cathedral steeple, 1373–1433*

131 *Lincoln Cathedral, central tower, 1240–1311*

132 *York Minster, south-west tower, 1432–74*

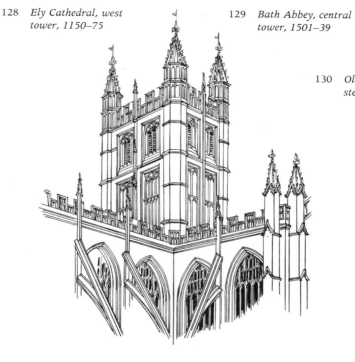

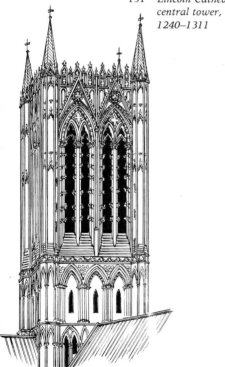

parapets and enriched porches while, in a number of instances, timber roofing was being replaced by stone vaults. Examples include *Lavenham Church*, Suffolk, *St Mary's, Taunton, St John's, Glastonbury, St John's, Cirencester* (127) and *St Peter's, Tiverton*.

Building materials for churches varied greatly from region to region. Stone and granite were used where available. Flint was extensively employed and the flints were now more carefully selected and graded for size. Flush-work was introduced into East Anglian building; stone blocks were cut into thin slabs for economy of the imported material and the flints were arranged round them to produce patterns between the panels, but they were set flush with the stone not raised above it. Elaborate designs were produced, especially on porches and towers as at the Suffolk churches like Eye and Woolpit. The method spread to other counties – Essex, Sussex, Wiltshire and Berkshire. Brick was used less than other materials, as yet, but it is particularly to be seen in the counties just mentioned because of lack of stone. For the same reason, timber was widely used in these regions.

Windows

During the Middle Ages window designs followed one predominant trend: they became larger. In the same period, the pattern of stonework which held the glass in place underwent many changes, with a general tendency to become more intricate and decorative. It is probably easier to date or identify the style of a Medieval building by its window openings than by any other single factor. This is because the designs changed frequently; the development was steady and in one coherent movement. Thus each period is known for its characteristic pattern and construction. This is not to say that window design all over the country at any given date would be identical; it was, naturally, in the large and important buildings that new trends first appeared.

Romanesque windows had been small, partly for defensive reasons and partly so as not to weaken the wall structurally. With the introduction of the pointed arch and the development of skill in masonry and engineering, window openings in the *thirteenth century* became larger and more numerous. The lancet style takes its name from the window pattern of the time, when *lancets*, or narrow windows, whether singly or in groups, were evolved. Such lights had narrow, pointed heads (133). Many famous grouped lancet windows survive; even better known than those from *Hereford Cathedral* (1220) are the beautiful north transept windows in *York Minster*, the 'Five Sisters', each of which is 50 feet high and 5 feet wide, (*c*.1250). These also represent the finest example of grisaille glass which was developed at this time. This glass gives more light to the interior than the earlier, richer glass work. In grisaille, the plain glass is painted delicately with a floral pattern in grey monochrome. At York, red and blue glass strips are incorporated.

It was in the lancet period that *tracery* – the carved stone mouldings containing the glass – was developed. The idea evolved from the grouping of two or more lights under one arch. This created a space above – the spandrel – which presented an awkward feature of design. This was overcome by carving it into quatrefoil or trefoil shapes. These were pierced and thus the earliest form of tracery, called *plate tracery*, was created. In this type of work the stonework is comparatively solid and the circular, cusped holes are pierced in it. A superb example is at *Lincoln Cathedral*, *c*.1220 (139).

By the Decorated Gothic period, *bar tracery*, where the stonework is much narrower and in 'bars' while the volume of glass is larger, became fully developed. The window area was now much larger and wider and was encompassed by an equilateral arch. The window was divided vertically by stone mullions, giving five, seven or even nine lights; the head was then decoratively designed. Such designs varied according to date, at first generally *geometric*, based on circles, trefoils and quatrefoils and later *curvilinear*, wherein the bar tracery divided the window head into flowing, flame-like shapes based on the ogee form. Many magnificent windows of both types survive, for instance, at *Lincoln* and *Carlisle Cathedrals* (134), *Melrose Abbey* in Scotland (166), *Exeter Cathedral* (137), *York Minster* and the chapter house at *Salisbury Cathedral*. The tracery of this time is especially suited to the circular, rose window, usually to be seen on the transept façades. One of the most beautiful of these is the 'Bishop's Eye' at *Lincoln Cathedral*, *c*.1325 (138).

The last phase of tracery design comes with Perpendicular Gothic work. Here the window is divided vertically by mullions and horizontally by transoms into panels (135). The proportions of the window are wider and the head may be enclosed by an obtuse arch or by the flatter, four-centred arch.

134 *Carlisle Cathedral, east window, c.1350*

133 *Oundle Church, lancet window, c.1200*

136 *St George's Chapel, Windsor, west window, c.1485–1509*

138 *Lincoln Cathedral, rose window, c.1325*

135 *York Minster, east window, 15th century*

137 *Exeter Cathedral, west front, 1328–75*

139 *Lincoln Cathedral, plate tracery, c.1220*

The number of lights is greatly increased as, for example, at *St George's Chapel, Windsor*, where there are 75 lights in the main window area (136). A particularly fine early instance is at *Westminster Hall* in London. The same theme continued into Tudor Gothic buildings, where sometimes the arch was replaced, or was enclosed by, a rectangular panelled window area as at *Bath Abbey*.

Doorways and Porches

The shape and proportion of *doorways* developed in a similar way to window design and this makes the doorway another suitable feature on which to base recognition of a period or style. Slowly, openings became larger and the arch mouldings surmounting them passed from narrow pointed form to equilateral, to obtuse, to four-centred. The more important early Gothic doorways were encompassed by an equilateral arch head. This was deeply recessed and richly moulded, with splayed sides. The shafts are often of contrasting material – Purbeck grey marble being the most common – to the capitals and bases. Some doorways have foiled heads, carved in cinquefoil or trefoil forms. Beautiful examples include *Ripon Minster* (143), *Salisbury* and *Chichester Cathedrals* (142) and *Bolton Priory Church*.

Fourteenth-century doorways are generally wider, covered by an obtuse arch, and can be very rich in carved ornament and quantity of mouldings (140). More actual *doors* survive from this time, made of wood with elaborate scrolled ironwork furniture. *Perpendicular Gothic* doorways often possess a square hood-mould over the obtuse or four-centred arch. The space between the square and the arch – the spandrel – is filled with carved stone decoration in the form of tracery, heraldic motifs or foliage. Doors are panelled rather than decorated with iron. In the late fifteenth century and Tudor times such panelling was usually in carved linenfold pattern. *Tudor* doorways have four-centred arches and decorative arch mouldings but plain jambs, often without shafts. Outstanding examples of fifteenth- and sixteenth-century doorways include *King's College Chapel, Cambridge*, *Magdalen College Chapel, Oxford* and *Chester Cathedral*.

Most large churches and cathedrals have *porches*. On the west front these are frequently in triple form, with the central doorway larger than its flanking companions. From the fourteenth century onwards, such buildings also have porches on the south and north transept façades – in single form but canopied and projecting. The most elaborate porches date from the fifteenth century, when they were often added to an existing building. They are profusely ornamented with sculpture, panelling, tracery and pinnacles. In architectural detail these porches display the characteristics of their time as at *Salisbury* (142) and *Lincoln Cathedrals* (Early English), *Gloucester* (141), *Canterbury* and *Chester Cathedrals*, *Lavenham Church* and *St John the Baptist, Cirencester* (127) (Perpendicular Gothic).

Towers and Spires

The tall graceful spire set upon an elegant tower is typical of the Early English period. This architectural feature is essentially Gothic in inspiration and spans the whole Medieval era. A spire has no constructional purpose; indeed, it presents structural and aesthetic problems, without performing any function save looking beautiful and acting as a landmark. To Gothic builders, the need to create churches of elegance and grandeur dedicated to the glory of God and to draw attention to these creations was so profound that hundreds of churches, from small parishes to great cathedral dioceses, boasted their spires and many still do. In general, the taller spires are to be found in the flatter, eastern part of the country, where they are visible for miles, and the smaller, sturdier towers in the hills and mountains of the west.

The chief structural problem of a spire is to accommodate its octagonal form on top of a four-sided tower. The union, especially in early examples, is often awkward; both visually and structurally unsound. Some steeples collapsed soon after building. Two common designs were the parapet and the broach. In the former instance, the parapet acted as support and also covered the junction; in the second type, squinches across the corners of the tower supported the other four sides of the spire and from these squinches pyramidal buttresses, called *broaches*, were built up the spire sides (124). An impressive early example of this is *St Denys' Church* at *Sleaford* in Lincolnshire, where the spire of 1220 is set upon the earlier tower of 1180.

In the fourteenth and fifteenth centuries the parapet design was more common. By this time the

140 *Lincoln Cathedral, the Judgement Portal*

141 *Gloucester Cathedral, south porch, c.1420*

142 *Salisbury Cathedral, west front portal, c.1258–66*

143 *Ripon Minster, west front, c.1220–50*

tower was extended upwards at the four corners by crocketed stone pinnacles which then buttressed the spire by means of arches in flying buttress manner. *St Patrick's Church* at *Patrington*, Yorkshire (126) and *St Wulfram, Grantham* are fourteenth-century churches of this type and *St James' Church, Louth*, Lincolnshire is an excellent fifteenth-century specimen.

England is rich in Gothic towers. Especially fine are the early example at *Ely Cathedral* (128), the fourteenth-century ones at *Salisbury* (99), *Lincoln* (131), *Hereford* and *Wells Cathedral* and the Perpendicular Gothic designs at *Gloucester Canterbury* and *York Cathedrals* (132), *St Botolph's Church, Boston* (125), *St Mary's, Taunton* and *St John's, Glastonbury*.

Abutment, Vaults and Roofs

These parts of a Medieval structure are essential and interdependent factors in the whole scheme. Abutment is the necessary corollary to secure the stability of a building which is roofed by a stone vault; with timber roofing its presence is less vital. The Gothic architectural form evolved because it became essential, due to fire hazard, to roof large churches with stone instead of timber. Such vaults required the flexibility inherent in the pointed arch (see page 38); the resulting vaults became ribbed structures, rising higher and covering wider spans, and these in turn demanded more extensive, carefully engineered abutment.

The *barrel vault* had been used by the Romans and, throughout Europe, in Romanesque architecture. Satisfactory for narrow spans, such as church aisles, the barrel vault, exerting the immense thrust which it does along its whole length, was dangerously unsuitable for the wider spans of the high vaults of nave or choir. It was for these spans (of which Durham Cathedral is an early example, see page 19) that the *ribbed vault* was evolved. In general, the ribbed vault and the pointed arch were developed at roughly the same period and both are typical of Gothic, rather than Norman, architecture. In a ribbed vault a framework of stone ribs is supported during construction upon wood centering until the spaces in between are filled with stone panels. The whole construction is lighter than the barrel vault and more flexible in design.

The resulting outwards and downwards thrust was counteracted by the development of the *abutment system*, which provided strengthening of the wall from the exterior face at the point where the greatest thrust was to be expected. Trial and error established this to be just below the springing line of the vault on the interior wall face. The *flying buttress* system was evolved to produce this strengthening at the specific point. It serves a dual purpose: the counter thrust at a given place on the exterior wall surface conveys the vault pressure away from the building and down to the ground and also, by means of a heavy pinnacle above, helps to offset the vault thrust (116).

The earliest Gothic vaults were ribbed designs in quadripartite pattern, with four ribs crossing diagonally to make four compartments. In the fourteenth century more complex vaults were designed by introducing intermediate ribs called *tiercerons*, which extended from the vault springing to the ridge rib, as at *Exeter Cathedral* (100, 101, 120). This style is typical of the earlier fourteenth century, but soon the *lierne vault* was developed. In this the lierne ribs extended in any direction from the structural ribs and might join any other rib. Lierne vaults became very complex as, for example, at *Wells* (115), *York* (104), *Gloucester* or *Winchester* Cathedrals; some patterns are described as star or stellar vaults.

In Perpendicular Gothic work the *fan vault* – a peculiarly British design – was evolved from the desire for a vault which would accommodate ribs of different curves as they sprang from the capital. The radiating ribs of the fan are of equal length and the bounding line is in the shape of a semi-circle. The whole group of ribs is made into an inverted concave cone. The radiating ribs are crossed by lierne ribs so that the complete surface is then, like the windows and walls of the time, panelled and cusped. Superb fan vaults can still be seen at *Henry VII's Chapel* in *Westminster Abbey* (121), *St George's Chapel, Windsor, King's College Chapel, Cambridge* (112) and *Bath Abbey* (118). Typical of Perpendicular architecture is the smallest possible wall area with large windows and extensive vaults; the necessary complement to this is an equally extensive flying buttress structure. A pinnacled flying buttress is set between each window. The characteristic forest of decorative, vertical stone pinnacles blending with the lines of delicate stone arches all diminishing in perspective along the façades is characteristic of such fan-vaulted structures (109, 111, 116).

Of equal interest in Medieval architecture is the contemporary evolution of the open *timber roof*, which provided the alternative method of interior roofing. Because of the fire risk, stone vaults were built where possible, but timber roofs had to suffice in areas where stone was not readily available and for smaller buildings. Most cathedral and abbey churches had timber roofs originally, but these were gradually replaced by vaults during the Middle Ages. The cathedrals which today retain timber roofing have had this renewed more than once and original timber ceilings are rare in such structures. The existing wooden covering is generally of boarded, ceiled type, often painted in coloured designs. *Ely Cathedral* nave is still roofed in this manner.

The decorative, open timber roofs are to be seen in parish churches and in secular architecture. Like the vaults, early designs in the thirteenth century were simple, generally of collar-beam type. These evolved slowly via tie-beam structures to the beautiful, complex hammerbeam roofs of the fifteenth century, of which many superb examples survive. The structure and development of such roofs is discussed more fully in Chapter 4 on Secular Medieval Architecture (page 76). By the fifteenth century the craft of the woodworker had reached a high standard. In East Anglia and neighbouring areas, where stone was not easily available, the hammerbeam roof was especially used for parish churches, where it was more suitable than the tie beam since it provided less visual interruption for the congregation. Among the many surviving examples of high standard are *South Creake Church* and *Trunch Church* in Norfolk, *Woolpit* (119) and *Needham Market* in Suffolk and *March Church* in Cambridgeshire. Tie-beam roofs can be seen at *Addlethorpe* in Lincolnshire and *Walpole St Peter* in Norfolk, while the arch-braced design is used at *Sparham* in Norfolk.

Capitals, Piers and Bases

These, together with ornament and mouldings, provide a useful means of identifying a period in Gothic architecture. The designs changed quickly and characteristically. The general trend between 1150 and 1550 was towards slenderer piers, grouped capitals and tall bases. Early English piers are clustered with shafts which are often of contrasting colour and material; dark Purbeck marble was frequently used for this on important buildings, as at *Salisbury Cathedral*. Capitals are moulded or foliated and are surmounted by a round abacus, unlike the Norman square one. Foliated capitals are carved stiffly, the stalks standing out from the capital bell and, later, falling in heavy clusters. These designs are vibrant and three-dimensional; beautiful examples can be seen in the chapter house and transept of *Southwell Minster* (147, 150) and in *Lincoln Cathedral* (144, 145).

Fourteenth-century piers are often designed on a diamond-shaped plan, with a central shaft surrounded by slenderer ones (148). Foliated capitals are carved naturalistically, with shorter stalks and a profusion of flowers and fruit; *York Minster* nave has some typical examples (149). Perpendicular piers are slenderer still and the vaulting shafts continue up the front and back of the piers in an unbroken line from ground to vault. Many capitals are plainly moulded; in larger buildings they are carved, but these are more stylised than before, lower in relief and include figures and foliage. Bases are tall and slender and often bell-shaped with an octagonal plinth below. *Winchester Cathedral* nave illustrates these (146).

Mouldings and Ornament

Early English mouldings are deeply cut, giving strong shadows. Ornament is restrained and only a few mouldings are decoratively carved, unlike the richly ornamented Romanesque arch mouldings. The most typical Early English ornamental motif is the *dogtooth*. This is a small pyramidal form cut into four leaves and repeated (165). Diaper decoration (161) and crockets (157) are also typical (164). The most usual motif of the Decorated period is the *ball flower*. This is a globular form with the flower partly opened to show a small sphere (160). Crockets are richly carved in vine motifs (155). Mouldings most often used are the ogee and the roll. Perpendicular design is distinguished by its panelled forms on all surfaces. Finials and crockets are finely carved, using animal and human figure designs as well as plants (151, 152, 153, 154, 157, 158). Mouldings are shallow and broad.

144   *Lincoln Cathedral, choir capital, from 1256*

145   *Lincoln Cathedral, choir capital, mid-13th century*

146   *Perpendicular pier base*

147   *Southwell Minster, transept capital, 13th century*

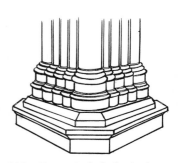

148   *Exeter Cathedral, pier base, c.1335*

149   *York Minster, nave capital, c.1310–20*

150   *Southwell Minster, chapter house, 13th century*

151 St Peter's Church,
     Tiverton, 15th century

152 Lavenham Church,
     Suffolk, crocket,
     15th century

153 Stone ornament, 15th century

156 Exeter Cathedral, west front
     screen, c.1350

154 Thaxted Church,
     gargoyle, 15th century

155 Winchester Cathedral,
     crocket, 14th century

158 Thaxted Church,
     gargoyle, 15th century

157 Early English crocket

159 Stone finial,
     15th century

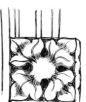

160 Ball-flower ornament,
     14th century

163
Dripstone,
14th century

161 Diaper decoration,
     14th century

162
Exeter
Cathedral,
west front
screen

164 13th-century ornament

165 Dog-tooth ornament, 13th century

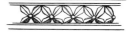

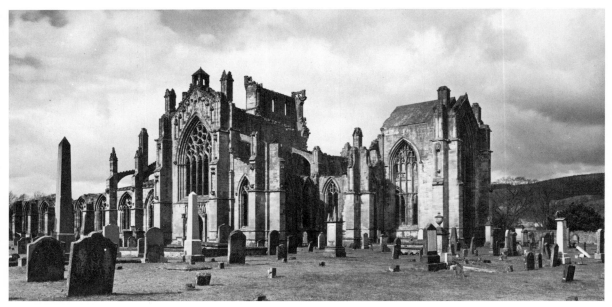

166 *Melrose Abbey, Roxburghshire, c.1390–1540*

167 *Jedburgh Abbey, Roxburghshire, 12th and 13th centuries*

168 *Elgin Cathedral, Morayshire, from 1224*

169 *Dunblane Cathedral, Perthshire, 13th century*   170 *Glasgow Cathedral crypt, 13th century*

CHAPTER FOUR

The Gothic Style:
Secular Architecture
1150–1550

Not many secular buildings have survived intact from the early Middle Ages. The great majority were constructed of wood and plaster, wattle or thatch and were rebuilt over and over again during the centuries, when either they were destroyed by fire or replaced by a larger, more modern structure. The survivors are mainly stone castles or fortified large houses. The later Middle Ages, from about 1400 onwards, present a different picture. Increasingly, throughout the fifteenth century and under the early Tudors, reflecting the growing wealth of the country, elaborate buildings were designed in more permanent materials. We have inherited a range of these, constructed for a variety of purposes. There are inns, guildhalls, university and school buildings, town and country palaces and houses, castles, bridges and tithe barns.

Such secular work was built from a variety of materials, depending upon the availability in the region concerned. The chief are stone, brick, timber with plaster and/or brick and flint. Stylistically the buildings show the same characteristics at any given period as those described in Chapter 3 on Ecclesiastical Architecture. Elaborate decoration and carving as well as stone vaults and rich, timber roofs can be found in secular work just as in ecclesiastical, but, in the smaller, simpler structures such as the average town or country house, ornamentation was at a minimum, coloured glass uncommon and tracery limited.

The Medieval Town

London was the Medieval capital as it had been in

Roman times. It was the only large city in the country but, even here there were gardens and orchards within the walls. A contemporary account, written about 1160,* describes the impressiveness of the Tower of London, its walls and bailey rising from deep foundations, the 'mortar being mixed with the blood of beasts', and of two other strong castles on the west side, linked by a continuous high great wall round the city, containing seven double gates and towers at intervals. The writer also refers to the river Thames as 'teeming with fish' and describes the expanding 'populous suburbs'.

Other towns in Britain were small by modern standards. There were only a few of any size; these included *York, Bristol, Norwich, Southampton* and *Lincoln*. An average town would only have 3000 to 4000 inhabitants who were thus able to enjoy the advantages of both town and country. Houses had gardens, orchards and paddocks, so town dwellers supplied their own food while their pigs and poultry wandered at will as in a rural area. The surrounding country was easy of access and citizens often owned cattle and held arable tenements outside the walls.

On the debit side the streets were narrow, poorly paved or cobbled and sloped towards the centre, where flowed the open drain. Horses, carts and people shared the same roadway. The streets were unlit, dirty and insanitary and all the prevailing smells from slaughter houses, tanneries and breweries may have been different from but were more powerful than the

---

* Preface to the biography of Thomas Becket, by William fitz Stephen.

diesel fumes we complain of today. Steep Hill in Lincoln gives a good impression of a Medieval street since it is reserved for pedestrians, being too narrow and precipitous for wheeled traffic (though, of course, it is not dirty or insanitary). The Jew's House here (93) has already been mentioned. It is suggested that the Jews were among the first to build stone houses in our towns in order to give themselves fireproof protection against their debtors.

The greatest hazard to Medieval towns was always the danger of fire. After the passing of the law of 1189, making it compulsory to build at least the lower party walls of stone, conflagrations were reduced and there was less danger of fire spreading. Defence was also a vital question for towns, which were all surrounded by city walls and, in larger instances, by a moat also. These walls were studded at intervals by watch towers and fortified gateways (171, 206). Sites for important towns were carefully chosen, partly for defensive purposes and partly for fresh water supplies and easy transport facilities. The latter were generally by river or sea. The town was also planned so that the streets, with their open sewers, drained off into a water course. *London* had been chosen by both Romans and Saxons as well as the Normans as a suitable capital site on the river Thames. *Edinburgh* was selected for its easily defensible natural site on a narrow ridge above the plain with precipitous rock sides as fortification. It also has convenient access to the Forth Estuary and so to direct sea routes. *Stirling* likewise is a natural acropolis.*

The layout of towns in different parts of the country varied according to geographical factors. Some were sited adjacent to a river, to a harbour, on a defensive rock or ridge, in the shadow of a protecting castle, abbey or cathedral. Town planning was also affected according to the foundation date of the settlement. Those which originated in Roman times, such as Colchester or Chester, were on a rectangular plan, built with city walls which had an entrance gate on each face. Those of Norman origin generally grew up more haphazardly round the great castle or cathedral as a focal centre. Medieval foundations of thirteenth- and fourteenth-century origin were often more

symmetrical, with wider main streets, intersecting at right angles. Many such towns exist on the Continent but few have survived unaltered in England. *Winchelsea* is one of these, planned as a seaport by Edward I, on a new site, as the sea had encroached on the old town; three of the town gates still exist. Another town founded by Edward is *Kingston-upon-Hull*, where a harbour was made at the point where the river Hull flows into the Humber estuary. The harbour was completed in 1299 and roads were built across the low-lying marshes to the present-day suburbs (then villages) of Hessle, Anlaby, Holderness and Cottingham. The *Church of the Holy Trinity* survives from the fourteenth-century Medieval city, as do also gatehouses and part of the town walls. Good examples of such gatehouses can also be seen at *Canterbury* (172) and *Rye*.

In the fifteenth century increased wealth flowing from the prosperity of the cloth and wool trades caused expansion of old towns and the founding of new ones. The *Cotswolds* and *Essex* were two such areas of expansion where some beautiful stone and timber houses of this time survive. Newer towns, such as *Wakefield* and *Halifax*, were flourishing while rising villages destined to become great cities were developing fast; Manchester and Birmingham were two of these.

The *market* was an important function in the life of all towns, large and small. The bigger population centres had a square laid out in the middle of the town, on which the chief streets converged. The church was usually set at one corner of the market place. In less pretentious towns the hub of life was the High Street, where were to be found the principal buildings – guildhalls, church, large houses. Halfway along such High Streets the road was widened for a short stretch and here was held the market. Several towns still possess such characteristic Medieval streets. *Edinburgh* is one example, with its Grassmarket and Lawnmarket; *Elgin* is another. *Market crosses* survive in a number of towns, generally today a bone of contention between traffic engineers and conservationists. Beautiful late Medieval stone examples include those at *Chichester* (176), *Salisbury* and *Winchester*.

---

* The Greek word meaning literally the city upon a hill. A defensive concept used by many earlier civilisations from the Ancient Greeks to the Medieval and Renaissance Apennine cities of Italy.

Castles

The years 1275–1350 were notable for the building of

MEDIEVAL TOWNS

172 *Christ Church,
Canterbury,
gateway, 1517*

171 *York city walls
and Minster*

173 *The Shambles, York*

174 *The Guildhall,
Lavenham. Half-
timber, c.1529*

175
*The George and
Pilgrims Inn,
Glastonbury, c.1475*

176 *Chichester
market cross*

many castles which are termed 'Edwardian', after Edward I, who was responsible for the erection of a number of them in order to consolidate his domination of Wales and Scotland. Earlier castles had consisted of a central keep surrounded by an enclosed area of land, which was defended by a fence, a moat and a gatehouse. Edwardian castles were concentric, that is, there is no reliance upon a central strongpoint or keep, but the castle consisted of rings of walls, one built inside the other, defended along their whole lengths by fortified towers. These mural towers were designed to provide covering fire against the attacker from every point of the compass. No part of the structure was then weaker than another and there were usually three defensive walls, each thinner than the Norman ones.

The concentric system was being used in England before Edward became King, but it was developed under Edward and his name is associated primarily with such Welsh and border examples as *Caernarvon, Conway, Beaumaris* and *Harlech* (179).

Such castles, which were new structures, needed no keep. The central space was an open courtyard where was constructed domestic accommodation comprising the separate buildings of the great hall, the chapel and those for living space. Between the inner and second ring of walls were built other necessary structures and in the outer bailey was room for garrison buildings, stables, cattle and villagers. Beyond the outer wall was a moat, defended by a strong gatehouse or barbican. Typical is *Beaumaris Castle* on the Island of Anglesey, where the moat is still water-filled and the mural towers are in good condition (177). *Caerphilly*, in South Wales, remains one of the finest of the concentric castles in Britain, though partially ruined. It has a rectangular inner ward of 70 by 53 yards, with a drum tower at each corner and a gatehouse in the centre of each end wall. The hall, 72 by 33 feet, is flanked by a chapel and private apartments. The second ward is 106 by 90 yards, its walls descend some 20 feet into the water; use has been made here of the lake, supplemented by a man-made moat. A third ward is defended by gatehouses, towers and portcullis and was connected to the second by bridges (184).

In a number of cases Norman castles were converted into concentric designs. Here, the central keep was retained for accommodation and as a final strongpoint and the curtain walls with their mural towers, gatehouses and moat were built around the exterior of the original castle. The *Tower of London* is one such example, where the *White Tower*, the original keep (83), is now surrounded by many other towers and walls. On the borders of England and Wales are *Goodrich Castle*, Herefordshire and *Chepstow Castle*, Monmouthshire. At Goodrich Castle (183), the original Norman keep (84) can be seen inside the later walling on the right side of the bailey. Fig. 178 shows a view of Chepstow Castle from the bridge over the river Wye. The strategic defensive character of the site can be judged; built as it is, the castle occupies a ridge whose cliffs drop sheer into the valley of the fast flowing river. The Norman keep, called the great tower, is marked 'A'. It has been added to later, as can be seen by the presence of Norman and Gothic fenestration. The great gatehouse (B), the main entrance to the castle, was built 1225–45 and the great tower (Marten's Tower) (C) in the years 1270–1300. In Scotland there was a similar development at *Bothwell*, Lanarkshire and *Kildrummy*, Aberdeenshire. Such castles had the best of both worlds, a spaciousness of living accommodation unknown to the Normans; yet, if the concentric system failed, the keep or donjon remained as a last line of retreat.

Fourteenth-century castles which were built as part of a town's defences, as opposed to the single unit out in the country, were designed in a rather different form. In North Wales there are two famous instances of this type: *Caernarvon* and *Conway*. These are roughly rectangular in plan and have strong mural towers set round one chief ring of walls. It is necessary for such castles to be built on commanding and, if possible, impregnable sites. Caernarvon, with polygonal towers, is almost encircled by the river estuary (182); Conway, with circular towers, rises steeply above the harbour's edge.

By 1375–80 the quadrangular plan began to supersede the Edwardian concentric arrangements. *Bodiam Castle* in Sussex is an excellent example of such castle building. It is approached over an oak bridge, which spans the moat, to the octagon. During the approach, the intruder would be under fire from the towers and would then have to pass the barbican, cross a ten-foot moat over which a drawbridge could be dropped as required, and storm the main gatehouse. This was fitted with three portcullises with their individual doors and chambers (181). Bodiam still presents the

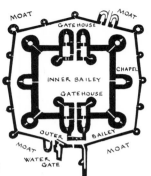

177   *View and plan, Beaumaris Castle, Anglesey, 1295–1325*

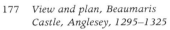

178   *Chepstow Castle, 1067–1300*

179   *Great gatehouse and outer gate, Harlech Castle, Wales, 1286–90*

181   *Main entrance, Bodiam Castle*

180   *Bodiam Castle, Sussex, 1385*

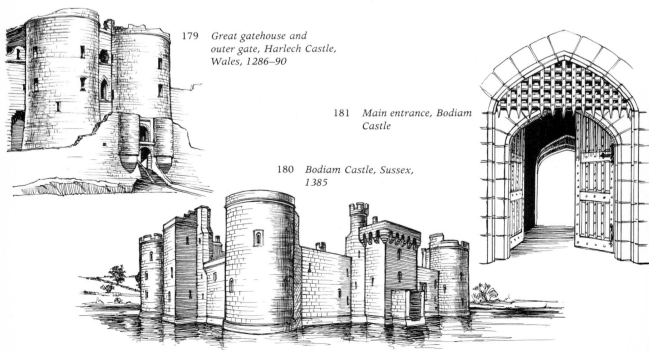

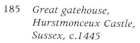

184 *Caerphilly Castle, Glamorganshire, late 13th century*

185 *Great gatehouse, Hurstmonceux Castle, Sussex, c.1445*

183 *Goodrich Castle, Herefordshire, 12th century to 1300*

182 *Caernarvon Castle, North Wales, 1283–c.1330*

shell of a great castle. Its outer walls, lapped by the moat, are in good condition (180). The barbican is in ruins but the main gatehouse is well preserved. On entering one steps into a quadrangular court surrounded by buildings and towers and containing the great hall, chapel, private chambers and kitchen. Other fifteenth-century castles include *Hever, Warwick* and *Hurstmonceux*. This last named is a fine example of brickwork and the gatehouse is especially well preserved (185).

Gatehouses were important centres of defence in the fourteenth and fifteenth centuries. A large castle or city wall system might have several, but generally there was one principal gatehouse, larger and stronger than the others. Outside this, across the moat, was a further gatehouse, the barbican, which was the outer point of protection from attack and which could be abandoned if necessary. Gatehouses were generally built on rectangular plan and were flanked by drum towers which might contain staircases. At ground level the gatehouse was defended by one or more portcullises and beyond this was an oak double door. The portcullis was of iron or oak with iron spikes. It was suspended by ropes or chains, fitted into side grooves. The chains were worked by a winch or were fastened to a counterpoise. The portcullis chamber, from where it was worked, was above. Gatehouses were built to defend city, castle, university and domestic house entrances (172, 179, 185, 186, 192, 206, 213).

Palaces

Medieval palaces survive only fragmentarily; until 1500 precedence was given to ecclesiastical structures and important palaces have mainly been rebuilt or replaced. Of the *Royal Palace of Westminster*, the Medieval hall adjoins what is now the Houses of Parliament. *Westminster Hall* was built in 1097–9 and from about 1178 was used primarily as Courts of Justice and for royal and parliamentary occasions. It was also the scene of state political trials such as that of King Charles I in 1649. The hammerbeam roof was erected during the reconstruction of the hall under Richard II in the years 1394–1401. It is a tremendous span for an open timber roof – 69 feet; the structure, design and carving are all magnificent.* Of *Eltham Palace*, Kent, the great hall survives. This is also roofed by a fine hammerbeam structure, though the

span is only half that of Westminster Hall. It dates from 1475–80 and is lit by Perpendicular traceried windows on all sides (188).

It was in the sixteenth century, under Henry VIII, that the secular age of building began to replace the ecclesiastical. After the Dissolution, many monastic properties, their lands and wealth, accrued to the State and Henry apportioned them to his supporters. The most famous palace of these years is *Hampton Court*, of which the Tudor part still remains, adjacent to and blended skilfully with Sir Christopher Wren's seventeenth-century additions. Hampton Court was begun by Cardinal Wolsey in 1514. It was not intended as a palace but as a large house to be lived in by a wealthy churchman. It was consequently laid out on a domestic and university quadrangular-court plan. After Henry VIII took over Hampton Court from Wolsey in 1525, he made it into a palace, but the collegiate scheme was retained, only on a more splendid scale. The style is Tudor Gothic, and the structure largely in brick with stone facings and tracery.

Wolsey had made, as was the custom of the time, a rough design himself, then contracted artisans for each trade to carry out the work. It was entirely executed by Englishmen except for some of the ornamental work, which was done by Italians. An example of this is in the terracotta portrait roundels on the gateway (186) by Giovanni da Maiano and the plasterwork ceiling and frieze in the small linenfold-panelled room known as Wolsey's Closet. This suite of rooms survives much as Wolsey left it. Henry VIII's chief contribution to the palace is the great hall of 1531–6 with its notable hammerbeam roof (187) which was the creation of James Nedham. This roof is in direct line of descent from Westminster Hall, but at Hampton Court the decoration is richer, and the emphasis on the four-centred arch and on horizontals and verticals is stronger. Hampton Court is also famous for its beautiful river façade (186, 189, 190) and Tudor kitchens.

Of Henry's other palaces, *Whitehall* in London was largely destroyed in the seventeenth century. Here also Wolsey had begun work and Henry took it over. *St James's Palace* in London was built 1532–40 and the gatehouse survives. *Nonsuch*, in Surrey, was

---

* Some of the timbers have been replaced over the years owing to decay and insect attack on the originals, but the form is unaltered.

186 *(above left) The great west gatehouse,*
Hampton Court Palace, 1515–25

187 *(above) The great hall hammerbeam roof,*
Hampton Court Palace, 1531–6

188 *Great Hall, Eltham Palace, 1475–80*

189 *Finial,* 190 *Chimney stack,*
Hampton Court *Hampton Court*

Henry's most extravagant and fantastic palace. Our knowledge of it is confined to drawings and descriptions for it was demolished about 1670. Begun in 1537, it represented a stage in Henry's continuous rivalry with Francis I of France and the French influence on its design was strong. Both French and Italian craftsmen worked in it and there was extensive Renaissance detail on a fundamentally English structure.

In *Scotland*, although in the fifteenth and sixteenth centuries there was the same general tendency towards building palaces which were more domestic and less military than earlier in the Middle Ages, the pace of change was slower than further south. Paradoxically, in the royal palaces at *Falkland* and *Stirling* the façades display some of the earliest attempts in Britain to design on Renaissance lines, not just decoratively, but as a coherent structure. This lead was not taken up and it was the seventeenth century before the concept was generally followed. Only slowly was the Medieval castle, with its great hall, chapel, kitchens and living rooms incorporated into a single palace instead of remaining separate buildings inside the castle bailey. The great hall at *Linlithgow Palace* is an example of the newer trend, though that at *Stirling*, before its eighteenth-century mutilation a magnificent late Gothic hall comparable to Westminster, was built originally as a separate structure.

Houses

The majority of Medieval houses were built of wood and most have perished. This is particularly true of houses in *towns* where space was more limited and constant rebuilding on the same site took place over the years. Also the congestion of narrow streets and overhanging upper storeys caused the loss of many hundreds of Medieval timber houses by fire. Most of the Medieval houses which survive are of timber and plaster, or timber and brick structures in the country, or houses of brick, stone or flint. As it was the wealthier citizens who could afford to build in more permanent materials, extant Medieval houses are mostly of manor house design or are smaller fortified houses.

In the early Middle Ages the main concern of the larger house owner or builder was protection against the marauder and so houses were fortified. They were defended by outer walls, a moat – which was spanned by a drawbridge – and protected by a portcullis and one or more gatehouses. The walls were battlemented with a parapet behind and were also machicolated. Such houses, built before 1400, were planned round an open courtyard, generally in two or three storeys. The windows were small for defensive reasons, and on the lower floor were often only slits. This semi-basement floor, the undercroft, was used for storage of food and household necessities which would be needed in times of siege, while the living area was above, reached through a front door or porch via a flight of stone steps. This door generally led into the hall, the most important room in the house.

The *hall* was two storeys high and had an open timber roof; the wood, brick or stone floor was covered in rushes and the walls painted or partly covered by wool hangings or tapestry. Bright colours were used. It was a large room, up to 40–50 feet long and, as in Norman times, was used as a general living room by everyone in the house. There was little privacy: everyone needed somewhere to keep warm, to enjoy recreation, to eat and to sleep. Most often there was a central hearth where massive logs burned, supported on iron fire dogs. The smoke escaped through a hole in the roof which was covered by a louvre. Some halls had wall fireplaces with stone hoods which directed the smoke upwards and outwards through the wall. There were no chimneys at this stage.

At one end of the hall was a raised platform called a daïs, on which was set the lord's table and canopied bench. Also at this end there was usually an oriel or bay window, which gave more light to this end of the hall and provided a decorative feature with its vaulted ceiling and coloured glass. At the other end of the hall were the 'screens'. These were in the form of a passageway divided from the main hall by a wood panelled partition in which door openings were made. From the other side of the screens, openings led into the buttery, pantry and kitchen. The wooden kitchen* was, at this time, often in a separate building due to fear of fire and the screens provided a covered way through which to bring the food into the hall. They

---

* An interesting stone kitchen survives at *Glastonbury Abbey*, Somerset. The Abbot's kitchen here is square with an octagonal roof and louvre above for the escape of smoke and steam. It had several large fireplaces and ovens.

191 *Great Hall with screen and gallery. Based on Haddon Hall, Derbyshire*

192 *Gatehouse entrance, Oxburgh Hall, Norfolk, from 1482*

193 *Manor House, Lower Brockhampton, Herefordshire, c.1400*

194 *Manor House, Boothby Pagnell, Lincolnshire, c.1180*

195 *Athelhampton, Dorset, from c.1485*

also prevented draughts from the front porch reaching the hall itself. Above the screens was often a gallery where minstrels played (191, 203).

Staircases to provide access from the hall to other parts of the house were either stone spiral ones, as in castles, when they were constructed in a turret or tower, or wood ladders. Very common were exterior staircases of stone steps built up the side walls of the house (194).

Good, typical examples of *manor houses* of the years 1180–1400 include the stone one at *Boothby Pagnell*, Lincolnshire, c.1180 (194), the early brick example of *Little Wenham Hall*, Suffolk, 1270–80 (196, 199), *Old Soar* at Plaxtol, Kent, c.1290, *Markenfield Hall*, Yorkshire, c.1310 and *Penshurst Place*, Kent, c.1340, all in stone. At Penshurst, there have been several later additions and alterations to the house, but the superb fourteenth-century hall survives, with its central hearth, daïs and open timber roof. Fig. 203 represents the hall as it would have looked in 1340.

The half-timber little manor house at *Lower Brockhampton*, Herefordshire, c.1400 (193) is particularly interesting for the survival of the separate gatehouse still spanning the moat. There is a fine timber-roofed hall and minstrel's gallery in the house itself. An unusual stone, tiny manor house is in the main street at *Tintagel* in Cornwall. This fourteenth-century building is long and low, covered by a slate roof. Inside, there is a parlour, a bedroom above it and a galleried hall.

The open *timber roofs,* used to cover both church naves and great halls, were the wooden counterparts of the stone vault. As time passed and the timber roofs of large churches were replaced with vaults, the domestic roof remained of wood, but the construction became more complex and ornamental. The British developed these designs as did no other nation; they extended from the tie-beam structures of the twelfth century to the final phase of the gilded, painted and angel-sculptured hammerbeam roof.

The Medieval roof (see Glossary) was gabled at each end with a fairly steep pitch. A long beam – the ridge purlin – extended horizontally along the ridge from one end of the hall to the other and further beams (purlins) were set at intervals parallel to it, down the pitch from apex to wall. Rafters were inserted across these at right angles, supported on the wall plate (the horizontal beam at wall level) at the bottom and attached to the ridge purlin at the top. The wall plate itself was secured by stone corbels.

The earliest and simplest design was the tie-beam roof. Here, a massive beam was thrown across the hall from wall plate to wall plate to counteract the outward thrust on the walls. It was pinned to the wall plates and usually curved slightly upwards in the centre. A central *king post* (or two queen posts) and side struts were often supported on the tie beam to strengthen the structure (191, 203, 207). Developing from this came the *trussed rafter roof* and *collar-braced* design. These obviated the tie beam and gave better visibility and more height to the room. In these, curved collar beams or straight struts braced and strengthened the rafters and purlins (198, 203).

The *hammerbeam roof* was evolved at the end of the fourteenth century. It consists of a series of horizontal hammerbeams which are extensions inwards, like abbreviated tie beams, and vertical hammer posts. The hammerbeams are supported on braced corbels and are usually decoratively carved with angels, animals or birds. The hammer posts support the appropriate purlins. The whole roof was originally brightly painted and gilded. The complete, rigid system of timbers was tenoned and pinned to provide a stable structure against the outward thrust of the rafters. External abutment was used as necessary (187, 188). In a double hammerbeam roof there are two sets of hammerbeams and posts, one above the other (119).

On the first floor of a house was generally to be found a smaller chamber, the withdrawing room or *solar*, which was a retreat for the lord and his family from the noise and bustle of the hall. Often there was a tiny rectangular window, called a squint, where the lord could look through from the solar to the hall below to see what was happening there. Several houses retain these as, for example, Penshurst and Great Dixter manor house in Sussex. A typical solar is illustrated in Fig. 198.

By the fifteenth century there was less need for fortification, so the extra available space provided more privacy in the form of bedrooms and reception rooms. The hall was still the principal room of the house, but was used less than formerly by the family themselves. The central hearth gave way to wall fireplaces with roof chimneys (191). The moat was still often retained, but the drawbridge and portcullis were replaced by a bridge leading to an elegant gate-

197 *Stoneacre, Otham, Kent, c.1480*

196 *Little Wenham Hall, Suffolk, c.1270–80*

198 *Manor House solar, c.1475–85*

199 *Plan, Little Wenham Hall*

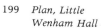

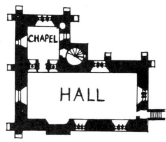

200 *Chimney stack, Hengrave Hall, Suffolk, 1525–38*

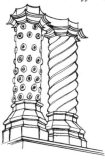

201 *Linenfold panel, c.1510*

202
*Oriel window,
Compton Wynyates,
Warwickshire,
c.1530*

203   *14th-century hall based on Penshurst Place, Kent*

204   *Tudor parlour, c. 1530, based upon the Abbot's room, Thame Park, Oxfordshire*

house, which accommodated a chapel in an upper room (192). Such fifteenth-century houses were spaciously laid out round a courtyard and have roof-lines of various levels broken by tall chimney stacks and gabled ends. There are stone, brick and half-timber examples. The stone and brick ones have Perpendicular Gothic window openings and project-ing porches. Timber houses have carved corner posts, barge boards and corbels. Of the many existing houses, interesting stone ones are *Compton Castle*, Devon, fourteenth and fifteenth centuries, *Cotehele Manor House*, Cornwall, 1485–1539, *Lytes Carey Manor House*, Somerset, 1343–1450, *Great Chalfield Manor House*, Wiltshire, c.1480, *Athelhampton*, Dor-set, fifteenth and sixteenth centuries (195) and *South Wraxall Manor House*, Wiltshire, fifteenth century. *Oxburgh Hall*, Norfolk is a fine moated, brick house (192) and *Ockwells Manor House*, Berkshire, 1466, is built from timber and brick. There exist a variety of half-timber houses, large and small. Of particular interest are *Stoneacre, Otham*, Kent, 1480 (197), *Rufford Old Hall*, Lancashire, 1463–1505, and *Great Dixter Manor House*, Sussex, mainly fifteenth century.

The houses of the first half of the sixteenth century represent a transitional stage between the Medieval pattern and the Elizabethan great house. The years 1530–50 were a time of energetic house building, from large mansions to small homes. As Henry VIII re-allocated the monastic property, wealthy land-owners built fine houses on their newly acquired estates. The need for defence continued to decline and these houses were more spacious, with larger win-dows (202), better staircases and with chimneys (200), gables and cresting finally replacing Medieval cren-ellation. Timber was becoming more costly as a result of centuries of felling without replanting. On the other hand, brickwork skills were developing and brick houses, decorated with terracotta, were typical of Tudor building. Inside, the flat, wood and plaster ceiling replaced the open timber roof, and walls were covered by a wood and decorative plaster frieze and, below this, oak panelling where the linenfold panel was most often seen (201, 204). Imposing houses of this time include *Sutton Place*, Surrey, 1523–5, *Barrington Court*, Somerset, c.1530, *Coughton Court*, Warwickshire, *Hengrave Hall*, Suffolk, 1525 (200), *Horham Hall*, Essex, 1502–20, *Stoke-by-Nayland*, Suffolk and *Compton Wynyates*, Warwickshire (202). Many structures of different kinds survive from

the energetic building activities of the later Middle Ages. These comprise buildings in towns such as guildhalls and inns and, in the country, farming structures such as barns and dovecotes, also bridges, and buildings for education at the universities and schools.

The *Guildhalls* of *London* and *York* were superb examples of their kind, but both have been altered over the years and largely rebuilt after devastation in the Second World War. From a rural area, the half-timber Guildhall survives at Lavenham, Suffolk (174). In *York*, the *Merchant Adventurers' Hall* retains its timber roofed hall and undercroft (207). Several fifteenth-century inns exist and are still functioning as hotels and public houses. The *George Inn* at Glas-tonbury is a stone example of 1475 (175), as is also the *Angel Inn* at Grantham. In half-timber work there is the *Mermaid Inn* at Rye and the richly ornamented *Feathers Inn* at Ludlow (205).

Several fine Medieval *barns* exist. These were built in stone or wood and had open timber roofs like the houses. Larger examples were divided into nave and aisles as in a church and were strongly buttressed on the exterior. Of especial interest are the tithe barn at *Bradford-on-Avon* and the abbey barn at *Glastonbury*, both of the fourteenth century (210). From the fifteenth century we have those at *West Pennard*, *Abbotsbury* and *Ashleworth*, all in the west country.

There are many Medieval *bridges* still spanning rivers in different parts of the country. Surviving examples are of stone or brick and have one or more round or pointed arches. The roadway rises to the centre, unlike Roman ones which were flat. Medieval bridges were constructed on timber piles, which were reinforced with iron and driven into the river bed. A starling of piles was built round each main pile and filled in solid. The starling tops were boarded and a stone platform was laid to support the actual bridge, which was constructed of ashlar blocks laid with mortar. Excellent examples can be seen at *Aylesford* (209) and *East Farleigh* over the Medway, *Radcot* and *Newbridge* over the Thames, *Bakewell* over the Wye, the *Clopton Bridge* at *Stratford-upon-Avon* and the beautiful round-arched 'Old Brig' of the fifteenth century at *Stirling*. Many bridges were built with a chapel on them, where a priest would bless travellers, hold services and collect alms. One of these bridges survives at *Bradford-on-Avon* (211). In troubled areas, military bridges were common, where a forti-

206   *The city walls and Micklegate Bar, York, 1198–1230*

205   *The Feathers Inn, Ludlow, c.1520–30*

207   *The Merchant Adventurers' Hall, York, 1357–69*

208 Monnow Bridge with military gateway, Monmouth, late 13th century

209 Aylesford Bridge, river Medway, 14th century

210 The Abbey Barn, Glastonbury, c.1330

211 Chapel Bridge, Bradford-on-Avon, 14th century

212 *Corpus Christi College, Oxford, early Tudor*

213 *Trinity College, Cambridge, the Great Gate, 1518*

214 *Christ Church, Oxford, Tom Quad, early Tudor*

215 *Magdalen College, Oxford, c.1490–1509*

216 *Gateway decoration, St John's College, Cambridge, early Tudor*

fied gatehouse controlled the passageway at the centre of the bridge. The *Monnow Bridge* at *Monmouth* is one of these (208).

At *Oxford* and *Cambridge Universities* the Medieval halls of residence give a clear impression of the house plan of the Middle Ages as they contain a great hall, chapel and rooms grouped round one or more quadrangles with gateways set at the entrance and exit of each. Remains of Medieval work is considerable and some is of finest quality Gothic architecture, such as *Magdalen College* façade and tower (215), *Merton College* chapel and *New College* chapel, all at Oxford. In the sixteenth century, under the early Tudors, *Trinity College* was founded in 1546 at Cam-

bridge when much of the Great Court was built, including the hall and chapel as well as the Great Gate (213). The decorative gateway to the outer court at *St John's College* also belongs to this time (216). At Oxford, Cardinal Wolsey founded his 'Cardinal College', now *Christ Church*. As at Hampton Court, Wolsey began building and Henry VIII took over. He moved the see to Oxford and called the college 'The House of Christ's Cathedral in Oxford'. It is still known as 'The House'. The Tom quad, with Tom Tower, was largely built at this time, but Wren completed the work in the seventeenth century (214). Front quad at *Corpus Christi College* is typical early sixteenth-century workmanship (212).

PART TWO

CLASSICAL DOMINANCE

CHAPTER FIVE

Elizabethan and Jacobean
1550–1625

Shakespeare's England was a 'golden age' for the country. By 1565 the struggles, both religious and economic, of the mid-century had abated, if they were not fully resolved. Medieval restriction was over and industrialisation had not yet begun. Most people lived in villages and small towns and, though not all were wealthy, extreme poverty was much rarer. Apart from the intermittent rumblings from Spain, the country was at peace and a middle class was establishing itself. The yeoman farmers were evidence of this change, as were also the houses built by middle class people in town and country. This was a phenomenon unknown in feudal Europe. The English had forged for themselves an individual freedom not, even now, available to many nations of the world.

At this time also the United Kingdom was taking a shaky step nearer towards its future foundation. Wales, long the land of conflict between Marcher Lords and the Celtic Welsh, was now peacefully amalgamated with England under the Crown. The monarchy itself was of Welsh (Tudor) line and the union of the two countries, effected militarily under Edward I, became a reality under Elizabeth.

In the north, in the borders and in Scotland, it was a different story. The region was poor, feudality persisted and there was a religious problem. Many years had to pass before the Union was achieved.

Elizabethan England, while enjoying its 'golden age' at home, encouraged the exploration overseas of the mariners who travelled the oceans of the world, extending English influence and bringing back fruitful contacts, trade and merchandise. In turn, this led to increased prosperity at home.

Elizabethan Towns

The population of England and Wales was growing. By the end of the sixteenth century it is thought to have passed four millions, as opposed to the two to two-and-a-half millions of Medieval times. Most people lived in rural areas, cultivating the land or tending sheep; cottage industries supplied the local needs. Even town dwellers spent part of their time in agricultural pursuits. Towns were still small but were larger than their Medieval counterparts. The average town now had about 5000 inhabitants, most of whom had ample living space, including gardens, orchards and farmsteads. About 20,000 people lived in each of the important towns of the country – York, Norwich and Bristol – other than London.

London was much the largest of these towns, becoming more important all the time and one of the greatest in Europe; by 1600 it had about 200,000 inhabitants. It was a microcosm of the nation, reflecting the changes which had taken place. This could be seen in the disappearance of the great monasteries and the importance of secular building and activity in contrast to the Medieval ecclesiastical. The City of London was now an essentially merchant community of great power and wealth, while the buildings of the monarchy and aristocracy were outside the city boundaries, in Whitehall, Westminster and beyond.

London was said by travellers to be the cleanest city in Europe, but by twentieth-century standards it would be considered filthy. The refuse littering the streets and the stench from the open drains and slaughterhouses had not improved since Medieval days. The city was still walled and with its famous gates – now just districts to us – Aldersgate, Cripplegate, Bishopsgate, Oldgate, Moorgate, Newgate, Billingsgate, all clearly named from their locality. London Bridge, the only one across the Thames until the eighteenth century, had been built in stone between 1176 and 1209, replacing the earlier, timber ones. It was a remarkable structure for its period, supported upon 18 stone piers, which were built on to oak planks and bedded in pitch. The bridge, with the starlings which protected these piers from the scour of the strong tide, acted as a dam, holding back the ebb tide. It was this, together with the lack of embankmentation, which caused the river to freeze over in cold winters. The roadway was supported on the piers, which were connected by pointed arches of differing size to accommodate vessels of varied tonnage. On the road were constructed houses and shops whose rent paid for the upkeep of the bridge. They suffered destruction by fire from time to time and were rebuilt, generally larger than before. In Elizabethan times, though the bridge roadway was 20 feet wide, only 10–12 feet of passageway remained and the houses jutted outwards over the river. On iron spikes, at the Tower end of the bridge, the decapitated heads of traitors were left to dehydrate slowly as a warning to others (217).

Stone houses were slowly replacing timber ones, but the great majority were still of half-timber with the upper storeys projecting to nearly meet across the narrow streets. Fire continued to be a great hazard in towns. Houses were often extended vertically instead of laterally as the population grew larger. This was especially so in London and in the north of the country. In Scotland the tradition of the tower house led to easy acceptance of such building. Edinburgh, in particular, was noted until the late eighteenth century for the tall tenement houses, many of which survive in the Old Town (219).

The market was still an important feature of town life, taking place in a market square or a widened section of the High Street. Shops were few, the needs of the community being served by the craftsman working in his house, travelling fairs and the market. The tolbooth, especially in Scotland, survives in several instances as a picturesque feature of the town High Street. As the name implies, this was the place where taxes and tolls were collected: it was the customs house. Medieval and Elizabethan ones were

tall buildings with a belfry and a clock and containing a court room, toll room and cells below for debtors. The buildings later developed into the town hall. The Canongate tolbooth of 1591 is an existing example in Edinburgh (218).

The Architectural Style in Britain 1550–1625

This was a time of energetic building activity, not of cathedrals and chapels, but of great country houses. From the aristocracy to the merchant and yeoman there was a deep desire to create a new, more spacious home, in keeping with the new spirit of the age, displaying the affluence of the owner. Throughout Europe the Renaissance ideals in philosophy, literature and the visual arts were now established. Britain came late to the field; Medievalism had lingered long here. In literature the English were a leading force, but in architecture they were backward. The aristocracy travelled abroad, particularly to France and Flanders, saw the new classical forms replacing the old Medieval ones, and returned to build their own new architecture. But the British interpretation was not pure classicism. In England, the established tradition for asymmetry, the gabled manor house, the mullioned window, the disinterest in sculpture was still strong. Protestant England still had little contact with Catholic Italy and few of the Italian artists who came westward to France extended their travels to England. The English architecture of these years is a blend of three sources: the Italian Renaissance, the French châteaux of the Loire valley and the Flemish decorative style, and all this is grafted upon an essentially English foundation of the Medieval manor house. The results are vital and plastic, a new English art form, national and different from that of much of Europe.

Classical Architecture: Origins, Greece and Rome

In Britain, as in Western Europe, there have been only two basic styles of architecture until the modern building of the twentieth century: Gothic and classical. Each has been subject to development and variation on its main theme, each enjoyed a period of some hundreds of years in which the development took place, and each was the subject of nineteenth-century revivals. Gothic architecture flourished

217 *View of London from the south bank of the Thames, early 17th century (after Hollar)*
A *Old St Paul's Cathedral*   E *Guildhall*
B *St Laurence Poultney*   F *St Dunstan-in-the-East*
C *St Andrew's, Holborn*   G *London Bridge*
D *St Michael*

during the Middle Ages – some 400 years in Britain – and the Renaissance re-initiated classical design. In Britain, coming late to this new classical form, the sixteenth century was a time of tentative experiment. Classical tenets were only established in the seventeenth century when they became the accepted mode of building.

An important distinction between Gothic and classical building is that the former is indigenous to north-west Europe, including Britain, and grew up steadily and nationally in each area, while the latter was an importation, first from Rome, then Greece. Because the climate of these countries is different

from that of Britain, adaptations had to be made, but the style remained basically the same. In beginning a study of the architecture of Renaissance Britain, it is helpful to look at the origins of the classical forms. Historically, Greek architecture is the prototype upon which Roman work was based, but the rediscovery and importation of these styles into Renaissance Europe worked in reverse. Greece was under the subjugation of the Turkish Empire; it remained unknown to and unvisited by the West for another two centuries. The architecture of Ancient Rome was studied by the Italians in the fifteenth century and by England much later. For some time it was believed

throughout Western Europe that Rome was the originator of the style; the Italians were jealously proud of this supposed fact.

What is commonly described as the *architecture of Ancient Greece*, the Hellenic building style, emerged from archaic beginnings about 700 BC and reached its zenith, in beauty and quality, in the mid-fifth century BC. The Ancient Greek civilisation continued until 146 BC, when Greece became a subject state of Rome. Many fine buildings date from the later years, but the later fifth-century work was never surpassed. The Greek style of building was simple in line and form and of limited design, whatever the purpose of the structure. It is a *trabeated* type of architecture and this is fundamentally different from the Gothic *arcuated* style. Medieval construction was based upon the arch, at first round then pointed, then from this

developed the vault supported on piers. In classical architecture, based upon the trabeated form (from Latin *trabes* = a beam), the construction is of a post-and-lintel type, consisting of vertical supports (the columns) and horizontal beams or blocks of stone or marble. From the early discovery that a lintel stone supported on two columns could form an opening, the colonnade evolved, in which a row of columns would carry a long, extended lintel and this became the exterior elevation of a building. In the Greek climate, an outdoor life was usual and colonnaded buildings provided shade from the sun as well as fresh air.

The beauty of Greek architecture derives, not from its variety of forms, but from its subtle and detailed attention to proportion and line. The Greeks developed a system of *orders* wherein the proportions of

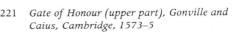

219   *John Knox's house, High Street, Edinburgh, 1490 and later*

218   *Canongate Tolbooth, Edinburgh, 1592*

221   *Gate of Honour (upper part), Gonville and Caius, Cambridge, 1573–5*

220   *Queens' College, Cambridge, mid-16th century*

the individual parts were studied and crystallised. Each order consists of a column, sometimes a base, a capital and an entablature. The entablature is the group of horizontal mouldings which is supported, as was the original lintel, on top of the columns. It, in turn, is subdivided into three basic parts: the *architrave*, above this the *frieze* and, at the top, the projecting *cornice*. In each order the types, proportions and decoration of the mouldings, the proportion of the column, the relationship of width to height and to the base, the capital and the entablature, all are regulated. The quality of Greek building varies, from the ordinary to the magnificent, according to the architect's subtle interpretation of these rules.

There are three Greek orders: *Doric, Ionic* and *Corinthian*. The Greeks preferred the Doric which, especially on the mainland, features in the majority of the best Greek buildings (222). The most famous of all, the *Parthenon*, is in this order. Built in the finest period, 447–432 BC, it is today partly ruined; in Fig. 224 it is shown restored. Much of the sculpture from the pediments and the interior frieze is in the British Museum in London. The Parthenon shows the chief features of the *Doric Order* (222, 224): a sturdy column, fluted but without base, a plain architrave and a deeply projecting cornice, with the intervening frieze enriched by alternate triglyphs and metopes. The former are vertical bands of stone and the latter alternating panels in which are set decorative sculptural groups. At either end of a Greek temple there is a triangular *pediment* which has similar mouldings to the cornice and is decorated in the tympanum with sculpture. The timber roof was covered with marble tiles. The Doric capital is simple; it has a square top member, the *abacus*, and below this the *echinus* with narrow rings cut in rows beneath (222).

The *Ionic Order* (226) has a narrower column shaft and a moulded base, a capital with curved side scrolls, called *volutes*, and a frieze which is usually decorated along its whole length by relief sculpture; the cornice projects less strongly. Near the Parthenon, on the Athenian Acropolis, is a beautiful example of the Ionic Order – the Erechtheion – also built of the local, white marble (227). The third order, the *Corinthian* (228) was rarely used by the Greeks. It is similar to the Ionic except that the capital is bell-shaped, with small volutes at the four top outer corners, and the bell is clothed in two rows of acanthus leaves curling over and outwards.

The *Roman civilisation* lasted several hundred years, overlapping the Greek one by a long time, but achieving its best architectural work between the first century BC and the third century AD. The Romans also built in the trabeated style and used the orders, adapting the Greek Doric, Ionic and Corinthian (226, 228) and adding two more, the *Tuscan* and the *Composite*. The first of these was similar to the Doric; the Composite has a capital which possesses some Ionic and some Corinthian features (225). The chief differences between Greek and Roman architecture are:

1. The Greeks used one order per façade. The Romans often used several, one above the other, as in the Colosseum (230).
2. The Greeks built primarily in the trabeated manner. The Romans also used arcuated methods and combined both forms in one building. This too can be seen in the Colosseum (230), where arches are structural and the orders decorative.
3. Roman orders and ornament are generally coarser and heavier than the Greek. The Romans preferred to use the Composite and Corinthian Orders (223, 225, 226, 229).
4. The Romans were great builders and engineers, famous for their concrete vaults, public baths, bridges and aqueducts, as well as temples. The Greeks were perfectionists of the subtleties of the simple classical temple form.

The Sources of the English Classical Style of 1550–1625

Of the three classical sources which formed the English style of these years, the influence of the purer classicism of the Italian Renaissance was weakest. The knowledge of the English builders came from books of drawings and designs, the impressions of the aristocratic travellers who returned to commission their homes and the craftsmen who came to work in England from the Continent. Though the purer Italian classical model was available in the publications of Vitruvius, Palladio, Alberti and others, the English were more drawn towards the French and Flemish interpretations. Great landowners visited France and Flanders more widely and they could see from the châteaux of de l'Orme and Bullant, Lescot's work on the Louvre and, in Flanders, Floris' Town Hall at Antwerp and de Key's at Leiden, what the finished

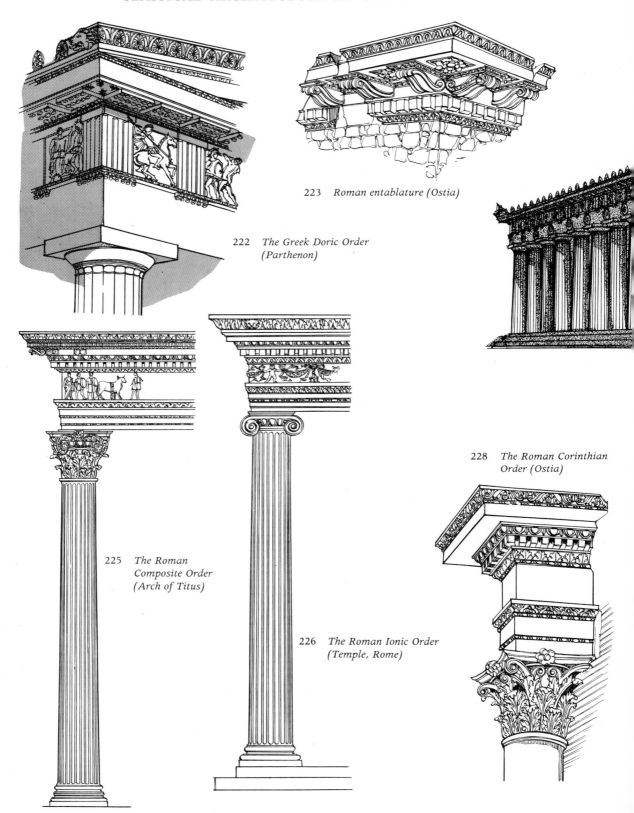

222   *The Greek Doric Order (Parthenon)*

223   *Roman entablature (Ostia)*

228   *The Roman Corinthian Order (Ostia)*

225   *The Roman Composite Order (Arch of Titus)*

226   *The Roman Ionic Order (Temple, Rome)*

224   *The Parthenon, Athens (restored), 447–432 BC*

227   *Greek ornament (Erechtheion, Athens)*

229
Roman ornament (Trajan Forum, Rome)

230   *The Colosseum, Rome, AD 70–82*

structure should look like. Few of them, at this stage, reached Rome or Florence. It was seventeenth-century England which returned to Palladio and Vitruvius through Inigo Jones.

Elizabethan England absorbed all the decorative possibilities of the new style from French and Flemish sources and interpreted them from the pattern books. Builders took their designs from Serlio's treatise, from de Bry and de Vries and from the German Dietterlin. In 1563 the Englishman John Shute published his *Chief Groundes of Architecture*, showing the five classical orders, based on Serlio's work. The Flemish pattern books on ornament were riotously ornate and the Elizabethans absorbed with enthusiasm the strapwork and cartouche designs, the ornamented orders, the decorative cresting and gabling. They incorporated these into their buildings, caring little and understanding less if their orders were wrongly proportioned and, from a classical viewpoint, wrongly employed, since they were added to a fundamentally Medieval building as decoration, not construction.

There were no architects yet in the modern understanding of the term. Surveyors and builders made 'platts' and 'uprights' (plans and elevations) but, in general, a building was designed as it progressed, with the prospective aristocratic owner explaining what he wanted, instructing his master mason on these lines and giving him some books on classical orders and decorative design to work from. Thus, at *Burghley House*, built largely in the 1580s, it was William Cecil, Lord Burghley who was largely responsible for the form of the house. He supplied his master mason with French architectural books and employed Flemish craftsmen.* He was the first of many aristocratic architectural dilettanti.

---

* Such craftsmen, masons, carpenters, glaziers, plasterworkers etc., were directed by a master of their trade, with the whole building operation supervised by a master mason or surveyor. The names of most of these are not known. Records are not generally available and Queen Elizabeth, unlike her father, inaugurated little building work herself, so royal records are few. The exceptions include *John Thorpe* and *Robert Smythson*. Thorpe was employed for some time at the Office of Works and, while there, made many drawings of the houses being built at the time and these are now in the Soane Museum. Smythson is thought to have been connected with the direction of three of the great Elizabethan mansions: Longleat (231), Wollaton and Hardwick. He was buried at Wollaton (235).

The Great Houses

The wealth of the Elizabethan and Jacobean era, architecturally, was funnelled into domestic construction. Few churches were erected and there was little civic or university building. It is the great houses which represent the architectural expression of the age. The aristocracy, who commissioned and partly designed them, vied with one another to create palaces suitable for the monarch, accompanied by her court retinue, to visit on her annual summer progress. For such a purpose and such a monarch a house had to be great indeed, both impressive and capacious. Each subject tried to outdo his predecessors when building a new house, in style, ornamentation, splendour and scale.

The House Exterior

The *plan* of these mansions varied, but there was a growing acceptance of a greater symmetry (the influence of the Renaissance), also a preference for a more compact house built round an open, rather than a closed, four-sided court. Early in the 1560s, the *E-plan* house was developed. In this, wings were extended forwards at each end of a rectangular house, while in the centre the short stroke of the E was provided by a projecting entrance porch. The house was then symmetrical, with the hall, solar and other reception rooms on one side of the porch and the screens passage and offices on the other. Often the latter would be given an oriel or bay window, extending much of the height of the house, to balance that of the hall. *Cobham Hall* in Kent has this type of plan. The *H-plan* then evolved from the E-plan design. Here, the side wings were extended as far to the rear as to the front. In the later decades of the century, a greater perfection of symmetry was achieved; bay window matched bay window, gable matched gable, chimneystack matched chimneystack. *Montacute House* is a classic example (238) as also is *Longleat* (231).

Window area increased in proportion to the wall rather as it had, a century earlier, in ecclesiastical building. Now the country was at peace, defence and fortification were unnecessary and advances were being made in the production of window glass. The notable change that this brought about prompted the contemporary jingle that at *Hardwick Hall* (Derbyshire), there was 'more glass than wall'. The skylines

231 *Longleat House,*
Wiltshire,
1550–80, stone

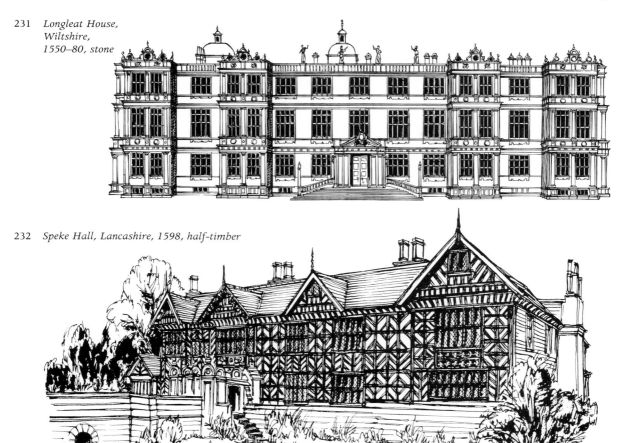

232 *Speke Hall, Lancashire, 1598, half-timber*

233 *Trerice Manor House,*
Cornwall, c.1573, stone

234 *Crathes Castle,*
Kincardineshire, c.1590

235   *Wollaton Hall, Nottinghamshire,*
      1580–8, stone

236   *Craigievar Castle, Aberdeenshire, c.1620*

237 *Little Moreton Hall, Cheshire, 1559–80, half-timber*

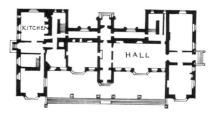

238 *Plan, Montacute House, Somerset, 1588–1601*

239 *Elizabethan main chamber, c.1575–80*

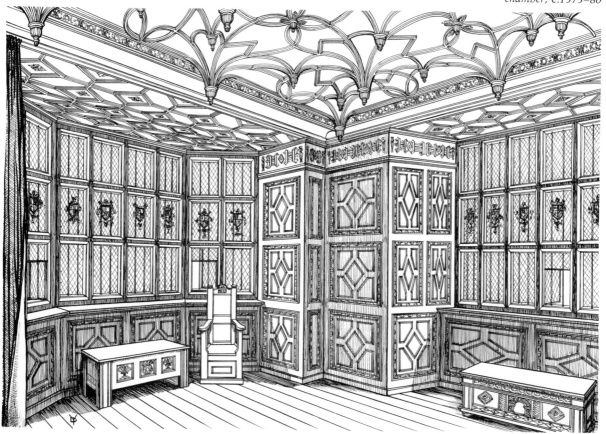

of these houses are one of their most attractive and characteristic features. They are varied and lively in silhouette, illustrating more the traditional English Medieval manor house than the new Renaissance concepts, which tended to horizontal rooflines, broken only by few classical stacks. The skylines of Elizabethan and Jacobean great houses were a riot of cresting, projecting, curving gables and decorative chimneystacks of the greatest variety in design. Often grouped in two, three or four columns, these stacks were ornamented in differing patterns and shared the same base and cresting. They represent the outrageous English adaptation of the classical coupled columns stripped of their classical characteristics.

The *entrance porch* or frontispiece was an Elizabethan development from the early Tudor gatehouse. As the main entrance to the building it was the focal centre for the employment of new Renaissance forms and ornament. Here the designers interpreted the classical orders and used them, not as structural elements, but in ornamental manner. The entrance porch generally had two or three storeys, each usually with single or coupled columns or pilasters. There was little attempt to study the correct classical proportions or forms, but the Elizabethan application of the classical tenets shows great vitality and richness of ornament inspired by Flemish sources. Two or more orders were used unrelatedly in one porch. Interesting *Elizabethan* examples include those at *Cobham Hall*, Kent (242), *Keevil Manor House*, Wiltshire and *Studley Priory*, Oxfordshire. *Jacobean porches* were even richer and more impressive, as at *Hatfield House*, Hertfordshire (246); *Bramshill House*, Hampshire (244), *Charlton House*, Greenwich (245) and *Audley End*, Essex (243).

The House Interior

At the same time as the need for defence declined, there was evinced a greater desire for privacy. The purposes of different rooms in a house altered and more and smaller rooms were included in the plan. The use of the *hall* as a living and sleeping room was abandoned. Elizabethan halls are smaller and of one storey only. They have flat ceilings decorated all over with plaster panels and strapwork, enriched with floral, animal and heraldic motifs. Some are in high relief and many are pendant designs (239, 247, 248, 249). The walls are panelled in wood, but here the

linenfold panelling of early Tudor times has been replaced by simple moulded and beaded panels, plain or inlaid with coloured woods and ivory (239, 241). There is a deep frieze of plaster, decorated and often painted, like the ceiling.

In Jacobean houses the whole room was beginning to be designed as one unit in classical form, with pilasters and columns dividing the sections and with windows, doorways and chimneypieces as focal centres (249). The classical details were still inaccurate by Italian Renaissance standards but the format was being accepted and interiors, like exteriors, were being planned as a whole to include all architectural motifs and details as part of the scheme. The hall screen was, in these years, still of wood but now very richly carved. Some examples, like those at *Audley End* and *Knole*, are most ornate and extend from floor almost to ceiling in a riot of Flemish mannerist treatment (241). Among the fine examples of hall plaster ceilings are the ribbed designs at *Knole House*, Kent, *Levens Hall*, Cumbria, the strapwork ceiling at *Hatfield House*, Hertfordshire and the pendant form at *Dunster Castle*, Somerset and *Trerice Manor House*, Cornwall (247). The hall floor was of stone, brick, wood or tiled. There were one or more wall fireplaces, generally two-tiered and an integral part of the architectural scheme of the room; they too were ornately carved in Flemish mannerist pattern (241, 266).

The Medieval solar had now been replaced by several reception rooms of which the main chamber (great drawing room) was the largest. Generally on the first floor, this had an architectural and decorative scheme second only in richness and quality to the hall. It was not so lofty and there was no carved screen, but the ornamentation and treatment of windows, ceiling and walls was similar. The floor was of wood (239, 249). Good examples include *Athelhampton House*, Dorset (248), *Montacute House*, Somerset, *Speke Hall*, Lancashire, *Hatfield House*, Hertfordshire and *Levens Hall*, Cumbria (253). Small parlours were in use by different members of the family and for dining privately.

Bedchambers were now more common, though they were still passage rooms; as there were few corridors, the bedrooms were actually a wide passage divided up and having a door at each end, which led into the adjoining rooms. The Tudor wing at Hampton Court Palace is of this design. As this system was draughty,

240 *Castle Ashby, Northamptonshire, c.1624, brick and stone*

241 *Jacobean hall, Audley End, Essex, 1603–16*

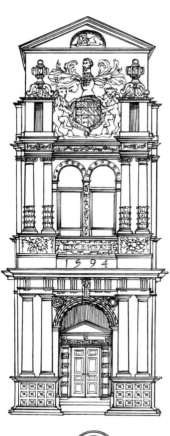

242   *(far left) Cobham Hall,
Kent, c.1594*

243   *(left) Audley End,
Essex, 1603–16*

244   *(below left) Bramshill Hous
Hampshire, 1605–12*

245   *(below centre) Charlton Hou
Greenwich, 1607–12*

246   *(below) Hatfield House,
Hertfordshire, 1611*

247   *Ceiling, Trerice House, Cornwall*

248   *Ceiling, Athelhampton, Dorset*

249   *Jacobean drawing room, c.1615–20*

the vast four-post bedstead, with its ornately carved headboard, posts and canopy frame and enveloping curtains and frill, provided a cosy room within a room. Many examples of such bedsteads survive in museums, such as the Victoria and Albert Museum in London, and in a number of houses in different parts of the country, for example, *Rufford Old Hall*, Lancashire and *Oxburgh Hall*, Norfolk. These bedsteads were so costly and so important that they were willed from father to son over several generations as one of the most precious of family possessions.

A new type of room which originated in the sixteenth century was made fashionable by the Elizabethans: this was the *long gallery*. It was located on the first or second floor of the house and extended along the whole of one long façade. Some galleries are as long as 170 feet but are quite narrow, about 20 feet wide and only 15 feet high. This long, narrow room had windows on three sides, on the two short ones and on the outer, long side, while on the fourth, inner side were two or more fireplaces. The purpose of the gallery was to provide plenty of space in which children could play and adults sit and talk, listen to music, stroll about or play games, in the winter months, without getting in one another's way or on their nerves. Modern multi-purpose, open-plan living rooms have a similar theme; the drawback to these is that they are not 170 feet long and the occupants, while not as numerous as in an Elizabethan long gallery, often get in one another's way. Long galleries survive in many great Elizabethan and Jacobean houses though some, as at Syon House, have been redesigned in a later age to alter the appearance of the proportions. Among the beautiful galleries are those at *Knole House*, Kent, *Hatfield House*, Hertfordshire, *Ham House*, Surrey, *Little Moreton Hall*, Cheshire, *Montacute House*, Somerset, *Hardwick Hall* and *Haddon Hall*, both in Derbyshire.

The third characteristic feature of these houses, together with the porch and the long gallery, was the *staircase*. It was not until the second half of the sixteenth century that this became a distinctive feature in the aesthetic design of a house as well as a means of access from one floor to another. Elizabethan staircases were of oak, solidly built and designed in generous proportions to accommodate the farthingale skirts of the ladies of the family. They were constructed in short flights of six to ten stairs and were called *dog-legged* because each flight returned back

alongside the one immediately above and below it. At the top and bottom of each flight was a massive newel post, decoratively carved in panels and surmounted by a finial. Each newel was joined to the next by a heavy, moulded handrail and an equivalent baulk of timber, the string, ran parallel, joining the treads. Ornamented balusters connected the two (251).

By the Jacobean period the staircase had evolved into a magnificent feature and a number of these survive, at *Hatfield House* and *Knole* for example (250, 252). Though still of oak and solidly built, these staircases were constructed round an open well, taking up much more space than the Elizabethan dog-legged type. The treads are broad, the flights short and the ascents easy. Some of the newels, especially the finials, are beautifully and interestingly carved (250, 252, 264).

Examples

There are a number of great houses of Elizabethan and Jacobean times in different parts of Britain which have survived with only marginal alterations since they were first built. Changes in furnishing, furniture, heating and lighting have been made to all those which are still lived in and restoration has taken place, but most give a clear picture of what such houses would have been like. The large mansions were generally built of stone or, at least, of brick and stone. Of particular interest among these are *Hardwick Hall*, Derbyshire, 1591–7, *Cobham Hall*, Kent, 1594–9 (242, 260), *Longleat House*, Wiltshire, 1550–80 (231, 263), *Montacute House*, Somerset, 1588–1601 (238), *Wollaton Hall*, Nottinghamshire, 1580–8 (235, 261), *Hatfield House*, Hertfordshire, 1607–12 (246, 252, 254), *Castle Ashby*, Northamptonshire, c.1624 (240, 256), *Burghley House*, Northamptonshire, c. 1585, *Bramshill House*, Hampshire, 1605–12 (244), and *Knole House*, Kent, c.1605 (250). Other large houses retain certain features of note from this time, such as the hall at *Audley End*, Essex, 1603–16 (241) and the long gallery at *Haddon Hall*, Derbyshire, 1585.

Of the smaller houses in stone and brick should be noted *Keevil Manor House*, Wiltshire, *Cothelstone Manor House*, Somerset (257), *Brereton Hall*, Cheshire, c.1586, *Fritwell Manor House* (258) and *Studley Priory*, both in Oxfordshire and all Elizabethan. From

250   *Jacobean staircase, Knole, Kent, c.1605*

251   *Elizabethan dog-legged staircase*

252   *Carved oak staircase, Hatfield House, 1607–12*

253   *Drawing room doorway, Levens Hall, Cumbria, late Elizabethan*

254   *Entrance doorway, Hatfield House, Hertfordshire, c.1607–12*

255   *Half-timber gable and window, Little Moreton Hall, c.1580*

256   *Bay window, Castle Ashby, Northamptonshire, c.1624*

257
Stone gable and window, Cothelstone Manor House, Somerset

258   *Window, Fritwell Manor House, Oxfordshire, stone*

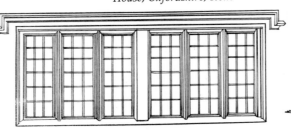

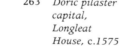

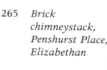

259   *Carved oak pilaster and panelling, c.1600*

260   *Porch detail, Ionic Order, Cobham Hall, 1594*

261   *Timber roof of hall, Wollaton Hall, 1580–8*

262   *Elizabethan carved panelling*

263   *Doric pilaster capital, Longleat House, c.1575*

264   *Jacobean carved oak staircase finial*

265   *Brick chimneystack, Penshurst Place, Elizabethan*

266   *Carved stone fireplace with carved oak mantel, c.1600*

267   *Wood panelling, Chastleton House, c.1610*

268   *Detail, hall screen, Knole House, Jacobean*

269   *Carved wood corbel bracket, Queens' College, Cambridge*

the Jacobean period are *Charlton House*, Greenwich, 1607–12 (245) and *Chastleton House*, Oxfordshire, 1603–12 (267). There are many beautiful half-timber houses dating from this time. These are to be found chiefly in the areas with little stone available, in Cheshire, Lancashire, East Anglia and Kent. Of particular interest are *Little Moreton Hall*, Cheshire, c.1559–80 (237, 255), *Rumwood Court, Langley*, Kent, Elizabethan, and *Speke Hall*, Lancashire, c.1598 (232).

The development of the plan of the great house in *Scotland* was different from England. Whereas south of the border the house plan was being opened up from the restricted courtyard and defensive features were being abandoned, the more troubled conditions and economic weakness of Scotland caused land-owners, large and small, to cling to the *tower house design* until well into the seventeenth century. The tower house had been the most characteristic type of domestic building for the upper classes in Scotland since the twelfth century. It was a compact, easily defensible residence with small land area and small windows yet, with its height, it provided adequate domestic comfort. Similar in outward form to the Norman keep, it attracts no special attention in early Medieval times but, by the end of the sixteenth century, it presents a contrast to the Elizabethan mansion. These years represent the Indian summer of the Scottish baronial style, when a number of fine houses were built in this manner of which several survive in the north-east around Aberdeen. Of particular interest are *Crathes Castle* (234) and *Craigievar Castle* (236), which both exhibit the characteristic corbelled turrets with pointed roofs, small windows and a tall, graceful silhouette.

The seventeenth century brought several attempts to follow the new fashions in Renaissance mansions. One example is the reconstruction of the *Palace of Pinkie* in Midlothian by the Earl of Dunfermline, begun in 1613. The ambitious plans for a grand courtyard house were not completed but, in the two ranges which were built, there was included a long gallery. Renaissance decoration and fenestration have been employed and earlier Scottish characteristic forms blend with these in a not unattractive manner. Another interesting courtyard building was the *Earl's Palace* at *Kirkwall* in Orkney, which dates from about 1600–5. This included some palatial apartments on the first floor, one of which was a large hall. It was a characteristically Scottish building despite clear influence from both France and England.

CHAPTER SIX

Inigo Jones and Wren
1620–1700

Inigo Jones 1573–1652

In Britain, architectural style had developed steadily and logically from Romanesque, through the various stages of Gothic to Elizabethan and Jacobean Renaissance forms, based upon Flemish mannerism but imposed upon a Medieval base. In the 1620s it was Inigo Jones who brought the Italian Renaissance to Britain and, in so doing, created a stylistic revolution. This was almost 100 years after the French architects Lescot, Bullant and de l'Orme had been experimenting with Italian Renaissance forms in their châteaux in France. Being so long delayed, the movement in England burst forth, fully mature, in Jones' *Queen's House* at Greenwich, clearly following the Italian villa pattern developed by Palladio at Vicenza. The Queen's House is the English interpretation of the Palazzo Chiericati; this is no copy, though, but an original design, restrained and characteristically national. The French architects had absorbed the Italian Renaissance form slowly, moving step by step from the purely decorative approach to the fully comprehended constructional one, treating the building as a whole, a considered classical scheme. Inigo Jones, coming much later on the scene, took the complete step in one stage, alone, the first English architect in the Italian Renaissance meaning of the term.

Inigo Jones was born in London, the son of a cloth maker. His father was poor and the young Inigo's education was scanty; he was largely self-taught. He became known first as a painter and designer of costumes and décor for Court masques. It was in 1611 that he was appointed Surveyor to Prince Henry of Wales. After the prince's premature death, Inigo Jones took the opportunity offered to him by Lord Arundel to tour Italy and France in search of works of art. He took full advantage of this chance to see for himself works of the Renaissance of which he had read. He spent one-and-a-half years travelling, studying, making drawings and measurements of both the antique Roman buildings and the Italian and French examples based upon them. For Englishmen this was a completely new idea; up to that time Renaissance styles and forms had been taken from the books published on the Continent and the results of these third- and fourth-hand studies were to be seen in Jacobean building.

One of the chief sources of information in Italy for the earliest Renaissance buildings, such as Brunelleschi's and Alberti's designs in Florence, were the works of *Marcus Vitruvius Pollo*, the Roman architect and engineer who wrote on the designs, proportions and basic principles of classical architecture in the first century BC. His manuscripts were discovered in AD 1414 and, from that time, provided invaluable material for Italian and other Continental architects on the Roman architectural style of the late Republican period. Drawings and descriptions were given by Vitruvius of the orders, ornament, building methods and materials used by the Romans at his time.

By the early seventeenth century Italian architects did not all follow closely the precepts laid down by Vitruvius, but one of them based his work closely upon Vitruvius' books. This architect was *Andrea Palladio* (1508–80) who, in turn, published in 1570 his drawings and designs. Inigo Jones was much impressed by Palladio's books 'I Quattro Libri dell' Architettura' and 'L'Antiquità di Roma' and took copies* with him to Italy where he checked, in situ, the measurements and drawings against the actual remains and buildings. When he returned to Britain he showed in his own work that, despite the strong influence of Palladio and Vitruvius, he was no mere copyist. Inigo Jones was a highly original architect, always intent upon studying for himself at source, then evolving his personal designs.

Although few buildings designed by Inigo Jones survive and much of his work on great schemes,† such as Whitehall Palace, was never carried out or has been destroyed, his importance in the history of English architecture cannot be too strongly stressed. He was the first English architect to work in the wider manner on the pattern set by the Italians, from Brunelleschi and Alberti onwards, and later by the French, led by such men as de l'Orme, Bullant and Lescot. These Renaissance architects were rarely masters of only one profession, most were either painters, sculptors, mathematicians, for example, as well as architects. They did not design only a part, or even the whole, of a building as the Medieval men had done, leading from their position as master masons, but envisaged an extensive scheme and controlled the operation of all the artisans employed on the project, responsible only to the client.

Inigo Jones' fame as the first Englishman to practise architecture in this manner is assured, even though the Banqueting Hall is all that survives from the ambitious Whitehall Palace scheme. However, the Queen's House (270) was begun a little earlier, in 1616, and so is the prototype in Britain for a pure classical building. Designed on Palladian villa lines for Queen Anne of Denmark, James I's consort, work was held up when she died. The building was completed later, in 1635, for the next Queen, Henrietta Maria and this

little masterpiece owes its survival to the intervention of a third Queen, Mary II, who insisted on its retention in the Greenwich Hospital scheme of the later seventeenth century.

Both the Queen's House and the Banqueting Hall (1619–22) are based directly upon Italian Renaissance forms and owe nothing to the mannerism of Flanders and Germany. They were a revelation to both patrons and architects in Britain at this time and though Flemish design, in domestic architecture in particular, continued until the mid-seventeenth century, Inigo Jones' structures set a pattern which provided a basis for the work of Wren, the Baroque school and the golden age of eighteenth-century British classicism. Both buildings have simple exteriors, the orders on the façades being used in designs which are symmetrical and compact. The Banqueting Hall (273) uses two orders, one above the other in Roman manner, Ionic below and Composite above, the only other decoration being in the classical window openings with their alternate triangular and rounded pediments and the balustraded parapet. The Queen's House (270) is plainer still with a rusticated lower storey and the Ionic Order confined to the central block. Inside, the chief room is the hall, a forty foot cube, which is surrounded by a gallery giving access to the queen's apartments.

Inigo Jones was involved in two town planning schemes in London which, although only fragments survive, illustrate his early acceptance of the concept of designing classical architecture as a scheme for streets and squares, not just a single building. In this he was developing the theme put forward by Italian architects in cities such as Rome and Pienza. The scheme for laying out Covent Garden was sponsored by the Earl of Bedford and the King and Council in 1630. It is thought that Inigo Jones designed the piazza lined with houses of classical design and with St Paul's Church built on the west side. Nothing of the original work remains, but the church was later rebuilt in the original style. Lindsey House in Lincoln's Inn Fields shows his ideas for the terrace form of architecture, developed on a large scale in the eighteenth century. Here is a giant Ionic Order* spanning two floors with parapet above. The whole order is of low projection and is purely decorative;

---

* Inigo Jones' annotated copy of Palladio has been preserved.

† Inigo Jones held the post of Surveyor-General from 1615 to 1642. It is a great loss to English architecture that so little of his work survives from this long period of office. This is chiefly due to the fact that Parliament permitted so little to be spent on civic and official building and there was even less ecclesiastical construction. From these years of office, only some 20 buildings are known to have been designed by him and of these only half-a-dozen survive.

---

* A concept first used by Michelangelo in his palaces on the Capitol Hill in Rome.

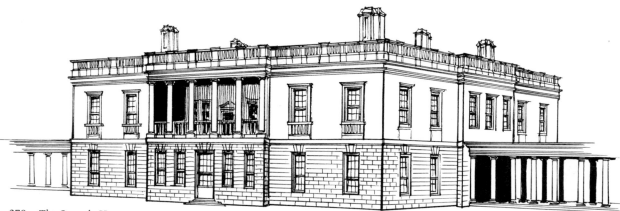

270   *The Queen's House,*
Greenwich, 1616–35

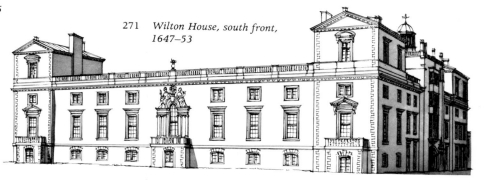

271   *Wilton House, south front,*
1647–53

272   *The Double Cube*
Room, Wilton
House, Wiltshire

the elevation is completely symmetrical.

Towards the end of his life Inigo Jones rebuilt part of the great house at *Wilton*, assisting the Earl of Pembroke. His court life and his office of Surveyor-General had ended with the advent of the Civil War and at Wilton his south façade (271) and the two superb cube rooms, part of the seven apartments, remain as testimony to this fine achievement of his last years. The exterior is simple, without orders, but with a central great window flanked by sculptured figures. Inside, in contrast, are sumptuous apartments.* The Double Cube Room (272) measures $60 \times 30 \times 30$ feet. The walls are white with gold enrichment and hung with Van Dyck portraits. Between these are carved oak decorative drops of fruit and flowers depended from scrolled cartouches. The carved wood doorcase is of the Corinthian Order, the doors panelled with acanthus decoration (277). The painted ceiling is deeply coved and has a central oval panel. The chimneypiece is of white marble carved in scrolls and swags. Here is a classical Renaissance apartment to hold its own with any Continental equivalent.

Domestic Building 1620–1650

Although Inigo Jones had brought the Italian Renaissance to Britain and this had a lasting effect upon architectural development, its influence until 1650 was small. Building in these years was plainer than Elizabethan and Jacobean work; it was nearer to Renaissance forms but it still reflected Flemish gabling and brickwork more than Italian classicism.

Brick was popular for building at this time; it was beginning to replace timber as the most commonly used material, partly due to an incipient shortage of wood and partly for its greater suitability to Renaissance design. Brick is cheap and durable but builders discovered, as Medieval builders in the Baltic coastal regions of Europe had found in the fifteenth century,

that it is not a material adaptable to rich or precise decoration. So English and Flemish brickworkers developed their own forms of expression in the medium, this time in classical not Gothic idiom. They introduced classical ornament in brick (or in stone sparingly used for decoration only), as well as pilasters, doorways, window frames and pediments (288). The techniques of Flemish brickwork were also established at this time, such as *Flemish bond* construction, where alternate 'headers' and 'stretchers' were used on all courses and *gauged* bricks were employed, that is, bricks cut exactly to the required size instead of the joint fillings being thickened to make up space.

Brick was especially utilised in domestic work and the Flemish influence was paramount here, illustrated in the curving Dutch gabling and decorative chimney stacks. A classic example of this style is the red brick *Kew Palace* (278) in Kew Gardens, with its typical rectangular sash windows and three-storey entrance with orders in brick. Houses which display similar characteristics, either entirely in brick or with stone-faced decoration include *Raynham Hall*, Norfolk, 1635–6 (279), *Swakeleys*, Middlesex, 1629–38, *Broome Park*, 1635–8 and *Quebec House* at *Westerham*, both in Kent.

University Building 1620–1645

Although the work was generally in stone, college building at *Oxford* and *Cambridge* in the first half of the seventeenth century shows many of the same characteristics and Flemish derivations as can be seen in the domestic field. The theme is classical and it is of a purer form than it had been in the sixteenth century, but *Canterbury Quad*, for example, built 1632–6 at *St John's College, Oxford*, is typical in its Flemish strapwork and other ornament. The colonnades on the west and east sides are each centred by an elaborate frontispiece incorporating respectively the statues of Charles I and his queen (301). Another Oxford structure typical of the time is the *Bodleian Library* tower. This was part of a major project for the Oxford Schools inaugurated by Sir Thomas Bodley in 1613. The tower is its most outstanding part. It is called the Tower of the Five Orders, as each of these is incorporated into the design; the tower is part of a quad surrounded by three-storey buildings (332).

The use of the classical idiom for constructional as well as decorative purpose and comprehension of the

---

* This is characteristic of Inigo Jones. He held strong views on the place of ornament in architecture and interior decoration. These are illustrated in his own words 'Ye outward ornaments oft to be sollid, proporsionable according to the rulles, masculine and unaffected.' This was his intention for the treatment of exterior façades. The interior was much richer but still controlled, unfussy and never overdone.

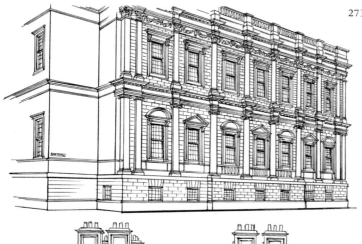

273 *The Banqueting Hall, Whitehall, London, 1619–22, Inigo Jones*

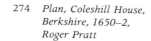

274 *Plan, Coleshill House, Berkshire, 1650–2, Roger Pratt*

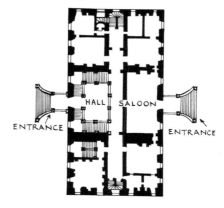

275 *Eltham Lodge, Kent, 1664, Hugh May*

276 *Thorpe Hall, Northamptonshire, south porch, c.1656, John Webb*

277 *Doorway, Double Cube Room, Wilton House*

278   *Kew Palace, 1631*

279   *Raynham Hall, Norfolk, c.1635–6*

280   *Dining Room based upon Thorpe Hall,
Northamptonshire, c.1655–65*

classical concept of a complete entity was clearly not yet understood, except by Inigo Jones. The front quad at *Oriel College, Oxford*, for example, as well as *Brasenose College Chapel*, also the chapel at *Peterhouse, Cambridge* show a blend of Gothic fenestration and detail with Flemish gabling and classical columns. A quieter, more serious approach is to be seen in the two ranges of this period in the *Clare College* quad, *Cambridge*, the east range built 1638–41 and the south 1640–2. The work is by *Thomas Grumbold*, who was also responsible for the beautiful *Clare Bridge* over the Cam, 1638–40, the oldest of the Cam bridges at the University.

Domestic Building 1650–1690: Dutch Palladianism and the 'Wren' Style

Between 1650 and 1670 a more symmetrical and purely classical house was evolved. This is often termed a 'Wren-style' house, incorrectly because the design was developed before Wren was practising as an architect and also because he designed little domestic work. Of the architects who contributed towards the purer classical trend in house design were *John Webb* (1611–74), a pupil and assistant to Inigo Jones, *Sir Roger Pratt* (1620–84) and *Hugh May* (1622–84). Much of Webb's work was for Inigo Jones' projects and his work closely followed that of his master; *Thorpe Hall*, Northamptonshire, *c.*1665 is one example (276, 280). Pratt's most famous house was *Coleshill*, Berkshire (1650–2), which was tragically destroyed by fire in 1952 (274). Hugh May's best known house is *Eltham Lodge* (275) in Kent, built in 1663–4, which closely resembles the Mauritshuis in the Hague (1633). Indeed, this style of building originated in the Netherlands and is in essence Dutch Palladianism. The style is so-called because the basis of design is that of Andrea Palladio. These seventeenth-century houses were strictly classical in theme, but with classical orders and ornament adapted to Flemish, and so later English, domestic needs.

Such houses were built of stone or of brick with stone dressings. In broad lines the Italian classical pattern was adhered to, with stress on the horizontal emphasis and a complete symmetry on each elevation and in the whole concept. The plan was a rectangle with an entrance in the centre of each of the long façades (274). There was a semi-basement floor and, above this, divided from it by a string course, was the principal floor called by the Italians the *piano nobile*; this was given prominence in position and proportions. Above was a further main floor and then a cornice and central pediment, balustrade and hipped roof with dormers and plain classical chimneystacks. The centrally placed entrance doorway was approached by a flight of steps to first floor level and led into the entrance hall (276, 284). An order might or might not be used, in column and pilaster form; it generally spanned two storeys (275). Larger houses had projecting side wings added to the rectangular block and a slightly advanced porch and central feature. The skyline was then sometimes broken by a lantern or cupola. *Belton House*, Lincolnshire, 1685–9, is a classic example of such a design (282).

The garden was by now becoming an essential part of the house scheme and the preference for an apparently casual, natural landscaping was beginning to be followed, in contrast to the formal layouts of the Continent, especially in France and Italy. Larger gardens could include a vegetable and orchard section as well as trees and flowers.

In the *house interior* the hall and main reception rooms (280) were placed on the *piano nobile*, with the long gallery and bedrooms above (285). Bedrooms were now chambers in their own right and no longer part of the passage; they were larger and had more furniture as well as a fireplace for heating. Kitchens were also now part of the house, even though generally situated a long way from the dining room, in whatever part of the house they could be fitted. The principal apartments had priority of position and their aesthetic appearance, on the exterior as well as the interior, was of prime consideration to the architect, who rated his clients' comfort and convenience, as well as that of their staff, as of secondary consideration.

The design and treatment of ceilings and walls had changed from Jacobean models. The ceiling and frieze were still of plaster, but a centrepiece – oval, circular or rectangular in shape – had replaced the all-over panels and strapwork. Ornament in this centrepiece was classical and naturalistic, using leaves, fruit, swags, *putti* and animals all in high relief. The cornice was enriched with classical ornament and the area between this and the centrepiece was often coved (280, 285). The central and other ceiling panels were, in large houses, painted with allegorical or historical scenes.

281 *Uppark, Sussex, south front centrepiece, 1688–90, William Talman*

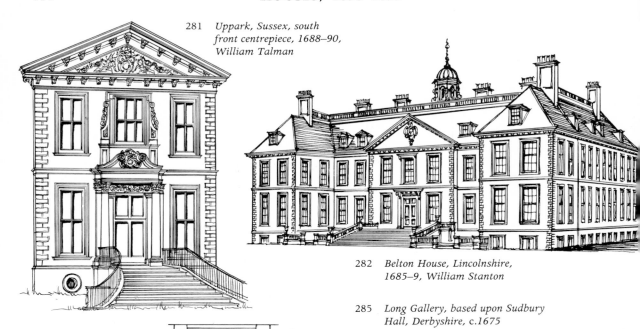

282 *Belton House, Lincolnshire, 1685–9, William Stanton*

285 *Long Gallery, based upon Sudbury Hall, Derbyshire, c.1675*

283 *Petworth House, Sussex, window, 1688–9*

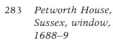

284 *Manor House, Princes Risborough, Buckinghamshire*

Panelling still covered most wall surfaces but, by 1660, the whole room was designed as a single classical unit. The panelling was in oak, cedar or fir and was treated as an architectural order in correct proportion and detail. Columns and pilasters were sometimes used, in which case they were spaced round the room and extended from dado rail to cornice, with plinth below and entablature above. Doors, windows* and chimneypiece were inserted into the scheme, generally flanked by columns or pilasters and decorated in the classical manner. Between these features were rectangular panels, sometimes raised from the background by bolection moulding frames (280, 285). The woodwork was left its natural colour or was painted in white or light shades. Mouldings were carved with classical ornament, most usually egg and dart, acanthus leaf or bead and reel designs (see glossary). There was much decorative carving in the Grinling Gibbons manner framing mirrors, paintings, panels and doorways (299, 300).

The heavy oak staircase was built until the later seventeenth century, though in the middle years a continuous carved scroll and acanthus balustrade replaced the solid balusters (293). *Ham House* in Surrey has a particularly fine example (1638) as also does *Eltham Lodge*, Kent (1664–5). From the 1670s this scroll type of balustrade was replaced by slenderer, barley-sugar twisted balusters (286). Carving in panels and finials was rich and varied all the century (289, 290, 298). Interesting houses of the period include *Fawley Court*, Oxfordshire, 1684–8, *Fenton House*, Hampstead, 1693, *Honington Hall*, Warwickshire, 1685, *Petworth House*, Sussex, 1688–9 (283), and *Uppark*, Sussex, 1688–9 (281, 297).

The union of Scotland and England under one crown from 1603, when James I of England and VI of Scotland, son of Mary Queen of Scots, succeeded Elizabeth, had little effect on architecture. Classical design had only briefly touched Scottish building traditions and, despite a slow abandonment of defensive features, there was no enthusiasm for the symmetrical, rectangular house. Scottish designers held firmly to the courtyard house in the years before the Restoration. Greater consideration was given to symmetry and there was a new mode in decoration which, like the Elizabethan of the previous century, was based upon mannerist ornament found in German and Flemish pattern books. Both on exterior and interior surfaces there appeared strapwork, cartouches, grotesques and heavily ornamented orders.

The outstanding building of the Scottish Renaissance style, a prototype for later structures here, is *Heriot's Hospital* in *Edinburgh*, built between 1628 and 1650. A square construction built round a square court, this is a strong, impressive building, Renaissance in symmetry and decoration, based, it is likely, on an Italian pattern-book drawing but retaining its Scottish baronial turrets and some Gothic fenestration in the hall and chapel ranges. Another large building, constructed later in 1679–90, but on a similar plan and grouping, is *Drumlanrig Castle*, Dumfriesshire (303). The entrance façade is more richly ornamented than Heriot's Hospital. It is approached by a curving double staircase, like that at Fontainebleau, and the house is carried on an arcaded lower storey, above which giant Corinthian pilasters extend through the first and second floors. Scottish-style turrets are still to be seen on the square corner towers.

It was not until after the Restoration that a purer form of classical architecture penetrated to Scotland and the architect, in the Inigo Jones sense of the term, made his appearance here. The later seventeenth century did not produce any architects of the stature of Inigo Jones or Wren, but the work of *Sir William Bruce* was competent and interesting in that he was able to combine a purer classicism with the Scottish vernacular so that the results were not merely vapid tracings of the Italian Renaissance. In 1671 Bruce was appointed King's Surveyor; his most important work in this office was the reconstruction of the *Palace of Holyroodhouse* in *Edinburgh*. This was not an easy task as he had to incorporate Medieval structures like the remains of the beautiful old church as well as parts of the later palace. Set against the background of King Arthur's seat and the Holyrood Park, the palace is now an impressive building, symmetrical, with its great corner towers still capped by conical turrets, but with a classical coupled-column entrance (302). Inside is the open, arcaded classical court on Roman Renaissance pattern. A further Scottish feature is in

---

* The casement window continued in use until late in the seventeenth century, but the frame, transom and mullion were of wood and built into the brickwork or stone surround. By 1680 the sash window was well established and rapidly superseded the casement pattern in general use.

286   Carved wood staircase, 1670–5

287   St Andrew-by-the-Wardrobe, London, doorway, Wren

288   Balls Park, Hertfordshire, doorway, c.1640

289/290   Staircase finials

291   St Lawrence Jewry, London, window, Wren

292   St Paul's Cathedral, London, window, Wren

293   Carved scroll-balustrade staircase

294   St Margaret Lothbury, London, doorway, Wren

296 *St Martin Ludgate, London, door-head, Wren*

295 *Hampton Court Palace, section of screen on Thames-side, Jean Tijou*

298 *Eltham Lodge, Kent, staircase panel, 1665*

297 *Uppark, Sussex, doorway detail, 1688–9*

299 *Carved decoration, Grinling Gibbons*

300 *Marble fireplace and, above, Grinling Gibbons' carved picture surround*

301 *St John's College, Oxford. Canterbury Quad, frontispiece, 1631–6*

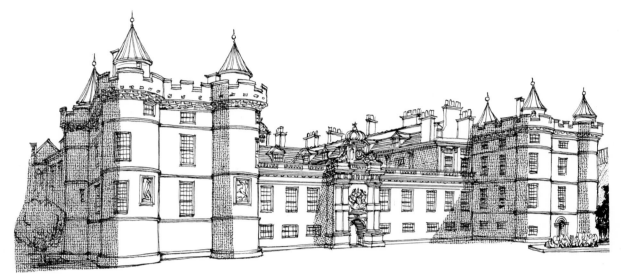

302   *Palace of Holyroodhouse. Architect, Sir William Bruce. Builder, Robert Mylne 1671–8*

303   *Drumlanrig Castle, Dumfriesshire, 1679–90*

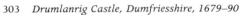

evidence in the dormers and chimneystacks which break the courtyard skyline.

Another impressive classical building can be seen in the house which Bruce built on his own estate of *Kinross* in 1681. He was also responsible for much of the new great mansion of *Hopetoun* near Edinburgh, but his work here has been obscured by the later reconstruction by the Adam family (pages 149, 174).

Sir Christopher Wren 1632–1723

The Restoration of the Monarchy under Charles II in 1660 caused a vigorous reaction in England. The return of a young monarch who was half French and had spent much of his life up to this time on the Continent inevitably introduced an influence which violently contrasted with the Puritanism of the Commonwealth administration. The new court and aristocracy were outward-looking, young and lively. The resulting effect on the arts, painting, sculpture, architecture, music and literature, was considerable. An English Baroque expression in these arts was tentative but perceptible. The current trends in Italy and France now introduced into Britain were having an effect. It was also an age of men of outstanding quality of genius, in science as well as the arts. In the years 1660–90 such men included, apart from Wren, John Milton, Isaac Newton, Robert Hooke, Grinling Gibbons, John Dryden, Henry Purcell, John Thornhill and Robert Boyle.

The name of *Sir Christopher Wren*, Britain's leading architect, is more familiar to the public than that of any other architect and his reputation, unlike that of any of his successors, has stood uniformly high ever since his death. To say that his work dominated the architecture of Britain during the second half of the seventeenth century is no exaggeration, for he was the vital force in all the important architectural schemes of the period, directing, influencing, controlling both the design and execution of large projects such as the rebuilding of London after the fire of 1666 and the layouts at Hampton Court, Greenwich, Chelsea and the universities. He was fortunate also in that when he was beginning to practise, great opportunities opened up before him, largely due to the Great Fire of London. He obtained commissions for civic and ecclesiastical building as a result and he was able early to establish his reputation for original design. Other architects, such as Inigo Jones and

Robert Adam, had the ill-fortune to miss such opportunities. It has been mentioned that Inigo Jones was the first British architect in the modern sense of the term, and Wren followed in this tradition and fully established it, that is, as the designer of a building project who supervises all aspects of the work from its early sketches to final completion.

Christopher Wren was born at East Knoyle in Wiltshire on 20 October 1632. His father was rector of Knoyle while his uncle, Dr Matthew Wren, was also a churchman, later being consecrated Bishop of Ely. The young man was brought up in a High Church tradition with a university background. From an education at Westminster School he went on to Oxford University, where he graduated in 1651 and obtained his master's degree in 1653.

It was soon apparent that the young man was outstandingly brilliant. 'That miracle of a youth', as John Evelyn described him in 1654, was chiefly interested at this time in science. It was here that he found full expression for his inventive mind, developing theories and experiments while still at college on some 50 different problems in the fields of astronomy, physics and engineering. This was a time when experimental science was becoming of interest all over Europe. The Royal Academy of Science was established in Paris. In England, Wren joined with Robert Boyle, the physicist, Dr Wilkins, Warden of Wadham College, Oxford, Dr Scarburgh, the mathematician and others to form the Philosophic Club of Wadham. This club applied itself to a study of science and philosophy and soon its members included Isaac Newton, John Evelyn and Robert Hooke; later, it became the Royal Society.

Wren was over 30 when he launched himself, almost casually, into architecture. At 25 he had been appointed to the chair of Astronomy at Gresham College, London and at 26 returned to Oxford to become Savilian Professor of Astronomy. This background was an unusual one, even in the seventeenth century, as preparation for an architect and his scientific training had a profound effect upon his approach to architecture. He had the faculty of envisaging an extensive scheme as a whole before work was begun and, to the constructional problems of roofing large spans, providing sound structures for support and buttressing, he brought his fresh, technical approach.

It is not known exactly when Wren became

interested in architecture. In 1661 Charles II invited him to supervise the fortification of Tangier. This he declined. His first essay into architecture was to design and build a traditional classical chapel for *Pembroke College, Cambridge* (1663), at the request of his uncle, now the Bishop of Ely. It is a competent building, illustrating a certain inexperience. His second attempt was much more original, the *Sheldonian Theatre* at *Oxford*, 1664 (334). He based his design upon a Roman theatre which he had studied in Serlio's book on architecture. The prototype had been open to the sky and Wren had problems in covering the English counterpart without using supporting columns which would obstruct the view, He solved this, typically, and with the aid of his colleague, the Professor of Geometry, Dr Wallis, by means of a timber trussed roof to carry the ceiling.

Unlike Inigo Jones, Wren made only one short trip abroad. His first-hand knowledge of Continental architecture was limited and, although he studied Italian and French designs, his aim always was to produce classical buildings suited especially to his own country and this is clearly displayed in the essential Englishness of Wren's work. His great fertility of imagination enabled him to design endless variations upon the classical theme to meet this need. In 1665 he went to France on holiday and spent some months visiting châteaux and staying in Paris. In the city he met Bernini who was there to present his designs for the Louvre. Wren also saw the Palace of Versailles and, in Paris, was especially impressed by Le Vau's Collège des Quatres Nations. Wren never reached Italy but brought back a quantity of books and engravings. He had extended his architectural horizons and enriched his appreciation. In 1666 came the turning point and opportunity of his life, the event which was probably what sparked off his decision to make architecture his career.

The Rebuilding of London

In his diary, John Evelyn records for 2 September 1666 – 'This fatal night, about 10, began the deplorable fire near Fish Street in London'. Many attempts had been made since the Act of 1189 to enforce diverse laws making it compulsory to use stone, at least for party walls, in London buildings. By 1666

most of the houses, at least, were still of timber; the streets were narrow and the upper storeys projected almost to meet in the centre of the road. The local outbreak in the baker's shop in Pudding Lane was burning brightly by 1 a.m.; augmented by a strong wind and following upon a long, hot, dry spell of weather, the city was overwhelmed by a rapid conflagration. The fire moved swiftly, encouraged by the early spread among the crowded timber houses towards the Thames wharves, which were stocked by inflammable goods, also by the destruction of the water-wheel by London Bridge, which cut off the water supply to the neighbouring city areas.

London burned for four days, at the end of which time, as is shown in the City Surveyor's report, 273 acres had been destroyed within the city walls and 63 acres without. Among the buildings lost were 87 churches and 13,200 houses in 400 streets and courts. Only one-fifth of the walled city still stood.

Charles II set up a royal commission to organise the rebuilding of London. On 13 September the Royal Proclamation announced that the city would be rebuilt in brick and stone on a new plan with wider streets. Wren was appointed principal architect to be assisted by Hugh May and Sir Roger Pratt in conjunction with the city delegates, Robert Hooke, Peter Mills and Edward Jerman. Wren's plan for the new city, which had earned him the task of carrying it out, was a classical one which not only incorporated ideas from Ancient Rome but also features from his recent observations in Paris. It was a geometrical gridiron plan with focal centres (*rond-points*) to pinpoint important buildings such as St Paul's, the Guildhall and the Mint. These were linked by main thoroughfares which gave vistas to and from them. The city churches were given suitable positions and in front of St Paul's Cathedral was to be a long, wedge-shaped open space. A key point of the plan was a wide embankment quay along the Thames from Blackfriars to the Tower based on that bordering the Seine in Paris (304).

The plan was approved by King and Parliament, but foundered on the commercial interests of the city which refused to yield up part of its rights for the good of London. Only a dictatorship or an absolute monarchy, as in Napoleon's Paris, could have pushed through a scheme which ran counter to so many individual interests. The city buildings were re-erected on the same blackened sites and the narrow

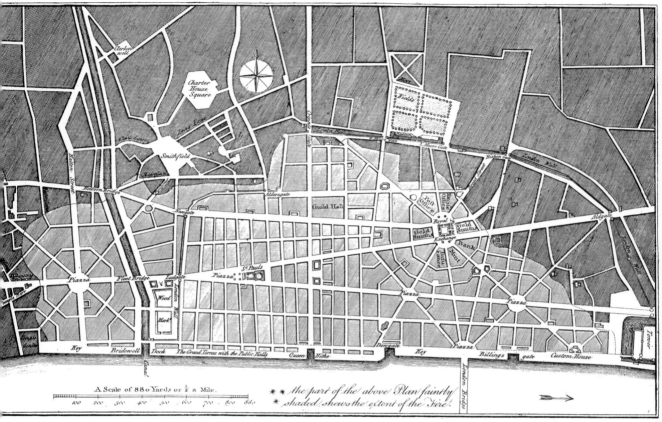

St. Christopher Wren's Plan for Rebuilding the City of London after the dreadfull Conflagration in 1666.

304   Wren's plan for London, 1666

streets remained unaltered.*

Despite the abandonment of his plan, Wren's part in the rebuilding of London was a large one. Some of his colleagues fell by the wayside but, assisted ably by Robert Hooke, he spent many years on the task of reconstruction, notably on 53 churches, which replaced the 87 lost, and on St Paul's Cathedral. Though his city layout was frustrated, a great advance in building construction was effected as a result of the fire. A new structural standard was set up for domestic building in brick and the timber-gabled pattern was abandoned. This was widely reflected in other towns in Britain and, over a long period, was profoundly effective.

The City Churches

In 1670 a tax was ordained by Parliament to be collected on sea coal arriving at the Port of London. The income derived from this tax was designed to pay for the rebuilding of the city churches and St Paul's Cathedral. In the years 1675–1705, which roughly covered the building enterprise, the money raised paid for the fabric of the churches, while the parishes assumed responsibility for the interior decoration and fittings.

Even in a career so full of great schemes and original architecture, Wren's city churches are out-

---

* Students of twentieth-century architecture might care to draw a parallel with the fate of Sir Patrick Abercrombie's plans after the Second World War.

305   *St Andrew-by-the-Wardrobe*

306   *Plan, St Stephen Walbrook*

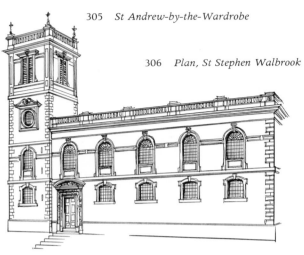

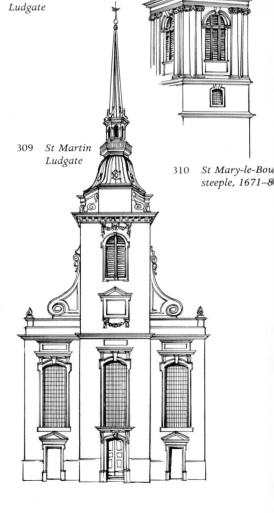

307   *Plan, St Martin Ludgate*

308   *St Bride, Fleet Street, 1670–84*

309   *St Martin Ludgate*

310   *St Mary-le-Bow steeple, 1671–8*

311   *St Stephen Walbrook,*
       1672–9

312   *St Benet,*
       Paul's Wharf

313   *Plan, St Lawrence Jewry*

315   *Plan, St Mary-le-Bow*

314   *(far right) St Edmund
       the King, Lombard
       Street*

316
*St Magnus the Martyr,
1670–1705*

standing. They illustrate, perhaps more clearly than any other examples of his work, his fertility of imagination, his ability to solve the most intractable of problems of site, limitation of space and variation of style. None of the churches is quite like any other; they are nearly all classical in conception, though one or two were designed in Gothic to harmonise with remains. The sites are most varied and few are level or possess any parallel sides of equal length (306, 307, 313, 315). *St Benet Fink*, for example, was decagonal in plan, few churches possessed a right-angled corner, and at *St Benet, Paul's Wharf* the site was so steeply inclined that even in this small area there was a variation of 10 feet in height (312).

Wren's qualities of versatility and inventiveness are nowhere shown more clearly than in his designs for the church steeples. He had no English classical precedent to work upon and many of the designs are in classical form and ornament based upon Gothic construction. Of the tall steeples *St Mary-le-Bow* is probably the most beautiful (310, 315). The gradual build-up from square, pilastered tower and decorative parapet via a central, colonnaded drum to a slender obelisk is perfectly proportioned and gives to London an impressive, though delicate, landmark. Of scarcely less originality is the wedding-cake steeple of *St Bride* in Fleet Street (308) and the design of *Christ Church*, Newgate Street, with its diminuendo in four-faced pattern. Interesting and unusual are the tall towers surmounted by bell towers and lanterns. These vary from the lofty *St Magnus the Martyr* (316) and the delicate *St Martin Ludgate* (296, 307, 309) to the plainer *St Margaret Lothbury* (294) and *St Edmund the King* (314). Many churches have simple towers such as *St Clement Eastcheap, St Benet, Paul's Wharf* (312), *St Andrew-by-the-Wardrobe* (287, 305) and *St Andrew Holborn.**

Wren varied his building materials to give colour and interest to the churches. He used Portland stone and brick, together and separately, and most churches had lead belfries and gilded vanes and crosses. In general, he designed the churches on the lines of the Roman basilica, for which he drew freely upon

Vitruvius and Serlio. He bore in mind that these were Protestant churches being erected on what had been mainly Catholic sites. He wanted the pulpit to be visible and audible from all parts of the building in order to establish a rapport between preacher and congregation. Also, and partly for this reason, most of these churches have light interiors with large, flat-topped or round-headed classical windows filled with plain glass in contrast to the darker, more mystical Catholic equivalents.

Some of the churches are large and richly decorated, others are small and simple. Some are finer than others, partly on account of the amount of money available, but also because Wren was more closely connected with the supervision of some churches. He gathered a team of craftsmen to work with him and some of the carving, glass and ironwork is superb. Two of the richest interiors were *St Lawrence Jewry* (291, 313), the Guildhall church, and *St Bride* (308) both, sadly, gutted in the Second World War and both now restored. *St Stephen Walbrook*, near the Mansion House, was one of the larger, richer city churches and apparently used by Wren as a 'trial run' for St Paul's. His design incorporates a central dome as well as a corner steeple. The dome is carried on eight arches supported on columns (311).

The rebuilding of the city churches occupied many years and much of Wren's long life. The first church to be restored and re-opened was *St Mary-at-Hill* in 1678, the last was *St Michael Cornhill* in 1721. Wren was then 89 years old.

St Paul's Cathedral

The Medieval cathedral was not destroyed in the Fire, as were so many churches, but the damage caused to an already ailing, neglected building was, in the end, fatal. The Church Commissioners insisted on repair of the fabric but, after the collapse of extensive sections of masonry, they had to give in and asked Wren to design a new cathedral.

St Paul's is Britain's only Renaissance Cathedral. Wren made several designs for it. He was determined that it should be classical and he was strongly influenced by Michelangelo's work on St Peter's in Rome (317, 319). His favourite design, undoubtedly of greater aesthetic and dramatic quality than the final building, was the Great Model Design, made in 1673 (320, 323). It was of Greek cross pattern, with four

---

* It is thought that Wren possibly realised that in later years his church steeples would be hemmed in by commercial structures. Certainly his focal interest in the designs and the principal ornamentation is on the upper, final stages and the lower storeys of the tower are plain.

equal arms, raised on a podium, totally symmetrical and with an immense central dome, 120 feet in diameter, crowning the structure. The project was rejected by the Church Commissioners as breaking too radically with the tradition of cathedral building in England. They wanted a cathedral with a tall spire like the previous one. Also, ecclesiastically, they wanted a Protestant cathedral not one which savoured so much of Rome. They complained that the floor space was inadequate and that there must be a long nave and choir.*

Wren made further attempts and in the final design compromised with an impressive, high, exterior dome on a colonnaded drum. The cathedral is built on orthodox Latin cross plan with long nave and the dome set over the crossing (292, 318), though a break with tradition was made in the large space under this dome (321). The west façade is symmetrical and classical, using coupled Corinthian columns in two stages with central pediment (324). The façade is nonetheless traditionally British in its twin western towers which, despite the Medieval theme, are Baroque in treatment (page 134).

Although Renaissance classical architecture had been introduced into Britain by Inigo Jones, *St Paul's Cathedral* was the first importance instance in the country of domical construction. The dome, as a structural and decorative feature, is the only major factor in the Renaissance architecture of Europe not to have been revived from Roman origins. The Romans had extensively developed stone and concrete vaulting but had not pursued the possibilities of the dome. The Pantheon dome for example is built on walls of circular plan and the problems of constructing a circular dome upon a square supporting structure were not investigated. In Renaissance and, even more widely, in Baroque European architecture, the dome was a vital structural and decorative feature. It was taken from the Byzantine development of the dome, which was one of the most important contributions of this eastern empire centred on Constantinople. The Byzantine domical structural design was, in turn, evolved from much earlier

buildings in the Middle East, in Anatolia, Persia and Syria.

The Byzantine contribution was the *pendentive*, which is a satisfactory method of carrying a circular dome upon piers which stand on a square plan, and the system will support large domes. The classic early example in Istanbul is that of Santa Sophia. It was on this pattern that Italian Renaissance architects based their domes; St Peter's in Rome is of this type (317). Fig. 325 illustrates the evolution of the pendentive from the early squinch methods. In 'A' is shown the construction of a circular dome on circular walling as at the Roman Pantheon built by the Romans. This presents few problems. In 'B' the dome is supported on walls on a square plan. Here an octagonal base is provided by building across the angles of the square. The squinch method in 'C' is where an arch or series arches span the angles. This method is used in many Roman and Byzantine examples, but none of these will support a large dome or one constructed upon piers or columns.

In a pendentive method of construction the triangular spaces between the square section and the circular base of the dome are built as if they are parts of a lower and larger dome so that their section is like that of an arch carried across the diagonal of the square space to be covered. This lower dome possesses a horizontal section which is concentric with the plan of the intended dome. As the lower dome is too large to fill the square space, it is cut off in vertical planes formed by the four walls of the square. When the four remaining parts of the lower dome have been built high enough to form a complete circle within the walls of the square, this circle provides the basis for supporting the actual dome. This is shown in 'D', while in 'E' the dome is set in position above its lower dome, that is, the spherical triangles which are called pendentives. In 'F' is shown the typical Renaissance or Baroque dome, carried on a drum (pierced by windows), standing on the pendentives. Internally, pendentives are decorated by paintings or mosaics as in St Peter's (317) and in St Paul's in London (322).

In *St Paul's Cathedral* the dome is set over the crossing of a traditional, Latin cross plan. It is upheld by eight massive piers standing on the floor which, in turn, support the eight arches from which spring the pendentives and dome upon its drum. Each pier is faced with pilasters in the Corinthian Order which is used throughout the cathedral (322). Wren designed

---

* It is interesting to compare Wren's Greek cross plan (320) with that of Michelangelo for St Peter's (319). Here also, after Michelangelo's death, the nave arm was lengthened, on ecclesiastical insistence, to make the design a Latin cross one.

319   Michelangelo's plan,
      St Peter's, 1547

320
Wren's Great Model
plan, St Paul's, 1673

DOME

317   St Peter's Basilica, Rome. Transept and crossing,
      mainly by Michelangelo, 1547–64

318   St Paul's Cathedral,
      London, from the
      south-east. 1675–1710.
      Wren

322 *St Paul's Cathedral, London, the crossing, Sir Christopher Wren*

323 *The Great Model design for St Paul's, 1673*

324 *St Paul's Cathedral, west front, 1675–1710*

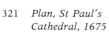

321 *Plan, St Paul's Cathedral, 1675*

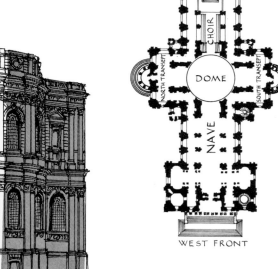

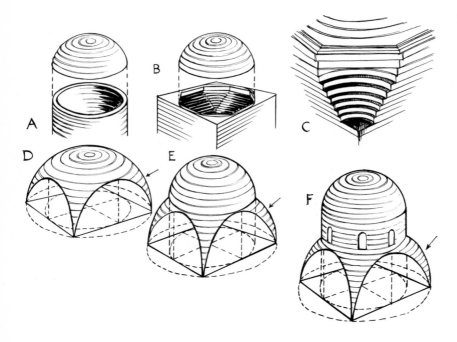

325   *Development of the Byzantine*
       system of Dome Construction
    A   *Dome over circular drum*
    B   *Dome over square – squinch*
        across corners to make
        octagon
    C   *Squinch*
    D   *Pendentives used – single*
        dome with pendentive and
        dome part of same
        hemisphere
    E   *Dome, a hemisphere set*
        above pendentives –
        compound design
    F   *Dome raised on drum*
        above pendentives –
        compound design

an impressive exterior dome surmounting a drum surrounded by a colonnade of Corinthian columns. This created for him a difficult construction problem as a hemispherical dome appears, on the interior, to be dark and too lofty. He dealt with the difficulty by building two domes,* an outer, taller one and an inner, shallower one, with a framework between. A brick cone surmounts the inner dome and supports the heavy lantern, the cross of which is 365 feet above the ground (318, 324).

The standard of craftsmanship in St Paul's is of a high order. The workers in different fields were selected from the best available in the 35 years of construction of the cathedral. These craftsmen also worked with Wren on the city churches, at Hampton Court and at Greenwich. Chief amongst the craftsmen of St Paul's are *James Thornhill* (painter), *Jean Tijou* (ironworker), *Joshua Marshall* (mason) and the carvers and sculptors *Jonathan Maine, Francis Bird, Caius Gabriel Cibber* and *Grinling Gibbons*.

---

* The idea of a double dome was not new. It was used in Byzantine building and in Renaissance Italy as at Brunelleschi's cathedral dome in Florence and Michelangelo's St Peter's in Rome. Wren's supporting structure was somewhat different.

Wren's Secular Designs

Apart from university work, there were three other great schemes of these years with which Wren was concerned: at Hampton Court, Greenwich and Chelsea. *Hampton Court Palace* had been built in Tudor brickwork for Henry VIII (page 72) but by the late seventeenth century was in a neglected condition. William and Mary decided to use the palace once more and asked Wren to rebuild and enlarge it. Due to the queen's death and also shortage of funds, the original scheme for demolition was fortunately amended, so the retention of the Tudor palace, incorporated into Wren's designs, has resulted, despite the blend of styles, in a harmonious whole. Wren's contribution to Hampton Court, carried out between 1689 and 1701, includes the grand entrance hall and staircase and new suites of chambers. The exterior of these façades are treated in his familiar manner of rose-coloured brick, with Portland stone for parapets, windows, columns and carving. Wren had used this attractive combination of materials so far only experimentally on one or two of his churches. This was the first example on a large scale and it was a great success (326).

The outstanding craftsmen of the day are seen at

their best at Hampton Court. There is Tijou's wonderful staircase in the entrance hall, his gates and grilles and, particularly, his Thames-side screen (295). *Jean Tijou* was a French ornamental ironworker who came to England in 1689, having fled from France in the Huguenot exodus. He was a prime mover in the revival of interest in ironwork in England in the seventeenth century. In the extensive schemes in hand at St Paul's, the city churches and Hampton Court Palace, he found full scope for expression in his medium. His influence on English ironwork was great. His own work was often ornate and freely scrolled; later, eighteenth-century ironworkers followed his lead, though in a more restrained manner suited to the age. Apart from Hampton Court Palace, Tijou's best work can be seen in St Paul's Cathedral in the circular stair in the west tower, the wrought-iron window coverings and in a number of screens and grilles.

The grand staircase hall at Hampton Court Palace is also noted for the frescoes on its walls and ceiling by *Antonio Verrio* and his colleagues. There are, too, some fine examples of the woodcarving of *Grinling Gibbons*. The story of how, in 1670, John Evelyn discovered this young man in a cottage carving a version of Tintoretto's crucifixion, is well known. Grinling Gibbons was one of the most gifted of all the craftsmen who worked with Wren. He carved in stone and worked in bronze, but his métier was really wood. In this medium he established a unique style in which he strove to recapture the realism and vitality of natural forms as portrayed by the great flower painters of the day. His work revolutionised the carving which was then being done in St Paul's and elsewhere. Hitherto the floral designs had been tightly packed and formally arranged. Gibbons carved almost in the round, with projecting sprays of leaves, flowers and fruit, rapturously flowing and laid with apparent casualness here and there, each being clearly detached from the other. This high relief work threw deep shadows on to the background and on to the other carved forms so that the whole design came alive and was vividly real (299, 300). This shows most clearly in his carving on the stalls and organ case in St Paul's.

The *Royal Hospital* at *Greenwich*, 1660–1714 (later the Royal Naval College), benefited from the experience of the greatest architects of the seventeenth century in Britain. The overall design was by Wren, but Hawksmoor and Vanbrugh (page 136) carried out

a considerable part of the scheme and showed their respect for their colleague by interpreting the design in his manner, not their own. William and Mary decided to build at Greenwich a naval counterpart to Chelsea Hospital. They gave the site and commissioned Wren to design the project, which was to be on an ambitious scale as a fitting tribute to Britain's sea power.

Wren faced the problem that he had to incorporate in his scheme both Inigo Jones' Queen's House (page 108) and the Charles II block already built by John Webb in 1665. The final design was planned with buildings on two sides of an open vista which terminated in the Queen's House (see plan 328). Wren was not fully satisfied with his scheme, for he felt, as have many later critics, that the Queen's House was too small in scale to terminate the vista suitably. Wren, assisted by Hawksmoor, supervised the work until 1702, when Vanbrugh took over. The hall dome and colonnade was completed by 1704 and the chapel side in 1716 (329). Despite criticisms of Greenwich Hospital, such as that the imposing colonnade vista leads nowhere and the unsatisfactory design of the dome drums, there is a grandeur and spaciousness about the complete scheme which strikes the beholder, especially when disembarking from the Thames pier. The approach by river towards the elegant domes and colonnades, retreating in perspective towards the distant classical prototype of the Queen's House, is a dramatic one. The layout spans English classical architecture from its first exponent, Inigo Jones, to the leader of the Baroque school, Sir John Vanbrugh.

The work of *Sir James Thornhill*, the painter, is displayed in the grand manner at Greenwich, where he painted the walls and ceiling of the great hall. His style was sympathetic to the large-scale allegory and his work was predominantly Baroque. At Greenwich the scale was especially suited to him, as was also the dome of St Paul's, where he painted scenes from the life of St Paul. He found full expression for his preference for Baroque when he later worked on the great hall at Blenheim (page 136).

Sir Stephen Fox, while Paymaster-General of the Army, was the chief promoter of the scheme to build the *Royal Hospital, Chelsea*, an idea suggested by Les Invalides in Paris, which had been founded in 1670. Here Wren, who was commissioned to design the scheme, had no restrictions of space or existing

326   *Hampton Court Palace, Middlesex, south front, 1689–1701, Wren*

327   *Cupola, Chelsea*

328   *Sketch plan of Greenwich layout*
  A   *King Charles' block, Webb, 1662–9*
  B   *Queen Anne's block, Wren, Hawksmoor, 1696–1729*
  C   *Chapel, begun Wren, Int. 1779–89*
  D   *Hall, Wren, 1698–1705*
  E   *Queen Mary's block, 1699–1752*
  F   *King William's block, 1698–1723 (part Vanbrugh, 1701)*
  G   *Colonnades, begun 1699*
  H   *Queen's House, Inigo Jones, 1616–35*

329   *Chapel dome and colonnade, Greenwich Hospital (C and G on plan)*

THIS DISTANCE IS NOT TO SCALE

MAIN ROAD

E G G F

C   D

B   A

RIVER THAMES

330   *Royal Hospital Chelsea, river front, 1682–92, Wren*

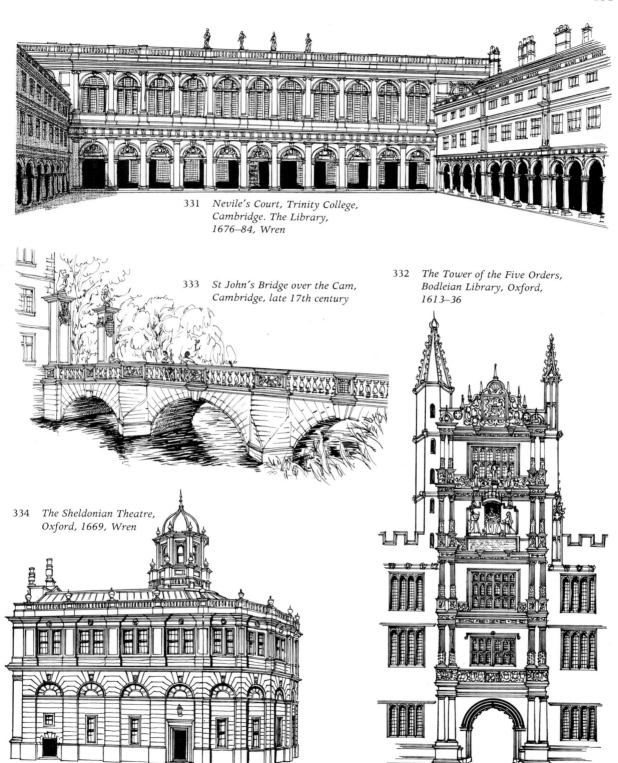

331 Nevile's Court, Trinity College, Cambridge. The Library, 1676–84, Wren

333 St John's Bridge over the Cam, Cambridge, late 17th century

332 The Tower of the Five Orders, Bodleian Library, Oxford, 1613–36

334 The Sheldonian Theatre, Oxford, 1669, Wren

335   *White Horse Close,*
Canongate, Edinburgh.
17th century, redeveloped
1965

336   *Town Hall,*
Abingdon,
Berkshire,
1677–80

337   *Custom House,*
King's Lynn,
1681, Henry Bell

338   *Market House, Tetbury, Gloucestershire, 1700*

buildings and was presented with a site which extended uninterruptedly to the river. The layout of this army hospital, which was built in the decade 1682–92, is simple. It forms three sides of a quadrangle open to the river. In the centre block are the hall and chapel with a cupola set over all (327). The Doric Order, in giant form, is used in the central portico. The whole design is quiet and restrained, carried out in red brick and stone (330).

The Universities 1660–1690

Wren also made the chief impact in this field of work during these years. Apart from Pembroke College Chapel and the Sheldonian Theatre, already mentioned (page 120), he completed Tom Tower at *Christ Church, Oxford* in 1681–2 in Gothic style (214) and

designed the chapel and other building at *Emmanuel College, Cambridge,* 1666–73. His finest work at Cambridge is the *Library,* occupying one side of Nevile's Court at *Trinity College.* Built 1676–84, the library is a masterpiece of simple perfection in composition. It is a long rectangular building of two storeys surmounted by a parapet. The Doric Order is used in the lower storey, which has an open arcade, and the Ionic Order above it, flanking the window openings. The statues surmounting the parapet of the façade representing Divinity, Law, Physics and Mathematics, are the work of the sculptor *Caius Gabriel Cibber,* a Dane who also worked with Wren at St Paul's and elsewhere (331).

The interior, completed in 1695, is superbly decorated by Grinling Gibbons' carving, especially on the bookcase panels.

CHAPTER SEVEN

The English Baroque
1690–1730

In art and architecture, Italy was the source of the Baroque as it had been for the Renaissance. The underlying force of the Baroque movement was also based upon a new process of thinking, this time not towards Humanism but from Humanism back towards the Church. A deep feeling had arisen: a desire for a re-introduction of spiritual values; evidence of man's need for belief in something greater than himself. Among other Orders in the sixteenth century, the Jesuits were instrumental in re-establishing a Christian way of life more suited to the contemporary world than the outgrown Medieval concept. The Roman Catholic church, aided by the revitalised gaiety and pageantry of its building, made much of the opportunity to attract people back to its fold. Bernini, the greatest of the Baroque artists, was a master of the dramatic form and lighting effects so typical of the Baroque interpretation of the current Christian approach.

From Italy the Baroque architectural forms spread throughout Europe, but the style was suited chiefly to the southern, Latin peoples of Catholic faith. This was partly for its religious significance and partly because it is an extrovert, rich, colourful form. In the greyer, Protestant north – in Britain, northern Germany, Holland and Scandinavia – it gained only a foothold; there classical architecture remained for much of the eighteenth century, cool and aloof, in straight lines and pure tones. Apart from Italy, Baroque architecture is found in its more vigorous and characteristic manner in Southern Germany, Austria, Switzerland, Czechoslovakia, Hungary, Spain and Portugal.

One of its predominant characteristics is a free use of curves (within the classical framework of orders and ornament). These curves, often of whole walls and ceilings, advance from convex to concave. It was Robert Adam (page 173) who, describing Baroque design as a feeling for 'movement', quoted St Peter's in Rome as the prime example. He referred to the balance and contrast of the convexity of Michelangelo's dome in relation to Bernini's concave piazza colonnade. Another important feature of Baroque architecture, especially of the interior, is the dramatic lighting effects in painting, sculpture and architecture, since all three arts are always fused in Baroque to blend into a unified creation. The favourite ground plan is oval as this lends itself to a maximum feeling for movement. Rich, sensuous vitality in colour, form and light is the keynote of Baroque work in all media.

Although several theories have been put forward for the origin of the term Baroque it is thought that the most likely is that it derives from the Portuguese word *barocco*, meaning an ill-formed, imperfect or grotesque pearl. It was first applied in a derogatory sense rather in the same way that the word Gothic was coined earlier (page 37). This was a reference to the strange, curving, sometimes bulbous shapes to be seen in this type of architecture. In the nineteenth century such design was looked down upon as being simply a late, decadent form of Renaissance classicism. It is less than 100 years since Baroque design was recognised as a style in its own right.

Baroque architecture in England takes a diverse form. The curves are only occasionally to be seen, but the movement, violent and discordant, is present, evidenced in the strong massing of shapes, dramatic light and shade and large scale grandeur. The Baroque school was short-lived here; by 1730 it was over and the British returned to a Palladianism first introduced by Inigo Jones, its order and tranquillity more suited to the temperament of the people than the emotional violence and voluptuousness of Baroque.

Different in interpretation though it may be, the later work of Wren, that of Talman and, especially, the designs of Vanbrugh, Hawksmoor and Archer cannot be termed anything other than Baroque for the buildings display the chief characteristics of the concept. Wren's designs showed a tendency towards Baroque in his late seventeenth-century work. The west towers of *St Paul's Cathedral*, for instance (324) and, even more, the domes and colonnades at *Greenwich* (329) are plastic and vibrantly alive. But Wren's Baroque was always restrained and controlled; classicism was paramount over extravagance. The designs never got out of hand. In this, as always, Wren was essentially English.

The end of Wren's career was unhappily beset by jealousies and intrigues. The old man had lived too long; new ideas in architecture were being put forward and the next generation of architects wanted a different approach. In 1714, when Queen Anne died, Wren was 82. He had led the architectural field in all principal appointments for nearly 50 years and younger men, who had worked for and with him, such as Nicholas Hawksmoor, were breaking new ground. George I, who acceded in 1714, preferred the newer approach. As Wren did not resign his Surveyorship, he was somewhat shabbily relieved of his post in 1718 on the pretext of a minor disagreement about the completion of St Paul's. His dignified acceptance of the situation was made in these words: 'having worn out by God's Mercy a long life in the Royal Service and made some Figure in the World, I hope it will be allowed me to die in peace'. This he did at the age of 91 in 1723.

Sir John Vanbrugh 1664–1726

Of the new generation of architects who worked in the English Baroque style, so different from the restrained and delicate classicism of Wren, Vanbrugh was the most colourful. Like Wren he came to architecture in his thirties, but his training and experience for it were in total contrast. Vanbrugh was of Flemish descent and this comes through in his work, seen in the extrovert robustness, elaboration and a tendency to coarseness of architectural form. In his youth he studied art in France, then spent some

time in the army, after which he launched himself into a successful career as a playwright.

In 1699, at the age of 35, Vanbrugh turned to architecture. He had studied building on the Continent and his first attempt at design was the stupendous mansion which he built for the Earl of Carlisle, *Castle Howard* in Yorkshire. Work was begun in 1701 and, like all Vanbrugh's conceptions, was in the grand manner with an enormous frontage and impressive hall. Castle Howard set the pattern for his designs, which were not rigidly defined blocks as in the seventeenth century, but grouped buildings of forceful, powerful masses, often discordantly contrasting with one another. Some of the work is coarse, particularly the detail, but Vanbrugh was a master of three-dimensional form in stone, adept at creating exciting, if violent, patterns in light and shade in settings of grandeur. His Flemish ancestry shows in his Baroque treatment of classicism, in the robustness of his porticoes, towers and wall articulation.

At *Castle Howard* the central block is surmounted by a large drum and cupola which dominate the structure (339). Inside, the great hall (341) is square, its giant Corinthian pilasters supporting the arches upon which the drum rises. The hall itself is spacious and imposing but the interior dome above is lofty and narrow (only 27 feet in diameter and 77 feet above floor level); the price that has been paid to achieve the impressive exterior silhouette.* On the north elevation of the house (346) curving arcades advance to bound a great open court on either side of which are extensive groups of buildings which accommodate kitchens,† stables, laundry, etc.

The creation of *Blenheim Palace*, Oxfordshire, 1705–22, was Vanbrugh's supreme triumph. A present from a grateful nation to the Duke of Marlborough, this immense structure seemed to be designed especially for display, rather than comfort and convenience. With Castle Howard and the later Seaton Delaval (1720–9), these houses were the last of these gigantic residences which became obsolete because of their sheer size and cost; they represent domestic architecture in the palatial grand manner.

This combined palace and castle also presented

---

* Wren's solution of this problem is discussed on page 128.

† As can be seen in 346, the kitchens were almost as far as possible from the dining rooms. In an age of ample supplies of servants this was not regarded as a problem.

339 *North front, 1699–1712, Sir John Vanbrugh*

340 *Park gateway*

341 *Entrance hall*

Vanbrugh with his greatest difficulties. The militant Duchess of Marlborough made no secret of her disapproval of the choice of architect and the design. Her relations with Vanbrugh steadily deteriorated during the years of building until Vanbrugh was finally excluded from his own work and the house was completed by Hawksmoor after the original architect's death.

Blenheim Palace as it stands today, in the superb setting of its park at Woodstock (342), is a remarkable house, both for its colossal scale and the superb Baroque treatment of its weighty and conflicting masses. The great centre block with its Corinthian portico is theatrical, even ostentatious, but its scale is absorbed in the greater compass of the complete frontage, extending to 856 feet (344). The centrepiece is connected to the massively castellar side pavilions by curved colonnades of Doric columns. Beyond these, forming the side wings of the *cour d'honneur*, are the stable and kitchen courts surrounded by their groups of buildings (342). Though quite different from the Italian Baroque of Borromini or Bernini – for there are few curves or undulations – the conception of Blenheim could be described by no other term than Baroque. Surprisingly, in contrast to the Baroque treatment of rustication, pediments, portico and colonnades, the detail is often simple as, for example, in the plain window openings (350). Inside are the superbly decorated great hall and reception rooms, decoration which includes especially the magnificent ceiling and wall paintings by *Sir James Thornhill* and *Louis Laguerre*.

Vanbrugh's architectural career was less than 30 years, much shorter than Wren's. Apart from Castle Howard and Blenheim, he was appointed to succeed Wren as Surveyor at *Greenwich Hospital* in 1716 and worked there until he died 10 years later. In the same years, apart from continuing at Blenheim, he built *Seaton Delaval*, the house at *Eastbury* in Dorset and his own house at Greenwich. This, *Vanbrugh Castle*, was begun in 1716 and is a Baroque version, very personally Vanbrugh, of a Medieval castle with towers and machicolations. In this, his own house, Vanbrugh had no fractious client to placate and he was able to explore his own ideas without hindrance.

House Design 1690–1730

Though such palatial residences as Castle Howard and

Blenheim were not typical of the larger country house of these years, they exercised a certain influence. From 1700 the rectangular block with slightly projecting wings, typical of the Dutch Palladian house, gave place to a main rectangular block which was extended towards a three-sided forecourt by curving or straight colonnades which, in turn, connected to side wings or grouped buildings. The principal floor, the *piano nobile*, was given precedence of space and size and much of the plan of the rest of the house was sacrificed to the height and nobility of the reception rooms on this floor. Here were to be found the hall and saloon; an exterior staircase led to the front door at this level.

The outstanding example of the large house of these years is *Chatsworth* in Derbyshire. Here the work of the main block, encompassing the courtyard, was carried out in stages and by different architects. The south façade (1686–96), by *William Talman** is correctly classical while *Thomas Archer's* north front (1705) is more Baroque, with a semi-elliptical bow section. In plan, Chatsworth comprises a great block of apartments disposed round an inner courtyard. Inside there can be seen some of the finest staterooms in England, also a chapel. No expense was spared to obtain the services of the most eminent artists and craftsmen. There are magnificent wall and ceiling paintings by *Antonio Verrio, Louis Laguerre* and *Sir James Thornhill*, while the woodcarving in particular is superb. The whole richly decorated and finished interior was carried out with great care over a long period (345, 347).

Typical of the smaller *town house* design is the rectangular block of *Mompesson House* in Salisbury. Here is a two-storeyed house with equal prominence given to the windows of both floors. Above is a cornice and hipped roof with dormers and chimneystacks. The decorative classical doorway provides the centre focus. Another example is the Headquarters of the National Trust, *No. 42, Queen Anne's Gate in London* (348).

The interior decoration of the main reception rooms and hall of such medium-sized houses had become plainer. The plaster ceiling was now enriched by simple low relief ribs and the walls were plainly

---

* Talman is also known for his work at Dyrham Park, Gloucestershire, where he rebuilt the earlier manor house between 1692 and 1704.

342 *Aerial view of house and park, 1705–22, Sir John Vanbrugh*

344 *Entrance front portico*

343 *Frontispiece gateway*

345   *Chatsworth House, Derbyshire. The west front*

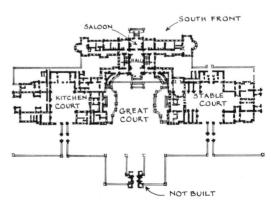

346   *Plan, Castle Howard*

347   *The State Bedroom, Chatsworth*

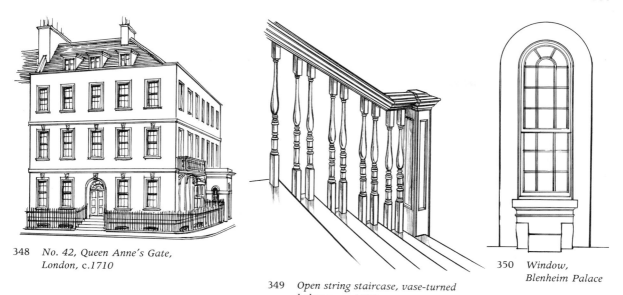

348 *No. 42, Queen Anne's Gate, London, c.1710*

349 *Open string staircase, vase-turned balusters, c.1700*

350 *Window, Blenheim Palace*

351 *Queen Anne Dining Room, 1702–10*

panelled. Some examples were designed with an order, others were without. The polished wood floor was now adorned by a rug or two, though these were still imported and costly,* but furniture was becoming more varied and there was a greater variety of pieces. The windows were of sash design and the doors wood-panelled (351). Staircases, still of wood, had more delicate balusters, vase-turned or barley-sugar twisted. The balustrate was now of open string design, that is, the balusters were set immediately into the stairs instead of the earlier model where they were inserted into a baulk of timber called the string; this was a closed string design. The handrail was now finely moulded and finials were rarely seen (349).

Nicholas Hawksmoor 1661–1736

Hawksmoor spent his whole life in the study of building and architecture. At the age of 18 he came to London and began to work for Wren, at that time as his domestic clerk. He assisted Wren on many projects and quickly absorbed the skill and knowledge needed to make his help invaluable. He was engaged on work at *Chelsea Hospital* (page 129), *the city churches* (page 121), *St Paul's Cathedral* (page 124), *Hampton Court Palace* and *Greenwich Hospital* (page 128/9). In 1705 he became the Deputy-Surveyor of Works for Greenwich. About 1700 Hawksmoor came into close association with Vanbrugh and worked with him on the Vanbrugh great houses.

Despite this long and close association, first with Wren and then with Vanbrugh, Hawksmoor developed his own style and in the first 35 years of the eighteenth century carried out a great deal of his own work, chiefly in ecclesiastical and university projects. Though entirely English in origin, Hawksmoor's Baroque designs were as controversial and forceful as Vanbrugh's. By the time he came to build his famous London churches and university courts he was an architect of great experience and long training. His Baroque work is entirely original; no-one having seen and studied a Hawksmoor church could possibly mistake this style for that of any other architect. Some of his churches, also his university work at All Souls, for instance, have a strong Gothic flavour. Indeed,

this Medievalism is an integral component of English Baroque, unique to this country.

In 1706 Hawksmoor designed the stone house at *Easton Neston* near Towcester. This, his one large domestic building, was articulated with a giant order of Corinthian pilasters standing upon a rusticated base. There is a beautiful staircase inside; also some wall paintings by Thornhill.

In 1711 an Act of Parliament was passed providing for the building of 50 new churches to minister to parishioners in the expanding suburbs of London. This was the first large-scale church building scheme since Wren's rebuilding of the city churches. These were to be new structures in the contemporary architectural idiom. In the first 30 years of the eighteenth century only a dozen churches were built under the Surveyorship of Hawksmoor and William Dickinson, though the latter was soon replaced by Gibbs (page 147) and then by James (page 159 and 360). The largest contribution, six churches, was made by Hawksmoor and his reputation as an architect stands in no small measure upon these highly original, individualistic designs. They are all different and all show vitality and power. They lack grace and delicacy, it is difficult to see beauty, but they are compelling and arouse admiration (albeit sometimes reluctant) and refuse to be ignored. As four of them are in London's East End and one in the City, it was inevitable that they should have received severe damage from bombing in the Second World War. Due to their massiveness of design and construction, much of the exteriors survived except for *St Alphege, Greenwich*, 1712–14, which was reduced to a shell.

St Mary Woolnoth, 1716–27 (353), is the only city church among the six. It is a most original design set upon a square plan. It has a solid-looking rectangular tower with Corinthian columns in the centre stage. Much of the lower section of the church is rusticated. *St Anne's Limehouse*, 1712–14, has a tall semicircular porch at one end. The tower rises by diminishing stages to a final, multi-sided upper feature. *St George-in-the-East*, 1715–23, whose interior was badly damaged, also has a multi-sided top feature. *Christ Church, Spitalfields*, 1723–9 (354) is the most individualistic of the East End churches. Here a rectangular, classical tower of great width ascends to a Medieval-type spire. The projecting porch below is of powerful design in the Doric Order, the entablature

---

* Carpet weaving was carried on in England from 1700 onwards and Wilton carpets began to be made.

352 *Church of St George, Bloomsbury, Hawksmoor, 1720–30*

353 *St Mary Woolnoth, Hawksmoor, 1716–27*

354 *Christ Church, Spitalfields, Hawksmoor, c.1725*

355 *All Saints' Church, Oxford, Dean Aldrich, 1709*

356 *All Souls' College, Oxford, Hawksmoor, 1716–34*

357   *Queen's College, Oxford, front quadrangle,*
      Hawksmoor, 1709–59

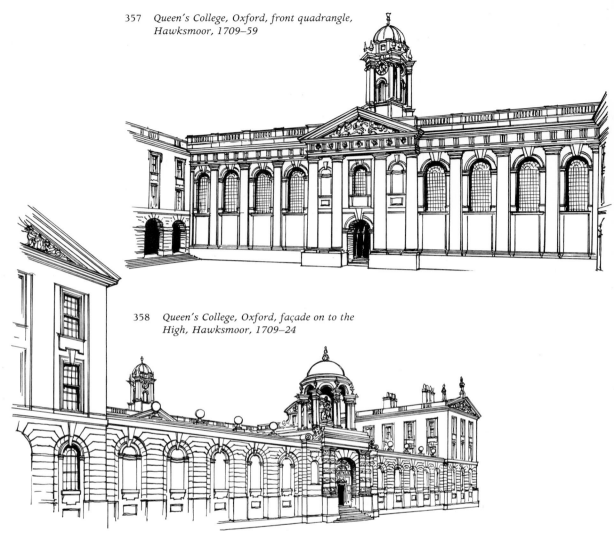

358   *Queen's College, Oxford, façade on to the*
      High, Hawksmoor, 1709–24

359   *Christ Church, Oxford, Peckwater*
      Quadrangle, Dean Aldrich, 1705–11

broken by a semi-circular arch. All of these Hawksmoor churches are very large buildings and *St George, Bloomsbury*, 1720–30 (352) the only church of the six in London's West End, is no exception. Erected on a square plan, it has a giant Corinthian portico raised on a podium, approached by steps. The tower is set at the side of the church and the steeple rises in stepped pyramidal form to the statue of King George at the top.

Hawksmoor's ecclesiastical work was obviously so original and of such telling standard that, when Wren died in 1723, Hawksmoor was appointed Surveyor at *Westminster Abbey*. Under his Surveyorship the western towers, long under discussion, were at last designed and built. The towers are hardly pure in style but they have now become a familiar and affectionately regarded London landmark.

University Building

Dr Henry Aldrich made extensive architectural contributions to *Oxford* while Dean of Christ Church. At *Trinity College* he designed the chapel (c.1690), a successful and charming work much in the style of Wren. Inside is some exquisite carving by Grinling Gibbons. In addition to the Fellows' Building at *Corpus Christi* (1706–12), Aldrich also designed the *Peckwater Quad* at *Christ Church* in 1705–6. Here, he planned three almost identical sides, pilastered in the Ionic Order. Each side has a centrepiece with pediment above. The result is dignified and monumental, if a little monotonous (359). The fourth side was completed after his death in 1710.

In Oxford he was also responsible for the *Church of All Saints* (355). Built 1707–10, this church is not of the stature of Wren's or Hawksmoor's work but does provide a link between the two periods of ecclesiastical building. The steeple is reminiscent of St Mary-le-Bow though the lower part of the church has a tall portico nearer to Hawksmoor. The rectangular, galleried interior has suffered from nineteenth-century restoration.

The most important Baroque work carried out at the Universities in these years was Hawksmoor's extensive rebuilding of *Queen's College*. By 1670 the Medieval buildings here had become dilapidated and, as the college was now wealthy, it was decided to rebuild on an ambitious scale. *Nicholas Hawksmoor*, entrusted with the task, began by building a fine

Library, which was influenced to no small degree by Wren's Library at Trinity College, Cambridge, but it is differently proportioned. The library at Queen's has a central pedimented feature with the order confined to this while the remainder of the façade is astylar.

In 1709 Hawksmoor continued his work at Queen's by beginning the scheme for rebuilding the *front quad*. The plan conceived the erection of a hall and chapel as a symmetrical block with a residential wing on each side advancing towards the High Street; the fourth side of the quad, fronting the High was then completed by a screen and gateway. The hall and chapel block has a central pedimented feature in the Doric Order and Doric pilasters are continued across the whole elevation. In the centre rises a cupola reminiscent of Wren's design at Chelsea Hospital (357). The screen fronting the High has tall terminal pavilions, each pedimented, and these pavilions are connected by a rusticated screen, punctuated by ten niches. The centre gateway, flanked by coupled, rusticated Doric columns, is covered overall by a large cupola (358).

Another work by Hawksmoor at Oxford is the *Clarendon Building*, built as the University Printing House in 1713–14. It is a robust classical structure on Roman lines with a giant Doric portico.

Hawksmoor was also responsible for the rebuilding of *All Souls' College* in the years 1716–34. Christopher Codrington, Fellow of the College, left his library and money for housing it to his college. It was decided to rebuild the quadrangle with the library on the north side and a hall and chapel on a different elevation. Hawksmoor was asked to make and carry out designs for this, but whereas at Queen's College the Medieval buildings had been demolished to make way for a classical scheme, at All Souls' he was asked to design in Gothic to fit the existing work. This he did, so the whole quadrangle is in Gothic pattern. An arcaded screen with central gateway fronts the High while, on the fourth side, he designed two large towers planned on the model of a Medieval gateway, but there is no gateway here. This is not Gothic architecture, but the Medieval spirit with Baroque display and scale of power. The design has no Medieval humility but is majestic architecture on cathedral scale (356).

360   *St George's, Hanover Square, London, John James, 1713–14*

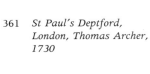

361   *St Paul's Deptford, London, Thomas Archer, 1730*

362   *St John's Church, Westminster, Thomas Archer, 1714–28*

363   *Birmingham Cathedral tower, Thomas Archer, 1709–25*

Thomas Archer 1668–1743

The last member of the triumvirate of English Baroque architects had a different preparation for his career from either Vanbrugh or Hawksmoor. Archer's training was the classic approach followed by most eighteenth-century architects. He was educated at Oxford, then studied on the Continent for four years, seeing at first hand in Italy the ancient classical buildings as well as the work of contemporary Italian architects. This preparation gave him advantages in breadth of vision and knowledge of the wide spectrum of classical design. Unfortunately much of his work has been lost or altered but we still have his north elevation at Chatsworth with its pilastered bow front.

The chief remains of Archer's work are in ecclesiastical architecture and here he displays a greater variety and sensitivity in design, though less self-conscious individuality, than his two colleagues. In 1709–15 he designed the Church of St Philip in *Birmingham*, now the *Cathedral*. This is a large, simplified Baroque structure, still finely sited in the centre of the city. The tower is of especial interest. Its four faces are concave with belfry openings flanked by coupled Corinthian pilasters; the cupola above is gracefully proportioned (363).

The other two churches for which Archer is known are in marked contrast to one another. *St Paul's Church, Deptford*, 1730, is a graceful building of considerable beauty standing in pleasant garden surroundings in a drab district of London. The body of the church is solid and powerful, fronted by a Baroque Doric portico, but above rises a slender, delicate steeple after the style of Wren (361). The *Church of St John* in Smith Square, *Westminster* was less fortunate in that, unlike St Paul's, it did not escape the bombs of the Second World War. It was gutted in 1940 and stood a stark, burnt-out shell for many years before it was rescued and restored to its original condition in 1964–9. It is now used as a concert hall. There is nothing delicate or reminiscent of Wren about St John's. It is a massive, uncompromising Baroque church standing four-square, with its corner towers and matching elevations filling completely the London square which it occupies. Like Vanbrugh's Blenheim and Hawksmoor's Christ Church, Spitalfields, St John's is an individual, powerful building, handled with vitality (362). Inside the church is more traditional, designed and decorated in the Roman Baroque manner with barrel vaulted ceiling supported on giant Corinthian columns. The wood side galleries are carried on Ionic columns.

CHAPTER EIGHT

Gibbs and the English Palladians 1710–1760

Judged by the standards of today, the eighteenth century appears a time of great contrasts. Magnificent mansions and houses were built in gracious parkland, but sanitation, hygiene and convenience received scant attention. The sons of the wealthy took the Grand Tour to enlarge their appreciation of the arts; the majority of the population had little education at all. Medical science made slow headway against the people's strong belief in superstition, witchcraft, magic charms and home remedies which were thought to cure anything from rheumatism to venereal disease. Vast quantities of food were consumed by the upper classes, but the poor in town slums starved. Improvements in agriculture were producing better bread, more meat and a better standard of food for the majority of people, yet over-eating by the wealthy caused them indigestion and, in many cases, shortened their lives.

Yet, in domestic architecture and the arts, the eighteenth century was Britain's 'golden age'. It is not easy to explain exactly why these years were so propitious to the creation of beautiful buildings, superbly decorated with such a high quality of craftsmanship in all fields. It was not simply because Britain was wealthy and under no threat. Victorian Britain was even wealthier and at peace for most of the nineteenth century, yet few art historians would suggest that here was a 'golden age' in their subject. Partly it was an accident of time in that the condition of architecture and the visual arts had reached this stage of high achievement after climbing up to this peak over the previous centuries. There had been a steady development in the classical arts since the time of Elizabeth I, but probably the most important factor in creating the most suitable climate for the flowering of these arts was the patronage of the aristocracy.

In Britain, the aristocracy functioned better as patron of the visual arts than even the monarchy had done in earlier years, for the monarch and his court had one viewpoint; the aristocracy was multiple. Some monarchs had good taste and were knowledgeable and interested in the arts; others had not and were not. The aristocracy, at their stage of development in the eighteenth century, were, on the whole, knowledgeable and had good taste. They were numerous and so could employ large numbers of architects, artists and craftsmen in all the allied trades and, due to their extensive European travels, knew exactly what they wished to create and possess. They demanded the highest standards, wishing to emulate the great palaces and houses which they had seen abroad and each to build one in the latest fashion greater than that of his acquaintances. To get what they wanted, unlike the middle classes and bureaucratic governments of the twentieth century, they did not count the cost. Indeed, it was not unknown for the head of an eighteenth-century aristocratic family to almost bankrupt the estate in order to create the mansion set in its parkland.

This supremacy in standards set an example to the less wealthy professional and middle classes. Their houses, decoration and contents were not so ambitious or costly, but their quality, though plainer, was in good taste. In a Britain where the industrial revolution had not yet swept skilled workers into the towns, country craftsmen of intelligence worked with care and devotion to produce things of beauty, whether in furniture, furnishings, pictures, silverware or ceramics. The simple builder based his designs for windows, doorways and ceilings upon the handbooks of architecture and decoration produced by the great architects of the day. The proportions and detail of these were laid down for him, meticulously worked out and evolved from 100 years of English experimentation in classical architecture.

James Gibbs 1682–1754

Gibbs was one of the architects whose books influenced later architects and builders, not only in Britain but also in America. His own work was not mainstream, for that was developing into Palladianism by 1720. Neither was he an English Baroque architect of the Vanbrugh/Hawksmoor school. Gibbs was always an individualist, his work influenced by different schools and especially by Wren, but he remained all his life, architecturally, 'the man who walked alone'. Paradoxically, it was Gibbs' books which had the widest influence, especially on the other side of the Atlantic where, on the eastern seaboard, 'Gibbs' churches, houses and colleges abound, though generally built in wood rather than stone. The two books which were especially known were his *A Book of Architecture*, published 1728, and *Rules for Drawing the several parts of Architecture*, 1732.

James Gibbs was one of the outstanding architects of these years. Though not an innovator, he showed brilliance of technical skill in the handling of his materials and in architectural design. He left his native Scotland when still a young man and spent some time travelling on the Continent. Later he was accepted in Rome at the Studio of Fontana, who was then at work on St Peter's. Gibbs worked in Rome during the years 1707–9 and this gave him the advantage over his British colleagues in that he had studied both in practice and theory at the fountain head.

In his first important commission after his return to Britain, the *Church of St Mary-le-Strand* in *London*, Gibbs' design showed his debt both to Roman Baroque and to Sir Christopher Wren. The body of the church was influenced by the years in Rome and the steeple reflects Gibbs' admiration for Wren's city

churches (366). Gibbs continued his ecclesiastical work by completing the neighbouring church of *St Clement Dane* (a Wren church to which Gibbs added the steeple) and by designing the smaller church of *St Peter* in Vere Street, *London*.

In 1722–6 he built his masterpiece, *St Martin-in-the-Fields* in *Trafalgar Square*, which was one of the most important buildings of the time and certainly the finest church. Its influence was deep and widespread; copies and designs obviously inspired by it can be seen in England, but even more so in the United States, where a number of churches in different States were erected to Gibbs' designs. St Martin-in-the-Fields is fronted by a magnificent Corinthian portico and this order is continued round the building in pilaster form. Gibbs broke with tradition here in his construction of the steeple. In order to save space and provide a compact design, he built the tower inside the west wall so that it emerges from the roof immediately behind the portico. This is in contradistinction to Wren and Hawksmoor, who always designed the tower to stand with its base visibly upon the ground. Gibbs had first experimented with a similar scheme in St Mary-le-Strand, where the steeple appears to grow out of the body of the church. Both this building and St Martin's were strongly criticised by the classical purists, but Gibbs' churches are structurally sound and have been judged aesthetically satisfactory by later generations. In the steeple itself, the Ionic and Corinthian Orders are used; the handling owes much to Wren's designs (365). Inside, the church has five bays and is aisled. The ceiling has an elliptical barrel vault, the decoration of which was carried out by the Italian stuccoists *Artari* and *Bugatti* (364).

James Gibbs' contribution to domestic architecture was not extensive. He designed the attractive *Sudbrooke Lodge* in *Petersham*, Surrey in 1718 and the larger house at *Ditchley* in Oxfordshire in 1720. His main field of work, apart from his churches, is *university building*. In his *Radcliffe Camera* at *Oxford*, built between 1739 and 1749, he returned to Roman Baroque in a bold, exuberant cylindrical structure surmounted by a cupola (371). At *Cambridge* Gibbs, like his later colleague Robert Adam (page 183), devoted much time and effort in an attempt to complete the great quadrangle at *King's College*. In both cases – Gibbs in the 1720s and 1730s and Adam in the 1780s – the architect was commissioned to design a comprehensive scheme for the great quadrangle and a

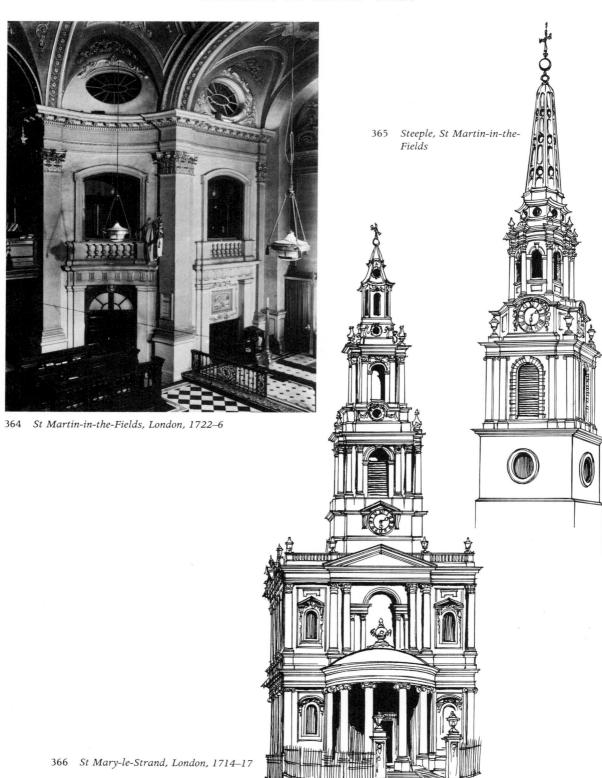

364   *St Martin-in-the-Fields, London, 1722–6*

365   *Steeple, St Martin-in-the-Fields*

366   *St Mary-le-Strand, London, 1714–17*

university library and administrative centre. These were two different schemes but, since the sites were close together, it was considered advantageous for the architectural layouts to have homogeneity.

For both architects the problem was the great Medieval chapel. Since the fifteenth century the large quadrangle had been dominated by this building, regarded by architects and university authorities as sacrosanct, yet how to marry it with an eighteenth-century classical scheme? (373). The chapel is on the north side of the quadrangle; Gibbs' solution was to design the hall opposite, on the south, with a great portico to face the chapel. On the east and west sides he would build classical, plainer blocks. His adjacent layout was for an open court lined by blocks on three sides to serve as administrative buildings and the university library. Only the *Senate House*, 1722 (368) was built in this latter court and the *Fellows' Building*, 1724, on the west side of the great quadrangle (372, 373), both restrained classical structures of high standard. Due to endless university wrangling, nothing further was achieved and the architect was shabbily treated (as was Adam later). Gibbs received only £100 in lieu of fees for the Senate House, which cost £13,000 to build.

Scotland

The paths of England and her northern neighbour had continued their separate ways despite the union of the Crowns under James I and VI. The political Union of 1707 was different. This was a watershed and, though until after the 1745 rebellion the changes were not marked, in the second half of the century the prosperity of Scotland began to revive.

Eighteenth-century Scotland produced some fine architects, but in the years until 1760 most of them still found career prospects to be more advantageous in England. James Gibbs was one of these, though he did return to his home town of *Aberdeen* towards the end of his life to build the West Kirk on the site of the nave of the Medieval *Church of St Nicholas*. Another Scottish architect was Colen Campbell, the designer of Palladian buildings (page 156) in England, whose publication *Vitruvius Britannicus* had a widespread influence in advising upon correct classical proportion and detail.

Meanwhile, in Scotland, in the years 1710–60 architects continued to pursue their own indigenous course. Sir William Bruce was followed by James Smith and Alexander MacGill, but the chief architect of this time was *William Adam* (1689–1748), father of the famous architect of the later eighteenth century, Robert Adam (page 173). William Adam was the son of a stone mason and, after initial training from his father worked for Sir William Bruce. Adam was energetic, a business man who made himself proficient as an architect, becoming in his middle years the man best known in his profession in Scotland. Most of the nobility and gentry went to him for new houses and alteration to existing ones. He was appointed Master Mason in North Britain to the Board of Ordnance and carried out a great deal of work in the building of forts in the Highlands.

Most of William Adam's civic work has been destroyed or altered; it is in his country houses that his style of building can still be seen. This is based chiefly upon the English work by Vanbrugh and Gibbs. Adam was attracted by powerful designs, Baroque in their massiveness and curves, also their monumentality. He used Palladian ornament and façade treatment, but in general the English Palladian school was too formal and prescribed for him. His best and most typical work can be seen at Hopetoun, the Drum, and Duff House.

Hopetoun House had been built for the Earl of Hopetoun by Sir William Bruce and Adam had assisted there as a young man. After Bruce's death Lord Hopetoun asked Adam to extend the building and bring it up to date in the modern architectural idiom. This Adam did, though the work was accomplished so slowly that both architect and patron died before it was completed. The remodelled Hopetoun House is on the grand scale, with an entrance elevation extending over 500 feet and fronted by green lawns and gravel drives. The approach view (376) offers an impressive pile-up of grey masonry; a great centre block, quadrant colonnades and terminal pavilions. A giant Corinthian Order spans the *piano nobile* and the second storey, taken up in Doric form in the pavilions. This is in the Palladian manner, but the skyline and the sweeping convex and concave contrasting curves of bays and quadrants are Vanbrugh-inspired Baroque, as is the weightiness of the whole composition. Most of the exterior was finished in the 1740s. The interior work, of the highest quality, is by Robert Adam, who took over in 1750.

367   *The Horse Guards, London,*
      William Kent, 1745–58

368   *King's Parade, Cambridge. Note*
      'A', The Senate House, James
      Gibbs, 1722–30 and 'B' The
      Church of St Mary the Great,
      1478

372   *Fellows' Building,*
      King's College,
      Cambridge, James
      Gibbs, 1724–30

373   *Panorama of buildings of King's and Clare*
      Colleges seen from the banks of the River Cam,
      Cambridge. 'A' Clare College. 'B' The Chapel,
      1466–1515. 'C' The Fellows' Building, James
      Gibbs, 1724–30

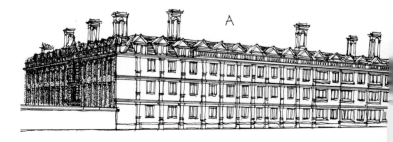

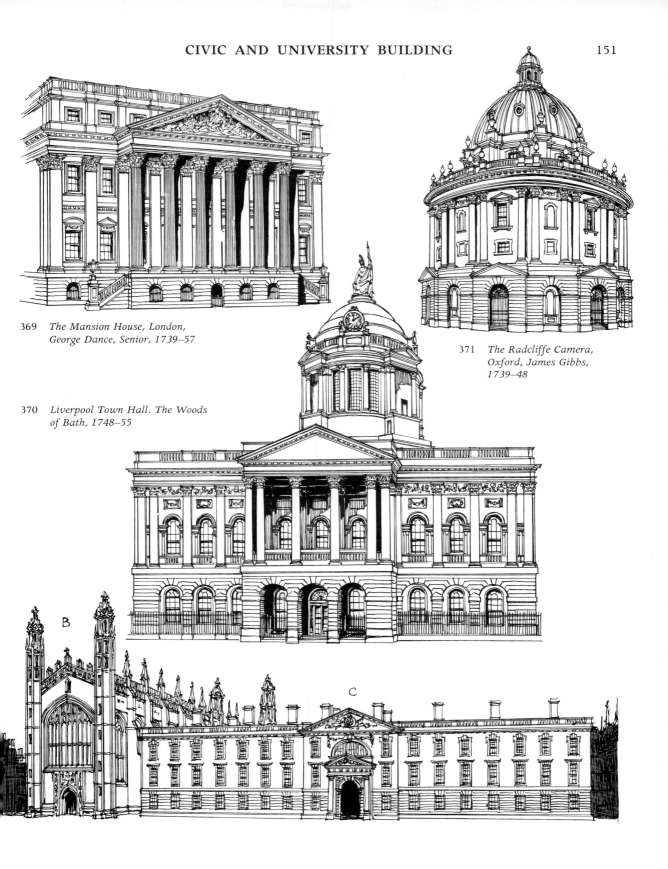

369 The Mansion House, London,
George Dance, Senior, 1739–57

371 The Radcliffe Camera,
Oxford, James Gibbs,
1739–48

370 Liverpool Town Hall. The Woods
of Bath, 1748–55

374   *Duff House, Banff, William Adam, 1730–9*

375   *Exterior staircase balustrade in iron. Stoneleigh Abbey, Warwickshire, Francis Smith, c.1720*

376   *Hopetoun House near Edinburgh, William, John and Robert Adam, c.1723–54*

William Adam was engaged at the same time on *Duff House*, near Banff. Despite the present state of the house* and the fact that the screen walls and pavilions were never built, Duff House remains the most impressive of Adam's works. Its vast block stands monumental and richly articulated in its dignity and grandeur (374). The house was designed in 1730 as a central, four-storeyed block with corner towers in the Scottish tradition, with central pediment and double curved approach staircase. It was intended to be connected to two-storeyed pavilions by quadrant screen walls. The uncompromising single large block, about 100 by 80 feet in plan, cost over £70,000, mainly because of the ready-worked stone brought by sea from the Firth of Forth. There is a rusticated lower storey; a giant Corinthian Order in pilaster form spans the next two floors with attic and balustraded parapet above.

The Palladians

Baroque architecture in Britain had been an implant, anglicised, but still of foreign origin. In the 1720s it was replaced by something much more English: *Palladianism*. The architectural pendulum had swung back to the correct Roman precepts of Palladio and away from the romantic English concepts of Wren and the rumbustious massing of form and ornament of Vanbrugh and his colleagues in Baroque art. All these variations of classical design were based upon Italian and Ancient Roman classicism but, whereas Wren, Vanbrugh and Gibbs had broken away from the rigid classical rules and had imprinted their own individuality and nationality, thus using the style and not permitting it to govern them, the Palladian school, which held the field in England from 1720 until 1760, returned to the more austere rendering of their ideal. This was a quiet, restrained classical form with little decorative enrichment apart from the orders; its lack of ostentation and dignified treatment were clearly attuned to the English taste.

This had a three-fold basis. First the work of

Andrea Palladio, the sixteenth-century architect of Renaissance Italy after whom the movement was named; secondly, the designs of *Vitruvius*, the architect of Republican Rome on whose precepts Palladio had based his work; and thirdly, *Inigo Jones*, the seventeenth-century English interpreter of the architectural expression. Palladian architecture was not quite like any of these, as a later copy is rarely the same as its prototype. In exteriors it was generally colder and more austere, but interior schemes often reached heights of splendour reminiscent of the great Roman baths and halls which inspired them.

The outstanding contribution of the Palladian school was in *country house* building. The exterior of these houses was generally plain and monumental, almost severe. A rectangular central block would be connected to side pavilions by low galleries and colonnades. The whole scheme was symmetrical, with careful attention to Roman classical proportion, orders and detail. The ground floor was rusticated and, above this, as in Inigo Jones' time, the *piano nobile*, the main floor, was much taller than the others. The entrance front generally faced north or east and on the opposite long side was the garden façade. Both long elevations generally had a central classical portico, commonly in the Corinthian Order, with a pediment above the entablature. This austere, symmetrical exterior was decorated only by rectangular sash windows and a balustrated parapet.

Great Palladian houses appear to be four-square, solid and indisputably English. What makes them into masterpieces, on the exterior, is the siting and surroundings, for the parkland and gardens are in contrast and thus complementary to the architecture. The Palladian house was carefully set on rising ground or at the foot of a vista or by a stream or lake. The peculiarly English park* was then laid out round it, with sweeping lawns, great spreading trees and studiously natural landscape, decorated by pseudo-classical temples and sculpture. *William Kent* and, later, *Lancelot (Capability) Brown*, became famous as the chief exponents of this type of landscaping – Brown made lakes from streams, and moved whole hillsides to where he needed them to create his effect. This treatment is indigenous, very different from French or Italian gardens based on the geometrical formalities at Versailles. It was envied and copied

---

* The building now belongs to the Ministry of Works, who are restoring it to its former condition. In the last 50 years Duff House has been used as a hospital and later by the army. Little remains of Adam's decorative interior schemes, though the structure is largely sound. The original staircase balustrade has disappeared, also all the furniture and nearly all the fireplaces.

---

* A rarity in Scotland in these years.

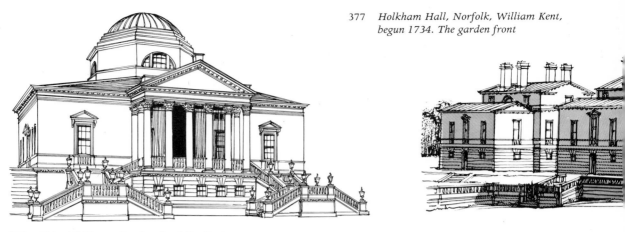

377   *Holkham Hall, Norfolk, William Kent, begun 1734. The garden front*

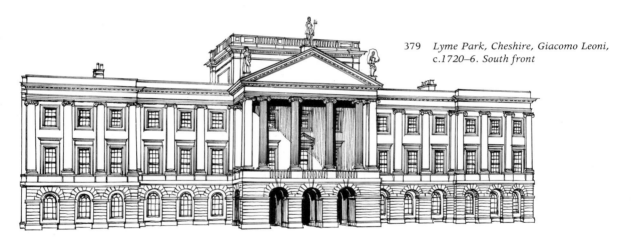

378   *Chiswick House, London, Lord Burlington, 1727–36*

379   *Lyme Park, Cheshire, Giacomo Leoni, c.1720–6. South front*

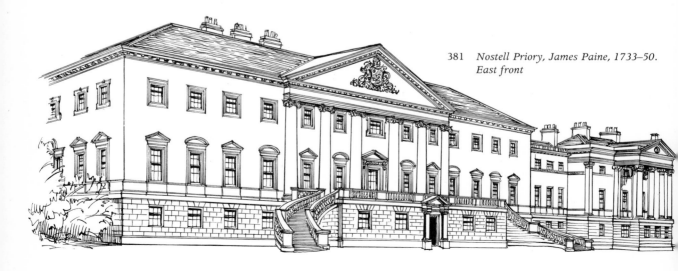

381   *Nostell Priory, James Paine, 1733–50. East front*

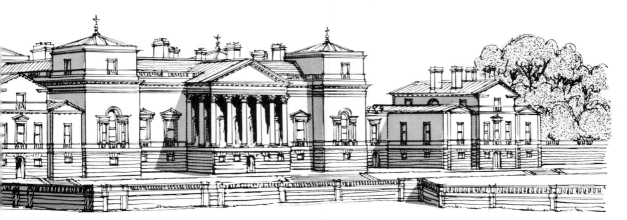

380   Holkham Hall, plan
      principal floor. A Hall.
      B Saloon. C Gallery.
      D State Bedroom.
      E Drawing Room.
      F Dining Room.
      G Library Wing. H Guest
      Wing. I Chapel Wing.
      J Kitchen Wing.

382   Holkham Hall, the hall

later by other European nations, notably by Catherine the Great of Russia.

All over England, in towns but more so in the country, Palladian houses were built – from large mansions to small houses and terraces. Most of the work was by builders who based their designs on houses they had seen or on drawings from books on architecture by men like Campbell (*Vitruvius Britannicus*), Kent (*Designs of Inigo Jones*), Lord Burlington (*Fabbriche Antiche*) and Vardy (*Designs of Inigo Jones and William Kent*), also a translation by Dubois, illustrated by Leoni, of Palladio's *Quattro Libri dell' Architettura*. There were not, as yet, many architects, but there was an informed aristocracy who sent their sons on the Grand Tour of Europe to study its classical sites and buildings for two or three years. On their return these men became patrons of practising artists and architects. One of the great noblemen of this type, leader of the Palladian movement, was Lord Burlington. He designed some buildings himself and was the patron of several of the most outstanding Palladian architects, including *William Kent* and *Colen Campbell*.

The *Earl of Burlington* (1694–1753) went to Italy as a young man in 1714–15 and, on his return, became extremely interested in the work of Palladio as he studied Campbell's *Vitruvius Britannicus*. He returned to Italy in 1719 and spent some months in Vicenza to see Palladio's work *in situ*. He met William Kent in Rome, brought him back to England and employed him at Burlington House in Piccadilly to carry out decorative painting. He employed Campbell there also to transform the house design.* The two best-known examples of Lord Burlington's own work are the *Assembly Rooms* in *York*, a rendering of a Palladian basilica, and *Chiswick House* in *London*, which he modelled on Palladio's Villa Capra near Vicenza. The Chiswick villa, built 1727–36, has only two porticoes (as opposed to Palladio's four) and the chief of these is approached by an Italianate exterior double staircase. The dome, which covers the hall, is shallow, carried on a hexagonal drum (378).

Colen Campbell (d.1729) also built a version of Palladio's Villa Capra at *Mereworth* in Kent in 1723. This rendering is nearer to the prototype, being a square block with four identical porticoed elevations

and a central drum and dome covering a vast interior hall. The design built by Palladio was suited to the Italian climate, where the idea was to avoid the sun by moving around the hall, to the rooms leading off it, according to the time of day and the shade required. In England the result is magnificent but draughty.

Little is known of Campbell's early life until he was commissioned by Lord Burlington to remodel Burlington House in 1717. In 1715 he had brought out his *Vitruvius Britannicus*, in which he published a series of plates of works by English architects including many of his own designs. It was this publication which attracted Lord Burlington's attention to him. Although his main purpose was to advertise his own work, Campbell performed a considerable service to architecture by the publication of so many plates of important buildings. Among Campbell's other work was *Wanstead House* in Essex, 1720, a large Palladian structure with a 260-foot frontage (demolished 1824) and *Stourhead* (383) in Wiltshire, built 1721–4. His most beautiful house is *Houghton Hall* in Norfolk, designed in 1721 for Sir Robert Walpole and built between then and 1730. This very large house, comprising a central block connected to pavilions by colonnades, extends over a frontage of 450 feet. The architect died before completion and the interior decoration was undertaken by William Kent and the stuccoist Artari. The great stone hall, inspired by Inigo Jones' Queen's House at Greenwich, is in the Roman tradition of splendour, with its first floor gallery, classical doorways, chimneypiece and coved ceiling ornamented with gambolling *putti* (384).

William Kent (1685–1748) was the personality of the Palladian school. A Yorkshireman, he came to London and then went on to Italy to study painting. He lived in Rome for nearly ten years, copying paintings for English patrons until, in 1719, he met Lord Burlington and returned with him to Burlington House to pass the rest of his life there. At first he was employed to carry out decorative painting but under Lord Burlington's guidance he turned to architecture and, through his patron's influence, acquired important commissions and became the fashionable architect of the 1730s and 1740s.

Kent's chief domestic commission was *Holkham Hall* in Norfolk, which he designed in 1734 (380). This, the most famous of all Palladian mansions in England and the home of the Earl of Leicester, lies in magnificent grounds laid out by Capability Brown

---

* Gibbs had worked on the house, also Lord Burlington himself, but much of this was altered in the rebuilding in 1866.

383   *Stourhead, Wiltshire. 1718–22. East front, wings added, c.1800*

384   *Houghton Hall, Norfolk. The stone hall, 1721–30*

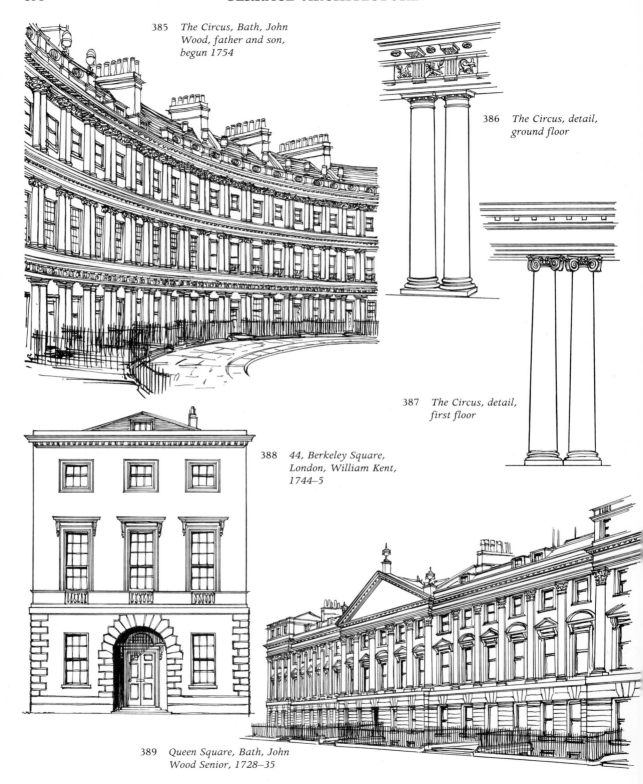

385   *The Circus, Bath, John Wood, father and son, begun 1754*

386   *The Circus, detail, ground floor*

387   *The Circus, detail, first floor*

388   *44, Berkeley Square, London, William Kent, 1744–5*

389   *Queen Square, Bath, John Wood Senior, 1728–35*

with lawns, trees and a lake. The exterior of the house is severe and symmetrical (377), but the interior is in complete contrast. The main achievement of Palladian domestic architecture (apart from the setting) was in the interiors and Holkham shows this in its finest form. The hall (382) is based on Roman basilican plan but, in its decoration and order, owes much to the Temple of Fortuna Virilis in Rome. The hall is built in Derbyshire marble in shades of cream and white, marked in red and has Ionic colonnades standing on a tall plinth broken by a central staircase which approaches the apse; behind this the doorway leads into the magnificent saloon. The plaster ceiling of the hall is beautifully designed and coffered; it has a decorative centrepiece enriched with classical ornament. William Kent believed in the practice, unusual at this date, of the architect designing not only the structure of a building but also all the detail of doorways, windows, ceiling, chimneypieces, furniture and furnishings. Holkham is a superb example and is so finely proportioned that it is difficult to credit the great size of the doorways, for instance, until someone stands in the opening and the height can be judged. The saloon ceiling and doorcases are excellent examples of Kent's best work. In 1742–4 he designed *No. 44, Berkeley Square* in *London*. This was a successful attempt to make a lavish home inside the greater restrictions of a town terrace house (388).

There were a number of other architects of quality designing in these years, most of whom followed the Palladian line. One of these was the Venetian *Giacomo Leoni*, c.1686–1746, who came to England to superintend the publication of an English edition of Palladio, which appeared in 1715–16 in two volumes; Leoni supplied the illustrations to Dubois' translation. In 1726, sponsored by Lord Burlington, Leoni published his three volume translation of Alberti on architecture. Leoni remained in England until his death and designed a number of houses in Palladian style. These include *Clandon Park*, near Guildford, 1731–5, *Queensberry House* near Burlington House in London, 1721, which was altered in 1792 and his south front additions to *Lyme Park* in Cheshire, 1720–30 (379).

Also working in Palladian style were *Isaac Ware*, d.1766, *Henry Flitcroft*, 1697–1769, and *John Vardy*, d.1765. Ware's best-known work is *Wrotham Park*, Middlesex, 1754; he also designed a number of houses in the West End of London. Henry Flitcroft's chief

building is the *Church of St Giles-in-the-Fields* in London, now dwarfed by the adjacent Centrepoint building. St Giles owes much to Gibbs' St Martin-in-the-Fields, also to the Wren city churches. Vardy worked for many years in the King's Works at Greenwich, Hampton Court Palace, Whitehall and Kensington and was closely associated with William Kent. It was in this capacity that he built the Horse Guards in Whitehall to Kent's designs after the latter's death (page 164). By mid-century the Palladian school was consolidated by a second generation of architects led by *Sir Robert Taylor* and *James Paine*, whose work was largely carried out in the 1760s (page 171). Typical of Paine's designs was *Nostell Priory* in Yorkshire, where he built the east front in 1733–50 (381). The wing on the right was added by Adam in 1765.

A further group of architects working at this time were designing in a manner which adhered less strictly to the Palladian code. *John James*, 1672–1746, had carried out work both at Greenwich Hospital and St Paul's. He contributed one church to the 1711 Act group of churches. This was *St George's, Hanover Square* in London, 1713–14 (360). It has a giant portico of Corinthian columns and a cupola-topped tower. James also completed Hawksmoor's Church of St Alphege at Greenwich.

George Dance the Elder, 1698–1748, was Clerk of the City Works in London from 1733 until his death. His best-known building in the city is the *Mansion House*, 1739–53 (369), with its fine portico of Corinthian columns crowned by the sculptured pediment. Dance built a number of churches in *London* which include *St Luke, Old Street*, 1732 (394), *St Leonard Shoreditch*, 1736–40 (392), *St Botolph, Aldgate*, 1749–50, and *St Matthias, Bethnal Green*, 1741. St Leonard's is the most successful design of these, its steeple owing something to St Mary-le-Bow.

Outside London there were a number of architects designing work of good quality, sound construction and varied design. These provincial architects tended to work in a small area, their contribution confined to a certain town or group of towns. Notable among them is *John Bastard* in *Blandford*, Dorset, where he built much of the new town after the old one had been largely destroyed by fire in 1731. The *Church* here, 1731–9, is a good example of his work (391). At *Worcester, Thomas White* designed the *Church of St Nicholas*, 1726–30 (396) and the *Guildhall*, 1719–22,

390   *Carved decoration, 1754–60*

391   *Blandford Church, Dorset,*
John Bastard, 1731–9

392   *Clock ornament, St*
Leonard's Church,
Shoreditch, George Dance
Senior

393   *Daventry Church, William*
and David Hiorn, 1752

396   *St Nicholas' Church,*
Worcester, Thomas White,
1726–30

394   *Doorway, St Luke's*
Church, Old Street,
London, George Dance
Senior, 1727–33

395   *Parapet, Daventry Church*

while *William* and *David Hiorn* worked in *Daventry*, where they built the church in 1752 (393). These provincial architects were influenced in their church design chiefly by Wren and Gibbs rather than Hawksmoor or the Palladians. This is evident especially in the steeples, but also in the interior decoration as at *Great Witley Church*, for example, built 1735.

House Interiors

The principal rooms in the large houses of the period were on the *piano nobile*. The living rooms led off a large, imposing, central hall, which was entered from the portico or main doorway approached by a single or complex exterior staircase (377, 381, 383). These *living rooms* would include a dining room (399), a small and large drawing room or saloon (402), a library, powder closets and, upstairs would be bedrooms (401) and dressing rooms. Kitchens and servants' quarters were relegated to basement and attics or, in large houses, to the wings or terminal pavilions connected by lower ranges to the central rectangular block. The Palladian tradition in great mansions was to house kitchen and service rooms, as well as stables, in these wings. The inconvenience of receiving one's food cold after being carried such distances from kitchen to dining room was not considered of importance; servants were in plentiful supply and the prestige and splendour of the house was the prime consideration.

There was now greater variety in the forms of interior decoration. This was classical in design, generally correctly proportioned and detailed in the Palladian tradition but the *walls* could now be covered and ornamented in several ways. *Wood panelling* was still employed; pinewood, cedar and, later, mahogany, were carved in classical schemes and ornament, the cheaper woods often painted in white or light colours (398, 399). Alternatively, *stucco-* ornamented walls were fashionable, again in classical decorative form, with the plaster enrichment added, then painted and gilded, to the wall surface (402). In the 1750s rococo decorative motifs began to replace the earlier Baroque and Palladian ornament. The newer designs incorporated scrolls and shells, flowers, ribbons and birds in a delicate, elegant composition. In some apartments, especially bedrooms, the walls were draped with *hangings* as far down as wainscot

level. These were plain or richly patterned in velvet, silk or damask (401).

From about 1745 a fourth alternative wall covering was provided by the introduction of *wallpaper*. At first this was imported from the East, being mainly of Chinese origin. It was sent in strips about four feet wide, several of which made a complete landscape or garden picture. Early English wallpapers were painted or stencilled attempts to imitate the more costly damask or velvet hangings of formal floral design. After 1754 printed patterns were in use; *John B. Jackson* of Battersea was a pioneer in this field. He published a report of his experimental work in 1754, giving data on his wood-block printing method. Many of his designs were representations of sculptured classical figures, made in monochrome, for those who could not afford the marble realities. Later wallpaper designs were of landscapes, floral designs and imitations of famous landscape paintings by artists such as Canaletto, Poussin or Lorraine. Wallpapers were not stuck to the wall. As they were so costly, they were mounted on canvas to a wood frame, attached to the wall by wooden wedges so that new paper could be put up without destroying the old. Some of these papers have been preserved in museums as they were not subject to damp and dirt from the walls.

Floors were of polished wood and *carpets* and rugs were still only seen in the principal reception rooms of large houses as they were as yet very expensive. Most of these carpets, which only covered the centre of the room, were imported, though needlework carpets were made in England. Carpet-knotting had lapsed in England in the later seventeenth century, but was revived as an industry in the middle of the eighteenth century when firms with names such as Wilton, Axminster and Kidderminster were started up (399, 401, 402).

The drawing room (402) or saloon was the main chamber of the house and was decorated and furnished in the most lavish manner. It generally faced south and was used for leisure. A massive cornice ran round the room and the white plaster ceiling was decoratively enriched. The chief feature of one wall was the chimneypiece, which extended from floor to cornice as a two-stage design as the overmantel was replaced by a carved framed mirror or picture. Rococo mirror frames were complex designs, usually gilded and with holders for a number of candles

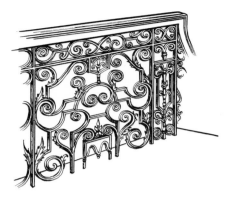

397   *Marble staircase, iron balustrade*

398   *Panel wall decoration incorporating candle holders. Carved painted and gilded wood, c.1756–60*

399   *Dining Room, c.1730*

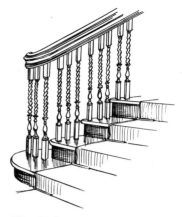

400 *Mahogany staircase,
twisted balusters, c.1715*

401 *Bedchamber, 1740–50*

402 *Drawing Room, 1750–60*

whose flames, reflected in the glass panels, increased the illumination of the room (402). Eighteenth-century interior décor made extensive use of large mirrors as well as carefully designed crystal chandeliers for this purpose. Six-panelled doors were most usual, with classical motifs in the carved panel borders. The sash windows reached from cornice to wainscot. They had large rectangular panes in wood frames. They were curtained by velvet or damask, looped up with tassels and cords and hung from a pole often hidden by a pelmet and crowned by an elaborate carved and gilded pediment. The *dining room* was less lavishly decorated but was similarly designed in a classical scheme (399). The principal feature of the bedroom was still the large four-poster bedstead, whose posts were now often in the form of classical columns (401).

A house would have one or two *staircases* according to size. The main staircase would be of stone if stucco decoration was used on the walls of the well and generally of wood if panelling was employed. Balustrades could be of wood or iron. In wooden ones the balusters, in open string design, were turned, usually in barley sugar twists (400). The wrought-iron balustrades were in scrolled design fitted to a mahogany handrail at the top (397). In the vogue for Chinese decoration of the mid-century, fret designs of wood balustrades were popular.

The furniture, furnishings and ornaments in the Palladian house were of a superb standard of craftsmanship. This was the age of beautiful silverware, of pottery and later porcelain and of the emergence of the great cabinet makers. *William Kent* designed much of the furniture used in his houses. This was in large pieces in carved mahogany or gilding and gesso was added to ornament a cheaper carved wood. Heavy marble tops were used on tables.

While William Kent was the chief designer in the years 1727–40, the following twenty years were dominated by *Thomas Chippendale*. Also a Yorkshireman, Chippendale came to London and later set up his shop in St Martin's Lane in 1753. He published his 'Director' the following year which contained designs for all kinds of furniture in the three basic Chippendale styles based on Gothic, Rococo and Oriental. These were his chief sources of inspiration, but all Chippendale furniture is unmistakably English in design. Chippendale's influence was far-reaching and he established the importance of the designer/cabinet-maker in the eighteenth century. He was

followed in the later decades by other famous designers such as Adam, Hepplewhite and Sheraton.

Building in Towns

The population of Britain was rising slowly. At the beginning of the eighteenth century it is estimated that there were five and a half million inhabitants in England and Wales. Towns were spreading outwards, especially London, whose wealthier citizens were moving westwards from the city and building spacious new houses in the villages of Chelsea and Kensington, as well as northwards and eastwards in Hampstead, West Ham and Walthamstow.

The City was the most densely populated area in Britain. It was not just occupied by day, as in modern times. The merchants and shop-keepers lived at their place of business with their families and servants. It was the nobility and professional men who had moved out, away from their crowded houses to take up residence in Piccadilly, St James's Square, Covent Garden and Westminster.

Town houses in these areas did not follow so closely upon the Palladian theme as the country residences, but some of the fashion trends in design were applied. The town house is, of necessity, restricted in site and so is taller and narrower, but there is the same insistence on predominance for the *piano nobile* where, if an order is used, it extends up from the first floor through two or three storeys to support the entablature above, which might be surmounted by an attic. If there is no order, its non-existence is noted by a string course at first floor level. This Palladian style of town house was in general use in London and other large towns from about 1730 onwards. Examples from these years include *Leoni's Queensberry House*, 1721, and *Kent's 44, Berkeley Square*, 1744–5, (388), both in *London*, and *68, The Close* in *Salisbury*, c.1735–40.

There are not many civic schemes surviving from this period. The outstanding example of Palladian building in this field (apart from the Mansion House, page 159), is the impressive layout of the *Horse Guards* in *Whitehall* (367). It was designed by *William Kent* in 1745, on similar lines to Holkham Hall, though the Horse Guards is largely rusticated and is surmounted by a clock tower. It was completed by Vardy after Kent's death.

Street Planning and Terrace Architecture

The idea of designing town houses by the street, or even round a whole square, had been initiated by Inigo Jones in Covent Garden (page 108). The experiment of making a uniform Palladian treatment of a street of houses tended to lapse after Inigo Jones' time and owners had their town houses built individually on similar, though not identical, patterns. From about 1730, town expansion began to go forward at a speed which made it architecturally desirable to treat the terrace houses as one façade. Ground landlords started to let their sites in a larger block instead of space adequate for only one or two houses. A few streets and squares in London were built with a repetitive Palladian façade as, for example, in Grosvenor Square, but the primary experiment at this time was in Bath.

In the early years of the eighteenth century *Bath* was still a small town. It was between 1720 and 1730 that the value of its waters was re-discovered and they were popularised for their medicinal properties. With royal patronage Bath soon became fashionable as a summer health and amusement resort. The leading figure in the consequent replanning and enlargement of the town to meet the new needs was *John Wood* (1704–54). He had already designed buildings in London and in the north of England, but in 1727 moved to Bath where he spent the rest of his life. By his work he helped to revive the popularity of Bath stone from the local quarries. He had a masterly conception of town planning in terraces, streets and squares. He did not visualise town houses simply as individual units but as part of a complete architectural layout for the city.

Wood's first important project in this manner was in *Queen Square* which he built in 1728–35. The entire square is designed in Palladian manner; the terraces are three-storeyed with rustication on the ground stage and, above the string course the *piano nobile*, its tall windows surmounted by alternating triangular and curved pediments. There is then the second floor with entablature above supported on giant pilasters which span first and second floors. The roof contains an attic stage. In Queen Square Wood did not simply repeat this Palladian formula from end to end of the terrace. He treated the whole façade as a palace with shallowly-projecting end pavilions and a central pedimented feature. These sections are marked by the use of columns instead of pilasters. The houses on each side of Queen Square became, together, the façade of a large country mansion (389).

John Wood carried out further Palladian building in, for example, *South Parade* and the country house of *Prior Park* in Bath, 1735, and, in civic work, *Liverpool Town Hall*, 1748–55 (370). His most spectacular achievement was his design for the *Circus* in Bath. He had discovered something of the Roman history of the city and planned ambitious layouts on Roman lines including a sports arena and a forum. The Circus is based on his ideas for a sports arena. This scheme was abandoned owing to the unsuitability of the English climate, but the form of the layout is the same. Here is a circle of 33 houses divided at three points by incoming streets. The design for the houses is repeated in identical manner all round the circle and comprises three stages using three different orders: Doric on the ground floor, then Ionic and Corinthian at the top (385–7). This simple but great conception was not completed in John Wood's lifetime, but work went on into the 1760s under his son, also John Wood.

The influence of these examples of terrace architecture in Bath was far-reaching. It encouraged architects in London and other towns such as Brighton, Cheltenham, Bristol and Hastings in the later eighteenth and early nineteenth centuries to develop the theme in their rapidly expanding urban areas.

CHAPTER NINE

The Classical Revival 1760–1790

Artistic exposition diversified in the second half of the eighteenth century. Its expression continued to be primarily classical, but eclecticism now had a wider base; the rigid rules of Palladianism were relaxed. This spirit of experimentation with new sources and ideas was the result of the expansion of the time; experienced geographically in extended travel overseas to more distant countries; and in the greater wealth at home which devolved from the current revolutions in both agriculture and industry.

The industrial revolution is sometimes thought of as being a nineteenth-century phenomenon, but even as early as 1760 its impetus was gathering momentum (438). The agricultural revolution in Britain belongs to the same period of development and it is no coincidence that both movements evolved at this time, for both arose in response to the need to provide food and employment for a population now fast increasing. It would have been impossible in the eighteenth century to bring enough food from overseas for this growth of population, stimulated by better conditions of medicine and hygiene. There was a move to farm the great estates more efficiently and smallholders were incorporated into larger units. At the same time thousands of acres of land, previously covered by woodland and heath, were enclosed to become productive arable fields. It is estimated that two million acres were added to the country's farming resources during the century. In addition the introduction of the scientific rotation of crops and pasture led to better yields and fatter stock.

All over the country on these medium-sized and large estates owners were ploughing back their profits into land and buildings. The ambition to own a beautiful house in fine parkland and grounds, prevalent in the years before 1760, culminated in the succeeding thirty years. This was the greatest age of country house building in Britain. The custom grew of sending the sons of great and aristocratic families on the Grand Tour of Europe. Greater distances were covered and two or three years were spent instead of only one in France and Italy, the travellers staying part of the time as guests of friends and relatives and the remainder in inns and rented lodgings. They collected antique and Renaissance sculpture, paintings, books, coins and ceramics and brought them back to decorate their homes. Often it became necessary to build new galleries and libraries to house these treasures.

Travel by the nobility and also by architects and artists led to increased knowledge. Interest was aroused in visiting Greece, Dalmatia and even lands as far away as Syria. In England the *Dilettanti Society* was formed to encourage such original research. It published papers and commissioned and financially supported expeditions by members. Among these was *Robert Wood* who, accompanied by Bouverie and Dawkins, went to Palmyra (Syria). In 1753 he published the result of their studies and drawings made there in *The Ruins of Palmyra*. His second expedition produced *The Ruins of Baalbec* (1757). *James Stuart* and *Nicholas Revett* followed, also under the society's aegis. They went to Pola (now Pula in Yugoslavia), then to Greece where they studied at Corinth and Athens. They returned in 1755 and, in 1762, published their *Antiquities of Athens*.

Other expeditions and other publications came from different countries. Notable were de Caylus' *Recueil d'Antiquités Egyptiennes, Etrusques, Grecques et Romaines* (1752), Le Roy's *Ruines des plus beaux Monuments de la Grèce* (1758), Winckelmann's *History of Ancient Art* (1763) and Dumont's *Temple of Paestum* (1764). This widening of the field for classical research made clear to both patron and architect in western Europe that Greece, not Rome, was the fount of the classical form and that, in many instances, the Greek was purer and more beautiful. The Greek/Roman controversy raged hotly and protagonists in the 'battle of the styles' took up indefatigable stands on one side or the other. In retrospect, the controversy appears to have been much ado about nothing. Both architectural forms were classical, with one derived from, then developed further than, the other. Why not use the better examples from both? This, of course, is what the great architects of the age did.

One factor which excited interest and controversy was the discovery of the *Greek Doric Order*. Ever since Brunelleschi in the fifteenth century, the *Roman Doric* or Tuscan had been the model, based on Vitruvius and the ruins of Roman buildings, then reiterated in succeeding publications through the sixteenth and seventeenth centuries. This order has a much slenderer column than the Greek version and also a moulded base. The drawings now seen, in the books published by those who had studied on the spot, showed the Doric Order of the Parthenon (222, 224), without base, fluted, with a more subtle echinus moulding to the capital than the Roman (which has a semi-circular section) and, most notable, a sturdier column and deeper entablature, giving different proportions of height and width to the order. This Greek Doric version horrified the Palladians and they were even more shocked when they saw drawings of the archaic period temples of Paestum and Sicily, which predate the Parthenon by a hundred years or more. For these earlier temples have even shorter, stockier columns and immensely large capitals supporting a weighty entablature. They are the most powerful-looking Doric buildings in western Europe. The English adherents to the Roman style, in the second half of the eighteenth century, led by Sir William Chambers, thought this work primitive and barbaric.

The pro-Greek faction of the later eighteenth century tended to go too far the other way, feeling that everything Greek was better than anything Roman. But even they did not value, as we do today, the great period of Greek sculpture and decoration. We consider this to be the fifth century BC, rating high the Parthenon sculptures, also earlier archaic work from Olympia and elsewhere. The Greek enthusiasts of the eighteenth century were more impressed by the later Greek work of the second or first century BC. In decorative fields they used designs from Greek vases and, mistakenly believing them to be Etruscan, incorporated their motifs into interior decoration and detail. Wedgwood used these sources, so did Adam. Indeed, the new pottery manufactory established by Wedgwood was named by him 'Etruria' and Adam proudly refers to his new 'Etruscan' motifs and colours of red, yellow earth and black.*

One European country did not acknowledge Greek originality for some time. This, naturally enough, was Italy. As publication after publication appeared, piling up the weight of evidence, the Italians found their champion in *Gianbattista Piranesi*, the Venetian artist who became famous for his drawings of classical ruins. In his publications *Le Antichità di Roma* (1748) and *Della Magnificenza ed Architettura de' Romani* (1763), he attempts the defence of Roman architecture against the Greek, asserting that the latter was more ornate and decadent.

The Greek/Roman controversy occupied the mainstream of architecture in the years 1760–90. On the periphery the widening ripples of the movement towards a climate of change could be discerned in other artistic expression. In mid-century there was, for many years, a fashion for Chinoiserie. This had been seen in Chippendale's furniture (page 164) and even so serious a protagonist of the Roman Palladian school as Sir William Chambers† published his *Designs of Chinese Buildings* and built the Pagoda in Kew Gardens (411).

A more fundamental movement was that of the Romantics. In England this took the form of a rebellion against the rigidity of Roman Palladianism

---

* Another source of these motifs for both men was the Roman art excavated at Herculaneum and Pompeii in the mid-century. Similar colours and decorative forms were found here, inspired originally from Greek sources.

† As a young man Chambers had worked for the East India Company in whose employment he travelled in Bengal and China.

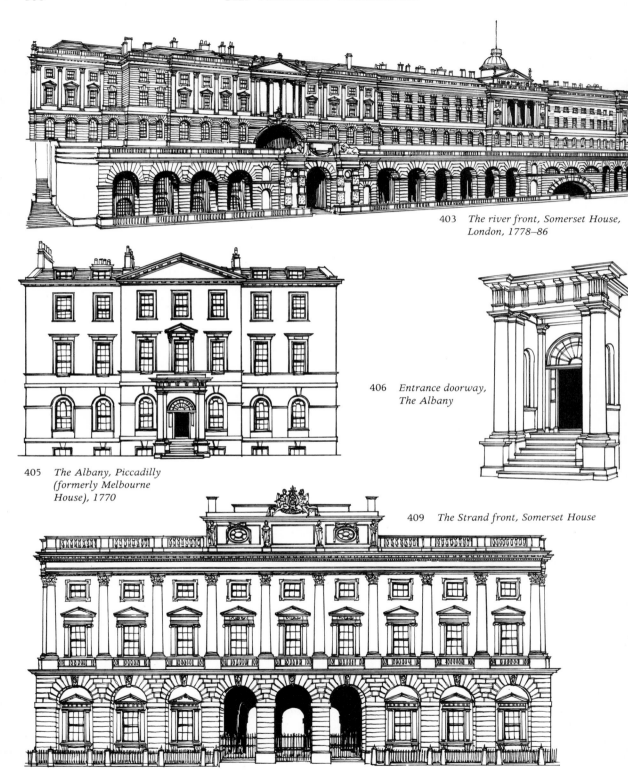

403   *The river front, Somerset House, London, 1778–86*

405   *The Albany, Piccadilly (formerly Melbourne House), 1770*

406   *Entrance doorway, The Albany*

409   *The Strand front, Somerset House*

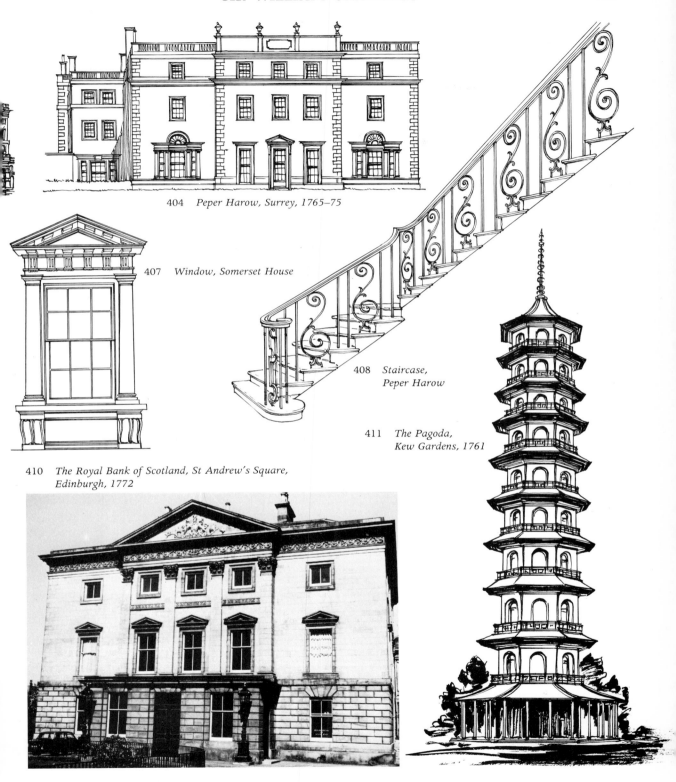

404   *Peper Harow, Surrey, 1765–75*

407   *Window, Somerset House*

408   *Staircase,
Peper Harow*

411   *The Pagoda,
Kew Gardens, 1761*

410   *The Royal Bank of Scotland, St Andrew's Square,
Edinburgh, 1772*

and against the dogma of reason. In the eighteenth century it was largely a literary force; its architectural expression was small. In Britain, Medievalism and the associated Gothic architecture had never completely died. Classical design had dominated the building scene for over two hundred years but the tiny flame had flickered intermittently. There were the few Gothic structures by Wren – Tom Tower at Oxford, some city churches – Vanbrugh's own house at Greenwich, Kent's contribution at Hampton Court Palace and Gloucester Cathedral. Hawksmoor had introduced his own brand of Gothic/Baroque at All Souls' College, Oxford and in the western towers of Westminster Abbey.

All of these examples are in the realm of literary Gothic; they have little in common with the Medieval spirit and lack comprehension of the building style, but they kept the feeling alive and provided the rebel outsiders' expression in a classical age. In the eighteenth century it was *Horace Walpole* who introduced the conception of a Gothic country house. His villa at *Strawberry Hill* where he enlarged and Medievalised the existing cottage in 1750 aroused widespread interest and controversy. In this Strawberry Hill Gothic, as it came to be called, he insisted on authentic Medieval forms for the interior rooms, decorating them with cusped and crocketed arches and panelled ceilings. The results are charming and delicate, full of the essence of good eighteenth-century craftsmanship and elegance but with nothing of the Medieval spirit. Strawberry Hill provides, though, the essential link between the Middle Ages, the Baroque/Gothic form and the final nineteenth-century revival.

Sir William Chambers 1723–1796

Two architects dominated the work of the 30 years after 1760. Both were Scots and they were exactly contemporary, living and dying within a year or so of one another. These men, William Chambers and Robert Adam were, however, in their work and in their personalities, total contrasts. *Sir William Chambers*, though of Scottish stock, was born in Gothenburg in Sweden. He spent much of his boyhood in Yorkshire but returned to Sweden, where he joined the East India Company at the age of 17. After extensive travels, he left the Company when he was 25 and went to Paris to study architecture. He stayed there for a year then continued to Italy where he

spent five years. In 1755 Chambers returned to England and set up practice. He was successful almost from the start of his career, progressing steadily from honour to honour. He became tutor to the Prince of Wales who, later, as George III, in appreciation made him architect to the King. He became Comptroller in 1769, was knighted in 1770 and was appointed Surveyor-General in 1782.

One of Chambers' early commissions was to lay out the *Gardens* at *Kew* and to ornament them with pavilions and temples in classical and oriental manner. Between 1757 and 1763 he did this, designing the Pagoda (411), the classical Orangery, some temples and alcoves. All his life Chambers was a staunch adherent to the Palladian tradition and continued to design, in strictly Roman classical form, work of the highest standard and finest proportions. It is a mark of the age that even Chambers should pay deference to the prevailing mood which demanded a touch of Romanticism in various forms, whether Chinese, Gothic, Indian or Greek; his pagoda was an instance of this.

In 1759 Chambers published his first edition of *A Treatise on Civil Architecture*. He compiled the work from many of his own first-hand studies in addition to works by Italian architects such as Bernini, Peruzzi, Palladio, Vignola and Scamozzi. The work includes whole designs and a wealth of detail on classical forms in doorways, window openings, ceilings and chimney-pieces.

Chambers was a proud, sensitive, reserved and humourless man. He was ambitious and convinced that his views on classical architecture were the correct interpretation for English architects. He resisted all incursion into the Greek form of classicism and rigidly adhered to the pure Roman Palladian form. His detail, ornament and proportions were meticulously correct; his work was sincere, intellectual and of cold, though superbly high quality. His houses, in particular, illustrate his Palladian viewpoint. Among his town houses there exists *Albany, Piccadilly*, formerly Melbourne House, 1771–3 (405, 406), also the two examples in *St Andrew's Square* in *Edinburgh*, one of which now belongs to the Royal Bank of Scotland, 1772 (410). His country house style can be seen at *Peper Harow* in Surrey, 1765–75, where the house, set in beautiful grounds, is now a school. It is a simple three-storeyed design with slightly projecting central block (404, 408). In

Scotland, he designed the mansion of *Duddington* in Midlothian in 1763–8; this house also possesses a beautiful staircase.

Chambers was the leading government architect of his day and in this connection was the architect of *Somerset House* in 1778–86. For a number of years a scheme had been discussed to house several government departments together in one building in the centre of London. The site was decided, that of the old riverside palace, which was demolished, giving a new site with a magnificent south front facing the river of 800 feet in length and a much narrower north elevation facing the Strand of about 135 feet, roughly in the centre of the long façade. This presents a two-storey elevation to the Strand with rusticated arches on the lower stage and the Corinthian Order in column form above. The entrance is placed centrally, comprising three round-arched openings. A balustraded parapet surmounts the cornice (407, 409).

The entrance leads into a central court which has a Corinthian pavilion in the middle of each of three façades. In the central façade, opposite to the main entrance, is a principal feature which also forms the focal centre for the river front; it is surmounted by a pediment and dome.

Somerset House is one of London's finest waterfront monuments, but it presented a number of problems which Chambers solved satisfactorily. One major difficulty of design was the site itself, being of such unusual shape, with one long façade and one short. Also, the river elevation would be lapped by the water as there was then no embankment. Chambers dealt with this difficulty by building a masonry platform above tide level, on which was constructed a basement storey for warehouses and offices. This was then fronted by a rusticated masonry arcade pierced by arches. The façade was divided into three blocks with a central archway and two side watergates so that the tide was controlled by the water's entry into these archways. At that time the building must have had a much more impressive appearance, as contemporary drawings show; now, much of the height has been lost to the modern roadway and embankment.

The river façade has a certain monotony (especially since the addition of the wings in the nineteenth century) and the dome in the central court, while satisfactory when viewed from the court or from the Strand, is inadequate when seen from the riverside.

The building is finely constructed in Portland stone, beautifully finished and with ornament and decoration of high quality. It is an excellent and typical example of Chambers' work.

Palladian and Neo-Classical Architects

In Palladian design, *Sir Robert Taylor* (1714–88) and *James Paine* (1716–89) continued their work in this tradition. Much of Sir Robert's time after 1760 was spent on designs for the *Bank of England*,* for whom he was chief architect. Apart from this, he is noted for his smaller houses: *Ely House*, Dover Street in *London* (1772) and *Asgill House, Richmond*. His chief large country house was *Heveningham Hall* in Suffolk. The north front (412) shows a traditionally Palladian treatment, with its large central block and two side pavilions connected by lower ranges. A giant Corinthian Order spans the two upper storeys, while below the projecting sections are rusticated. The complete elevation is monumental and extensive, handled in faultless Palladian proportion. In 1780 Sir Robert Taylor was responsible for the design of the bridge at *Maidenhead* in Surrey. It is a long stone bridge with balustraded parapet, mellowed attractively in its Thames-side setting.

Like Taylor, *James Paine* was a Palladian in the Burlington tradition. After Nostell Priory (page 159), he designed *Thorndon Hall*, Essex (1763–9) and *Wardour* in Wiltshire (1770–6). Towards the end of his life, while High Sheriff for Surrey, Paine designed a number of *Thames bridges*: those at Richmond, Chertsey, Walton and Kew. The first two of these have survived and that at *Richmond* is especially fine. It was built in 1780–3 of Portland stone and has five arches (435).

Although considered a provincial architect, for most of his extensive practice was carried on in the north of England, the work of *John Carr of York* was in no way inferior to that of the London architects of this group. He began his career as a mason but entered architectural practice soon after 1750. Like Taylor and Paine he was a Palladian architect and had worked under Lord Burlington for some time. Much of his work is in the domestic field of country houses. He designed *Harewood House* in Yorkshire (1760) and built the north front before Adam took over; he built

---

* Little of this work has survived.

412　*Heveningham Hall, Suffolk, north front,*
1778, Sir Robert Taylor

413　*Denton Hall, Yorkshire, 1770–80, John Carr*
of York

414　*Fairfax House, York, 1770, John Carr of*
York

415　*The Assize Courts, York, 1777, John Carr*
of York

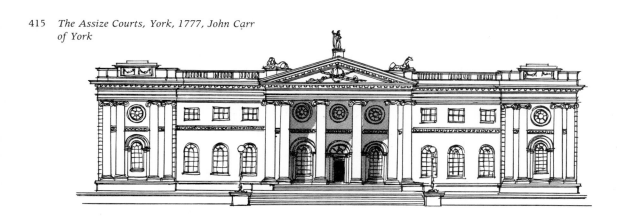

the east front of *Wentworth Woodhouse* in the same county (1770) and *Lytham Hall* in Lancashire (1751–64). Among his smaller houses are *Denton Hall*, Yorkshire 1770–80 (413) and, in *York*, his own house *Fairfax House* 1770 (414). Also in York is his *Assize Courts* 1776–7 (415). Among his churches is *Horbury Church*, Yorkshire (1791), which has a tall, classical steeple, and Ionic lateral porch. Carr's work was always well-proportioned in sound classical tradition and he performed a great service in building so much architecture of high standard in northern cities.

George Dance II (1741–1825) was one of a younger group of architects. Son of George Dance the Elder (page 159), he succeeded his father as Clerk of the City Works in London. He was an original architect following closely neither of the main classical factions of his day, but designing according to the individual commission in hand. Much of his work has been lost, especially in London. The two chief examples were the Church of *All Hallows*, London Wall, which was badly damaged in 1940–1 and *Newgate Prison* which he designed in 1769. This building was one of the most original of the eighteenth century. Built over the years 1770–82, it was an impressive structure with dramatic though austere and even grim qualities. The main composition consisted of unbroken, windowless walls, entirely rusticated; this gave an awesome appearance to the place. In the centre was the keeper's house with entrance lodges on either side. The windows here gave contrast to the enormous area of wall between. The prison was burnt by the Gordon rioters in 1780, later rebuilt but finally demolished in 1902 to make way for the Central Criminal Courts.

In *Scotland* the Palladian, and later the neo-classical, line was being followed, as in England, but still with the incorporation of vernacular features; *Culloden House*, Inverness-shire, c.1788 is typical. The neo-classical approach is to be seen in *James Playfair's Cairness House* in Aberdeenshire, built from 1791. Father of W. H. Playfair of Edinburgh's New Town (chapter 10), James Playfair was noted, as in this instance, for his bold eclecticism in classical elements combined with Egyptian forms.

Robert Adam 1728–1792

Although the work of Robert Adam is two centuries old, it has taken the greater part of this time for a balanced assessment of it to evolve. The fluctuations of critical opinion have been extreme and long lasting. For much of the nineteenth century his name was reviled or ignored. He was mistakenly believed to have based his ideas only upon his studies of the Palace of the Emperor Diocletian at Split. He was also erroneously credited with the inferior work of his host of imitators. In a violent reversal of taste, the *fin de siècle* re-discovered him. Everything was then by Adam, all the work of his contemporaries and successors. In the 1920s he was thought to be a firm of decorators referred to as 'Adams' and there was confusion; was there one Adam or several?

Today the name of Adam is a household word. Everyone interested in the arts, interior decoration and furnishing has heard of him. The public are not so clear about what he did. He is thought to have designed thousands of fireplaces, painted ceilings, made furniture, fire irons and door knobs. How has the reputation of one of Britain's greatest architects become inextricably associated with door knobs and fireplaces?

It is a tribute to Adam's popularity and importance that his services were sought by the richest and most influential people in the land. Such families have so far, in the main, survived the vicissitudes of world wars and penal taxation in death duties and Adam rooms are still in their possession. Since most of the houses are now open to the public we can see for ourselves what his contribution to architecture and decoration was. It is a sobering thought that he decorated all these great houses – some 37 of them – not including the ones which have been demolished – in only 30 years. His tremendous capacity for concentrated work was equalled only by his almost invariably high level of artistry.

Adam began practice in London in 1759 and from then onwards he poured out a tremendous number of very personal designs. He was an eclectic, using many classical sources, fusing them into a quality entirely Adam. His concept of 'movement' came from the Baroque features of Borromini and Bernini. He absorbed Kent's, Gibbs', Vanbrugh's plastic massing of blocks and columns. His early ceiling designs, especially, were rococo. From the beginning, even before he set out on his Grand Tour, he knew himself to be (as he was) an innovator not a copyist. His sense of the romantic, his feeling for elegance were instinctive. They led him to gauge unerringly what the aristocratic owners of houses in Britain would want in the 1760s and he used this personal intuition to combine the architectural themes with motifs from his own archaeological studies in Italy and Dalmatia. He added to these the experience of other men, favouring especially Wood's drawings of Palmyra.

Robert Adam was born at Kirkaldy in Fifeshire on 3 July 1728, the second son of William and Mary Adam. He spent his early childhood in this coastal town on the Firth of Forth then, when he was 11, the family moved to Edinburgh, where William Adam established his architectural practice (Chapter 8). In a family of 10 children there were four Adam brothers, all of whom followed their father into the practice of architecture. The eldest, John, remained all his life in Edinburgh, working first for his father, then competently taking over the practice on the latter's death in 1748.

William Adam sent his sons to the local high school in Edinburgh and Robert and James to university there. Robert attended from 1743, when he was 15, but his studies were interrupted by the '45 rebellion, after which he was ill and never returned to the university nor graduated. He began work with his father's firm and, between 1750 and 1754, carried out architectural commissions in Scotland with John and James. It is interesting to see the work which the brothers achieved in completing the interiors at *Hopetoun House*, which William had been working upon; also in building *Dumfries House* in Ayrshire (1754). The exterior here is straightforwardly Paladian, but inside, as in the red and yellow drawing rooms at Hopetoun House, the décor is already, despite the inexperience of the young architects, beginning to display the breakaway from Palladianism towards a lighter, rococo touch.

In 1754 Robert Adam set off on his Grand Tour with Lord Hopetoun's younger brother, the Hon. Charles Hope. Adam was away for over three years in France and Italy*. He carried out an energetic programme of work, never wasting time and knowing that this was his one great opportunity to amass the knowledge in notes and drawings to carry out his lifetime's career.

---

* For students who are interested to read a first-hand account of Adam's life in France and Italy, H.M. General Register House in Edinburgh is custodian to the letters which Robert Adam wrote home to his family between 1754 and 1758 (about one letter per week) and which belong to Sir John Clerk of Penicuik. The letters may be consulted in the Register House or photostat copies ordered from there.

This first-hand experience added to his outstanding abilities enabled him to create the 'Adam style'.

Robert Adam returned to Britain in 1758, set up practice in London and, within an incredibly short space of time, became the fashionable architect of the day. By 1762–3 his services were in great demand and in the 1760s he produced his finest work.

Partly due to his success and partly to his temperament, which was self-confident, sometimes impatient, always wanting to tackle something new and on the grand scale, the 1770s were less fortunate for him. His phenomenal success had encouraged many imitators, none of whom possessed his fertility of imagination or quality of originality. Submerged under quantities of work, he experimented with mass-production schemes, which lowered his standards, particularly in stucco ornamentation. Financial problems arose from his impatience to get on with the work, allied to inadequate business judgement, as at the Adelphi. This, combined with what was taken to be his patronising attitude in his preface to the *Works in Architecture* of 1773, acquired for him enemies as well as envious colleagues. The last decade of his life saw him designing more and larger commissioned projects, many of them doomed to sterility as they foundered upon financial inadequacy or bureaucratic opposition.

Adam's great ambitions were to create a new, personal style, which he did, and to complete at least one great public building scheme. In this last respect he suffered as Inigo Jones had done (page 108). He evolved scheme after scheme, all manifesting careful thought, professional presentation and a high standard of individual solution. In the 1780s, little of this was carried out and he died at 63 while engaged on a number of such problems.

Visiting Syon House, Osterley, Kenwood or Kedleston one can see different interpretations of classical design. Adam was always searching for something new and suitable for a given commission and environment. Like Sir Christopher Wren, he found new solutions to differing problems but, also like Wren (page 120), his work, though variable, is instantly recognisable as his own. He created a new form of classical design, of world-wide influence, especially in the U.S.A., France and Russia, but particularly suitable for British houses; as British as Capability Brown's landscaped parks.

He was convinced by his research in Italy, as was

416 *Sculptural panel, Admiralty Screen, Whitehall, 1760*

417 *Porch, Chandos House, London, c.1770*

419 *Ground Plan, St James's Square house*

418 *No. 20, St James's Square, London, c.1775*

420 *Fitzroy Square, London, from 1790*

Piranesi, that the Romans had never abided by rigid rules such as those which the Palladians followed,* but had adapted their classical orders to need and scale. Adam did this too. He would take an order, re-create its proportions and decoration, alter the accepted rulings and the result would have more of the essence of the source material than anything seen in Britain in the first half of the eighteenth century.

It is widely known that Adam designed everything in a house down to the smallest detail in order to achieve homogeneity, so much so that we tend to remember the detail rather than the whole. His interiors varied from delicate stucco arabesque-covered walls and ceilings to the Roman grandeur of the columned hall at Kedleston or the palatial richness of the ante-room at Syon. He included colour in a number of his designs; many of these can be studied in the Soane Museum and they show a grading of light ground colours with, often, white stucco ornamentation. Gilt is used sparingly.

What Adam admired most in building was movement. He achieved his interpretation of this by light-ness: an ethereal quality, especially in his interiors. The fact that there are fewer exteriors by him was because he was so often asked to alter, enlarge or redecorate an existing building. At Bowood, the Admiralty Screen, Fitzroy Square and in Edinburgh he showed himself equally an exterior architect.

To sum up Adam's work in a phrase or with a label is not easy; the most appropriate is probably 'romantic classicism'.

One of Adam's first patrons was Admiral Boscawen, who in 1759 commissioned him to design the stone screen to front the *Admiralty Building* in *Whitehall*; also to redecorate the principal apartments in his own house at *Hatchlands* in Surrey. In these early works Adam did not play safe by designing in the traditional manner. He took this first opportunity to carry out his own ideas; a similar marine element of decoration appears in both commissions (416, 423). The decoration at Hatchlands is immature in comparison with the great interiors of the 1760s, the stucco is still in fairly high relief and the motifs large scale, but the Adam treatment is already recognisable. *Shardeloes*, Buck-inghamshire (1758–63) illustrates the next phase,

still using high-quality materials and craftsmanship, but in more delicate vein.

Adam's work can be neatly categorised into three decades, each showing a change of mood and approach. The *1760s* were the years of his greatest success and of his best quality work. This was the decade of the great country houses, of which Syon and Kedleston are the masterpieces; only slightly less superb are Harewood, Osterley and Kenwood; while there is a great deal of fine work surviving at Bowood, Compton Verney, Croome, Mersham-le-Hatch, Newby and Nostell.

Adam drew on many sources for the designs in these houses, believing that the mode should be suited to the commission, which is why his work appears to be varied. For his palatial style he drew on the grandeur of Imperial Rome found in thermal baths and triumphal arches and the late Roman work which he had studied at Diocletian's palace in Split. For more intimate apartments he adapted the delicate stucco and fresco wall decoration he had seen at Herculaneum and which his brother James later recorded at Pompeii. He also used the purity of Greek ornament and orders, Byzantine richness of colouring and, in his exteriors, his feeling of movement from Italian Baroque.

At *Syon House*, Middlesex, there is great variety in the five state apartments which he designed *en suite* round the square courtyard of the former Medieval religious house, but the palatial theme is uppermost (426). The *great hall* is cool Roman grandeur, all in cream, white and black. It is modelled on a Roman basilica, with apses at both ends; one is coffered, the other screened and containing the steps up to the ante-room, made necessary by the differing floor levels. The Roman Doric Order (Adam's favourite for entrance halls) is used.

In each of the five rooms Adam needed to appear to change the actual dimensions since they were quite unsuited to be eighteenth-century aristocratic apart-ments. In the hall he reduced its apparent length by the apses and the height by the richly decorated, deeply beamed ceiling. The adjoining *ante-room* he adapted to appear a cube by his disposition of the columns outlining a square floor area and by their advanced entablatures with gilded, life-size antique figures above. The eye is so absorbed by the riot of colour in this room, the gold and white of the ceiling,

---

* Palladianism stemmed from Vitruvius who lived in the first century. The Roman Empire lasted until the fifth century and the style developed greatly in these years.

421   East portico, Osterley House,
      Middlesex, from 1761

422   Sculptural detail, fireplace,
      20, St James's Square, London,
      c.1775

424   Doorway, red drawing room,
      Syon House, Middlesex, from
      1762

423   Drawing room ceiling detail,
      Hatchlands, Surrey, 1759–62

425   *Ceiling detail, gallery, Harewood House, Yorkshire, 1759–71*

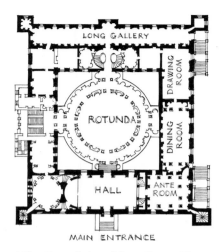

426   *Ground plan of Syon House. The rotunda and other parts (left white) not built*

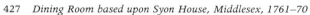

427   *Dining Room based upon Syon House, Middlesex, 1761–70*

the brilliant scagliola floor,* the gilding and the *verde antico* marble of the columns that it does not notice that the room is actually 36 × 30 feet and only 21 feet high.

A further illusion was created by Adam in the gallery. This Jacobean long gallery, 136 feet long by 14 feet wide and 14 feet high, was an absurd shape for a Georgian apartment. It could not be altered so Adam equipped it as a library but decorated it for use in its original capacity, for entertainment, chat and gaiety. His ceiling design of circles, octagons and squares makes the apartment appear wider and shorter. The wall articulation, treated classically in the Corinthian Order throughout, also seems to shorten the excessive length. The whole apartment is decorated in very low relief.

The other two great rooms at Syon, the gold and white *dining room* (427) and the richly red *drawing room* (424) are both superb Adam interiors.

At *Kedleston*, Derbyshire, the house had been designed and partly built by *James Paine*, who had completed the north entrance front. The plan of this Palladian house was a central rectangular block with four pavilions connected to it by curved arms (429). On the north façade Paine had built the house largely according to plan, with a heavy Corinthian portico above a rusticated basement. Adam was called in to design the south front and decorate the apartments.

Here, he pursued his theme of 'architectural movement'. The single block again has a rusticated basement, but with curving stairways to the entrance on the piano nobile. The central feature is a triumphal arch, modelled on that of Constantine in Rome, and the low dome of the saloon rises unobtrusively behind it (431). The design can only be seen in truncated form† for Adam had planned curving colonnades to corner pavilions, balancing those on the north side. His idea was to obtain his 'movement' by the Baroque

theme of convexity moving into concavity, here based upon St Peter's in Rome.

There are many fine state rooms at Kedleston, the *library*, the great *drawing room, dining room, music room* and *state bedroom*, all Adam interiors of high quality. What are remarkable though, and quite unique, are the vast Roman hall and the circular saloon. The *great hall*, on the *piano nobile*, is designed on the lines of a Roman atrium, dedicated to honouring the ancestors of the house and decorated with their statues, arms and trophies. It is an enormous apartment, lit solely from above, like the Pantheon in Rome; there are three elliptical oculi in the ceiling. The 16 vast monolithic columns and four half-columns are of local alabaster, which is cream with reddish-brown markings. Their Corthinthian capitals are in white marble and support a white entablature with dark green frieze. There are two magnificent wall fireplaces in the hall, each of white marble with, above, stucco relief sculptural decoration framing a circular painting. The grate, fire-irons and fender, in burnished brass and steel, are of Adam's finest quality.

The circular *saloon*, leading out of the hall, is 42 feet in diameter and 55 feet high. It is beautifully proportioned and decorated, from the octagonal coffering of the dome to the walls, doorways and paintings. The cast-iron stoves are, in particular, exquisitely ornamented; they are part of Adam's hot-air heating system.

Harewood House in Yorkshire also displays the Adam grand manner. The house was largely built by *John Carr* of York and Adam's exterior work on the south front was altered by Barry in the nineteenth century. Some fine interiors remain which include the hall, gallery and music room. This is one of Adam's best Doric halls, though quite different from Syon; it is smaller and more warmly treated. The entablature has a striking frieze of ox skulls and the walls are decorated with some beautiful relief panels.

As at Syon, the gallery is long and narrow: 77 × 24 feet and 21 feet high. Again, the cleverly patterned ceiling, comprising octagons, lunettes and circles all ornamented in Adam low relief stucco in motifs of griffins and arabesques with painted and sculptured panels (425), helps to detract from the apparent length of the apartment. The gallery is especially noted for the successful co-operation between Chippendale and Adam. Chippendale made most of the furniture and the three great Venetian windows have curtain boxes

---

* A favourite Adam theme was to repeat or create a similar design in floor covering to that of the ceiling above. At Syon in the ante-room this is in scagliola. At Saltram and Harewood, for example, it is in the form of a carpet woven to Adam's design.

† The high cost of the interior apartments which, at Syon, curtailed the building of Adam's rotunda over the central courtyard, at Kedleston forced the cancellation of the building of the wings and pavilions. Exterior work at Kedleston does, however, include the beautiful three-arched bridge (436).

428   *Dining Room based upon Saltram,*
       Devon, 1768–9

429   *Ground plan of Kedleston Hall*

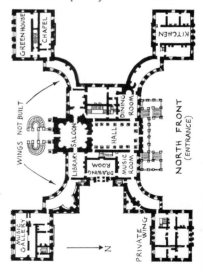

430   *Town House Reception Room,*
       1771–4

431

431 *South front, Kedleston Hall, Derbyshire,*
     1760–8

432 *Door furniture, Saltram*

433 *Apse decoration, the library, Kenwood House,*
     London, 1767–8

434 *Fireplace detail, saloon, Nostell Priory,*
     Yorkshire, from 1766

433

432

434

and valances carved in wood. They are so realistic that they are generally thought to be curtaining. The pier glasses between the windows, with console tables beneath, are superb.

The *music room* is charming and still possesses its original carpet which echoes the ceiling design. It shows a circle within the square room and a central star surrounded by paterae and swags. These circular paterae reflect the Kauffmann medallions in the ceiling. The wall decoration here is classic Adam: rectangular panels of stucco design alternating with Zucchi paintings of Piranesi-type ruins.

Osterley and Kenwood show Adam in more intimate mood. *Osterley Park* is only a few miles from Syon. Here also the architect took over an existing house, this time Elizabethan. His contribution to the outside is the magnificent portico on the east (421), which is thought to owe something to the Temple of the Sun at Palmyra while the detail is like that of the Erechtheion in Athens. The Osterley portico is approached by a grand staircase of 20 steps which raise the open courtyard beyond the colonnade to *piano nobile* level in the house. The whole of the interior of Osterley, except the gallery, was decorated by Adam and there are many apartments arranged round the courtyard. Those of greatest interest are the *hall*, the *drawing room*, the *library*, the *tapestry room* (its walls covered by tapestries), the *Etruscan room* (so-called because it is decorated in Adam's 'Etruscan' manner) and the *state bedroom*. In all the rooms, as well as the fine *staircase*, the decoration of ceilings and walls is elegant and in low relief, the colours are subtle and harmonious and the doorcases, windows and chimneypieces part of the general scheme.

Kenwood House in Hampstead was remodelled in 1767–8. It is the *library* here which is of especial interest; the apartment was designed not only for displaying books but also as a room for entertaining. The rectangular form is shortened by an apse at each end fronted by a screen of Corinthian columns supporting only a bar entablature which does not hide the exquisite decoration of the semi-dome of the apse (433). This apsidal finish to one or both ends of a rectangular room was a favourite Adam device (see Syon dining room, 427), altering proportions as he needed and giving interest and mystery to the apartment. The Kenwood library ceiling is shallowly barrel vaulted and decorated all over with low relief stucco and painted oval and lunette panels. On the exterior,

Adam built the north portico which is derived from that at the Erechtheion, in Athens. The Greek detail is finely designed and carved.

Of the other houses of the 1760s which survive, of especial interest is the Diocletian Wing at *Bowood*, Wiltshire, 1761–71, the saloon at *Nostell Priory*, Yorkshire, 1766 (434), the gallery at *Croome Court*, Worcestershire, *c.*1760 and the hall, staircase, library tapestry room and sculpture gallery at *Newby*, Yorkshire, 1765–83.

Adam produced two widely known publications, the first the result of his studies in Split in 1758 entitled *Ruins of the Palace of the Emperor Diocletian at Spalatro in Dalmatia* (1764) and, in 1773, Volume One of *Works in Architecture of R. and J. Adam*. Both these were quality productions with fine engravings and careful text (451). The second publication was a presentation of the Adam designs and volume one was followed by others.

The decade of the *1770s* was a less harmonious one for Robert Adam. Pressure of work caused him to lower his superbly high standard of craftsmanship; his work became thinner, the decoration so low relief as to be almost spidery; the plastic quality of 'movement' waned. He carried out a great many commissions of which the chief were his town houses, the Adelphi project and country houses at Saltram and Mellerstain.

Adam's *London houses*, of which only a few remain, were planned to give accommodation for lavish entertainment and maximum privacy for the owner behind a narrow façade. Behind this front was a carefully planned suite of rooms of different shapes and sizes integrated with an originally designed staircase and landings. Such town houses are today converted into clubs, business, office and university accommodation. The two outstanding examples are 20, St James's Square and 20, Portman Square.

The house in *St James's Square* was built in 1772–3. Both this and the adjoining no. 21 belong to the Distillers' Company, who have duplicated Adam's façade across both houses, making an impressive front. The lower storey is rusticated, broken by windows and two beautiful doorways. The first and second floor are then spanned by a Corinthian Order in pilaster form, with attics and dormers above (418). The ground floor plan (419) is typical of the Adam town house and has close affiliations with the Pompeian town house.

Both houses suffered great damage in the Second World War, but have now been restored carefully and accurately to Adam's designs in the Soane Museum. There are many beautiful rooms here, typical of his decoration in this decade. The outstanding parts of the house (no. 20) are the *staircase* (443) and *well* and the first floor *withdrawing room* (now the board room). The hall rises to the full height of the house, but the single staircase ascends, as was eighteenth century custom, only to the first floor,* where it ends in a balustrated landing. The well is lit at the top by a decorative oval fanlight. The staircase balustrate has a mahogany handrail and a delicate iron balustrade. In the withdrawing room there is a segmental barrel vaulted ceiling decorated rather as in the Kenwood library. The doorcases, doors and marble mantlepiece are of fine quality (422).

No. 20, Portman Square, now the Courtauld Institute of the University of London, has a plain astylar exterior in brick and a delicate pedimented Doric porch. The interiors are of high quality, especially the *music room* on the first floor. Of unusual design is the *staircase* which is set in a circular well. It ascends from the ground floor in one central flight, then divides at the half-landing into two branches, which sweep round the well to the first landing. The balustrade is similar to that at St James's Square. On the first floor the walls are decorated with gravure paintings in monochrome; above are sculpture-filled niches and doors leading into the rooms. Higher up is an Ionic colonnade extending to a stucco decorated drum and then a low-domed, delicate, circular lantern with graceful ironwork decoration. The staircase well is tall and not extensive but the Adam design makes the utmost of the available area, giving an impression of much greater spaciousness than actually exists.

Chandos House, at the end of Queen Anne Street, was built 1770–4. Its chief feature is the elegant porch (417).

The two interesting country houses of this decade are *Saltram* in Devon and *Mellerstain* in Berwickshire. At Saltram the *saloon* and *dining room* survive; notable here are the original carpets. They reflect closely the respective ceiling designs (428).

The new house at *Mellerstain* had been begun in 1725 by William Adam, who built the two wings.

---

* A secondary staircase continued up to the other floors, generally on the rear side of the house.

These remained separate for 40 years until Robert Adam was asked to complete the work. The house is in fine condition. The *library* is the finest room with an especially beautiful ceiling.

In the *1780s* Adam's enthusiasm and originality returned. The linear, sometimes fussy decoration of the 1770s, together with the low-relief exterior façades disappeared. Adam rediscovered his zeal for architectural plasticity. His exteriors once more displayed movement; they were characterised by the vitality of their monumental designs. Interior schemes were simpler; there was less of the spider's-web tracery of Portman Square and more of the rich interplay of colour and form that had been seen in the 1760s.

This was the decade of the great projects, large schemes which took a great deal of time to work out in detail and many of which were not built. *Cambridge University* was one of these where Adam, like James Gibbs before him (page 147), made designs for completing the great quadrangles at King's College. At *Bath*, a similar story resulted in Pulteney Bridge (page 190), and at *Edinburgh* the New Town worked out so carefully by Adam, was largely built after his death (page 210 in Chapter 10).

For much of the 1780s Adam was a commuter between London and Scotland. He carried out extensive plans and designs for London streets (page 192), but also undertook many commissions in Scotland. In *Edinburgh, H.M. General Register House* was built to designs which he had made in 1772. The Princes Street elevation has only been slightly altered and, inside, the rotunda retains its Adam decoration. He was commissioned to design new buildings for *Edinburgh University* in 1785. His plans here were for a college built round two quadrangles with a monumental entrance and elegant dome above (440). Work was begun in 1789, but only the entrance section was achieved before financial problems and the Napoleonic Wars delayed the project for 20 years. The façade on to South Bridge is much as Adam designed it (441), though the dome is not; this is a typically nineteenth-century version. The rest of the University, completed by W. H. Playfair, was constructed to a much more limited plan differing considerably from Adam's design.

Elsewhere in Scotland Adam's work in the 1780s extended to country houses as far as the Highlands. He built several projects in *Glasgow* and then worked

435   *Richmond Bridge, Surrey, 1774–7, James Paine*

436   *Bridge in the grounds of Kedleston Hall, Derbyshire, 1758–70, Robert Adam*

437   *Pulteney Bridge, Bath, from 1770, Robert Adam*

438   *Ironbridge, Coalbrookdale, Shropshire, over the Severn, 1779. First iron bridge in the world*

439   *Culloden House, Inverness-shire, c.1788*

440   *Adam's design for ground floor of*
      Edinburgh University, 1789

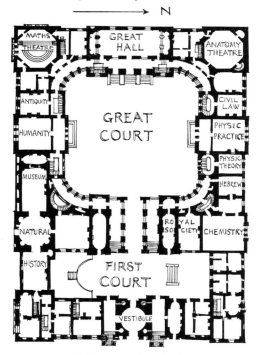

441   *Entrance to Edinburgh University on South Bridge*

on *Yester House* and *Gosford House* in East Lothian and a new house at *Newliston* in West Lothian.

At this time Adam was also designing in a castellar Medieval style related, in a Romantic manner, to the literary Gothic movement combined with the Scottish vernacular theme which had never quite died out. He set a pattern which a number of Scottish architects emulated. The chief example of this type of house is *Culzean Castle* in Ayrshire (1776–92), now the head-quarters of the Scottish National Trust. Here Adam, who was commissioned to enlarge and modernise an existing castle which was of traditional Scottish keep type, designed a boldly massed structure full of 'movement'. Culzean has a magnificent situation, built on the edge of a bluff overlooking the sea which washes the foot of the precipitous basalt cliffs 150 feet below. The architect has produced a fine stately home, romantic Medieval on the exterior and classical Adam within. The outside is dramatic and powerful (442); inside is an unusual layout (445), of which the *circular saloon* and the oval *staircase well* are exceptional. Adam designed the great drum tower on the seaward side of the house as a classic example of 'movement'. He then took advantage of its form to create this unusual circular room. The six tall windows give a breath-taking view of sea and sky with a backcloth of the mountains of the Western Isles. Ceiling and carpet designs are Adam's, not identical but of one theme. The oval stairwell is on Italian Renaissance-villa pattern, with cantilevered stairs and a balustrade curving round the well; the three orders in column and pilaster form are used, one on each floor (444).

Craftsmen of the later eighteenth century

The quality of craftsmanship which decorated the buildings of the second half of the eighteenth century was superb and has never been surpassed in England. The work carried out by painters, stuccoists, metal workers, sculptors, carvers and cabinet-makers was by men who worked with many different architects. Adam employed a number of them and without the high quality of their work he could not have achieved his magnificent interiors. None of them worked solely for Adam; they also decorated apart-ments for Chambers, Taylor, Paine, Wyatt and many other architects. Many of them came from the Continent, some were British.

Of the painters, *Angelica Kauffmann* was the best known and most colourful character. Born in Switzerland, she achieved the unusual honour, for a woman, of becoming a founder member of the Royal Academy. She had wit, charm and gaiety; she married twice, her second husband being *Antonio Zucchi*, also a talented painter. Other painters who carried out a great deal of decorative work included *Giovanni Battista Cipriani*, *Francesco Zuccarelli* and *William Hamilton*.

Some artists worked in several media, for example *Biagio Rebecca* who imitated classical sculptural reliefs as well as painted decoration. *Francesco Bartolozzi* was an expert at reproducing antique designs in engravings. An Italian of great charm, he earned large sums for his superb plates which appeared in many books published by architects. He spent the money as fast as he earned it and consumed vast quantities of alcohol and snuff, yet lived to the ripe old age of 88.

The outstanding stuccoist was *Joseph Rose*, whose superb quality of work can be seen at Syon and Harewood. Among the best sculptors and carvers were *Michael Spang*, *Thomas Carter* and *Joseph Wilton*. The chief craftsman in metal was *Matthew Boulton*; he developed the use of ormolu, widely used by Adam, especially at Syon on chimneypieces and doors.

The name of *Josiah Wedgwood* needs no introduc-tion; Wedgwood pottery is as well-known today as it was in the eighteenth century. Josiah was an energetic visionary, a shrewd businessman and a craftsman dedicated to raising the standard of his product. He aimed at purity of earthenware and made it into a work of art suitable for a queen's table, whereas previously it had been the poor relation of porcelain in the ceramics industry. *John Flaxman*, the sculptor, worked for Wedgwood for many years and modelled the famous classical friezes, medallions and plaques, many of which still ornament Wedgwood jasperware. These plaques were also incorporated in the decor-ation of furniture and chimneypieces in eighteenth-century houses.

Chippendale had set the pattern for the quality designer/cabinet-maker. Adam also designed furni-ture for his interiors and the two men worked together on a number of commissions. *John Linnell* and *William France* also worked in this field, for instance, at Kedleston and Kenwood.

442 *Culzean Castle, Ayrshire, 1771–92*

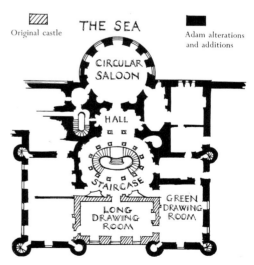

443 *Staircase, 20, St James's Square, London, c.1775*

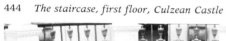

444 *The staircase, first floor, Culzean Castle*

Original castle   THE SEA   Adam alterations and additions

CIRCULAR SALOON

HALL

STAIRCASE

LONG DRAWING ROOM

GREEN DRAWING ROOM

445 *Sketch plan of first floor of Culzean Castle*

448   *The Guildhall, 1775, Thomas Baldwin*

449   *The Pump Room and Colonnade, 1786–99, Baldwin and Palmer*

446 *Pulteney Street with the Holbourne of Menstrie Museum in centre distance, 1785, Thomas Baldwin*

447 *Bath Street, 18th century, Thomas Baldwin*

450 *Lansdown Crescent, 1789–93, John Palmer*

Terrace Architecture and Town Planning

In 1760 it was still *Bath* which led the way in the design and construction of town houses in streets and crescents. Civic planning on a large scale was carried on here for the remainder of the century. The contours posed problems, with the city centre on the low-lying land flanking the Avon and the hills rising, sometimes steeply, around. The architects who designed the new town not only dealt with this problem, they took advantage of it. There were built curving terraces and crescents on the edges of these hill crowns, giving fine vistas of both city and countryside. In Bath the architecture is Palladian, well built in stone, and the conception is on the grand scale.

The work of John Wood (see Chapter 8) was continued by his son, also *John Wood*, who built the most impressive of the hill-side terraces, that of the *Royal Crescent* (1767–75). Here Wood showed himself like his father and John Carr of York, not only a provincial architect, but one whose work ranked with much of the best building created by London architects. The Crescent forms a gigantic arc following the edge of the crown of the hill, high above the city. The Ionic Order is used, with 114 columns fronting 30 houses, which present a uniform façade constructed on a major axis of 538 feet. The elevation is 47 feet high, comprising three storeys. The giant order of engaged three-quarter columns spans the first and second floors, with entablature and parapet above. The whole Crescent, although now partly internally adjusted to provide more up-to-date accommodation, is almost unchanged on the exterior; it remains one of the finest examples of terrace building in Britain.

A number of other superb terraces and crescents survive in Bath, though not quite so extensive in scale. Of special interest are *Lansdown Crescent*, 1789–93, designed by *John Palmer* (450) and *Camden Crescent*, 1788, by *John Jelly*. There is also some high quality civic work in the centre of the city, built over a number of years but of the same stone and a similar architectural style. The *Pump Room* and colonnade of the famous baths was rebuilt in 1786–8 by *Thomas Baldwin* (449), although the interior was completed by John Palmer a little later. Baldwin also designed the *Guildhall* in 1776 (448). It contains a large banqueting hall of 80 by 40 feet with an elaborate stucco patterned ceiling; the Corinthian Order is used in fluted columns standing on pedestals round the room.

Robert Adam was asked by Sir William Johnstone-Pulteney to design a new town as a suburb of Bath at Bathwick on land owned by his wife. Divided from the city by the River Avon, in the 1760s this could only be crossed by a ferry. Adam designed the *Pulteney Bridge*, which he based upon the Ponte Vecchio in Florence, a roadway lined by shops on either side. This delightful bridge survives, somewhat altered (437), but nothing was built of the rest of the scheme, though the existing Pulteney Street (446) was laid out on the site of Adam's chief artery to the suburb.

In the later decades of the century *London* slowly began to follow Bath's example in laying out town houses in streets and squares. The most impressive instance of this, the Adelphi project, is now lost to us. It was a gigantic speculative enterprise undertaken by all four of the Adam brothers in 1768. The idea arose from Robert's ambition to build a great civic scheme. Not being commissioned to do this, the brothers undertook it on their own, and it proved so vast a project that it was unsuitable financially for private means. Despite near tragedy, the brothers extricated themselves by their own acumen, their personal fortune, a public lottery and the help of influential friends. The accommodation which they built was in great demand from the time that it was finished until its demolition in 1937. The buildings were all continuously occupied for nearly two centuries as the houses and offices for which they were designed.

The Adelphi site was an area bordering the north side of the Thames called Durham Yard. There was in 1768 no embankment and where the Victoria Embankment Gardens are now laid out was a pestilential stinking area of mud which was covered at high tide. The Durham Yard site lay behind this, extending from the present Savoy Place to the Strand and from York Buildings to Shell Mex House. The scheme was to embank or drain the Thames edge and build up a Royal Terrace above vaulted arches which would be used as warehouse storage. It was hoped that the government would take over these vaults and it was their failure to do this which caused the financial crisis.

The scheme was carried out fully between 1768 and 1774. It was designed in the form of palace façades to the river, high up to give a magnificent view and to provide houses and offices there of great beauty and amenity, including stabling, water supply, heating,

451   *The Royal Terrace as it was in 1774*

452   *Doorway, No. 7, Adam Street*

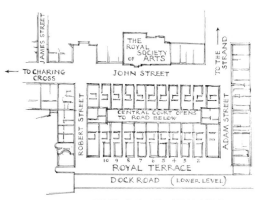

453   *Simplified sketch plan, upper level, 1774*

etc. There were two streets parallel to the Strand and cross streets at the ends (453). This was to be a great Roman palace and the similarity of its theme to the southern colonnaded wall of the Palace of Diocletian in Split was obvious to everyone, even though the architectural style was quite different (451).

The streets were all named after the Adam brothers; the name Adelphi, chosen by them, is derived from the Greek word ἀδελφοι (brothers). The cost was incredible. Architecturally the Adelphi set a pattern for town terrace building for the rest of the century. The Adam style of ornament was applied to the exterior of the building in the form of low relief projection of pilaster and entablature also in ornamental forms of carved and terracotta enrichment.

Almost the whole scheme was demolished in 1937. This act was summed up by Sacheverell Sitwell[*]: 'The Adelphi wilfully and of cupidity was pulled down. Willing hands did more damage to London than a German land-mine'; and by Dr Pevsner[†]: 'In London, the principle of the palace façade for a whole row of houses was introduced by Robert Adam in his Adelphi (that magnificent composition of streets with its Thames front known all over Europe, which was destroyed, not by bombs, but by mercenary land-owners just before the War)'.

The Royal Society of Arts building survives in John Street and the façade of No. 7 Adam Street shows the typical pilaster and ornamental treatment used on the façades of the less important houses (452).

The Adam brothers also undertook two other schemes in *London* of speculative building by streets and squares. In *Portland Place* Robert Adam planned a *Grande Place* on the Continental pattern surrounded by individual palaces, each different and specially designed for a wealthy patron. He interested a number of the wealthy aristocracy, but the American War of Independence, which began in 1775, curtailed the desire for financial speculation and the scheme was shelved. The houses, which were built a decade later, on either side of Portland Place, still a stately thoroughfare, were handled by James Adam. They are monotonous in their repetition and, due to inadequate supervision, they came as near as Adam work ever did to slap-dash standards.

Fitzroy Square was designed by Robert Adam in 1790, but was built after his death. The south and east sides (420) were constructed largely to his designs, which show a bold massing in the central block and terminal pavilions. The interiors have been altered.

---
[*] Sacheverell Sitwell, *British Architects and Craftsmen*, Batsford, 1948.

[†] Nikolaus Pevsner, *An Outline of European Architecture*, Penguin Books, 1961.

CHAPTER TEN

Late Georgian and Regency
1775–1830

The term 'Regency' in Britain is, like that of 'Queen Anne', a misleading one for it is used in the arts and architecture to describe the years from about 1790 to 1830, that is, the intermediate time between the end of Georgian Britain and the beginning of Victorian. The actual Regency – that of the Prince of Wales, later George IV – lasted only from 1811 until 1820, but the term is used here in its architectural sense. This is very much a transitional period between two different social structures. Georgian Britain had an agricultural economy, controlled by a privileged aristocracy; Victorian Britain saw the growth of industrialisation, the rapid spread of towns and the consequent depopulation of the countryside. Architecturally, as well as economically and socially, the Regency is a time of transition and a pause between two divergent ideologies. In Georgian Britain classical architecture was built for the well-to-do patron and displayed superb design and craftsmanship. Victorian Britain saw the establishment of the speculative builder, suburban expansion and the decay of taste. It also witnessed the end of original architecture in the re-emergence and adaptation of every previous style.

Although it had been developing since the mid-eighteenth century, industrialisation did not, before 1830, produce the full impact of the changes inherent in this revolution. The great engineers – Telford, Stephenson, Rennie and Brunel – were building their bridges and aqueducts, but the railway system had yet to come and the condition of the roads, though improving, still hindered easy travel.

In general, in *industrial building* traditional ma-terials and structural methods were still employed. The silk mill in 457 is typical: a brick construction in simplified classical form. Bridges, too, were mainly of the elegant, classic design, little changed, except in their simplicity, from earlier eighteenth-century examples. The stone bridge at *Cambridge* by *Wilkins* (455) and that by *Soane* at *Tyringham* (456) are two beautiful instances of this.

Ironwork, generally wrought iron, had been used as a building material for a long time, but it was only in the late eighteenth and early nineteenth century that architects and engineers began to use it on a large scale. An early instance is the *Ironbridge* at *Coalbrookdale* (438) in Shropshire, over the River Severn. This was the first bridge in the world to be made almost entirely of iron and reflects Britain's position as the earliest industrialised nation. The bridge was built in 1779 and is now scheduled as an ancient monument. It is constructed of five parallel arch ribs almost 200 feet in length. The spandrels are filled by circles and ogee arch heads while the roadway above is made from cast iron plates of two and a half inch thickness. The bridge, which took only three months to build, weighs 400 tons.

In the early nineteenth century many bridges were made of iron as the development of cast iron proceeded apace. They became less traditional in design and were adapted to the characteristics of the newer material. An early instance is the remarkable structure of the *Pont-Cysylltau aqueduct* in the Vale of Llangollen. Built by Telford in 1805, it has an iron superstructure carried on stone piers, spanning over 1000 feet of countryside (454).

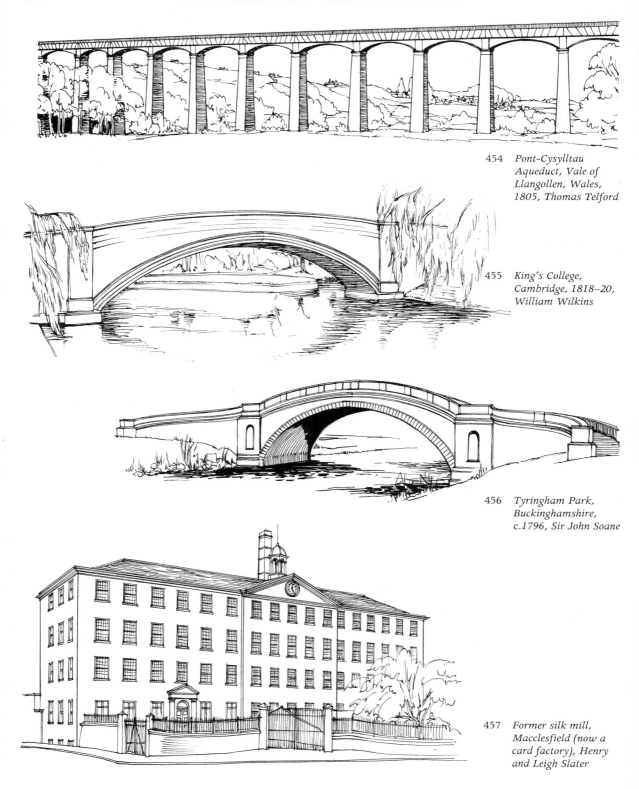

454   Pont-Cysylltau
Aqueduct, Vale of
Llangollen, Wales,
1805, Thomas Telford

455   King's College,
Cambridge, 1818–20,
William Wilkins

456   Tyringham Park,
Buckinghamshire,
c.1796, Sir John Soane

457   Former silk mill,
Macclesfield (now a
card factory), Henry
and Leigh Slater

Iron was being used more and more extensively in all kinds of building, both decoratively and structurally, though up to 1830 this was mainly as decoration in canopied balconies, railings and staircase balustrades. It was a prime characteristic in Regency terrace building in particular, and superb examples of the craft survive in many parts of the country, in London, Brighton and Hove, Bristol, Cheltenham and Edinburgh (462, 466, 478, 487–92, 494, 496, 503, 507).

Late Georgian Building

In the 1770s and 1780s there were a number of architects designing in neo-classical form in a similarly elegant and eclectic manner to Robert Adam. Some of these were copyists and adapters of the Adam style, but Holland, Leverton and Wyatt were quality architects in their own right.

Henry Holland (1745–1806) designed entirely in classical style; his work was meticulous in its interpretation and detail and he preferred, in general, the simpler, subtle Greek forms to the more ornate and heavy Roman. Unfortunately most of his work has been lost, in particular his Carlton House in London and Pavilion at Brighton, both of which were commissioned for the Prince of Wales and were redesigned later by Nash. In common with other eighteenth-century architects, Holland undertook speculative building in London where he developed an area of land in *Chelsea* and laid it out in an estate which he called *Hans Town*. This comprised the streets known today as Sloane Street, Hans Place and Cadogan Place.

In 1771 Holland went into partnership with Lancelot (Capability) Brown and built a number of country houses for which Brown laid out the grounds. One of the best of Holland's surviving houses is *Southill* in Bedfordshire, which he built for Samuel Whitbread. It is typical of his work, tasteful and restrained, exquisite in detail and excellently planned. Colonnades of coupled Ionic columns connect the centre block to the two wings, all of which are pedimented, and the Ionic Order is repeated on the south façade of the main block (458).

Thomas Leverton (1743–1824) was a less original architect and patterned his work closely upon Adam and Wyatt. This has a delicate, tasteful quality which can be seen in his town houses and terraces in *London*. Here he created some beautiful interiors in romantic classical manner, with fine stucco decoration and elegant staircases with iron balustrades. Typical are several houses in *Bedford Square* (461) where No. 1, in particular, has a beautiful staircase and domed entrance hall. Of his country houses, *Woodhall Park* in Hertfordshire (1778–82) survives. An interesting feature here was the 'Etruscan' style entrance hall, with fluted ceiling and white walls decorated with painted medallions in red, yellow and red-brown. The curving staircase had a delicate, iron balustrade (462). The stairwell was stuccoed in decorative panels in the Adam manner while the domed ceiling was fluted in a fan design.

James Wyatt 1746–1813

A member of a large family of builders and architects, James was the most gifted and best known. A man of unusual talents, he experimented with all possible styles of architecture and excelled at a number of them; he is considered by some critics to be a mere copyist and by others a brilliant originator. Early in his career Wyatt was hailed as a genius. At this time Robert Adam was at the height of his fame and Wyatt began to design in the Adam manner. Infuriated, Adam complained in his *Works of Architecture* of plagiarism. Wyatt had spent some years in Italy where he had made measured drawings of St Peter's and the Pantheon. He returned to England to win the competition for the rebuilding of the *Pantheon* in Oxford Street in *London*. Designed for concerts and masquerades, it was a large, aisled hall under a giant cupola. It had a hemispherical dome like its prototype in Rome, but the decoration reflected that of Adam. The building* created a sensation when it was opened in 1772. It was a great success architecturally and functionally and established Wyatt's reputation. Aristocratic patronage began to flow in his direction.

Wyatt went on to design a number of country houses in the Adam manner and in Greek Revival form. At *Heveningham Hall* he continued the work of Sir Robert Taylor (page 171) and redecorated the interior, which possesses some fine, delicate craftsmanship (466, 467). His beautiful Orangery here has an elegant semi-circular portico (465). Heveningham is mainly in the Adam manner; in a more Greek vein

---

* The Pantheon was burnt down in 1792. It was roughly on the site now occupied by Marks and Spencer's Stores.

458 *Southill, Bedfordshire, 1796–1803, Henry Holland*

459 *Boodle's Club, London, 1780, John Crunden*

460 *St Pancras' Church, London, 1819–22, W. and H. W. Inwood*

461 *Bedford Square, London, 1774, Thomas Leverton*

462 *Woodhall Park, Hertfordshire, 1778–82, Thomas Leverton*

463 *The Radcliffe Observatory, Oxford, designed by Henry Keene, 1772, completed James Wyatt*

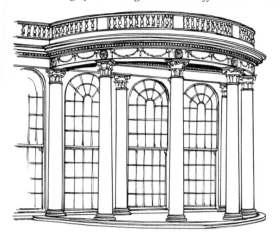

464   *Fonthill Abbey, Wiltshire, 1795–1807*

465   *The Orangery, Heveningham Hall, Suffolk, 1790–1800*

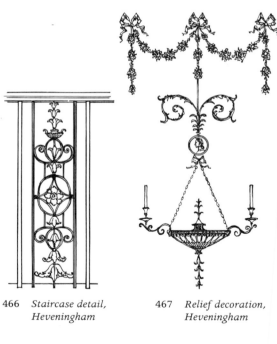

466   *Staircase detail,*
       Heveningham

467   *Relief decoration,*
       Heveningham

468   *The hall, Dodington Park,*
       Gloucestershire, 1798–1808

Wyatt built the *Radcliffe Observatory* at *Oxford*, originally designed by Henry Keene and based upon the Tower of the Winds in Athens (463).

In the early nineteenth century Wyatt turned to both Greek classicism and Romantic literary Gothic. *Dodington Park*, Gloucestershire, is a dignified Greek classical house with a large Corinthian portico and, inside, a great hall (using the Composite Order) and an imposing double staircase (468). The detail work here in ceilings, friezes and doorcases is of high standard in the best Wyatt tradition. He also designed the church at Dodington on Greek cross plan.

Wyatt built a number of Gothic houses which, like Strawberry Hill (page 170), were picturesque and Medievally romantic. *Ashridge Park*, Hertfordshire, the best known of the survivors, has a central hall taking up the whole height of the tower. The most spectacular essay into Gothic must have been *Fonthill Abbey*, Wiltshire, which he designed for the wealthy William Beckford in 1795. This immense house (464) was cruciform in plan and over 300 feet along. The tower, constructed over the crossing, ecclesiastical fashion, rose to 270 feet and, inside, the great hall was 80 feet high. At one end of this a flight of steps ascended to a saloon built under the tower. The Gothic detail (as at Strawberry Hill) was authentic. Mr Beckford was so anxious for the house to be completed that he ordered work to be carried out in shifts round the clock. Due to inadequate supervision, specified support arches to the tower were not built and some years later it collapsed in a gale and the house was afterwards demolished.

Regency Building

From the 1790s onwards the regurgitation of previous architectural styles really begins. But in the years before 1830 this is a light-hearted, still romantic affair; new sources of inspiration are tried out, tossed around and abandoned in favour of something else. It has nothing of the seriousness of Victorian eclecticism. Regency architects experimented with these architectural forms in order to create something of their own and in no case was the Regency version a close copy of the original; it was an idea, a conception to be played with. Because of this the resulting Regency architecture is interesting in its own right, suited to its time and, to us, attractive to look at and functional to use. The sources of material employed

at the time were classical, based on Greece and Rome; Gothic, still of a Romantic type, but becoming more Medieval in spirit; Italian Renaissance and Baroque and Oriental, primarily Indian.

In the years 1790–1820 there were two outstanding architects whose work dominated the time as, a generation earlier, the scene had been dominated by Chambers and Adam. Similarly, these later architects, Soane and Nash, were as great a contrast to one another in both architecture and personality as their predecessors had been.

Sir John Soane 1753–1837

Soane was the son of a bricklayer, born near Reading. He determined early in life to become an architect and this dedication to and love of architecture stayed with him strongly all his 84 years. He was articled to George Dance, then to Henry Holland. He won both gold and silver medals at the Royal Academy Schools and went to Italy on the Travelling Scholarship from 1778–80, where he studied in Rome, Paestum, Pompeii and Sicily.

Soane was the last of the line of completely original architects, which had begun with Inigo Jones. He used many styles for inspiration, mainly neo-classical, generally Greek, but he also took structural ideas and decorative treatment from Byzantine sources. Like Wren and Adam before him, he fused these sources into an architectural style which was personally Soane and characteristically English. In his later work, the austere simplicity of his barely ornamented masses foreshadow modern architecture, but for over 100 years no designer in England took up his lead.

In 1788 Sir Robert Taylor died and Soane was appointed to succeed him as Surveyor to the *Bank of England*. He held this post until 1833, during which time he carried out extensive schemes in London. At the Bank he developed his personal style. The work was monumental, stripped of all superfluous ornament, partly Greek, partly Byzantine, relying on simple, pure lines and fine proportion. Soane was never content with less than perfection; he paid meticulous care to detail as well as design.

His exterior work to the Bank of England was in the *screen wall* with which he surrounded the awkwardly triangular site. The wall had to be secure from attack and so was windowless. Soane avoided monotony, using a stylised Corinthian Order articula-

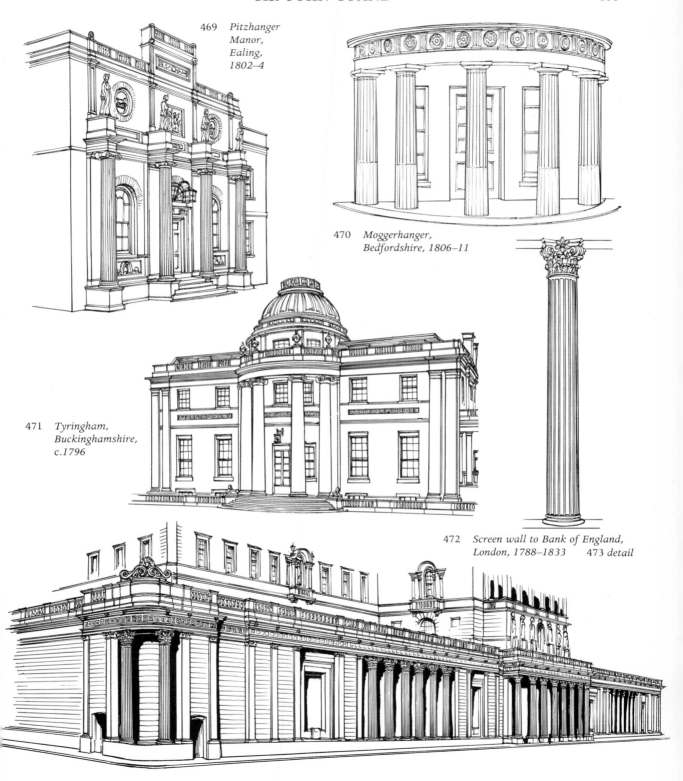

469 *Pitzhanger Manor, Ealing, 1802–4*

470 *Moggerhanger, Bedfordshire, 1806–11*

471 *Tyringham, Buckinghamshire, c.1796*

472 *Screen wall to Bank of England, London, 1788–1833* 473 *detail*

tion in the form of the Temple of Vesta at Tivoli. Even today, when the balance and proportion of the screen wall has been ruined by the vast twentieth-century superstructure, Soane's design has dignity and interest (472, 473).

His greatest originality at the Bank was in the interior halls which he lit from above with glass domes and lunettes, supporting these on austere arches and vaults, their mouldings and ornament reduced to a minimum.

It was no doubt at Paestum and Sicily that Soane began to appreciate the beauty of the monumental, archaic Doric Order. These same, sturdy, fluted columns without base, supporting a heavy abacus and entablature, which had horrified both Adam and Chambers had an austere power which appealed to Soane. He used this on the house at *Moggerhanger* in Bedfordshire (470) in 1806. At *Tyringham* in Buckinghamshire, he preferred a lofty Ionic portico leading the eye upwards to the simple cupola (455, 471).

Of greater originality were Soane's own two houses, the town house at *13, Lincoln's Inn Fields* in *London*, built 1812–14 and now the Soane Museum, and *Pitzhanger Manor, Ealing, c.*1802, his country house, now the public library (469). The former is handled in low relief with typical Soane incised decoration, while the latter is fronted by four Ionic columns with their own entablatures and pedestals. Both houses are ornamented by Soane's favourite draped figures based upon the caryatids from the Erechtheion south porch. The severe *Art Gallery and Mausoleum* at *Dulwich** (1811–14) owes little to classical architecture or, indeed, any earlier style. It is original Soane in brick with austere lines and simple masses. Apart from a rare note of detail here could be a modern building of the inter-war years.

John Nash 1752–1835

An exact contemporary of Soane, Nash was a contrast to him in every way. He was not austere or restrained but an enthusiastic extrovert. Whereas Soane's architecture was personally original, Nash's was not. Like Wyatt, Nash was a man of his age; he designed in all styles of the picturesque and romantic. He dabbled in Gothic, the Italian Renaissance, Palladian

and Greek; he built rustic-cottage country houses, castellated mansions and picturesque villas.

He was also attracted by the possibilities of Indian design and took the opportunity to experiment with his ideas when he was commissioned by the Prince Regent to build the Pavilion at *Brighton*. The royal pavilion here was originally designed by *William Porden* and built 1803–5. This had an Indian flavour, clearly influenced by *Sezincote*, designed a few years earlier for Sir Charles Cockerell who insisted on this style. Porden's building later became the *Dome Concert Hall* and Nash designed the present, colourful *Royal Pavilion*. He began the work in 1816, and, though originally planned to be in Indian style, Nash mixed his sources of design and the building might more accurately be described as 'Indian Gothic' with a flavour of Chinese, especially in the interiors (486).

John Nash's contribution to architecture lies not in his eclectic experimentation nor in the originality of his classical, design but in his brilliance as a town planner. His extensive Regent's Park terraces, the old Regent Street and Carlton House Terrace represent a far-reaching achievement in town planning, of modern dimensions carried out in a picturesque version of eighteenth-century classicism. Here was the logical continuance of the work and schemes of men like John Wood.

Nash was given a unique opportunity in 1811 to design and carry out this extensive London scheme. This was made possible by the availability of the land at the same time as a period of prosperity and energetic support from royal patronage. With this combination of circumstances Nash was enabled, between the ages of 60 and 80, to build a considerable proportion of his great scheme. The layout comprised a large area covering Regent's Park, St James's Park, Regent Street and Trafalgar Square.

In 1811 Marylebone Park property reverted to the Crown. It consisted of farmland which it was intended to develop and the Prince Regent enthusiastically backed the idea of a lavish scheme to enhance his capital. Both Nash and Leverton were asked to design a plan. Leverton's was not very original and consisted of an extension of the eighteenth-century conception of domestic squares. Nash's ideas were far more extensive and revolutionary. He set out a whole garden city for the well-to-do in the centre of the metropolis. The scheme included a park with graceful villas, a lake, a canal, crescents and terraces and focal

---

* Now rebuilt after war-time destruction.

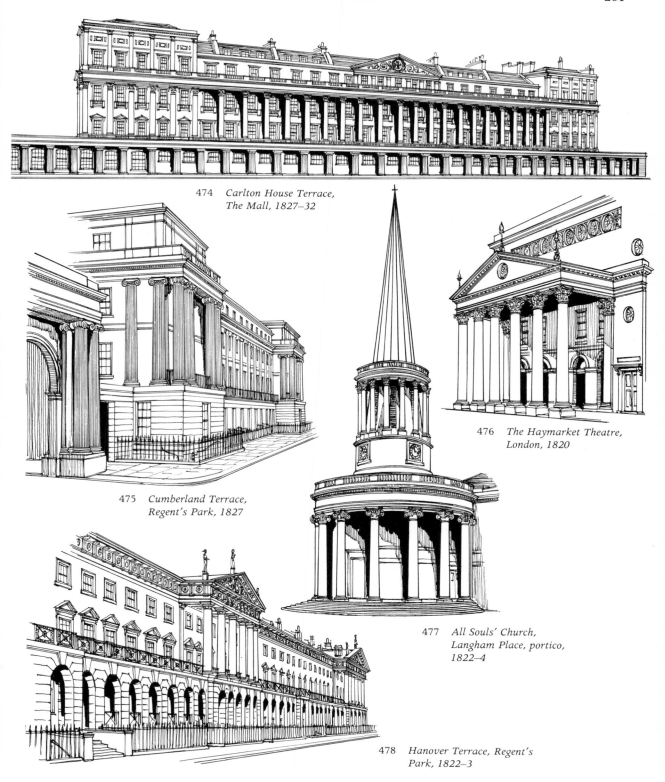

474   Carlton House Terrace,
The Mall, 1827–32

475   Cumberland Terrace,
Regent's Park, 1827

476   The Haymarket Theatre,
London, 1820

477   All Souls' Church,
Langham Place, portico,
1822–4

478   Hanover Terrace, Regent's
Park, 1822–3

centres such as Trafalgar Square. The *pièce-de-résistance* was to be a royal route from the Prince Regent's Park, where a summer palace was to be built, to his Carlton House in the Mall via the future Regent Street.

Nash's scheme was accepted and he began work in 1812. When he died, 23 years later, much of his vast concept, in which he energetically participated to the end, had been realised. He was forced, during these years, to forego some of his best ideas such as the double circus, many of the villas and their gardens and the Summer Palace. Regent's Park today represents only a section of his original plan and Regent Street has been totally rebuilt, though it retains its unusual quadrant line. But the terraces have largely survived and are probably appreciated more now than when they were built. In that age of critical architectural appraisal, some of the slap-dash detail and proportions which the builder had carried out from Nash's sketchy drawings, and without adequate supervision, were deplored. Today, restored and adapted to modern use, the Regent's Park Terraces display an architectural splendour against a background of mediocrity of building.

The crescents and terraces were built over a 20-year period. The earliest was *Park Crescent*, begun in 1812. It was planned as a circus but only half was built. It is a simple but impressive layout with its colonnade of coupled Ionic columns. Fronting the park are the palatial, imposing terraces of which *Cumberland Terrace* is the most monumental (475). Also impressive are *Hanover*, *Cornwall* and *Chester Terraces* (478). In the years 1827–32 Carlton House in the Mall was demolished and Nash replaced it with *Carlton House Terrace* (474), and St James's Park was laid out.

Regent's Park was the northern end of Nash's royal mile and Carlton House the southern. Between the two he designed the great boulevard which, commencing with Park Crescent, would sweep down Adam's Portland Place towards Oxford Circus, continue as Regent Street with the quarter circle (the Quadrant) at the lower end to bring it into line with Lower Regent Street and so to Waterloo Place. There were problems with commercial interests in Regent Street as Nash insisted upon absolute symmetry of architectural design in the Quadrant and in the Lower Regent Street approach to Carlton House. But these were overcome and the scheme was architecturally and financially successful. Nash also built *All Souls'*

Church at the northern end of Regent Street. It is an unusual design and aroused controversy for its circular porch and spiked spire (477).

In 1825 Nash was creating a new scheme aimed to connect Bloomsbury and Whitehall, with a link to the Regent Street scheme by means of Pall Mall. A new square was formed at the north end of Whitehall called, from 1831, *Trafalgar Square*. Except for St Martin-in-the-Fields, the buildings were all erected there after Nash's death by other architects. The development of the square enabled St Martin's to be viewed clearly for the first time.

Of Nash's other work in *London*, the exterior of the *Haymarket Theatre* (476) survives much as he designed it, also the *United Service Club* in Pall Mall (1828). Nothing remains from his ill-fated project of Buckingham Palace except for the beautiful *Marble Arch*, which he had based upon the Arch of Constantine in Rome and planned as a triumphal entrance arch to the palace forecourt.*

William Wilkins 1778–1839 and Sir Robert Smirke 1781–1867

These two architects belong to the next generation. Together they were responsible for the bulk of architectural commissions between 1825 and 1840. They typify their time, their work being sound, authentic in whatever style was considered suited to the individual commission – Gothic or classical in Greek or Roman form, excellently constructed and executed. By eighteenth-century standards their buildings are not inspired; they lack the originality of a Soane and the brilliance and sense for design in the mass and on the grand scale of a Nash. In comparison, though, with Victorian building, their contribution gains in stature and accomplishment.

William Wilkins was the son of an architect. He was educated at Cambridge and returned there later to carry out extensive commissions. After a period of study in Europe he published his *Antiquities of Magna Graecia* and established a reputation as an enthusiastic Greek revivalist. In *London*, Wilkins built *St George's Hospital* at Hyde Park Corner in 1827–8 and, in 1832, his best-known structure, the *National Gallery* in Trafalgar Square (Chapter 11, page 219).

---

* The Marble Arch was set up in its present position in 1851.

Sir Robert Smirke was the son of an artist and began his architectural career as a pupil of Soane. Like Wilkins, he spent some time studying in Europe, after which he began work as a convinced Greek revivalist. He acquired an exceptionally large London practice, much of which was concerned with public building. Smirke's work was almost all based upon Greek classicism; it is academic, well designed and often monumental, but rarely uplifting. His best known building is the *British Museum* (Chapter 11, page 219), but he also designed the *Royal Mint* (1809) and the *College of Physicians* in Trafalgar Square (1824–7). Here he used his favourite Greek Ionic Order as he did also in his *Shire Halls*, for example that at *Gloucester* (1814–16).

Churches

Comparatively little church building had been carried out since the impetus given by the 1711 Act providing for the erection of churches, in which Hawksmoor had been the leading spirit (page 140). By the early nineteenth century the population had increased and had been re-distributed. New centres of population had been formed by the migration of workers from country to town. To meet this situation in 1818, the Church Building Society was formed and, with Parliamentary support, a Church Building Act was passed, which provided that £1,000,000 should be spent to build new churches. The money would be allocated under the supervision of the Church Commissioners, since which time these churches have been referred to, generally in a derogatory manner, as the Commissioners' Churches. Some years later a further £500,000 was allocated and the total number of churches constructed was eventually 214, of which 174 were Gothic (see Chapter 11). The majority of these churches are in the London suburbs and in the industrial areas of Yorkshire, Lancashire and the Midlands. Few of them are aesthetically or architecturally attractive; they are nearly all large, capable of holding big congregations and most were cheaply built. In the years 1818–30 there were no terms of reference as to style and the early examples were in Greek classical form. Later the Gothic Revival movement gained ground, especially for ecclesiastical building (page 221).

The Church Commissioners were advised in their selection by a board of three architects: Nash, Soane and Smirke. All of these built one or more churches, but none of them was very interested or helpful in this project of mass production churches. They were individualists, successful and busy. No real leader emerged and it is inevitable that later generations should compare this situation and its results with the two previous opportunities which had occurred; the first after the Fire of London in 1666, when Wren had designed his 50-odd churches (page 121) and the second in 1711, when Hawksmoor and his fellow architects had stepped into the breach. Now, lamentably, there was no Wren, Gibbs or Hawksmoor and, at the same time, the Commissioners were asking for as large a church as possible to be built for as little of the taxpayers' money as possible. This injunction (so familiar today) was hardly likely to produce a St Bride's or St Martin-in-the-Fields.

A few of the earlier classical churches are exceptions to the general uninspired mass of those built in the first half of the nineteenth century; those designed by the Inwoods are amongst these. In particular, *St Pancras'* Church, London, built 1819–22, is one of the exceptionally fine Greek Revival churches and ranks with St Martin's as a great success (463). The design for the church was by *H. W. Inwood*, who had travelled for a short while in Greece and returned to win the competition at the age of 24. He and his father, W. Inwood, were partners and they built it together. The church has an unusual steeple which is based upon the Tower of the Winds in Athens, the motif being repeated in diminishing scale. The body of the church is based upon the Erechtheion in Athens, with fine detail in the Ionic Order. The design comprises a large hall with an apse at one end and the tower and portico at the other. Inside, the simple, galleried hall has a flat ceiling and rich Greek decoration. The church was costly – some £70,000 – over four times the cost of an average Commissioners' church.

Another delightful Inwood church is *All Saints'* at *Camden Town*, 1822–4. This has a tall, semi-circular portico, still in the Greek Ionic Order, and a slender, cylindrical tower. Here too the detail is delicate and finely executed (480).

Sir John Soane's contribution to the Commissioners' churches does not show his work at its best. He built three in London, *Holy Trinity, Marylebone* 1824–5, *St Peter's, Walworth* and *St John's, Bethnal Green*, 1824–5. Holy Trinity is a classical design with Ionic

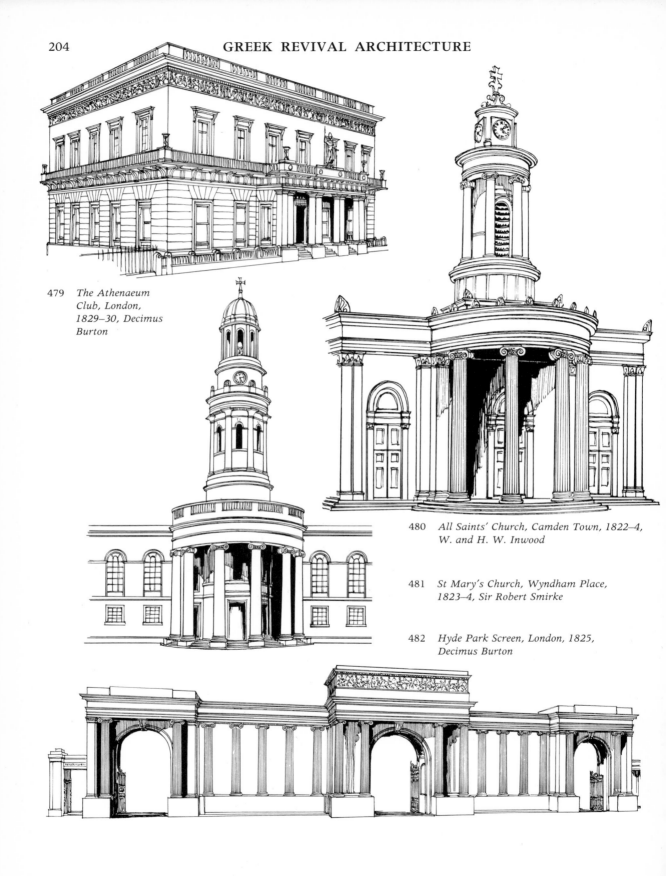

479 *The Athenaeum Club, London, 1829–30, Decimus Burton*

480 *All Saints' Church, Camden Town, 1822–4, W. and H. W. Inwood*

481 *St Mary's Church, Wyndham Place, 1823–4, Sir Robert Smirke*

482 *Hyde Park Screen, London, 1825, Decimus Burton*

porch and a traditional Corinthian tower. St John's is a more original, typically Soane design with tall, simple, round-headed windows of Gothic, plate traceried quality but with a classical doorway; the interior has been altered.

John Nash's church, *All Souls'* in Langham Place, has already been referred to (page 202). The circular porch here is of Roman Ionic design, boldly Baroque in its deep shadows and curves. The drum, below the spire, is encircled by a colonnade of Corinthian columns (477).

Sir Robert Smirke designed a greater number of churches for the Commissioners than his two colleagues. They are all on Greek Revival pattern and remarkably similar to one another. Typical is *St Mary's* in Wyndham Place in *London*, 1823–4 (481). The church is built on a terminal site on the Portman Estate and has a fine semi-circular Ionic portico. The tower is too lofty and somewhat repetitive. Similar are *St Anne's, Wandsworth*, 1820–2, *St Nicholas', Strood* and *St Philip's, Salford*, 1825.

Apart from the work of these architects, *Thomas Hardwick's* parish church of *St Marylebone*, 1813–18, is an imposing classical example, and a more delicate design was provided by *James Savage* in *St James' Church, Bermondsey*, 1827–9. Savage designed several classical churches for the Commissioners and he was also responsible for an early Gothic one, *St Luke's, Chelsea*, 1820–4 (484). Although this shows a certain lack of experience in building in Gothic, it represents a serious attempt to construct a Perpendicular Gothic church with stone, not plaster vaults, and the concomitant abutment system. It is a large, costly church with pleasing silhouette and good detail.

University Building

William Wilkins was the main contributor in this field, designing in both classical and Gothic styles. *London University* was founded at this time and Wilkins designed it in 1827–8. Now University College, the structure is fronted by an impressive Corinthian portico raised on a great podium with approach steps.* The dome is set above and to the rear. This was a new university building, erected in the centre of a great city and a break was made from the Oxford and Cambridge tradition of court plan-

ning. Here was envisaged no chapel but a central, large assembly hall with flanking libraries, museums and other accommodation. The portico was built with its entrance steps and, inside, the vestibule and grand staircase, but, strangely, the assembly hall was not carried out.

Still in classical vein, Wilkins designed the building for the new *Downing College* at *Cambridge*. A Greek Revival work, the Ionic Order from the Erechtheion is used on an austere, rather conventional structure. Not far away is his attractive, single-arched, stone bridge over the Cam at King's College (454).

In the 1820s Wilkins turned to Gothic. At this time architects still approached this style of work in a romantic manner, though it was being taken more seriously than in the eighteenth century. In 1822 Wilkins submitted a design for the completion of the great court at *King's College, Cambridge* which, despite the elaborate plans of Gibbs and, later Adam, had still not been completed (pages 147, 183). Other architects submitted designs, some classical, some Gothic. It was decided to use Gothic in order to harmonise with the Medieval chapel and Wilkins' plan for a long screen fronting the main road with a centrepiece formed by the principal entrance gateway, was accepted (483). He also built the Gothic Hall, where he broke with tradition by setting his great oriel window half-way along the elevation instead of at the daïs end.

At *Corpus Christi College* in Cambridge Wilkins designed the *New Court* in 1823–30 in Perpendicular Gothic style. The whole new quadrangle is laid out as one unified scheme which comprises library, hall and chapel. It is here that Wilkins' Gothic can best be judged as he had a free hand in a new layout. The results are pleasing and the Medieval spirit is not lacking.

Also in Gothic vein is *Rickman** and *Hutchinson's New Court* at *St John's College* nearby, built 1827–31. This is in Perpendicular design too, but is warmer and more romantic than Wilkins' somewhat classical Perpendicular. There is a screen wall with central gateway and terminal features with centrally placed

---

* The side wings were added after Wilkins' time.

* This is Thomas Rickman (1776–1841) who published in 1817 *An Attempt to Discriminate the Styles of English Architecture*, where he gave to Medieval building the classifications of Early English, Decorated and Perpendicular (page 40).

483   *King's College, Cambridge, screen and gateway, 1822–4, William Wilkins*

484   *St Luke's Church, Chelsea, 1820–4, James Savage*

485   *St John's College, Cambridge, 1826, Rickman and Hutchinson*

486   *The Royal Pavilion, Brighton, 1816–20, John Nash*

Perpendicular oriel windows. The Perpendicular Gothic bridge, the 'Bridge of Sighs', so-called after its Venetian prototype, is by the same architects. It is a single-arched bridge and the whole scheme, with the court is undoubtedly Rickman's most successful achievement (485).

Town Planning and Terrace Architecture

Already in the later decades of the eighteenth century the Industrial Revolution had begun to cause a slow but steady migration of workers from country to town. In agricultural areas unemployment was forcing whole families to move to towns to find work in the new factories. At the same time better standards of medicine and hygiene were enabling more children to survive to adulthood and the population began to increase sharply; by 1801 it had risen to nine millions. The 20 years of war with revolutionary and Napoleonic France interrupted building programmes for new housing which soon became acutely necessary and municipal corruption and lethargy had never been greater. The slum conditions in large towns, bad in the eighteenth century, because of these varied factors deteriorated further.

Although in these years conditions of living in towns were now extremely bad for the poor, the development of civic planning and housing for the well-to-do was extending rapidly. Throughout this this period the standard of building was high; many acres of land were covered by, in the main, fine, solid graceful structures, laid out in streets and squares. Portland stone was used for larger buildings and brick, covered in stucco and painted the colour of stone, for the terraces and smaller houses. The name of John Nash is closely associated with this increase in stucco-covered façades.

Apart from the need for civic building and housing for the increasing population in London and the manufacturing towns, other small centres of population were expanding rapidly because of leisure interests. These were the spas and seaside resorts. Bath was the chief eighteenth-century example (Chapter 9), but during the Regency it was followed by such spa towns as Cheltenham and Tunbridge Wells. Along the south coast, continuing upon the popularisation of Brighton by the Prince Regent, came the extension of Hove, Hastings and St Leonards.

London

Here, as in other large cities, the quality terrace architecture built in the eighteenth century has been demolished on a widespread scale. Of the few examples which survive, with the exteriors at least mainly as they were built, are part of *Fitzroy Square*, designed by *Adam* (Chapter 9) and *Bedford Square*, where much of *Leverton's* work remains (487). A few of *Holland's* houses exist from his *Hans Town* development, but it is difficult to visualise the original scheme. *The Paragon* at *Blackheath* is a variant on the usual terrace; it consists of classical blocks connected by curving Doric colonnades (493).

It was from 1800 that the steady but accelerating growth of the capital began to transform London from a normal city surrounded by pleasant villages into a sprawling metropolis. In 1800, most of the suburbs which we now think of as near to central London were yet villages: Hampstead, Highgate, Blackheath, Putney, Chelsea. Between 1800 and 1835 were developed much of London's West End, Bloomsbury and Belgravia. The architectural standard was still good and the amenities excellent. The classical form of terrace architecture prevailed. The terraces varied from whole streets to small blocks and were curved or straight.

Apart from John Nash's Regent's Park scheme (page 200), the two men chiefly responsible for the building enterprise of these years were *James Burton* (1761–1837) and *Thomas Cubitt* (1788–1855), both of them speculative builders, not architects. Burton was a most enterprising and successful man. He developed much of *Bloomsbury*, taking over sites and letting out some work to other builders, although supervising the whole himself.

His son, *Decimus Burton*, the architect, designed much of the work for his father and also worked with Nash on the Regent's Park terraces. Decimus Burton is especially known for his *Hyde Park Corner screen*, with its graceful Ionic colonnade (482) and for the arch which he had designed as a triumphal entrance to the park. This was based upon the Arch of Titus in Rome and a sculptured quadriga was intended to surmount it.* Decimus Burton also designed the

* The arch was later moved to the top of Constitution Hill and its angle to the screen altered. The present quadriga was set in position in 1912 and replaced the earlier equestrian statue of Wellington.

487 *Bedford Square, London, 1780, partly by Thomas Leverton*

491 *The Promenade, Cheltenham*

492 *New Steyne, Brighton*

493 *The Paragon, Blackheath, c.1790*

494 *Lewes Crescent, Kemp Town, Brighton, H. E. Kendall*

488   Royal Crescent, Brighton

489   Belgrave Square, London,
1825, George Basevi

490
Lansdown Parade,
Cheltenham

495   Pelham Crescent, South Kensington, 1820–30, George Basevi

496   Brunswick Terrace, Hove, 1825, Wilds and Busby

Athenaeum Club in Pall Mall (479). It is interesting to note here, as well as on the Hyde Park screen and Nash's United Service Club, the Greek sculptured friezes extending round the buildings. These were all inspired by the arrival of sections of the Parthenon frieze (the Elgin marbles), which had been acquired for the nation in 1816.

Thomas Cubitt continued Burton's work from the 1820s onwards. He is, perhaps, more famous particularly as the founder of the first modern-style building firm. Until Cubitt's time, work in different trades had been sub-contracted – bricklaying, masonry, carpentry, etc. – and, whereas the system had worked well enough until 1800, when large-scale development was involved, as the nineteenth century required, it showed itself inefficient and slow. Cubitt bought land and workshops and set up a firm which included all craftsmen necessary to the building trade, on a permanent wage basis. To keep his firm financially solvent he had to provide continuous work for them. This he did by large-scale speculative building. His standards in building and architecture were high, far above those of the men who followed him. Sometimes he had to sacrifice aesthetic needs to financial and domestic ones; here was the beginning of the devaluation of architectural standards, a devaluation which has continued uninterruptedly ever since.

Despite this, Cubitt performed a great service to London. Many of his houses, squares and terraces still stand; as fine, elegant and sound as they were over 100 years ago. They expose as inferior much of the later phases of development which surround them. All his life Cubitt used his influence to combat the abuses of architecture, building and living standards to which speculative building is heir. He was especially interested in drainage and London's sewage arrangements, and constantly worked to improve these. His own houses were soundly built, pleasant to live in and created to last, not just for the moment. He supplied first-class amenities in the way of land drainage, sewage, lighting and roads.

Cubitt began his development at *Highbury Park* and *Stoke Newington*, then moved on to *St Pancras* in Tavistock Square, Woburn Place and Euston Square.* The façades of his houses were in stucco in Greek

classical style. His most extensive and best-known enterprise was his creation of *Belgravia*. When Buckingham Palace was designed from Buckingham House he realised that the area was suitable for wealthy development. He leased an area of swampy ground from Lord Grosvenor and converted it into aristocratic squares. *Belgrave Square* is typical, designed by *George Basevi*. The square is lined with classical terraces with single, large houses set at the corners (489).

George Basevi (1794–1845) had been a pupil of Soane. In a short working life he designed a great deal of terrace housing in London. Apart from Belgravia, where he worked for Cubitt between 1825 and 1840, he helped to develop South Kensington, where his *Pelham Crescent* survives (495).

Edinburgh

Scottish cities such as Glasgow, Aberdeen, Dundee and Elgin were expanding as were the English ones. At Edinburgh the final achievement of the New Town was, perhaps, the most notable because of the long delay and the extended period in which the city had been restricted to its Medieval compass.

In the mid-eighteenth century Edinburgh was still confined within its city walls, built entirely on the narrow ridge which extended from Holyrood to the Castle and which contained only one main road, the royal mile. The whole of Edinburgh was packed into this strip, one mile long and about a sixth of a mile wide. Because of this the city, in the three previous centuries, had had to extend upwards. Tall, stone tenement blocks, eight to ten storeys high, were squeezed together with narrow passages (wynds), three to five feet wide, between. These wynds are still there in the old town, with their steep steps and slopes and metal handrail up the centre, like their counterparts in Montmartre.

From early in the eighteenth century it had been decided to build a new town north of the city. In order to do this the North Loch had to be drained. This was a lake bordered by marshes, noisome and pestilential and made even less salubrious by the tanneries and slaughterhouses which by tradition lined its edges. It covered the area now occupied by the Waverley Station and Princes Street Gardens as far as the Castle Rock. The loch was finally drained in 1763 and a plan for the town chosen by competition

---

* Considerable loss was occasioned here in 1961, together with the great Greek Revival Euston Arch, designed by Hardwick 1838, when the new Euston Station was built.

in 1767. This plan by *James Craig* was comprehensive, but work was painfully slow. Between 1780 and 1792 *Robert Adam* carried out countless surveys and designs for the new town, but the municipal delays were endless and frustrating.

From the plan (498) of the centre of present-day Edinburgh, it can be seen that, having drained the North Loch, bridges had to be built to span this area and the Cowgate, which were steep valleys flanking the main ridge of the old city where the royal mile (High Street and Canongate) runs. The *North Bridge* was built to the designs of *Robert Mylne* and *John Adam* in 1772 and the *South Bridge* and the university façade on it to Robert Adam's in 1788.*

With the opening of the bridges the New Town could be built. It was to be laid out on grid-iron pattern in classical style within a rectangle of 4000 by 1100 feet. The main thoroughfare, George Street, was to run east/west along the ridge parallel to Princes Street and the royal mile (498). There would be a square at each end, Charlotte Square on the west and St Andrew's on the east. Most of the town was laid out after Adam's death, but the north side of Charlotte Square was built to his designs (499), as was H.M. General Register House in Princes Street.

Costs were mounting and there were delays due to the Napoleonic Wars. After 1815 the speed of building accelerated and a new generation of architects created the Greek Revival New Town, the 'Athens of the North' as it was termed. Far less fine in individual buildings than Adam's designs and architecture, the New Town nevertheless was a tremendous achievement, creating, as in Bath, a homogeneous scheme in one style and material. The city had, at last, awakened to the advantages of its topography and had utilised this to the full instead of complaining, as people had in the previous century, of not possessing a city built on flat land where it was easy to expand.

St Andrew's Square was completed as was Charlotte Square. Here, unfortunately, St George's Church, which had been planned by Adam to dominate the west side of the square, was finally built by and to the designs of *Robert Reid* (1811–14) and is an anti-climax. The terraces were completed and the Calton Hill – Edinburgh's acropolis – was covered by Greek

monuments like a weighty northern Athens. On the lower slopes of the hill stands the best Greek Revival building in the city, the *Royal High School* (1829) by Thomas Hamilton (500).

In Princes Street, at the intersection of the Mound, were built Edinburgh's chief Grecian structures, the *Royal Scottish Academy* (1823–36) and the *National Gallery* (1845), both by *W. H. Playfair*, who contributed so greatly to Edinburgh's expansion in these years, including completing the University. A fine vista showing the topography of Edinburgh and the New Town development in juxtaposition with the old can be seen from the top of the Scott Monument in Princes Street (501, also see 498).

Resorts and Spas

The seaside resort of *Brighton* and *Hove*, popularised by the Prince Regent and developed from the village of Brighthelmstone, was laid out between 1800 and 1850. From Hove to Kemp Town, some three miles of sea front stand as a magnificent tribute to the terrace building of these years. There are gaps where later development has intervened, but a great deal survives. Here is the culmination of Nash's Regent's Park terraces; there is no local feeling present. The work is mainly painted stucco-faced, as in London.

Many architects contributed to the Brighton and Hove scheme. Of particular quality and distinction is the great length of *Brunswick Terrace* (496), built by *Charles Busby* and *Amon Wilds*, divided into two sections by *Brunswick Square*, by the same architects. Nearby is *Adelaide Crescent* by *Decimus Burton*, while at the other end of the sea front, are the magnificent terraces and squares at *Kemp Town* (494). Of outstanding quality also is the *Royal Crescent*, on more intimate scale, with its dark brick contrasting harmoniously with the white painted woodwork and iron canopies and railings (488). At *Hastings* and *St Leonards* there was considerable expansion also. *James Burton* and his son *Decimus* designed and built much of the fine architecture here, though less has survived than at Brighton.

Cheltenham was developed as a spa in the early nineteenth century as Bath had been in the eighteenth (490). The architect most closely associated with this was *John Buonarroti Papworth* (1775–1847), much of whose work was for Cheltenham. The son of a builder, he worked in an architect's office in London before

---

* The North Bridge was replaced in 1896 and only the engineering of the South Bridge survives; the street façades are modern.

497 *The Regent Bridge*

498 *Simplified plan of c.1790. Shaded area represents the low ground originally covered by the North Loch water and marshlands: now the site of Waverley Station and railway, Princes Street Gardens, the Mound and art galleries. The Mound was created from earth excavated from the New Town*

A Charlotte Square
B North side built to Adam's designs
C St George's Church
D Adam houses in Queen Street
E St Andrew's Church
F St Andrew's Square
G The Royal Bank of Scotland
H H.M. General Register House
K North Bridge
L The Tron Church
M St Giles' Cathedral
N South Bridge
O The University
T The Castle

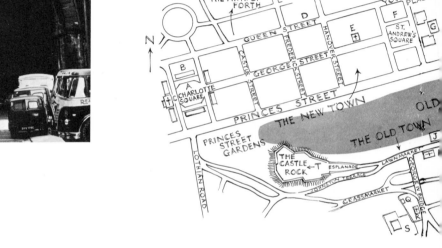

499 *Charlotte Square, 1791, Robert Adam*

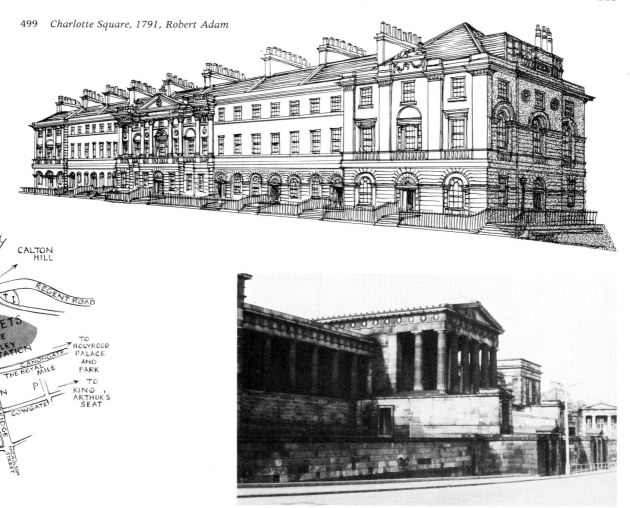

500 *The Royal High School, 1829,*
Thomas Hamilton

501 *Panorama seen from top of Scott Monument*
   A Church of Tolbooth St John
   B Outlook Tower
   C New College and Assembly Hall
   D Castle
   E National Gallery of Scotland
   F Royal Scottish Academy
   G St Cuthbert's Church
   H St Mary's Cathedral
   I Princes Street
   J St George's Church

502   *Ickworth, Suffolk,*
       1796–1830, Francis
       Sandys

503   *Staircase with iron*
       balustrade, 1790–1800

504   *Bryanston Square, London*

505   *Dining Room, c.1795.*
       Style of James Wyatt

506 *Seaside terrace house, c.1800*

507 *Serpentine scroll balustrade, c.1800*

508 *Dining Room, 1811—20*

beginning practice there himself, where he became a versatile architect. In Cheltenham he laid out the *Montpellier* and *Lansdown Estates* in mainly Greek classical style. *John B. Forbes* also contributed a great deal to the city's expansion. He initiated the *Pittville Estate*, building the *Pump Room* there in 1825–30, which like Papworth's Montpellier Pump Room is fronted by a colonnade with a rotunda rising behind. It was a great assembly hall based on Roman bath plan, but is Greek Revival in style in the Ionic Order.

At Brighton and Cheltenham, as also at *Tunbridge Wells*, where *Decimus Burton* designed the *Calverley Estate* for his father *James Burton* to build, there are many examples of decorative ironwork, wrought and cast. The variety of design in balconies, railings and canopies is infinite and the craftsmanship excellent (488, 490, 491, 492, 494, 496).

The House Interior

Ceilings and walls were most commonly stucco-decorated with classical motifs, using white and light colour shades. The ornament was similar to that which Adam had initiated, but in low relief, and it became more sparing towards the end of the century (505). Cast iron, used previously for utensils and implements, was employed more widely. It was decoratively handled and appeared in staircase balustrades, fire grates, fireplaces and stoves (507, 508). Coloured and white marbles were still widely employed, as also was scagliola. This was made from gypsum, glue, isinglass and colouring to imitate marble. It was very hard and could be polished. It was cheaper, also more plastic than marble for use as inlay so it could be used in table tops, columns and chimneypieces as well as floors.

In the later eighteenth century *staircases* were more often of stone or marble, with iron balustrade and mahogany handrails (462, 466, 503). The circular or elliptical stairwell plan was fashionable so that the staircase swept down in unbroken line from top to bottom of the house. Adam, Chambers and Wyatt had set the pattern which continued into Regency houses (507).

The doorcase was still of classical design; in large houses it was flanked by columns and surmounted by a pediment. Doors were solid, of polished mahogany, panelled and decorated with brass or ormolu. Early nineteenth-century doors were panelled in low relief. The tall, sash windows had narrow glazing bars (505). Bow windows were fashionable in the Regency (506). Some were round in section, others segmental (508).

There was a feeling of lightness in Regency houses, both in atmosphere and colour. The large windows were draped with light-coloured silk, linen or chintz curtains, often striped or delicately sprigged to echo the gowns of the day. The curtains were held back from the window to permit the light to enter the room. Wallpaper was, by 1800, the most usual wall-covering. Papers were light and gay to blend with curtains and upholstery. Stripes were fashionable, often satin-grounded, also in flock papers as well as some in imitation of marble (508).

Mirrors were still an integral part of the interior décor. They increased the illumination of the room and were decorative. All the furniture designers of the eighteenth century had made them. They had carved frames and a large area of glass divided into smaller panels by the curving frame design and incorporating candle holders. Regency mirrors were typically circular with convex glass. The frame was ornamented by balls and was surmounted by an eagle or scroll (508).

There were a number of famous furniture designers and cabinet makers who followed on from Chippendale and Adam. The two outstanding names were *Thomas Sheraton* (1751–1806) and *George Hepplewhite* (d.1786). Sheraton's furniture is noted for its apparent fragility. He had a preference for inlaid or painted furniture rather than carved decoration. Hepplewhite is known for his shield and oval-backed chairs. His furniture was also delicate and he used similar motifs to those of Adam, though he also included his 'Prince of Wales' feathers'. *Thomas Hope*, the interior decorator and furniture designer, published his *'Household Furniture and Decoration'* in 1807. This reflects his studies and travels in Greece, Sicily and Egypt and, though his work followed French Empire styles, his Regency furniture was strongly influenced by Greek and Egyptian motifs. These included sphinxes decorating the backs and arms of chairs.

PART THREE

THE AGE OF REVIVALS

CHAPTER ELEVEN

The Nineteenth Century
1830–1900

It is only now that a balanced evaluation of Victorian architecture is being made. In the first half of the twentieth century historians were too close to the previous age to assess its contribution fairly. Most condemned the work as derivative, mass-produced and in poor taste. A few, in contrast, praised fulsomely. Certainly the Victorians perpetrated much ugly, tasteless building, permitted largely uncontrolled expansion by private speculators and created for posterity immense areas of slums; but they also constructed buildings which have endured; developed a complex and extensive system of railway, road and canal communications; experimented successfully with methods of mass production in building materials; explored the possibilities of iron, glass, steel and pre-fabrication and last, not least important, created a quantity of fine architecture.

Despite continued demolition of nineteenth-century work, we still possess a great deal because so much was built. Indeed, more buildings were constructed in the nineteenth century than in all the previous ages added together; this is one of the reasons for the low standard of much of the work. It was in the years 1830–1900 that the effects of the Industrial Revolution snowballed; the movement of peoples from country to town accelerated and the higher birth-rate and better medical care raised the total number of people to an undreamt of level. To provide houses, factories, schools, colleges and civic buildings for this increased population a tremendous building drive was necessary.

Two major results of this – problems which still trouble us today – were the mass-production develop-

ment of the building industry and speculative expansion. In the early nineteenth century craftwork and hand-made decoration, furniture, etc., were still common. By 1900, ceiling plaster ornamentation, wainscot mouldings, fireplaces and decorative motifs of all types were mass-produced and applied ready-made to both outside and inside of a building. A hardness of finish and sameness of design invaded more and more the domain previously governed by aesthetic considerations; a process which has culminated in the module-based glass and concrete box architecture of our own day.

At the same time, unscrupulous members of the community, present in every age, were cashing in on the desperate need for housing. Speculators bought land on the outskirts of industrial cities and built houses, packed densely in the familiar back-to-back style of the northern and Midlands towns of the 1860s. Sanitation and amenities were totally inadequate; life was a misery for thousands and their standards of health and hygiene appallingly low. The ravaging of the British landscape by bricks and mortar in ugly shapes and monotonous rows had begun, to continue almost uninterruptedly until the present time. As the buildings rose so smoke from the myriads of coal-burning chimneys blackened their surfaces and polluted the atmosphere to create the 'peasouper' fog for which British cities were known throughout the world.

But not all Victorian town housing was of slum potential. Between the two extremes of large houses and back-to-back dwellings was also created a quantity of middle class homes. These too were often built in terrace rows. Though not usually beautiful, they were well constructed and many of them still stand and make good homes today. They contain large, well-designed and proportioned rooms. Architecturally the better examples followed the current fashions of the time. Of early Victorian schemes in *Islington, Milner Square* by *Gough* and *Roumieu*, 1841–3, (512) is an example of a simplified, classical pattern, while *R. C. Carpenter's* Lonsdale Square*, 1838, is in the current Perpendicular Gothic mode (511). Later in the century, terrace building for the well-to-do was more commonly on a Baroque classical theme with French-style mansard roofs or Flemish gables. In London, *Albert Hall Mansions*, 1879, a brick block of flats and *Grosvenor Place*,† 1865–75, are typical (513).

By 1850 there were appearing, in Europe as well as England, philanthropists, visionaries and architects of social purpose, ahead of their time and current thinking. In Germany there was Krupp at Essen, in England Sir Titus Salt in Yorkshire. Such men built 'ideal townships' for their workers, with housing, shops and amenities near to the factories. These were the pioneers of the new town or garden city concept of the twentieth century.

Saltaire was the first example of a 'New Town' in Britain. *Sir Titus Salt*, the Bradford mill-owner, built a new Italianate mill on the banks of the River Aire a few miles from the city and, around it, houses, a hospital, library, church, institute and almshouses for his workers. Each house had a parlour, kitchen, pantry, cellar, three bedrooms and outside toilet. Built of stone, in terrace form, the streets were named after Sir Titus' large family of children: Titus, Caroline, George, William, Henry, etc. (509). Though lacking some of the 'mod cons' expected in a new town of 1975, these houses were well built. They are pleasantly situated and were palaces compared to the slums in which other Bradford workers lived at the time.

A similar scheme, on a smaller scale, was initiated at *Copley*, a village near Halifax, where a Grecian-style mill and about 100 houses were built to the designs of *W. H. Crossland* in the 1860s. These stone houses are simple, late Gothic in design.

Later, a housing experiment was carried out at *Bedford Park* in *London*. Here was no industrial centre or industrialised founder. In 1876 *Mr J. T. Carr* initiated the construction of a housing estate to be built centred round a church, general stores and club. Several architects worked on the project over many years: *Norman Shaw, Maurice Adams, E. J. May* and *Sir Ernest George*. The houses are of brick, semi-detached and in terraces, suitable for families of moderate income. They have gabled roofs and many are built in Shaw's Queen Anne and Dutch manner (510).

In style the Victorian age was one in which previous designs were revived. There was not a single earlier style which architects did not emulate and adapt to their use. The two fundamental types of building – classical and Gothic – were used in all their forms. Classical architecture was designed in Greek, Roman, Italian and French-Renaissance clothing, while Gothic appeared in all its guises from Romanesque and Lancet to Perpendicular and Tudor. Many architects designed in both classical and Gothic form, suiting the style to the building. Although there was no rule, classical forms were preferred for civic and public building – government offices, town halls, university colleges – and Gothic for ecclesiastical and domestic work. This was particularly so before 1855–60, after which time the Gothic Revival became stronger than the classical faction and Gothic town halls, station façades and academic buildings appeared all over the country.

In the 1830s the leading architects continued to design their important structures in Greek Revival manner. *Sir Robert Smirke's British Museum* (517) is an impressive example, with its tremendous south front of 48 Ionic columns. The building is constructed round an open quadrangle and the Ionic colonnade continues round it. It was *Sidney Smirke*, Sir Robert's younger brother, who covered in the quadrangle with a cast iron dome to create the reading room in the 1850s. *William Wilkins* built the rather less successful National Gallery in Trafalgar Square (1832–8) and *George Basevi* began his *Fitzwilliam Museum* in *Cambridge* in 1837; this has a fine Corinthian portico.

Charles R. Cockerell (1788–1863) succeeded Soane as architect to the *Bank of England* in 1833. Whereas Taylor and Soane had both contributed chiefly to the London headquarters, Cockerell made his reputation in building branch banks in large industrial cities. Of

---

* Carpenter's finest work is Lancing College chapel (515), built in Decorated Gothic style in 1854–5.

† Being demolished piece-meal and replaced by modern buildings.

509   *Titus Street, Saltaire, Yorkshire,*
1854–70, Lockwood and Mawson

510   *Bedford Park, London, from 1876*

511   *Lonsdale Square, Islington, 1838,*
R. C. Carpenter

512   *Milner Square, Islington, 1841–3,*
Gough and Roumieu

513   *Grosvenor Place, London,*
c.1867–75

similar Greek Revival design are those at *Bristol, Plymouth, Manchester* and *Liverpool* (516). Apart from the banks and insurance offices, Cockerell was also responsible for the *Taylorian Museum* (the Ashmolean) at Oxford (1840–5).

The outstanding classical building of the nineteenth century is *St George's Hall* in *Liverpool*, designed by an architect who died of tuberculosis at the early age of 34, *Harvey Lonsdale Elmes*. The structure was planned to incorporate a great central hall for concert performances flanked by the crown court on one side and the civil court on the other. The building occupies a fine site in the centre of a great square in the city and is a remarkable design for a young and inexperienced architect who had never visited Italy or Greece. The exterior is in Greek classical form in the Corinthian Order (514), while the interior is the essence of Roman grandeur based upon the great vaulted Baths of Caracalla.

In Gothic design the most outstanding and most popular structure is the *Palace of Westminster*. It is fortunate that such a building was designed in the 1830s before the Gothic Revival had gathered momentum. In 1834 the old Palace was destroyed by fire. It was decided that the new Palace should be Gothic in style to harmonise with the nearby Westminster Abbey and that it must incorporate the Medieval Westminster Hall and St Stephen's Chapel from the old Palace. *Sir Charles Barry* (1795–1860) won the competition and the first stone was laid in 1840.

At this time the fashionable interpretation of Gothic was in the Perpendicular form. This attracted Barry also because it would harmonise most closely with the Henry VII Chapel of Westminster Abbey opposite and because he was in sympathy with the chaste, rectilinear simplicity of the style. Barry's handling of the design problems was masterly. He retained Westminster Hall and, in the centre of his new building, made an octagonal chamber with lantern above; a chamber which gives direct access through St Stephen's Hall to Westminster Hall. At the southwest corner is set the Victoria Tower and, at the opposite end of the Palace, the more delicate Clock Tower (containing Big Ben). The finest view of the limestone building is from the river (518, 519).

Because of his close connections over so many years with the Palace of Westminster, Barry is often thought of as a Victorian-Gothic architect, but he carried out a great deal of work in the 1830s and much of it was in classical idiom; he was a man of his age and believed in suiting the style to the commission. His *St Peter's Church* at *Brighton* (1823–8) is Gothic, but in the *Royal Institution, Manchester* (1824–35 and now the City Art Gallery), the *Treasury Buildings* in *Whitehall* (1846) and his London clubs, the *Reform* (1837) and the *Travellers'* (1829–31), he used either Greek or Italian Renaissance classical. He also remodelled a number of large houses in classical and Elizabethan design.

Although he lived until 1860, Barry was not a Gothic Revival architect. His work was authentic in style and structure but his attitude to Gothic was nearer that of earlier designers. The Gothic Revival was seriously established in Britain by the idealists and thinkers rather than the architects. The movement was espoused by men who advanced it on moral and theological grounds. They were desperately sincere and had a deep belief that only a man moral and good in heart could design great architecture and that an immoral man could only create inferior work. They also believed that the Middle Ages was the greatest period of human endeavour and of the human spirit and that the arts and architecture which emanated from that time were the most beautiful. They aimed to recreate such architecture. They had a horror of architectural sham and thought that any material which had not existed in the Middle Ages should not be used in Gothic Revival ones. They abhorred the work of the years 1780–1840 when architects had used plaster to surface vaulting and incorporated iron as column structure.

One important influence of this type was the *ecclesiological movement*, which emanated from Oxford and Cambridge. Ecclesiologists believed strongly that, not only was Gothic the true style, especially for ecclesiastical architecture, but it must be late thirteenth-century Gothic or 'Middle Pointed' as they termed it. Another forceful influence was *John Ruskin*, the art critic. He was one of the most fervent prophets of the Gothic Revival and, by his works, especially the *Seven Lamps of Architecture* and the *Stones of Venice*, spread and popularised it.

The third important protagonist was *A. W. N. Pugin*, who was writer, decorator and architect. In his *Contrasts: or a Parallel between the noble edifices of the fourteenth and fifteenth centuries and similar Buildings of the present day. Shewing the present decay of Taste,*

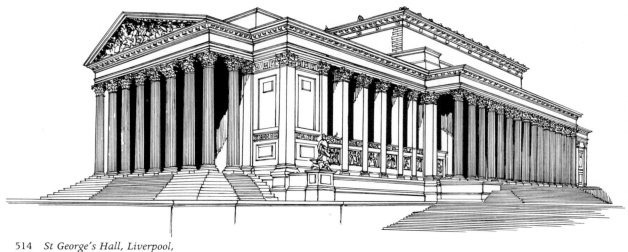

514 *St George's Hall, Liverpool,*
1839–54, Harvey Lonsdale
Elmes

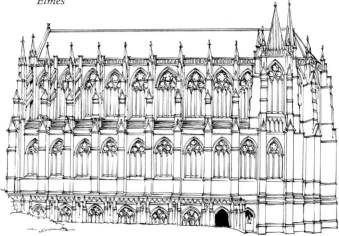

515 *Lancing College Chapel, Sussex,*
1854, R. C. Carpenter

516 *The Bank of England, Liverpool,*
1845, C. R. Cockerell

517 *The British Museum, London,*
1825–47, Sir Robert Smirke

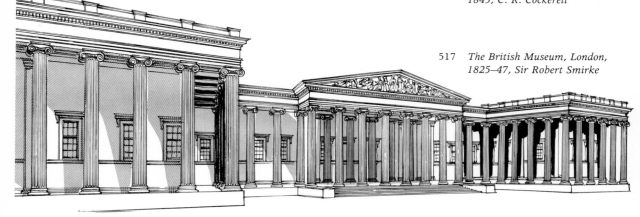

518 *The Palace of Westminster,*
1836–65, Sir Charles Barry

519 *Detail, Palace of Westminster*

520 *Bristol Cathedral, west doorway,*
1868–88, G. E. Street

521 *St James the Less, Westminster,*
1858–61, G. E. Street

he sought to prove the inferiority and immorality of Renaissance architecture by showing drawings, beautifully executed, of a fine Medieval structure side by side with an inferior standard nineteenth-century classical one. Pugin worked unceasingly, writing, drawing and designing. His output was enormous. He followed his 'Contrasts' with The True Principles of Pointed or Christian Architecture, where he tried to show that the decorative features of a Medieval building are essential parts of it, not a veneer. Unlike his early nineteenth-century predecessors he understood fully Medieval structural principles and put these into practice in his churches such as St George's (now the Cathedral), Southwark (1848), the Roman Catholic Cathedral of Birmingham (1839–41), St Giles', Cheadle (1841–6) (523), St Marie's, Derby (1838) and St Augustine, Ramsgate (1846). He designed a number of houses also, but his chief monument is his work on the Palace of Westminster, where he collaborated with Barry and made all the designs and supervised the work for the ornament, stained glass, fittings and furniture (519).

Shortly before his death Pugin arranged the Medieval Court for the Great Exhibition of 1851. He undertook the work with his usual passionate enthusiasm, although he did not scruple to make clear his scorn and contempt for the building itself: 'a greenhouse', he called it.

The question may be asked: 'What is the fundamental difference between the architecture of the Gothic Revival and that of the Middle Ages?' It is clear that there are differences, but these are not easy to define. The chief of them is in the craftsmanship. Medieval work evolved over hundreds of years. A large body of craftsmen spent their lives carving, modelling, painting and working in plaster, glass, iron or wood. In the nineteenth century, after several hundred years of classical design, there were no craftsmen in Gothic architecture. Barry and Pugin had to train a new school of craftsmen to build the Palace of Westminster. Their work was excellent but, after 1850, the pace of work accelerated and demand far exceeded the supply of all forms of craftsmen. So means of mass-production of decorative features had to be developed. It is this which gives the hard, repetitious finish of a nineteenth-century finial or capital. Medieval buildings took many years to erect: nineteenth-century ones could be completed in months.

Another difference is in spirit. Medieval building arose from the religious feeling of its time. In the nineteenth century religious fervour was strong but it was not the sole basis for life. Lord Clark* expresses this feeling vividly: 'Although the saints in a modern Catholic image shop are extremely virtuous, they are obviously the product of an utterly worldly civilisation, whereas the gargoyles of a Medieval cathedral, though monsters of vice, are alive with the spirit of a truly religious age.'

The Gothic Revival in Britain was at its height from 1855–85. Termed the High Victorian Gothic period, its chief designers were Street, Waterhouse, Scott and Butterfield. These architects, and many others, covered the country with Gothic structures: town halls, hotels, administrative centres, university and school buildings and railway stations. The ecclesiological doctrine had now triumphed, indeed the pressure from the society's influential members upon architects to toe the line or else forego the commission had been great. As time passed, earlier Medieval sources were sought; Barry's Palace of Westminster had been derived from Perpendicular Gothic, High Victorian design was based on 'Middle Pointed' and then Lancet and even Romanesque, though many buildings also incorporated a dash of Venetian, Flemish or French flavour.

George Edmund Street (1824–81) was a deeply religious man, an ecclesiologist and a believer in the theory of the indissolubility of a clear conscience and a great architect. His work was strong and uncompromising, with a fondness for colour and polychromatic patterning. His Church of St James the Less in Westminster is typical, built in red and black brick and with a richly decorated, dark interior (521). Street's best known work is the Law Courts in the Strand (1868–82); he spent many years also in Medieval restoration work as at Bristol Cathedral (520).

Alfred Waterhouse (1830–1905) carried out many larger projects in industrial cities. They are monumental, polychromatic, boldly three-dimensional and arouse strong feelings in the beholder. The harsh colours of his red, yellow and black bricks, ornamented with terracotta, have matured to a softer blend with the passage of time and structures such as the Natural History Museum and Prudential Assurance

---

* Kenneth Clark, The Gothic Revival, John Murray, 1962.

Building in London and his *Town Hall* in *Manchester* are more tolerantly, even affectionately, regarded than they were 30 years ago (524).

Sir George Gilbert Scott (1811–78) represents the quintessence of the Gothic Revival. Less original than his colleagues, he was responsible for the greatest number of buildings and for popularising the movement. He believed in it implicitly and was a great admirer of Pugin. Hardworking and sincere, he was the founder of an architectural dynasty which spread over a century. His output was tremendous; he was engaged on and responsible for some 730 buildings, many of which were pedestrian. Of particular interest are some of the structures which have aroused controversy over the years but are now returning to favour, such as the *St Pancras Station Hotel* façade (522), the *Albert Memorial* and the *Foreign Office* in *Whitehall*.

William Butterfield (1814–1900) was the architect most revered by the ecclesiologists. A reserved, arrogant, deeply religious man, most of his work was ecclesiastical, in churches and universities. His style was highly individualistic, characterised by strong massing, lofty steeples and stronger and harsher polychrome colouring than that of any other architect. He did not believe in painted colour, but used durable materials for his ornament: mosaic, tile, brick, marble and alabaster. *All Saints', Margaret Street* is typical of his churches and *Keble College, Oxford* his best work (525). The chapel here aroused fierce controversy for many years, but opinion has mellowed as has, fortunately, his harsh polychromy.

A vital, far-reaching contribution to architecture was made by the nineteenth-century development of the potentialities of *steel, iron* and *glass*. The great engineers of the first half of the century such as *Telford, Rennie, Stephenson* and *Brunel* had shown by their bridges and aqueducts what could be done with iron and steel. Pioneering examples which survive include the *Clifton Bridge* over the Avon gorge at *Bristol* (528) and those at *Conway* (529) and the *Menai Straits*. Not only were these structures great technical achievements, they also rank among the finest aesthetically; as innovators and designers the Victorian engineers led the architects.

The nineteenth century was the *railway age* and in this field engineer and architect worked together to provide a previously undreamt of comprehensive transport system for everyone, as well as creating the railway termini – the 'cathedrals' of their time. The technical advances in the production and use of cast iron spread over into the terminus buildings. Railway architecture was in classical, and later, Gothic style, but its structural basis was iron. Many of the best examples, such as Euston Station, have been demolished, but much of the iron structure at Paddington survives; also the façade at King's Cross (526).

Another famous 'cathedral' of the nineteenth century was the structure of glass and iron designed to house the Great Exhibition of 1851. Dubbed '*The Crystal Palace*' by Punch, it has been known by this name ever since. In 1850 a competition was held which included the proviso that it must be possible to dismantle the building and re-erect it elsewhere. This precluded the use of traditional building materials and the competition was won by *Sir Joseph Paxton*, who was not an architect but a gardener and glasshouse designer. His Crystal Palace was a pre-fabricated glasshouse of vast dimensions (530). It was erected in Hyde Park for the exhibition in less than five months. 1851 feet in length, it contained 900,000 square feet of glass in a metal framework supported on over 3000 iron columns. In 1852 it was dismantled and re-erected at Sydenham where it was in popular use until its destruction by fire in 1936.

The Crystal Palace was bitterly criticised at the time by many architects, as well as by both Pugin and Ruskin, to whom a pre-fabricated building constructed by mass-production methods was anathema. But it was an important innovation both for the use of the materials and the structural methods employed and pointed the way towards modern techniques.

Large country and town *houses* were still being built during the nineteenth century by all the leading architects of the day who designed these in the current mode. *Barry* built and re-designed a number using, for the example, the Elizabethan style at *Highclere Castle* in Hampshire (1842–4) and Italian palace design at *Bridgewater House* in *London* (1849); *Harlaxton Manor*, Lincolnshire, by *Anthony Salvin* (1831–55) is typical of the Perpendicular Gothic phase and *Pugin's Scarisbrick Hall*, Lancashire (1837) has an ecclesiastical flavour.

At the same time the rapidly growing and well-to-do middle class was building its houses. These were of considerable size, good construction, solid and complacent. The family of substance, from 1855 onwards, seemed to find in the 'Medieval' architec-

522   *St Pancras Station Hotel,*
1865–75, Sir George Gilbert Scott

523   *St Giles' Church, Cheadle,*
1841–6, A. W. N. Pugin

524   *Manchester Town Hall, 1869,*
Alfred Waterhouse

525   *Keble College, Oxford, 1868–82,*
William Butterfield

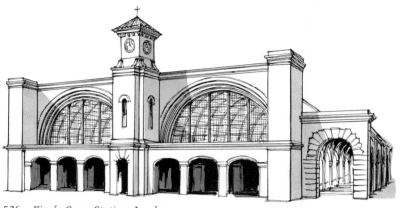

526 *King's Cross Station, London,
1852, Lewis Cubitt*

527 *Seaside Ironwork, Brighton*

528 *Clifton Suspension Bridge, Avon
Gorge, 702 ft. span, 1836–64,
I. K. Brunel*

529 *Conway Road Suspension
Bridge, 1826, Thomas
Telford*

530 *The Crystal Palace, Hyde
Park, London, 1850–1,
Sir Joseph Paxton*

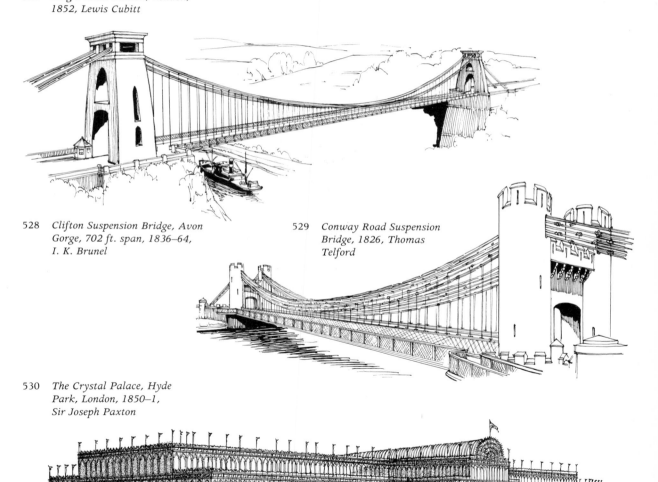

tural style the answer to its desire for romantic building and artistic expression. These Gothic houses were mass-produced, built of ornately decorated polychrome brick and stone. Simplicity of line and ornament was rare. They were often a mixture of Medieval styles; a single house might contain features of early Gothic and Tudor with Flemish sixteenth-century gabling.

Many examples of such houses survive, now divided into several flats, on the inner ring of such cities as London, Oxford, Reading, Manchester or Edinburgh (538). The main floor, the Georgian *piano nobile,* is approached via a flight of steps to the front porch; there is a bay window at one side, extending downwards to the floor below, which is the half-basement or area storey. Generally there are one or two floors above the first and attics and dormers in the roof. Victorian town houses are tall rather than wide and steep gables and chimney stacks break the skyline. Coloured brick is used in yellow, red and black, with brick and stone dressings round the Gothic windows. The Medieval-style capitals, columns and ornament were factory-produced and appear hard and bulbous.

In the 1860s the romantic absorption with the Middle Ages was giving to some painters, designers and architects a longing to get away from Victorian overdecoration, spurious materials and mass-production. *William Morris* (1834–96) particularly abhorred the trend towards mechanisation and tried to re-establish the quality of craftsmanship and simplicity in design. When he married in 1859 he commissioned his friend, the architect *Philip Webb,* to build his home in traditional materials in English farmhouse style. This was the *Red House* at *Bexley Heath* in Kent.

Unable to find the designs of textiles and furniture that he wanted he designed these himself and, with his friends, for instance Edward Burne-Jones, founded the firm of Morris and Co., which became known for quality design and workmanship in the making of textiles, wallpaper, furniture, coloured glass, murals and weaving. The well-to-do flocked to buy the firm's products, but Morris, the Socialist, was bitterly disappointed that the cost of producing articles by the individual craft method could not compete with the mass-produced item and so put his work out of reach of the average buyer.

Morris' ambition to elevate the craftsman again to the position which he had held in Medieval society failed – the clock could not be put back – but his re-introduction of quality design and the use of genuine materials slowly began to influence a new generation of architects and designers.

Especially in domestic architecture a number of these men began to design in simpler style, using traditional materials. The buildings were still 're-vivals', but of a plainer type evidencing quality of taste. *Philip Webb* (1831–1915) was followed by the most versatile of these architects, *Norman Shaw* (1831–1912), who adopted a number of differing styles to suit the client of a town or country house, demonstrating both his astounding adaptability and his instinct for tasteful design and good craftsmanship. In particular, he is noted for his houses based upon sixteenth-century half-timber work (536) and Flemish brick-work with terracotta ornament (532). He also developed a Dutch Palladian style as at *Bryanston* (531) and a Queen Anne town house pattern as at No. 170 Queen's Gate (1888) in South Kensington. Shaw was not only a domestic architect; he carried out a quantity of civic and public building as in, for instance, his insurance blocks in Pall Mall and, the best-known, *New Scotland Yard**** where he experimented with Scottish baronial style in polychrome banding of Dartmoor granite with brick (535).

With the last decade of the century the work of Voysey and Mackintosh presaged the development of modern architecture. *C. F. A. Voysey* (1857–1941) was not only an architect, but designed also wall-papers, fabrics and furniture. His work was plain with clean lines in traditional materials. His houses were also traditional, but the plan was informal and the elevations unsymmetrical. The walls were rough-cast in white, the ceilings low and the roofs long and sloping with lean-to buttresses. His window openings are characteristic, plain and rectangular casements with leaded lights. Typical are his own home, 'The Orchard' at *Chorleywood* (533) and the pair of terrace houses in London (537).

Voysey's houses, though modern in their simplicity, were still traditional. The work of the Scottish architect *Charles Rennie Mackintosh* (1869–1928) more nearly heralded the functionalism of the twentieth century. His *Glasgow School of Art* (1896–1909) was designed on stark, uncompromising lines

---

* The Embankment building, not the modern structure in Broadway.

531 *Bryanston House, Dorset, 1890, Norman Shaw*

532 *Ornamental detail, 196 Queen's Gate, London, 1875, Norman Shaw*

533 *'The Orchard', Chorley Wood, Hertfordshire, 1898–9, C. F. A. Voysey*

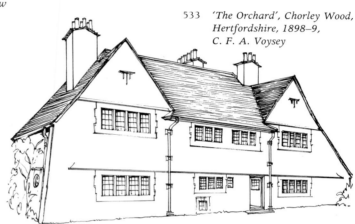

534 *Bishopsgate Institute, London, 1893–4, C. Harrison Townsend*

535 *New Scotland Yard, London, 1886–90, Norman Shaw*

536 *'Wispers', Midhurst, Sussex, 1875, Norman Shaw*

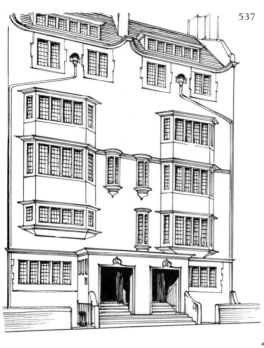

537 *14–16 Hans Road, Kensington, 1891, C. F. A. Voysey*

538 *Gothic suburban house, 1860–70*

539 *Early Victorian drawing room, c.1840–8*

which owed nothing to the past. His decorative work and furniture showed the influence of Art Nouveau, as does also the work of C. Harrison Townsend (534).

From 1835 onwards the *rooms* of a house were crowded increasingly with furniture, furnishings and ornaments. Colour schemes became darker and the light was obscured more and more by curtains and fringes. Fig. 539 shows an early Victorian drawing room where this trend has begun. The wallpaper is still light-coloured and striped and the ceiling white and plain but the Victorian furniture is heavier and more ornate than that of the Regency, and the room is more crowded with pieces, including the typical papier mâché work. The room is lit by gas, supplemented by candles and wall mirrors are now small and ornately framed.

By 1855–60 all surfaces were decorated. Carpet, wallpaper and furnishings were designed with large floral motifs in strong, dark colours and the paintwork was usually a heavy brown. The grate was of black-leaded cast iron and the chimneypiece above a complex polished mahogany or painted wood erection draped with fringed and tasselled velvet, its shelves and nooks overflowing with bric-à-brac. Long lace curtains hid the windows and these were flanked by heavy velvet or brocade ones to be drawn at dusk. There was a profusion of brass, porcelain, glass, papier mâché, lace and tatting – all demanding hours of housework, from a large, easily obtainable staff.

In the last decade of the century in the interior of the house, like the exterior, overdecoration was controlled. Eighteenth-century revivals in décor and furniture followed quickly upon one another. There was a vogue for neo-Adam decoration and imitation Sheraton and Hepplewhite furniture. There were still too many pieces filling the available space, but the intolerable clutter and obsessive ornamentation was abating.

PART FOUR

MODERN ARCHITECTURE

CHAPTER TWELVE

The Twentieth Century

British architecture, like that of Western Europe, had been a story told in two styles only: Gothic and classical. The twentieth century has produced something quite different which is international and owes nothing to its predecessors. Modern architecture is the term universally applied to this style of building which evolved in a number of countries after the First World War and which has culminated in the current designs of glass, concrete and steel based on module construction presently being erected all over the world. No-one has yet suggested a better name to describe these structures which appear to have no link with past styles.

There were four primary causes for the emergence of modern architecture:

1. The nineteenth-century population explosion in Europe which, together with the effects of the Industrial Revolution, made urgently necessary an increased rate of building for all purposes.
2. The development of new building materials and methods.
3. The deep desire of architects, designers and artists for a change of style.
4. The extensive destruction in two World Wars which necessitated the rebuilding of whole towns as well as particular sites.

Although the third point is a valid one, the development of modern design became inevitable chiefly from the pressure engendered by points one and four. This pressure hastened the development in materials and technology which made it possible to erect cheaply by mass-production methods and pre-fabricated systems on a large scale. Together these factors have brought about a transformation in the building scene and have killed for ever the architec-tural industry founded upon craftsmanship and an aesthetic basis.

Before the emergence of the modern movement, the strange ephemeral episode of *Art Nouveau* manifested itself. Appearing in a number of European countries from 1890, it had burnt itself out by 1914. It was a decorative rather than an architectural movement though it showed itself in early twentieth-century building design. Though short-lived and limited in its scope, it is important historically in architecture as an early attempt to break away from eclecticism. It was not entirely successful in this but manifested a deeply-felt striving to do so. The chief materials used in Art Nouveau were iron and glass, also faïence, terracotta and veneers. In England the decorative forms were applied in interior decoration in fabric design and stained glass. Architectural examples on the fringe of the movement included *C. Harrison Townsend's Whitechapel Art Gallery*, 1900 and *Bishopsgate Institute* (534), both in *London*, and *C. R. Mackintosh's Glasgow School of Art* (page 228).

Art Nouveau was in part an escape for architects who wished to break away from eclecticism but who also shied away from industrialisation and technology. They preferred the world of the individual, the crafts-man, the cottage industry. It was an extension of the ideas of Morris and Ruskin. Based upon backward-glancing, it could not last. The First World War finally broke down the illusions and post-1918 architects were either eclectics or modernists.

Apart from the small voice of Art Nouveau, archi-tecture in Britain until 1914 was eclectic, largely a continuation of late Victorian work. Based upon classical or Gothic prototypes, more often the former, some of the best works evidenced a robust baroque theme inspired by the building of the Grand and Petit Palais in Paris at the turn of the century. Of this type, the extensive layout of the *Cardiff City Centre* (543, 544), the *Central Hall, Westminster* (545) and the *town hall* at *Deptford* (540) all by the firm of *Lanchester, Stewart and Rickards* are excellent examples. Well designed and finely detailed, the city centre in Cardiff, in particular, has stood the test of time well.

At the turn of the century, the work of Voysey, Shaw and Mackintosh had put British architecture in the vanguard in Europe. It looked as though Britain would continue to lead when, due to her pre-eminence industrially, she developed an early use of steel frame construction for buildings. But this was not to be and the possibilities of a new architectural style based upon steel girder construction were not followed up. Instead, the traditional stone façade was used to clothe the steel structure so that, in appearance, there was no difference between such buildings and nineteenth-century ones. The *Ritz Hotel* in *Piccadilly* and the *Morning Post Building* in the *Strand* were both built in 1906 by *Mewès and Davis* with steel framing, but the Ritz in particular is faced with a heavy stone façade more Renaissance than modern.

Building impetus gathered force after the First World War and there was great activity in Britain in the years 1920–9. Designs continued to be traditional, the workmanship was of good quality but architects were reticent about moving into new fields. The trend towards a modern architecture was solely in the simplification of the classical or Gothic form. Buildings became plainer with large areas of empty wall scarcely enriched by sculpture or any other ornamentation. Vacuity was mistaken for simplicity. In the classical field the early work had been led by such men as *Sir Aston Webb* (Victoria and Albert Museum, Cromwell Road façade, 1899–1909, Admiralty Arch, 1910, Buckingham Palace façade), *Sir Reginald Blomfield* (the Quadrant, Regent Street) and *Sir Guy Dawber* and *Sir Ernest Newton* in domestic building. This was all competent, traditional classicism in the English vernacular. In the 1920s architects such as *Vincent Harris, Herbert Rowse* and *Sir Herbert Baker* contined the theme, the work still competent but becoming more aridly unoriginal as time passed.

The outstanding figure of the time was *Sir Edwin Lutyens* (1869–1944). His work was also traditional, generally on a classical basis, streamlined and simplified, yet definably personal. He worked in all fields: civic, housing, ecclesiastical. Like Wren, Adam and Shaw he handled the simplified classicism of his day in the specifically English manner, yet placed his own original mark upon it to make it recognisably Lutyens. His earlier work was in country house building where, following in the tradition of Shaw and Voysey, he used brick, half-timber and stone in pleasing, spacious designs suited to the individual commission. Typical are *Heathcote, Ilkley*, 1906, of local stone, *The Deanery, Sonning*, 1899–1901 and *Tigbourne Court, Surrey* (547, 549) in brick.

Lutyens built few town houses (36, Smith Square, Westminster is a survivor), but his work in *Hampstead Garden Suburb*, begun 1908, shows his traditional brickwork. Here he built the pleasing churches and Institute Buildings in the centre of the estate (572). His low-cost council scheme in *Page Street, Westminster* (548) is a more original housing complex. Here he used light grey bricks, Portland stone and white cement to produce a chequer-board pattern in successive rectangular blocks on courtyard layout. The effect is austere, modern and non-eclectic, apart from the white painted sash windows. It is one of his most original works.

In the early 1920s Lutyens turned to large civic schemes and developed his classical theme. One of his best works is *Britannic House* in Finsbury Circus in London (546). Typical of his simpler, more streamlined approach is the *Reuter Building* in Fleet Street. He built a number of these large, plain classical structures, particularly as architect to the *Midland Bank*.

Another traditionalist was *Sir Giles Gilbert Scott* (1880–1960), grandson of the nineteenth-century Sir George. In a large number of churches, work on abbey, cathedral and university chapel restoration and building, Scott evolved a simplified Gothic style as Lutyens had done in classical form.

His outstanding contributions were in widely different fields: the Anglican Cathedral of Liverpool and in power station design. Scott won the competition for *Liverpool Cathedral* in 1901 at the age of 21. It is a fine design: Gothic in modern dress. It is a red sandstone building with a high vault and impressive tower. The high cost and difficulty of finding sufficient funds and skilled labour has delayed its completion, but now the nave is the only part unfinished. The last of the great Gothic-style cathedrals, it is perhaps an anachronism, though a worthy swan song.

541, 542
*London Life Assurance
Building, 1924,
W. Curtis Green*

543　*Cardiff City Centre*

540　*Deptford Town Hall,
London, 1902, Lanchester,
Stewart and Rickards*

544　*Central Wesleyan Hall,
Westminster, 1906–12,
Lanchester and Rickards*

545　*The City Hall, Cardiff City
Centre, 1897–1906,
Lanchester, Stewart and
Rickards*

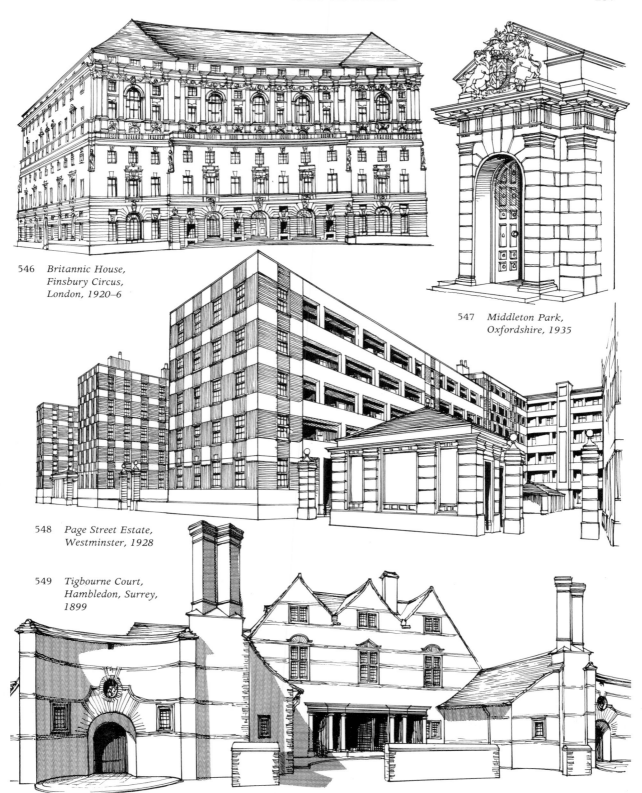

546 *Britannic House,
Finsbury Circus,
London, 1920–6*

547 *Middleton Park,
Oxfordshire, 1935*

548 *Page Street Estate,
Westminster, 1928*

549 *Tigbourne Court,
Hambledon, Surrey,
1899*

Scott's Medieval design in his churches is less interesting, though it is typical of the period (551). Other architects followed in this style of emasculated Gothic from *Sir Edward Maufe's Cathedral* on Stag Hill at *Guildford* (553) and his *Church* of *St Thomas* at *Hanwell* (1933) and the *Church* of *St Wilfred* at *Brighton* by *Goodhart-Rendel*.

In 1929 Scott set the pattern for *power station* design in Britain with his brick building at *Battersea* on the Thames in London. He continued with this type of work till late in life; at the age of 79 he was consulting architect for the nuclear power station at Berkeley. In 1937–52 he built the new *Waterloo Bridge* in London and was later consultant for the Forth Road Bridge near Edinburgh.

Although genuine modern architecture did not appear in England until the 1930s, a few structures showed indications and a slow trend towards its adoption. *Adelaide House* at London Bridge (1924) and the *Kodak Building* in Kingsway (1911), both by Sir John Burnet's firm, are early examples of steel framing with the structure visible and marked in the façades. There followed the plain block architecture, superficially modern in appearance but still with classical window openings, shorn of mouldings and ornament. *Senate House* at *London University* (1933–7), *Shell Mex House* (1929), *Broadcasting House* (1929) and *Bush House* (1925–8) all in *London*, are typical. The best example of this type is *Broadway House*, the headquarters of the Transport Executive by *Sir Charles Holden* (1929), though at *Swansea*, *Sir Percy Thomas* built a new civic centre as interesting and characteristic of its period as the earlier Baroque layout at Cardiff (559).

The Modern Movement

A few architects were experimenting with new ideas before 1918, but in general it was an inter-war creation. These modern architects rejected ornament; in reaction to nineteenth-century overdecoration and eclecticism they produced buildings which were stark, denuded of softening enrichment. They were concerned with the proper use of material and architectural structure.

It is paradoxical that the centuries where men had the original thought and courage to defy the tradition of the established architectural schools should mainly have been among those which, in the 1920s and 1930s,

submitted to totalitarian government. Such totalitarianism made it impossible for these original artists to work, so they emigrated, suffered in prisons and camps, died or submitted to dictation in their work. These countries – Germany, Italy and the U.S.S.R. – produced more than half of the original thinkers and designers of modern architecture.

Many of the leaders of modern architecture were born in the decade 1880–90. A large proportion of them lived to a considerable age and, like Mies Van der Rohe, Gropius and Le Corbusier, continued working and creating interesting designs until very recently at the end of their lives.

There are many 'isms' to which modern architecture has been subject in its evolution since 1920. These are often incomprehensible to the layman, in themselves difficult to define and explain and represent the stages through which many of the architects passed, often quickly and without regret. Expressionism was current just before and after the First World War, then came Constructivism, but it was Functionalism which was chiefly associated with the movement in the 1920s. This, the need for a building to be designed suitably for its purpose, had always been a tenet of good architecture, but one which had to a certain extent been lost sight of in nineteenth-century eclecticism. The leaders of the modern school were impressed by the theme of structure, of making it visible and unashamed, not covered by a classical or other façade. They were intrigued by the new technology and by engineering projects and the shapes evolved: spheres, cylinders, cones, cubes. They worked out the economics of building in these forms, endlessly repeated to facilitate cheap production. Their careful idealistic schemes became lost under the calculations of accountants, the mass of buildings required, under municipal and parliamentary authorities and the amount of money available, so that everything became subject to the theory that if a building were efficiently designed for its purpose it must, willy-nilly, be beautiful. Early essays on these principles, especially in housing, were disappointing. The results showed plain concrete blocks, relieved only by a railing or a gate. Stark simplicity was characteristic, but before long architects learnt to handle the new materials and to adapt to the new freedom of design. For centuries architectural proportions and form had been governed by structural means. Steel and concrete building meant

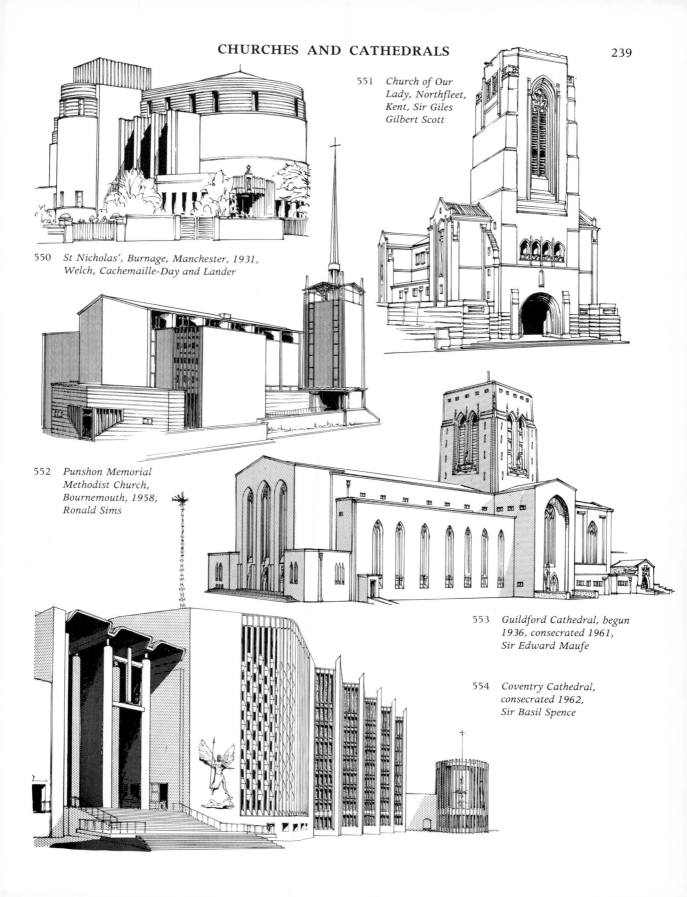

550 *St Nicholas', Burnage, Manchester, 1931, Welch, Cachemaille-Day and Lander*

551 *Church of Our Lady, Northfleet, Kent, Sir Giles Gilbert Scott*

552 *Punshon Memorial Methodist Church, Bournemouth, 1958, Ronald Sims*

553 *Guildford Cathedral, begun 1936, consecrated 1961, Sir Edward Maufe*

554 *Coventry Cathedral, consecrated 1962, Sir Basil Spence*

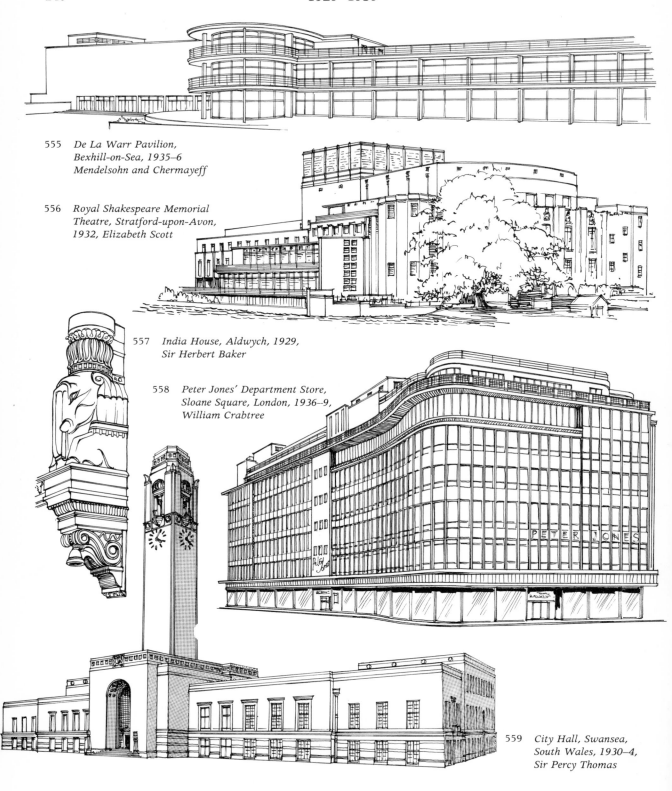

555   De La Warr Pavilion,
      Bexhill-on-Sea, 1935–6
      Mendelsohn and Chermayeff

556   Royal Shakespeare Memorial
      Theatre, Stratford-upon-Avon,
      1932, Elizabeth Scott

557   India House, Aldwych, 1929,
      Sir Herbert Baker

558   Peter Jones' Department Store,
      Sloane Square, London, 1936–9,
      William Crabtree

559   City Hall, Swansea,
      South Wales, 1930–4,
      Sir Percy Thomas

that many of the old concepts of weight, support and strength were outdated. The architect was now free to design heights, spans and loads far greater than had previously been known. Only slowly did most of them take full advantage of this opportunity.

In the U.S.A. architects such as *Frank Lloyd Wright* and *Louis Sullivan* had been experimenting for some time with these new concepts and structures. In France *Le Corbusier* was developing his 'Urbanisme' theories; in Italy *Terragni* was at work. In Russia there were *Lissitzsky* and *Melnikov*, in Switzerland, *Moser* and in Holland, *Oud* and *Dudok*. In Europe, probably the most influential centre was the Bauhaus.

It was in 1919 that *Walter Gropius* was appointed at Weimar to head the Art College which developed into the *Staatliches Bauhaus*. Here he was able to put into practice his strongly held ideas. He was so successful that this small college, which trained only a few hundred students in the short years of its existence, became architecturally world famous, a Mecca which attracted architects, artists and students from all over Europe. Artists of such stature as Paul Klee from Switzerland and Vassili Kandinsky from Russia were two who joined this orbit.

Gropius' idea was to set up an institution where students in all the arts and crafts could study and learn one from another. He abhorred the artificial barriers which existed between artists and craftsmen and between artists practising in different media. He saw them all as interdependant. He felt that the manual dexterity in the craft was as vital and necessary as the mental contribution of the designer. So every Bauhaus student, whatever his field of work or talent, took the same workshop training. He saw and studied what was necessary for the complete design. When qualified he was able to comprehend and oversee all the aesthetic and constructional processes in his field.

In these theories Gropius was returning, as William Morris had wanted to do, to the Renaissance architects' comprehension and facility in all the visual arts, but, unlike Morris, he did not want to set the clock back, but embraced with enthusiasm all the advantages of modern technology, adapting and utilising them to the needs of architectural design.

Genuine modern architecture was unusual in Britain before 1945. The few examples which were built were chiefly by the European architects who fled from their own countries in the 1930s and came to seek political asylum in Britain. Although some would have liked to stay in the country, mainly they emigrated further, mostly to the U.S.A., because the architectural opportunities in England for modern architecture were so limited. The British profession was still dominated by the traditionalists.

Walter Gropius himself came in 1934. He designed one or two buildings, notably *Impington Village College*, Cambridgeshire with Maxwell Fry and departed for the U.S.A. in 1937. *Erich Mendelsohn* also came from Germany, in 1933. He built the *De la Warr Pavilion* at *Bexhill-on-Sea* (555) in 1936 with *Serge Chermayeff* (from the Caucausus), then went to Palestine and later to the U.S.A. *Berthold Lubetkin*, also from the Caucausus, founded the firm of *Tecton* which built the *Highpoint Flats* at *Highgate*, also the *Finsbury Health Centre*, both in 1938. *Peter Behrens*, who came from Germany, built one of the first modern houses in Britain as early as 1926. This is *'New Ways'* in *Northampton*, which is a starkly plain block with a triangular metal-framed window extending vertically the full height of the house above the severe canopied doorway.

The lead given by these Continental architects encouraged modern building in Britain. In the 1930s, slowly, some of the younger architects broke away from the traditional school led by Lutyens and Scott to design functionally in steel, concrete and glass. At first a modern design was produced in brick in plain blocks constructed on steel framing. *Sir John Burnet's Royal Masonic Hospital* at Ravenscourt Park (1930–3) is a purpose-built structure of this type; so also were *Sir Charles Holden's* new *London Underground Stations* as, for example, the circular one at Arnos Grove (1932).

Much closer to the Continental functionalist pattern was the new *factory* for *Boots Pure Drug Company* at Beeston by *Sir Owen Williams*. The site of 236 acres was acquired in 1927 near Nottingham on the River Trent. Williams designed two sections of the pharmaceutical factory, the 'wets' and the 'drys', the former for liquids, creams and pastes, the latter for powders and tablets. Completed in 1932 and 1938 respectively, these two structures are based on the unit dimension system in steel and concrete with an immense area of glass curtain walling under a cantilever roof construction.

A parallel structure was designed by *William Crabtree* in *London*. Equally ahead of its time in

Britain this is *Peter Jones' department store* (558). Reminiscent of Mendelsohn's earlier work in Germany, the façade is wrapped round the structure in a curving glass and steel front, almost Perpendicular Gothic in its reticulated panelling.

Architecture since 1945

The pattern had now finally changed. No building had been carried out for six years and vast areas of destroyed and damaged property needed replacing. No longer were traditional architectural methods adequate, so in Britain, as elsewhere in Europe, the international style was accepted and followed. Within a decade a new problem emerged, that of reconciling the needs of pedestrians and motor vehicles for space in the city streets.

Since 1950 a tremendous quantity of building has been carried out. The town planner has become an important factor in the scheme and, both in reconstruction and in new layouts, the scale encompasses wider areas of land and groups of buildings for different but related purpose.

Despite the international character of modern architecture, national traditions still make themselves felt, based, as they always have been, on climate, resources, individual life style and economic necessity. Thus, although modern architecture everywhere is based on module construction and the same materials of glass, steel, and concrete are used, there are differences between the work of countries and areas. For example, due to an advanced steel industry, British modern architecture follows that of the U.S.A. and Germany in steel-framed building, which means designs based upon the rectangular block, then glass curtain-walled or concrete faced. In Italy or Spain, for instance, where steel is less readily available, there is greater stress upon reinforced concrete, often designed in parabolic curves and vaults. Again, in Mediterranean countries, glass curtain-walling is less suited to a hot, sunny climate and the traditional desire for colour is seen in bright mosaic and painted exterior murals.

In order to carry out the immense building programme needed after the War, standardisation of design and form was inevitable. This, together with the quantity of structures completed, has led to monotony. As more and more of the architecture of the past centuries is demolished to make way for present needs this monotony increases. A visit to some of the cities of West Germany, where the original buildings were almost 90% destroyed – West Berlin for example – shows that no matter how high the quality of the modern work, if there is little leavening provided by older structures, there is a chilly uniformity to a city which is entirely newly built.

It is not always easy to blend the architecture of previous centuries with modern work. It was possible to build new structures in the seventeenth and eighteenth centuries side by side with those of the fifteenth and sixteenth. The style may have been different but the material and scale was the same. Nothing can blend successfully a 200-foot modern tower with the intimate Medieval or classical structure. A visit to the City of London, where office blocks rise far above dainty Wren steeples or to St Giles' Circus where Centrepoint stands alone, incongruously overshadowing the pre-war structures limited by the 100-foot cornice line, shows the incompatibility of such a marriage. At least the re-emergent cities of Essen and Düsseldorf do not have this problem.

Typical of major structures erected in the first decade after the war are the Royal Festival Hall and Coventry Cathedral. Neither of these is out of scale with surrounding buildings and, though modern in treatment and structure, there is nothing aggressively different about them. The *Royal Festival Hall* was the permanent building which stemmed from the Festival of Britain held in 1951 to commemorate the Great Exhibition of 100 years earlier. Designed by the L.C.C. architects *Robert Matthew* and *Leslie Martin* (560), the hall has been a great success. Simple, and due to the austerity of the period, perhaps a little clinical in appearance, it is functional and pleasant inside, well heated and ventilated, and with an acoustic system which totally shuts out the noise of the adjacent railway yet retains that of the concert performer. The auditorium (seating nearly 3500) is the principal feature of the Royal Festival Hall. The site was restricted, so it is raised on stilts above two foyers, on different levels, where concert-goers can stroll and view the river during intervals. The auditorium is sealed within an outer envelope which includes restaurants bars and a theatre.

Coventry Cathedral (554) is very much a product of its age. It is a modern building wherein have been employed modern methods of construction and

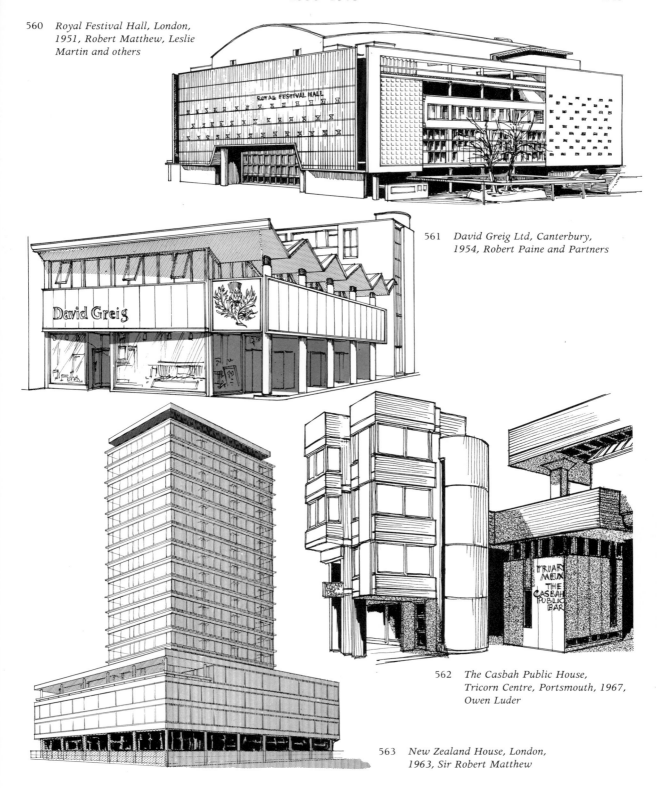

560 *Royal Festival Hall, London, 1951, Robert Matthew, Leslie Martin and others*

561 *David Greig Ltd, Canterbury, 1954, Robert Paine and Partners*

562 *The Casbah Public House, Tricorn Centre, Portsmouth, 1967, Owen Luder*

563 *New Zealand House, London, 1963, Sir Robert Matthew*

decoration. But, as the architect, *Sir Basil Spence*, has stated it is a traditional cathedral in plan, scale and materials. It is completely different from its Medieval and Renaissance predecessors yet its interior has that quality essential to all cathedral churches, the power to move and uplift the human spirit. On the exterior of this not large building of pinkish-grey sandstone the sole sculptural decoration is provided by *Sir Jacob Epstein's* bronze 25-feet high group of St Michael and the Devil. The work, which is one of the sculptor's last but finest, is ideally placed, set off by the great expanse of plain sandstone around it. Inside, of supreme quality, is the gloriously coloured 195-light baptistery window by *John Piper* and the two chapels. The focal centre, above the altar, is the tapestry of Christ by *Graham Sutherland*. The glass entrance screen, engraved by *John Hutton* (as at Guildford) gives a fairy-like quality to the end of the cathedral. It screens and protects from the outside but does not cut off or obscure. There is no full stop here, only a gossamer barrier between the new cathedral and the remains of the old.

In the years 1955–65 architecture became more modern and large scale. *New Zealand House in London* by *Sir Robert Matthew* is a good example of the tower block rising from its podium on Le Corbusier-type pilotis (563). The *Millbank Tower* (1963) by *Ronald Ward and Partners* is a loftier structure, it having been possible to retain the height of the original design due to the open site on the Thames embankment. The *B.B.C. Television Centre* is an interesting building by *Norman and Dawbarn*. This is circular in plan with a hollow centre and subsidiary blocks radiating from the external circle. It was the first attempt to provide studios purpose-built for television. The exterior is largely brick and glass; inside is a variety of colour and texture of which the highlight is the great abstract mural by *John Piper*.

Many new *hotels* have been built in the 1960s, especially in London. These are of varied design, in tall blocks and in long, low masses. In several instances the circular theme has been used; typical are the *Ariel Hotel* at London Airport, 1961, *Russell Diplock Associates* and the *Grand Metropolitan Hotel* in Knightsbridge, 1974, which is rather like a circular Centrepoint and by the same architect (*Seifert*).

More original than Coventry in its design and imaginative use of modern structural opportunities is the *Roman Catholic Cathedral of Liverpool*, built

1962–7 by *Sir Frederick Gibberd* to replace Lutyens' abandoned design.* It is constructed on circular plan – the centrally planned church of the Renaissance ideal – but this is no eclectic building. It is like an immense marquee with a glass lantern and metal crown above (564). The cathedral is built on the immense podium of its classical predecessor and has an outside sacrament chapel and altar where open air services are held. Inside, the cathedral emanates, by the handling of its spatial features and both the natural and artificial lighting, the spiritual quality to be felt in the great Medieval cathedrals. There is no white light. The natural lighting comes entirely from the lantern, of which the glass ranges through all the spectrum colours, and from the narrow strips of glass in the nave walls. Chapels are inserted into these walls all round, squeezed in between the great sloping buttresses which offset the thrust of the 2000-ton lantern. The lighting is rich and glowing, even on a dull day; in sunshine, it becomes magical. The altar is set in the centre of the grey-patterned floor. Round it are concentric rings of pews and, above, is suspended the delicate, metal baldacchino.

Sir Frederick Gibberd also designed the smaller but interestingly original new public library at *Redbridge* in London. This again is centrally planned, with high and top lighting.

The expansion of higher education since 1945 has led to a tremendous quantity of building for universities and technical colleges as well as new schools. Much of this work is pedestrian and, in the last decade, economy has dictated the architectural terms. Work of high quality at the *established universities* would include *Arts Faculty* buildings (1961) by *Casson* and *Conder* at *Cambridge*, also *Fitzwilliam House* (1961) by *Denys Lasdun* there (565) and, in more 'brutalist' form, the new *Churchill College* (1964) by *Richard Sheppard*. *Manchester University* pioneered the concept of a large, unified student community and there are some interesting buildings in the layout at Owen's Park student village.

Some original architectural designs have been carried out at *Durham University*. In the buildings fronting the A1 trunk road the façades have been kept

---

* This was designed by Lutyens in 1929 and intended to be an immense neo-classical cathedral. Due to the Second World War, the death of the architect and accelerating costs, the project was abandoned when only the crypt and sacristy had been built.

564 *Metropolitan Cathedral of Christ the King, Liverpool, 1962–7, Sir Frederick Gibberd*

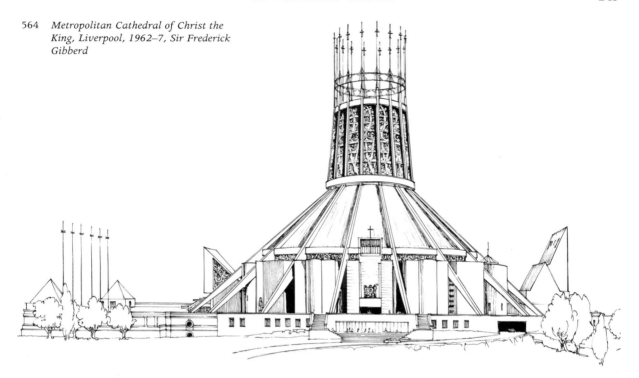

blind to cut out noise and dirt and advantage is taken of the natural lighting on the opposite elevation. Dunhelm House at the university is an interesting design reminiscent of Le Corbusier's Convent of La Tourette at Eveux-sur-l'Abresle. It is one of a number of buildings which, in the 1960s and 1970s, lean towards the 'brutalist' approach. Brutalism has not been a new replacement movement, indeed it was more an innovation of the 1950s than the 1960s, but the precepts of its exponents, usually the younger architects, took time before they were accepted and carried into practice, and then chiefly for public and university building. Such work is forceful and honest in its use of materials: concrete, slatted or boarded, brick, steel and/or glass. The main point is, that the materials should be used plainly and openly and should not be a disguise for something else. Brutalist form shows itself in powerful, simple, logical patterns, in massive, thrusting design. Although the theme owes much to Le Corbusier, it also stems from the pioneers of similar ideals in the 1920s and 1930s, such as Terragni of Italy and Mies Van der Rohe of Germany.

The *new universities* gave the greatest opportunities to the architect-planner. One of the earliest of these,

Sussex University, is built on a fine site of rolling country between the Downs and the sea at Falmer. The chief architect, *Sir Basil Spence*, has used a brick and concrete format, combining the two media skilfully in an arcaded style. This can be seen in the first building constructed, Falmer House, 1962–3, which has a central court in traditional British university pattern. The flattish arches are repeated, though the balance and proportion differs on each of the three floors (566). The architect's Meeting House is also interesting; of the two floors, the lower is designed for relaxation, the upper as a circular chapel. The work at Sussex is an example of 'brutalist' design in the more traditional materials.

York University has not only been constructed on a new site, but it has been extensively landscaped and the water-logged ground drained to provide a most attractive artificial lake around which the colleges are planned (567). The buildings are well and pleasantly designed and include some unusual structures such as the central hall with its roof suspended from an A-frame. Designed by *Sir Robert Matthew*, the university was begun in the early 1960s and work still continues.

Brutalist design has been used in public and

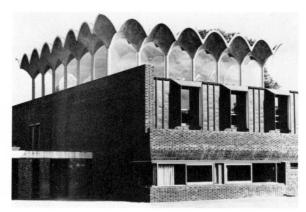

565 *Fitzwilliam House, Cambridge. Hall and library, Denys Lasdun*

566 *Courtyard, Falmer House, University of Sussex, founded 1961, Sir Basil Spence*

567 *University of York, founded 1961, Sir Robert Matthew*

568 *University of Salford, Manchester, 1961, Noel Hill*

general building. *Queen Elizabeth Concert Hall* on London's riverside is one stark and controversial example. An imaginative use of boarded concrete is to be seen in the *Tricorn Centre* at Portsmouth. Designed by *Owen Luder*, this town planning scheme is unashamedly plain, making no attempt to be elegant or finely finished. Its success is achieved by contrasts in shape and the play of light and shade one upon another and against the sky. Built on several levels, it is a breakaway from modern boxed-in architecture. It comprises a covered market with lorry space, a multi-storey car park, a piazza, a public house and flats. Typical of the interiors is the Casbah Public House (562), its ceiling decorated in black dull-surfaced material in square blocks and the walls wood-slatted and scarlet-painted. The scheme is warm and cosy, yet thoroughly modern.

Housing: Garden Cities, Flats, Housing Estates and New Towns

These are the four chief means by which individuals and corporate bodies both private and municipal, have sought to house a rapidly rising population in the twentieth century, in a manner which would be a social improvement upon the terrible conditions of the previous century. The ideas of such industrialists as Sir Titus Salt were carried to a further stage in the *garden cities* of the years 1900–40. The aim of a garden city was to create a new centre of population in a planned housing area which would also contain amenities such as churches, shops, schools and clubs and would produce a self-supporting community in the cleaner rural air with a higher proportion of open space per house than had been the case in nineteenth-century industrial towns.

Ebenezer Howard was one of the original proponents of the idea and published his plans in a book in 1898. He intended the land on which the town was built to be owned by or held in trust for its community and he wanted adequate land space to provide a rural belt between the town and other urban areas. It was an attempt to call a halt to the increasing urban sprawl of the great cities.

The Garden City Association was formed and a company established. The two examples which were built were *Welwyn* and *Letchworth*, both in Hertfordshire. Letchworth is larger, comprising about 4500 acres of which 1500 are used by the town and 3000

kept as a green belt. The factory area is apart from the town but readily accessible. In both towns the buildings are traditional, in brick, clapboard and half-timber and there is great variety in size and design of house from terraced cottages to large, detached villas. The houses have gardens and the roads are tree-lined. In the centre of the town are broad avenues with shops, council offices, a theatre and civic buildings (570).

At the same time a number of industrialists were establishing their own model housing estates adjacent to, but not an integral part of, their factory area. *Bourneville* stems from Cadbury and Rowntree built theirs at *York*. The most extensive and impressive was Lord Leverhulme's *Port Sunlight* in the Wirral of Cheshire. The Lever factory was built in 1888 and the housing estate has developed since then for the firm's employees. Architecturally the estate is successful. There is great variety of materials, styles and scale of buildings and no overall architectural monotony. A number of well known architects in the domestic field contributed to the scheme, such as *Sir Ernest George*. Most of the houses are simple in brick, stone, or half-timber with pargetting. There is also a church, an art gallery, schools, a cottage hospital, library, bank, fire station, post office and shops (573).

In municipal schemes the *London County Council* was the largest organisation in the field and a number of cottage estates were built. These were much more cramped than the garden cities, with a high density of population per acre and no green belt between one suburban estate and another. Also, these were dormitory suburbs and workers had to travel, often long distances, to their jobs.

It was after 1930 that the congestion in large cities became so acute that it was realised that flat accommodation represented the only way to solve the housing problem; the garden city had only touched the fringe of this. Two of the chief difficulties in designing good accommodation in flats are to permit adequate ingress of light and to cut out noise. Most council schemes did neither. The usual layout in the 1930s was for access by galleries, that is an open corridor along one façade of the block. Each corridor was reached by open staircases. There was no privacy from the noise of people approaching other flats and the gallery above cut out the light from the windows of the gallery below. Large numbers of these depressing, noisy blocks were built in these years.

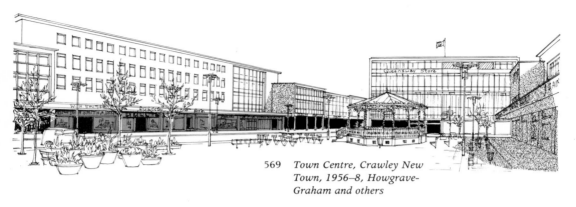

569   *Town Centre, Crawley New Town, 1956–8, Howgrave-Graham and others*

570   *The Parkway, Welwyn Garden City, begun 1920, Louis de Soissons*

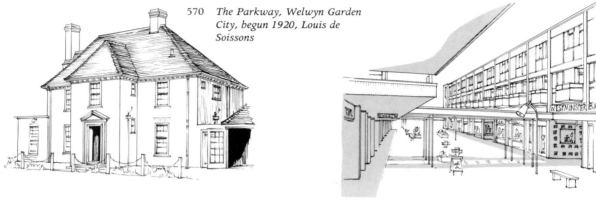

571   *Pedestrian shopping precinct, Stevenage New Town, 1960*

572   *Central Square, Hampstead Garden Suburb, begun 1906*

573   *Brick and half-timber building including bank and library, Port Sunlight Estate, Cheshire*

Lutyens' low-cost flats at *Page Street* have been referred to (page 235 and 548). Of a high architectural standard and in luxury class but still of corridor access design, *Wells Coates* built the simple concrete *Isokon Flats* at Hampstead (574). In a balcony design in modern construction *Maxwell Fry* built *Kemsal House* in 1936. This was a low-cost block in Ladbroke Grove in *London* which was of advanced design for its time. *Tecton's Highpoint Flats* (page 241) were in the luxury class and are one of the earliest of the tower blocks (though small by post-war standards).

After 1945 the proportion of municipal housing increased, accelerated by the urgent demand created by war damage. The character of such housing had now altered and was both more enlightened and more catholic in interpretation. *London County Council*, having the largest housing problem on its hands, has, naturally, built some of the largest and most comprehensive of such schemes. The best of these is the *Alton Estate* at *Roehampton*. The open site is a magnificent one: on high ground with views in all directions, it adjoins Roehampton village and Wimbledon Common. Designed by the Housing Division of the L.C.C. Architects' Department under *Leslie Martin* and *Whitfield Lewis*, the estate is a mixed development with an informal layout incorporating eleven-storey blocks, four-storey maisonettes and two-tier terrace houses. The landscaping has been imaginatively carried out, taking full advantage of the natural beauties of the site; the only serious deficiency was the lack of foresight in considering provision for private cars.

Of different design, in a more heavily populated district of London, *Drake and Lasdun* evolved the 'cluster block' layout* in *Bethnal Green*. Here, four rectangular blocks are connected to a core by bridges. The structure, in reinforced concrete, has the advantage of easy ingress of light and air as well as being a more interesting building design (576). In the *Pimlico Housing Estate* in Churchill Gardens, *Powell and Moya* evolved an original heating system by using the exhaust heat from Battersea Power Station on the opposite side of the river to supply an estate of 1600 dwellings. The green glass tower, some 140 feet high, is the centre of the plant for the heating system.

---

* In recent years this interesting scheme has been emulated in Moscow as ideal for giving maximum light and air in crowded urban areas.

An interesting estate outside London which helped to pioneer the 'brutalist' architectural idiom, is the *Park Hill Estate* at *Sheffield*. Developed by the City Architects' Department, this is built on sloping ground so that at one end buildings are composed of 14 storeys and at the other of only four or five. The plan includes shops, pedestrian walks and play spaces. The structure is of reinforced concrete with brick panels. It is an imaginative and ingenious architectural scheme, but the extensive use of concrete in the South Yorkshire climate lacks colour and interest and has not weathered well.

The equivalent development after the Second World War to the Garden City theme after the First, was the *New Town* idea. With Lord Reith as its Chairman, the New Town Committee was set up in 1945 to suggest guiding principles upon which the theme might be developed. The New Towns Act of 1946, which followed, provided for 20 such towns to take the overspill from large cities, especially London, and that they should not adjoin the city in question. Planning was quickly implemented on the first sites: *Hatfield, Stevenage* and *Hemel Hempstead* in Hertfordshire, *Crawley* in Sussex, *Harlow* in Essex. Others, like *Cumbernauld* near Glasgow, followed later. The New Towns have been a success despite problems of resettling urban populations and providing interest and entertainment for the young. Each New Town comprises a town centre with large shops, car parks, civic and cultural buildings, amenities, schools and colleges. Adjacent residential areas have schools, churches, public houses, community centres and sports facilities. The architecture is entirely modern but varies greatly from one part of the country to another, using indigenous materials and methods of building. Probably the most successful examples are those set in the more rolling, varied landscapes such as Crawley in Sussex and Cumbernauld in Scotland (569, 571).

Houses

In the years up to 1918 large houses were still being built for well-to-do clients. Among the architects practising in this field *Sir Edwin Lutyens* was the foremost. Continuing in Shaw's and Voysey's tradition, Sir Edwin designed many such houses using different styles in brick, stone, wood and slate. They all have dignity, good proportions, restrained, elegant detail

574   *Isokon Flats, Hampstead,*
      1933–4, Wells Coates

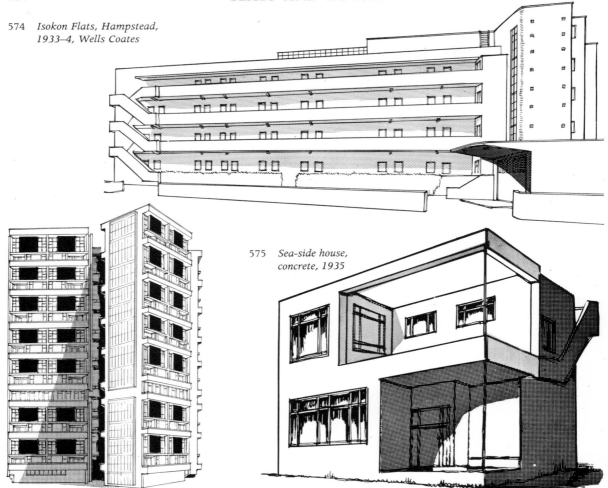

575   *Sea-side house,*
      concrete, 1935

576   *Claredale Street,*
      Bethnal Green.
      'Cluster' design,
      1958, Drake and
      Lasdun

577   *Drawing Room,.*
      1928–35

and a high standard of craftsmanship.

Interiors of the time were much plainer than Victorian ones, with less elaborate wallpapers and carpets, a smaller quantity of furniture and fewer ornaments. The Art Nouveau influence showed itself for a brief decade in wallpaper, furniture and stained-glass design.

The inter-war years produced few good houses from an architectural, aesthetic or comfort standpoint. It was a negative time, when reaction against over-decoration, overfurnishing and dark, rich interiors had set in and little that was positive took its place, with a resultant emptiness in exterior designs and interior decoration.

The bulk of domestic building was of a speculative nature and was put up on a vast scale in town suburbs. Mock Tudor or fifteenth-century beams, consisting of wood less than one inch thick, superimposed upon brick and plaster, attempted to give the impression of character, originality and wealth. The term 'stockbroker Tudor' has now become one of disapprobation but, in their time, such houses in the desirable areas on the fringe of suburbia were eagerly sought after.

A few British architects in the 1930s followed the lead of the émigré Continental ones and designed houses on functionalist lines (575). *Maxwell Fry's* 'Sun House' in Frognal Way, Hampstead, 1935, is one of these, where the architect made full use of the new materials and modern structure in his flat roof and cantilevered balcony.

On the interior, the *dernier cri* in design was also for the plainest of décors (577). The walls were distempered or papered in cream or white, carpets were unpatterned, chairs of functional design were covered in plain wool or velvet. An electric bar fire, set in a cream, stucco-finished fireplace, had replaced the old coal-burning grate, and electric light the gas mantle. Plainness was everywhere. Vacuity was accepted as simplicity and, though the ordinary person without intellectual pretensions did not go to such extremes even his drawing room scheme was carried out in cream or beige, neutrally if not emptily. The reaction from Victorianism was extreme; every attempt was made, if distemper was not used, to find a wallpaper with an indiscernible pattern and furnishings of like kind.

Since 1950 interiors have become more colourful again. Man-made fibres have made possible furnishing materials of bright, washable designs for curtains, chair covers and even carpets. An informal open-plan style has brought more variety to interior design and walls and ceilings can be painted, papered or even left in natural brick or stone. Modern home design and forms of heating have brought light and warmth to the contemporary home.

Glossary

The bold reference figures in brackets refer to line drawings in the glossary.

Abacus The top member of a capital, usually a square or curved-sided slab of stone or marble (**584, 586**).

Abutment Solid masonry acting as support against the thrust or lateral pressure of an arch (**581, 583**).

Acanthus A leaf form used in classical ornament (**586, 594**).

Acroteria Blocks resting on the vertex and lower extremities of a pediment to carry carved ornament (**584**).

Ambulatory A passage or aisle giving access between the choir, with high altar, and the apse of a church.

Antefixae Carved blocks set at regular intervals along the lower edge of a roof in classical architecture.

Anthemion A type of classical ornament based upon the honeysuckle flower (**594**).

Apse Semi-circular or polygonal termination to a church most commonly to be found in the eastern or transeptal elevations.

Arabesque Classical ornament in delicate, flowing forms, terminating in scrolls and decorated with flowers and leaves (**589**).

Arcade A series of arches open, or closed with masonry, supported on columns or piers.

Arch A structure of wedge-shaped blocks over an opening which support one another by mutual pressure (**578**).

Architrave The lowest member of the entablature (**584, 587, 588**).

Arcuated construction Where the structure is supported on arches.

Arris The vertical sharp edges between the flutes on a column (**584**).

Articulation The designing, defining and dividing up of a façade into vertical and horizontal architectural members

Ashlar Hewn and squared stones prepared for building.

Astragal A moulding at the top of the column and below the capital.

Astylar A classical façade without columns or pilasters.

Attic A term applied in Renaissance architecture to the upper storey of a structure above the cornice.

Bailey A court enclosed by inner or outer walls of a castle or by any of its defensive circuits.

Baldacchino A canopy supported on pillars set over an altar or throne.

Barbican Outer defence to a city or castle. Generally a double tower over a gate or bridge.

Barge board Ornamental carved wood boards on the exterior gable beams of a roof (**602**).

Barrel vault A continuous vault in semi-circular section, like a tunnel (**599**).

Bascule A type of drawbridge raised or lowered with counterpoise.

Basilica In Roman architecture a hall of justice and centre for commercial exchange. This type of structure was adapted by the early Christians for their church design. It was a rectangular building generally with an apse at one end. It was divided internally into nave and aisles by columns, not piers, and these supported a timber roof. The basilican plan continued in use for several centuries.

Bay Compartment or division in a building. Term applied particularly to cathedrals where bays are marked by vaulting shafts and pillars (**583**).

Bolection moulding A curved moulding generally used to raise one surface, such as a panel, above the remainder.

Caisson *see* Coffer.

Cantilever A specially shaped beam or other member (e.g. staircase tread) supported securely at one end and carrying a load at the other free end or with the load distributed uniformly along the beam. A cantilever bracket is used to support a cornice or balcony, etc. of considerable projection. The cantilever principle is frequently adopted in designs of large bridges, e.g. the Forth Railway Bridge, near Edinburgh.

Capital The crowning feature of a column or pilaster 584, 586, 587).

Cartouche Ornament in the form of elaborate scrolled forms round shields, tablets or coats of arms.

Caryatid Sculptured female figure in the form of support or column.

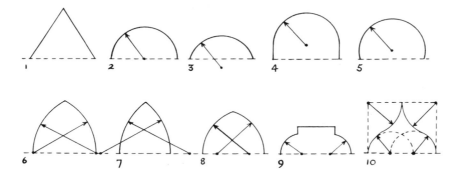

578   *The Arch*

1	Triangular	7	Pointed – lancet
2	Round – semicircular	8	Pointed – obtuse
3	Round – segmental	9	Shouldered
4	Round – stilted	10	Ogee
5	Round – horseshoe	11	Four-centred
6	Pointed – equilateral		

579   *Wall sets-off*

580   *Quoin stones*

581   *Buttress sets-off*

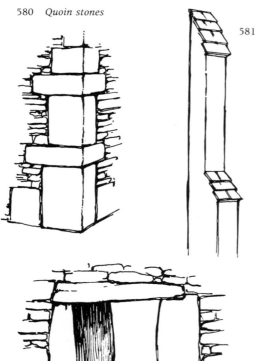

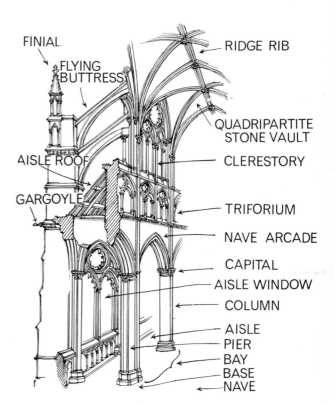

FINIAL

FLYING BUTTRESS

RIDGE RIB

QUADRIPARTITE STONE VAULT

AISLE ROOF

CLERESTORY

GARGOYLE

TRIFORIUM

NAVE ARCADE

CAPITAL

AISLE WINDOW

COLUMN

AISLE

PIER

BAY

BASE

NAVE

582   *Lintel*

583   *Gothic construction*

Ceiling cove Curved part of a ceiling where it joins the wall.

Centering A structure, usually made of timber, set up to support a dome, vault or ceiling until construction is complete.

Chamfer An angle which is cut off diagonally. The cut can be straight or concave.

Chevet Term given to circular or polygonal apse when surrounded by an ambulatory from which radiate chapels.

Chevron ornament Romanesque decoration in zig-zag form.

Cinquefoil Five-leaf tracery opening.

Clerestory The upper storey of a church generally pierced by a row of windows (583).

Coffer Panel or caisson sunk into a ceiling, dome or vault – often ornamented (585).

Collar beam Curved tying beam in a timber roof.

Corbel table A projecting section of wall supported on corbels (carved blocks of stone or wood) and generally forming a parapet.

Cornice The crowning member of the classical entablature (584, 588).

Coupled columns In classical architecture where the wall articulation is designed with the columns in pairs.

Crocket A projecting block of stone carved in Gothic foliage on the inclined sides of pinnacles and canopies (596).

Crossing The central area in a cruciform church where the transepts cross the nave and choir arm. Above this lofty space is generally set a tower, with or without a spire.

Cruciform A plan based upon the form of a cross.

Cupola A spherical roof covering a circular or polygonal form.

Curtain wall In modern architecture this term is in universal use and commonly describes an external non-loadbearing wall composed of repeated modular elements generally of glass in metal framing. These are prefabricated then erected on the site.

Cusp Point forming the foliations in Gothic tracery.

Cyma A moulding in a section of two contrasting curves – either cyma recta or cyma reversa – used especially in classical architecture (588, 594).

Dentil Classical form of ornament (587).

Domical vault A vault covering a square or polygonal compartment and shaped like a dome.

Drum The circular or poly-sided vertical walling supporting a dome.

Drum tower Round tower.

Echinus A curved, moulded member supporting the abacus of the Doric Order. The term is derived from the Greek *echinos* meaning sea urchin. The curve resembles the shell of the sea urchin (584).

Engaged column A column (in classical architecture) which is attached to the wall so that only a half to three-quarters of its circumference stands visible.

Entablature The top portion of an architectural order which consists of horizontal mouldings. These are divided into the architrave which surmounts the capital, then the frieze and last, and uppermost, the cornice (584, 588).

Entasis Taken from the Greek word for distension, is an outward curving along the outline of a column shaft. It is designed to counteract the optical illusion which gives to a shaft bounded by straight lines the appearance of being curved inwards, i.e. concave.

Fillet A narrow flat band which divides mouldings from one another; also separates column flutes (588).

Finial Ornament finishing off the apex of a roof, gable, pinnacle, newel, canopy, etc. (583).

Flute Vertical channelling in the shaft of a column (584, 587).

Frieze The central member of the classical entablature (584, 587, 588).

Frontispiece The two- or three-stage entrance feature applied to the principal façade of a court or building.

Giant order Used in later classical architecture wherein the order spans two storeys of the façade.

Greek cross plan A cruciform plan where the four arms of the cross are of equal length.

Guilloche Classical ornament in the form of an intertwined plait (594).

Guttae Small cones under the mutules and triglyphs of the Doric entablature (584, 590).

Hammerbeam Horizontal beam in timber roof situated as a tie beam but in two sections with main opening in the centre (605, 608).

Hammer post Rests on the inner side of the hammerbeam (605, 608).

Impost The horizontal stone or mouldings on top of a pier from which the arch springs (595).

Intercolumniation The space between columns.

Intersecting vault Where two vaults, either of semi-circular section or of pointed form, meet and intersect one another at right angles. Most usual instance is in the crossing of a church where the transepts cross nave and choir (601).

King post (also queen post) Vertical post extending from ridge to tie-beam centre to support the latter. Queen posts are in pairs (604).

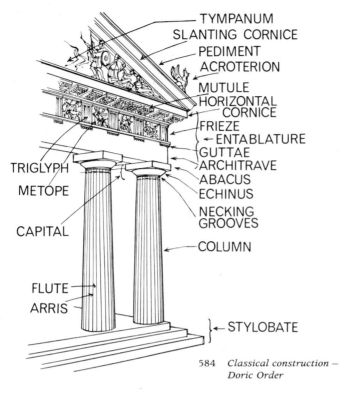

TYMPANUM
SLANTING CORNICE
PEDIMENT
ACROTERION
MUTULE
HORIZONTAL CORNICE
FRIEZE
ENTABLATURE
GUTTAE
ARCHITRAVE
ABACUS
ECHINUS
NECKING GROOVES
COLUMN

TRIGLYPH
METOPE
CAPITAL

FLUTE
ARRIS

STYLOBATE

584   *Classical construction –*
       Doric Order

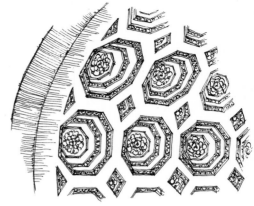

585   *Coffered vault*

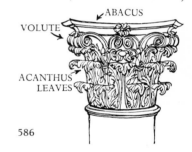

CORINTHIAN CAPITAL
(Ancient Roman)

ABACUS
VOLUTE
ACANTHUS LEAVES

586

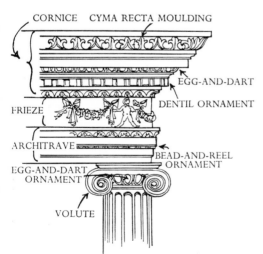

CORNICE   CYMA RECTA MOULDING
EGG-AND-DART
DENTIL ORNAMENT
FRIEZE
ARCHITRAVE
BEAD-AND-REEL ORNAMENT
EGG-AND-DART ORNAMENT
VOLUTE

THE IONIC ORDER
(Ancient Rome)

587

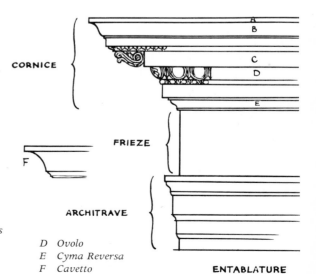

CORNICE
A
B
C
D
E
FRIEZE
F
ARCHITRAVE
ENTABLATURE

588   *Classical mouldings*
       A   *Fillet*
       B   *Cyma Recta*
       C   *Corona*
       D   *Ovolo*
       E   *Cyma Reversa*
       F   *Cavetto*

589 *Arabesque and griffin ornament*

590 *Greek Doric entablature*

KEY or FRET PATTERN

PATERA

591 *Classical ornament*

592 *Trefoil*

593 *Quatrefoil*

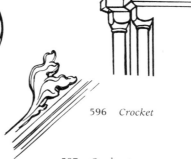

595 *Impost mouldings*

596 *Crocket*

597 *Oval patera*

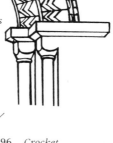

594 *Classical ornament*

EGG and DART

LEAF and DART

BAY LEAF GARLAND

GUILLOCHE

PATERA

FRET

ACANTHUS

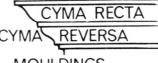
CYMA RECTA
CYMA REVERSA
MOULDINGS

598 *Gothic mouldings*

← Bead and reel

← Anthemion

← Bead and reel

Lantern Structure for ventilation and light. Often surmounting a dome or tower.

Latin cross plan A cruciform plan where the nave is longer than the other three arms.

Lierne From the French *lier* = to tie. A short, intermediate rib in Gothic vaulting which is not a ridge rib nor rises from the impost (609).

Lintel The horizontal stone slab or timber beam spanning an opening and supported on columns or walls (582).

Lunette A semi-circular panel, often ornamented in the form of stone, wood or glass.

Machicolation A parapet in medieval fortified buildings with openings between supporting corbels for dropping missiles upon the enemy.

Metope The space between the triglyphs of a Doric frieze. Often decorated with sculptured groups or carved ornament (584, 590).

Module A unit of measurement based on proportion by which the parts of a classical order are regulated. Generally taken from the half-diameter of the column at its junction with the base. In modern architecture, a standard unit adopted for the convenience of mass production.

Monolith Single, standing stone.

Monolithic column One whose shaft is of one piece of stone or marble in contrast to one made up in hollow drums.

Mullion Vertical bar dividing the lights in a window.

Mutule Blocks attached under Doric cornices from which the guttae depend (584, 590).

Necking The space between the astragal of a column shaft and the actual capital.

Ogee moulding A moulding incorporating a convex and a concave curve.

Order In classical architecture the order comprises the column and the entablature which it supports. The column is divided into base, shaft and capital (584).

Pediment The triangular feature in classical architecture which resembles the Gothic gable. Supported on the entablature over porticoes, windows and doors (584).

Pendentive Spherical triangles formed by the intersecting of the dome by two pairs of opposite arches, themselves carried on four piers or columns.

Peristyle A row of columns surrounding a temple, court or cloister, also the space so enclosed.

Piano nobile An Italian Renaissance term meaning literally the 'noble floor'. In classical building it is the first and principal floor.

Pier A solid mass of masonry between windows, also support for a bridge and masonry from which an arch springs (583).

Pilaster A column of rectangular section often engaged in the wall.

Piloti A term in modern architecture taken from the French word for pile or stake. Introduced by Le Corbusier in his designs of flats and houses supported on columns or piles.

Plinth Lowest member of base or wall; sometimes divided into stages (598).

Podium A continuous projecting base or pedestal.

Portcullis A strong, heavy frame or grating of oak or iron, made to slide up and down in vertical grooves at the sides of a castle gateway.

Quatrefoil Four-leaf tracery opening (593).

Quoin External angle of a building (580).

Relieving arch A relieving or discharging arch or slab is constructed to prevent the weight of masonry above it from crushing the lintel stone below.

Ridge crest Exterior ridge or upper angle of roof.

Ridge pole, purlin or piece A baulk of timber extending along the internal ridge of a roof on which the upper ends of the rafters rest (604).

Rotunda Building of circular ground plan often surmounted by a dome; a circular hall or room.

Rubble work Stones of irregular shape and size used although generally roughly in cube or block form.

Rustication A treatment of masonry with sunk joints and roughened surfaces. Used in classical architecture.

Set-off Sloping or horizontal member connecting the lower and thicker part of a wall or buttress with the receding upper part (579, 581).

Shaft The column of an order between capital and base (584, 587).

Shingle Oak tile.

Spandrel Triangular space formed between an arch and the rectangles of outer mouldings as in a doorway. Generally decorated by carving or mosaic (605, 608).

Solar Medieval term for an upper room, usually the private sitting room of the owner of the house.

Squinch Arches placed diagonally across the internal angles of a tower or base of drum to convert the square form into an octagonal base to support an octagonal spire or circular drum.

Starling Pointed mass of masonry or wood projecting from the pier of a bridge.

Stilted arch An arch having its springing line higher than the level of the impost mouldings. It is then connected to these mouldings by vertical sections of walling or stilts (578).

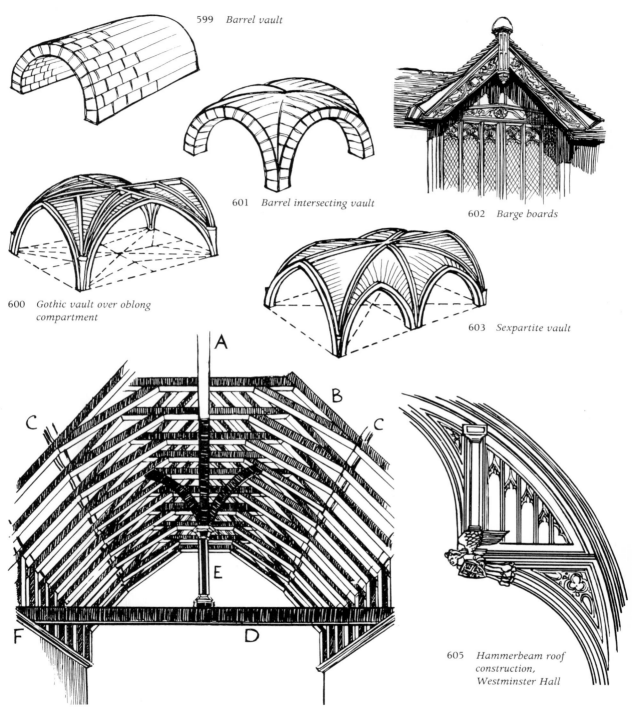

599 *Barrel vault*

601 *Barrel intersecting vault*

602 *Barge boards*

600 *Gothic vault over oblong compartment*

603 *Sexpartite vault*

605 *Hammerbeam roof construction, Westminster Hall*

604 *Timber roof*
    A Ridge purlin   *D Tie beam*
    B Rafter   *E King post*
    C Purlin   *F Wall plate*

606   *Groined vault*

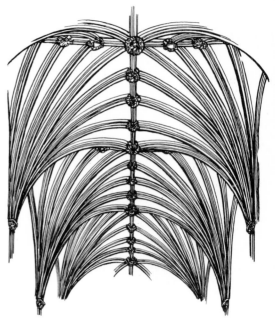

607   *Ribbed vault*

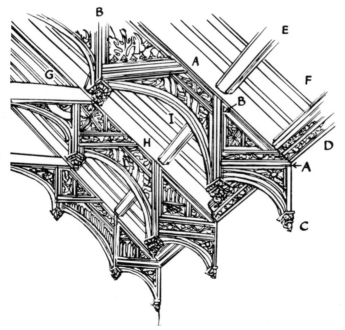

608   *Double hammerbeam roof*

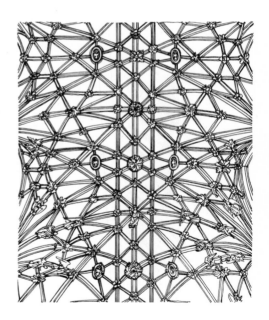

609   *Lierne vault*

Strapwork A form of ornament using straps or lines of decoration intertwined and forming panels. The straps are flat with raised fillet edges. Used on ceilings or walls, especially in early Mannerist type Renaissance work in Flanders, Poland and Britain.

String course A moulding or projecting course set horizontally along the elevation of a building.

Stucco A plaster used for coating wall surfaces for moulding into architectural decoration or sculpture.

Stylobate A basement, generally of three steps, supporting a row of columns in Greek temple design (**584**).

Swag A drop type of decoration composed of ribbons, flowers and fruit.

Tie beam A horizontal or slightly arched beam connecting the principal rafters of a roof (**604**).

Tierceron A third rib in Gothic vaulting.

Trabeated construction A structure composed of horizontal lintels and vertical posts as in Greek architecture (**584**).

Tracery The ornamental stonework in the head of a Gothic window.

Transept The arms of a cruciform church set at right angles to the nave and choir. Transepts are generally aligned north and south.

Transom Horizontal bar of wood or stone across a window or a door top.

Trefoil Three-leaf decoration used in Gothic architecture, particularly in window tracery and panelling (**592**).

Triforium The central, or first floor stage, of a Medieval church between the nave arcade and the clerestory. The triforium is usually arcaded and may have a passage behind at first floor level extending continuously round the church (**583**).

Triglyph The blocks, cut with vertical channels, which are set at regular intervals in the frieze of the Doric Order (**584, 590**)

Tympanum The triangular space between the sloping and horizontal cornices of a classical pediment (**584**).

Undercroft The chamber partly or wholly below ground generally in a Medieval building. In a church this would be a crypt, in a house or castle it would be used for storage.

Vault Arched covering in stone, brick or wood (**583, 599–601, 603, 606–7, 609**).

Vaulting bay The rectangular or square area bounded by columns or piers and covered by a ribbed or groined vault (**583**).

Vaulting boss A carved decorative feature set at intervals in a ribbed vault to hide the junctions between one rib and another (**607, 609**).

Vault springing The point at which the vault ribs spring upwards from the capital, corbel or arch impost (**583. 607**).

Volute A spiral or scroll to be seen in Ionic, Corinthian and Composite capitals (**586, 587**).

Voussoir The wedge-shaped stones which compose an arch.

Wall plate Horizontal timber extending lengthwise on top of the wall immediately under a timber roof (**604**).

Wattle-and-daub Walling made from vertical timber stakes woven horizontally with branches and reeds. The whole is then surfaced with mud.

Bibliography

A select list of books recommended for further reading

General

ALLSOPP, B., *A General History of Architecture*, Sir Isaac Pitman and Sons Ltd, 1960

ALLSOPP, B., BOOTON, H. W. and CLARK, U., *The Great Tradition of Western Architecture*, A. and C. Black, 1966

BATSFORD, H. and FRY, C., *The English Cottage*, B. T. Batsford Ltd, 1950; *The Cathedrals of England*, B. T. Batsford Ltd, 1960

BRAUN, H., *The Story of the English House*, B. T. Batsford Ltd, 1940; *Elements of English Architecture*, David and Charles, 1973; *English Abbeys*, Faber and Faber Ltd, 1971

CAMESASCA, E., *History of the House*, Collins, 1971

CLIFTON-TAYLOR, A., *The Pattern of English Building*, Faber and Faber Ltd, 1972; *The Cathedrals of England*, Thames and Hudson, 1967

COLVIN, H. M., *The Biographical Dictionary of English Architects 1660–1840*, John Murray Ltd, 1954

COOK, G. H., *The English Cathedral*, Phoenix House Ltd, 1957

COOK, O. and SMITH, E., *English Abbeys and Priories*, Thames and Hudson, 1960

CRUDEN, S., *Scottish Abbeys*, H.M. Stationery Office, 1960

COX, C. and FORD, C. B., *The English Parish Church*, B. T. Batsford Ltd, 1954

CROSSLEY, F. H., *Timber Building in England from Early Times to the end of the Seventeenth Century*, B. T. Batsford Ltd, 1951; *The English Abbey*, B. T. Batsford Ltd, 1949

DUNBAR, J. G., *The Historic Architecture of Scotland*, B. T. Batsford Ltd, 1966

DUTTON, R., *The English Country House*, B. T. Batsford Ltd, 1949

FLETCHER, B., *A History of Architecture*, The Athlone Press, 1975

GIBBERD, F., *The Architecture of England*, The Architectural Press, 1965

GLOAG, J., *Guide to Western Architecture*, George Allen and Unwin Ltd, 1958

GLOAG, J. and BRIDGWATER, D., *A History of Cast Iron in Architecture*, George Allen and Unwin Ltd, 1948

HARRIS, J. and LEVER, J., *Illustrated Glossary of Architecture 850–1830*, Faber and Faber, 1964

HARVEY, J., *The English Cathedral*, B. T. Batsford Ltd, 1956

HUTTON, G. and SMITH, E., *English Parish Churches*, Thames and Hudson, 1957

ISON, L. and W., *English Church Architecture Through the Ages*, Arthur Barker Ltd, 1972

JORDAN, R. FURNEAUX, *A Picture History of the English House*, Edward Hulton, 1960

KERSTING, A. F. and DUTTON, R., *English Country Houses in Colour*, B. T. Batsford Ltd, 1958

KIDSON, P. and MURRAY, P., *A History of English Architecture*, George G. Harrap and Co., 1962

LINNELL, C. L. S. and KERSTING, A. F., *English Cathedrals in Colour*, B. T. Batsford Ltd, 1960

LITTLE, B., *English Historic Architecture*, B. T. Batsford Ltd, 1964

MANSBRIDGE, J., *Graphic History of Architecture*, B. T. Batsford Ltd, 1967

MARÉ, E. de, *The Bridges of Britain*, B. T. Batsford Ltd, 1954

MEYER, P. and HURLIMANN, M., *English Cathedrals*, Thames and Hudson, 1950

NELLIST, J. B., *British Architecture and its Background*, Macmillan and Co. Ltd, 1967

OGILVIE, V., *The English Public School*, B. T. Batsford Ltd, 1957

O'NEIL, B. H. ST J., *Castles*, H.M. Stationery Office, 1954

PETZCH, H., *Architecture in Scotland*, Longman Group Ltd, 1971

PEVSNER, N., *Buildings of England*, Penguin Books Ltd

POTHORN, H., *Styles of Architecture*, B. T. Batsford Ltd, 1971

PUGIN, A. W. N., *The True Principles of Pointed Architecture* (Reprint of first edition of 1841), Academy Editions, 1973

RUSKIN, J., *The Stones of Venice*, William Collins Sons and Co., 1960; *The Seven Lamps of Architecture*, The Noonday Press, U.S.A. (new edition), 1961

SIMPSON, W. D., *Castles in England and Wales*, B. T. Batsford Ltd, 1969

SORRELL, A., *British Castles*, B. T. Batsford Ltd, 1974

VALE, E. and KERSTING, A. F., *A Portrait of English Churches*, B. T. Batsford Ltd, 1956

WARE, D., *A Short Dictionary of British Architects*, George Allen and Unwin, 1967

YARWOOD, D., *English Houses*, B. T. Batsford Ltd, 1966

Saxon and Romanesque

ALLSOPP, B., *Romanesque Architecture*, Arthur Barker Ltd, 1971

BLAIR, P. H., *An Introduction to Anglo-Saxon England*, Cambridge University Press, 1956

CONANT, K. J., *Carolingian and Romanesque Architecture*, Penguin Books, 1966

FISHER, E. A., *The Greater Anglo-Saxon Churches*, Faber and Faber Ltd, 1962

STOLL, R., *Architecture and Sculpture in Early Britain*, Thames and Hudson, 1967

Medieval and Gothic

BRAUN, H., *An Introduction to English Mediaeval Architecture*, Faber and Faber Ltd, 1951

BROWN, R. A., *English Medieval Castles*, B. T. Batsford Ltd, 1954

COOK, G. H., *English Monasteries in the Middle Ages*, Phoenix House Ltd, 1961

FRANKL, P., *Gothic Architecture*, Penguin Books, 1962

HARVEY, J., *The Gothic World*, B. T. Batsford Ltd, 1950; *The Master Builders,* Thames and Hudson 1971; *Henry Yevele*, B. T. Batsford Ltd, 1944; *Gothic England*, B. T. Batsford Ltd, 1948; *The Mediaeval Architect*, Wayland Publishers, 1972

RICKMAN, T., *An attempt to Discriminate the Styles of Architecture in England from the Conquest to the Reformation*, John Henry and James Parker, 1862

STEWART, C., *Gothic Architecture* (Simpson's History of Architectural Development), Longman Green and Co. Ltd

WEBB, G., *Architecture in Britain in the Middle Ages*, Penguin Books, 1956

WRIGHT, J., *Brick Building in England, Middle Ages to 1550*, John Baker, 1972

Elizabethan to Wren 1550–1700

ALLSOPP, B., *A History of Renaissance Architecture*, Sir Isaac Pitman and Sons Ltd, 1959

BRIGGS, M. S., *Wren the Incomparable*, George Allen and Unwin Ltd, 1953

DOWNES, K., *Christopher Wren*, Allen Lane, the Penguin Press, 1971

DUTTON, R., *The Age of Wren*, B. T. Batsford Ltd, 1951

FURST, V., *The Architecture of Sir Christopher Wren*, Percy Lund Humphries and Co., 1956

GIROUARD, M., *Robert Smythson and the Architecture of the Elizabethan Era*, Country Life Ltd, 1966

HIND, A. M., *Wenceslaus Hollar and his Views of London and Windsor in the Seventeenth Century*, The Bodley Head Press Ltd, 1922

HUGHES, J. Q. and LYNTON, N., *Renaissance Architecture* (Simpson's History of Architectural Development), Longmans Green and Co. Ltd, 1965

LEES-MILNE, J., *The Age of Inigo Jones*, B. T. Batsford Ltd, 1953; *Tudor Renaissance*, B. T. Batsford Ltd, 1951

PEVSNER, N., *Studies in Art, Architecture and Design* (2 vols.), Thames and Hudson, 1969

SEKLER, E., *Wren and his Place in European Architecture*, Faber and Faber Ltd, 1956

SITWELL, S., *British Architects and Craftsmen 1600–1830*, B. T. Batsford Ltd, 1948

WHIFFEN, M., *Stuart and Georgian Churches 1603–1837*, B. T. Batsford Ltd, 1948

WHINNEY, M., *Wren*, Thames and Hudson, 1971

The Eighteenth Century

ADAM, R. and J., *The Works in Architecture of Robert and James Adam*, Alec Tiranti Ltd, 1959

DAVIS, T., *John Nash*, David and Charles, 1973

DOWNES, K., *Hawksmoor*, Thames and Hudson, 1969

EDWARDS, A. T., *Sir William Chambers*, Ernest Benn Ltd, 1924

FLEMING, J., *Robert Adam and his Circle*, John Murray Ltd, 1962

HARRIS, J., *Sir William Chambers*, A. Zwemmer Ltd, 1970

HUSSEY, C., *English Country Houses, Early Georgian 1715–60*, Country Life Ltd, 1955; *English Country Houses, Mid-Georgian 1760–1800*, Country Life Ltd, 1956; *English Country Houses, Late Georgian 1800–1840*, Country Life Ltd, 1958

JOURDAIN, M., *The Work of William Kent*, Country Life Ltd, 1948

LEES-MILNE, J., *The Age of Adam*, B. T. Batsford Ltd, 1947

STROUD, D., *George Dance Architect 1741–1825*, Faber and Faber Ltd, 1971; *Henry Holland*, Country Life Ltd, 1966

SUMMERSON, J., *Architecture in Britain 1530–1830*, Penguin Books, 1969

WITTKOWER, R., *Palladio and English Palladianism*, Thames and Hudson, 1974

YARWOOD, D., *Robert Adam*, J. M. Dent and Sons Ltd, 1970

The Nineteenth Century

BARMAN, C., *An Introduction to Railway Architecture*, Art and Technics Ltd, 1950

BLOMFIELD, R., *Richard Norman Shaw*, B. T. Batsford Ltd, 1940

CLARK, K., *The Gothic Revival*, John Murray Ltd, 1962

COOK, J. M., *Victorian Architecture*, Johnson Reprint Co. Ltd, 1971

FERRIDAY, P., *Victorian Architecture*, Jonathan Cape, 1963

GOODHART-RENDEL, H. S., *English Architecture since the Regency*, Constable and Co., 1953

HITCHCOCK, H. RUSSELL, *Early Victorian Architecture in Britain* (2 Vols), Architectural Press Ltd, 1954; *Architecture, Nineteenth and Twentieth Centuries*, Penguin Books, 1958

HOBHOUSE, H., *Thomas Cubitt the Master Builder*, Macmillan, 1971

HOWARTH, T., *Nineteenth and Twentieth Century Architecture*, Longmans Green and Co. Ltd, 1959

MEEKS, C. L. V., *The Railway Station*, Architectural Press Ltd, 1957

PILCHER, D., *The Regency Style*, B. T. Batsford Ltd, 1948

POPE-HENNESSY, J. and WILD, H., *The Houses of Parliament*, B. T. Batsford Ltd, 1945

PUGIN, A. W. N., *Contrasts* (Repub.) Leicester University Press, 1969; *Specimens of Gothic Architecture* (2 Vols), M. A. Nattali, 1825

RICHARDS, J. M. and MARÉ, E. de, *The Functional Tradition in Early Industrial Buildings*, Architectural Press Ltd, 1958

STANTON, P., *Pugin*, Thames and Hudson, 1971

STROUD, D., *The Architecture of Sir John Soane*, Studio, 1961

TURNOR, R., *Nineteenth Century Architecture in Britain*, B. T. Batsford Ltd, 1950

Twentieth Century and Modern

BANHAM, R., *The New Brutalism*, The Architectural Press, 1966; *Guide to Modern Architecture*, The Architectural Press, 1962

BENNETT, T. P., *Architectural Design in Concrete*, Ernest Benn Ltd, 1927

BIRKS, T. and HOLFORD, M., *Building the New Universities*, David and Charles, 1972

BUTLER, A. S. G., *The Architecture of Sir Edwin Lutyens* (3 Vols), Country Life Ltd, 1950

DANNATT, T., *Modern Architecture in Britain*, B. T. Batsford Ltd, 1959

GROPIUS, W., *Scope of Total Architecture*, George Allen and Unwin, 1956

HATTRELL, W. S., *Hotels, Restaurants and Bars*, B. T. Batsford Ltd, 1962

HARVEY, W. A., *The Model Village and its Cottages, Bournville*, B. T. Batsford Ltd, 1906

HOWARTH, T., *Charles Rennie Mackintosh and the Modern Movement*, Routledge and Kegan Paul Ltd, 1952

HUSSEY, C., *The Life of Sir Edwin Lutyens*, Country Life Ltd, 1942

LE CORBUSIER, *Towards a New Architecture*, The Architectural Press, 1970; *The City of Tomorrow*, The Architectural Press, 1971

PEHNT, W., *Encyclopaedia of Modern Architecture*, Thames and Hudson, 1963

PEVSNER, N., *The Sources of Modern Architecture and Design*, Thames and Hudson, 1968

PRICE, B., *Technical Colleges and Colleges of Further Education*, B. T. Batsford Ltd, 1959

RICHARDS, J. M., *An Introduction to Modern Architecture*, Penguin Books, 1956

WHITTICK, A., *European Architecture in the Twentieth Century*, Leonard Hill Books, 1974; *Erich Mendelsohn*, Leonard Hill Ltd, 1956

WEBB, M., *Architecture in Britain Today*, Country Life Books, 1969

Regional

BOOTH, P. and TAYLOR, N., *Cambridge New Architecture*, Leonard Hill, 1970

COBB, G., *The Old Churches of London*, B. T. Batsford Ltd, 1948

COOK, G. H., *Portrait of St. Alban's Cathedral*, Phoenix House Ltd., 1951; *Old St. Paul's Cathedral*, Phoenix House Ltd, 1955; *Portrait of Canterbury Cathedral*, Phoenix House Ltd, 1949; *Portrait of Durham Cathedral*, Phoenix House Ltd, 1948

COURLANDER, K., *Richmond*, B. T. Batsford Ltd, 1953

EDWARDS, T., *Bristol*, B. T. Batsford Ltd, 1951

GODFREY, W. H., *A History of Architecture in and around London*, Phoenix House Ltd, 1962

HICKMAN, D., *Birmingham*, Studio Vista, 1970

ISON, W., *The Georgian Buildings of Bristol*, Faber and Faber Ltd, 1969; *The Georgian Buildings of Bath*, Faber and Faber Ltd, 1969

JESSUP, R. F. and F. W., *The Cinque Ports*, B. T. Batsford Ltd, 1952

JOWITT, R. L. P., *Salisbury*, B. T. Batsford Ltd, 1951

KERSTING, A. F. and DICK, M., *Portrait of Oxford*, B. T. Batsford Ltd, 1956

KERSTING, A. F. and LITTLE, B., *Portrait of Cambridge*, B. T. Batsford Ltd, 1955

LAMBERT, S., *New Architecture of London*, The Architectural Association, 1963

LINDLEY, K., *Sea-side Architecture*, Hugh Evelyn, 1973

LITTLE, B., *Birmingham Buildings*, David and Charles, 1971; *Cheltenham*, B. T. Batsford Ltd, 1952; *The Three Choirs Cities*, B. T. Batsford Ltd, 1952

MARGETSON, S., *Regency London*, Cassell, 1971

RODGERS, J., *York*, B. T. Batsford Ltd, 1951

SHEPHERD, T. H. and ELMES, J., *Metropolitan Improvements*, Jones and Co. 1828

SMITH, R. A. L., *Bath*, B. T. Batsford Ltd, 1948

SPENCE, B., *Phoenix at Coventry*, G. Bles Ltd, 1962

SUMMERSON, J., *Georgian London*, Barrie and Jenkins Ltd, 1962

Index

Buildings are generally listed under the names of towns or villages and persons under the surname. Illustration references are printed in bold type.